PUTTING THE PEOPLE LAST

Government, Services and Rights in Victoria

Edited by
Michael Webber with Mary L. Crooks
The Victoria Foundation for Public Policy
Promoting justice in economic and social policy

HYLAND HOUSE

First published in Australia in 1996 by
Hyland House Publishing Pty Limited
Hyland House
387–389 Clarendon Street
South Melbourne
Victoria 3205

National Library of Australia
Cataloguing-in-publication data:

Putting the people last: government, services and rights in Victoria.

ISBN 1 875657 81 9.

1. Public welfare—Victoria. 2. Education and state—Victoria. 3. Medical care—Victoria. 4. Medical policy—Victoria. 5. Civil rights—Victoria. 6. Victoria—Social policy. 7. Victoria—Politics and government—1990–. I. Webber, M. J. (Michael John).

361.6109945

Typeset in Australia by Hyland House Publishing
Printed in Victoria by East Side Printing

Contents

Introduction

Michael Webber

The Liberal–National Party government was elected to power in Victoria in October 1992. The government has claimed to be repairing an alleged financial mess left by the Cain–Kirner Labor governments and to empower consumers by giving them freedom to choose among service providers. In industry after industry—education, health, electricity, water, metropolitan transport are just the most prominent examples—the government has cut expenditure 'in order to reduce debt', has pushed schools, hospitals, the SECV and Melbourne Water into more corporate forms of organisation, and has begun the formal privatisation of the utilities. Not content with the power of its legislative majorities, the government has also set about limiting the rights and responsibilities of Victorians. In all of this, private interests—the interests of businesses and the rich—have been put ahead of the interests of ordinary Victorians. The public interest has been put last in the past three years.

This book tells the story of these changes. No one volume—or at least, no volume that could be carried—could set out the full story of the alterations that Kennett's government has wreaked on our state. What the writers do try to tell is:

- what changes have been imposed on the state since October 1992
- what justification has been provided by the government and its apologists
- why the changes have actually been implemented and
- their effects on people's lives.

These stories are told in four parts. A series of essays by a number of authors describe, explain and document the changes made in our state over the past three years. They all provide the information that Victorians need to understand what Kennett's government has done and why. In the first part we tell the story of education—what has happened, why and with what effects. In the second, the tale is health. The third part of the book examines more generally what privatisation is about, what the experience of privatisation in other countries has been, and describes in some detail what is happening to our electricity industry. Finally, we turn to Victorians' civil rights and their government. As I say, these are only examples; there were plenty of others to choose from. Despite their variety, these stories tell common, sorry tales.

Tale 1: our rights are being reduced. Of course, our rights are being reduced legally, as the Kennett government has restricted the right to strike, abolished the Accident Compensation Tribunal, limited access to government documents under freedom of information legislation, abolished the position of the Commissioner for Equal Opportunity, increased police powers and sacked local councils. But our rights are also being diminished in more insidious ways: the privatisation of utilities takes them out of the public realm and so excludes the public from decision taking. We are being redefined as consumers—of health, education and the range of privatised services—making choices as if health and the rest were cans of beans on a supermarket shelf. In the past, when the services were public, argued over and debated in the public realm, we helped shape the kinds of choices that we were offered. Just as our civil rights are being eroded, so are out political and social rights.

Tale 2: the level of service is being reduced. Our taxes have risen faster in Victoria than elsewhere in Australia, but we are getting less and less for the expenditure. Schools have fewer teachers and cleaners; hospitals provide less services and for shorter and shorter stays; the electricity industry cuts off more and more people from electricity supply; the water supply industry no longer maintains a system of public parks for our free enjoyment; we have a lower level of access to legal protections. We begin to see some of the effects: the real price of water has risen (the bills might have remained the same, but we have to pay to use the parks now); school retention rates have begun to fall; schools have closed; specialist teachers in schools are fewer. Other effects will take longer to show up statistically.

Tale 3: justifying all of this is the ideology of competition and the market. Increasingly since the early 1980s, the New Right in Australia has been arguing that governments have little or no role in providing public services: services should be provided by private corporations, acting in competition with other providers. If providers are in competition and if the public is free to choose who to patronise, then—it is argued—we will get the lowest prices and the highest quality service. Just as we do in commercial television. This argument is true under certain conditions, but none of the ideologues who plague our newspapers and airwaves pay much attention to working out whether those conditions apply in the 'markets' for education, health, electricity, water, transport and the like. And, of course, the conditions do not apply.

Tale 4 is a more cynical story. Privatisation—like building roads commercially and charging tolls—presents an opportunity for profit. In the past, banks made profits out of utilities—by providing or organising loans for interest or a fee. Now, though, many more corporations can get to the trough and can extract more. Money is to be made in lawyers and 'consultants' fees, organising the sales; in buying utilities cheaply and reaping the windfall gains as their share prices rise; by concentrating service on those most easily served and ignoring those who are difficult or expensive to provide for; and by dividing the market and offering different levels of service to people with different abilities to pay. We used to own those assets. Now we pay for the right of foreign corporations to make money out of them.

In all, over the past three years, the interests of the public have been put last. Our rights have been circumscribed; our services impoverished; our stock of assets sold off to mates.

About the Authors

Bob Carter was born in Ballarat and grew up in the Latrobe Valley. He currently teaches at Bairnsdale Secondary College and is a member of the Australian Education Union (Victorian Branch) Council. Bob has been actively involved in community campaigns to halt the privatisation of our public utilities.

Meredith Carter has been the Director of the Health Issues Centre since June 1992. The Centre is an independent research group with a national reputation for its recommendations for health sytem reform from a consumer perspective.

Dr Ken Coghill is a Visiting Fellow at the Monash University Graduate School of Government, with responsibilities for postgraduate research and teaching in relation to democratic governance. He has been Member for Werribee in the Legislative Assembly, Parliament of Victoria 1979–96, including serving as Speaker 1988–92 and as Parliamentary Secretary of the Cabinet 1982–88. Prior to his parliamentary career, he was a councillor of the Rural City of Wodonga and worked as a veterinary surgeon in the Department of Agriculture, Victoria.

Mary L. Crooks lectured at Phillip Institute of Technology from 1978–86. She has worked in several areas at state government level, more recently as Chair of the Social Justice Consultative Council (1989–92). Mary was one of the founding member of the Victoria Foundation and is now its convenor.

Dr John Ernst is Associate Professor in the Department of Urban and Social Policy at the Victoria University of Technology. He has a long interest in the economic and social consequences of privatisation as well as in the political philosophies that have generated the push to privatise. He is the author of *Whose Utility: The Social Impact of Public Utility Privatisation and Regualtion in Britain* (Open University Press, 1994).

Bill Hannan is a Melbourne writer who has published extensively on education, including *Democratic Curriculum* (Allen and Unwin, 1984). He was a seconday school languages teacher in Victoria and worked for many years in the teachers' union movement. He was Chair of the State Board of Education and Director of Curriculum in Victoria in the 1980s.

Catriona Larritt is a postgraduate student at the Department of Geography and Environmental Studies, University of Melbourne. Her current research focuses on gender relations and the Australian environmental movement. She has worked as a tutor and is also a keen athlete.

Andrew Refshauge is Deputy Leader and Minister for Health in the New South Wales Labor government. He is a qualified medical practitioner.

Terri Seddon is an Associate Professor in the Faculty of Education, Monash University. She has completed historical studies of restructuring in the 1930s depression and contemporary studies of restructuring in teachers' work, curriculum, school organisation, policy and educational governance. She has authored three books on this work: *A Curriculum for the Senior Secondary Years* (with Professor Christine Deer) (ACER, 1992), *Contest and Beyond: Reframing the Theory and Practice of Education* (Falmer, 1993) *and Whatever Happened to Teacher Award Restructuring* (ACER, in press).

John Thwaites is Shadow Minister for Health in Victoria. He is the Member for Albert Park. He hold degrees in Law and Science and prior to entering Parliament he was a barrister.

Michael Webber is Professor in the Department of Geography and Environmental Studies at the University of Melbourne. He was a co-founder and is the Deputy Convenor of The Victoria Foundation. He had published widely on the topics of industrial policy, industrial restructuring and the implications of industrial change for ordinary people. Recent books include *Global Restructuring: The Australian Experience* (with R. H. Fagan) (Oxford University Press, 1994).

Lessons About Education
Schools in Victoria's Future

Mary L. Crooks, Terri Seddon and Bill Hannon

Contents

'To Market, to Market'

The Radical Right Experiment with Victoria's State Education System

Mary L. Crooks

INTRODUCTION

In 1992, before the coalition government came to power in Victoria, the State had a very good school system built by successive governments over the previous three decades. Despite an erosion of education resources in the 1980s, Victoria's education system had achieved international acclaim in curriculum design and in the way it addressed the needs of a diverse student population. The quality and quantity of staffing was good and morale was reasonable (Marginson 1993a).

There had been a steady increase in the retention rate to year 12, which was over 85 per cent in 1992, the highest of any Australian state. Victoria had also enjoyed the best teacher–pupil ratios in Australia for the previous twenty years. Both of these features were commented on by the Independent Review of Victoria's Public Sector Finances (1992) as contributing to a high standard of provision of government services.

The state system had benefited from a twenty year history of devolution in education, in which parents, teachers, their representative organisations and those working in the education bureaucracy had worked hard in partnership to implement a devolved model of educational governance which reflected a commitment to cooperation between schools, to equity and access, to school-based decision making and to parental participation (Seddon 1994; see also the following paper by Terri Seddon).

So, in 1992, the state's education system was in pretty good shape. And we all know the adage 'if it's not broken, don't fix it!' What, then, explains the fact that this very same system is now undergoing the most radical transformation ever? Why? What is the need? What are the sorts of outcomes we can expect from such change?

The terms of the education debate imposed by the coalition government are that we had a debt and fiscal 'crisis' caused by the previous Labor government; we had 'overspent' in the major portfolio areas such as education and health; our class sizes were luxuriously too small by interstate comparison; teachers had 'captured' the decision-making process to the detriment of the system; we spent more on education than states like Queensland so the system was clearly plagued by inefficiencies; and we spent too much on teacher salaries. The major steps taken by the coalition government have been construed as unavoidable and all absolutely necessary if our state finances were to be restored—over 200 'non-viable' schools closed; 8000 teachers removed from the system and a level of expenditure cuts unprecedented in the state's history.

Apart from poignant stories in the print media about school closures, and some concern about the dislocation and pace of change, the coalition's education policy has been subjected to little public and media scrutiny. Yet the answer to what is happening to Victoria's schools does not simply rest with expenditure cuts, school closures and reductions in teacher numbers. Nor does it lie in the so-called debt 'crisis' which allegedly necessitated unprecedented expenditure cuts. The Kennett government's program for state education is only manifestly about these changes. Deeper down, the ideological agenda has been to transform Victoria's education system into a market-based model of education. Educational services are to be defined in market terms; only products passing through the market are to have real value; schools are to be seen as commercial enterprises, to be run on a business footing and pitted against one another in winning market share.

This paper seeks to identify and detail the ideological agenda of the coalition government as it forces change on to what was a reasonably functioning and well-regarded system. The paper focuses initially on the emergence of Radical Right thinking in Australia since the late 1970s, for it is in this particular development that we can discern a very different policy prescription for state education from what had been so far applied.

Against this backdrop, the paper explores the evolution of the Victorian Liberal Party's education policy throughout the 1980s and early 1990s. This history is instructive for it shows how the education policy—in a series of subtle but important ways—underwent a radicalisation to the extent that it came to mirror, by the early 1990s, a Radical Right agenda for change.

Indeed, by the time the coalition government came to power in 1992, it is possible to discern a substantial confluence on educational policy between the Liberal Party and the thinking of right wing think tanks in the United States, the United Kingdom and those in Victoria such as the Institute of Public Affairs and the Tasman Institute. This harmony of ideology and policy direction was further demonstrated and affirmed by the Kennett government's Commission of Audit which reported in 1993.

The coalition's market experiment with Victoria's state education system is now in place. A Schools of the Future framework for state education is steadily being implemented. Competition, efficiency and autonomy are now being set as the cornerstones of the system. 'Self-managing' schools and 'global budgeting' have been ushered in at the same time as the education sector has experienced great expenditure cuts and dislocation. The first attempt at statewide assessment (the Learning Assessment Project) has been introduced. After eighteen months or so, it is now possible to identify some of the major impacts of this two-pronged approach to education in Victoria. Indeed, some of these impacts take the form of reversals—in class sizes and student retention rates in particular. It is also possible, especially in view of overseas experience, to identify the crucial shortcomings of a 'market determined' model of state education.

ASSAULT AND CAPTURE: THE RADICAL RIGHT'S PRESCRIPTION FOR PUBLIC EDUCATION

As we illustrated in the first *Bulletin* of the Victoria Foundation (Crooks & Webber 1993), the late 1970s saw the emergence of an aggressive neo-classical economics in Australia and other countries in the developed world. It came to be reflected in Australia by a more public doctrine of 'economic rationalism'.

The emergence of 'economic rationalism' in Australia

The public embodiment of this neo-classical economics, or economic rationalism, lies in the belief that the free market is the best way to transact any activity. Open competition in a free market generates the greatest efficiency, it is claimed. The role of government is limited to creating and protecting free markets. Undue government activity, especially of a sort which creates 'distortions' and 'inefficiencies', is not welcome.

The economic rationalist agenda in Australia in the late 1970s and 1980s revolved around a series of interrelated beliefs and policy objectives. These objectives included the complete dismantling of tariff barriers; the deregulation of financial and labour markets; the reduction of trade union power; the privatisation of state-owned enterprises; a reduction in the size of government and minimisation of government outlays; lower and less progressive taxation; and the meeting of welfare costs by the user-pays principle.

The development of this economic rationalist ideology occurred through a number of strategically important avenues of power and influence—key Commonwealth ministries (Treasury, Finance and Trade); the major political parties; the leadership of several major corporations; academic economic commentators in the mainstream print media; and a clutch of right wing think tanks around the country, including the Institute of Public Affairs, based in Victoria.

Indeed, in large part the neo-conservative upsurge lay in the development of these right wing think tanks in Anglo-Saxon economies. As Carey (1987: 12) points out, these think tanks of the right were well resourced. They had at their disposal millions of dollars with which to fight, and win, the battle of ideas—money solicited largely from powerful and influential corporate backers keen to see their corporate interests defended.

Carey (1987: 13) instances the recent history of the Heritage Foundation in the United States as evidence of this strength:

> The Heritage Foundation, established in 1973, coordinates a 'resource bank' of 'a thousand academics and several hundred other policy research groups'. In 1985 its budget was $11 million ... Moreover, 'at least twenty-five other noteworthy public-policy groups,' *Atlantic*

Monthly reports, 'have been formed or dramatically expanded [since 1975]; nearly all are anti-liberal'.

It is a mistake, argues Manne (1992: 30) to underestimate the role played in our public life of the 1980s by these think tanks: 'Most citizens are at a loss when it comes to economics ... Economic rationalism, in Australia as elsewhere in the Anglo-Saxon world, was sucked into (an) ideological vacuum'.

The Radical Right recasting of public education

The Radical Right's assault on education is premised on the system being in 'crisis'. Public education is presented as suffering a dreadful malaise, a system in decline which enjoys less and less community confidence. Alarms are raised about educational standards. The Radical Right then recasts public education. It replaces the notion of 'public good', 'universalism' and 'access' with a lexicon embracing competition, efficiency, autonomy and entrepreneurialism.

Applied to such areas as education, the Radical Right holds that state provision of merit goods is destined to be inefficient. It is not surprising then, that the central conclusion drawn by the Institute of Public affairs (1992: 17) in its assessment of Victoria's education system was that:

> There is scope to achieve substantial improvement in the efficiency with which (educational) services are delivered without reducing the quality of education ... Furthermore, the ... unnecessarily high expenditure in education is ... the illegitimate outcome of pressure group tactics in 'capturing' the bureaucracy and budget process.

The Radical Right argues that while some government funding is necessary, this does not mean that government needs to deliver the educational services. The separation of funding and delivery of government services is justified on a number of grounds (Moore 1994):

- •the establishment of a competitive framework is likely to maximise efficiency and quality
- •there is less risk of 'capture' by special interest groups
- •there is less risk of political intervention in political administration.

The ideological attraction of a free market model sees educational services, therefore, defined in market terms, as a commodity no different from others traded in the marketplace. Only products passing through the market have real value; schools are seen as commercial enterprises, to be pitted against one another in winning market shares. Through this process of market production and exchange, students (the 'customers') and parents (the 'purchaser' of the services) seek customer satisfaction. All parents, it seems, have the same capacity to fund increased school costs; all can find the 'best' school for their children.

In Australia a premeditated assault on state education took place. This was highlighted in an interview published in the *Sydney Morning Herald* in 1985 in which Hugh Morgan—Western Mining Corporation's managing director and a leading New Right figure—outlined a political strategy:

> The main objective was to capture the public policy agenda ... What Morgan wanted to see on the agenda was four issues: the size and role of the public sector, the power of unions, industrial deregulation, and the education system. (Marginson 1993b: 5)

The arguments about public education were advanced by the think tanks from the mid 1980s onwards. The degree of consonance from country to country is considerable, reflecting an explicit and aggressively promoted internationalised ideology.

A spread of countries

In essence, the Radical Right arguments revolved around a constellation of fundamental ideas which, although allowing for some differences in emphasis and coverage, spread with a remarkable similarity across such Anglo-Saxon economies as the United States, the United Kingdom, New Zealand and Australia. These key beliefs, on this international scale, are nicely illustrated in the following excerpts:

1. Schools should be 'subject centred' and not 'child centred' wherein the basics are firmly established and educational energies are not directed at ideologically dubious pursuits such as 'peace studies'.

> I've seen an explosion of programmes packed with suppressiones veri and suggestiones falsi, presupposing legitimately controversial conclusions as their forgone conclusions. (Flew1991: 21)

> Two slogans ... of educationists in recent years, ... continue to distract teachers: the slogans of 'relevance' and 'multiculturalism'. Too often the pleas for 'relevance' ask us to measure the value of a subject by the current perceptions of those who have yet to understand it. 'Life Skills' or 'Peace Studies' may look fascinating to the child who comes to them for the first time, and who experiences the thrill of lessons entirely adapted to his own emotional repertoire. (The Hillgate Group 1986)

2. There is little incentive to improve education as long as there is a 'monopoly provision' of public schools, which is also buttressed by special interest groups (such as teacher unions).

> The current near monopoly of the public schools, buttressed by the power of the teachers' unions, provides little incentive within the education establishment of ways to improve education. Education must be opened to competition through a system of tuition tax credits and

vouchers ... The success of such programs, which would have to meet the exacting demands of parents, would spur other programs to emulation and would drive out those that are ineffective. (Gardner 1985)

The state educational system as we know it is not only a monopoly provider: it is dominated by the powerful bureaucratic interest groups entrenched in certain teacher unions, in Local Education Authorities and in the Department of Education and Science. These groups ... will provide the major obstacle to any reform ... It is therefore necessary to have a clear grasp of fundamental principles, and to be prepared to defend merit, standards and achievement against those who promote mediocrity in the name of 'social justice'. (The Hillgate Group 1987)

3. That the education system would benefit immensely from being opened up to competitive pressures. Parents should be able to choose the schooling for their children, as they choose any other consumer product.

Genuine competition will of course be painful at first, for those whose incompetence will be revealed by it. But good teachers will soon be sensible of the rewards, and in time their pay and conditions will be so transformed as to enable them to enjoy once again that professional and social status which is theirs by right ... As the bureaucracies dwindle, so will the money available to spend in schools increase. And as school expenditure increases, so will teachers begin to enjoy their new-found responsibilities. (The Hillgate Group 1987)

The important feature ... is that it is the parents who decide, through their patronage, how much money a school should receive ... Moreover, all who receive the benefits of state education will have a 'right of exit'— either to other state schools or to private schools—which will be something more than a merely nominal freedom. The beneficial effect of this on state education is obvious: schools will have to work in order to stay in business, and the worse their results, the more likely they will be to go to the wall. (The Hillgate Group 1986)

4. It does not automatically follow that the state should provide the education, least of all to manage the schools; autonomy for schools is crucial to the quality of school organisation and educational outcomes.

Even if one accepts the need for compulsory education, and the convenience of universally 'free' education—that is, taxation-funded schooling for all—it does not follow that the state has to provide the education, least of all to manage the schools. State-funded education need not be state-run education.

The mistake our forebears made was to assume that if there were to be universal, 'free', compulsory schooling, then the government had to provide the schools ... There is no reason to suppose that governments are better at running schools than the private sector. (Sexton 1990) *Stuart Sexton wrote this paper in his capacity as Director of the Education Unit of the right wing Institute of Economic Affairs in London.*

Except under special conditions, we believe the existing institutions of democratic control are simply inconsistent with the autonomous operation and effective organisation of schools. Bureaucracy is unambiguously bad for school organisation. But bureaucracy is not the most fundamental impediment to more effective schools. That distinction belongs to direct democratic control. (Chubb and Moe 1990)

The comparative failure of the government school system thus derives importantly from the lack of management autonomy at the level of individual schools. School principals have far too little power and responsibility for the services they are supposed to deliver. (Institute of Public Affairs 1992)

5. There needs to be a winding back of the education bureaucracy and in particular, a stop to the control exercised by special interest groups.

An ominous offshoot of this increased centralisation has been the use of the federal bureaucracy as a base from which powerful and unaccountable special interest groups have operated. The loss of local control of schools to those groups has eroded the flexibility needed to respond to local situations. (Gardner 1985)

For the past ten years the education system has largely been run by unions and education bureaucrats (including ex-union activists) on the basis of negotiated industrial agreements which severely limit the capacity to make discretionary budget decisions and which have been negotiated on a basis that gives educational and/or budgetary objectives a lower priority than union objectives. (Institute of Public Affairs 1992)

The major problem facing the funding of Victorian school education is long term, excessive influence by teacher unions over government decision-making. Such capture of the education system ... has led to far more generous student teacher ratios in Victoria than in the rest of Australia. (Victorian Commission of Audit 1993: 27)

The Radical Right thrust into public education has enjoyed a strong measure of success in the United Kingdom, the United States, New Zealand and now in Australia. In a carefully crafted attack, public education debate has been recast to reflect the Radical Right's preoccupation with efficiency, competition and autonomy. The Victorian coalition government in its approach to state education provides one of the clearest demonstrations of this ideology at work. Yet this particular emphasis of the coalition in its education policy is relatively recent, a feature explored in the following section.

THE RADICALISATION OF THE VICTORIAN COALITION'S EDUCATION POLICY

In the decade or so prior to their electoral win in 1992, the Victorian coalition's education policy was documented at five key points—a White Paper in 1980, an Education Policy (1982), *A New Liberal Policy for Primary and Secondary Education* (1984), *Raising Standards: Education and Training Policy* (1988) and, finally, *Education: Giving Students a Chance* (1992). Careful reading shows a subtle but important shift in this education policy.

The early 1980s—advocacy of a humanised system

The White Paper of 1980 was a major treatment of the then Liberal government's policy on state education and it was to serve as the principal reference point in further policy development in the early 1980s. It advocated reorganisation of the system, a devolution of authority and an enlarged role for regions of schools. It also argued for a devolved system of decision making in a clear and single administrative system as a replacement of what was perceived to be a cumbersome bureaucracy. It emphasised the need for responsiveness to local needs and aspirations, for consultation, participation and improved efficiency.

In the education policy document released in 1982 by the Hon. A. J. Hunt MLC, the Liberal Party noted the continued progress in every aspect of school education in Victoria:

> At every level, teacher–pupil ratios have improved and class sizes have declined. As a corollary, face to face teaching hours for teachers have declined substantially in secondary and technical schools, providing more time for preparation and correction of work and for individual attention to students.

> By world standards, our schools are extremely well staffed and teachers enjoy excellent conditions. Taken over all, the sum per child spent in Victorian State schools on teaching is greater than in any other Australian State.

> The professionalism and dedication of the vast bulk of our teachers is of the highest order, and the standards of curriculum relevance, development and presentation are second to none.

> Educational standards are progressively increasing and more young people today are better educated than ever before. Standards of literacy and numeracy of children at given levels in our schools are steadily improving.

Despite this progress, the 1982 policy document noted a significant concern. It referred to, but declined to specify, the vested interests in Victoria which had continually throughout the 1970s belittled each advance. The persistence of the attacks had, it claimed, damaged public confidence in state education and affected the morale of parents, principals and teachers. Our system, the policy document claimed, provided a 'damn good education, and there was a need for a united show of faith and confidence and support for the achievements of public education in Victoria' (page 3).

The further improvements to be sought revolved around the expansion of the building program, the provision of ancillary staff, recognition of the need for shared specialists for smaller primary schools, a review of allowances, and a new mechanism for participation and consultation designed to provide an effective voice in the decision-making process for all those interested in education.

There were further organisational developments set in train by the White Paper's advocacy of decentralised, devolved educational decision making. The offices of the minister and of the Director-General would be incorporated at Nauru House to provide for a streamlined administration. A widely representative Victorian education council and regional education councils for each of the 12 regions were seen as important mechanisms to improve community input into public education.

The establishment of an Institute of Education Administration at Geelong provided training in administrative skills. Managerial skills would also be provided by a number of staff places at the Administrative Staff College at Mt Eliza and particular stress would be placed on enabling women to attend these courses so that they might fill senior administrative positions (page 10).

Guidelines for core curriculum would be established by committees including teacher representatives, regional personnel, members of the community and education department professional staff. These guidelines would provide a policy framework in curriculum within which teachers would develop detailed programs for use in their schools (page 11).

The overall effect of the new administrative structure would be to 'humanise the whole system and make it more responsive and effective' (page 10).

The interests and commitments were addressed further in the Liberal Party's education policy of 1984 which was released by the then Leader of the Opposition, Mr Jeff Kennett. The basis of education policy, it claimed, lay in a high standard of physical, educational and environmental resources, the development of vocational skills and the qualities of good citizenship. Equal opportunity was essential along with the highest possible professional standards (page 6).

Six key areas were identified in the determination of policy for primary and secondary education:

•departmental structure—school, regional, central

•buildings and facilities

•staffing

•industrial relations

•equal opportunity and curriculum development

•freedom of choice in education and government assistance for non-government schools.

School councils would play a significant but not exclusive role in the determination of staffing patterns and in the development of general policies and facilities for the school (page 11).

A Liberal government would strengthen role of the principal. In terms of curriculum (within overall State guidelines), staff management, and matters of professional judgment within the school, the school principal would have the final decision. Where the principal and council are unable to agree on matters, the issue would be referred to the department for resolution (page 11).

The 1984 policy recognises that a free state education system does mean that all teaching and essential aids are the responsibility of the state. Parents and school communities, however, would be encouraged to raise school standards and increase learning opportunities through their own initiatives and resources wherever possible (page 12).

With respect to class size, the policy proposes a desirable objective for an overall class size limit of 25 pupils but a maximum class size or inflexible staffing formula would not be imposed. The policy would be to increase substantially the school retention rate and to provide adequate staff to cater for the increased school population level in the higher classes (page 16).

Increased funds would be made available for non-teaching staff in all schools. Individual school councils would have the maximum degree of freedom and discretion to determine the best use of their entitlement as between the various classes of ancillary staff available to them having regard to the special needs and special interests of the school (page 16).

The document notes that the most important ingredient for a successful education system is a good teacher and that the efforts of a good teacher are likely to be maximised in a friendly atmosphere and conducive environment where incentives are provided for promotion, service opportunities and a higher level of performance (page 17).

Industrial peace in Victorian schools was recognised as fundamental to the best interest of pupils. Goodwill, fairness and justice must be the basis of all agreements made with teacher organisations (page 17).

The 1984 policy document emphasises freedom of choice in education. Primarily, it interprets this by endorsing a dual system of schools in which parents have maximum choice between state and independent schools. It goes on, however, to assert that both government and non-government schools should be encouraged to be pacesetters in new initiatives and educational development. There should be diversity of educational choice at all schools. To facilitate this choice within the state system, the Liberal Party committed itself to progressively remove all zoning and embark on a program to develop 'cluster group' schools to meet the requirements of academically gifted children on a regional basis (page 29).

The late 1980s—a system in crisis

Four years later, in a policy document called *Raising Standards* (1988) the Liberal Party argued that our education system was in crisis. After six years of Labor, large sections of the government school system were allegedly in chaos. There was a loss of confidence in school standards and discipline. The Labor government was hamstrung by indecision and union influence (page 1).

Under a Liberal government, the education system would, among other things, aim to foster diversity and choice within Victoria's education system; and would encourage and reward teachers' commitment and let them get on with the job (page 2).

There was key weaknesses, it says, in the school system. There was no guarantee that all schools were giving adequate priority to teaching children the basics; there had been a proliferation of subjects, many of which were regarded as soft options, limiting students' prospects in further education, training and the work force; and there were no satisfactory mechanisms in place for determining educational standards. An effective system for assessing student achievement was lacking. The means of identifying children at risk and assisting them were undeveloped (page 3).

A Liberal government would make mastery of the basics the focus of school education by introducing programs ensuring literacy and numeracy for all, by establishing a priority curriculum and instituting statewide testing (page 4).

The Liberal government would devolve effective power to schools. It would extend the concept of school based selection of principals to advanced teachers and senior teachers (page 11).

School councils representing the local community would be responsible for framing school educational policies within statewide guidelines and goals. Their role would be primarily strategic rather than operational. Councils would be accountable to the minister, and be responsible for:

- determining the broad curriculum objectives of the school

- developing a discipline code

- setting an appropriate dress code for the school

- monitoring school budgets and their management

- controlling buildings and grounds where community use is involved

- general development of school grounds and buildings, including the ability to carry out capital works with ministry assistance where appropriate

- furnishing and servicing of buildings

- ensuring that government/ministry policy is observed on all matters pertaining to education, safety and health of students.

Councils must genuinely reflect the broad community interest. Department of Education employees should constitute no more than 40 per cent of the membership of school councils. Adequate provision should be made to coopt interested parties from the wider community, including representatives of employer groups and trade unions.

Principals are seen as a key to a school's success. The Liberal government would give principals the central role in the education system that their educational leadership demands.

The school principal would be accountable to the Minister of Education, and be established by statute as the school council's chief adviser. Subject to the council's general policies and the ministry's directions, the principal would manage the affairs of the school. While industrial agreements with the teacher unions would be maintained, the fetters on principals performing their proper role would be removed. The agreements would be confined to matters affecting terms and conditions of employment.

In managing the affairs of the school, the principals would be expected to consult and involve the school's staff and be responsible for:

•managing and deploying teaching and ancillary staff

•employing non-teaching staff

•chairing the advanced teacher and senior teacher selection committees

•staff development and the introduction of an annual inschool system of feedback to teachers on their performance

•assigning higher duties allowances subject to ministry guidelines

•determining, together with the education ministry's regional office, the assistance that the educational support centres will provide

•student management and welfare services

•curriculum development and delivery

•discretionary funds of significant size.

The 1988 policy document also emphasised the need for greater choice and opportunity. The school system, it says, must provide for a diverse population of students with differing needs and desires. Some of these arise out of curriculum requirements, some out of location and some out of particular abilities or disabilities. It argued that the Labor government's policies of shutting schools and forcing schools into similar moulds, combined with restrictions on school enrolments, had reduced opportunities for students.

The Liberal government would encourage diversity and choice so that schools would be free to develop their own specialties and students would be able to attend the school that most suits their needs and aspirations.

This would be achieved by:

•ending Labor's policy of closing schools because of financial considerations despite the school's educational viability

•supporting schools in developing their own specialties—such as sports, music, academic studies or practical or technical subjects

•supporting single sex schools where they are viable and desired

•ending zoning restrictions

•encouraging school councils to publicise their school policies and the qualities their schools offer (page 13).

1992—Diversity and choice as the hallmarks

The 1992 policy of the Liberal Party took the themes in the 1988 document several steps further. It argued that the Labor government had attempted to use the education system, and in particular curriculum, to further its political objectives. Too much emphasis had been placed on teaching students process at the expense of knowledge. Instead, students were to be encouraged to develop a critical understanding and appreciation of our society's cultural heritage; and emphasis would be placed also on the development of literacy and numeracy skills and the learning of basic science concepts. The policy committed the coalition to empowering the community by:

- encouraging parents and students to choose the school that best meets their needs
- ensuring that all schools teach students to a high standard of literacy and numeracy
- having school communities manage resources provided directly to them—not consumed by a central bureaucracy
- letting school communities select their own staff so that teachers will become true professionals
- requiring school councils to establish a 'school charter' that sets out the educational aims of the school and provides accountability to parents.

Diversity and choice would become the cornerstones of education in Victoria. There would be more opportunity to offer the type of educational program that best meets the needs of each individual student. A Liberal–National coalition would reward excellent teachers, that is, recognise higher skills and quality teaching with higher remuneration; schools would be able to appoint business managers and support staff, leaving teachers to concentrate on teaching and educational activities.

School councils would establish a school charter, monitor and evaluate the performance of the school; determine curriculum objectives; approve school budgets; have the major role in selecting the school principal; establish a code of conduct and dress code; and control the development and service of school buildings and grounds.

In the early 1980s the Liberals spoke of the benefits of small class sizes, of participation and consultation, of equal opportunity and integration of children with special needs; of simplifying the administrative system; of providing incentives to teachers for promotion, service opportunities and a higher level of performance. By 1992, however, the Liberal Party policy emphasis was on such things as parental and student choice in selecting the school that best met their needs; letting school communities select their own staff; appointing business managers; increasing the power of principals in their managerial capacity; and increasing the responsibility of school councils for framing the educational policies of the school, within broad guidelines.

Through much of the 1980s, the education policy prescription of the Liberal Party reflected a set of interests and concerns which sit comfortably with a liberal/conservative philosophy. By the time the coalition parties came to power in 1992, however, their education policy had taken on a number of subtle but significant policy shifts. Competition, autonomy, choice and efficiency were central values. Consumer sovereignty was a guiding principle. There was a concern over standards; the system was perceived to be in crisis. In effect, the coalition parties had adopted the rhetoric of the Radical Right. It remained to be seen whether their rhetoric would be matched by action.

SCHOOLS OF THE FUTURE

A market experiment is now undrway in countries such as England and New Zealand. The innocuously titled approaches (e.g. *Tomorrow's Schools* in New Zealand, *Better Schools* and *Choice and Diversity* in Britain) embrace the essence of the Radical Right position on public education. Victoria's Schools of the Future is no exception. The main features of the experiment are now outlined.

The experiment in outline

In January 1993, just four months after the Coalition came to power, the Directorate of School Education released its framework for state education. Entitled *Schools of the Future,* this preliminary paper outlined the essentials of the proposed new system and schools were given until 19 March 1993 to decide whether they wished to participate in a pilot program.

The preliminary paper was seen as 'the first stage of a process to help schools determine their own futures as we move towards the 21st century'. In a preface, the minister outlined the challenge as he saw it:

> Quality education is all about people—students, teachers and the principals who lead them, not the vested interest groups to whom 'the system' was captive for so long ... The Schools of the Future concept has no intrinsic value in itself. It is solely a means of helping to build that team in and around a school, so as to constantly improve the quality of the education available to each student in that school.
>
> The future is for you and your students, if you have the will to grasp it. (Department of Education 1993)

The mission of the Schools of the Future program was identified as giving students access to a high quality education which will maximise their potential for the future. The program's objectives were four-fold:

1. to encourage continuing improvement in the quality of educational programs and practices in Victorian schools so as to enhance student learning outcomes

2. to actively foster the attributes of good schools in terms of leadership, school ethos, goals, planning and accountability process

3. to build on a statewide framework of quality curriculum, programs and practices, and

4. to commence immediately a pilot program to develop administrative arrangements and determine the phased implementation of the Schools of the Future concept over the next three years.

A high quality education will only be achieved, the paper argued, if schools are able to build a team of teachers who are committed to quality teaching in the classroom and to helping each student maximise his or her potential.

The best circumstances in which to build such a team are those where a school has control over its operations and future. This is the underlying purpose of the Schools of the Future concept, wherein:

- parents would be able to directly participate in decisions that affect their child's education

- teachers would be recognised as truly professional, able to determine their own careers and future and with the freedom to exercise their professional skills and judgment in the classroom

- principals would become true leaders in their school with the ability to build and lead their teaching teams

- communities, through the school charter, would be able to determine the future destiny of the school, its character and ethos

- within guidelines, schools would be able to develop their own curriculum programs to meet the individual needs of students and

- schools would be accountable to the community for the progress of the school and the achievements of its students. (Department of Education 1993: 3)

School curriculum

Within a broad curriculum and standards framework established by the Board of Studies, Schools of the Future would be able to develop their own distinctive programs to take account of the particular aspirations of their communities, the interests of their students and the talents of their teachers.

Each school is considered to be unique and is best placed to make decisions about teaching and learning programs and what is needed to support them. It is envisaged there will be different approaches to learning and teaching and these approaches would continue to change in response to new knowledge about learning and teaching and advances in technology.

Such programs may shape a distinctive school profile within the wider community. Indeed, it is envisaged that some Schools of the Future would become centres for particular fields of learning, for example, science, languages and music.

The organisation of work for teachers and students should reflect these advances, and not be constrained by outdated and restrictive assumptions related to standard class sizes, types of groupings, building spaces and rigid timetables. Such restrictive assumptions have limited teachers' freedom to explore options for better quality outcomes for their students for too long.

It would provide a framework for the allocation of resources within the school and would be the starting point in the regular review process. It was intended to be an enabling rather than a constraints document.

Code of conduct

School councils of Schools of the Future would be required to develop and approve a code of conduct as part of their school charger. The code of conduct would set out not only the behaviour expected of students, but sanctions in dealing with disruptive behaviour.

School councils

All of the powers currently held by school councils would continue in arrangements for Schools of the Future, notably in their authority to determine the educational policies of the school within guidelines. These powers would be extended to include those related to the employment of non-teaching staff and the contracted services of teachers for particular projects. (Department of Education 1993: 4)

Parents and other members of the school community would play a more significant role in decision making in Schools of the Future. The principal would be a voting member of the council. The principal would be the executive officer of the council and, as well as providing professional advice to the council, would be responsible to the council for implementing the decisions of the council.

The chairperson of the school council would not be an employee of the Directorate of School Education.

It is intended that the school councils of Schools of the Future would normally have from six to twelve members, with employees of the Directorate of School Education having no more than one-third of the membership. There would be provision for the council to coopt members of the community with special expertise. (Department of Education 1993: 9)

Principals

In Schools of the Future the principal's role as an educational leader would continue to be strengthened. Principals, as leaders of their teams, would consult and seek advice from members of the team on a range of issues from time to time.

As an officer of the Directorate of School Education, the principal (or head teacher) is responsible to the Director of School Education who is responsible to the minister for the provision of quality public education. The principal as executive officer of the school council is responsible to the council for implementing the policies made in accordance with the school charter. (Department of Education 1993: 9)

Financial management

Each School of the Future is to receive a budget fairly determined from a formula. The aim is for each School of the Future to have complete control over its financial resources and to have the capacity to plan how these resources will be used across the full range of staff, services, equipment and supplies.

Resources will be allocated to Schools of the Future according to an equitable formula based on their profile of student learning needs and other factors which cause one school to differ from another. In this way (subject to the obvious limitations of available places) students and parents who opt for programs at a particular school can be assured that the school of their choice would be adequately funded. In turn, schools would be encouraged to offer quality, diversity and choice in their programs.

A variety of factors would determine the size of the school grant. The largest portion of the grant will be based on relative costs of providing different kinds of educational programs. There will be a basic cost for a student in a regular program that does not require special needs' resources. Funding will increase where students require programs that are designed to meet learning disadvantage or major learning or physical disability. (Department of Education 1993: 12)

Salaries would continue to be paid centrally except for staff contracted to meet particular short term needs. The total costs of all staff will be a notional charge against the school's budget. An important aim of the pilot program would be to trial models and systems for effective and flexible management of available funds.

Schools would be supported by business managers or through access to business management services, to ensure that principals and teachers would be able to focus their energies on the teaching and learning programs of the school. Small schools or small schools in the same geographic location may share such services.

All school-generated funds may be used for appropriate purposes consistent with the school charter. They would be audited annually, a statement of which will be included in the school's annual report.

Schools may seek sponsorship and community support for purposes consistent with the school charter. (Department of Education 1993: 13)

Accountability and school review

An increase in authority and responsibility in a School of the Future requires an increase in accountability to the students, staff, parents, the local community, government and the wider Victorian community for the resources of the school as well as for educational standards. (Department of Education 1993: 5)

An accountability framework would be developed by the Schools Review Office having regard to the student assessment policies and procedures approved by the Board of Studies. This framework, together with the educational and financial performance reports prepared by schools, would form the basis for system-wide reports dealing with the effectiveness of schools, the quality of education programs, student learning outcomes, and the efficient and effective use of resources.

Schools of the Future would be expected to use their results, together with other information and data on the outcomes of their programs (gained from internal assessments or from sources such as reports to external funding bodies or projects conducted by the school), to report to their school communities on their school's performance against the objectives contained in their school charter. Measures of achievement would be based on the use of profiles and other approved assessment tasks as determined by the Board of Studies.

There would be provision within the school review process to survey teacher, student and parent views of the quality of service and teaching and learning conditions at a given school.

The findings of such satisfaction-level surveys would be available to the individual school and, on a consolidated basis, to the Directorate of School Education. (Department of Education 1993: 17)

People

When the Schools of the Future program is fully operational, all selection of staff would occur at the school level. However, teachers would continue to be employed by the Directorate of School Education. They would not be employed by their school councils.

Schools would have the capacity to select and employ teaching and non-teaching staff for particular projects or to meet other short-term needs. These people would be contracted to the school councils, according to policies and procedures for such arrangements.

Initial and ongoing training and professional development will be required for principals, staff and council members. Principals will receive high-level training in leadership and management.

Resource management

Major capital works and some aspects of maintenance for Schools of the Future would continue to be part of the central budget.

The school council of a School of the Future may contract educational support and other services from the public or private sectors. Additional to its current authorities for the acquisition and disposal of physical resources, the council of a School of the Future may make arrangements for a wide range of capital works and maintenance matters, the community use of buildings and equipment and the use of student support, educational and advisory and management services, subject to the policies of the Directorate of School Education and the policies and procedures approved by the school council.

Remote schools

The special needs of remote Schools of the Future would be recognised in the schools grant. Small schools would be encouraged to join clusters to share administrative and technological support.

Support for Schools of the Future

The budget of schools would be sufficient to cover the cost of obtaining highly skilled curriculum and support services. In the short term it is envisaged that school support centres would continue to offer such services. Over time, however, it is likely that a range of sources would be available, including support centres, school-based support centres offering services to other schools, access services offered by the private sector, and services offered by educational institutions in the tertiary or TAFE sectors.

Directorate administration

The central office of the system would be progressively reduced in the years ahead so that it becomes a strategic core. Functions to be performed would be largely restricted to matters related to the framework of policies, priorities and accountability, including the expert determination of equitable resource allocations to schools, and some personnel functions; the planning of major capital works and maintenance that cannot be controlled or predicted at the school level; school review; and policy guidelines and implementation procedures for Board of Studies accredited courses. Regional offices would be scaled down as the capacity for self management is taken up at the school level.

Competition, efficiency and autonomy enshrined

A revealing account of the 'new public sector culture' at work is given in the Department of Education corporate and business plans for 1994–96, copies of which were leaked to the public in the latter half of 1994. The Corporate Plan, for instance, argues that deregulation of the education and training system in Victoria will lead to new approaches to the design and delivery of education and training, especially through the private sector:

> The autonomy of education and training institutions will encourage their market orientation and lead to a competitive system which offers high quality provision through enterprising arrangement and programs. (Department of Education 1994c: 2)

Quality education and training is underpinned, says the Corporate Plan, by a combination of factors—excellent teaching staff, exemplary curriculum, high standard of facilities, intersectoral links, research, and by competitive institutions:

> Competition between providers is conducive to the provision of better, more effective and efficient education and training services which offer greater choice and opportunity. It will be developed by encouraging strong, independent leadership, best management practice and evaluation. (Department of Education 1994c: 12).

The 'market determinism' ethos which has taken a hold on the managers of the state's education system is further evidenced by the emphasis on key policy principles including the empowering of 'consumers' (i.e. parents/children); a 'preference for market mechanisms'; the creation and maintenance of a 'devolved, open, competitive, quality education environment'; and the 'minimising of government bureaucracy'. (Department of Education 1994c: 10)

Against this background, with notions of competition, efficiency and autonomy firmly established as the new motive forces, it is not surprising to consider what the Department of Education identified as achievements in its presentation to the Budget Expenditure Review Committee of 18 July 1994. In an overview of the department, it said it has:

- implemented major changes in policy and service delivery, e.g.
  Schools of the Future
  college-based employment
  market driven arrangements for delivery of vocational education and training services
  rationalisation of schools
  registration of private providers
  dual recognition programs in schools and TAFE

- satisfied all budget and staff reduction targets

- established an Integrated Performance Management Framework to link progressively corporate, business and agency planning with resource management and individual officer performance across the department.

These achievements, it notes, have been delivered in a difficult industrial relations environment and in the context of the largest budget and staff reduction program in the department's history.

With respect to **resource management** achievements for 1993/94, the department noted that:

- expenditure was $23.9 million under the recurrent appropriation of $2880.7 million

- asset sales totalled $103 million

- a major rationalisation of schools was completed with 226 school sites closed since October 1992

- a major outsourcing program had begun

- 290 Vocational Education and Training Private Providers were registered.

On the matter of **service delivery outcomes** notable achievements were listed as:

- reform of the VCE

- implementation of the Schools of the Future program (first intake was 317 schools)

- expanded open learning through the use of satellite technology

- the abolition of compulsory unionism in tertiary institutions

•the introduction of a new performance based career structure for
principals.

Some of the challenges were nominated—including federal industrial
legislation and federal awards; the development of sound output/outcome
measures and benchmarking; the complete outsourcing of major systems;
and the organisational capacity to deliver quality services in the face of projected increases in government school numbers, possible further downsizing
to absorb leave loading, restoration of productivity dividend and possible
capital change.

In its draft Business Plan, the Department of Education identified six
management imperatives to translate its strategic goals into programs or outcomes. One of these is listed (page 9) as the need to 'achieve' the department's
contribution to Victoria's debt management strategy and *the return to AAA
Credit Rating*.

Certainly it should be acknowledged that a major portfolio area of the
state's budget such as education has to compete in the allocation of finite
resources and that financial strategies in the different budget areas will reflect
overall government priorities. Nonetheless, it is notable that the management
of the state's education system—which provides for the education of approximately 80 per cent of Victorian children—should be linked directly to securing favourable verdicts from private sector financial market analysts whose
primary concern is with conditions of financial investment. What the link
may suggest, however, is that the level of expenditure cuts to education (the
greatest in the state's history), has been one way in which the Kennett coalition government has signalled to the ratings agencies its aggression and pre-
paredness to cut state expenditure massively (irrespective of any other public
policy consideration of medium to long-term economic and social costs to
the community).

In sum, the Schools of the Future model embodies the key assumptions of
the Radical Right about public education that we have described earlier.
Practically, the model is remarkably similar to the recent experiences of countries such as New Zealand where, in response to the Picot Report and
Tomorrow's Schools, self management has been affirmed, regulatory boards
abolished, the education bureaucracy reduced, one line budgets introduced
and boards of trustees appointed to oversee local schools.

THE EXPERIMENT TAKES EFFECT: MAJOR IMPACTS

Prior to the 1992 coalition win, Victoria's state education system was well
placed by a number of important and telling criteria. It enjoyed a leading reputation on curriculum matters; the quality and quantity of staffing was good;
student retention to year 12 (85% in 1992) was the highest in Australia; the
state also enjoyed the best teacher–pupil ratios in Australia, and had done so
for twenty years; expenditure on schools per head of population ranked fifth
of all systems in 1992/93; per capita expenditure on students in government
schools ranked fourth of all systems in 1990–95; educational governance

reflected a partnership involving parents, teachers, their representative organisations and those in the bureaucracy:

> Despite problems at the top, state schooling blossomed in the ten years of Labor. Schools became vital sites for learning and social relationships and there was a strong sense of democratic involvement, curriculum innovation and program diversity within and between schools. Although schools did not eradicate educational inequalities, they reduced the barriers to a quality schooling for female, working class, non-English speaking and Koori students. (Brennan 1992: 7)

This is not to suggest the system was seen to be in perfect shape. There has been criticism, for example, of the fact that the state's expenditure on education was cut in almost every budget in the decade preceding the Kennett coalition government (Kronemann 1993). With the advent of the coalition government came a series of dramatic changes to the state's education system. What so far have been the major impacts?

A system cut to the bone

To date, neither the Minister for Education nor his chief administrator have recognised any need to assess the impacts of the changes they have made to the education system:

> I am not interested in output indices. (Mr Don Hayward *The Age* 21 September 1994)

> I am not particularly interested in assessing the impact of the cuts. (Mr Geoff Spring *The Age* 21 September 1994)

It is as well that others, however, have been moved to make such an assessment. After all it makes sense for Victorians to understand what is happening to their children's education system.

In 1993/94, an education consultant, David McCrae, undertook a survey of government schools to assess the impact of funding cuts. The survey involved a sample of 148 schools and follow-up interviews with fifteen of the principals who responded. Questions were asked about staff and student numbers, changes to teaching programs and their organisation, changes to support services within and without the school, and opinion about the most positive and negative features of the impacts of the cuts. A high rate of response came from secondary and P-12 schools (86%); less so from primary schools (61.4%).

The key findings of the survey can be summarised as follows:

- School grants had increased across the board and as such, physical and financial resources were not identified as a problem.
- The largest cut had occurred in staff entitlements and salaries. If the

1993 staffing levels had been maintained, there would have been 50 more teachers working in the 43 primary schools sampled and 159 more teachers in the 60 secondary schools.

•Over 40 per cent of secondary schools reported a current shortage of staff for particular areas, such as LOTE, physical education, art/craft, and technology studies.

•Administrative support staff changes were minor, although it appeared that the scale of demands in terms of both skill levels and quantum of work had increased very substantially.

•Using comparative data from the Australian Education Council, Victoria was now worse than the national average on staff–student ratios.

•To manage the cuts in primary schools the majority of primary schools chose to increase their class sizes, cut teacher administration and planning time (APT) allowances, and reduce or delete specialist programs.

•Class sizes in primary schools had increased. The largest grade reported was 38. There were five cases reported of prep classes of thirty or larger.

•The tack taken in secondary schools to manage the impact of the cuts was more complex. Most schools seemed to have chosen different configurations of class size increases, teaching allotment increases, time allowance reductions, and program reductions.

•The most negative impact of the cuts was most commonly believed to be the loss of staff and consequent increase in class size.

•There was a widespread fear among principals that global budgeting was simply another means of cutting funds and forcing schools into additional local fund-raising procedures.

In commenting on these findings, McCrae concluded that if the goal of the 1993/94 cuts was to decrease government spending on public education, then it has been conspicuously successful. If the goal was to get teachers working harder, it has been successful through increased class sizes and allotments and reductions in time allowances. McCrae notes, however, that this is not to say teachers are working more effectively, that students are learning more or are happier in their studies, or that the reach of education into the whole student population is increasing. If the goal was, at the same time, to maintain the quality of education in government schools, it has not succeeded. The loss of quality in Victoria's government schools is now evident, he argues, by reference to four key criteria: the reduced capacity for schools to provide individual attention because of increased class sizes and increased staff loads; reductions in the provision of comprehensive programs; the elimination in many schools of specialist options especially in such areas as music, art/craft, LOTE, sport, remediation, library and computers; and low morale and workplace duress for the state's committed and caring teachers. McCrae's conclusion is that:

> No enterprise can ... expect to reduce its resource base by 20 per cent and maintain the same level of productivity, and especially not in education ... The data show that there has been a major reduction in the quality of education able to be provided by Victoria's government schools, directly due to the impact of the cuts but also to the quality and style of management employed. (McCrae 1994)

A year later and the outcomes identified by the McCrae survey have worsened. The overall picture for the past two years reveals expenditure cuts of more than $400 million; 300 school closures; over 8000 teachers removed from the system (approximately 20 per cent); the removal of several thousand support staff; a marked increase in class size and pupil–teacher ratios across the state; and a decline in student retention to year 12.

The statistical story
On several key dimensions, the statistical data alone convey the story of major impacts.

Education as a proportion of budget sector outlays — Over the last decade, education's share of budget outlays has declined. In 1981/82, for example, education comprised 31.2 per cent of budget outlays compared with 22.5 per cent in 1994/95. Total outlays have decreased substantially under the coalition government, from $14,627.2 million in 1992/93 to an estimated $13,886.8 million in 1994/95 (Figure 1)

Per capita expenditure — Victorian expenditure has been above average, compared to other Australian government school systems, but it has not been the highest.

The per capital expenditure on students has now fallen below the national benchmark of $4421. In 1992, Victoria spent $4791 per student but by 1994 this had fallen to $4345. The DSE estimates that recurrent expenditure per student will fall by about $500 per student from $4791 in 1992, to $4300 in 1996 (Figure 2).

Capital Expenditure — Capital expenditure is down, from $291.3m in 1991/92 to $193.6m in 1993/94.

Enrolments — According to the Directorate of School Education 1995 Census, enrolments continue to decline, with 7110 fewer students attending government schools than in 1994 (Figure 3).

Special needs teachers — In 1992, under the previous Labor government, there were approximately 2000 special needs teachers allocated, with a promise of an additional 400 for 1993. When the coalition was elected, this total was cut by 80 per cent, and numbers dropped to approximately 500 (*VSTA News*, 10 February 1994).

Class sizes — Average class sizes in Victoria's government schools are now higher than at any time since 1984. Nearly 62 per cent of primary classes now have more than 26 students.

Figure 1: Education's share of the Victorian Budget

Sources: Victorian Budget papers, various years, Composition of Budget *Sector Outlays;* Victorian Budget Paper No 2, 1994/95, *Budget Sector Outlays by Purpose, 1990/91 to 1994/95.* (Presented in Kronemann 1995)

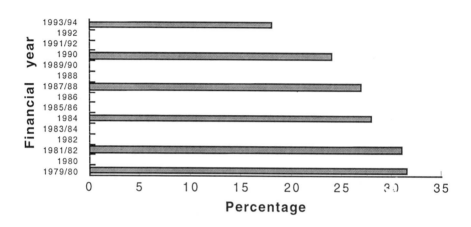

Figure 2: 1992/93 Expenditure on government schools per head of population

Source: Commonwealth Grants Commission, Report on General Revenue *Grant Relativities: 1994 Update.*

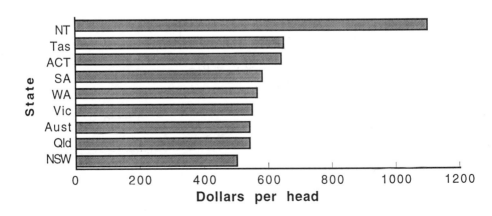

Figure 3: Enrolments in Victorian Government Schools February 1993 to 1995
Note: Total enrolments include special and language students.
Source: DSE, *Summary Statistics Victorian Schools*, February 1993; DSE, *Summary Statistics Victorian Schools*, February 1994 (presented in Kronemann 1995).

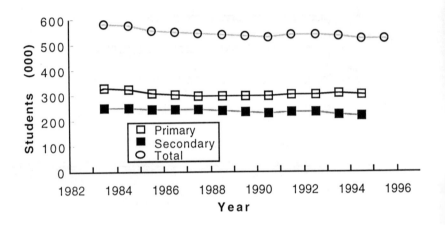

Figure 4: Victorian primary class sizes
Sources: EDV, *Compendium of Statistics*, various years; OSA, *MOET Facts and Figures about Victorian Schools*, various years; DSE, Facts and Figures about Victorian Schools, February 1993: 10, 22; DSE, *Summary Statistics Victorian Schools, School Education Victoria 1993—an overview*, 15, 18; DSE, *Summary Statistics Victorian Schools*, February 1994: 17 (presented in Kronemann 1995).

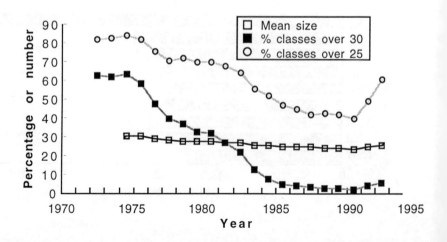

Figure 5: Victoria's retention rates
Sources: ABS cat no 4221.0 1993, *Schools Australia,* and earlier years; DSE, *Summary Statistics Victorian Schools,* February 1993 (presented in Kronemann 1995).

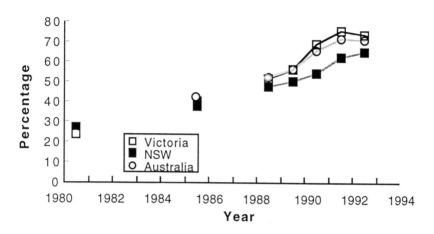

In 1992, student–teacher ratios in Victoria were 15.8 (primary) and 10.8 (secondary). In 1994, these ratios had increased to 18.7 (primary) and 12.3 (secondary), and are now above the national benchmark of 18.0 (primary) and 12.1 (secondary).

Student retention rate — Victoria's retention rates in 1981 were lower than those of NSW and lower than the Australian average.

Over the last decade, Victorian retention rates improved substantially and are now well above the Australian average, while NSW has fallen behind.

Within Victoria, February 1991 government school retention rates exceeded those in Catholic schools for the first time.

Since the Coalition parties won office in 1992 and executed their radical changes to the public education system, there has been a continuing downward spiral in retention rates, falling from 84.6 per cent in 1992 to 70. 6 per cent in 1995 (McMurdo, 1995:6). (Figure 5).

These statistics tell a revealing story. Victoria's state education system is now undergoing a dramatic winding back—not only in terms of expenditure, staffing and the number of schools but with respect also to class sizes and student retention rates. This is not, however, the full extent of the major impacts. The coalition's prescription for state education is now giving rise to deeper seated stresses and tensions in the system.

Emerging tensions in the system

By several key criteria, Victoria's state education system, in the throes of a market experiment, appears to be at risk. The expenditure cuts of the last two years have been of an unprecedented order; teaching levels have been gutted; class sizes are steadily on the increase; specialist options are a luxury item; the removal of over 4000 special needs teachers has hit regions of educational disadvantage; and morale is a problem. It is not only educationalists who express anxiety about the coalition's changes to the state education system:

> Sadly, not all governments are taking such a far sighted stance. In Victoria for example, we have seen a virtual decimation of the education system to the point where teachers and schools are stretched to the limit.
>
> The state government's practice of excluding interested parties, divide and rule can only lead to chaos. Vital support has gone from a number of areas for no other reason, in some cases, than political expediency. As a result, programs such as those offered by the Education Foundation and industry are having to help fill the large gaps left in the system, rather than enhancing and extending programs which should rightfully be funded by the state. (Ron McGimpsey, Managing Director, BP Australia Limited, Speech to Education Foundation Awards Ceremony, 21 June 1994)

But is the system overly stressed? After all, it may be that the program of the Kennett government is more complex in its impacts and that there are positive aspects of the changes that occurred. In this regard, it is helpful to consider a number of these changes in closer operational detail.

One of the major organisational changes of the DSE has been the closure of school support centres. Previously, these had operated on a regional level and housed a number of support services for schools such as speech therapy. With these centres gone, school principals now have to contend with the issue of replacement services. What has happened is that such services are provided at a district level, organised through district liaison principals. In this way, the service is still close to schools and convenient for students and teachers. Resources are still provided by the DSE. The district scale of activity makes sense and seems to enjoy the support of school personnel. Significantly, however, schools have had to take up the extra workload involved without any additional administrative support.

On another practical level, it seems clear that the power now vested with schools to handle physical maintenance can work to the school's advantage. Instead of relying on a cumbersome approach of the previous Public Works Department, schools can now decide what needs doing, which (local) contractor can do it and in accordance with the school's own time lines. This flexibility is already evidenced in the obvious physical improvements to the appearance of many of our schools. But is also worth noting that the decisions on physical works may well be driven by a belief that parents will choose schools on the basis of appearance rather than educational quality.

It seems, for example, that the 'Two for One—Administrative Upgrade Grants' have this improved appearance strategically in mind. With the closure of schools and subsequent sale of sites, the DSE upgrade grants are aimed at improving administrative areas, office reception areas and conditions for non-teaching staff. These areas are, of course, also the first point of contact (or point of 'sale') with inquiring parents and other members of the public. So while the system generally loses one-fifth of its teaching staff, many schools have taken up the grant offer to improve the school facade.

The question of curriculum services sheds more light on an emerging tension in the relationship between resources and service delivery. Previously supplied by the support centres, these services are now organised through the district model, with one consultant per district. Key Learning Area Networks are being set up, which district liaison principals are expected to encourage and support. Again, this change makes sense. There is a lot to be said for sharing professional, intellectual resources at a district level. But the flip side is that time release for the staff to attend such meetings (other than recently delineated district curriculum leaders) no longer exists and systemwide encouragement has gone. Teachers involved in the Learning Area Network, especially those who undertake a chairing role, can expect to do most of the organisation work, meet after school, and increase their workload considerably. With no money for replacement teaching staff, curriculum development becomes a voluntary commitment and part of an increased workload for school staff. Overall, the impetus for engaging in curriculum debate and development now lies squarely with the individual school—and curriculum development becomes one of the school's competing priorities. Potentially, such a curriculum model paves the way for schools to 'product differentiate' in much the same way as a company seeks to create and maintain market share for its products. The importance and commitment accorded by schools to curriculum development may help them to determine a 'niche market' with respect to the type of educational service they put on offer. For schools struggling with large classes, educational disadvantage and special needs among its students, as well as an overtaxed staff, the capacity to take a proactive role in curriculum development may be difficult.

The recurring theme is that the expenditure cuts to the education system militate against effective implementation of these organisational changes, however meritorious they might be. Schools are struggling to survive under the burden of large classes, increased workloads and inadequate resources. Instead of assisting school-based decision making and delivery of education locally, the DSE appears to have taken away from schools all the things that would help local delivery.

In effect, the state now provides a base level of funding but beyond this, schools are expected to deliver education in their areas with this amount, plus what funds they can raise locally. As a result, parents are now directly experiencing the pressure of government policy changes in a number of ways:

> The areas outside some of the ... classrooms are catchment areas for litter, dust and leaves. These areas are not the responsibility of the contract cleaners.
>
> If you could find some time to do some sweeping on a fairly regular basis (perhaps while waiting for children after school) could you please let me know. I'll supply the broom! (Inner urban primary school *Newsletter* 1995)

Hardly a week goes by without a further call to fundraising arms, a reminder of a working bee toward a major fundraising event or the need to return order forms for goods from which the school can siphon off a slim percentage:

> Our school community slogged for six months for a washed out fete on Saturday that raised $2500 towards much needed maintenance at the school. Meanwhile the Government that keeps shrinking our school's global budget spent $10,000 on a state reception for the Rolling Stones. Mr. Kennett, your priorities are obscene. (*Access Age,* 31 March 1995)

In short, whereas fundraising activity in the past was a way of putting some icing on the school cake, it is now the means to which schools are forced to resort in order to simply shore up their basic financial position. The entrepreneurial imagination now needed to be displayed by parents and school staff in soliciting local monies is now a clear manifestation as to how market principles have been embraced as the modus operandi for Victorian state education.

Riding with the rhetoric of 'self-managing schools' and in the face of inadequate resources, the DSE can, of course, adroitly adopt the old motto 'all care, no responsibility', for if schools now fail to deliver quality education, the fault is theirs alone.

This tension between the local 'devolved' school and the 'centre' is evident in other ways. On the one hand, the DSE speaks of partnership and the need to work as a team. Schools are to develop a charter which can be negotiated with the DSE and from which comes a guarantee of funding for the next three years. On the other, however, the DSE has imposed a Curriculum Standards Framework which specifies components such as two hours of physical education, two hours of sport and a language other than English (LOTE) which must be taught in all schools but leaves the schools to decide what has to be dropped in order to accommodate this prescription.

The recent furore over the Learning Assessment Project is particularly instructive. As soon as discontent surfaced among many of the state's primary schools and their school councils over the imposition of this statewide testing—to the point where schools indicated non-compliance, the DSE response was to put a structure in place whereby 'flying squads' would be sent in to recalcitrant schools to administer the test. That the DSE pulled back from such an intimidatory exercise is not the main point. What is more telling is that it seriously entertained such a proposition.

There is now more than a suggestion of a very untidy management relationship between the 'local' and the 'central' spheres—both of which are critical parties to educational governance in terms of devolved decision making and partnership in the education system generally. There appears to be little consultation by the minister or his bureaucracy with legitimate peak education bodies such as VICCSO or the Parents Federation. For the most part, the government chooses to ignore the input of teacher unions: since the coalition's Mr Don Hayward has been in the chair, the only official meeting has been a first course lunch with Mr Brian Henderson, then head of the VSTA, and Mr Peter Lord, president of the FTUV.

As well, the DSE has introduced Teaching Service Order 140 which prevents DSE employees from speaking freely to parents or school councils on matters of education policy. Public comment is defined by the Order as 'any comment, oral or written, which is made to any person not employed by the directorate'.

Significantly, in his assessment of the education cuts of Victoria's government schools, McCrae (1994) identified what might be the greatest cut of all:

> There have only been short periods in the past 20 years in Victorian government education when 'good authority' has been established between those in charge and those employed. 'Good authority' has little to do with resources. It is a reciprocal professional relationship where leaders are respected, their judgement trusted and their support for baseline necessities confidently assumed. The evident loss of 'good authority', and all that goes with it, could be the most damaging cut of all. Without it, Victoria's schools face a decrease or more of disruption and the establishment of alternative cultures of authority. This is widely known as anarchy and is caused by exceptionally bad management.

This loss of 'good authority' in Victoria's education system is sharpened by the knowledge that the skills of professional teachers and principals over the last decade had reached a fine edge. Anecdotally, it is recounted that when the Minister for Education, Mr Hayward, first spoke to principals, he was quick to assert the benefits to principals of coalition changes—'you'll be able to sack staff'. The ominous silence that greeted this stated benefit bewildered the minister. In short, he had not understood that many of those present had been powerful advocates of a culture of collaborative decision making which they themselves had helped to build and use to good effect in their schools and system management. To position the principal as the pivot, or some kind of feudal lord (and, paradoxically, as a line manager), is at the same time to overthrow a professional collegiate culture that was working well and, ironically, is what is now regarded more widely as 'industry best practice'.

In practice principals are becoming so overloaded with work as to deny them real opportunities for educational leadership. They have, it appears, been targeted by the DSE as a strategically important conduit through which to introduce the agenda of change. Through pressure on their time, principals are seen to be increasingly remote from their teaching staff.

While adopting the rhetoric of partnership and 'building teams in and around the schools', the DSE applies a structure for school-based decision making, promotions and teacher allowances which rest on hierarchical management assumptions, which affirm the power of the principal and constrain the possibility of effective team work in schools. One of the tragedies, in both the short and longer term, is that much of the sophisticated bank of skills built up around cooperative decision making has already been lost to the system by the departure of so many teaching professionals including principals. What remains, under the new management formulae, will continue to be eroded.

Looking over the events of the last two years, it may well be that it is still too early to identify adequately the impact of the coalition government's changes to state education. Indeed, the full range of effects of Victoria's 'market experiment' may not be known for some time. In this respect, however, we should be mindful of the weaknesses in the Radical Right's political and policy agenda and then ponder, in light of some emerging overseas research findings, what the future might look like if Victoria's market experiment with state education is permitted to run its course.

FUNDAMENTAL FLAWS IN THE RADICAL RIGHT EXPERIMENT

Stephen Ball (1993) has argued that reference to a 'market experiment' on public education is both appropriate and inappropriate. Appropriate because no-one, not even the politicians, know what is going to happen to education in the market place. There is a lot of blind faith around, and not much hard evidence. But, he says, the label is also inappropriate because most experiments are conduced through the careful collection and evaluation of data.

To a 'market determinist' it is axiomatic that the private market is a superior form of economic and social organisation. But as we argued in the first *Bulletin* (Crooks & Webber, 1993) of the Victoria Foundation, there are several fundamental weaknesses in the political and policy prescriptions of the Radical Right and they need to be understood and addressed in grappling with current issues and setting an alternative direction for state education.

Fundamental flaws

While the coalition government is brimful of confidence in the rightness of its actions, their public policy is deeply flawed on three counts:

- their preoccupation with 'the economy', divorced from any understanding of the social world

- their reification of the free market model and consequent lack of faith in the ability of public institutions to deliver useful services that people want

•their lack of concern and inability to deal with inequality and injustice.

The failure to comprehend the wide, complex and often unpredictable array of factors which make up human behaviour is evident in the Radical Right's approach to education. In reconstructing Victorian public education in terms purely of costs and benefits, the economic rationalist approach overlooks and discounts the reality that schools are a significant social institution that have 'non-economic' values and benefits which cannot simply be reduced to narrow market terms. As Marginson (1992: 8) argues, the social obligations of public education, such as the provision of universal literacy and access, appear only as costs and never as benefits. Similarly, the role of schools in their local communities, the social and educational outcomes of interactions between teachers and students, the social benefits of art, music or language are unaccounted for in an economic model. The only outcomes of education that are real are those which are measurable by economic criteria. If outcomes are not measurable, they are not real and so can be ignored. Thus cost cutters ignore their effects on unmeasured outputs. (Marginson, 1992: 17)

The reification of the free market model means that educational services are defined only in market terms; only products passing through the market have value; so schools are now seen as commercial enterprises, to be pitted against one another in winning market share. Through this process of market production and exchange, students (the 'customers') and parents (the 'purchasers' of the services) secure consumer satisfaction. Teachers and education administrators have no choice but to deliver the goods in this new system. By contrast under the old system, according to economic rationalists:

> There (was) little reason ... for the administrators of teachers to pay close and direct attention to the needs or criticisms of students or parents ... You cannot make a dog miaow or a cat bark. And neither can you make a monopolistic supplier of a service, one that does not even get its funds directly from its customer, pay close attention to its customers' wants. The only way to do so is to break the monopoly, to introduce competition, and to give customers alternatives. (Friedman & Friedman 1984: 153–5, quoted in Marginson 1992: 15)

It is on the question of justice and equity that the Radical Right flounders most noticeably. It conceived of individuals acting autonomously, without interference, to maximise their economic self-interest. Self-interest is held to include family and perhaps friends but goes no further. A broader solidarity is impossible (Marginson 1992: 11). With everyone intent on pursuing their own private interests, an 'invisible hand' (according to Adam Smith's famous dictum) somehow guides the market to ensure that outcomes are just.

Thus, there is no questioning in the minds of economic rationalists, that all people—irrespective of their sex, ethnicity, age or education—have the same unhindered capacity to negotiate the market: all employees can reach fair individual employment contracts with their employers; all families have the same capacity to fund increased kindergarten or school fees; all can find the 'best' school for their children; all can choose freely between public transport and private cars.

The Radical Right has no effective answer to the basic fact that some individuals are clearly better able to maximise their economic self-interest than others. This is nicely illustrated by the treatment of equity and education in the Kennett government's Commission of Audit. In supporting its scheme for 'competitive, self-managed schools', funded by 'output-related student unit sources' the Commission of Audit (1993: 40) recognised that:

> there are areas and parents with a lesser capacity to pay for locally-raised funds, and that to avoid major statewide disparities in educational opportunities, these may need generous funding supplementation by government.

The fact is that market prices ration according to tastes (what people prefer) *and* according to capacity to pay. Economic rationalism pays most of its attention to differences in tastes; it tends to ignore differences in ability to pay, for these are commonly ascribed to differences in productivity (and so are both natural and justified).

In the Victorian experience so far, the only tangible response to equity issues seems to rest with the Victorian equity program—in which Commonwealth funds are handed on through the state, to schools identified as disadvantaged. 'Social Justice' has disappeared from the lexicon, at the same time as four thousand special needs teachers have gone from the system. There appears to be no formal recognition of any need for systemwide provision for equity issues. Disadvantage is an individual matter, to be handled locally. There are disadvantaged individuals in Kew, so the argument seems to go, just as there are such individuals in Broadmeadows, or Footscray or Yallourn. As such, funding should be spread to allow for these individuals to be picked up in local responses. This atomistic view of disadvantage (there is no such thing as a 'disadvantaged community') probably helps to reconcile the fact that while one leading private girls school can employ half a dozen full-time staff to run its computer laboratory, a lap top program in a northern suburban state school is run by staff in their spare time.

There is already anecdotal evidence that under the Schools of the Future program schools are excluding students they see as too demanding of financial and teaching resources. The power to expel or simply say 'don't come back' is now vested by the code of conduct in the principal (students have a right of appeal, but only to the school council). Market pressures will surely force schools to push undesirable students out of schools and onto the streets (but off the statistical records of the DSE).

These weaknesses in the Radical Right approach are now becoming apparent after several years of market experimentation in such countries as the United Kingdom and New Zealand. New Zealand is now several years on from the Picot Report and *Tomorrow's Schools*. According to Beare (1995) there has been a steep climb in class sizes: classes of more than thirty students are now common. In 1991, zoning was abolished, so schools no longer have to guarantee a place to children who live nearby. In February 1995, primary school principals in Auckland voted not to admit students aged 5–7 years if they could not speak English. There are also signs of a 'white flight' from certain schools and an overloading of enrolment in middle class suburbs.

In reflecting on evidence from an evaluation of the changes in the United Kingdom, Stephen Ball (1993: 11) lists a series of research findings which begin to sketch some important market effects:

- Schools are paying a lot more attention to what parents want for their children's education. Or, more precisely, what schools *think* some parents want. Or, even more precisely, what schools think that *some* parents want. In a few cases, schools are engaging in crude forms of 'market research' or are consulting public relations firms, but for the most part the 'responsiveness' of schools is based upon impression or the emulation of rival. (All of this still begs the question as to whether parents always know what is best educationally for their children.)

- The publication of examination league tables and other performance indicators has meant that schools are increasingly keen to attract enrolments from 'motivated' parents and 'able' children who are likely to enhance their relative position in local systems of competition. In a sense, there is a shift of emphasis, from student needs to student performance; from what the school can do for the student to what the student can do for the school.

- In relation to the above, there is increasing evidence of a shift of resources away from students with special needs and learning difficulties. Well-established and proved systems of special education needs in schools are being dismantled or much reduced in size. Resources are being directed more towards those students who are most likely to perform well in tests and examinations.

- Generally, the role of special education needs work in schools is being played down. Schools which have histories of excellence in special education needs work are concerned that they will become labelled by parents as 'caring' rather than 'academic' institutions. One rather sad and dramatic comment from a special education needs teacher illustrates the climate of concern now in place in the education market:

We don't want to become a secondary modern, especially if the special needs department is so understaffed anyway. We can't cope with the numbers of students that need the help ... Next year, for instance, we're having a kid who's got Down's Syndrome. He's going to be joining us, and then there was another one with, not Down's, but something else, who also thought, ah, yes, Northwark Park, and we thought, well no, we can't take two. This is going to be enough having one child with that level of need and integrating. I mean it's such a new thing for us, we can't deal with two, we just can't handle it, we're going to be stretched enough as it is, but luckily the parents have decided to go elsewhere ... But we were beginning to think, oh my gosh, are we going to starting getting a reputation, ah yes, Northwark Park, they integrate students with these difficulties and then, you know, what effect does that have on the perception of parents with that school, when they come to want a school for their band one kid, do they send them to that school?

• Some of the money and energy previously devoted to educational endeavours like special education needs work is now focused upon marketing activities. Most schools have some kind of marketing or public relations committee. Brochures and prospectuses are glossier and more carefully thought out; logos, uniforms, headed paper, etc. are being planned to create a corporate image aimed at potential consumers. (Again, in some instances, public relations firms are brought in. The skills and knowledge of school governors can also be important in these areas.) Open evenings, items in the local press, newspaper advertising and school performances are now part of a marketing strategy. In some of our research, schools' staff are under pressure to change their style of dress to give a 'better' impression to parents. Hype, image and impression management are very much to the fore.

• All of the above are, of course, related to competition; to rivalry with local schools for student recruitment. Where there are large numbers of surplus places, the competition is intense and the 'responses' outlined above are clearer. Where places are filled, or where there are no nearby rivals, then the competition and the 'response' effects are more muted. In metropolitan areas where competition is at its most cut-throat, previous systems of cooperation and collaboration between schools have been severely curtailed and replaced by a climate of suspicion and hostility. Head teachers are beginning to talk about 'poaching', 'industrial espionage', 'knocking copy' and 'underhand moves'—always on the part of the other schools, of course.

• What the changes above amount to is a significant shift in the value framework of education. In the market, shrewdness, rather than principles, is rewarded. Long-held commitments and beliefs are being abandoned or compromised in order to ensure institutional survival. Commercial rather than educational principles are increasingly dominant in making curriculum, organisation and resource decisions.

• Part of this value shift is evident in the 'gap' which is opening up between the management and teachers in schools; a gap of values, purposes and concerns. Management is increasingly dominated by issues of marketing and recruitment and finance and budgeting. Teaching is dominated by delivery of the National Curriculum and sometimes, at least, the educational needs of individual students. The culture of school management is steadily becoming divorced from educational concerns. As one deputy head explained: 'the senior management team are no longer managing education but managing an educational institution'.

• On the other side of the market, the consumer side, some parents are clearly becoming more active in exercising the possibilities of choice (where they are available). Middle class parents in particular are exploiting the market in education and bringing their social and cultural advantages to bear. In general terms, the education market is geared to the consumption values and modes of the middle classes. Middle class parents are likely to have the knowledge, skills and contacts to decode and manipulate what are increasingly complex and deregulated systems of choice and recruitment. The more deregulation, the more possibility of information procedures being employed. The middle classes also, on the whole, are able and willing to move their children around the system.

• By contrast, we find that working class parents are likely to prefer the local school for their children. This in part reflects a limited knowledge of other schools and the economic and familial constraints within which choice of school is set. But locality is also a positive value for many working class parents. They want their children to go to a school which is easily accessible and does not involve long and dangerous journeys; a school where friends', neighbours' and relatives' children also go.

• The changes in school policies indicated earlier involve a shift in the range of choices now available to parents. Certain choices are being privileged. Parents who want a comprehensive school (using that term to represent a paradigm for a particular set of values and practices) may find their choice being squeezed out of the marketplace. Parents with children with special education needs will also find that some schools will give preference to other less expensive and less demanding children. In political rhetoric, the differences between choosing (making a choice) and getting your choice are systematically ignored. More specialisation and selection will mean more and more frustrated choosers.

• Paradoxically, one effect of emulation and rivalry (and of the system of published performance indicators) is a greater 'dull uniformity' among schools as they seek to play safe, emulate 'popular' rivals and compete for the same sought-after students.

Ball acknowledges that many of the issues are a lot more complex than he has been able to indicate here. But, he says the disciplinary effects of the market are clear, and the value shifts are marked. Whether all of this will lead to a raising of standards remains to be seen. It might, but, some people may want to ask, at what cost?

CONCLUSION: THE TASK AHEAD

It is clear that the Radical Right throughout the 1980s onwards, was able to conquer what Wilby and Midgley (1987) have described as the high ground of public debate in a virtually uncontested pre-emptive strike. And it is also clear in Victoria, that people with an abiding interest in and commitment to, a high quality state education system—parents, parent groups, teachers and teacher unions—have been to some extent caught off stride by this premeditated assault on public education and have been slow to come to terms with the nature of the assault and its likely short and long-term implications.

In the previous section, it was suggested that the recurring theme now evident in Victoria's government schools is of school-based devolution ('self - management') without adequate resources and other supports. On the surface, this is puzzling because surely the sensible course of action for the educational 'reformers' would be to put the resources in place which best assist the achievement of the desired goals of efficient, competitive, autonomous schools—particularly as these goals are feted as a new and better direction for state education. It seems however that the coalition government may well be caught between several conflicting objectives—the need to prove its fiscal virility by being seen to impose expenditure cuts of an unprecedented order; its ideological fixation with 'smaller government' and the user-pays principle; its interest in shifting responsibility for decision making onto schools (which then have to bear the brunt of problems and 'failures'); and its desire to impose a highly prescriptive and centralised notion of control.

In some major respects, we are watching a drama unfold in Victoria where the roles and dialogue have already been on stage elsewhere. As one eminent United Kingdom educationalist noted with anguish after only a few years of a Thatcherist program of educational change:

> all agree that major advances in education right across the board are necessary both to enhance the quality of life ... and to restore the country's economic and industrial position generally. There will be much to be done, and to be undone. The aim must be to build on (and recognise) the positive work of the schools, the teacher and the local authorities ... In place of the doctrinaire reliance on market forces to shape the future, we must substitute joint, cooperative effort by all concerned to build an educational environment directed to realising the full potentialities of all our citizens, whatever their age, gender, race or social class. Such must be the objective. (Simon 1992: 198)

The task ahead in Victoria is twofold. The market approach to state education is terminally flawed and will prove to be an inappropriate model. In rejecting this model, the solution does not rest in harking back to 'old' arrangements. Rather it lies in redefining the arguments, policies and financial commitments necessary to achieve strong and high quality state education with all of its attendant features—the restoration of universal access; the quest for excellence; a humane and equitable system; genuine partnership between schools, parents, students and teacher unions; and the creation of decent resource-sharing arrangements between schools.

REFERENCES

Ball S 1993 Market forces in education *Education Review* (National Union of Teachers) Vol 7 No 1 Spring

Beare H 1995 *The Age* 2 May

Brennan M 1992 What have we learnt in ten years? *Secondary Teacher* 1: 7

Carey A 1987 Conspiracy or groundswell? In Coghill K (ed) *The New Right's Australian Fantasy* Melbourne: McPhee Gribble

Chubb J and Moe 1990 *Politics, Markets and America's Schools* The Brookings Institution

Coghill K (ed) 1987 *The New Right's Australian Fantasy* Melbourne: McPhee Gribble

Crooks M 1994 *Victorian State Education: A System at Risk* Northcote: The Victoria Foundation *Bulletin of Society and Economy 4*

Crooks M L & Webber M J 1993 *State Finances and Public Policy in Victoria* Northcote: The Victoria Foundation *Bulletin of Society and Economy 1*

Dennison S R 1984 *Choice in Education* London: Institute of Economic Affairs

Department of Education 1993 *Schools of the Future: Preliminary Papers* Melbourne

Department of Education 1994a *Presentation to Budget Expenditure Review Committee* Melbourne 18 July

Department of Education 1994b *Draft Business Plan 1994–96* Melbourne

Department of Education 1994c *Draft Corporate Plan 1994–1996* Melbourne

Flew A 1991 Educational Services: Independent Competition or Maintained Monopoly? In Green D G (ed) *Empowering the Parents: How to Break the Schools' Monopoly* London: Health and Welfare Unit: 15–53

Gardner E M (ed) 1985 *A New Agenda for Education* Washington: The Heritage Foundation

The Hillgate Group 1986 *Whose Schools? A Radical Manifesto* London

The Hillgate Group 1987 *The Reform of British Education: From Principles to Practice* London: The Claridge Press

Independent Review of Victoria's Public Sector Finances 1992 Melbourne

Institute of Public Affairs 1992 *Schooling Victorians: Lessons for the Future* Melbourne

Kronemann M 1993 *Trends in Victorian Schools' Funding* Melbourne: FTUV Research Paper

Kronemann M 1995 *Victorian Government Schools: Trend Data* Melbourne: FTUV Research Paper

Liberal Party 1984 *A New Liberal Policy for Primary and Secondary Education* Melbourne

Liberal Party 1988 *Raising Standards: Education and Training Policy* Melbourne

Liberal National Coalition 1992 *Education: Giving Students a Chance* Melbourne

Lord P 1995 Schools' Out as Teachers Strike *The Sunday Age* 30 April

Marginson S 1992 Economic Rationalism in Education, Adelaide: Paper presented to the Rationalising Australia Conference Flinders University of South Australia 12 February

Marginson S 1993a The Kennett Government's Education Policies Melbourne: Paper presented to Australian Rationalists Conference November

Marginson S 1993b Free Market, Strong State *Frontline* October: 5–6

Manne R 1992 Wrong Way: Go Back *ABM* November

McCrae D 1994 Into the bone: The impact of cuts to Victorian school education 1993–94 Melbourne

McMurdo G 1995 Retention plummets *Australian Education Union News* 20 October Melbourne

Moore D 1994 Education: the Context of the State and Federal Economics Melbourne: Address to an Education Forum, Abbotsford May

Secretary of State for Education and Science and Secretary of State for Wales 1985 *Better Schools* London

Seddon T 1994 Devolution: Pressing Education beyond Politics This volume

Sexton S 1990 *New Zealand Schools: An Evaluation of Recent Reforms and Future Directions* NZ Business Roundtable December

Simon B 1992 *What Future for Education?* London: Lawrence and Wishart

Stone D Old guard versus new partisans: Think tanks in transition *Australian Journal of Political Science* 26: 197–215

Victorian Commission of Audit 1993 *Report, Volume Two*: 7–80

Victorian Secondary Teachers Association *News* 10 February 1994

Wilby P and Midgley S 1987 As the New Right Wields its Power *The Independent* 23 July

Devolution
Pressing Education Beyond Politics

Terri Seddon

> The commitment of all of us, whether parents, principals, or the
> Directorate of School Education, must be to help each Victorian student
> maximise his or her potential ... students must have access to a high
> quality education ... quality education is all about people ... it is not
> about 'the system', nor the vested interest groups to whom the 'the
> system' was held captive for so long ... Schools of the Future will enable
> teachers to better and more freely exercise their professional skills and
> judgements in the classroom ... Schools of the Future will enable princi-
> pals to become true leaders ... Schools of the Future will give the com-
> munity greater say in the present and future progress and direction of
> the school (Hayward 1993: 1).

The imagery of the Victorian government's 'flagship' policy, Schools of the
Future, is of a new initiative in decentralisation and devolution: a radical step
away from the educational governance of the past toward a brave new world
of local school management.

But, as most people know, Victoria has a long history of devolution in
education. For the last twenty years, parents, teachers, their representative
organisations and those within the education bureaucracy in Victoria have
been working toward a devolved model of educational governance.

Under the Labor government, Ministerial Paper 6 brought devolution to
its most refined level. It was termed the partnership model. This is because
the government, parents and teachers were brought together in a partnership
to work for the good of Victorian education. This partnership involved a
framework of negotiated agreements between the three major parties (government, parents and educators) which clarified a functional division of
labour in terms of decision making and responsibilities. The partnership
operated at both school and central levels to produce an educational provision which was in the interests of Victorian students.

At base this partnership was an organisational arrangement which allowed
the sharing of wisdom between those groups most concerned with children's
education. Parents could present their views of their own children's education
as well as expressing a distinctive parental view about children in general.
Teachers and educators offered a professional perspective on children and the
work of educating them. The government provided an orientation which was
informed by the double responsibility of both resourcing educational provision

and administering the public interest in education. Each partner provided a check on the others. It was an arrangement which not only enabled a productive sharing of views, but also tempered sectional interests.

Like all negotiated arrangements, the devolutionary partnership worked better in some parts than others. It depended, for its continuing relevance and fine tuning, upon a practical politics of constant renegotiation. But, importantly, it established a framework for agreement over what to disagree about, the appropriate forms of antagonism and the procedures for resolution. It was an imperfect instrument of educational governance but one that had a lot going for it, not least its flexibility and scope for renegotiation. For this it achieved international recognition as an innovative and effective approach.

The Schools of the Future program is not, then, an innovative approach to school governance, only a new model of devolution. The current Victorian government has not invented devolution but is denying the past and, worse, smearing those years of honest effort to create a workable devolved educational governance as the machinations of vested interests.

The new model of educational governance has three important features which distinguish it from the partnership of the past:

1. There has been a major redefinition of the players in educational governance.

2. The relationships between the players have been transformed.

3. The government seems confused about its own role in educational governance.

Let me address these in turn.

REDEFINING THE TERMS
There has been a wholesale redefining of the terms of the old educational partnership. Parents are now defined as *consumers* rather than *participants* in educational processes. They are expected to articulate their demands about education so that the demands can be met by education providers. By and large, the parents are not expected to be active participants in this process of determining the service to be provided, just like a supermarket shopper cannot determine the products on the supermarket shelves. Their activity is presumed to only extend to the choice of this or that can of fish, deodorant or school.

As consumers, parents have been set alongside other consumers of education's products: governments and industry. But parents have only a fraction of the resources of either governments or industry to make clear and publicise their wishes. Parents' links into the education policy process depend upon formal representative structures and if their representative organisations are denied, as in Victoria, the sources of influence are less extensive. The outcome is far from being a 'level playing field' in the capacity to express 'consumer demands'.

Redefining the parents as consumers has been paralleled by a redefining of teachers (educators) as *providers* in a service enterprise. Schools appear as *businesses* under the Schools of the Future program with the principal as managing director, the school council as board of directors, and teachers as workers. These relationships are clearly different to the relationships of the partnership model of devolution. A wedge has been driven into what had been a more or less unified education profession. The principal is to be the educational leader in the school, the executive officer of the school council and the central figure in staff selection. On his or her head rests responsibility and accountability for curriculum, resource and personnel management and school organisation. The teachers are supposed to just do the work, provide the teaching.

The third partner of old, the government, has also been redefined in recent years. The state, as a social institution, is made up of a number of different parts (e.g. the legislature, the judiciary, the bureaucracy, statutory agencies, etc.) whose relationships with one another are always characterised by enduring tensions and endemic conflicts. Usually these relationships are negotiated so that agreements about a functional balance of power is achieved. For almost 70 years, for instance, the Director of Education who was the head of the education bureaucracy was the pre-eminent force in Victorian education. Politicians generally rubber-stamped the policy and administration of the bureaucracy. In more recent years the functions of the Director of Education have been fragmented, the power of this position dissipated and finally, overturned in favour of an executive model of governance headed by the Minister.

It is this *executive model* which is so striking today. Firstly, the minister or political official is privileged over the administrative officials of the bureaucracy. Indeed, corporate managerialism has succeeded in not only subordinating administrative to political officials, but reconstructing them in their own image. Administrators are now most prized, and most highly paid, if they have substantive expertise in the political work of management, rather than being expert in the content, and the provision of *public* service, in an area.

The second shift toward an executive model is apparent within parliament itself. Traditionally, in governments derived from the Westminster system, there is an enduring, but usually productive, tension between the 'executive in parliament', that is, the MPs we elect to office in order to take care of the day-to-day affairs of state, and the 'sovereign in parliament' which since the expansion of the franchise has been 'the people'. As the protests over Albert Park Lake, the dismissal of local councils and school closures suggest, the executive political officials of the Victorian government are extending their executive role to new levels of leadership at the expense of the public's voice. Dissenters are merely dismissed as self-interested ratbags. The effect is to create a 'thin' democracy where 'the people's' role is merely to cast a vote and relinquish the management of public affairs to the executive political officials. There is a long history of criticism of such democratic tokenism, not least in the Liberal Party and its predecessors.

While Victoria provides good illustrations of executive government, it is important to remember that it is neither a purely Liberal, nor Victorian phenomenon. Corporate managerialism was introduced under Labor governments in Victoria and Canberra. The quips about 'President Keating' capture a popular truth that the federal Labor government has, in its own way, lost sight of the people. In education, this is evident in the ongoing criticisms of the consultative procedures being used by the federal government. The production of glossy documents, too-short time-lines and the release of major and controversial policies just before Christmas is taken as evidence that the federal government doesn't really want feedback on its policies except from a few favoured peak organisations and individuals.

In summary, the old devolutionary partnership was based on a sharing of wisdom between parents, teachers and government. The new Schools of the Future devolution brings together consumers, service providers and executive government in educational governance.

TRANSFORMING THE RELATIONSHIPS

As these redefined players of the educational partnership take on their new character, the relationships between them shift, as you see in Figure 1.

Figure 1: The redefined players and shifting relationships in devolution

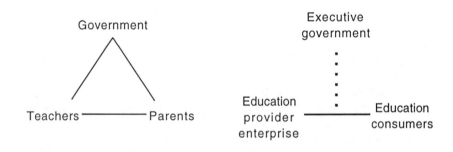

In the old three-way partnership, each player made a different, but equally significant, contribution to the provision of public education. The relationships between the players were roughly equal. This has changed.

Now what is privileged is the market relationship between the community of consumers and the provider enterprise. Parents' choice of school affects school enrolments and hence, funding and the viability of the enterprise.

This changes the responsibilities of the players in educational provision.

The responsibility of the consumers is to make known their educational aspirations and needs, and to ensure through their agency, the school council, that these consumer demands are integrated into school programs. The enterprise is responsible for providing attractive programs to ensure continued enrolments and school viability. To this end, the school can now pursue sources of funds which are additional to those provided by government and the traditional supplement, parental fundraising. As in other businesses, educational and financial decisions are the managing director's (principal's) responsibility.

But, having fanfared and launched Schools of the Future, the government now seems confused about its own role and responsibilities in the devolutionary model.

GOVERNMENT CONFUSION: REGULATION OR LINE MANAGEMENT?
Specifically, the government seems uncertain whether local management of schools is to operate on a regulatory or line management model of devolution. Figure 2 may clarify the distinction.

In the regulatory model the responsibility of government is to provide a framework within which education service provision and contractual market relationships can proceed. As the original Schools of the Future documentation indicates, this devolutionary model operates within statewide curriculum and resource frameworks but a school and its team of teachers has 'control over its operations and future' (Directorate of School Education 1993: 2). The model includes a commitment to fund the enterprise's current operations and future dreams, subject to a negotiated contract between the school and DSE in terms of service provision.

Figure 2: The government role: regulatory agency or line manager?

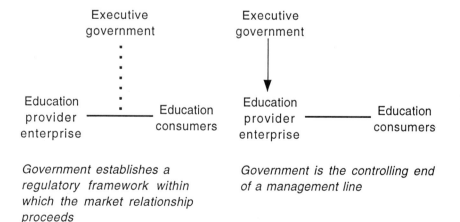

Executive government

Education provider enterprise ———— Education consumers

Government establishes a regulatory framework within which the market relationship proceeds

Executive government

Education provider enterprise ———— Education consumers

Government is the controlling end of a management line

But the practice of government over the last few years suggests that there is considerable confusion over what counts as 'regulation'. The promise of autonomy and funds in the regulatory model has been overshadowed as schools have been pressed toward 'autonomy' by edict. Schools must declare staff 'in excess of need' because the government has changed the staffing formula. Schools must close. Communities must decide which school must close. No, it's not *that* one that must close.

Increasingly the new devolutionary model seems less regulatory and more like a line management structure reaching from the minister to teachers in the schools. The policy frameworks become non-negotiable impositions on schools and their consumer communities. Such management shatters not only dreams, but operations.

Despite the rhetoric of devolution, this is a model of centralised control with decentralised administration of central demands. Its practical effect is to off-load administrative work, once done centrally, to the schools and particularly, the principals and school councils. Its financial effect is to reduce the education budget because, irony of irony, the administrative work of the public system of education is taken up by 'the people'; those school councillors who, unpaid, do this work of administration in their spare time, a kind of 'hobby'.

The long-term implications of these trends are difficult to identify with any certainty, although research is beginning to emerge from the United Kingdom and New Zealand which suggests some likely trends. By and large this research has focused on the implications of educational provision being organised on a market basis. It has documented the way schools tend to become sectional, catering either for the affluent middle class or for poorer working class communities, and has shown how the emphasis on educating students tends to be overtaken by entrepreneurial concerns: maintaining student numbers, seeking funds, marketing.

There is much less research which focuses on the political implications of the shift toward Schools of the Future styled market devolution. I want to finish this paper with a few preliminary comments on these matters.

DEVOLUTION: PRESSING EDUCATION BEYOND POLITICS
This Liberal government, like its Labor predecessor, has accurately recognised that educational decisions need to be made at the local level by those most affected by them. But local decisions do not stand alone. They are made within and, indeed, are shaped by the organisational framework of educational provision and governance which is decided centrally. Devolution is never only about relegating some decisions to schools so as to permit 'local' school management. Rather, devolution always involves, firstly, determining an appropriate division of labour and responsibility in educational decision making between local and central levels and between different agencies, and secondly, establishing an acceptable framework within which that local and central decision making can proceed.

My point is that alongside all the government's talk of devolving decision making and responsibilities to schools, there must be a set of assumptions about the decision-making powers and responsibilities of the centre which are not being so openly discussed.

Let us then begin to identify the political implications of School of the Future devolution and, particularly, the role of the centre in the new devolutionary model. My assumptions in this are that the Schools of the Future policy statement represents the Victorian Liberal Party's long-term goal in educational governance and that, as Minister Hayward and others assert, it is just unfortunate that policy implementation has coincided with cuts in funding. The implication of these assumptions is, therefore, that the line management features of contemporary educational governance are merely a transitionary political strategy for effecting change. Given these assumptions, a number of trends emerge.

It seems that the government's assumptions about the role of the centre in educational governance is shaped by a simple functional division of labour in which education is seen to be a purely local activity while the centre is understood as the site of government.

Education is presented as the local provision of a service to consumers. This local service provision is the responsibility of education enterprises, schools, and especially the principal who must develop and market the school's services to the parent consumers and must manage the teachers to provide that service.

The role of central authorities is government—not of education but of the state. The responsibility of government is leadership, or ruling, rather than ensuring participation in government. Education is only one aspect of the affairs of state and it must, therefore, be governed according to its 'rightful place' in that wider frame of reference. Cuts in funding can, therefore, be easily justified because the resources for public education must be subordinated to the government's work of debt reduction.

The consolidation of the government's arms length role in ruling education depends upon distancing the centre from the pluralist politics which has characterised education over the last twenty years.

This is served by the exclusion of parents and educator organisations from central decision making. Not only does this take the heat out of debates about educational provision, it also affirms that the roles and responsibilities parents and teachers are educational, and, therefore, purely local. If these groups attempt to participate in central decision making, they are presented as interfering in the processes of ruling which are not about education, but the affairs of state.

Arms length governance is also served by establishing abstract principles which regulate the practice and provision of education. In place of pluralist politics around issues of curriculum and resources, the government can appeal to seemingly neutral indicators, such as student enrolment and national benchmarks, as a basis for justifying funding decisions. After all, if parents choose to enrol their children in a particular school, and if funding is tied to each individual student, then the consumers are determining the viability of each educational enterprise. The government is only funding according to consumer demand. School curricula may be debated and fought over at a local level but the green light for action at a central level is given on the basis of bureaucratic procedures.

When such abstract indicators are enacted as routine procedures there is no scope for politics. Once indicators, frameworks and procedures are accepted as a legitimate basis for action, contentious issues of educational provision and practice are lifted above politics to the simple realm of apolitical administration.

The effect is to press education beyond politics of all but a local kind. This establishes a distinction between education and government, and links that distinction to different kinds of politics. The central politics of government appears dignified, ruling the affairs of state on the basis of a presumed legitimate power. By contrast the local politics of education appear as undignified squabbles, fights over access to decision-making processes, struggles to promote particular interests.

This distinction is further entrenched because education is understood in a narrow way. It is conceived, above all, as a labour producing industry, enhancing human capital by providing appropriate skills to appropriate individuals. Alongside this is an equally utilitarian, but more homely, family view of education as a children-socialising institution. What this framing does is focus on the benefit of education to individuals and de-emphasise the benefit of education to government. It neglects the broader role of education in creating a unique and creative culture and a capable and caring community.

The new model of devolution appears to push education beyond politics of all but a local kind. The implication is that our rulers and leaders will establish an acceptable central framework for decision making, and determine the range of issues which will be dealt with on a routine administrative level and those which can be the subject of practical politics at a local school level. The further implication is that our rulers and leaders know best; that there is no need for a sharing of wisdom in order to clarify problems or identify best solutions.

The trouble is that there seems to be little practical basis for this kind of return to a golden age when rulers were accepted as legitimately powerful and omniscient. After all, liberal democracy, with its institutionalisation of the sharing of wisdom, replaced feudalism.

It is difficult to see the pluralist politics of education dissipating to the extent that central decision making will achieve uncontroversial legitimacy. Politicians and governments are viewed with suspicion rather than trust. Interest groups have little to gain from subordinating their interests to the interests of governments. The smear of sectionalism can, of course, be applied all round.

There is already evidence that while governments seek to rule, they get an awful lot wrong. Governments tell us that we have to have cuts in educational expenditure and that we want reduced taxes. Yet in the most recent opinion survey on people's attitudes to education, health and social welfare, conducted by the Research School of Social Sciences at ANU, 77 per cent of people supported more spending on education. When offered a choice between reduced taxes and more spending on education, 44 per cent chose lower taxes but 54 per cent chose more spending on education.

The notion that national benchmarks justify cuts in Victorian educational funding is treated with derision. Queensland's cheaper education is not necessarily better. Queensland and Victoria have different histories, have different capacities and have made different contributions to national well being. The idea that benchmarks can be established which are authentic in relation to these different contexts is recognised as a piece of bean-counters' fiction which presumes that the distribution of dollars provides an adequate and meaningful basis for comparing apples and oranges. Incidentally, it also makes a mockery of claims about states' rights.

Furthermore, in the press to create an educational provision organised around individual interests, and oriented to socialising the young and vocationalising youth, governments are clearly overlooking the social *and economic* importance of culture and community which depends upon a shared education. They do not seem to realise that it is culture and community which provides the foundation for economic growth and market position in an information age, and is the basis for the creation of distinctive goods and services which can give competitive advantage.

The tragedy is that the government has lost sight of the role and purpose of public education in a modern economy. The Schools of the Future model of devolution takes us down the track of a thin democracy, ruled by men with simple world views and bully boy approaches. It subjects us to a policy regime which is systematically eroding the infrastructural basis of a vibrant economy which maximises and makes full use of its human resources. And, in its rush to rule, government will not hear that encouraging economic development and international competitiveness can never be reduced to just the support of individual, private, interests. It depends, rather, on the reconstruction of social solidarity through the formation of a lucky country culture, community and capacity which ensures the well - being of its people. And this is, fundamentally, what public education has always been about.

REFERENCES
Directorate of School Education 1993 *Schools of the Future: Preliminary Paper* Melbourne
Hayward D 1993 Introduction, in Department of Education *Schools of the Future: Preliminary Paper* Melbourne

Lying Low

Education Under Kennett

Bill Hannan

The education ministry under the Kennett government has kept a low profile, content to claim that all has been happening for the best in the best of all possible worlds. No doubt this seemed the best way to get through all the cutting exacted by the state Treasury: 270 schools, 8000 teachers, $370 million. It also reflects a poverty of ideas about managing a public school system.

The Kennett–Stockdale–Hayward school closures and staff cuts were managed as a blitzkrieg. Whether the right targets were hit may never be known. In the cases of Richmond and Northlands they manifestly were not. However, many schools needed to be closed or reorganised either for economic and demographic reasons or in order to provide a broader curriculum in languages, arts, technology and the VCE. Labor had recognised this but had temporised in the face of resistance from pressure groups. At all events, the schools have gone. The main question now is what sort of provision has grown out of this pruned system. Were the cuts merely wiping out waste or deliberately and permanently reducing the scale and scope of the public school system? Apart from having more devolved administration to handle, what will Kennett's Schools of the Future actually provide for the localities they serve?

The cutting is part of a total program of reducing and privatising the public sector. In general the benefits of privatising are said to compensate for the effects of the reductions. In the case of education, however, 'privatising' has to be translated into devolution of administration, via a program known as Schools of the Future. The coinciding of cuts with devolution necessarily hampers this program. To opponents of devolution, the program is simply a device to hide cuts and pass off responsibility for future shortages. Supporters have had to struggle with inadequate resources to implement what is a major change to a large centralised system. So far, the ministry has vacillated between handing over responsibilities to schools and hanging on to the right to issue directives on this and that from head office. It is still hard to tell when or whether the Schools of the Future will cross the line from being cut down and kicked about by head office to being empowered to make their own way within a reliable resource context.

CUTS

The cuts to staff and budgets in state schools have been described in ways that would have impressed Goebbels. It was not simply that the state budget had to be brought under control. Education, it was asserted, in common with other public services under Labor, had become fat and indulgent, and in particular a rort for the teacher unions. Public schools in Victoria would be brought back to the national average. Victoria would no longer stick out, red-faced, as the state that spends the most on public schooling. In the space of a couple of years Victoria fell to middle position in spending per student, and to the bottom of the scale for education spending per head of population. It should be noted that Australian averages are at the bottom end (14th out of 17) of OECD spending on education.

Any ill effects of this fall from waste, says the propaganda, will be absorbed, indeed turned to advantage, by the self-management gained under Schools of the Future. Freed of bureaucracy and in control of their own budgets, self-managing schools, it is claimed, will inevitably be more efficient. The cheapest will also be the best.

Schools of the Future has not figured much in public discussion of education. The government buys newspaper space from time to time to praise the program, and education writers recycle publicity material. This obscurity is not for want of fervour on the part of Brian Caldwell, the program's chief architect, and Max Sawatski, its chief huckster. In their incandescent prose, the program is already a world-beater:

> The power is on, the heat is up, and the excitement is running high—
> Victoria is about to embark on the most significant school reform effort
> yet witnessed in Australia, and perhaps the world. (Address to principals,
> undated)

The measure of reform in public education is improvement in students' learning across the full social spectrum. This is brought about by improvements in curriculum and teaching. Both curriculum and teaching are affected by school organisation, resources and systemwide patterns of provision. But in any good planning the exigencies of curriculum and teaching should call the tune.

Since most of the education budget goes on staffing, the large cuts demanded by the Kennett government had to come out of teaching and by extension, the curriculum. Cutting the bureaucracy—usually a popular move—is not enough. Even a large bureaucracy does not account proportionately for many people. Labor was able to shed bureaucrats, but not teachers. The coalition got rid of both. The numbers of bureaucrats will creep back, because the government has underestimated what it takes to run the kind of system they want, but the extra costs will not be noticed. The teacher cuts will be more enduring, for economic (and perhaps ideological) reasons, and will have a much greater effect on the quality of the system, that is, on its curriculum provision, its teaching and its students' outcomes.

If Labor were elected to government it would be under immediate pressure from much of its constituency to restore teacher numbers. It will have to make some increases immediately, but for both budgetary and electoral reasons it would probably not restore previous levels. At the least, it will have to restore staffing targeted for equity programs. At most it might strike an accord to work towards target staff ratios for a typical mix of general and practical classes. It should avoid locking the system into rigid maxima across the board, and try to tie improved staffing to improving student outcomes.

If the coalition is re-elected, it may cut teacher numbers further. Its proclaimed desire to improve buildings and equip schools with modern technology will not be met simply from savings or sales of closed schools. Theoretically, at least, the government has prepared the ground for further reductions. Research, its apologists have claimed, does not show that classes of thirty produce worse student outcomes than classes of twenty-five. The money wasted on low teacher–student ratios would be better spent on facilities or outside education. Many classes in Victoria have now climbed into the high twenties, and some into the thirties, but more teachers could still be shed to stay inside the 'research' figure of thirty. Subjects with small enrolments have often dropped out of school curricula already, but there is still scope for eliminating more.

The 'research shows' argument is a misuse of statistics. On the subject of class size, research offers no certain conclusions. The Director of the Australian Council for Educational Research, Professor Barry McGaw, has pointed out several times recently that we do not have enough evidence to say what the connection is between resources and student outcomes. This is not the same as saying there is no connection. Common sense and, on balance, international research, suggests that better resources should lead to better teaching, so long as the extra resources are used to improve students' learning rather than solely to improve teachers' conditions. Non-government schools, with control over their budgets, certainly act on this common sense view. To be taken seriously research would have to show unequivocally that common sense is mistaken.

The more common justification—that education was costing too much and had to take its share of the pain—had some merits. Greater efficiency was undoubtedly needed. At the very least, education had to learn to live within its budget. Labor had recognised this but was unable to enforce it. Schools stayed open that should have been closed or reorganised as part of more efficient units. Staffing formulae had to be made to work more efficiently. Smaller classes and so-called 'special needs' staffing allocations needed to be clearly directed towards improving student outcomes. There was room to cut, but efficiency alone cannot be honestly used to justify the scale of the Kennett cuts. Only a deliberate shift away from public provision can explain them.

In the short term, the quality of government schooling has undoubtedly been undermined by the Kennett government's blitz. However they might be rationalised in the long term, the cuts were too big and sudden for schools to absorb quickly or efficiently. Across the board cuts to staffing ratios do damage to the least wealthy schools that special program money does not make up. On their own evidence, the loss of morale among teachers and parents is great. The government is lucky that it has been let lie low.

Although it is hard in the short term to gather evidence of direct effects of resource changes on students' outcomes, some indicators are already there. Classes have grown larger overall by two or three students. Subjects with small enrolments have been dropped, but no plans made to provide for these in other ways. Since the government came to office, retention to year 12 has fallen. The government points out that there have been parallel drops across Australia in the same period, but in Victoria the drop in government retention is greater than in the comparable Catholic system, and it is greater in working class and rural regions than in the eastern suburbs.

To make long-term judgments about cuts to specific departmental budgets it is necessary to know something of a department's strategic planning. The decision to cut or add to a department's budget is made by central agencies—Treasury, Premiers, Finance—on general political and budgetary grounds. Departments can argue about the exact amount and timing, but essentially a figure is plucked from the air. The department then has to make it work—find the money and justify the cut publicly.

To keep the system working rationally when budgets change annually, or perhaps more often, departments have to plan. Whether the government of the day cuts teacher numbers or adds to them, the system itself has to have a view of optimum numbers for various elements of the curriculum. These tend to be argued about mainly in the industrial arena, as a question of teachers' conditions. From a planning viewpoint, however, they can only be sustained by reference to curriculum targets (that is, what and how we expect students to learn) and to the school structures best able to achieve them.

Plans of this sort have not been made public, and probably don't exist. They have been supplanted by talk about budgeting for Schools of the Future. Issues of flexibility, school level budgeting and local selection, all good things in themselves, have displaced discussion of curriculum provision, systemic structures, equity and the improvement of teaching. On present indications we can assume that the government intends to keep Victoria plugging along with or behind national averages; and we are asked to take it on trust that devolving administration to schools with fewer staff will improve student learning.

EQUITY

Any move to devolution in a large system necessarily raises the complementary question of systemic planning and regulation. In public education, at least three things call for central policies and enforcement: provision, enrolment and equity. Planned provision is needed to ensure that everyone will have access to a curriculum suitable to the times. Enrolment policies have to maintain balance and efficiency in the system as a whole. Equity programs are needed to redress significant differences in outcomes experienced by groups of students.

For twenty years Australians have accepted that different levels of funding are required for different school populations if educational opportunities are to be equal. Apart from this basic agreement, however, amounts, target groups, methods of distribution and methods of evaluating results have remained controversial.

There is still a long way to go. Research continues to reveal great inequities in educational outcomes, but it also reveals successes. In the growth of upper secondary enrolments over the past decade, Australia has witnessed an historic democratising of education, comparable to the foundation of public systems in the 1870s and the growth of junior secondary education in the middle of the century. We should remind ourselves that this latest advance, like its predecessors, was made possible by the willingness of governments to fund all comers and by the faith and skill of teachers. The Kennett government may well think that this last phase of democratisation should be kept in check lest it become a large and permanent burden on the state purse.

Some of this expansion has been made possible by programs directed to disadvantaged groups. Some large groups, however, continue to perform badly. Students living in poverty form the most notable group. Although girls perform well overall—partly at least because of special programs directed towards them—the sub-group of girls of low socio-economic status and non-English speaking background is still disadvantaged. In some areas of scientific and technological study girls are still notably low in numbers. Regional patterns of success continue to be biased in favour of areas of greater wealth. In general we are at a point where we have to scrutinise the effectiveness of all equity funding and in some areas make a bigger effort than has yet been made.

The Kennett government has proposed funding schools according to a Student Resource Index. In essence, this attaches different amounts of money to different types of student. A disabled student, for example, might need twice or three times as much funding as a typical student, non-English speakers would attract a loading, and so on. It is a rational scheme, likely to attract support from any colour of government.

The Index proposal suggests that the Kennett government accepts the principle of equity. But this is a hollow commitment if the base level of funding before any extra equity funding is applied is inadequate. In that case, differences in student performance could easily become greater in spite of differential funding. When there is not enough basic money to keep programs going schools take to raising their own from fees, donations and chook raffles. Since most disadvantaged students live in relatively poor suburbs, private fundraising naturally favours the better off. In practice, this could maintain the comparative disadvantage the Index is supposed to correct.

Of course, private fundraising is not supposed to happen in public schools: fees are not charged, levies must be voluntary. But this has long been a rhetorical position. If there is a fuss in the press, the right noises are made by the minister or department and the journalists do not persist. In any case it is impossible to stop voluntary activity. In principle, a self-managing system will encourage greater levels of private fundraising and sponsorship. Central authorities have to ensure that schools without significant private resources get enough to do a good job. The greater the cuts to the base, the greater equity funding must be.

Critics of an Index might also say that it puts too much trust in schools to use the money as intended; but this has been true of previous centralised systems too. Its greater weakness is that it may leave entirely to schools the task of developing and monitoring programs. Some schools of course will do this superbly, but the system also has a responsibility to spread good practice and help those schools that do not come up with the goods on their own.

Properly used, extra staffing—sufficient to halve class sizes in key elements of the curriculum and create one-to-one situations in programs such as Reading Recovery—is the most likely way to improve outcomes for disadvantaged students. If Victorian schools stay at about the same base level reached after the cuts of the past two years, the Resource Index will have to give more generous loadings for disadvantage than we have become accustomed to. The Kennett government has got away with more daring reversals of practice, but in this case its constituency comes from the wrong side of town.

STUDENT OUTCOMES

Finding out what works and helping schools in trouble require both schools and systems to monitor student outcomes. Conservative politicians and pundits enjoy sneering at the idea of equal outcomes (grey, socialist uniformity etc.), but equalising outcomes for identifiable groups is what equity programs are all about. To be content with providing only for equality of opportunity is to be irresponsible about public money. Eventually we need to know whether the group we spent the money on got something out of it, whether outcomes are beginning to equalise. Once we know that we can decide how to continue. Without any evidence, the programs are open to special pleading and capricious change.

How such monitoring and planning is to be done in the new system of self-managing schools with a skeletal centre, is not clear. Perhaps some consultancies will be let out to universities from time to time, but these may not be able to provide the long-term continuous monitoring that is needed. Under the Labor government this was being done as part of the Victorian Profiles Program. Had Victoria persisted with the national profiles project, it could have been done nationally.

The present ministry no longer seems committed to using profiles in these ways locally or nationally. Apart from lamely asserting that parents want the LAP tests, the Board of Studies has not made it clear how information from the LAP tests will be analysed. Despite denials, they will probably be used to monitor the performance of schools (what managers could resist the temptation?) but whether or how they will be used to monitor for equity has not been revealed.

Leaving aside the merits of differing sorts of data, the essential problem is absence of any consistent monitoring over time. This weakens a system's capacity to plan and to improve. Previous Victorian governments have nothing to write home about in this regard, but Labor did see the development of profiles for literacy and maths and took part actively in developing national profiles. The Kennett government tossed these aside for entirely capricious and ignorant reasons and introduced yet another, and inferior, instrument in the LAP. The responsibility now falls to outside researchers still pursuing this theme—particularly the University of Melbourne—to get their message through to government. Chopping and changing for trivial partisan reasons is a feckless way to conduct what should be seen as a core function of government; and especially so in a highly devolved system.

PRIVATISING

When Caldwell and Sawatski speak of 'new and creative ways of resourcing' schools, they are probably referring to the Student Resource Index, or perhaps global budgeting. But it is hard not to sniff also the Kennett government's enthusiasm for selling or reducing public assets. Caldwell and Sawatski's models are those of public systems and private corporations in the English speaking world. The Kennett government, however, adds its own flavour to management by appealing to small business principles.

The thinking is familiar by now. It is close to that of private school lobbies who appeal to concepts of individual rights: the right to choose, the right to consume the taxes you pay, to make sacrifices for your own children. Right wing pundits make parallel appeals: to freedom from social engineering by the state and the right to spend your own money to your own advantage.

These are all arguments that extend easily to the extreme position of treating education as a private good. If it is, there is no reason why schooling should not be entirely privatised, with governments merely varying assistance to users via tax concessions and subsidised vouchers.

The private view has always had a good run in Victoria, but until now has not become dominant. In the long term, a public view of education as a common cultural and economic good has prevailed, and led to universal public provision. The Kennett version of the private view, as revealed so far in relation to education, is perhaps a moderate and expedient one. It believes that a large dose of the private spirit into public services will improve their efficiency—to such an extent, in fact, that very large cuts will be absorbed.

To date this dose of private spirit has been embodied in transfers of administration to schools and of some services to the private sector. These are supposed to balance out the permanent reductions in funding for staff. They will not, however, meet the increasing demand to expand schools' curriculum offerings. Inevitably, government schools face pressure to raise private contributions.

At the same time funding levels for non-government schools are maintained on the double assumption that a strong private sector increases choice and saves government from paying out the full cost per student. In Health, it has become routine for the minister responsible for public provision to urge people to make more use of private services via insurance. There are many creative ways to apply the same sort of thinking to education.

Of course, it may prove politically impossible to privatise schooling more than it now is. It is more likely that the processes now being implemented—decentralising administration and squeezing resources—will be allowed to engender gradually greater degrees of inequality among schools. They are, however, processes that could be used to withdraw altogether from direct public provision. We may yet see a Kennett government trying to persuade Canberra to go along with a radical voucher or competitive tendering system for all schooling.

A long-term plan for public education in Victoria would have to envisage more spending than at present. School buildings have been in a bad way for a long time. Many of them are the products of the hurried expansion of the 1950s and 1960s and are beyond their use-by date. Even when they are kept in reasonable repair, which is costly, they are inferior to most of the public and many of the private buildings in the community around them. A modern curriculum requires expensive facilities for technology, the arts and recreation which many schools do not yet have. It also requires much more hi-tech equipment than most schools have.

Even if the basic level of staffing remains at the level it has been cut to—which is probable—additional staffing for remedial programs in literacy and numeracy and for other equity programs is needed. And to rise from the present low standard of provision for specialist studies in primary school—languages, arts, technology—extra staff will be needed at that level. There is of course a trade-off possible here in that more specialist staff could release classroom teachers for more individual or small group remedial teaching.

COSTS OF A SYSTEM

Ancillary staffing, for school administration, district services and statewide curriculum development will also have to grow to service the kind of system described for the Schools of the Future. Victoria is presently at the bottom of the national scale for numbers of non-teaching staff. Systems making fewer demands on schools have more staff to support school administration. Principals and senior teachers are spending more of their time administering. Many claim to be desperately overworked.

This seems at odds with the government's singling out of principals as the educational leaders of the system. On the other hand, a marketer-manager oriented towards customer satisfaction may be the government's idea of an educational leader.

The more autonomous schools are, the more administrative work is replicated, and the greater the demand on central authorities to produce and monitor clear-cut policy and guidelines. Maintaining a centralised curriculum provided by two separate and to some extent rival bodies—the

Directorate and the Board of Studies—sets up an inescapable demand for bureaucrats. For the moment the government is getting along, with the help of a compliant press, by declaring everything a success even before it has happened. In the longer run, the system will have to deliver. Boasts of cutting bureaucracy to the bone are good propaganda, but they are usually belied by creeping increases in bureaucratic numbers.

If general staffing is kept at its present level, much of the recurrent cost of schooling could be managed within the state budget. But some of the larger costs involved in capital works and equipment may be beyond state resources even in a long-range plan. A plan to improve the state's poor school infrastructure probably requires a deal with the Commonwealth. This in turn requires trade-offs, one of which would be Victoria becoming a more reliable participant in national curriculum, training and certification.

In recent years the Commonwealth has been trying to unburden itself of direct responsibilities for school education. This has been made easy by the reassertion of states rights by both coalition and Labor states. On the surface, this is a combination that could lead to still larger drops in resource levels for education. In reality, there is an in-built tension that keeps school education on the national agenda. The states do not get enough money to fund big improvements beyond recurrent expenditure and some capital spending, and the Commonwealth needs evidence that extra money is being honestly used. Crucially, it also wants state activity to advance national economic needs, especially at the point where school education overlaps its fields of training and higher education. Thus the two levels of government are inescapably drawn into accountability arrangements. Today this essentially means collaboration on curriculum and assessment. The Kennett government's distaste for national collaboration in these areas may be the one thing it shares with left wing lobby groups.

SCHOOLS OF THE FUTURE

In the Kennett scheme of things devolution compensates for the cuts and sets public schooling within the government's more general philosophical framework of privatisation and small government wherever possible. Right now, public schools cannot be privatised outright. If their framework of finance and governance were clearer, they could perhaps be put up for tender. And as they are, they can be made corporate, enterprising, autonomous, accountable and competitive as Schools of the Future.

In its pristine form, the Schools of the Future program was a total devolution from bureaucracy to schools. At his first meeting with general managers after the election of the coalition government, the new Director of School Education, Geoff Spring, told regional general managers that their task was to stay long enough to 'turn out the lights'. The system would consist of a tiny central office and about seventeen hundred autonomous schools. 'Consultants'—mostly school principals with contacts but no idea of running a large system—would have Schools of the Future up and running just as soon as they could clear bureaucrats out of their offices. The general managers began to calculate the scope of their packages. Some took them, but three years later the positions are still there—filled in some cases by the consultants.

The Kennett government's selling of their devolution reforms sometimes suggests that Victoria is being a world-class innovator. In fact devolution in education has been a fashion in the English speaking world for a good while. Mrs Thatcher espoused it. New Zealand made a thorough job of it. Edmonton, Alberta is much visited and praised. Even the highly bureaucratic systems of the United States have played with it. And, much closer to home, the Catholic Education Office of Victoria has operated a devolved system for ages—if anything they're trying to introduce some centralism.

The Cain Labor government made a couple of muddled attempts to devolve authority to schools. Under the first Minister for Education, Robert Fordham, the authority of school councils to establish school policy was affirmed especially in the area of curriculum. Resources, however, remained under central management by city or regional offices. Thus schools could teach what they liked but staff appointments and finances were directed from outside.

Under Ian Cathie, the minister's office and the bureaucracy became convinced that this ideological devolution should be turned on its head: that the curriculum should be centralised and resource management devolved. As part of a restructuring of the central and regional bureaucracies, a paper called 'Taking schools into the 1990s' was put out for discussion. It proposed a modest level of devolution of resource management. Given the reception it got from the education unions and parent and school council organisations, who were the chief sounding boards for Labor policy, it might as well have proposed sale by auction of the entire system.

From then on, devolution of school administration was an idea held by the bureaucracy and favoured by many secondary school principals but unacceptable politically. With John Cain ignorant about educational matters, and Joan Kirner strongly opposed to devolution of school administration, it would have got nowhere in cabinet even had it been raised.

The Schools of the Future program got round the problems of opposition by ignoring the opponents. In the circumstances this was sensible. More often than not the opposition had come from peak bodies—the central office rather than the school or school council—whose self-interest was both manifest and craven. But it has still been hard to introduce the program. Much of the difficulty has come from the fact of its being introduced simultaneously with enormous cuts. In the minds of many people in the schools it is simply a cover for cuts, a passing off of responsibility for shortages from the centre to the schools. But in part, the difficulty arises from the culture of the system itself which is accustomed to over a century of central administration and has very low levels of administrative staff.

These difficulties of introduction, combined with the low intellectual quality of public descriptions of the program, make Schools of the Future an insubstantial concept. It may amount to little more than some devolution of administration. The general proposition that greater local responsibility will lead to better overall management is probably right. But even if the Schools of the Future program is well enough handled to achieve this, where does that take us? Good management is a necessary objective for any system, and a difficult one to achieve in large systems. But it is not sufficient to define the system. Once you've got it, you realise it is something you should always have had in order to get on with the main game. Individual school management may be better more often than large scale system management, but only the extremely cynical would deny that they both aim to serve the same purposes.

These purposes are not defined by reference to the management system. The main game is to get the best possible educational outcomes for the greatest number of students. The prime definers of this are the quality of teaching and the curriculum. Other school systems express this purpose in terms such as New South Wales's 'Excellence and Equity'. Achieving high quality in outcomes across the whole spectrum of students is both a school and a system responsibility. Caldwell and Sawatski talk about 'real schools of the future within a real system of the future', but leave only a foggy idea of what the system is and how it is improved.

At the moment it is very hard to assess the claimed virtues of this particular devolution effort. Schools write charters allegedly tying them into a system. They continue to get directives from the centre on anything that might be politically troublesome—fees, uniform, student conduct, aspects of curriculum. How real are the charters on the ground? Can their observance be effectively monitored—a difficult task even in a centralised system? Are there any discoverable limits to central direction on matters that attract public notice?

The Kennett government, for its part, seems to see schools essentially as it sees other affairs of state: as businesses requiring to be managed within a market. The market, however, is internal. Unlike banks, for example, the competition is not among rival systems. In the Schools of the Future market, each self-managing unit competes with other units in the manner of small businesses. Some units will flourish because they offer a wanted product; others will decline.

The difficulties of this concept lie in the defining of the product and the allocation of responsibility. By taking a very active role in defining the curriculum, the government is trying to fix one aspect of the product, so that every unit will know what has to be delivered, but leave other key aspects of the product open so that units can compete for customers—or, to put it more favourably, customers can have a choice. Some of these choices may be entirely valid: between languages or art forms, for example, or between codes of student conduct. But many will come down more crudely to questions of quality. Which schools get the better results in the most common and decisive elements of curriculum? Where can you get the best teaching? Or if the teaching cannot be controlled, where can you find the most select student population?

These are old and sensible questions that have shaped the development of the public system for a long time. Public administrators can only answer them by guaranteeing a high level of quality across the whole system. If the differences are great and manifest, the system becomes unbalanced, inefficient and inequitable.

SYSTEMATIC PROVISION

In highly centralised systems, enrolment policies are rigid. Schools are zoned either to districts or to selected populations. In devolved systems, enrolment policies give way to provision policies. Schools of the Future falls between two stools: it leaves enrolment to the market, but is light on planning for provision.

Closing, or opening, schools in a district dramatises the basic responsibility of a public system: to provide a service to the whole community. A century ago this responsibility was fulfilled by the building of state schools in the most out of the way corners of the state. In the middle of this century, the focus of this responsibility to provide shifted to new suburbs and to the demand for high schools in old suburbs that had been provided only with technical and domestic arts schools. Today some of the old rural schools are being closed down on the (arguable) grounds that they cannot provide efficiently. More often, however, provision is an issue in secondary schooling, especially in the senior years.

Discussion of provision usually turns on questions of quality. The presence in Victoria of Australia's largest private school sector always makes the quality of state provision a lively issue. The Kennett government has given the issue an even higher profile by cutting both staffing ratios and school budgets. There is, however, a fundamental question of provision that underpins issues of quality, namely whether the provision meets basic curriculum necessities. It is one thing to make maths teachers work harder; but another thing altogether to provide no maths at all.

The reality is that Victoria's schools already provide very differently. Any vision of public education has to be clear about the nature of differences that will be tolerated or encouraged and the measures that will be taken to eliminate undesirable differences. Diversity in education is often linked rhetorically to choice, as though it always results in greater provision. But some forms of diversity—such as little maths or no languages in a local school—limit choice.

Under Labor the basic questions of provision were being tackled by the process known as school reorganisation or district provision. The alternate names reflected the program's dual purposes. One purpose was economic: small secondary schools, of which there were many, not only have to be maintained but also usually have a more generous supply of teachers. Further, many, like Northlands, are in bad repair, requiring much more than routine maintenance. But this purpose rode in tandem with an upfront and widely agreed curricular purpose: schools with small senior secondary sections could not offer a sufficiently broad VCE. Joan Kirner in particular had stressed that this second purpose had to be the ruling purpose.

Behind these two immediate purposes was the larger general aim to make government schools the dominant system, the standard against which others had to measure themselves. The power of the private interest in education is nowhere stronger than in upper secondary schooling. Powerful comprehensive government secondary schools could be created by reorganising. School closures under Labor were a by-product—necessary but secondary—of reorganising schooling into districts. A district would consist of a substantial senior college, three or four junior secondary campuses and their main feeder primary schools. Had they been formed, districts might have been about the size of an old municipality and be closely related to a TAFE college. They might also have run some first year university courses.

District colleges would have been serious rivals to private schools, and might in the longer term have led to substantial links with Catholic systemic schools. The few multi-campus schools that were set up, such as Sandringham Secondary College, are very strong schools capable of drawing students from non-government schools. They were the first sign that comprehensive government schools could achieve the kind of standing confined up till then to academically selective schools.

These were the plans slowly making their way through the Cain–Kirner ministries against the resistance of self-styled guardians of public schooling, such as VICSSO. This is what Labor meant by school reorganisation, and it is how closures were normally achieved. Indeed it is the only way closures could ever have got through the Labor governments of the period. The same pressure groups within the party that continued to slow down or nullify the reorganisation process could have killed off altogether a simple closures process.

The Kennett government pursued only economic purposes in its closures. The district idea has survived in an attenuated form, as an alternative to regions for supplying a few specialist services. The notion of a district as the focus of a comprehensive provision of curriculum vanished. In its place, schools with old, and often inadequate, curriculum profiles are to evolve into self-managing units which will compete in offering services to clients. The charters of the units will require common elements, but these elements do not in themselves add up to the overall provision that would have been required of a district.

The difference in the two approaches can be illustrated in the provision of the VCE. At the level of the whole system, including both government and non-government schools, the Board of Studies provides a framework which it believes, rightly or wrongly, to be comprehensive. The present framework includes a range of academic studies grouped in fields and arrangements for accrediting vocational courses devised in the TAFE system.

The Board of Studies, however, does not run schools. It simply sets out a framework from which schools or systems select. From the standpoint of students and their families the only useful question is what is actually provided in the schools that are reasonably accessible to them? For some rural students this may turn into a question of where they will live during term, but the great majority of families should expect to find what they want within reasonable daily travelling distance.

This was the premise on which district provision was based. It was argued that a complex of schools and colleges within a fairly large district could provide comprehensively for students seeking a variety of academic and vocational programs. Without a district approach it was apparent that the several schools within the district tended to compete with one another for clients by offering minor variations of a limited curriculum. At a local level, the Board of Studies framework became a context for competition rather than comprehensiveness. Essentially, schools offering a successful, but very narrow, academic curriculum were prospering and schools offering vocational or softer academic courses were declining. A few schools were attracting students by offering a broad range of both academic and vocational courses, but their location was a matter of chance—many students who might have wanted such schools would probably not even have heard of them. In Schools of the Future terms the system needed not only individual school charters but also coherent district charters. As we know, the Kennett government scrapped the district idea for education even though it saw it as useful in other areas of public provision such as health.

The need for provision on a district basis is particularly acute at the VCE level where the range provided for in the Board of Studies framework is very wide; but it is felt to some extent at all levels. Arts, music, languages, technology, sport are in demand throughout primary and secondary school, but they cannot be provided adequately by single schools with a few hundred students. Unless the system steps in with a wider model of provision, individual units have to find ways to grow in order to compete. Successful schools grow to meet the most popular demands; unsuccessful ones decline slowly. This can be dressed up as bracing competition, but as a method of shifting resources, it is wasteful in both economic and educational terms.

The Schools of the Future program seems to by-pass general issues of systemic provision. It rightly asserts that schools should be as self-managing as possible within a publicly accountable system, and that they should be responsive to their clientele. In principle, at least, the program has attended to these matters by reinforcing the historical tendency of Victoria to devolve authority and have schools work within overall system guidelines. But the Schools of the Future project shares with its antecedents one crucial failing: it does not adequately define its product, and cannot therefore plan to provide it comprehensively. Such a failing would promptly destroy any of the business operations that schools are now said to be analogous to.

Even if we accept the language of the times—the system supplies a service, the school is a locus of service delivery and the student is the client (arguable in a political system that depends on votes), we still have a mess if we cannot say what the service consists of within that context. 'Education' is too broad an answer. So is 'the Board of Studies frameworks'. This is analogous to BHP saying it deals in minerals and stuff. The company would only survive if the law obliged everyone to use minerals and stuff for twelve years of their lives. In the market they would have to define their product more sharply. In education, we have to know precisely what the units are supposed to deliver.

The Board of Studies framework is a pile of paper, not a delivered service to students. The school charters will be, in Caldwell and Sawatski's word, a 'theoretical strategic planning document' if the unit is not equipped to deliver the service imagined by the Board. And the fact is that most Victorian schools, even before the cuts, could not deliver. At senior secondary level, provision for vocational education was pathetic, languages close to non-existent, humanities virtually a private school preserve. At primary and junior secondary level, languages, arts, technology and sports ranged from thin to invisible. A school with plentiful provision in any one of these areas stood out.

There has been a decade of rhetoric about guidelines and strategic plans, but only the district provision idea was trying to come to terms with putting the service on the ground within reach of all students. Labor and its pressure groups variously promoted and resisted the idea. The coalition scrapped it. The best long-term approach would have been to combine the idea of systematic provision with school and district self-management and the present government's barge-in-and-do-it style. A combination of that sort would result in extensive reorganisation of government schooling, rather than simply self-management for the survivors. It would also probably have produced what the government says it is aiming for but not getting: better provision for less money.

Most Victorians would swap all the talk about best practice in Alberta and average practice in Australia for a scheme to have a public system competing successfully with private schools. If this idea has come to anyone in a position of influence, they must regret the opportunity passed up to achieve it. At the ministerial and governmental level there is not the least trace of such a vision. On the contrary, there has been a fall in public school retention and a rise in private school patronage figures. These draw defensive rather than competitive responses from government spokespeople. This is telling in a government that flatters itself on its love of competition and boasts of dedication to international best practice.

ENROLMENT

Uneven and unplanned provision highlights questions about enrolment. For a long time the Victorian school system had rigid enrolment policies. Schools had zones and every child within the zone was entitled to a place. The apparent assumption here was that every unit of the system—every school—offered a uniform standard of provision.

The appearance of uniform provision, however, had two large escape hatches at the secondary school level: at one end a system of secondary technical schools in parallel with high schools, and at the other end a clutch of selective high schools. Both of these descended from the early days of public education when it was hard enough to set up any sort of public secondary school let alone an open comprehensive system. Later, selective schools would be defended by their patrons on the grounds that they offered choice, excellence and even equity. But although successive governments tolerated their continuing existence—and from time to time basked in their prestige—further selective schools were not established. More importantly, following recommendations in the 1985 Blackburn Report, the technical and high school systems were merged. By the beginning of the 1990s, Victoria ostensibly had a comprehensive system.

This new system, however, used no zones. Through the 1970s and 1980s a general decline in overall student numbers combined with shifts in ideology to emphasise parental choice and by implication diversity of provision. Many schools had already tried to differentiate their programs to suit the students they had in their district. Now those needing to increase their enrolments changed both programs and style to suit the students they wanted to attract. With the Kennett closures, many of the least successful in this competition no doubt vanished, but the competition itself has not disappeared. Victorian schools continue to be diverse and the Schools of the Future program entrenches their need to remain competitive.

Since the 1970s, diversity and its partner choice have become sacred cows in education. The private sector is especially fond of milking them. The general ideology of government today—at least in the Anglophone world—has added competition to the holy herd. But what reality does this rhetoric stand for in education? Is the kind of diversity we have the kind we want in a public system?

Historically, selective schools, high schools and technical schools have formed an academic pyramid. Selective schools and high schools offered the same curriculum, except at times for Latin, but with better results in the selective schools. Technical schools offered a markedly different curriculum but one which was seen as suited to students of low ability.

When the Kennett government came into office, it had already been demonstrated by researchers that a typical school district in Victoria contained a predictable hierarchy of secondary schools (it is hard to get performance figures from primary schools, but those feeding popular secondary schools obviously tend to be in more demand). At the top of the pile and having trouble fitting applicants in was an academic high school, probably with a school uniform. Next was a high school offering a mixed curriculum, a bit lighter on academic subjects and correspondingly heavier on 'alternatives'. At the bottom and struggling to stay open was the old tech or the school that a few years earlier relied on STC for its enrolment.

Without any central direction, the general historical pattern founded on ability had cloned itself in each district across the system. The difference was that actual enrolment policies were covert. Overtly, the policy was one of open choice. But the pattern had many restrictive features: each separate offering was in itself narrow; some kinds of study could not be offered in any of the schools, some that might have been useful in particular schools could not be offered, and students were locked into a particular pattern with little chance of variation. In short, the choices were preset and the students had to fit them.

District provision set out to reconstruct this enrolment pattern, basically by putting the various academic, practical and vocational programs under one roof and incorporating feeder schools into a cooperative overall administration. Obviously this would not alter the forces that sustain the hierarchy of subjects but it widened the choice for any one individual without restricting specialisation.

Without this layer of planned provision, and of course without any zoning, schools are in an enrolment market. What will they sell? If the past is anything to go by it won't be diversity, it will be quality. Most people want an academic curriculum, some a vocational one, the latter sometimes as a fallback. If only one can be offered they will want the academic. For most families the choice will be between first or second rate academic. Despite all the national urging and local lip service, vocational education will continue to be the loser.

The aim of competition is presumably to raise general standards. By competing all will improve their quality. The drawback is that if standards become clearly different, no one will want the inferior variety. This is not a commercial service where quality can be offset against price. People want the best for their children, and they want it badly. Which is another way of saying they do not want diversity between schools, in programs, quality, cost or results. They want flexibility with quality wherever they live.

Public school enrolment policies also have to deal with young people who fall through the provision net: the truants, the kids who leave one school and don't turn up at another, the homeless who lack the support to get to school regularly, the difficult students a school wants to move on. Regional offices used to try to track these and make arrangements. District structures that enabled school and social agencies to work together would be the most effective set up. Even under the best arrangements, such students are hard to count, find and place. How Kennett's skeletal regions and districts handle the problem is anyone's guess.

CURRICULUM

To plan provision requires clear views about the school curriculum and its resourcing. In opposition the Liberal Party learnt that the surest avenue to publicity was through the curriculum. With the help of David Penington, it attacked the VCE remorselessly and hopped on any other curriculum band-wagon offering: standards of literacy, the content of English courses, propa-ganda in social studies, the ruination of mathematics, the decay of science, the neglect of genius and so on. In general, it rode the old conservative hobby horse that change in curriculum necessarily leads to decline in standards. While claiming concern for the fate of all students in a now universal school, it appealed to nostalgia for a familiar meritocratic curriculum.

Once the party came to office, however, the curriculum was no longer fair game for headlines. On the contrary, it has to be sustained, defended and kept up-to-date. Of necessity, most of the curriculum that was attacked so vehemently has now to be supported. It is hard to change curriculum even if you have good ideas. The Kennett government has few ideas, good or bad, on the subject.

Changes to the VCE curriculum mostly confirmed what was already in train, except for assessment where changes took the certificate backwards. A review of the way teachers' assessments were verified (by Brown and Ball, the latter now Executive Director of the Victorian Board of Studies) concluded that the process was unreliable. But the conclusion seems to have been fore-gone. The Director of ACER, Professor Barry McGaw, has since pointed out that the review evidence itself showed the verification process to be as reliable as other common forms of assessments for tertiary entrance. Other recent research confirms the reliability of teachers' assessments.

The Curriculum Standards Framework for the years P–10 differs little from any of its cousins or predecessors, local, interstate or national. The attempt to move into curriculum monitoring with the LAP tests was bun-gled. Dismantled literacy programs will have to be revived.

Essentially this means that what was already untidy, because it was in an early stage of transition, has become messy. Immense and necessary changes have been misunderstood, slowed down or derailed. Just as planned provision of the curriculum was cast aside in favour of chaotic petty competition, so the momentum of curriculum planning and development has drifted into a lame provincialism reminiscent of the early 1980s.

The Kennett government came to power as the last phase of a national curriculum was being worked on by all the states and territories. When the project was completed, nine months later, Victoria combined with other coalition state governments on the council of ministers to reject the work. The New South Wales Liberal minister, Virginia Chadwick, who had up till then strongly supported the national project, was forced to rescue what she could from what might have become outright rejection.

The rejection was motivated by a mixture of ignorance, anti-Labor senti-ment and states rights superstition. The national curriculum had in fact been developed jointly by the states and territories; but it was depicted as a Commonwealth product and thrown out. States would develop their own versions. The assumption that curricula developed state by state must, by right, be better than a curriculum developed by national collaboration was not questioned. States have the responsibility for running schools, and hence must devise their own curricula, runs the argument. A new Labor minister for education in NSW is the latest to repeat the argument.

The states rights position confuses management and curriculum. Certainly the prospect of Australian schools being managed by a Commonwealth department is appalling. Many, including the Victorian government, assert that management by a large state bureaucracy is bad enough. Common sense, experience and good management practice all point to small-scale management at district and school level. But it does not follow automatically from this that curriculum and teaching methods should be local matters, or even state matters.

Curriculum is no more a sensible states issue than railway gauges. The school curriculum is the means by which we ensure that young Australians are introduced to the nation's culture. Often the curriculum will merely complement the education provided by families and cultural groups, but in some respects it is the principal agency. A curriculum is what schools have in common, what makes it possible for students to move from one school to another and for all students to share in a national culture. It is a statement of what all young Australians should know and be able to do. In large measure it is already common to all states and territories. Early in the national curriculum project it became clear that state authorities, and in some cases, individual schools, had been toiling along producing, unknown to one another, the same curriculum. Same strengths, same high hopes, same warts, same anachronisms, same follies.

The incoming coalition ministry rationalised its rejection of national work by claiming that it was not good enough. Victoria, however, could not do better. The Curriculum Standards Framework developed by Victoria's Board of Studies is mostly a straight copy of the national frameworks, and where it diverges—in maths and science—indicates that the people doing the adaptation either didn't know what they were up to or were clumsily engaged in setting back the clock. Some changes—such as the elimination of outcomes for Australian history in junior secondary school—are a capitulation of management to professional nuttiness.

The successful critical talk of opposition has not yet shown a positive side in government. Resources for making significant improvement in curriculum are scarce. It probably takes a well-managed national effort to muster them sufficiently. More and more, state efforts reveal the thinness of provincial professional and political thought about curriculum.

The provincial curriculum not only sacrifices the advantages of having a common curriculum for all Australians, but also turns out to be inferior in quality. There appears to be nothing a provincial curriculum can do that a national curriculum cannot, except perhaps allow provincial politicians to grandstand for their supporters. A national curriculum on the other hand can be a focus for national cultural debate and for the pooling of scarce intellectual resources. As a side benefit it can also force provincial politicians and pundits to survive outside their little ponds. It is time for some of the strongest lobbies for national curriculum, which include business and the armed forces, to open their mouths again.

It must be remembered however, that the move to national collaboration was in its infancy. There was a very long way to go. The ordering of a common curriculum from prep to year 10 in eight areas, each with explicit lines of learning outcomes was novel and is still untried. To test and improve it requires five to ten year cycles of review and adjustment. Although all states seem to be pursuing much the same approach, their refusal to collaborate can only weaken the process, if not kill it off.

A NARROWING CURRICULUM

At the upper secondary level, national collaboration was even more immature. A statement of key competencies related to employment was produced, but it was sidelined as something relevant only to vocational training. Discussion of a national year 12 certificate was kept off the agenda.

The resistance of state boards of studies to opening the senior school curriculum to national discussion reflects the jealousy with which private school and university lobbies protect the processes of academic selection. These are not processes that can be tampered with lightly by any government. Their dominance, however, produces effects that governments cannot ignore: overheated demand for university places and the curriculum that delivers them, stunted development of vocational education and training, and inadequate curricula for a large proportion (perhaps half) of the senior school population. Some of these deficiencies, as we have noted, stem from inadequate school structures which cannot deliver even the curriculum that exists; but some are also built into the basic frameworks of the boards of studies.

These are national deficiencies, reflecting national uncertainty about the integration into senior secondary schooling of what used to be wholly quarantined in TAFE, junior techs and industry. They reflect also the limitations of depending on England and the United States for models. Scotland, France or Sweden would each be more instructive. Victoria has been nibbling at the task since the Blackburn Report of 1985, but in ten years has not produced much more than some dual accreditation of VCE and TAFE studies. These crediting arrangements have certainly benefited some students and schools, but they are circling around the basic question without landing. Why have divided curriculum and assessment arrangements (schools and TAFE) when the great majority of students are in school ostensibly studying for a single certificate? On this question the Victorian Board of Studies has barely kept up with the average national rate of inaction.

For the curriculum of prep to year 10, the eight areas of the national project have been accepted with minor variation in every state. In principle, at least, this puts an end to the divided curricula that prevailed, especially in secondary schools, well into the 1980s. In practice, large questions of provision and teacher development arise. The common curriculum implied by the adoption of the eight areas includes subjects that were previously elective or, particularly at primary level, not provided at all: languages, technology, arts. It also implies levels of achievement in the former core subjects of maths and English beyond those previously achieved by large groups of students.

Even the large number of school closures already made does not increase typical school size very much. The simultaneous cutting of general staff levels and reinforcing of the autonomy of small schools make it very hard to broaden the curriculum. Essentially, primary schools need more teachers, secondary schools need to be organised into junior and senior campuses, and both need effective ways of sharing resources.

Contrary to any idea of comprehensive provision, the present trend of government policy will require schools to select specialities that draw big numbers rather than offer a broad range. This will be presented as choice for parents and competitive opportunity for schools. Some will sustain languages, some not, some music, some not, and so on. Schools with superior private resources will offer more, thereby tacitly exemplifying the fact that those who can afford it prefer breadth of choice to a limited selection.

THE BASICS

In the matters of literacy and mathematics, the Kennett government offers an example of what guardians of traditional standards do when they get into office: they cut down special programs and introduce tests. This satisfies the instinct that educational problems arise from slackness in teachers rather than disadvantage in students, and more generally that differences in school performance are individually rather than socially based.

The government's cuts to staffing across the board inevitably cut also into early reading programs such as Reading Recovery and Reading Together which were building under the previous government's Literacy Strategy. In many schools, these programs had been made possible by rearranging allotments within existing staff levels. As general staff numbers drop, so does the school's capacity to allot teachers to intensive teaching or programs requiring extra administration. Remedial programs in maths had a much lighter grip on life than reading programs. They readily fall away as staff resources are squeezed.

In a field swept by the winds and sighs of pundits, cranks and quacks, it is necessary to keep on repeating basic facts about the so-called basics. The key fact is that we now need higher standards than we have ever demanded, simply because we expect virtually everyone to continue with literary subjects and maths through to year 12, and to develop high order skills in thinking. To this we need to add the indications from repeated research that a student's school performance is usually determined by their performance in reading up to about year 3. Maths we know less about, except that large numbers are performing poorly by the middle of secondary school. The demands made on all students now to think and communicate can only be satisfied from a strong base in early schooling.

How to raise universal standards in literacy and maths is a matter of continuing controversy. The suggestion implied in some critiques of modern methods that reading failure can be fixed by going back to the old methods which did not in fact work for everybody is plainly nutty. The best advice for class level teaching is to use a range of methods and where possible to include parents; but persistent trouble probably needs one-to-one teaching in regular, short doses. Hence the need for extra staff, and the vulnerability of literacy programs to general cuts.

If the Kennett government decides to restore some of the lost ground in these areas, it will probably claim another stroke of world leadership. Parents and other educators, however, will simply wonder why the government adopted such a chaotic approach to so central a problem.

The reason for the stop-and-maybe-start-again approach obviously lies partly in the government's slash and burn style. It may lie partly in the government's ideology of public administration, which avoids planning in favour of local management. It may also result from the fact that responsibility for curriculum is divided obscurely between the Board of Studies and the Directorate. As with many aspects of curriculum, improving standards in the basics requires systematic planning and some leadership. The present ministry seems to be preoccupied with resource and administrative questions and to be merely puddling along with its curriculum functions.

If the ministry wants more coherent planning it will probably decide to strengthen its curriculum and monitoring bureaucracy and shoulder aside the Board of Studies. The Board has been mediocre in most things and bungled the selling of the LAP testing. The hazard of such a territorial battle is that it draws private schools and universities out on the Board's side, but the Directorate can stake out a lot of ground by increasing its own resources and taking the initiative in strategic areas such as literacy, maths, vocational education, key competencies, accountability and national collaboration.

PARTICIPATION
A government committed to planning finds it necessary to consult with those affected. In educational matters this is often the whole community. An educated community expects to have an effective say in broad policy, as well as in the local things that affect their own children.

A rough summary of public consultation in education over the past decade is that Labor became entangled in it and Kennett got rid of it. Labor's school closures process, for example, was like the AFL's attempts to get mergers. No one could agree until everyone agreed. Kennett simply nailed up a list and cleared people out.

In government, both parties emphasised increasing the powers of school councils. This is essentially a representative solution, which allows for community consultation if the council wishes it. Over the 1980s many schools developed strong relations with their local communities. Whether increasing the management and budgetary powers of councils will change their relationship to the community remains to be seen.

Labor also stressed consultation at the central level, with unions and with the peak organisations of schools councils and parents club. Unions and central organisations from both government and non-government schools held positions on boards and committees as well as having direct access to the minister. This was often a cumbersome and obstructive way to conduct affairs. Representation even on high level boards was undermined by direct dealing between government and organisations, and consensus consisted of what was left after all dissent was removed.

But the Kennett government's dumping of all such consultation cannot be seen as a solution. The community as a whole—and not only parents—has a big stake in education and education in turn profits from a high standard of public knowledge of and debate about its programs and directions. At the least there needs to be sustained, open monitoring of trends in public services. The combination under Labor of statutory boards and freedom of information did not work well in practice but it would be useful to re-examine the elements. A board has to be clear of sectional influences and have the resources as well as the authority not only to comment but also to conduct its own monitoring and research.

The Kennett government is notorious for its secrecy, being more inclined to legislate to suppress information than to make it available for public debate. In education, the casualty of this approach is not only debate but also planning. Education is well beyond the stage where it can be improved by the simple application of policy and resources. Both policy and resourcing have to be grounded in thorough educational research. Claiming world leadership in wiping out bureaucracy is no substitute for maintaining a bureaucracy free to research the effects of what you are doing. There is not so much known about education that we can afford to do without what we have. Politicians cultivate electoral advantage by promising testing programs, but each incoming government has its own pet method. Continuity with previous administrations is last on their list. Each has to be persuaded over again to finance long-term and penetrating research. With a press interested chiefly in shocking findings, the public hears little of useful, continuing research and educational policy is only marginally influenced by it.

AN INADEQUATE PUBLIC SYSTEM

In 1996 we will see a change of minister—another from the coalition according to the opinion polls. A new ministry, even from the same side, may also see change in the senior bureaucracy. In a politicised public service entrenched bureaucrats are thought to have agendas of their own.

A new ministry is not likely to change the essential policies of the Hayward ministry. It may realise, however, that they are extremely limited, indeed that they are not adequate to the management of a public school system. Teacher numbers have been brought down to a national average and some administration has been devolved. Even if this puts us ahead of England, New Zealand and Edmonton, Alberta, it's nothing to write home about.

The real target is students' learning. The most obvious and undeniable fact about students' learning is that it can be improved by good teaching. Whether teaching is improved by getting schools to tighten their belts and manage their allotted resources is unknown. The Hayward ministry and its consultants and publicists have had no doubts on this largely unresearched matter. One supposes they have had a vision.

The greatest contribution a new ministry could make to the quality of public schooling would be to restore teacher numbers where they are clearly needed—notably in programs to improve literacy and maths—and to plan for the professional development of classroom teachers.

As the manager of a public system, a new ministry will inherit a nebulous set of arrangements described as self management. While each unit of the system will no doubt be managing in its own way, some excellently, some awfully, there will be no systematic pattern of provision across the state. Unless things change, the Board of Studies will go on publishing provincial versions of national frameworks, and schools will go on picking out the bits they can do, the bits they like and the bits they can raise extra money for. Nor will there be systematic patterns of enrolment or school accountability. Some schools will be more anxious to compete for particular populations than to provide for their locality. Students will continue to fall down the cracks between the schools that push them out and the schools that don't pick them up. Schools will continue to impose fees and the ministry to describe them as voluntary. Committees will continue to publish guidelines for school charters, school reports, school sponsorships, school uniforms—anything that can't be controlled or stopped, and therefore needs to be covered by policy.

If a new ministry wants to strengthen public schooling—and the commitment of the Kennett government to any form of public provision beyond a 'safety net' is questionable—there are some quick improvements that could be made. Improving teaching is slow, but planning for equitable and comprehensive provision on a district basis could be established in the lifetime of a government. So could a defensible return to a national agenda for curriculum, certification and vocational education. None of this strengthening would set back what the present government sees as its pace-setting reforms; indeed, they too would be strengthened. They are not even costly measures. What they need is commitment to public education, to a school system of the future.

A Health System in Crisis

Conflict and Ideology in Victorian Health Care

Meredith Carter, John Thwaites, Andrew Refshauge

Contents

A Revolution in Health Care

Commercial or Democratic?

Meredith Carter

Major changes have occurred in the Victorian health system since the change of state government in 1992. According to Dr John Paterson, the secretary of the Department of Health and Community Services, these changes reflect 'a philosophical revolution' in thinking about the role of government occurring worldwide. Looking at developments in other states and territories around Australia, it certainly seems that Victoria is by no means the only state affected by this revolution, although some of its principles may be applied with a greater degree of enthusiasm than is seen elsewhere.

A CORE VALUE: A DEMOCRATIC HEALTH SYSTEM

For the ordinary person trying to assess these developments useful first questions might be:

•What kind of health services do we want?

•How can we best achieve such a system?

While this might lead to concerns about who delivers those services, it is useful to start without any assumptions or stereotypes.

In answering the question 'What kind of health services do we want?' the World Health Organization (WHO) has suggested that an essential ingredient of the worldwide strategy of achieving health for all people is the massive involvement of the public, not just in the support and operation of health services but also in the decisions about the allocation of resources and the determination of priorities. The WHO argues that the target of health for all will be unobtainable unless radically different forms of health care are put into practice, permitting the development of health services that are people's services, responsive not only to people's needs in respect of health and development and encompassing more than just services designed and maintained by health personnel or focused solely on medical care. (WHO Study Group 1991)

In essence what this recognises is that people have interests in health care not just as the end users or 'customers' of health services but also as citizens and as taxpayers. As citizens, people are interested in the outcomes of health care, in planning and in resource allocation issues. As taxpayers people are concerned about the funding and costs of health care.

It is also useful to reflect on what the World Health Organization has to say about the future of health care. A recent editorial of *World Health*, the

WHO journal, suggests that three concepts must apply (Bryant 1994):

•Communities must endorse the concept of universal coverage or access to care.

•Communities must ensure that care is available according to need. Application of these concepts requires defining a population, assessing its needs and ensuring that all those who need it receive care in keeping with available resources

•Increasingly vital to the future organisation of health care is 'democratisation'. The concept of democratisation will feature in decision making at all levels of the health system: impacting on the relationship between doctors and consumers, communities and health services; and managers and policy makers.

It might be thought that these concepts or values underpin the kind of accountability most Australians might want from our health system and services. Through Medicare, Australian society has already endorsed the concepts of universal coverage and of medical services at least, provided according to need. Through the device of a Public Hospital Patient's Charter, the state and Commonwealth governments have also agreed on a statement of principles to underpin a more democratic relationship between individual patients and hospital service providers. Thus it may be useful to keep in mind the WHO concepts when assessing the 'philosophical revolution' in government as it applies to health services and whether the changes made in its name promote a democratic approach to health care—a people's health system.

COMMERCIALISATION AND MARKET SOLUTIONS

Key components of the revolution are the application of a commercial ethos and market solutions to the delivery of health services. The Victorian experience makes a useful case study for assessing these developments especially since the Secretary of the state Department of Health and Community Services suggests that Victoria is making an important national contribution to the re-evaluation of the role of government occurring in this country.

Underlying this re-evaluation are beliefs about how best to maximise the value of the taxpayer's dollar and how to obtain greater accountability from service providers for their use of that dollar. The Victorian government has been very explicit about its endorsement of applying a commercial approach to achieve these outcomes, including competition between the public and private sector in health care delivery as far as possible. A Department of Health and Community Services briefing note, written shortly after the change of government, suggested that:

the creation of equity between the public and private sectors means that public sector providers will need to move to a more commercial approach in their operations. The government has now created such a framework through the State Owned Enterprises Act and consideration must be given as to how such a commercial approach can be progressively implemented in the health and community services system.

The Victorian approach also includes attention to making services more 'consumer oriented' and in the health sector making them more 'patient focused' and sometimes even 'customer oriented'. The use of the term 'customer' is appropriate because the kind of consumer orientation envisaged tends to cast consumers in a passive role as the recipient of government services rather than a citizen entitled to actively participate in planning, monitoring and evaluating government services. This approach is somewhat limited in terms of encouraging actual consumer participation, or in many cases even maintaining funding to existing consumer organisations.

In the Victorian health sector there have been few if any areas of government or government funded activity left untouched. Some groups falling within the federal government's priority areas such as cancer, mental health and heart disease have been relatively protected from budget cuts. However, peak organisations such as the Victorian Alcohol and Drug Agencies Association (VAADA), community health centres, women's health services (including family planning clinics) and consumer organisations such as Health Issues Centre have all suffered severe cuts. Restructures, mergers, attempts to develop 'paying services' and other survival tactics have become commonplace.

Nor have hospitals been exempted from significant budget cuts. A new audit of Victoria's public finances was undertaken by a specially constituted Victorian Commission of Audit which reported at the end of April 1993. Although, like the immediately preceding audit of Victoria's finances, its methodology and findings have been criticised, key findings included statements that Victoria's hospitals are 9 per cent more costly to operate than their New South Wales counterparts. Solutions considered by the Commission included sales of public hospitals and nursing homes. This option was an attractive way to minimise recurrent spending and also attractive because

> experience has shown that corporatised or privatised entities can offer superior service quality, and yet deliver community service obligations by adopting effective, modern management models and focusing on customer service. (Victorian Commission of Audit 1993: 128)

Ironically, it is only a few short years since the Victorian Hospitals Association suggested in its discussion paper *Privatise Public Hospitals?*, that 'it is unlikely that any level of government would ... even consider the mass sale of public hospitals to the private sector' (Victorian Hospitals Association 1988).

The Commission of Audit concluded that unfortunately, present Commonwealth policies on the funding of public hospitals and a lack of incentives for people to take out private insurance provide major impediments to such proposals. Meantime then, the Commission proposed other recommendations consistent with the state government's commitment to making greater use of private facilities. Recommendations included:

- •privatisation of outpatients services to improve efficiency and reduce recurrent outlays by shifting costs to the Commonwealth budget
- •rationalising hospital services through joint or network arrangements between hospitals
- •competition between private and public hospitals in metropolitan and larger provincial centres
- •commercialising non-core services such as catering and cleaning in public hospitals (i.e. contracting out) and
- •reviewing nursing structures and numbers. (Victorian Commission of Audit 1993: 117–30)

Casemix funding, a strategy derived from the United States, is also seen to provide a stepping stone both to a more efficient public sector and to greater competitive activity between the public and private sectors, since it enables cost comparisons to be made more meaningful. Dr John Paterson has described casemix as follows.

> The idea was that if you are admitted for an ingrown toenail then the government would pay say $100 flat for that and for whatever followed from it. The government would no longer write an open cheque for as much as the doctor felt like earning from public patients on the day. It was an extraordinary good idea ... It is a wonderful technique for paying for output (but) not a health strategy in itself. (Paterson 1993a)

CASEMIX FUNDING

Casemix is the funding mechanism all states and territories have agreed to work towards over the life of the current Medicare Agreement. It was introduced first in Victoria, from 1 July 1993. The federal government says that casemix-linked funding should enable planners, providers and payers to better manage and distribute resources for patients. The Victorian government has also begun to develop an Epidemiology Unit to provide better statistical information about the health status and needs of the community and thus eventually provide a better base for determining what type of casemix should be purchased from Victorian hospitals.

As part of the new competitive environment, hospitals were told that they would have the autonomy from the state Department of Health and Community Services they had long sought but they were also told they would be made more responsible for their own decisions. In the Victorian Hospitals Association newsletter, the state Department Secretary invited hospitals to try his quick quiz titled 'Will you still be alive in 1995?' in order to assess their likelihood of survival in this new climate (Paterson 1993b). Financial incentives for hospitals to compete included access to a special pool of funds to reward those hospitals which took steps to cut their waiting lists. The pool was in fact funded by the hospitals themselves. Funds were reserved by the Department for additional throughput but hospitals were unable to draw on the pool if designated high priority patients were kept waiting more than a month for surgery.

This new regime was short lived. Hospitals showed themselves quite capable of competing and the bonus funding pool was soon under considerable strain. In addition hospitals were, not surprisingly, beginning to specialise in areas able to return a profit under casemix. For example, cardiac units began to proliferate. At the same time waiting lists re-emerged as a problem and 'shroud waving' attracted renewed attention in the media as the impact of budget cuts also began to take real effect. The government did not resile from competition but recognised the need to temper the process with planning. The Premier stepped in and announced yet another review under the aegis of a special Metropolitan Hospitals Planning Board.

The Planning Board reports seem to have turned to the proposals mooted by the Victorian Commission of Audit for inspiration. Public hospitals are to be corporatised to reflect more closely beliefs about the operation of the private sector. Melbourne's metropolitan hospital stock is to undergo 'reconfiguration' in networks governed by seven hospital boards. The existing forty or so boards were sacked. Presumably this will enable the rationalisation of the excess floor space the Commission of Audit (1993: 130) considered was provided in Victorian public hospitals and of the number of hospital establishments themselves.

There is no intention to include community members as such on the new paid hospital network boards which comprise people primarily selected for their business expertise. Legislation was passed to prohibit any appeals through the courts against these forced amalgamations. *The Age* newspaper editorialised on 12 May 1995, that this legislation may have been motivated by the 'urgency' of the task.

A BROADER SWEEP TO THE MARKET ETHOS
As in Victoria, corporatisation and privatisation in various guises is firmly on the agenda of health departments around Australia. Considerable media attention has been given to the strong trend across several states to privatise hospital outpatients services. Commonly this is achieved by the hospital ceasing to provide public outpatient clinics using doctors contracted to the hospital. The same services are then provided by the same doctors in their capacity as private clinicians in privatised consulting rooms. Alternatively, people are encouraged not to use outpatients and emergency services but to attend their local general practitioner instead. These are strategies which enable state governments to 'shift' the costs onto the federal budget because the federal government is responsible for payment for medical services outside hospitals.

Yet overall such practices are likely to increase the costs of such services to the taxpayer. In its 1995 survey of Australia, the OECD criticised this strategy, arguing that 'the driving force behind growth in health expenditures in Australian is volume growth in the fee-for-service sectors' (see Davidson 1995).

But cost shifting is simply one component across the spectrum reflecting a shift to a market approach to health. Strategies start with what might almost be described as *simple privatisation*. Examples of this include the federal government sale of some of its repatriation hospitals to private corporations. *Compulsory competitive tendering* and *contracting out* (particularly cleaning, catering and any other so called hotel services) are very much favoured in several states including Western Australia. Even the Australian Medical Association has concerns about any extension of these activities. Responding to an Industry Commission Inquiry into contracting out by public sector agencies, the AMA suggested that the quality, continuity and 'culture' of health care could suffer. The AMA also expressed concern at the impact on teaching and research when the key criteria for competitive tendering is price (*Medical Observer* 9 June 1995).

Senator Richardson, when he was federal Minister for Health, was keen to revive the strategy of buying beds for public patients in private hospitals where this would be useful to reduce waiting lists, but there has been little takeup of the money offered to implement this proposal.

More acceptable to the private sector have been complex partnership arrangements such as private operators building and running public hospitals. A notorious example occurred in New South Wales where the state government entered a 20 year contract with the Mayne Nickless hospital subsidiary, Health Care of Australia Limited, to build and operate the first private for profit 'public' hospital at Port Macquarie (Catchlove 1993: 2). As this enterprise was to be the only 'public' hospital in the region, it met with a storm of community protests before finally opening after protracted negotiations in late 1994. Ironically the battle over the three years since the initial agreement was signed in 1992 has led to a very detailed health service agreement including attention not just to costs but to quality. The agreement also builds in community participation by way of community advisory and monitoring committees.

THE CHALLENGE OF CHANGE FOR THE HEALTH SYSTEM

Few would disagree that changes to the hospital system are overdue. The dominance of hospitals in the health system and the bias towards funding for hospitals rather than community-based care has done little to alter the disparities in health outcomes between different groups in our community. As the National Health Strategy report *Enough to Make You Sick* (1992) demonstrates so clearly, poor health status is about poor socio-economic status. If you are a single mother, if you are Aboriginal, or if you are among the long-term unemployed then even if you eat well, you don't drink and you exercise appropriately, statistically you are still more likely to die at an earlier age than a person with the same level of risk factors who is better educated and on a higher income.

The dominance of hospitals has done nothing to ensure that the community is consulted about the shape of the health system or to ensure adequate care in the community. This is despite the fact that the chronic health conditions which are most prevalent such as hypertension, asthma, arthritis, diabetes, are amenable to treatment in the community. All too often, the need for acute, inpatient care represents a failure to provide adequate community-based care (Harvey 1991).

Health economist, Dr Terri Jackson, has pointed out that the dominance of the hospital system has done little to change a health system in which decisions about the shape of the system are made with little concern for the input of ordinary people. Her comment comes over and above the perspective of specific groups such as women users, or the cultural practices and beliefs of Aboriginals and Torres Strait Islanders or immigrants to Australia. Hospital dominance has left largely unchanged a system in which doctors still make most important decisions, too often ignoring the contribution of co-professionals and more importantly without really understanding the range of priorities and needs of individual patients (Jackson 1993).

So certainly it can be agreed that change in the hospital system and in the health system as a whole is overdue. However, is it a shift to a more commercial ethos that is needed? And what is it that suddenly makes change urgent? The concerns just outlined have been conspicuously absent. Rather the justification for much of this activity is that health care costs are rising, health care resources are scarce, private health insurance levels are falling and the population is ageing. Thus the argument goes, that the community just can't afford it all.

Yet according to the 1995 OECD survey Australia's health spending is around average for western countries at about 8.5 per cent while health outcomes (measured in terms of infant mortality, life expectancy and so on) continue to improve in line with those of other comparable countries. Interestingly, the Australian Institute of Health and Welfare (1994: 31) has reported that when we ask whether we are spending too much or too little or just about enough on health care, it is not possible to provide a simple answer. There is a growing debate about whether the level of health expenditure is in fact an important determinant of health in industrialised countries.

Resolving this apparently simple question relates to the difficulties of measuring overall health status and also the fact that there is no hard evidence as to the overall impact on health of most of the treatments and services delivered by modern health care systems. There is little evidence that increasing expenditure as a percentage of gross domestic product (GDP) would significantly improve overall health status. This is not, however, an argument that Australia is necessarily spending too much on health care.

Certainly Australia spends well below the 14 per cent (and rising) expenditure on health services in the United States, which relies heavily on market-based responses to the health needs of the American population. Health care costs have here been rising slowly (and this growth is much less dependent on the business cycle than are other sectors of the economy) but Australia's health spending has also been relatively stable over the years since the introduction of Medicare. Growth, where it has occurred, has been particularly in the private sector. For example, private hospitals grew at a faster average annual rate than recognised public hospitals by three percentage points between 1985/86 and 1990/91, and faster than total recurrent health expenditure (Australian Institute of Health and Welfare 1994: 11).

Thus, while there are pressures on Australia's health spending we can justifiably question where the notion of spiralling health care costs comes from. Why is there this popular notion of crisis needing to be solved with strategies such as competition, corporatisation and privatisation of public hospital services?

One way of understanding the genesis of these ideas and their ready ability to find support is to be aware that Australia's health arrangements are dominated by conflict (Health Issues Centre 1991). Governments as funding bodies and planners are on one side charged with responsibility to plan health service provision rationally and to contain costs. On the other side of this conflict, service providers of all kinds seek to attract more resources to the health system. Service providers can be defined broadly to include not only individual practitioners such as doctors or physiotherapists but also their associations and unions. Service providers also include the private hospitals, equipment and technology manufacturers, pharmaceuticals companies and private health insurers.

Taking just a couple of examples it becomes clear that a shift to the private sector certainly doesn't imply constraints on health costs, a cheaper or more efficient system. It is widely acknowledged that spending on pharmaceuticals, an almost entirely private sector industry, is rising at an astronomical rate and is a major driver pushing up the costs of health care.

Reflect too on private health insurance and the fall occurring in the number of people who still supplement their Medicare coverage with private insurance. It is interesting to note the views of the then assistant general manager of Medibank Private, Ian Wearne. Speaking to the 1992 Australian Private Hospitals Association General Congress, he commented that the major cause of the flow out of private health insurance is the price of the product. The major reason for the price is the rising costs of the benefits paid on behalf of members and there has been some deterioration in the risk profile of the remaining membership (mainly older people). However, the real concern today is that (medical and hospital) utilisation rates are increasing much faster than can be accounted for by the worsening risk profile alone. In addition none of the new technologies and techniques which were said to offer cost reduction have in fact delivered. For example, in-patient bed days continue to grow strongly while at the same time we have an explosion of so-called 'day surgery', much of which hardly qualifies as surgery in the true sense of the word. And while he said he didn't wish to be overly critical and was aware of many efficient private hospitals trying to contain costs, the hard facts were that more hospitals needed to see that income maximisation today could well threaten viability tomorrow.

It can be understood then that the notion of a crisis for some, represents an opportunity for others. Thus, as pressure is placed on governments to restrain or reduce taxation, constraints are imposed on the public sector, evidenced for example by waiting lists, and this creates new market opportunities. For private entrepreneurs, given guaranteed costs plus reimbursement offered by Medicare paying the lion's share of the bill whether a patient is treated publicly or privately, there are real opportunities in what has been described as 'medibusiness' and 'hospibusiness' (Scotton 1987).

It is also interesting to note the highly concentrated makeup of Australia's private hospital sector: 33 per cent of private hospitals are shared among just 10 corporations while 25 per cent of hospital beds belong to the Catholic Church. Private insurers also own a sizeable share of the private hospital industry (*Medical Observer* 31 March 1995). Certainly there is no current crisis in private hospitals, despite declining rates of private health coverage and this is partly because increasingly these hospitals are aligning themselves to meet state government needs. This is achieved in two ways:

- •by offering services or functions to supplement the public sector, and

- •by 'mainstreaming' or moving out of niche markets into the provision of the full range of hospital care (see Catchlove 1995).

These points underscore the political dimensions of health care spending. As has been noted elsewhere,

all decisions about health resources and their allocation remain essentially political decisions made by one group on behalf of another and framed within a particular set of beliefs. This is important because the implications are that increasing health costs are not always inevitable and health spending priorities can be changed. (Health Issues Centre 1991)

It is also important to understand the nature of federal–state relations in Australia as they impact on health and health spending. The federal government has very little constitutional power to direct health policy. Hospitals in particular are under the jurisdiction of the states—but the states have limited capacity to raise taxes and are also limited in what they can borrow. This is often referred to as 'vertical fiscal imbalance'. The states have the constitutional power but the federal government raises much of the money needed to run hospitals among myriad other spending priorities. Hospitals are funded under the Federal–State Hospital Medicare Agreement. And as the states are wont to complain, the federal department imposes a number of strings on the money it provides under this Agreement. One such string is that public health care in public hospitals should be absolutely free and available to all. The universal availability of care within a capped budget through Medicare is recognised internationally as a very effective way of constraining health costs overall but it is the states who must implement this policy and not sur-prisingly they find it difficult.

Thus sometimes moves associated with privatisation and commercialisa-tion are not so much about real cost savings as about cost shifting. A good example is the privatisation of outpatients services noted above. (Incidentally, this is also how the state government has saved costs in Work Cover. It is not so much that Work Cover has become more efficient, costing the communi-ty less, but that it has shifted much of the burden for compensating injured workers from the state system—Work Cover—onto the federal system—Social Security.)

Joint ventures with the private for-profit sector in hospital developments (e.g. Royal Melbourne Hospital: Catchlove 1993) are also seen as a mecha-nism for the states to avoid recurrent expenditure, especially upgrading of capital works (Victorian Commission of Audit 1993: 126). A Queensland Health Department policy on public–private partnerships in hospital ser-vices, released in 1995, is quite upfront about this.

It is true that although Australia's health spending is not high relative to the rest of the world there are pressures on the economy and we have a rela-tively young population so that as the population ages we need to look more closely at what we are buying for our health dollar if spending overall is to remain at a reasonable level. Added to these pressures are the pressures on the health budget arising as the various stakeholders in the health sector seek to maintain or increase the resources available to it. Finally, as the strength of the overall economy waxes and wanes further pressures are placed on gov-ernment capacity to meet increasing expectations. Thus it is not simply the states searching for ways to restrain costs. This was the main thrust of the fed-eral government's National Health Strategy Review conducted in the early 1990s.

Finally we need to take into account the difficulty of neatly distinguishing public and private in health care delivery in Australia. It is so intertwined that John Deeble, one of the architects of Medicare, has suggested that trying to distinguish between them is like trying to unscramble an omelette. (Deeble 1982)

The system as a whole is predominantly public both in terms of provision of services and financing. Hospitals are predominantly public with private hospitals traditionally small and concentrating on the more profitable and less complex surgery such as day surgery and maternity cases. There are of course major exceptions with some very large and well-equipped private hos-pitals but still relatively few with accident and emergency or intensive care facilities, for example. It is possibly not well known that public hospitals treat at least as many privately insured patients as do private hospitals (Owens & Scotton 1991: 200). Apart from hospitals

some 82 per cent of all medical services in Australia are provided by pri-vate medical practitioners and yet we have no means of requiring accountability for the quality and accessibility of these services (Moore 1993: 12–15).

This intertwining of public and private services has led many to suggest that rather than attempting to distinguish private and public service delivery it may be more useful to concentrate on the distinction between public and private financing of health care.

According to the National Health Strategy (1991), the balance between and the respective roles of the public and private hospitals reflect past and existing financing systems, rather than any planned or considered approach to creating an optimum system of hospital care (1991: 13). In Issues Paper No. 2 the Strategy argues that the key distinction between the two is no longer hospital ownership or the type of service offered. More important is the way the two systems are financed, in other words whether they are primarily paid for by public or private insurance, and who is entitled to access at what cost (1991: 112).

Recognising these realities the National Health Strategy put forward the view that government has a responsibility to utilise effectively all available health services to meet its obligations to adequately provide for the health of the community. In Australia this requires involvement of both public and private services given their extensive interdependence (1991: 12–14). The strategy therefore proposed the rationalisation of beds, facilities and the number of hospitals across both the public and private sectors (1991: 14), including adoption of the British purchaser–provider model. This would promote competition among providers but maintain the 'primacy of government for equity and efficiency reasons' (1991: 45).

Also seen by many as a step along the road to commercialisation, the purchaser/provider split is an idea borrowed from the National Health Service in the United Kingdom. The idea is that hospitals should cease to be directly run by the public service and should become corporate entities—independent business units which government can deal with at arms length. This distance is attractive because it begins to persuade people that decisions about what services are available in hospitals are nothing to do with government, although of course the government remains the major purchaser and hospital personnel may remain public servants.

Coupled with casemix benchmarks for payment, however, a purchaser–provider model can also give government much better control of how it wants to spend the health budget than the previous system of simple historical budgeting whether it buys from the private sector or from public services. However, within this model, sometimes also called the internal market, or managed competition, there is no necessary empowerment of consumers, whose only sanction if dissatisfied is to leave the service. There is of course very little choice when talking about hospitals, to go somewhere else.

HOW CAN WE ACHIEVE THE HEALTH SYSTEM WE WANT?
Return now to the questions posed at the outset of this discussion and concentrate on what kind of health system health care consumers want and how

to achieve adequate accountability from it regardless of whether the service provider is public or private. Clearly moves towards greater involvement of the private sector in health service delivery need not be dismissed out of hand. They do, however, raise serious concerns about how the primacy of government in ensuring equity and efficiency can be assured in a market environment and about how the interests of consumers as patients, as citizens and as taxpayers can be protected. This discussion has reflected some of those concerns.

In particular there must be greater awareness that though economic drivers may promote reform, consumers of health care are entitled to be regarded as more than simply passive customers of whatever health services are on offer. They are entitled to be full participants at all levels of decision making about how the health system should operate. What consumers do not need is a shift from a non-user friendly dead hand of bureaucracy style system with minimal accountability and consumer participation to a 'gee whiz' competitive market style system with just as little participation and accountability.

There are numerous ways in which people can participate in the health system and in which the health system and services could be more accountable to consumers. These begin with the micro level issues of access to personal treatment records and informed consent in the one to one relationship with individual providers such as doctors or physiotherapists, to the role of community advisory committees in health planning and of community members on boards of management of health services and on health department decision-making bodies.

At the organisational level steps towards a more democratic health system include greater attention to consumer protection and a more transparent and open exchange of information in the community including information about the outcomes of treatments and the performance of services. Thus for a health system in which health services are people's services, available and responsive to those who need them, a system which meets the WHO's prescription for the future and gives meaning to democratic principles of equity, openness, rational planning and participation, some of the key elements must be:

- •better information and education systems to communicate better with ordinary people about services, priorities and alternatives
- •a much broader definition and acceptance of consumer participation
- •much more attention to strategies for accountability of the health system to consumers, regardless of whether the services within it are delivered by public or private providers or hybrids of the two.

REFERENCES
Australian Institute of Health and Welfare 1994 *Health Expenditure Bulletin* December
The Age 1995 Editorial 26 May
Bryant J 1994 Editorial: the future of health care *World Health*

Catchlove B 1993 The view from the private sector *Health Issues* No. 37

Catchlove B 1995 The new face of private health care, In *The Lyncroft Report* June/July

Davidson K 1995 No healing here—the system's healthy *The Age* 14 June

Deeble J 1982 Unscrambling the omelette: public and private health care financing in Australia, In McLachlan G and Maynard A (eds) 1992 *The Public/Private Mix for Health* London: Nuffield Provincial Hospitals Trust

Harvey R 1991 *Making It Better* Melbourne: Issues Paper No. 8, National Health Strategy

Health Issues Centre 1991 *Who Controls Where the Health Dollar Goes?* Melbourne: Health Issues Centre

Jackson T 1993 Consumer support for casemix: walking the fine line *Health Issues* No. 37

Medical Observer 1995 AMA roundup, 9 June

Medical Observer 1995 Who owns the hospitals, 31 March

Moore K 1993 A health consumers' charter *Health Forum* 26

National Health Strategy 1991 *Hospital Services in Australia: Access and Financing* Melbourne: Issues Paper No. 2, National Health Strategy

National Health Strategy 1992 *Enough to Make You Sick* Melbourne: Research Paper No. 1, National Health Strategy

Owens H and Scotton R 1991 The economics of case payment, In Selby Smith C (ed) 1991 *Economics and Health 1990* Proceedings of the Twelfth Australian Conference of Health Economists

Paterson J 1993a Casemix funding: can your hospital survive in a competitive environment? *VHA Report* May

Paterson J 1993b Health and community services: a revolution in consumer focus *Health Issues* No. 37

Scotton R 1987 Contribution to Health Insurance Forum, In Butler J and Doessel D (eds) 1987 *Economics and Health 1987* Proceedings of the Ninth Australian Conference of Health Economists

Victorian Commission of Audit 1993 *Report* Melbourne

Victorian Hospitals Association 1988 *Privatise Public Hospitals?* Melbourne: VHA discussion paper

Wearne I 1992 Funding hospitals through private insurance *The Australian Private Hospital* November

WHO Study Group 1991 *Community Involvement in Health Development: Challenging Health Services* Geneva: World Health Organization Technical Report 809

Competition and Health Care

John Thwaites and Andrew Refshauge

A FREE MARKET IN HEALTH

Economic rationalists seem to believe that our public health system should be run on the same basis as a supermarket, car manufacturer or fast food outlet. This market-based approach has been adopted enthusiastically by conservative governments, partly for ideological reasons and partly as a means of making budget cuts.

In Victoria so-called market policies have been introduced with public hospitals competing with one another for patients and paid an income according to the number of patients treated. In New South Wales, market theories have been used to justify privatisation of hospitals and health services.

An approach suggested by some, including federal Labor MP Mark Latham is 'managed competition'. While the phrase may appear to be an oxymoron, the real question is how much management and how much competition? Latham (1994) suggests managed competition would involve competition between both public and private health institutions to win performance-based contracts from regional health authorities. This is similar to the system recently introduced in New Zealand where health providers can compete to win contracts to provide health services for regional authorities known as crown health enterprises.

The market-based approach in Victoria has been explicitly stated. In a speech made shortly after the introduction of casemix funding in Victoria in July 1993, the secretary of the Department of Health and Community Services, Dr Paterson (1993a), said:

> Within a short time the economics of the operations of public hospitals, individually and as a system, will become indistinguishable from that of Target, Safeway, General Motors Holden or McDonalds.

As we know in other manifestations, the market produces winners and losers. Dr Paterson (1993b) acknowledged this in another speech to hospital administrators when he said that the new system

> will produce marked structural changes to Victoria's acute health services accomplished through a price system ... will your hospital get rich through the new funding system, or are you a dead duck?

However the losers in the health care market are not only the hospitals which are not deemed 'efficient' enough to survive, but also the patients of those hospitals regardless of their health needs.

Similar problems arise under a system of managed competition when the contracts for providing health services expire. What if the local public hospital puts in a more expensive bid than a private hospital and the purchasing authority enters a contract with the private hospital to provide the public health services? Does the public hospital then close and sack its staff? What happens to the teaching and research activities undertaken by the public hospital? What happens to the services previously provided at the public hospital to low income or non-English speaking groups which may not be so profitable for the private hospital to provide? Will the public hospital be able to re-open two or three years later and take part in the next round of bidding? Of course not.

Alternatively, the private hospital may bid for only some of the public health services; most probably the more profitable elective surgery. The public hospital would lose more than the real cost of work done, and the marginal cost of the remaining services would be higher.

Competition and market policies don't have a very good record in health care. The United States has a competitive market system which is the most expensive and inequitable in the western world. The United States' experience demonstrates that the market approach to health care means

•losing equity of access to higher quality health services

•losing public control over hospital facilities

•losing public control over health planning

•greater health costs for the community (Refshauge 1992).

Similar problems are surfacing in Victoria and New South Wales following the introduction of market policies in health care. Australian states should be wary about embracing competition and market policies as the way to fix perceived problems in Australian health care. The cure may be worse than the disease.

IF COMPETITION IS THE SOLUTION, WHAT IS THE PROBLEM?

The proponents of competition in public health care see it as the answer to perceived problems in our health system being rising health costs, inefficient public hospitals, and long waiting lists (Moore 1992). Competition is said to increase efficiency whereas the traditional method of funding by fixed allocations to hospitals is said to simply institutionalise hospitals inefficiency (Latham 1994). How real are the problems to be 'solved' by competition and market policies?

Health expenditure

Health spending in total in Australia has remained relatively constant since 1984/1985 at around 8 per cent of gross domestic product (GDP). By comparison in the United States, with the most market-based system, health care costs have risen from 9.2 per cent in 1980 to around 13 per cent in 1992, and are continuing to rise (Refshauge 1992).

Interestingly, the area where health expenditure in Australia is rising most rapidly is not hospitals which have largely been funded according to traditional historical allocations, but medical benefits under Medicare which are paid on a fee-for-service basis to doctors operating in a private market.

Public hospital efficiency

The Victorian government has boasted of major productivity improvements in public hospitals following the introduction of casemix. However productivity in public hospitals has been improving significantly throughout Australia over the past decade including Victoria prior to the introduction of casemix. The latest survey of the public hospital system by the Australian Institute of Health and Welfare (AIHW) indicates that Australia's public hospitals treated more patients for less cost with improved efficiency between 1989/90 and 1991/92.

Furthermore, the evidence tends to suggest that Australian public hospitals operate at a similar efficiency level to private hospitals when adjustments are made for the teaching and other obligations of public hospitals (Kelly 1993).

Patient throughput and waiting lists

Competition and casemix are said to increase inpatient throughput and reduce waiting lists.

Hospital inpatient activity has been increasing substantially in Australia without market policies. The recent AIHW survey indicates that there has been a 2.7 per cent increase in the number of cases treated per year, adjusted for population growth, between 1989/90 and 1991/92 (*The Australian* 23 December 1994). In Victoria there was a 23 per cent increase in the number of patients treated between 1986/87 and 1990/91 (from 527,545 to 650,604).

The competitive environment in Victoria has provided an incentive to hospitals to artificially increase inpatient admissions by classifying procedures as inpatient treatments which previously were not recorded or were regarded as outpatient services. Such procedures include patients remaining in emergency departments for more than four hours, and pre-admission work-ups. The Kennett government has boasted of an increase of 60,000 inpatients in 1993/94, but this should be matched against the reduction in outpatients treated that year of 1,000,000.

The Kennett government has also boasted of a reduction in waiting lists under casemix. However, as the chief executive officer of a major hospital has observed, casemix has provided 'unambiguous incentives for self-control of waiting lists': hospitals are not paid casemix bonus money unless they can show a drop in more urgent waiting list categories (Stoelwinder 1994). As a result hospitals are re-categorising patients to less urgent categories. The waiting lists look better, but the patients are waiting just as long or longer in many cases.

In any event, on current projections the total number on waiting lists in Victoria is likely to be higher in June 1995 than it was in June 1992. Similarly, in New South Wales waiting lists have got much worse under the Greiner and Fahey governments.

NSW: PRIVATISATION OF HOSPITALS AND SERVICES

The Greiner and Fahey governments have pursued a policy of privatisation of hospitals and hospital services. What has been the experience of this policy there?

The first privatised hospital is at Port Macquarie. The hospital, which is operated by Health Care of Australia (a Mayne Nickless subsidiary), has recently opened after a political controversy stretching over two years. Mental health and community health services at Port Macquarie have also been privatised.

The Fahey government recently signed contracts for private operating theatres, pathology services and day surgery at the Prince of Wales hospital. The contract was awarded to a consortium of a small private hospital and a construction company. The offer made to the government by the consortium was a cheaper deal than that offered by the alternative bidder, the University of New South Wales.

A number of other hospital privatisations are proposed, and services such as radiology and pathology are also being privatised.

It is too early to determine the precise effects on access to health care as a result of the privatisation of the Port Macquarie hospital, and other privatised health services in New South Wales. Certainly pensioner and other groups are concerned that they will lose access to health services in the future, if they are seen as unprofitable, or the company running the hospital falls into financial difficulties.

However, it is already clear that the cost to taxpayers of the Port Macquarie project will be greater than a comparative public hospital. The state government will pay up to $1 million a month to 'rent' public hospital beds at the new hospital. The government will have to pay an 'availability charge' of $130 million for uninsured patients to use the hospital over the next 20 years. This is double the figure which had been given to the New South Wales Parliament's Public Accounts Committee when it investigated the cost of the private hospital last year. All up the private hospital will cost the taxpayer around $480 million as opposed to $420 million to build and operate a public hospital over the 20 year period.

VICTORIA'S HEALTH CARE SUPERMARKET

Victoria introduced its new competitive hospital system on 1 July 1993. From that date public hospitals have been paid according to a casemix formula. The same formula is used throughout the state for all hospitals. Essentially large city teaching hospitals are paid under the same formula as small rural hospitals.

Public hospitals are encouraged to compete with one another, and indeed with private hospitals, for patients. The government said it had no plans to close public hospitals, but if they are not sufficiently 'efficient', or fail to attract enough patients, they 'should not expect to survive' (Department of Health and Community Services 1993).

At the same time the government has introduced massive cuts of over $250 million to hospitals' annual budgets. As Professor Stoelwinder (1994), the chief executive officer of the Monash Medical Centre, has stated: 'Casemix funding provided the opportunity to obfuscate budget cuts in complex pricing structures, to dress them up as relative inefficiencies'.

Under the casemix formula, hospitals are paid a variable amount depending upon the number and types of cases treated (casemix) together with a fixed amount which includes payments to cover outpatients, teaching and accident and emergency. Hospitals are paid according to diagnostic related groups (DRGs). DRGs group similar episodes of care and assess them according to an average cost for that type of treatment. Accordingly, the hospital makes a profit if its treatment of a patient in a particular DRG is less costly than the average, and a loss if it is more costly. This provides a clear incentive to reduce the length of time a patient stays in hospital.

The so-called 'average cost' payment for a DRG is set by the government, and some DRGs are more profitable (i.e. the payment is greater than the cost) than others. There is, accordingly, an incentive to shift hospital activity towards the more profitable DRGs and away from less profitable activity.

Outpatients, accident and emergency departments, and teaching and research are not paid under a casemix formula. They continue to receive fixed grants but at much reduced levels. This also provides a significant incentive for hospitals to shift their activity from these less profitable areas to more profitable DRGs.

In the first year of casemix, hospitals were able to compete for funds from a casemix bonus pool which paid hospitals a bonus for patients treated above the target. However, in a major policy shift in October 1994 the government effectively abandoned this policy, and restricted major hospitals from access to further bonus payments. The competitive policy had got out of control and the bonus pool money was being sought at such a rate it would have been exhausted midway through the financial year.

PROBLEMS WITH THE MARKET EXPERIMENT IN VICTORIA

The market experiment with competition in health care in Victoria has not worked out as well as its proponents had hoped. The ideological market-based approach to health care has not only led to the closure of hospitals and health services, but also has affected the quality of health care, the type of services provided, and access to health services.

Access and equity

People who have lost access to health care in the new competitive environment in Victoria, include country people, older people particularly those suffering with multiple and chronic illnesses, and people needing outpatient services.

Professor Stoelwinder (1994) has raised concerns about the fate of small country hospitals in the competitive environment. He said of these hospitals: 'Under the current casemix formula their financial viability is threatened. Market rules implicit in the reforms dictate that they should have to close'. Six country hospitals were forced to close last year and a dozen more are under threat. The government has sought to avoid responsibility for these closures by saying they were hospital board decisions caused by the failure of the hospitals to attract sufficient patients. However the rigid market approach has failed to take account of the additional costs which country hospitals incur and the smaller populations they serve.

The question which is left unanswered is whether the people who live in the regions served by these closed hospitals should lose access to health care because the market deems their hospital inefficient.

It is not just people in country Victoria who are finding it harder to get access to hospital services. Older people and people with chronic illness generally take longer to treat and are not profitable under casemix. By contrast, hospitals are financially rewarded for treating uncomplicated short stay patients. As a result there is a market pressure for hospitals to increase activity in the profitable areas, and avoid older patients for whom they are poorly remunerated.

The market approach is being forced on hospitals' internal arrangements, with individual units operating as business centres and required to remain profitable under casemix. As a result these units are sometimes disinclined to take older patients with multiple problems, and the patients are left lying for up to two days on trolleys in hospital emergency departments unable to get admission to a hospital ward.

Outpatient services are paid under a fixed grant and accordingly there is no market incentive to maintain or increase the level of these services. There has been a major decline in outpatient treatments in Victoria under the new system, which particularly affects people from non-English speaking and low income groups who favour outpatient services (State shifts costs, *The Sunday Age* 14 August 1994).

The competitive environment has also led some hospitals to begin charging fees for allied health services such as physiotherapy. People who cannot afford the new fees simply miss out on the service. Community health centres have now also been forced to introduce fee charging as part of the 'user pays' approach to health care.

Competition is leading to a cost shifting by the state government onto patients and their families. As patients are discharged earlier, the burden of providing care is shifting from the state to family members, usually women. At the same time millions of dollars of health costs are being shifted onto the Commonwealth government (and taxpayers) as outpatient services are privatised and pharmaceuticals paid for through the Pharmaceutical Benefits Scheme rather than supplied by the hospital.

Quality of care

Doctors and health professionals in Victoria have raised serious concerns that the quality of health care in Victoria has declined as a result of the market-based approach to health care and massive budget cuts. Some of the major concerns about declining quality of health care include:

- maternity patients being discharged before proper lactation and assessment of the infant
- sick, elderly and complex medical patients who are discharged from hospital too early
- inadequate follow-up and continuity of care of discharged patients
- emergency department patients forced to lie on trolleys for long periods unable to get proper health care in a ward.

As hospitals are forced to compete to treat more patients at a lower cost, patients are being discharged 'quicker and sicker'. Many new mothers have indicated they felt pressured to leave hospital before they were ready. As an obstetrician in a public hospital observed:

> There is no doubt these women are receiving less nursing care, and are being sent home earlier than has happened in the past. There is evidence that women are experiencing more medical complications and problems associated with breast feeding and that more babies are returning to hospital with problems such as jaundice. (Duncan 1994)

Community nurses are saying that they are seeing more cases where people are being discharged with serious wounds that need medical attention. A report by the Council on the Ageing has indicated that elderly people are being discharged before they are ready (Elderly Health a Disaster, *Herald Sun* 25 September 1994).

A survey of admitting doctors conducted by the independent review of the first year of casemix funding in Victoria found that 56 per cent of admitting doctors believed there had been a change for the worse in the quality of clinical outcomes for patients in the year, and 39 per cent believed discharging patients too soon was the main reason. Only 1 per cent believed clinical outcomes had improved (Health Solutions 1994: 105).

A key problem which has been identified is the lack of continuity of post-hospital care. Hospitals now have a financial incentive to provide as many inpatient 'treatments' as possible but no financial incentive to care for patients after discharge. Proper health care should be concerned with the whole episode of care. The market approach tends to divide up the episode of care into units for which different health providers are paid a price. Each provider then has an incentive to pass on costs to other players in the system as much as possible.

Continuity of care is vital for satisfactory health outcomes, but continuity and quality of care is undermined if a market system provides incentives to shift responsibility and costs to patients, their families or other health providers.

Teaching, research and staff quality

It should be recognised that the high quality of health care in Australian hospitals is largely based on the high quality of their doctors, nurses and other health workers. Teaching and training in hospitals plays a vital part in maintaining this quality. It is difficult to assign a market price for such teaching in hospitals, and accordingly it also falls by the wayside as hospitals struggle to treat more patients for less cost.

The heads of the University of Melbourne Departments of Medicine at six major Victorian hospitals were so concerned about the serious damage to teaching and research in hospitals that they wrote a joint letter to *The Age* newspaper on 18 November 1994 saying that:

> The combination of output-related funding and gross reduction in budgets has affected these hospitals to such an extent that they will be scarcely able to carry out normal quality control procedures, let alone exercise the educational and research functions that are central to their position, which over time, contribute so greatly to patient care.

The consequences of the damage to teaching, will not show up immediately in short-term quantitative surveys such as unplanned patient readmissions. However, as the leading medical professors have noted, in the long term the result will be a serious lowering of standards in teaching hospitals.

Medical research similarly does badly under a market system. Victorian hospitals have in the past provided money for infrastructure costs for medical research such as laboratory equipment, staff salaries and electricity costs. However as the cool winds of competition blow through hospitals, this support is also under threat. This has led the director of a major Victorian medical research institution to say that the state government has 'washed its hands' of medical research through the casemix funding formula (Research chief warns: 'we'll pack our bags and leave, *The Sunday Age* 3 July 1994).

Another consequence of the drive to reduce costs in the competitive environment, has been that hospitals are relying on less qualified nursing staff. These nurses are cheaper in the short term, but unable to provide the same standard of care as more experienced and qualified staff.

Capital works—lack of planning in the competitive environment

When casemix was introduced, the Kennett government indicated that capital works and equipment funding would be linked to casemix. The government indicated that it was considering a 'capital charge' on hospitals under which the hospital would have to pay interest to the government on any capital funds advanced as though it were a business borrowing funds from the government. In other words capital and equipment were to be part of the new market theory where hospitals could use profits from trading for capital works, or alternatively borrow the money from government.

Capital works were not to be based upon the concept of need for health facilities, but rather on the business concept of a return on investment. The market approach to capital works has meant that the Department of Health and Community Services has carried out very little capital works planning in the first two years of the Kennett government, presumably leaving it to the market to decide where new hospital facilities would be built.

In December 1994, in a major policy switch, Mr Kennett appeared to abandon the free market approach to capital works, and said Victoria needed a 50 year hospital building plan. Presumably even the Kennett government has seen that the market would not supply new public hospitals in the growth areas, while it allowed or even encouraged the duplication of certain services as existing hospitals competed with each other for patients.

Proper planning for capital works allows consideration of social justice factors such as need, how far someone should have to travel to a hospital or health service and the appropriate level of access to health care for disadvantaged groups.

WHY THE MARKET FAILS IN HEALTH CARE

Historically governments have become involved in the provision of health care because the market has proved to be a failure in providing adequate health care for their citizens (Ernst 1993: 15).

Health care is not a simple commodity like a motor car or hamburger, and has characteristics which do not conform to those in the standard market transaction. A market approach to health care fails on a number of grounds:

- market forces fail to achieve access and equity in the delivery of health service

- certain key areas of health such as health prevention and education programs are under-supplied by the market

- consumers have insufficient knowledge of health products and options, and are in no real position to shop around; providers (generally doctors) not consumers dictate the pattern of demand

- the profit motive produces a number of perverse incentives which are undesirable and inefficient in terms of the overall health status of the community

- the required 'management' of competition in health care leads to considerable costs of regulation and administration.

Access and equity

Market forces fail to achieve access and equity in the delivery of health services. In economic jargon, horizontal equity cannot be achieved. The market allocates health services, not on need but on factors such as income, geographic location, access to information and power.

This system is best illustrated in the United States where over 30 million Americans are uninsured and have almost no access to health care (Refshauge 1992). Families needing urgent medical treatment have been bankrupted by its high cost. Many hospitals practise 'wallet diagnosis' where the patient's insurance status rather than health need determines the type of care given (Shirley 1993).

The system of managed competition in New Zealand has lead to the introduction of a range of new user charges in the health system. The effect of these user charges is greatest among the poor and sick (Baker 1993).

A system of managed competition, where public and private hospitals bid for contracts with regional health authorities, poses real risks for access and equity. Private hospital companies will naturally target the profitable segments of the market such as elective procedures on low risk patients. In order to compete on price, the public hospitals are likely to be forced to follow suit. Alternatively the public hospitals will remain as the care giver of last resort, dealing with the most expensive patients, and unable to compete when it comes to negotiating contracts with the regional purchasing authority. Health services and hospitals meeting the needs of poor people, the old and chronically ill, will inevitably become run-down and close.

Lack of access and equity may not be of such concern in the distribution of hamburgers and Holden cars, but it should be of the utmost concern in the distribution of health care, which is a basic human right and underpins social cohesion.

Under-supply of health promotion and prevention programs

Good health care is about much more than treatment of illness. Programs aimed at preventing illness and accidents and promoting good health are vital in maintaining a healthy community. They also make good economic sense by reducing hospital and medical costs.

However, the market fails again when it comes to health prevention and education programs. Because their benefits are widely distributed it is difficult to assign a market price or levy individual charges. A market system under-supplies or fails to supply altogether health promotion and education programs (Ernst 1993: 17). It is not surprising that a health promotion unit at Melbourne's largest hospital was an early casualty of the Kennett government's competitive system.

The benefits of good health care and prevention of illness are not limited to an individual consumer but spill over to the rest of society, for example by reducing infectious diseases or making the workforce more productive (Scott 1993). A market-based system, based on a price for individual services, will tend to undersupply public health care programs like immunisation and HIV/AIDS education, because individual recipients pay the full price while the rest of society receives the spillover benefits for nothing. Public health care programs are more valuable to society than they are to individuals; so society should be willing to pay more for them than are individuals; but such payment is impossible in a market-based system.

Consumers lack of knowledge and provider capture
In the standard market transaction, there is a reasonably clearly defined product or service and the consumer decides what to buy, pays the price and benefits. If necessary the consumer is able to shop around to compare price and quality (Southon 1994).

However, consumers of health services are in no real position to shop around. How many people just diagnosed with a brain tumour will research the death rate of their local hospital? the infection rate? the bed-day cost? Even if they wanted to, the information is not available (Refshauge 1992: 6).

In most medical situations, the consumer does not even decide what health service they want. It is normally the provider, the doctor, who diagnoses the condition and decides what treatment will be given. Because providers have more information than consumers, they have the ability to capture and control the system by supplying the services which suit them (Scott 1993). The potential for over-servicing is exacerbated by a market system which pays a unit price per treatment.

It may be argued that in a system of managed competition, the purchaser is not the individual patient, but rather a regional health authority on behalf of all consumers in a region. However, in such a system it is still the providers who largely decide what treatments will be supplied, and the incentive for over-servicing with a system based on a price per treatment remains.

Because of the particular nature of the health market, and the relative dominance of health providers, it should not be assumed competition will automatically lead to lower prices and improved efficiency. Specialists' colleges impose barriers to entry which protect specialists from competition. In many country regions it is very difficult to attract any doctors at all. Health care is not a buyer's market!

Under a system of managed competition, where providers can bid to supply health services to a region, what is there to stop a particular group of specialists agreeing to put in one joint bid and charging a monopoly price? Given the small number of specialists in certain fields, especially in country regions, this is not far-fetched. It is exactly what has happened in certain regions of New Zealand under the new competitive system. Perhaps competition will mean different regions bidding against each other to pay still higher prices to obtain the services of sought-after specialists.

The profit motive produces perverse incentives
The health sector is made up of people having the full spectrum of motives and attitudes from the altruistic to the greedy. A health system which puts a premium on values such as access, equity, and quality tends to encourage those with altruistic values. However a market system where the first priorities are price and profit produces perverse incentives which attract the greedy and are undesirable and inefficient in terms of the overall health status of the community. These perverse incentives include (Southon 1994):
- treating more profitable, less complicated cases

•shifting costs to other parties

•concentrating resources on coding and recording systems to maximise payments

•compromising quality in ways which are not easily or immediately detected

•rewarding clinical units on the basis of their commercial success rather than on quality or need.

All of these incentives have become apparent in the new competitive environment in Victoria as discussed above. The incentives are even stronger when competition is associated with major budget cuts as in Victoria.

In a system of managed competition where private and public hospitals are bidding against each other, even the altruistic institutions will be unable to avoid these perverse incentives if they are to compete on price. In the United States, non-profit hospitals which have failed to target the profitable sectors of the health market have been forced to close or have been taken over by private for-profit hospitals (Kawachi 1993).

Administrative costs and efficiency

It is a fallacy to assume that administrative costs will necessarily be less in a health system based on managed competition. A vast bureaucracy is required to 'manage' the competition. Additional administrative costs are also incurred by providers such as hospitals. Doctors in Victoria are claiming their time is increasingly being taken up with paperwork required by casemix (Farrell K, letter to editor *The Age* 20 July 1994). Clinicians have complained that resources previously devoted to direct patient care are now being diverted to the growing managerial structure including consultants in hospitals (Niall J, letter to editor, *The Age* 9 December 1994).

Some of the additional administrative costs incurred in a system of managed competition include (Southon 1994):

•the central administration must maintain and amend appropriate fee levels for hundreds of DRG categories

•the price paid for various items needs to be continually adjusted and refined to meet changing circumstances and address anomalies

•financial and management consultants need to be employed to structure the financial systems and maximise hospital income

•increased legal and quasi-legal expenses are incurred in setting up the purchaser/provider contracts

•auditors are required to check that individual providers are providing the contracted services, and not 'gaming' the system, or inappropriately cost shifting.

CONCLUSION

The market system purports to be value free, and to remove politics from health care. In fact purchaser bodies (whether they be regional health boards or the state government) exercise their values in the mix of services which they choose to purchase, and the price they are prepared to pay for such services. Nor can it be said that the market system removes politics from health care. Health is intensely political under any system. Where a government's political interests are at stake, for example in marginal seats, the 'invisible hand' of the market may in fact be guided by a government concerned about its future. The price paid by government is amenable to political manipulation and the Kennett government is making payments to certain hospitals which are more explicable on political than market grounds.

One of the real vices of the market-based system is that it tends to obfuscate these political decisions and mask basic values and policy decisions underpinning health care. If a policy decision is made that hospitals should concentrate on low risk elective surgery and not on assisting older people with chronic illness, then that decision should be explicit and not masked in a form of market theory which suggests that treatment of older people with chronic illness is somehow less 'efficient'.

The key objective in improving efficiency in health care should be to shift resources from the least cost effective to the most cost effective interventions and activities (Segal & Richardson 1994: 89). What is required is an analysis of the effectiveness of different types of intervention or activity in dealing with each health condition. It may be that for particular types of illness the most effective intervention is prevention and education programs at an early stage.

This type of analysis requires a level of planning which is not supported by a market structure. The market structure based on price competition does not provide the planning or analysis required, but leads to an excessive concentration on short-term profit.

As Allan Maynard, the Professor of Economics at the Centre of Health Economics at the University of York, England wrote in *The Lancet* (1992: 538):

> the central policy issue is not competition or regulation but the identification of the cost effectiveness of competing therapeutic interventions. Instead of wasting scarce resources on the redisorganisation of health care structures and the often ill-conceived expansion of management, greater efforts to identify good practice and create islands of rationality in the oceans of medical uncertainty would unite both clinical and non-clinical managers. Without this unity, together with increased evaluative research, planned markets (regulated competition) will exhibit the unwelcome characteristics of the past: Ill-informed choices fuelled by the rhetoric of self interest.

The market structure in health care is being trumpeted by economic rationalists who believe that the less government does the better, and a pseudo-market structure should be superimposed on those functions which government retains. However health care is a classic case of market failure and the evidence in the United States and elsewhere points to its numerous failings.

The market or competitive structure undermines the basic principle of universal access to quality health care and tends to mask fundamental policy decisions in health care. Most significantly it has been used to mask budget cuts by dressing them up as relative inefficiencies between hospitals. It is not value free in that it clearly favours certain medical interventions over other areas of health care.

Better policy decisions will be made if the principles and values underlying health care are explicit rather than pretending they are subject to the invisible hand of the market.

REFERENCES

Baker M 1993 User charges: bad medicine for health, in *Health Reforms: a Second Opinion* Wellington NZ: Wellington Health Action Committee

Department of Health and Community Services 1993 *Casemix funding for Victoria's Hospitals* Melbourne: Department of Health and Community Services

Duncan K 1994 Casemix critics *The Age* 15 July

Ernst J 1993 Steering the healthy course *Health Issues Journal* 37 December

Health Solutions 1994 *Independent Assessment of Casemix Payment in Victoria* Melbourne: Health Solutions Pty Ltd, December

Kawachi I 1993 The American connection, in *Health Reforms a Second Opinion* Wellington NZ: Wellington Health Action Committee

Kelly R 1993 Casemix funding and public hospitals: the end of politics?

Latham M 1994 Health's road to recovery *The Australian* 23 June

Moore D 1992 *Report on Victorian Public Health System* Melbourne: Institute of Public Affairs

Paterson J 1993a Beyond case payments: a new paradigm for Australian health and welfare, speech October

Paterson J 1993b Casemix funding: can your hospital survive in a competitive environment? *Victorian Hospitals Association Newsletter* May

Refshauge A 1992 *Health Privatisation: The US Experience*

Scott G 1993 Health in the Marketplace, in *Health Reforms a Second Opinion* Wellington NZ: Wellington Health Action Committee

Segal L and Richardson J 1994 Economic framework for allocative efficiency in the health sector *The Australian Economic Review*

Shirley I 1993 Wallet diagnosis and health, in *Health Reforms: a Second Opinion* Wellington NZ: Wellington Health Action Committee

Southon G 1994 A perspective on the Victorian health reforms *Australian Health Review* 17

Stoelwinder J 1994 Casemix payments in the real world of running a hospital *Medical Journal of Australia* 161

Sell Out!

Privatising Services and Utilities

Michael Webber, John Ernst and Bob Carter

Contents

Privatisation in Review

Michael Webber and John Ernst

There have been some 15,000 privatisations worldwide over the last two decades; privatisations across the globe may raise about $US800 billion in the next five years (International Financial Law Review 1994). Privatisation transfers government functions to private corporations, non-government organisations and the family. In the past ten years the policy of privatisation has spread to Australia and a particularly virulent form of it has appeared in Victoria. Why has this form of public policy appeared? What do the privateers seek, what are their ideological foundations, what are the characteristics of their argument? There is an immediate practical political issue too: what are we to think of the privatisation of the State Electricity Commission of Victoria?

Privatisation seems to have two origins. In the Anglo-American world, privatisation has long been a policy of conservative parties (e.g. the denationalisation of state-owned industries in Britain) but received a lot of impetus from the revolutions in politics wrought by Reagan and Thatcher. In the developing world, privatisation has been a policy advanced by monetarist interventions in the economies of countries (Pinochet's Chile was an early example) which have come under the influence of the World Bank and International Monetary Fund. The first privatisation push began when such sectors as banking, transport and heavy industry were removed from government control. Privatisation was later extended as public utilities were shifted from the operations of government. And now privateers argue that the state should even get out of such core arenas of well being as education, health and community services.

The arguments about the merits of privatisation range far and wide. To some, privatisation represents a quick fix, a means of reducing government debt (which is itself regarded as a bad). To others, privatisation is a means of attaining efficiency and competition: a way of making ourselves sufficiently productive to compete in the new global market place. Yet others are driven by ideology, by the attempt to create circumstances in which (some) people can maximise their personal freedom. Whatever these arguments, two facts are clear:

- privatisation is unpopular with most people where it has been tried

- there is little evidence that privatisation can accomplish any of the benefits claimed for it.

Instead, privatisation often leads to higher prices, less choice and less accountability—most notably for those who are vulnerable and disadvantaged. In the end, privatisation means that society loses control over its key assets.

To emphasise: privatisation does not achieve many benefits. In Britain productivity growth has been unrelated to privatisation (Bishop and Kay 1988). In Britain shares in companies being privatised have been offered at a discount (to make sure that investors are confident that the utility will indeed be sold) and so the major beneficiaries of privatisation have been those who bought shares—and contrary to common prejudice, this has not been the ordinary people (Bishop and Kay 1988). British consumers clearly have felt that the privatisation of British Telecom has been accompanied by a deterioration in service (Dunsire 1990). The Independent Review of Victoria's Public Sector Finances (Chapter 11) has a clear and comprehensive statement of the relative efficiency of Victoria's public commercial authorities.

Privatisation, then, is not simply a technical matter of efficiency and well being. Although the merits of privatisation are stated in terms of debt, efficiency and aggregate well being, the repercussions of privatisation extend much further. Privatisation represents a means of

- shifting control over production, public utilities, education, community services and health from those who have been elected on the basis of 'one person: one vote' to those who have been selected on the basis of 'one dollar: one vote'

- extending the array of activities in which private corporations can make profits

- shifting the burden of paying for utilities and social and community services away from those who can pay (corporations and higher income households) to those who need the services most

- shifting relationships in society from the personal, where integrity and ethics matter, to the market where all is free and supposedly equal exchange.

Privatisation is a key policy of the so-called 'New Right'. The New Right embodies

- a set of core values. Citizenship means the legal and economic rights of self-interested individuals. The central right of those individuals is freedom from coercion (not freedom to participate), particularly freedom to enjoy their property rights

- particular beliefs about the role of the market. In the market lives the holy trinity of New Right economic thought: voluntary exchange, competition and open access. The market is regarded as an unrivalled mechanism for production, distribution and exchange: it is efficient and impartial

- a vision that limits the role of the state.

The New Right criticises state intervention in the economy and society:

•The state produces worse outcomes than the market because planning requires more knowledge than people actually have, because it is outside competition and because state businesses are immune from market sanctions. Even private monopolies (perhaps regulated by the state) are better than publicly owned monopolies.

•Since bureaucrats are regarded as rational, self-interested persons, their policy making is interpreted as maximising personal benefits, such as building empires, rather than providing social benefits. So the state's bureaucratic methods are inherently inferior to those of the market.

•The intervention of the state is morally objectionable as an infringement of personal liberties.

It is less obvious what the New Right actually thinks that the state should do. Indeed there is some confusion between the non-interventionist theory of the New Right and the authoritarian practices of such governments as those of Margaret Thatcher and Jeff Kennett.

Privatisation is clearly connected to these three core values. Privatisation enshrines the principle of commodification—that all interactions between people are or really ought to be market-based exchanges. Privatisation can extend the property rights of (some) individuals and extend the range of operation of the market. And it takes the state out of a large arena of economic and social life.

This bald preference for markets over state provision of services provided the historic starting point for advocates of privatisation. But recent versions of privatisation theory take this initial position into more sophisticated theoretical territory. They distinguish between the state as enabler (the government steers the ship of state) and the private market as doer (the rowers!). It prescribes contracting out, splitting internal operating units and the like to enhance competition among service providers. Yet these new prescriptions suffer crucial flaws.

•There is no evidence to underpin their view that bureaucrats build empires at the expense of the public.

•The service providers must be monitored for compliance and their experience never forms part of the evidence used to evaluate and formulate policy.

•The model identifies no difference between public and private spheres: ideals of service and equity have no place in contemporary public sector management.

•The model asserts that the central relationship between a person and the providers of services is an individual and contractual one in what is essentially a market.

So privatisation is not simply about the transfer of ownership or the physical restructuring of such utilities as water and energy. Privatisation is also about redefining social relationships: it is founded on the paradigm of consumerism. We argue the contrary: citizenship implies a limit to commodification and commercialisation: the market cannot guarantee to provide basic welfare goods to all citizens as of right.

The proposed privatisation of the State Electricity Commission of Victoria exemplifies the interplay of ideology and evidence on a stage where our own important interests are at stake.

The privatisation of the SECV is only one among many undertaken or planned by the current Victorian government. It is especially significant, in size and by virtue of its strategic industrial and social position, but gas, water, transport as well as ambulance services, prisons, warehousing, computer facilities and the provision of support to schools and hospitals are among the targets for sale to those seeking to profit from the community's needs. Increased cost and/or reduced equity of access are probable consequences in each case. Exorbitant fees for consultants and excessive salaries and share deals for the new managers have been a feature of the Victorian experience.

The break-up and sale of the state's electricity industry runs counter to the legitimate interests and needs of the overwhelming majority of Victorians. The policy will weaken an efficient and strategic industry, increase income inequalities and reduce the government revenue that has to pay for services and works directed toward the common good. The government's plans are legitimised on the basis of facile assumptions and often erroneous descriptions of 'fact'. The Victorian community is best served by the retention of the electricity industry in the ownership of the community.

The Victorian power industry should be structured in a way that promotes efficiency and security of the electricity system. Horizontal and (at least partial) vertical re-integration is, therefore, called for. The challenge ahead is to maintain and extend social responsibility and efficiency in the public sector. Public ownership for communal benefit is legitimate. The profit motive is not the only source of human endeavour. We must increase, rather than reduce, the involvement of the community, as workers, service recipients and consumers, in planning and supervising community affairs.

REFERENCES

Bishop M and Kay J 1988 *Does Privatisation Work?* London: London Business School

Dunsire A 1990 The public/private debate: some United Kingdom evidence *International Review of Adminstrative Sciences* 56: 29–61

Independent Review of Victoria's Public Sector Finances 1992 *State Finance Victoria*

International Financial Law Review 1994 *Privatization: A World Privatization Guide* London: Euromoney Publications

Ideology and Interests
Privatisation in Theory and Practice

John Ernst and Michael Webber

TWO VERSIONS OF PRIVATISATION
Privatisation is not one single policy. There are two general forms of privatisation.

Privatisation mark 1
Privatisation mark 1 is prescribed by the New Right. It has:

- a primary stance: anti-state, and

- a major focus: load-shedding: sale, transfer or abandonment of state programs, defunding, and deregulation.

The case for this form of privatisation is summarised in the box on the next page. The case against this variant of privatisation is built around concerns for equity, service quality and choice.

There is little if any reputable evidence which shows that privatisation actually improves social justice outcomes. While it is possible in theory to admit the progressive potential of privatisation, it

> seems highly improbable. The same political forces that support privatization generally also support cutbacks in public spending for social welfare; the same arguments about incentives and efficiency used in favor of privatizing public services are also cited by those who want to terminate public financing for the services altogether (Starr 1989: 42–3).

The primary manifestations of *inequity* are:

- cream-skimming: the most profitable parts of the service system are bought and most attractive clientele are served by the private sector while the public sector has to service the more expensive or dependent client group, and therefore appears less efficient than the private sector. Contrast, for example, private and public nursing homes and prisons

- entrenched dual-track human services system: one a fast track (private) and the other unsealed and heavily pot-holed (public)

- locational disadvantage: the geographical distribution of services is uneven and not related to need.

The negative impact of privatisation on service quality is driven by the profit motive. In their analysis of the privatised system of health and community care in the United States, Stoesz and Karger (1991: 164) conclude that

> [t]he profit motive forces corporations into an industrial mode of production whereby the accepted measure of success is not the quality of services rendered, but the number of people processed.

Rationale for New Right privatisation·
- promotes freedom of choice

- provides service flexibility

- consumer empowerment/sovereignty (particularly through 'power of exit')

- productive efficiency (efficient management of resources) through 'market disciplines'

- allocative efficiency (efficient distribution of resources) through 'price signals'

- fiscal imperatives: present Victorian budgetary difficulties are simply an extreme expression of a common problem confronting contemporary governments—perennial difficulties meeting community expectations and balancing the books

- reduces government 'interference'

- reduces public sector trade union power.

Manifestations in policy in Victoria:
- closure of State nursing homes; construction of private prisons

- withdrawal of funding for community development programs and consumer advocacy groups

- changes in kindergarten and maternal and child health funding

- removal of planning and environmental controls.

Finally, choice may be illusory. Choice can only be effectively exercised when:
- there is more than one provider for the product or service

- consumers can obtain and evaluate information on the price and quality of service offered by providers

- consumers have the resources to choose between competing product/service providers.

In the field of human services, one or more of these preconditions is usually missing. The service is often provided by a monopoly, information on service quality is hard to obtain, there are barriers to using information effectively (e.g. among frail older people and people with intellectual disabilities), or information is too costly given consumers' financial resources. In most human services, supportive, timely and effective service delivery is more important to consumers than choice per se.

Privatisation mark 2

This more recent version of privatisation (which some even describe as 'post-privatisation') has received its fullest and most influential airing in David Osborne and Ted Gaebler's popular treatise *Reinventing Government* (1993). A rather more modest Australian expression of some of the ideas can be found in James Cox's CIS monograph *Private Welfare* (1992).

Privatisation mark 2 has evolved in response to the perceived need to reform non-detachable, non-saleable parts of the state (that is the rump of non-government business enterprises). This version recognises the importance of retaining significant policy and regulatory engagement in key public policy areas, like the human services. It also reacts to the failings of the hard-line denationalisation/deregulation and anti-state approach.

The pivotal shift in thinking under this new paradigm is the attitude and approach adopted towards government. To quote Osborne & Gaebler (1993: 23–4):

> our fundamental problem today is not too much government or too little government. Our fundamental problem is that we have the wrong kind of government. We do not need more government or less government, we need better government. To be more precise, we need better governance.

Or again:

> Conservatives have long argued that governments should turn over many of their functions to the private sector—by abandoning some, selling others, and contracting with private firms to handle others. Obviously this makes sense, in some instances. Privatization is one arrow in government's quiver. But just as obviously, privatization is not the solution. Those who advocate it on ideological grounds—because they believe business is always superior to government—are selling the American people snake oil. (Osborne & Gaebler 1993: 45)

This new version of privatisation has

•a primary stance: divide responsibility between the state and market/non-market sector by separating 'enabling' and 'doing'

•a major focus: efficiency through competition by means of

—contracting out

–contestability (via real or proxy forms of competitive tendering)

–creating internal markets by, for example, splitting purchaser and provider, and

–commercialisation, the incorporation of private sector values and approaches into public sector service systems (eg economic pricing, user pays, managerialism).

The following box describes the rationale for and major features of this version of privatisation theory.

Rationale for mark 2 privatisation:

- efficiency and effectiveness are raised by competition. The threat of competition ('contestability') in the public sector raises efficiency

- separating service provision from policy development divides effort along the lines of expertise and capacity, leading to superior focus, effort and outcomes

- importing the values and operations of the market into the public sector roots out waste, inefficiency and what Osborne and Gaebler call the 'bankruptcy of bureaucracy'

- shifting power from producers to consumers

     –encourages strong customer-orientation, customer surveys and letting customers choose their service providers

     –allows purchasers to evaluate more rigorously and gives them greater freedom to dispense with inadequate service providers.

Manifestations in policy—competition and contestability:

- compulsory competitive tendering in local government

- non-government organisations competitively bidding for work/contracts

- benchmarking (proxy or 'yardstick' competition)

- case-mix funding and 'internal markets' in health care

- rampant commercialisation.

A BRIEF CRITICAL HISTORY

Privatisation has come a long way since its modest and ugly beginnings in Pinochet's Chile in the mid 1970s, and its reach now extends to most of the developed and developing nations of the world. Along with its prolific growth over the years, the scope of privatisation has also widened to cover almost every area of public sector activity.

Everything, it seems, it up for grabs. Government-owned banks and airlines, already in competition with private corporations, are being sold.

Transport, water, gas and electricity suppliers—traditional government monopolies—are being sold to corporations that are attracted to the high profit, low risk and captive markets of these sectors. Now, core areas of the welfare state such as education, health, housing and community services and even roads are being drawn into this process through compulsory competitive tendering, contracting out, internal markets, users-pays and private sponsorship.

Privatisation policy, in Australia and elsewhere, has been built on a foundation of ideology and voodoo economics. Political pragmatism has been important too. Privatisation has often been sold as a short-term fiscal fix—by cashing in public assets or load-shifting. Also, in Victoria at least, the government has adopted the Thatcherite objective of using privatisation as a means of destabilising and immobilising the public sector trade union movement.

In addition to these political motives, there is in this country a disturbing degree of what might be described as *conviction privatisation*, the stuff that true believers are made of. True believers pursue privatisation for the higher goals of efficiency and competition. Of course, the rhetoric of efficiency and competition is standard in privatisation programs worldwide, as it legitimates and dresses up in purer purposes rather more mundane and self-serving objectives. But the problem in this country is that many policy makers seem actually to believe all the efficiency and competition rhetoric and hence are committed to privatisation more for this reason than any other. Paul Keating, the Victorian Treasurer Alan Stockdale, Peter Troughton (the head of the Victorian ESI Reform Unit), the Chairman of the Australian Competition and Consumer Commission, Professor Alan Fels, and Professor Fred Hilmer (the architect of framework under which state public utilities will be subject to national competition policy), are all apostles of conviction privatisation. However, since taking up the post of chairman of the NSW power giant, Pacific Power, Professor Hilmer seems to have changed his tune to some extent.

But neither ruthless political pragmatism, nor starry-eyed obeisance before the altar of Competition, fully explain the contemporary passion for privatisation. When the multiple layers of rationale and rhetoric are lifted, privatisation in all its nakedness is revealed as an ideological project. Privatisation forms the strategic vanguard in the battle to defeat the collectivist impulse and win hearts and minds for capitalism. Margaret Thatcher's rallying cry of 'rolling back the frontiers of the state' and her goal of 'popular capitalism' simply made explicit what many privatisation advocates have chosen to keep to themselves.

Elites and popularity

Privatisation policy is the archetypal example of elite policy making. Although it seeks to tap the prejudices of ordinary people—based on a wilful misreading of the mood and the values of the public—it does not originate in, nor interact with, popular opinion. Privatisation is initiated and sponsored by elites, to an agenda which serves their primary interests; with as little community knowledge of and input into the decision-making process as it is possible to get away with. And often it is relentlessly pursued regardless of whether it is supported by the population at large or not.

In reality, privatisation policy is notoriously unpopular, as survey evidence in Britain and Australia shows. The reason is simple: privatisation has not much more than hollow rhetoric to offer ordinary citizens, in exchange for the expropriation of part of their estate. Over the peak period of Margaret Thatcher's privatisation program (1986–90), opinion poll after opinion poll emphasised that the British were unconvinced by the government's pro-privatisation propaganda and that they much preferred continuing public ownership of the energy and water industries (80% in the case of water). Polls taken since privatisation show that privatisation remains more unpopular than ever (MORI 1993) and that the majority of the British public want the electricity and water industries renationalised.

Surveys of public opinion in this country show similar levels of support for the retention of public ownership and management of public infrastructure and essential services. The October 1994 Saulwick Age Poll found that at least two-thirds of people nationally supported public ownership and management of water, postal services and electricity (and the majority also favoured public control of airports and railways). An EPAC study (Withers et al. 1994) published around the same time, on public attitudes to government expenditure and provision, likewise showed that the vast majority of Australians support government provision of physical and social infrastructure (motorways: 82%, garbage collection: 75%, police services: 70%, hospitals: 67%, schooling: 64%, airlines: 63%).

The AGB McNair poll for *The Age* (4 February 1995)—in which almost two-thirds of people polled were opposed to the sale of the electricity industry—provided further confirmation of the fact that public utility privatisation is not popular. The Victorian government's commitment of public funds to an expensive propaganda campaign on the electricity sale was in itself a tacit admission of the deep unpopularity of privatisation. Yet it would be foolish to find much comfort in the tenor of popular opinion alone, for the history of privatisation shows that it not only succeeds in rolling back the state, it is also adept at rolling over people and democracy—particularly when they are quiescent.

The intelligent attitude of scepticism and caution that characterises the public view of privatisation, finds little resonance in the media, however. Here gung-ho, heroic and unsubstantiated accounts of privatisation abound. The fact that this occurs, despite clear evidence that there is a dark side to privatisation, says much about the representativeness and analytical power of the Australian media. But is also says something about the conventional measures used to evaluate privatisation. The focus has been on limited and short-term economic indicators and the social, environmental, or strategic impacts of privatisation have been largely ignored.

Efficiency

Yet even when measured in conventional economic terms, research shows that the efficiency outcomes of privatisation are mixed. The general conclusion of academic analysts seems to be that sometimes privatisation improves productive efficiency (Megginson et al. 1994), but in many instances it seems to make little difference (Dunsire et al. 1991; Jackson & Price 1994). Also the much-vaunted cost savings, which are commonly attributed to competitive tendering, are rarely matched in practice; and when they are, this may well be at the expense of service quality (Ernst 1994a).

In many instances, the really hard work of improving the productivity, performance and efficiency of government business enterprises—as well as the cruel work of retrenchment—is actually done when they are still in public ownership. In fact, aside from Eastern Europe, privatisation generally relies for its success on selling winners not losers. Undeniably, there has been a major lift in the economic performance of public utilities across Australia over the past five years, as reports produced by the Bureau of Industry Economics (1994), the Industry Commission, and even the Victorian government's own Independent Review of Victoria's Public Sector Finances (1992) and the later Commission of Audit (1993) have acknowledged. The fact that this widely-applauded transformation can occur under public ownership begs the obvious question: why is privatisation necessary at all?

Competition

Privatisation advocates in this country usually build their arguments on the view that Australia needs privatisation and reform of public enterprises to compete internationally. This view certainly drives the so-called National Competition Policy. Now if the keys to the international trading kingdom could indeed be found by privatising industries like energy and water, you would expect to find:

1. that utility charges for Australian businesses are inordinately high by comparison with our major trading partners, and

2. that utility charges among the world's most dynamic trading economies are much lower than Australia's.

But in the electricity industry, for example, the reverse is true—Australia's average price of electricity for industry is one of lowest in the world and is between one-half and one-third the price (depending on volume and state) of Japanese power (Bureau of Industry Economics 1994: 11). No, the road to international competitiveness is rather more complex than the simplistic nostrums of privatisation ideologues would have us believe!

Social justice

If evidence on the economic effects of privatisation is equivocal, the social impacts are much clearer. Privatising governments promise much, but the track record shows that privatisation does not usually deliver the goods in terms of choice, service flexibility, lower prices or better services. In many cases, it has meant higher charges and poorer services; invariably it has meant less control and accountability over how services operate. Ironically, on those rare occasions where there have been gains for ordinary consumers, these have been won not through the operation of market forces—as the rhetoric would have it—but through the intervention and action of public regulatory bodies. But these effective regulatory agencies have considerably more consumer protection teeth than are found in the jaws of the Victorian Regulator-General (Ernst 1994b).

Competition—and its allegedly miraculous works—occupies a pivotal place in the political marketing of privatisation policy. Experience internationally shows that for the great bulk of consumers it remains a fiction. Large industrial and commercial customers monopolise any competition gains that are made available through public utility privatisation. Captive domestic consumers then end up paying more than they should, usually because of inadequate price regulation and because they effectively subsidise the cheap pricing deals made at the competitive, high volume end of the market. The experience of countries like the United States and United Kingdom shows that competition as a motive force in the provision of human services is rarely possible and is even more rarely desirable.

International experience highlights one thing above all else: privatisation has marked distributional impacts on particular sectors of society. The privatisation of public utilities and human services has more often than not led to regressive and inequitable outcomes, where the most vulnerable and disadvantaged sectors of the community have been hit hardest. Over the period leading up to and following privatisation, essential services often become more difficult and expensive for low income groups to access. And in some instances, services are withdrawn altogether (Ernst 1994c). The sale of public enterprises widens the already great disparities of income and wealth characteristic of market economies. The transfer payment from general taxpayers to the select new owners of the water industry in Britain, to take a particularly notorious example, was in excess of £9 billion.

In their zealous pursuit of market-based alternatives to public provision, contemporary governments often overlook the obvious fact that the underlying dynamic of the market is driven by contest and inequality. Therefore, to rely on market (or quasi-market) forces alone for the production and delivery of essential and community services, is to expose the most vulnerable sections of the population to the chill winds of service access, based simply on market power.

Social justice should represent the central mission of community services, and be a central organising principle in providing essential public utility services. But in a market economy, unless governments supply the underpinning, in the form of adequate public financing and effective public regulation, the principle and practice of social justice collapse altogether.

It is unusual for government ministers and economic analysts, who blithely speculate on the outcomes of privatisation, to take account of anything other than the short, or at best the medium, term. Yet the evidence from elsewhere suggests that the privatisation of essential services and community services is likely to bring with it longer term social and economic costs.

One of most important of these costs is the loss of strategic control over key parts of the physical and social infrastructure—a major casualty of public utility privatisation in Britain. This was brought home most poignantly in the collapse of the domestic coal industry (and with it the destruction of dozens of mining communities) after electricity was privatised. And the environmental consequences of an energy policy, such as that in Britain which consists essentially of the dictum—*let the market rule*—are likely to prove equally damaging: private electricity utilities are forced by market considerations to use cheapest rather than greenest technologies and to maximise sales rather than conserve resources. The social balance sheet of a decade of service privatisation in Britain has yet to be fully tallied up, but the bleak outlines are clear for all to see: Britain is a darker, substantially more unequal and dangerously more fractured place than once it was.

Rolling back the privatisers

The brief and frenetic history of privatisation shows us too that the legacy of privatisation well and truly outlives privatising governments themselves. Privatisation offers a form of political immortality—perhaps this helps to explain its popularity among ambitious politicians. Once public utilities are sold or local government human service capacity is dissolved, it is a difficult, if not impossible, policy decision to reverse. The great political achievement of Margaret Thatcher was not that she survived for fifteen years as leader of that consummate boy's club, the British Conservative Party. No, her most remarkable achievement is that she has been able to reinvent herself in successive British governments—that of John Major and that of the Labour heir-apparent to the prime ministership, Tony Blair.

For political parties of the moderate Left, the financial and political complexities of returning essential services to public ownership have become too hot (or too costly) to handle. Instead they pin their hopes on making fundamental changes to the regulatory system; changes where, it is argued, action can be taken to ameliorate the worst effects of privatisation. Regulation—either in the form of independent regulatory bodies, or tightly monitored local government service contracts—can reduce some of the damage, of course; and it is for this reason that we need to influence the design and operation of the regulatory machinery. Yet in truth, this is really trying to close the public interest stable door well after the profit-hungry private horse has bolted.

Privatisation is also a matter of ideology. Privatisation has become the 'flagship' of the New Right approach to government. This approach has been advocated by Veljanovski (1987), Pirie (1988), Letwin (1988) and Redwood

(1988). The prescriptions of the New Right have come to dominate political discourse internationally over the last decade, though they have been implemented most completely in Britain, the United States and New Zealand.

Privatisation is, then, part of a theory of the New Right. Among the major intellectual strands of the New Right are eighteenth century *laissez faire* economics, public choice theory, libertarianism, and authoritarian conservatism. In this sense, the New Right is a theory against collectivism. What then are the central precepts of this elaborate intellectual counter to collectivism, which has dominated political thought and action for most of the first seventy years of the twentieth century?

There are three central elements of New Right theory:

- core values

- belief in the market

- critique of the state as economic agent.

Why the Ascendancy of the New Right?

- the failure of Keynesian demand management to deal with the volatile mixture of high inflation and high unemployment ('stagflation')

- the 'fiscal crisis' of the contemporary state: taxation revenues have not kept pace with demands on spending

- continuing international economic instability following the OPEC oil crisis in 1973

- the demise of United States economic leadership and

- the inability of 'social democratic' governments to adapt to national and global changes in economic and social development.

Core Values

New Right theorists frame their political and economic prescriptions around a set of core values concerning the human condition. The 'values centrepiece' in the New Right world-view is a concept of citizenship rights (Gamble 1988), built upon the trinity of individualism, freedom and property rights.

For the New Right, many social programs, particularly those with distributional intent, lead to the use of state coercion (e.g. taxation) and infringe individual property rights. Inequality in their view is a fundamental staple of a free economy and a free society, for without it the structure of property rights as well as the basis for economic growth and social advance is undermined:

> The range of what will be tried and later developed, the fund of experience that will become available to all, is greatly extended by the unequal distribution of present benefits; and the rate of advance will be greatly increased if the first steps are taken long before the majority can

profit from them. Many of the improvements would indeed never become a possibility for all if they had not long before been made available to some. If all had to wait for better things until they could be provided for all, that day would in many instances never come. Even the poorest today owe their relative material well-being to the results of past inequality (Hayek 1960: 44).

In other words, inequality is useful.

The New Right offers a concept of citizenship in the free market economy. The central point in New Right political philosophy is the individual in society. The notion of society itself is markedly problematic for New Right theorists. While the bald 'there is no such thing as society' view expressed by Margaret Thatcher may over-simplify the New Right stance, the treatment of society as a thing in itself is explicitly dismissed. The dimensions of citizenship are highly circumscribed, with a strong emphasis on economic and legal rights. What is noticeably absent is the sense of social citizenship. (Social citizenship refers to the rights and duties concerned with the welfare of people as citizens, taking welfare to include work, education, health and quality of life.)

Fundamentally, the individual is seen as **self interested** and **rational**. These characteristics make for self-conscious and purposive action on the part of individuals designed to further their own personal interests. Individual interests, however, cannot be satisfied in isolation and they inevitably require a degree of interaction with other self-interested and rational actors. Within a social context made up of such individuals, the maximisation of personal interests is supposed to be best achieved through an explicit form of voluntary exchange and cooperation. This is the logic that underpins the concept of the free market.

The individual in interaction with others is (like the market) largely self regulating. There is little need for externally imposed constraints and controls—with the exception of a system of rule compliance to ensure that everyone plays fair. While law and order are integral to the effective operation of individual voluntary exchange (particularly to preserve and protect property rights), the emphasis must invariably be on maximising personal freedom. For radical liberal theorists, the operation and allocational efficacy of the free market—which for them is very much a metaphor for life generally—is profoundly retarded if the scope for individual action is unnecessarily constrained.

Freedom (or liberty) is a concept which occupies a salient place in the pantheon of liberal values. Yet as many critics of New Right philosophy have asserted, for all its rhetorical importance, freedom is perceived in a limited and negative way. Freedom, in the sense of **absence of coercion**, rather than freedom as opportunity to participate (economically, politically or socially), is the paramount objective of liberal politics.

Essentially, the onus is on the individual to create their own opportunities through market-related exchanges. As long as they are free from unjustifiable constraint in accessing the market, the allocation of rewards in this process is seen to be fundamentally fair, despite the fact that rewards will often be unequal:

> It cannot be denied that the Rule of Law produces economic inequali-ty—all that can be claimed for it is that this inequality is not designed to affect particular people in a particular way. (Hayek 1986: 59)

The suggestion that the outcomes of the invisible hand of the market should be moderated through external action, to create opportunities for particular groups in society, is perceived as a direct threat to the inviolable freedom of others to maximise their return from market exchanges, as well as a basic infringement of **property rights**.

The right to hold, use and dispose of property (physical, human, infor-mational or otherwise) is the central dynamic in the New Right's social order. Any attempt to interfere with individuals' right to accumulate and use the property they legitimately acquire through market interactions (apart from basic levels of taxation to finance law and order, defence and the provision of public goods) is viewed with abhorrence by the New Right.

According to the New Right, private property should form the dominant form of tenure in a free market economy. There should be as little recourse to common property as possible. Almost by definition, common property is intrinsically inferior as a mode of ownership to private property. Privatisation serves this argument in two important ways. First, it shifts the locus of own-ership away from 'dysfunctional' state forms and second, through the sale of shares in privatised enterprises, it extends individual property rights.

The role of the market

> ... the competitive market has several features which render it uniquely congenial to a liberal individualist society. The coordination it effects among human activities is, firstly and above all, non-coercive. Each agent adjusts his plans to the plans of others by reacting to the informa-tion about others' preferences and resources that is transmitted to him through price signals ... It is a form of coordination which is finer than any achievable by central planning and one which at no point abrogates the liberty of individuals. (Gray 1986: 69)

The market—built on a foundation of voluntary exchange, competition and open and unrestricted access—is universally viewed in New Right thought as an unrivalled mechanism for efficient production, distribution and consumption. By actively facilitating competition it ensures that a close relationship exists between (i) the need for goods and services and their production and (ii) the cost of producing goods and services and the prices charged for them. Remarkably, according to free market advocates, this pattern of communication and signalling is achieved naturally and spontaneously, without the need for elaborate and formal systems of coordination and planning (Adam Smith's 'invisible hand').

The virtues of the market are held to reside not only in its efficiency, but also in its impartiality. The free market is seen as neutral, in that it doesn't discriminate among individuals on anything other than economic grounds (such as the saleability of their product). As suggested earlier, the outcomes of market processes will often be unequal, but this is seen to have little to do with the internal working or logic of the market itself. The essential amorality of the free market in New Right thought is outlined by Gamble (1988: 53):

> A significant feature ... is the abandonment of the claim that the pattern of rewards and incomes which is the outcome of markets is in any sense just. Hayek denies that the question has any relevance. The set of general rules that define the market order can be considered just but not the outcomes themselves, because these depend on luck, chance, accident, effort, skill, inherited wealth, inherited talents and many other factors. For ... many of the New Right the market is a lottery.

The New Right claims that the operation of the free market is aloof from questions of morality or justice. So, to intrude upon the value neutrality of the market is to disrupt the incentive structure, which acts as the dynamo for competition, efficiency and economic growth. Intrusion also politicises the market by coercing it to discriminate in favour of particular groups, on the basis of some externally imposed set of moral criteria. The denial of market injustice represents a significant divergence of New Right theory from traditional conservative thought, which recognises the need to offset instances of market failure.

Whether this highly idealised model of the free market bears any relation to the way in which contemporary capitalism actually works is hardly explored by New Right theorists. Yet the New Right world view is a long way removed from the transnational, corporate oligopolies that dominate the international economy in the late twentieth century. In practice, to the New Right, capitalism in whatever guise is seen as somehow expressing free market principles. The fact that this is patently not the case in many instances is either blithely ignored, or tendentiously argued away by the assertion that, for all its flaws, contemporary capitalism still represents a vastly superior mechanism for production and distribution than any alternatives.

Monopolies act as a constraint on the free play of market forces, and this is recognised by New Right theorists. The enforcement of competition law and the proscription of monopoly practices by the state are viewed as necessary in order to protect the integrity of the market economy. The existence of natural monopolies in areas such as electricity distribution and water supply confronts the New Right with the unenviable choice of public or private monopoly. In that choice, private monopoly is to be preferred because a state monopoly is protected against both potential competition and effective criticism and because the state itself becomes more identified with the interests of those who run things than with the interests of the people in general (Hayek 1986). It is generally accepted, however, that private monopoly over essential services needs to be publicly regulated. So, again: privatise where possible, regulate where necessary.

The role of the state

> Privatisation is at the vanguard of a world-wide movement in thinking and politics about the legitimate role of the state in an industrial society of the 1980s. Socialism in whatever form has both lost the battle of ideas and been forsaken as a practical solution to the immediate industrial problems that most economies are now confronting. (Veljanovski 1987: 204)

The New Right's views on the state are altogether more ambiguous than its concept of the market. They are, though, built on a criticism of the post-war social democratic state (Dunleavy & O'Leary 1987: 47):

> State intervention ... in practice produces worse results than do market solutions ... administrative and bureaucratic methods are inherently inferior to markets as a means of allocating resources; and because it is objectionable on moral grounds.

Given the New Right's deification of the market, it is hardly surprising that an alternative to market-based production and distribution would be seen as less efficient and effective. And much of the case against the involvement of government as a producer is built around this central belief. However, some analyses of the detrimental effects of state involvement in the economy adopt a more developed position. In particular, they draw attention to

1. **the problems of planning.** Centralised planning assumes a level of skill that human beings generally don't possess. Given the limits on human knowledge, attempts to plan amount to little more than the tyrannical imposition of the views and vested interests of senior bureaucrats on the majority.

2. **the absence of competition.** The effective monopoly of many state-based enterprises enables them to remain unreceptive to preference and price signals; they place consumers and potential competitors in a disadvantaged position.

3. **the comparative performance of state-run enterprises.** The absence of competition and the lack of a sanction (bankruptcy or hostile

takeover) are adjudged to be the cause of the poor performance of public enterprises relative to private sector firms. Although the evidence on the comparative performance of public and private enterprises in the utility sector is inconclusive, this does not inhibit critics of the public sector from using this line of reasoning as a supposed empirical buttress to their arguments.

These arguments are given a hard edge by public choice theory. The starting point for public choice analysis is that actors in the public sphere—officials and politicians—exhibit the same rational, utility-maximising behaviour as that expressed by individuals in the private market. Hence, in contrast to classical public administration dictums, public sector actors are seen to be essentially motivated not by obscure notions of public service, but by self interest.

The argument runs that there is little reward for productivity and efficiency in the public sector. So factors such as size of organisational territory and budget become the performance criteria. Dunleavy and O'Leary (1987: 114) amplify this interpretation:

> The key difference between firms and state agencies concerns what it is that their managements try to achieve. In private firms (even those which are inefficiently run), decisions are still made with a view to increasing profits, since managers' earnings are often profit-related. But in government agencies bureaucrats' welfare is more likely to be closely linked with the size of their budget than the earnings of their bureaux. Increased appropriations create more jobs for government officials, improve promotion prospects, strengthen demand for their services, make it easier to run agencies and improve their prestige and patronage abilities ... Hence the central objective of all government officials is to maximize their agency's budget.

Furthermore, public choice theorists claim that politicians purchase electoral support by trading ever-escalating promises, without serious consideration of their public expenditure impact:

> why did the economists of the thirties, forties, fifties, and into the sixties take the Keynesian theory of policy seriously? Why did they fail to see the elementary point that elected politicians will seek any excuse to create budget deficits? (Buchanan 1989: 21)

Voters, it is said, effectively conspire with politicians in this fiction that the ante can continually be raised, because they don't directly relate the costs of the promised additional programs to the taxes they pay. Hence the affection in New Right circles for public financing devices—such as the community charge—that draw a strong link between consumption and taxation.

The conclusion that public choice theorists arrive at from all this is that the failings of democratic government as manager of the public purse are so deeply entrenched and pervasive that government should be entrusted with as few responsibilities as possible. For the New Right, public choice theory makes its critique of the state morally satisfying. This benefit is derived from being able to tunnel under the moral high ground traditionally held by advocates of collectivism, that public sector activity is informed by a commitment to public service and by pursuit of the public interest.

The empirical validity of public choice theory of administration has been subjected to increasing challenge by political scientists in recent years:

> the great majority of empirical researchers are by now agreed ... that the hypothesis concerning the predominant role of self-interest in Western politics cannot be upheld (Lewin 1991: 98), and ... the appeal of budget-maximizing models has not been grounded on detailed empirical support. (Dunleavy 1991: 223)

Much has been made of the differences between radical liberals and conservatives over the appropriate role of the state (Hayek articulates the lines of division in his Postscript to *The Constitution of Liberty*, 'Why I Am Not a Conservative'). What then are these contrasting viewpoints on the state?

Put simply, the logic of the pure radical liberal view on the centrality of the free market suggests that the state has a marginal role to play. Because the market in its free and unfettered form is the most efficient vehicle for production and distribution, the state should have minimal presence in the market. Equally, most of the current set of non-market functions performed by the state (such as social welfare, environmental protection and corrections) could quite easily be converted into market transactions by handing them over to the private sector. The primary legitimate role for the state under this view is that of protecting private property through the provision of law and order.

> Its major function must be to protect our freedom both from the enemies outside our gates and from our fellow-citizens: to preserve law and order, to enforce private contracts, to foster competitive markets. (Friedman 1962: 3)

As a model of a role for the state in contemporary western society, the radical-liberal view is grossly under-developed. Its lack of intellectual substance can, with some validity, be parodied as 'the state is the collector of residue activities spurned by the market'.

In the conservative world view, the state occupies a clear and unequivocal position as the defender of traditional values, authority and social order. Without a strong and omnipresent state, representing ruling class interests, society would dissolve into anarchy and chaos. To be sure, in this view, the core function of the state is to protect property rights. However, the conservatives accord the state a dominant, positive role and give it entry into the private domain of relationships and values (such as the family) even at the expense of individual liberty: 'In general, it can probably be said that the conservative does not object to coercion or arbitrary power so long as it is used for what he regards as the right purposes' (Hayek 1960: 401).

Yet as Gamble (1988: 28–9) states:

> The idea of a free economy and a strong state involves a paradox. The state is to be simultaneously rolled back and rolled forward. Non-interventionist and decentralized in some areas, the state is to be highly interventionist and centralized in others. Others argue that centralised and assertive intervention is required in the short- and medium-term to clear the way for the full flowering of a free market economy; and that intervention by the state is necessary to sustain a free market economy. These arguments recognise that the state performs an important function as a facilitator of, and residual support for, the market economy.

Privatisation and contracting out occupy a centrally important place in the New Right project for structural social change. For they simultaneously enshrine the principle of commodification as the basis of individual interaction in society (premised on market-based exchanges), extend individual property rights, promote the ascendancy of the market, and crystallise the shift in the role of the state from producer to enabler.

THE NEW GOVERNANCE

The privateers mark 2 advocate an entrepreneurial, 'New Governance' approach. The assumptions and elements of this approach must not go unchallenged. Here we take on

- the ideas of public choice theory
- issues in separating policy and provision
- the culture of contracts
- the convergence of public and private sectors
- implementation.

The public choice underpinning

The edifice of *entrepreneurial government* ('active government without bureaucratic government' according to Osborne and Gaebler (1993: 284) rests on the foundation of public choice theory. In the public choice view of the world, public policy is essentially an unholy alliance of politicians, bureaucrats and interest groups who separately and collectively conspire to feather their own nest at the expense of the public.

The failings of government are contrasted with the self-evident virtues of the market in New Right philosophy. The entrepreneurial government thesis is built around a sanitised and romanticised view of the market and the superiority of market values. The market becomes the model for measuring success and for determining the rules of the game, in the public as well as the private sector.

The British political scientist John Kingdom captures this sense of dichotomy and convergence, when he says, in his polemic on Thatcherism (1992: 76):

> Where the market, like a stern schoolmaster, brings out the very best in the human spirit, the institutions of politics have the edifying quality of Dicken's Fagin. For this reason the public choice theorists expend much of their energies in seeking to redesign the state, trying assiduously to remould the clay in the image of the market.

The roots of the new managerialism currently permeating federal and state public services are planted in this sort of soil.

The seductive thing about the public choice view of the world is that it touches that nerve of anarchism in all of us and conforms to popular stereotypes of grasping politicians and empire-building bureaucrats. But does it actually provide an explanation of the day-to-day workings of government?

The Victorian government through its recent policy initiatives has answered in the affirmative. As we have seen, academic political scientists have, however, not shown anywhere near the same level of confidence in the claims of the public choice school.

Separation of policy and provision

Public choice theorists advocate the separation of policy and provision. The state should set policy; private businesses should provide services. It is argued that separation:

1. allows agencies to focus on what they do best

2. improves accountability by clarifying the 'principal–agent' relationship. Janet Chan (1992: 243) writes of prisons that '[b]ecause of the necessity of drawing up contracts which specify standards of performance, obligations and safeguards against abuse, privatisation could well result in a more accountable operation than the publicly-run prison system allows'

3. forces agencies to focus on planning, development and evaluation rather than service delivery.

Yet each of these arguments is partial:

1. Public accountability is reduced if private service agencies operate in commercial secrecy, outside the direct scrutiny of government and without the overlay of ombudsman protection.

2. The 'principal–agent' problem may well become worse if agents know more than principals and if contractual time lines and rigidities slow changes in policy. The costs of monitoring compliance are almost certain to be higher.

3. The argument that separation strengthens policy development ignores the fact that policy development needs to be attuned to service experience. The separation of service and policy may exclude consumers' voices from policy development.

Also governments need directly to engage as service providers to provide a form of public counterpoint and comparison to private and other forms of human services provision. Cavanagh (1993: 14) argues that '[w]ithout direct government participation, some service needs will simply not be brought into the political arena to create the necessary pressure to ensure that a service, at an adequate standard, will be provided'.

The separation of policy and provision may constrain what have become known in Australia over recent years as *community service obligations* (CSOs). CSOs are the requirements that public utilities provide services to everyone—including disadvantaged members of the community—even though the cost of providing that service may not be completely recovered. Competition and contestability radically alter the way that CSOs are costed and financed (often in the past they were financed internally and not costed), and they raise doubts as to whether CSOs can and should be delivered at all.

The suggestion that governments might fund CSOs by separate allocations to providers is not as straightforward as it appears at first glance. The boundary between CSOs and corporate social responsibility is by no means clear-cut. Watson and Johnson (1993: 225) put the problem succinctly: '... all enterprises in competitive and monopolistic markets carry social costs and there is a difficulty in identifying what is exceptional in the social costs dealt with in any specific case'. There is a clear danger that privatised enterprises may attempt to fill the loosely woven CSO basket with all sorts of items, which they will declare as purchases, not of their own, but others' making.

The culture of contracts

Market government establishes a quite different relationship with its citizenry than social democratic government. The relationship is individual in focus and contractual in character, as opposed to being collective, non-specific and open-ended in its delineation of rights and responsibilities. The 'contract culture', based on transparent, defined relationships, is also mirrored at the agency level; as for example in the interaction between government departments and non-government organisations.

The terms of the relationship between citizens and agencies of the state have in the past often been vague. Hence a more contractual basis can bring gains in accountability and quality of service (as, in some instances, under the Citizen's Charter in Britain). Indeed as Ian Harden points out in *The*

Contracting State (1992: 69), the contractual approach if '... taken seriously ... requires the state to do more, not less. Guaranteed legal rights to public services are not cheap and are unlikely to be paid for wholly by efficiency savings'. Rarely are they taken this seriously, of course. And in the present fiscal environment, they are much more likely to be used to delimit and exclude than the reverse.

More fundamentally, the contract culture of the *Reinventing Government* paradigm mandates a set of relationships which mirror market transactions. The world, including the political domain, is regarded as one of buyers and sellers (or purchasers and providers). As in the market, individual transactions and individual claims are recognised to the exclusion of collective action and group claims. This atomises collective needs and reduces the scope for joint action designed to influence the process of democratic decision making.

One illustration of this is found in the way that governments are abandoning the structures of community consultation developed during the 1970s onwards. Now governments obtain feedback (and consumer 'voice') through market research surveys and opinion polls. This acts to control and centralise the agenda-setting in public policy, for as Anna Coote (1992) has pointed out,

> market research ... avoids any danger of individuals getting together as groups of citizens, or any obligation to enter into dialogue or to negotiate with them. It keeps power in the hands of the body commissioning the research, which remains free to formulate the questions, interpret the answers and decide what to do about the results.

Contracts clearly designate purchaser and provider, customer and service deliverer. But in areas of the human services this simple and clear relationship is often opaque and confused. It is often difficult to determine who exactly the customer is and as a consequence to decide who exactly are or should be the parties to the contract. Customer and service user are not necessarily the same.

All this suggests that the metaphor of contracts is rather more complex and problematic than the advocates of entrepreneurial government generally admit. The contract culture, at the agency level, may well result in better targeted and performance-conscious services and government. But at the same time, it is likely to reduce agency autonomy and independent advocacy, and what Lipsky and Smith (1990) call the civic virtues of non-profit organisations. The contractual approach has the potential to turn independent agencies into passive agents, and like the changes occurring in the way that governments go about obtaining consumer views on services, it tends to concentrate and centralise power in the policy process.

Convergence of public and private sectors

Campaigns to reinvent government seek to apply the principles of private sector management and to inculcate a commercial, competitive ethos into the public sector. As Sullivan (1992: 219) says, 'the monopoly of welfare services by welfare state agencies is replaced by a policy and service framework indebted to market theory'. This represents possibly the most significant transformation in the character of contemporary government.

The language of 'customers', 'unit costs', 'benchmarking', 'managed competition' and 'contestability' has become a significant part of the contemporary lexicon of the public sector. It symbolises how market values and processes are incorporated into the machinery of government. Through privatisation and commercialisation the boundaries and characteristics of public and private sectors become more and more blurred, and ultimately converge.

In an increasingly commercialised public sector, government may have its hand on the tiller, but the direction and pace of travel is heavily influenced by the charts and compasses supplied by the private sector and in accord with the currents directed by the market.

The view of 'government as business' and the unfiltered application of private sector management techniques (some of which are seen as having little currency in the best parts of the private sector) are likely to retard the attainment of important equity outcomes. And they will ultimately erode the collective good and public stewardship functions central to the meaning of government.

Common, Flynn and Mellon (1992: 134) refer to the process of 'agencification' under the Next Steps Initiative in Britain and argue that it

> may divorce public sector managers from previous public sector values like equity and integrity. They have a clearly delimited role and deliver according to their circumscribed responsibilities ... these managers have been unable to define any real difference between public and private sector management. We believe that there are and should be differences.

Public sector management should be distinguished from the private sector on several significant counts (Alford 1993):

- the public sector produces **'public values'**: promotes equity and protects the collective interest (e.g. about the environment and international relations), as well as market ones

- the public sector operates in a **complex decision-making environment**: usually manages many and diverse stakeholder interests and often considers short, medium and long range effects of decisions (intergenerational equity is one example). In contrast, the decision context of the private sector is usually more time-limited and its stakeholders confined to shareholders, employees and customers

- the public sector's effectiveness often relies on the **cooperative**, as opposed to the competitive, participation of others. Competition has a dysfunctional effect if applied inappropriately in the public sector:

examples include service duplication, loss of scale economies, the dismantling of collaborative institutional arrangements and the focusing
on marketing at the expense of service delivery

•the public sector uses diverse resources to achieve its policy ends,
involving not only public money, but significantly, **public power** as
well. The responsibility and leverage that attends the state's monopoly
on legalised coercion distinguishes government fundamentally from
business.

But in challenging simplistic formulations of entrepreneurial government
it is easy to be misunderstood. This is not to argue that the old bureaucratic,
inefficient, producer-led culture which characterised some parts of the state
system is congruent with the more assertively consumerist and rights-orient-
ed climate of the 1990s. Complacent indifference towards the performance
of the public sector is not an intelligent or persuasive response to the problems of contemporary governance. But then neither is blind faith in market
analogues and market surrogates.

In reality, neither bureaucratic nor market modes of human services provision (and this country has had considerable experience of both) have really empowered service users. The key to successful public sector provision in
the future does not lie in adopting an inappropriate, and potentially damaging, private sector management template, but in developing a form of practice that marries conventional notions of efficiency with the particular
demands and challenges of the citizenship model of governance. As
Common and his colleagues (1992: 137) put it: 'The real trick is for public
sector managers to preserve **public** values while producing efficient and effective services'.

Implementation

What will be the extent of real, as opposed to rhetorical, consumer choice in
internal markets under managed competition? Will it simply be a case of
'same choice, different face', replacing public with private monopoly.
Common et al. (1992) use the delightful phrase 'playing at shops' to describe
this fiction of consumer choice. A study completed in 1992 for the Joseph
Rowntree Foundation in Britain assessed early evidence on contracting out
local authority community care services. In the main contracting out has not
raised consumers' choices: 'In all but two of our cases, respondents said the
contract did nothing to increase user choice of service' (Common & Flynn
1992).

There remains the danger of **cream-skimming**. Examples are raised by Le
Grand (1992: 19) in relation to:

•the National Health Service, where fund holding GPs might manipulate their patient lists in order to choose the 'best' patients, and

•the recent education changes, where there are 'preliminary signs of ...
schools setting up formal or, more commonly informal, means of

selection [of the most academically able students]'

A **cost-benefit analysis of contracting out** services would need to balance:

- the size, if any, of cost-savings through contracting out, which generally range from an upper 20 per cent to 6 per cent at best

- the effort involved, which includes the costs of contract monitoring and enforcement in 'high risk' and sensitive areas of service provision

- the distributional consequences of changes in employment conditions, which are likely to be different for senior managers and front line staff.

Finally, the entrepreneurial/market-based approach is more likely to reinvent problems (such as inequality and social disharmony) than to actually reinvent government, if it is used by governments as a backdoor way of load-shedding, and as a strategy for saving expenditure. This appears to be the substantial attraction of the New Governance paradigm for the present Victorian government.

CONSUMERISM OR CITIZENSHIP?

Privatisation, corporatisation, and micro-economic reform have become bywords in the political and bureaucratic management of public utilities in Australia. While Victoria has won the mantle of privatisation pace-maker among the states, energy and water utilities in every state in the Commonwealth are being subjected to various forms of restructuring. A significant part of the momentum for this change has come from the federal government and its agencies, like the Industry Commission and the newly formed Australian Competition and Consumer Commission.

Privatisation of public utilities involves more than transferring ownership and restructuring water and energy industries. It also seeks to redefine the relationship between the individual and the state, and in particular the way in which individual and social needs for essential utility services are met. At its heart, the privatisation project is founded on consumerism.

In contrast to the present situation, which is characterised by the New Right as begrudging and inefficient service delivery under conditions of public monopoly, ordinary consumers are promised choice, better services and new rights. To use the borrowed language of the Victorian Treasurer, utility consumers are to be empowered.

But is the paradigm of consumerism appropriate to public utility services? For public utility services are different from other commodities in the market place. These differences include:

- energy and water are 'merit' and collective goods

- demand for essential utility services is price and income inelastic, and

- domestic supply of water and energy is a network or natural monopoly

Consumerism also fails to address the central issue of access.

Consumerism and its limitations

Consumerism is built on the central dynamic of commodification, designating most forms of service and exchange as commodities which can be priced and sold. Virtually all human needs are translated into individual wants. Market-based interactions become the primary mechanism for satisfying these wants. Consumerism gives expression to the idea of the individual in the marketplace.

Consumerism articulates a set of procedural rights designed to protect the individual in the market and supposedly to make the consumer sovereign. These rights are **choice, information, the power of 'exit'** and the ability to seek **redress** in the event of service failure (through, for example, complaints procedures and compensation measures).

The effectiveness of consumerism as a principle for public utilities rests on the extent to which choice and exit rights can be realised in practice. The other rights are secondary and contingent, whose power is only realised once the choice and exit conditions are met. For example, the right to information has little meaning if a consumer cannot choose between different service options and providers. Equally, it's no use being able to complain if the complainants cannot take their business elsewhere or substitute one product for another.

In Britain, the choices available to domestic consumers of electricity, gas and water services are no greater now than they were before the industries were privatised. Yet, since consumers cannot choose between different water or energy service providers and cannot substitute one utility service for another, they cannot exercise their power of exit. In effect, ordinary British consumers today have about as much chance of using the key lever of consumer sovereignty as did their seventeenth century travelling forebears looking to hire a horse from the Cambridge carrier, Mr Hobson: he indeed offered a choice—the one nearest the door, or nothing!

Equity

Even if competition and choice actually emerge in the domestic utilities sector in the future, will this lead to a consumerist nirvana and will it eliminate the need for most forms of public regulation? And what is likely to be the distributional impact of utility companies competing for the business of domestic consumers?

A certain scepticism about the virtues of competition might be derived from the observation that historically the competitive market place has done little to promote access and equity in any sphere of human consumption. Privatisation of the utility industries raises more specific concerns, too.

Ordinary consumers lack information in their dealings with utility providers. Consumers' lack of information would need to be removed if competition is to benefit domestic consumers. Consumers will need to be markedly more informed about the utility market place, as well as their own pattern of consumption and expenditure than they are now. In contrast to the supermarket or shopping mall, where the array of consumption choices is visibly laid out before prospective purchasers, utility consumers will need to go to some trouble to become more fully informed. For some consumers, these transaction costs will outweigh the benefits gained in terms of price or service quality. For others, either because of disability, language, or the sheer complexity of the task, the opportunity to shop around for utility services is effectively foreclosed.

The received wisdom in competition theory is that if there are multiple and competing suppliers then almost invariably prices decrease. But for some consumers of utility services, competition is likely to have the opposite effect. This will almost certainly be the case for consumers in rural Australia. The removal of uniform tariffs is inevitable, as the public monopoly practice of internally subsidising loss-making sectors is abandoned by profit-making corporations. Under a competitive regime, utility tariffs for customers who have hitherto benefited from cross-subsidies would almost certainly increase, unless public expenditure maintains a level of uniform pricing. On the other hand, the removal of cross-subsidies may provide a welfare gain (in the form of lower prices) for consumers who live in areas where the distribution and supply costs are relatively low. From an equity perspective, the winners and losers from these tariff adjustments will be defined indiscriminately, without reference to ability to pay or social impact.

There are other negative by-products of competition. These include:

•a decline in overall service quality (as competitors strive for price advantage by reducing costs)

•the abandonment of special services targeted at groups in the community with particular needs, such as older people and people with disabilities and

•a reduction in research and development effort.

Some consumer organisations in Britain argued along these lines in their recent defence of the monopoly of British Gas in the domestic gas market.

The elevation of choice as an end to be valued in itself needs to be questioned. Water and energy services are not like commodities traded in the local market or the shopping town. People obviously cannot select their utility services on the basis of an immediate visual evaluation of price and quality. More importantly, consumers are likely to want a utility service that is reliable, safe, and value for money, rather than fine graduations of choice.

Even if the conditions of actual, as opposed to rhetorical, choice and exit rights were to be satisfied in the future, there would remain the fundamental flaw in the consumerist paradigm; namely its failure to address **access/entry** rights.

Access to water and energy services, sufficient to meet personal and household needs, is one of the fundamental human requirements. Yet clearly, the capacity to access utility services is not shared equally by all individuals and households. There are disparities in ability to pay for energy and water. In addition, higher energy costs are imposed on many low-income households as a result of their living conditions (poorly insulated housing, expensive forms of heating, inefficient appliances: Boardman 1991).

In the face of these structural barriers to entry and access, the consumerist paradigm is mute. Procedural rights and protections—like effective complaint mechanisms and guaranteed standards of service—are important, but in themselves they are insufficient. A panoply of procedural rights is largely ineffective in assisting consumers negotiate their way through the utility service system when, at the core is the fundamental problem of fuel or water poverty—as the regulatory bodies in Britain are finding out.

British experience

Within the circumscribed frame of reference set for them, the utility regulators in Britain have made, generally speaking, a positive contribution to the welfare of ordinary consumers. The procedural rights that domestic consumers have achieved in recent years are generally superior to those offered during the decades of nationalisation in Britain. These gains have not been delivered by the operation of the market, as the thesis of consumerism asserts, though; they have been delivered, ironically, by public regulation of the market.

However, the British regulatory system has been ineffectual in two areas.

1. It has not dealt with the problems of access and equity: there are rising numbers of households living in fuel and/or water poverty.

2. It has not coped with the utility's **collective goods**: for example, in not constructing a framework for managing such negative externalities as CO_2 emissions.

Yet to blame the formal regulatory bodies for these omissions is really to expect too much of the regulatory apparatus. Responsibility for vital social, economic and environmental policies about the public utilities ought to be the preserve of democratically elected governments, not of quasi-independent, regulatory bureaucrats. However, the loss of strategic control over primary areas of infrastructure is the first—and arguably the most significant—casualty of public utility privatisation. Privatisation casts important questions of public policy adrift from the democratic process.

Consumerism, it is important to recognise, is essentially an expression of a negative, one-dimensional view of citizenship. It constitutes a repertoire of individualistic protections for those able to make their way in the economic system. It undercuts the very notion of public utilities in the sense of collective provision for the collective good. For a more positive framework of social, as well as consumer, protection we need to look elsewhere.

An alternative: Social citizenship

By the social element I mean the whole range from the right to a modicum of economic welfare and security to the right to share to the full in the social heritage and to live the life of a civilised being according to the standards prevailing in the society. (Marshall 1992: 8)

Marshall did not allude specifically to energy and water services in his account of the evolution of citizenship rights, but their importance in present-day society places them firmly within the last part of his definition: 'to live the life of a civilised being according to the standards prevailing in the society'. In his recent essay, Citizenship, Rights and Welfare, Raymond Plant (1992: 16) updates Marshall's concept of social citizenship by arguing that it

> implies some limit to commodification and commercialisation, in the sense that the basic welfare goods to which individuals have rights are not ultimately to be subject to the market mechanism, since the market cannot guarantee the provision of these goods, as of right, on a fair basis to all citizens.

Social citizenship recognises substantive as well as procedural rights (Plant 1991). It mandates public policy and utility industry action to ensure that access rights are guaranteed and protected. Because social citizenship, in contrast to consumerism, recognises **collective** as well individual rights and responsibilities, it firmly locates strategic decision making on the utility industries firmly within the domain of democratic accountability and public policy.

So what specifically would be different about public utilities under the social citizenship view?

First and foremost, a social citizenship approach to utility services would be built on a framework of **public ownership** of the natural monopoly elements of the public utilities. This would require the public to own the entire transmission network and domestic distribution sectors of the energy and water industries; although in the case of the domestic distribution, this need not be in the form of centralised management and control. The ownership status of the other parts of the utility industries should be considered on a case by case basis. The criteria for decision making about their future should be framed by notions of social as well as economic efficiency, and must consider the longer range public interest.

The social citizenship approach seeks to capture some of the gains of **independent regulation**, although public regulation would be more active and equity oriented than now. Regulators should designate general consumer-oriented service standards and set social and environmental performance targets aimed at promoting best practice within the utility industries.

One of the most enduring and disingenuous myths perpetrated by the public utility industries is that they are a set of economic services, with no mandate, nor responsibility, for social welfare. But as the Sheffield welfare rights activist, Martin Fitch (1992: 5), has cogently asked, 'what is it that these providers of essential services supply if not welfare? Enjoyment of the services of the water, fuel and telecommunications utilities is the foundation of well-being—of welfare—in modern societies'.

The current obsession with expunging all cross-subsidies in the public utilities is impracticable, commercially absurd, and in the context of their social function, irresponsible. This does not necessarily mean, of course, that the utility industries should be obliged to provide open-ended **community service obligations** (CSOs) and cross-subsidies. But it does necessitate a less purist approach to the internal allocation of costs. It is usually argued that measures aimed at giving financial assistance to low income consumers are better handled through the taxation/social security systems rather than by internal price manipulation, for the reasons that this is more distributionally progressive, is more transparent, and is likely not to reduce efficiency. However, this view overstates the progressivity of the tax system, and understates the progressivity of some forms of tariff-setting (such as rateable value). And transparency has a weakness: external, government-provided concessions and subsidies are rudely exposed to the vagaries of budgetary and cost-cutting processes.

Whatever the decision on the treatment of CSOs, the social citizenship paradigm would control utility tariffs tightly and would constrain the utilities' ability to generate excessive revenues. In Britain, shareholders have been the primary beneficiaries of unanticipated cost savings.

REFERENCES

Alford J 1993 Towards a new public management model: beyond 'managerialism' and its critics *Australian Journal of Public Administration* 52: 135–48

Boardman B 1991 *Fuel Poverty: From Cold Homes to Affordable Warmth* London: Belhaven Press

Buchanan J M 1989 *Essays on the Political Economy* Honolulu: University of Hawaii

Bureau of Industry Economics 1994 *International Performance Indicators, Electricity Update* Research Report 54 Canberra: AGPS

Cavanagh J 1993 Can children's rights be served by a privatised welfare system? *Public Issues Forum:* Autumn 11–16

Chan J B L 1992 The privatisation of punishment: a review of the key issues *Australian Journal of Social Issues* 27: 223–47

Common R and Flynn N 1992 What's in the contract? *Community Care* 6 August 1992

Common R, Flynn N and Mellon E 1992 *Managing Public Services: Competition and Decentralisation* Oxford: Butterworth-Heinemann

Coote A 1992 (ed) *The Welfare of Citizens: Developing New Social Rights* London: IPPR/ Rivers Oram Press

Cox J 1992 *Private Welfare* St Leonards: Centre for Independent Studies

Dunleavy P and O'Leary B 1987 *Theories of the State: The Politics of Liberal Democracy* Basingstoke: Macmillan

Dunshire A 1990 The public/private debate: some United Kingdom evidene

International Review of Administrative Sciences 56: 29–61

Ernst J 1994a Privatisation, competition and contracts, in Alford J and O'Neill D (eds) *The Contract State: Public Management and the Kennett Government* Geelong: Deakin University Press 101–35

Ernst J 1994b A licence to exploit *Frontline* June 1994

Ernst J 1994c *Whose Utility? The Social Impact of Public Utility Privatisation and Regulation in Britain* Buckingham: Open University Press

Fitch M 1992 Public utilities, regulation and the welfare of 'difficult customers', Sheffield: unpublished manuscript

Friedman M 1962 *Capitalism and Freedom* Chicago: University of Chicago

Gamble A 1988 *The Free Economy and the Strong State: The Politics of Thatcherism* Basingstoke: Macmillan

Gray J 1986 *Liberalism* Milton Keynes: Open University

Harden I 1992 *The Contracting State* Buckingham: Open University

Hayek F A 1960 *The Constitution of Liberty* London: Routledge Kegan Paul

Hayek F A 1986 *The Road to Serfdom* London: Ark Paperbacks

Jackson P M and Price C M (eds) 1994 *Privatisation and Regulation: A Review of the Issues* London: Longman

Kingdom J 1992 *No Such Thing as Society?* Buckingham: Open University Press

Le Grand J 1992 Paying for or providing welfare?, Paper delivered at Social Policy Association Annual Conference, Nottingham (July)

Letwin O 1988 *Privatising the World* London: Cassell

Lewin L 1991 *Self-Interest and Public Interest in Western Politics* Oxford: Oxford University Press

Lipsky M and Smith S R 1990 *Government Provision of Social Services Through Nonprofit Organisations* Canberra: ANU Urban Research Unit Working Paper 21

Marshall T H 1992 Citizenship and social class, In Marshall T H and Bottomore T 1992 *Citizenship and Social Class* London: Pluto

Megginson W L, Nash R C and van Randenborgh M 1994 The financial and operating performance of newly privatized firms: an international empirical analysis *The Journal of Finance* XLIX: 403–52

MORI 1993 *Electricity Services: The Customer Perspective* Report prepared for the Office of Electricity Regulation, London

Osborne D and Gaebler T 1993 *Reinventing Government: How the Entrepreneurial Spirit is Transforming the Public Sector* New York: Plume

Pirie M 1988 *Privatization* Aldershot: Wildwood House

Plant R 1991 Social rights and the reconstruction of welfare, In Andrews G 1991 (ed) *Citizenship* London: Lawrence and Wishart

Plant R 1992 Citizenship, rights and welfare, In Coote A (ed) *The Welfare of Citizens: Developing New Social Rights* London: IPPR/ Rivers Oram Press (1992)

Redwood J 1988 *Popular Capitalism* London: Routledge

Starr P 1989 The meaning of privatization, In Kamerman S B and Kahn A J

1989 (eds) *Privatization and the Welfare State* Princeton: Princeton University

Stoesz D and Karger H 1991 The corporatisation of the United States welfare state *Journal of Social Policy* 20: 157–71

Sullivan M 1992 *The Politics of Social Policy* Hemel Hempstead: Harvester Wheatsheaf

Veljanovski C 1987 *Selling the State: Privatisation in Britain* London: Weidenfeld and Nicolson

Victorian Commission of Audit 1993 *Report of the Victorian Commission of Audit Volume 2* Melbourne

Watson G and Johnson M 1993 Pricing: cheap water or an environmental perspective, In Johnson M and Rix S (eds) 1992 *Water in Australia: Managing Economic, Environmental and Community Reform* Leichhardt: Pluto 212–34

Withers G, Throsby D & Johnston K 1994 *Public Expenditure in Australia* Economic Planning Advisory Commission Paper No. 3, Canberra: AGPS

Selling the SECV
Flaws of Economic and Social Logic

Bob Carter

PRIVATISING THE SECV

The Victorian electricity supply industry has since the 1920s been government owned. It is centred on thermal generating stations that use brown coal in the Latrobe Valley 150 kilometres east of Melbourne. The State Electricity Commission of Victoria (SECV) was established in 1921 under the chairmanship of Sir John Monash to enable Victoria to take industrial and community advantage of the vast, cheap and easily accessible deposits of brown coal (lignite) in the valley. Electricity production by the SECV, being reliable, relatively cheap and readily available virtually throughout the state, has been a significant factor in Victoria's pre-eminent industrial position in the nation.

Brown coal remains, at 84 per cent, the dominant source of energy for electricity. Gas-fired or gas-turbine stations provide peak and intermediate load equal to about 8 per cent of electricity. Hydro-electric installations supply 5 per cent of power at peak demand. About 2 per cent of total electricity production comes from net purchases from interstate and co-generation.

An integrated grid supplies virtually all inhabited parts of the state. All but a few industrial, commercial and domestic electricity consumers are connected. Power is purchased

•directly from the SECV or

•indirectly, through 11 publicly owned municipal electricity undertakings (MEUs).

Connected to the grid is a large aluminium smelter in the far west of the state serviced by a purpose-built 500kV transmission line.

The past several years have seen large-scale and continuous changes in the structure, operations and staff levels of the SECV. During the 1980s the commission began remoulding itself into a more commercially oriented, profit-reporting organisation. In this corporatisation the SECV established semi-autonomous business units dealing with each other in a commercial relationship. From 1984 it declared an operating profit and, under the Public Authorities Dividend Act, provided a dividend to the state. This dividend has built to over $200 million per annum over the last few years.

Along with these developments have been dramatic and accelerating reductions in the commission's workforce. From a peak of some 23,000 employees in 1983/84, numbers have dropped, most particularly during the past four years, to less than 12,000 in 1993. Estimates as low as 7000 have been quoted for total employment in 1995. Modern plant, particularly power stations, is not labour intensive and methods of applying labour to tasks have been improved. At the same time, staffing has been reduced by contracting-out work and abandoning non-essential (e.g. municipal) functions.

The economic and social ramifications of the commercial focus have been most keenly felt by the SECV's workforce and the Latrobe Valley community. Unemployment is stubbornly high and property values have crashed (Munro 1995). There is a high demand for welfare relief. A round of second-level redundancies has begun as contractors shed workers who had followed their jobs into the contractor firms. The training role formerly performed by the SECV is not being taken up by the contractors whose view is narrow and short term.

The SECV and the New Right
The SECV has been in many ways a remarkably successful organisation. It has exploited Victoria's brown coal and transformed it to community and industrial benefit. This has been achieved, however, at considerable cost to the Latrobe Valley environment and to the health of valley workers and residents.

The SECV has underpinned the state's industrial development and provided cheap and reliable domestic electricity. It has proved itself, moreover, a highly competent commercial enterprise. As a government-owned monopoly, however, it affronts New Right philosophy and economic rationalism.

The electricity supply industry, as historically constituted, fails the economic rationalist test on all counts. It is a monopoly; it is government owned; it is subject to government regulation and it discriminates in price among classes of customers. As such, it attracts a lot of attention from the free-marketeers. Its disaggregation and privatisation are aims close to the heart of the economic rationalist.

The Victorian Coalition government has reflected many of the policies and programs advocated by the proseletisers of the New Right—the Institute of Public Affairs (IPA), the Tasman Institute and the Industry Commission. The advocacy of the New Right can be seen in areas including health, transport, education, industrial relations and in staffing levels in the public service. The Victorian government has proved itself to be a willing experimenter in New Right policy implementation. It is not alone among Australian governments in this. It is, however, the most enthusiastic and adventurous.

The Coalition Prescription
The Victorian government proposes, and has implemented the first stages of, revolutionary changes to the structure, operation and ownership of the Victorian electricity supply industry. Claiming to improve the efficiency of the industry and reduce debt, it plans to disaggregate (break-up) the industry and create a private market in electricity.

In broad brush terms it plans to follow the advice of the IPA and Tasman

Institute and the policy prescriptions of the federal Industry Commission. The Office of State Owned Enterprises (ESI Reform Unit) in the Victorian Department of the Treasury has, along with an unknown number of private sector consultants, undertaken the detailed planning. Treasurer Stockdale has been the political and public voice.

Initially, the generation, grid transmission and distribution functions were separated. There was a generation company and a transmission company, while five companies, three metropolitan and two rural, absorbed the former SECV and municipal electricity business roles in distribution. An eighth company became responsible for operating a wholesale electricity market and for system security (Department of the Treasury 1994a).

When the corporation was first broken up, a single company, Generation Victoria, controlled all generation. This company was further disaggregated in early 1995. Separate companies took control of:

1. Loy Yang A and the Loy Yang open cut mine

2. Yallourn W and the Yallourn mine

3. Hazelwood Power Station and the Morwell mine

4. the gas-fired stations, Jeeralang and Newport

5. the Victorian hydro-electric facilities.

The Snowy Mountains hydro scheme is to remain a joint undertaking of the Victorian, NSW and Australian governments.

The newest thermal plant in Victoria, Loy Yang B, is owned 51 per cent by the United States company, Mission Energy and 49 per cent by the SECV. A publicly owned company, SECV Shell, will acquire, under an existing contract with Mission, Loy Yang B's output and pay for Loy Yang B's capacity (Department of the Treasury 1994b).

The state's electricity transmission grid has been put into the hands of Power Net Victoria (PNV). The grid company is to act as a neutral carrier that owns and controls lines above 66kV that supply power from the generators to the five distribution companies. It is intended that it remain in public ownership.

Victorian Power Exchange (VPX) (the Pool) provides system security and operates a wholesale market by processing bids and settlements and ensuring that market operations do not threaten the safety or security of the supply. VPX is to be funded by the industry. The government intends that it be eventually owned by industry interests (Department of the Treasury 1994b).

Electricity is be traded in both wholesale and retail markets. In the wholesale market, the generators will sell to electricity distribution businesses and large industrial or commercial consumers. In the retail market distribution businesses will sell to end-use customers.

Larger consumers will operate in an unregulated competitive market (if their load exceeds a designated level, reducing to 50kW in mid 1998) through contracts or purchases on an energy spot price market, the Pool.

Other consumers 'will be captive to the distribution business responsible for the area in which they are situated'. This latter part of the market is to be subject to regulatory powers (Department of the Treasury 1994a).

While there is still uncertainty over timing and the ultimate number and arrangement of generators, the government intends to privatise all but the grid company and SECV Shell over the next few years. The development of the market is to be staged. Customers, according to their demand, would enter the market progressively between 1994 and 2000. After this date the theoretic ability would exist for all customers to make bids for purchase, through VPX, from the generators or any of the distribution companies.

Prices charged to customers will be controlled until they enter the competitive market. 'By the year 2000', states the Office of State Owned Enterprises, 'the retail sector is expected to be highly competitive, with the exception of very small customers where metering and administration costs may result in limited choice'. After this date these captive customers will have to rely on the Office of the Regulator General for price protection. These very small customers number almost two million: all of Victoria's residential consumers and many small businesses! (Department of the Treasury 1994a).

The reconstruction of Victoria's electricity industry is justified by the assertion that competition and private ownership are needed to raise efficiency.

- The Industry Commission, in its 1991 report on Australian electricity generation and distribution, argued that disaggregation, corporatisation and privatisation would unlock maximum efficiencies through exposure to the disciplines of the market (Stretton 1991).

- The Office of State Owned Enterprises report of February 1994 prefaces its description of electricity supply industry (ESI) reform with the assertions that a

  competitive and privatised ESI will ultimately achieve ... better investment decisions ... because of competitive market pricing and private sector capital market disciplines ... improved use of existing assets ... enhanced incentives for reducing operating and capital costs (and a) closer matching of supply and demand. (Department of the Treasury 1994a)

- The Tasman Institute and the IPA in *Project Victoria* (1991) advocated corporatisation/privatisation of the ESI. They saw it leading essentially towards a 'user pays' system ... a greater focus on commercial performance and a reduction in political interference. (Tasman Institute 1991: 18)

While government statements on cross-subsidy of consumers have been tentative beyond guarantees of uniform domestic tariffs to 2000 and a less-than-CPI price cap over this period, the concern with distortions on the demand side is shared by the Office of State Owned Enterprises.

Retail prices are currently uniform within each customer class. However, cross subsidies between customer classes are being progressively removed in an effort to ensure that electricity tariffs reflect costs. Cross subsidies provide the wrong signals to consumers, creating inefficiencies within the market and advantage one group at the expense of others. (Department of the Treasury 1994a: 24)

Victoria's electricity industry, according to the Office of State Owned Enterprises, 'remains relatively costly, inefficient and unresponsive to customer needs'. This is the result, it says, of excess capacity and an unfair tariff structure. It bemoans also the lack of competitive pressure needed 'to stimulate innovation, commercial investment decisions, world standard productivity and (to) maximise value for customers'. (Department of the Treasury 1994a: 1)

Prescription and Prejudice

Any attempt at a reasoned and temperate response to the plans for electricity industry reconstruction is complicated by the nature of the arguments. They have three elements.

- **The extremely theoretic nature of the economics.** Rather than judge economic arrangements by result, by whether they deliver what is desired by the community, New Right rationalist economics evaluates in terms of how closely those arrangements conform to a theoretical model. It matters little whether an industry is efficient, whether it performs a strategic industrial and/or social role. If it fails to fit neatly with models of competition, private ownership and is encumbered by government interference, regulation or protection it must be deregulated, privatised, made to conform.

- **The value system which accompanies it.** The leadership of the state coalition government accepts the prescriptions of the New Right because the prescriptions fit their preferred view of the world. Free markets, individual endeavour, taxation as an evil, government as an interference, the superiority of private over public enterprise: New Right theory gives such values validity. They are made not only laudable, but unquestionable.

- **The often blandly erroneous assertions which are laced into the argument.** The industry is portrayed as inefficient, unresponsive and lacking in initiative. Later we examine, and refute, such assertions. The point to be noted is the need for the New Right to see the industry in these terms.

EFFICIENCY AND COMPETITION

The government's actions and proposals are, as we have seen, justified on several grounds. Central to these grounds are the arguments that privatisation and the break-up of the industry will increase the efficiency with which electricity is delivered. In part, those efficiencies will be gained by creating a competitive structure for the industry.

Efficiency

The subject of the Victorian electricity industry's efficiency is replete with assertion. Admittedly, efficiency is difficult to measure and compare but such radical changes must prove their case. Claims such as 'relatively costly ... inefficient' need to be scrutinised as do the scenarios for efficiency gains 'like nothing else we've seen' arising from competition and privatisation (federal Treasurer Willis, quoted in *The Age* 8 March 1994). So, what is the situation and what is the potential for improvement?

While the evidence reflects differing interests and intents, claims of gross inefficiency do not stand up to investigation. Indeed, on a number of indices the very opposite is true. An Industries Commission investigation in 1991 placed Australian electricity prices below nine major industrialised nations' prices (Stretton 1991). According to a more recent study, large industrial users in Melbourne pay, at an average 5.4 c/kWh, significantly less than those in Brisbane and Perth and less than industrial prices in New Zealand, Canada, the United Kingdom, the United States or Japan (NUS International, quoted in *The Age*, 14 August 1993).

A 1992 EPAC study found that, while Victoria's system was below average in technical efficiency, it was among the world's best in the economic use of resources. It showed also that rates of return on capital and rates of profit achieved by the SECV in the late 1980s and 1990s fluctuated around 12.5 per cent and 15 per cent respectively (Clare & Johnston 1992). Strong productivity growth has continued in Australia's government business enterprises (3.1 per cent each year between 1981/82 and 1990/91 compared with 0.2 per cent for the Australian economy overall). The SECV has, in some aspects, led this growth. For instance, electricity output per employee grew 17 per cent in the decade to 1990/91.

A detailed international study compared the performance of some 100 utilities involved in generation, transmission and/or distribution (Electricity Supply Association 1994). Australian utilities were compared with principally private sector, urban-oriented, utilities in the United States as well as utilities in Canada, the United Kingdom, Europe, Japan, Thailand, Taiwan, Greece and South Africa. The study was undertaken by London Economics. It found:

- The SECV is below other Australian generators in technical efficiency, rating 0.86 compared to 0.99 in Queensland, 0.95 scored by Pacific (NSW) and 0.87 for Australia. The international sample averaged 0.90.

- On efficiency of resource use, however, the SECV, 'with a score of 0.95 achieves ... a level which places it in the top 10 per cent of utilities with cost minimising input ratios and comparable to the average of the frontier (best practice) utilities'.

•To the extent that Australian utilities fall below frontier achievement, it is 'the relative cost of capital per MW of capacity installed which may be a constraint to Australia's comparative performance'. These capital costs include the combined impact of construction costs, inflation and interest rates.

•In transmission, Victoria and WA fall below the Australian and international average efficiencies. This partly reflects long-distance, high-voltage transmission to such large volume consumers as Alcoa.

•When comparing technical efficiency in distribution, Victoria (excluding the MEUs) scores 0.85, above both the Australian and the international sample which score 0.83 and 0.81 respectively. This is significant since the distributors against which the SECV was ranked were generally United States private utilities servicing large urban centres with dense consumer networks.

The data used in this study were compiled in 1991. The study describes an industry which is far from languishing in lethargy, an industry which in its particular operating environment holds up extremely well in international comparison.

The notable productivity increases in the Victorian ESI over recent years indicate that the relative position of the industry may have improved and suggest that achievable rates of return and profitability have still to be reached. While it is debatable whether rates of return are the only or best indicators of a healthy and socially responsive utility, it remains to be proved that disaggregation and sale to private owners are the most likely way of achieving them.

Competitive markets?

We are asked to accept massive changes in the structure and ownership of the electricity industry on the basis of the efficiencies and reduced prices we are told competitive markets will deliver. The view of competition is, however, significantly flawed.

It is difficult to see the owners of generating units, stations or groups of stations being equal competitors given the age of Hazelwood and the particular designs and capabilities of the gas-fired and· gas-turbine stations. Hazelwood might produce for purchasers a viable rate of return but only if it is sold for less than it is currently worth within an integrated system.

An owner of Jeeralang and Newport would, presumably, desire to use their generating capacity to a greater extent than now. The gas stations now meet peaks in demand, because they can come on-line rapidly. Rather than levelling the peaks in system demand, new owners would want a more predictable and constant revenue producing market. Not only would this role waste finite resources, it would prevent the state system from responding to short but critical unexpected peaks or breakdown of other units in the system.

Victoria currently possesses some excess generating capacity. Competition among independent generators trying to sell this excess may provide some of the price-reduction disciplines sought by the proponents of a restructured industry. It is likely, also, to lead generator companies to seek to raise total consumption of electricity. The environmental implications are obvious.

This very excess removes for a long time the threat of entry of competitors, a crucial element of competition. Prices above marginal cost and the sheltering of inefficient users of resources, do not exist in a text book competitive environment. In such cases, according to the theory, lower-price competitors move into the market. Generating plant, however, comes in large, expensive increments. Entry into the Victorian market with a greenfield plant would entail significant risks. It could be accomplished only over some years of planning and construction. Excess capacity and the massive and risk-laden capital expenditure necessary to enter the Victorian market make a threat of entry, other than through the national (eastern) grid, empty.

The competitive Victorian electricity industry, as envisaged, falls well short of the model competitive market. There would be minimal threat of entry. The independent generators would be using plant of differing ages and technical efficiency and varying supply-niche attributes. The number of firms within the market would be limited: in generation, no more than seven (including Loy Yang B and the Snowy Mountains); in distribution, five. The likelihood of compartmentalisation of the market is high as is corporations' ability to agree tacitly on prices. Regulation of the market further erodes the purity of the model. It may be socially desirable, and may provide protection and some degree of certainty and security, but it is not Adam Smith!

Among the problems confronting the designers of Victoria's reconstructed electricity industry are two particular contracts. They govern the supply of power to Alcoa's Portland aluminium smelter and the price and volume of electricity bought off the majority privately owned Loy Yang B power station. (There is no mention in the government documents of Alcoa's Point Henry smelter in Geelong, although supply arrangements for it are similar to Portland's.)

At Loy Yang B, Mission Energy is in the early days of a 33-year contract to supply 20 per cent of the state's capacity at a reported 40 per cent premium over current prices. The Loy Yang B units are the state's newest and most efficient and were purchased at an allegedly discount value (Davidson 1994a, 1994b).

In the case of Alcoa, the SECV is contracted to supply electricity at prices which depend on Loy Yang A's rate of return on capital, world aluminium prices and the costs of the dedicated transmission line. Through a flexible tariff arrangement the contract recognises profit and loss periods for the supplier to assist Alcoa through depressed market conditions (Government of Victoria 1984). The contract has 20 years to run. Through the trust which holds the government interest in the Portland smelter, the SECV has been compensated by the government for its losses (the price has not covered SECV's costs for much of the life of the flexible tariff arrangement: *Independent Review* 1992: 144–8).

The government's proposed solution to these two problems is to maintain them as public liabilities. Supply to the Portland smelter (and Point Henry?), purchase of Loy Yang B's output and payment for its capacity have been transferred to SECV Shell, a publicly owned remnant of the SECV (Department of the Treasury 1994b). The purchase of the dearest electricity and capacity in the state and the sale (at least for some periods) of electricity at a loss are burdens to be borne by the public while profitable operations move into private hands.

Under such an arrangement SECV Shell would, obviously, soon collapse. The government appears to have made some allowance for this in designing a franchise fee to be levied on the distribution businesses which supply smaller, captive customers. For how long, and to what extent, the public would be protected against these losses is unclear. In a disturbingly equivocal tone the Office of State Owned Enterprises states that 'provision has ... been made for Government to charge' such a fee. 'Government has stated', it goes on, 'that the objective of this fee is to partially or completely recover expected losses' (Dept of the Treasury 1994b: 80). Whether this means that government compensation of SECV Shell for losses arising from the aluminium flexible tariff will cease, to be picked up by the franchise fee, if implemented, is not clear from the Office of State Owned Enterprises documents.

The stated rationale is to 'ensure that the market was not distorted by non-commercial transactions in any way'. While these arrangements certainly remove gross anomalies from the proposed market they also starkly reflect the government's attitude to public, as compared to private, interests.

VIABILITY, PRICE AND BENEFITS
A host of additional questions can be raised about the disaggregation and sale of the SECV. These questions concern:

- the viability of a disaggregated industry

- the price at which it could be sold

- the distribution of benefits from the sale.

Having disposed of the arguments about efficiency and competition, we now examine evidence about these questions.

Reconstruction
A disaggregated electricity industry will prove less viable and efficient than a vertically and/or horizontally integrated industry.

Arguments about economies of scale are easier to put than to prove but, certainly, there is considerable professional support for maintaining at least a fully integrated thermal generation industry (see Colebatch 1993 and Lloyd 1994). A Generation Victoria briefing paper asserted 'electricity was heavily influenced by economies of scale'. It claimed that 'smaller individual units would probably face higher, not lower, costs, and the higher risks of smaller companies would bring higher costs. Instead of the projected price falls, it suggested prices would rise' (as related by David Walker, *The Age*, 20 September 1994). Such views seem to be given substance by the London Economics study referred to earlier. On the basis of its international survey it states that 'utilities owning more stations tend to have higher efficiency scores, suggesting that there are some important scale effects' (Electricity Supply Association 1994: 28).

Private corporations pay higher prices to borrow capital than do public borrowers. Combined with a reduction in scale and the privatisation of risk, the implications are that the industry is moving in the direction of lower efficiency, lower rate of return and higher costs.

The government's planned disaggregation of the industry may, in fact, jeopardise the financial viability of the generators. Such a scenario is noted by the New York credit ratings agency, Moody's, which warns that the Victorian market may not be capable of supporting disaggregation to the extent planned (Moody's 1994). At 4.5 million people the Victorian market is relatively small to support five competing generators. The public will be left with unsold investments—presumably the older and less efficient plants.

The proposed eastern states electricity grid assumes an ambiguous position in planning. The Tasman Institute (1991) argued that Victoria's electricity industry needs to improve its efficiency to compete with interstate suppliers. Yet the grid is also talked down by reconstructors, described as not fully defined, 'in important respects ... not accepted in principle' and having, in the foreseeable future, 'low interconnection capacity' (Dept of the Treasury 1994a: 10). Interstate electricity trade is said to demand reconstruction and to pose little threat to a partitioned Victorian industry. The Office of State Owned Enterprises foresees devaluing of Victorian assets to ensure profitability in interstate competition.

To the extent that an eastern grid is realised it may provoke effective interstate competition. Competition may take the form of NSW's Pacific Power dumping excess capacity. Electricity transmission remains relatively inefficient (power is lost as distance increases and the infrastructure is expensive); so differences in the cost of generation have to be large to cover costs of transmission. Even so, an integrated Victorian industry would be in a stronger position than a disaggregated industry to cope with cross-border incursions. The Office of State Owned Enterprises implies as much.

At what price?

The argument that privatisation is necessary to retire state debt is misdirected if not disingenuous. Premier Kennett, in early 1995, claimed that there was 'no alternative', that the state could not afford to service the SECV debt. He cannot, surely, expect to be taken seriously. The SECV has, for many years, met out of its operating revenue all commitments on debt. It has adhered to a policy of no new debt since 1990 and, over recent years, made significant inroads into the repayment of debt. Above and beyond this it has produced respectable profits and provided increasing dividends to the government of Victoria.

While debt cannot justify sale of electricity assets, it is pertinent to examine whether the Victorian community would be likely to get value for the assets.

The assets are likely to be more valuable to the community than they are to private investors. There are several reasons for this:

- •Private corporations pay higher interest rates for borrowed capital than do public operations. Moody's (1994) assesses stand alone generators as having a higher credit risk than vertically integrated utilities which are able to mitigate the various risks inherent in the industry.

- •Private corporations pay Commonwealth company taxes. At approximately 33 per cent, an immediate one-third of value is taken from the ownership of the industry assets between them being publicly and privately owned.

What private investors would be willing to pay would, therefore, be less than the current asset value, unless the prospective buyers believed they could make considerable gains in profitability.

Proceeds to the community from privatisation are reduced, moreover, by the transaction costs. Payments to lawyers, consultants, brokers and the like could subtract between 5 per cent and 10 per cent of receipts before it is available to repay debt or to be turned to other community purpose. R G Walker (1994) reports costs of between 2.8 per cent and 11.2 per cent in United Kingdom privatisations. The NSW GIO privatisation cost $71 million (almost 6%) of proceeds. The complexity of the plan for the SECV does not suggest a cheap privatisation!

The value of the Victorian electricity assets are in the region of $10 billion with an underlying debt of perhaps $7–8 billion. Given the factors affecting private capital, there must be some doubt that sufficient revenue would be raised to meet this debt through sales. Government advisers have suggested that this value could rise to between $15 billion and $18 billion since investors expect to improve efficiency and therefore future rates of profit. However, the Victorian industry is already, in the context in which it is operating, an efficient and profitable one. The gains from competition are likely to be illusory and a disaggregated industry risks real losses in efficiency and productivity. Interested investors can hardly be expected to be naive. The higher sale price would seem, therefore, fanciful unless the prospective owners believed they were able to raise prices sufficiently instead of reducing costs.

A recent paper has investigated a range of scenarios to illuminate the financial implications of privatisation (Walker 1994). Due to the interest and tax effects mentioned above, and the high rates of return expected by equity investors, the value of the output of a privatisation enterprise to private owners is less than it is to the public while in public hands. The findings of the study were that 'the maximum likely ... bid ... would be in the range of 57 per cent—78 per cent of the retention value' to the community in terms of the stream of income which would be otherwise derived. And, as the author of the paper makes clear:

> If the proceeds of privatisation go toward the repayment of debt, or the purchase of new infrastructure which will not produce equivalent cash flows, the likely outcomes may be higher deficits, or the need to raise additional revenues via taxes. Or, various current services to the community will need to be pared back or abandoned.

Conclusions such as these take us into the discussions of the equity of privatisation. If the Victorian community is going to lose from the break up and sale of the SECV, the losses will be suffered through reduced asset prices or raised electricity prices, or both. If, as Walker argues, the sale of assets does not compensate for the lost flow of receipts, the community loss will be in the form of reduced public sector services and/or in tax increases necessary to maintain such services. If electricity prices rise it is unlikely that the impact will be neutral in an equity/distributional sense.

For whose benefit?

A principal justification of the privatisation of electricity industries is to eliminate cross-subsidies to consumers. The Industry Commission has argued that Australia has too high a cross-subsidy between large industry and domestic consumers and that not only is this an unwarranted impost on business, but confusing and debilitating to the electricity industries' economic performance (Stretton 1991 and *The Australian* 16 March 1994). Utilities would operate best, the commission believed, if they adopted straightforward commercial objectives and this, it argued, was best done by privately owned commercial organisations.

The Office of State Owned Enterprises describes a competitive electricity industry, in which 'the Government will identify and protect ongoing community service obligations and concessions by separating them from the commercial aspects of the industry' and in which wrong price signals are eliminated (Dept of the Treasury 1994a: 3, 24). At base, CSOs bring to the fore the debate over utility production, whether water, gas, electricity, telecommunications are to be seen as commodities like any other in the market place or whether suppliers are responsible for access, equity and distributional impacts.

There is significant cross-subsidy within the Victorian electricity system (as there is in most electricity supply systems throughout the world). The principal beneficiaries are large and high voltage consumers and domestic, particularly rural, consumers (SECV 1993a). In a competitive market, with no cross-subsidies and CSOs, customers' benefits are determined by their relative power in the market, unless the regulator constrains the corporations' marketing.

The Victorian parliament has passed three pieces of legislation to specify forms of regulation:

- the *State Owned Enterprises Act 1993*
- the *Electricity Industry Act 1993* (plus an amending Act in 1994), and
- the *Office of the Regulator General Act 1994.*

The Office of the Regulator General Act seeks 'to create an economic regulatory framework ... which promotes and safeguards competition and fair and efficient market conduct'. The office obtains its specific regulatory powers from the Electricity Industry (Amendment) Act. While the regulator is bound by statements of government policy from the Governor in Council, the office is:

- enabled to regulate the tariffs that apply to ordinary consumers (who operate without a market contract and not on the spot market)

- given the mission of

  – promoting competition throughout the industry

  – maintaining an efficient, economic and financially viable industry, and

  – protecting the interests of consumers in regard to price, safety, reliability and quality.

The legislation does not attempt to ensure any welfare result other than that which fits comfortably within the competitive market world view of the economic rationalist. The only direction which might be said to have a social relevance is the Regulator's objective 'to protect the interests of consumers with respect to electricity prices and the safety, reliability and quality of electricity supply and to ensure that users and consumers benefit from competition and efficiency'. As Ernst (*The Age* 27 May 1994) has pointed out, the legislation 'gives little attention to social regulation' and is 'far weaker than the equivalent systems in the United Kingdom and United States'. Yet even the stronger British system of regulation has been unable so far to protect consumers from profiteering by the private electricity companies (Helm 1994).

The architects of electricity industry reconstruction have accepted the position put forward by the Industries Commission: the price of electricity in Australia is weighted unfairly and inefficiently on the side of small and domestic consumers; the benefits derived from exploiting the natural and capital resources of the industry need to be realigned; distribution must become more socially efficient or rational.

COMMUNITY EFFECTS

The reconstruction of the Victorian electricity supply industry, already in train and planned over the next few years, is not in the interests of the Victorian community. It is based precariously on theory and driven by a determination to fit the industry into a narrow vision. It puts at risk, in the name of efficiency and productivity, an industry which already ranks well on both these scores. The proposals seek to redistribute the benefits derived from Victoria's capital and natural resources. They demand inordinate faith in the theory of the market and in the mechanisms of competition.

An efficient and socially oriented electricity supply industry is to be highly valued. Its future lies most securely in public ownership and integration and in community-based supervision of the use of the state's resources. This way avoids some of the implications for the Victorian community of the coalition prescription for the Victorian electricity supply industry.

The environment

The burning of brown coal to generate electricity has a range of environmental and health impacts which are locally and globally significant. These include the emission of greenhouse gases, discharge of particles and sulphur dioxide into the atmosphere and salt into water. Significant demands are made on land and on water supplies. Power stations are implicated in the formation of ozone.

The SECV has undertaken a range of technological, research and demand moderation initiatives which have aimed to reduce environmental ill effects or have had this as an incidental outcome. Particle and other emissions were significantly reduced by cleaner generating plant and preventive technologies. Research was conducted and/or supported by the SECV into the global carbon budget, reafforestation, alternative and renewable energy technologies, land rehabilitation and noise reduction.

The size and accessibility of the Latrobe Valley coal deposits makes it unlikely that they will be abandoned as an energy source in the foreseeable future. Despite the environmental problems in using them, they will remain Victoria's dominant source of power for large volume, base-load generation. The SECV saw the mitigation of the effects of brown coal use as part of its responsibility as a public utility. We cannot be assured that the same view would be taken by a disparate collection of private generators.

The installation and use of the most environmentally efficient technology can be expensive. It can have adverse effects on profitability. Absolute emission levels can be set by the EPA but public utilities have the capacity to improve on those levels, even at some cost to profits. The public is able to trade-off productivity and dividends against cleaner air and water. Such a trade-off is unlikely by a private sector generator that answers to shareholders and competes for market share.

Few private companies would undertake a program designed to reduce demand for their product. The SECV, however, did just that between 1990 and mid 1994. Through the Demand Management Action Plan (DMAP) the SECV actively encouraged and assisted customers to moderate their demand for electricity by raising their energy efficiency.

DMAP entailed expenditure by the SECV ($14.4 million in 1990/91) and reduced revenue (a net reduction of $10.4 million in 1990/91). The revenue loss in that year as a result of DMAP was just under 1 per cent of total revenue. While the total cost of DMAP to the SECV over this period was $24.8 million, a net benefit of $43 million accrued to the Victorian community (SECV 1993b). While DMAP's focus was primarily economic, the environmental gains from moderated demand are obvious. DMAP was abandoned in June 1994. This, according to the 1994 Report of Electricity Services Victoria, was done 'in the light of ESI restructuring'.

The message is clear. The aims of DMAP were community objectives; they are not compatible with the aims or the approaches of a privatised industry. For demand moderation the community will have to rely on the government or the regulator general. Yet the government is marketing the industry to private buyers on the basis of profits waiting to be reaped.

Social infrastructure

The interest of a private owner of part of an electricity industry is in the profit to be extracted from it. The role of management is to serve that interest to the best of its ability. These interests and roles are not usually identical to the interests of the Victorian community. From this arise many of the potential problems and risks inherent in breaking-up and selling-off the SECV.

The principal interests of the Victorian community in the electricity industry include:

• electricity at reasonable prices for domestic, industrial, business and community consumers and assured supply to all domestic and community users regardless of economic disadvantage

• benefits from the use of the assets of the industry and from the exploitation of Victoria's resources, shared among the whole Victorian community

• safe and reliable supply with minimum disruption

• employment and economic advantages for Victoria and Australia, gained by an electricity industry which is able and willing to respond to opportunities and community/social priorities

• assistance with social and industry policy and planning

• the cleanest environment reasonably possible.

The government's plans are not likely to reduce prices but are likely to make it difficult to meet community service obligations. The use of electricity assets and Victoria's natural resources for economic and social ends expresses itself not only in terms of the pricing of electricity but also in the way profits are distributed. A disaggregated, privatised electricity industry threatens to reduce the ability of the community to take advantage of opportunities to minimise environmental outcome. In similar ways, the community's other interests in the electricity industry are placed at risk.

The electricity industry can best play a strategic role in the state's industry and social planning if it is integrated and publicly owned. The SECV has historically fulfilled that role. Victoria's brown coal resource has been the basis of Victoria's industrial development; it is unlikely that the resource would have been developed had the government not established the commission in 1920 and then encouraged and underwritten it. Significant technical problems inhibited the use of brown coal; from a commercial viewpoint the risks in trying to exploit brown coal were high. Monopoly and the spreading of risk across the whole community enabled the venture to be undertaken.

This is not only of historical interest. Social and industry policy can best be implemented when infrastructure—roads, communications or power supplies—can play the appropriate and required role. The community cannot simply rely on the interests of investors to supply this infrastructure. Private generators and distributors are likely to be less, rather than more, flexible in installing and locating plant and in using developing technologies since they are risk averse.

> In fact, it can be argued that in a real world of high levels of uncertainty in the energy sector as a whole, large, integrated, publicly owned electricity enterprises employing large capitals and diverse technologies are essential to spread the risks of operating in such an environment.
> (Johnson & Rix 1991: 133)

The coalition's model for the Victorian electricity industry will reduce Victoria's ability to plan an economic and social future. It will effectively take out of public hands one of the most important levers available for social and economic planning.

Victorians have a legitimate interest in the reliability of their electricity supply. The high standards of reliability achieved by the SECV have been a result, not only of technical expertise, but also of an integrated generation system consisting of a number of generators of varying attributes operating as an entity. Each unit in the SECV's system fulfilled a role: base loads were supplied, regular and unexpected peaks were met and breakdowns were rapidly compensated.

The disaggregated industry cannot guarantee such performance. Plant is not likely to exist to take up peaks, expected or otherwise, or to come on line in the event of major plant break down. All generators will want their plant operating at peak capacity as often as reasonably possible; reserving, or readying, plant in case your competitor is down for a hour or more is not in the individual generator's best interest. Coming on line at all, at a particular time, may not suit a generator's economic or engineering plan. A significant increase in black-outs and brown-outs would come with the territory of a privatised, disaggregated Victorian electricity industry.

There is another risk to the Victorian community. Premier Kennett has stated that electricity assets would be sold only if an acceptable price can be obtained. Some of the assets may not be sold. Such an outcome poses dangers for the Victorian community. Imagine the situation, a few years hence, where two or three generators have been sold and the metropolitan distributors are controlled by foreign power companies. The remainder—older, less productive remnants, including SECV Shell—languish in public ownership, unsaleable. The sales have retired only part of the SECV debt. Some billions of dollars of debt remain but the remnant publicly - owned industry cannot produce a profit because it owns the high cost distribution networks and uses the oldest generation plant in the state. Large private profits are repatriated to the United Kingdom, France or the United States. The remaining public assets are stranded and, along with the remnant debt, are a liability on the Victorian budget, public sector and community, drawing funds away from urgent needs.

A social dividend

Averaging around $100 million per annum through the mid and late 1980s the Public Authority Dividend paid by the SECV reached $210 million in 1992. Generation Victoria, National Electricity and Electricity Services Victoria (the three businesses created in the original break-up of the SECV) made a combined profit (before tax and interest) of $1.3 billion in the year 1993/94. They generated dividends to the Victorian government of $20 million in the case of Generation Victoria and $185.8 million from Electricity Services Victoria. National Electricity, the grid company, was the source of $46 million. The government-owned electricity businesses therefore provided over $250 million to be used to provide public services and building and maintenance of public assets. From July 1993 the electricity businesses had also to make tax equivalent payments to the government.

Industry experts are confident of prospects for even higher profits over the next few years: dividends and tax equivalent payments of at least several hundreds of millions per year would be available to the government. At the same time the industry has been able, and could continue, to meet all interest payments on its debt and progressively reduce its overall debt level.

Government business enterprises (GBEs) are not solely, or even predominantly, about making profits. There are other reasons for their existence and other priorities which they need to fulfil. If a GBE can, however, fulfil these priorities, both economic and social, and as well provide funds for other community purposes it becomes a valuable asset indeed.

Government can obtain funds to operate public sector services and undertake public works through taxation and charges, from fees charged for services provided and through the earnings of GBEs. To dispose of government business enterprises, for no good reason other than ideological myopia, is contrary to the best interests of the Victorian people, particularly those who already gain least from the use of the state's resources and wealth.

REFERENCES

Clare R and Johnston K 1992 *Profitability and Productivity of Government Business Enterprises* EPAC Research Paper No 2

Colebatch T Power structure will not survive: expert *The Age* 25 February

1995

Davidson K 1994a Fantasy's power can sometimes shut out the real world *The Age* 10 March 1994

Davidson K 1994b Power industry: One into six doesn't go *The Age* 3 September 1994

Department of the Treasury (Victoria) 1994a *Reforming Victoria's Electricity Industry: Stage Two*

Department of the Treasury (Victoria) 1994b *Reforming Victoria's Electricity Industry: A Competitive Future for Electricity—A summary of reforms*

Electricity Services Victoria 1994 *Annual Report—Year ended 30 June 1994*

Electricity Supply Association of Australia 1994 *International Performance Measurement for the Australian Electricity Supply Industry 1990–1991*

Generation Victoria 1994 *Annual report 1994*

Government of Victoria 1984 *The Portland Aluminium Smelter Government Statement* Economic Strategy for Victoria No. 3

Helm D 1994 British utility regulation: theory, practice and reform *Oxford Review of Economic Policy* 10: 17–39

Independent Review of Victoria's Public Sector Finances 1992 State Finance Victoria

Johnson J and Rix S 1991 *Powering the Future: The electricity industry and Australia's energy future* Pluto Press

Lloyd B 1994 Short circuit of sense in power sell-off *The Age* 9 March 1994

Moody's Investors Services 1994 *Challenges of Restructuring the Australian Electricity Sector: Credit Risks With Precedent* Sydney

Munro I 1995 Power struggle in the valley of doubt *The Age* 12 February 1995

National Electricity 1994 *Annual Report 1994*

Parliament of Victoria 1993 *Electricity Industry Act 1993 No. 130/1993*

Parliament of Victoria 1994a *Office of the Regulator-General Act 1994 No. 42/1994*

Parliament of Victoria 1994b *Electricity Industry (Amendment) Act No. 53/1994*

State Electricity Commission of Victoria 1993a *Annual Report: 1992–1993*

State Electricity Commission of Victoria 1993b *The SEC—A Case Study*

Stretton R 1991 Power—and more cost—to the people *The Bulletin* 8 October 1991

Tasman Institute and the Institute of Public Affairs 1991 *Project Victoria: Victoria An Agenda for Change* Melbourne: Tasman Institute

Victorian Auditor-General's Office 1993, Special Report No. 24: *Open Cut Production in The Latrobe Valley*

Walker D 1993 Bright sparks who lead the charge for change *The Age* 7 March 1993

Walker R G 1994 Privatisation: a reassessment *Journal of Australian Political Economy* 34: 27–52

The Erosion of Civil and Political Rights in Victoria

Catriona Larritt and Ken Coghill

Contents

Acknowledgements. Catriona S. Larritt would like to thank Michael Webber and Mary Crooks for their thoughtful criticisms of earlier drafts of this paper. Also, she is grateful to Mr Paul Chadwick, Dr Chris Corns, Professor Arie Freiberg and Ms Moira Rayner for reading different parts of the paper, and to Mrs Pamela Larritt and Mr Stuart Wood for reading the entire paper.

Victoria on the Move, Move, Move

Catriona S. Larritt

INTRODUCTION

In December 1993, approximately 100 baton-brandishing police, flanked by mounted police, clashed with peaceful protesters at Richmond Secondary College in Melbourne. The protesters had occupied the buildings for almost one year in opposition to the Kennett government's closure of the school as a co-educational facility. The police were ordered to remove the protesters to enable contractors to commence renovations for a new girls' school. The police intimidated and forcefully removed many of the protesters, causing considerable public concern. It was questioned whether Victoria Police were adequately trained and equipped to cope with peaceful demonstrations and public protests (Kingston 1993). Mr John Halfpenny, (then) Secretary of the Trades Hall Council, blamed the Kennett government for encouraging police brutality and suggested that 'these scenes people will be seeing on television as a result of this morning's assault on the pickets are the sorts of scenes we are used to seeing in other countries, like some despotic regime in South America' (cited in Painter 1993: 1). It is often difficult to balance freedom of expression and political protest and police control over public demonstrations. It appears, however, that the police used excessive force to remove the protesters and threatened the right of individuals to demonstrate peacefully against a political decision (Goldberg 1994).

Graphic images of police forcefully subduing a political protest do not sit easily with the common perception of Australian society. Australia is usually perceived to be a liberal democracy with a political culture which respects fundamental rights and freedoms (O'Neill 1987; Jones 1990). The notion of 'fundamental rights and freedoms' has been influential in all genuine democracies, but there is little agreement about the specific content of such rights and freedoms (Cooray 1985). For practical purposes, however, a distinction may be made between civil and political rights and socio-economic rights.

Civil and political rights include the right to freedom of expression, the right to freedom of association, the right to a fair trial and the right to peaceful assembly. Ideas about these 'classical' rights originated from seventeenth and eighteenth century political philosophers and have been developed over many centuries. Civil and political rights are essentially negative, functioning as restraints upon government actions (Legal and Constitutional Committee 1987). The most common contemporary declaration of civil rights and political freedoms is the *International Covenant on Civil and Political Rights*. This covenant was adopted by the United Nations in 1966 and ratified by Australia in 1980. It contains 22 articles guaranteeing substantive civil and political rights (Box 1). These rights and freedoms, however, are not absolute. For example, Article 21 of the covenant enables the peaceful right of assembly to be restricted in order to protect national security, public safety, public order, public health or morals or to ensure the recognition and respect for the rights and freedoms of others.

In contrast to civil and political rights, socio-economic rights include the right to strike, the right to work, the right to an adequate standard of living, the right to health and the right to education. The Legal and Constitutional Committee (1987) suggested that socio-economic rights are sometimes labelled 'new' rights because of their recent and non-universal development. Socio-economic rights require positive government actions to ensure their implementation and are often difficult to enforce. Socio-economic rights have been enshrined in the *International Covenant on Economic, Social and Cultural Rights* which was adopted by the United Nations in 1966 and ratified by Australia in 1975. The central concern of this paper is the state of civil and political rights in Victoria.

Fundamental rights and freedoms in Victoria have not been enshrined in a bill of rights in the Victorian Constitution as they have been in, for example, the United States. Instead, in accordance with English tradition, civil

---

Box 1: Selected Articles of the International Covenant of Civil and Political Rights

Article 6	the right to life
Article 7	the right not to be subjected to torture or cruel, inhuman or degrading treatment or punishment
Article 8	the right against slavery or compulsory labour
Article 9	the right to liberty and security of the person, including the right against arbitrary arrest, detention or imprisonment
Article 10	the rights of prisoners
Article 12	the right to freedom of movement
Article 13	the rights of aliens
Article 14	legal process rights, including the right to a fair trial, to trial without undue delay, to adequate legal assistance, to be presumed innocent until proven guilty
Article 17	the right to privacy
Article 18	the right to freedom of thought, conscience and religion
Article 19	the right to freedom of expression
Article 21	the right to peaceful assembly
Article 22	the right to freedom of association
Article 26	the general right against discrimination

and political rights in Victoria have been protected by common law as developed by judges when they decide cases and by the self restraint and democratic spirit of the parliament (Commonwealth of Australia 1987; Bailey 1990; Weeramantry 1990). Flaws do exist in these historic institutions and civil and political rights have been breached under both coalition and Labor governments. However, it appears that the rights and freedoms of Victorians have largely been respected. The Statute and Law Revision Committee (1979: 3) postulated that 'the state of fundamental rights and freedoms was fairly satisfactory in Victoria'. More recently, the Legal and Constitutional Committee (1987: 61) concluded after reviewing the state of human rights in Victoria that 'it would appear that the civil and political rights of the average Victorian are, on the whole, reasonably well protected'. Similarly, it was stated in the summary of this committee's report that 'Victoria has a proud record in acknowledging and protecting human rights. Compared with other places, Victoria has been a leader in protecting these rights' (Legal and Constitutional Committee 1987: ix).

The coalition parties were elected to power in Victoria on 3 October 1992. The Kennett government immediately embarked on a radical program to rescue Victoria 'from the brink of financial and social disrepair' (Office of the Premier 1994: 2). The Kennett government has radically restructured the economy. It has diminished the current account deficit, dramatically decreased government expenditure and reduced the ratio of debt to gross state product. The Kennett government has also implemented many other significant changes. It has abolished the Law Reform Commission, restricted the right to strike, abolished the Accident Compensation Tribunal without reappointing its judges to an equivalent court, restricted access to government documents under freedom of information legislation and placed senior public servants on five year contracts with a one month termination notice. The Kennett government has limited the Supreme Court's jurisdiction to review ministerial and parliamentary decisions, abolished the position of Commissioner for Equal Opportunity, tipped the balance of power in discrimination complaints in favour of the respondent, altered sentencing practices, changed the public prosecution system, increased police powers to obtain names and addresses, fingerprints and forensic samples, and introduced a new offence of loitering by convicted sexual offenders. It has sacked local councils, appointed unelected commissioners who are answerable to the executive government itself, delayed democratic elections for most local councils until 1997 (after the next state election) and avoided scrutiny and debate of legislation by incorporating substantive law as subordinate legislation. Most of these changes have been implemented without consultation.

The nature and implementation of the Kennett government's actions have been well documented by the media. Additionally, some commentators have produced in-depth analyses of particular changes. For example, Fox (1993) examined the Kennett government's reforms to sentencing practices, while Corns (1994) explored the changes to the public prosecution system.

However, the impact of the Kennett government's actions on the civil and political rights of Victorians has received remarkably little attention (the exceptions being short, largely descriptive articles by Bernstein (1994), Wallace (1994), Zifcak (1994) and the Australian Labor Party (1995)). This is surprising given the number of the Kennett government's changes which appear to affect such rights. This paper begins to correct this neglect by examining the effects of some of the Kennett government's actions on civil and political rights and then attempting to explain how and why such changes have been implemented. The vast nature of 'rights and freedoms' coupled with the quantity of changes that the Kennett government has made mean that there are many pieces of legislation, policies and practices which could be analysed. A decision was made to focus on the impact of five different pieces of legislation enacted by the Kennett government on civil and political rights. These include the:

- *Sentencing (Amendment) Act 1993* which alters Victorian sentencing practices

- *Crimes (Amendment) Act 1993* which increases police powers to obtain names and addresses, fingerprints and forensic samples

- *Freedom of Information (Amendment) Act 1993* which alters the accessibility of government documents

- *Equal Opportunity (Amendment) Act 1993* which changes the operation of anti-discrimination legislation

- *Public Prosecutions Act 1994* which reforms the public prosecution system.

The decision to analyse these five pieces of legislation means that other Kennett government changes and their impact on civil and political rights remain unexplored. This reflects a limitation of space rather than an attempt to diminish the importance of other changes or their repercussions.

OUT OF SIGHT AND OUT OF MIND: *SENTENCING (AMENDMENT) ACT 1993*

The coalition parties vowed to bring law and order into line with community expectations during their 1992 election campaign. Protection of the community and the rights of victims were primary concerns. The Kennett government's first step towards achieving this goal was the enactment of the *Sentencing (Amendment) Act 1993* which increases the custodial sentences for serious sexual offenders and serious violent offenders and empowers courts to impose indefinite sentences on persons convicted of serious offences (Box 2). The *Sentencing (Amendment) Act* highlights the Kennett government's disregard for community consultation and disrespect for principles of justice which ensure basic civil and political rights.

The Kennett government introduced the Sentencing (Amendment) Bill into the Legislative Assembly on 28 April 1993. Opposition to the contents of the Bill and the manner in which it was introduced were immediately

---

Box 2: *Sentencing (Amendment) Act 1993*

•Amends the *Sentencing Act 1991* and the *Crimes Act 1958* and repeals the *Community Protection Act 1990*.

•Emphasises community protection as the main purpose of sentencing serious sexual offenders and serious violent offenders and overturns the principle of proportionality in certain cases.

•Increases the prison sentences of serious sexual offenders and serious violent offenders by one-third by abolishing remissions.

•Provides that the sentences of serious sexual offenders will usually be served cumulatively.

•Empowers courts to impose indefinite sentences on serious offenders.

---

voiced. The most prominent opponents were the Victorian Council for Civil Liberties, the Law Council of Australia, the Law Institute of Victoria, the Victorian Bar Council, the Victorian Criminal Justice Coalition, the Legal Aid Commission, the International Commission of Jurists and the (then) Human Rights Commissioner, Mr Brian Burdekin. The Scrutiny of Acts and Regulations Committee, an all-party parliamentary committee responsible for establishing whether legislation and regulations violate rights and freedoms, held a public hearing on 10 May 1993 and commented that public interest in the Bill was acute (Scrutiny of Acts and Regulations Committee, 1993a). Mr Desmond Lane, a barrister, argued that:

the bill was prepared in secret and revealed to nobody outside the Government, until it was introduced only last week. Despite this, the Attorney-General had admitted that she intends to ram it through the Parliament this month, no doubt to avoid public debate, which is the community's only defence against such arrogance. (Lane 1993a: 12)

Similarly, Mr Robert Richter QC, (then) Vice President of the Victorian Council for Civil Liberties, stated that:

the Attorney-General refused to consult with the community in relation to her law and order package. And the Sentencing Bill remains 'non negotiable' despite the fact that her own Scrutiny of Acts and Regulations Committee, who gave only 45 minutes consideration to the issue have warned that it might 'trespass on the rights and freedoms of individuals. (Victorian Council for Civil Liberties 1993a: 1)

The Kennett government curtailed parliamentary debate on the Bill and rapidly passed it in the Legislative Assembly and the Legislative Council. The *Sentencing (Amendment) Act 1993* was assented to on 1 June 1993 and the whole Act commenced operation on 15 August 1993. Professor Richard Fox of Monash University stated that only two of the 24 amendments made to the legislation as it passed through parliament addressed the central concerns of its opponents (Fox 1993).

The *Sentencing (Amendment) Act 1993* ignores the sentencing principle of proportionality as a restraint on both excessive and lenient punishment in certain cases. The principle of proportionality provides that the seriousness of the punishment should be related to the seriousness of the offence. In other words, the punishment must fit the crime. Proportionality is one of many principles which should be considered in the fair sentencing of offenders. Other principles include punishment, deterrence, rehabilitation, retribution and community protection. However, the *Sentencing (Amendment) Act 1993* provides that community protection must be the primary purpose for which the sentence is set for a serious sexual offender or a serious violent offender. A sentence which is greater than that which is proportionate to the gravity of the offence may be imposed to achieve this goal. The Scrutiny of Acts and Regulations Committee (1993a) was concerned that in overturning the principle of proportionality, sentencing would become arbitrary. The committee thus concluded that the Act may trespass unduly upon rights and freedoms. The practice of 'warehousing' offenders in custody for longer than appropriate, in the name of community protection, may be referred to as 'incapacitation' (Fox 1993). Fox (1993: 401) argued that:

> the danger of abandoning the restraining influence of proportionality in favour of incapacitation, even selective incapacitation, is that the latter is both inefficient and seductive. Even if limited to serious 'dangerous' offenders, the inevitable problem with incapacitative strategies is that of being unable to identify, with sufficient confidence, those likely to recidivate as to justify their detention for periods beyond the normal maximum applicable to the offence.

Abandoning the principle of proportionality thus undermines fair sentencing and establishes a dangerous precedent. Incapacitation is seen as a solution to crime, which it is not. Conceivably, such a 'solution' could be extended to apply beyond serious sexual offenders and serious violent offenders.

The *Sentencing (Amendment) Act 1993* also empowers courts to sentence a serious offender, over 21 years of age, to an indefinite term of imprisonment, regardless of the maximum penalty prescribed for that offence. The Act provides that a court may impose an indefinite sentence on its own initiative or on application from the Director of Public Prosecutions. An offender would be sentenced indefinitely if the court was satisfied to a 'high degree of probability' that the offender represented a serious danger to the community because of his or her character, past history, age, health or mental condition or the nature or seriousness of the offence. The onus of proof lies with the prosecution. An offender sentenced indefinitely would serve a nominal sentence (equal in length to the non-parole period that would have been imposed had the offender been sentenced for a fixed term) before having his or her sentence reviewed by the court which imposed the original sentence. If the court decided that the offender was no longer a danger to the community, then the indefinite sentence would be suspended. The offender would then be subject to a five year reintegration program run by the Adult Parole Board and would remain in prison as though he or she had been sentenced for a further five years. If the court remained convinced that the offender was still a serious danger to the community, then the offender would remain incarcerated for another three years, followed by another review.

The Scrutiny of Acts and Regulations Committee (1993a) considered that the three-year interval between reviews was too long and that indefinite sentences may trespass unduly on the rights and freedoms of serious offenders. Provisions for indefinite sentencing overturn the general principle that an individual will not be imprisoned unless a court has been convinced beyond reasonable doubt that the individual has committed an offence. Instead, serious offenders may be indefinitely imprisoned because they might commit a crime. There is much scepticism about whether predictions of future dangerousness can be accurately achieved. Indeed, Fox (1993: 410) argued that:

> if such predictions cannot be made with a high level of accuracy, then it is arguable that the extended detention of offenders beyond their nominal sentence in reliance of poor predictive skills is, of necessity, arbitrary. Arbitrary imprisonment, not for what the person has done, but for what he or she may or may not do, is seen as a threat to basic human rights.

The power to detain offenders beyond that which is proportionate to the crime may be necessary in extreme circumstances in order to protect the community from physical violence. However, the Kennett government has applied this proposition too widely. Indefinite sentencing is a dangerous extension of the *Community Protection Act 1990* which applied specifically to Mr Garry David.

CONTROLLING THE CRIMINAL ELEMENT: *CRIMES (AMENDMENT) ACT 1993*

The second aspect of the Kennett government's election commitment to establishing a 'safer Victoria' was to increase police powers. This was achieved with the *Crimes (Amendment) Act 1993* which increases police powers to obtain names and addresses, fingerprints and forensic samples and creates a new offence of loitering by sexual offenders (Box 3). It is often difficult to balance police investigative and law enforcement powers with individual rights, freedoms and privacy (Rozenes 1992). However, the Kennett government has increased police powers at the expense of the rights and freedoms of all Victorians, especially children. Mr Robert Richter QC postulated that the:

> dramatic extension of police power by the Victorian government exposes the community to the possibility of unfettered abuse at the hands of the

Victoria Police ... The effect of the [legislation] will see Victorians crimi-
nalised without any possibility of holding police accountable. (Victorian
Council for Civil Liberties 1993b: 1)

Box 3: *Crimes (Amendment) Act 1993*

•Amends the *Crimes Act 1958.*

•Increases police powers to obtain the names and addresses of persons
reasonably suspected of having committed or about to commit an
indictable or summary offence, or who may be able to assist in the
investigation of an indictable offence which has been committed or is
about to be committed.

•Empowers police (by consent or with a Children's Court order) to
fingerprint children aged between 10 and 14 years (i) suspected of
having committed or (ii) having been charged with or (iii) having
been summonsed to answer charges for an indictable or summary
offence.

•Empowers police to use reasonable force to fingerprint adults and children over 15 years (i) suspected of having committed or (ii) having
been charged with or (iii) having been summonsed to answer charges
for an indictable offence or summary offence.

•Empowers police (with a Magistrate's Court order or where a suspect
has given informed consent) to conduct forensic procedures if there are
reasonable grounds to believe that the procedure would confirm or dis-
prove the involvement of a suspect in the commission of an indictable
offence and if the suspect (i) is believed to have committed or (ii) having been charged with or (iii) having been summonsed to answer for
charges for an indictable offence.

•Creates a new offence of loitering by sexual offenders.

•Clarifies provisions relating to escape from custody.

The first Crimes (Amendment) Bill was introduced by the Kennett
government into the Legislative Assembly on 19 May 1993. The Bill was
originally planned for the spring session of parliament, but was leaked to the
media in April 1993. The content of the Bill caused significant community
concern. The Victorian Council for Civil Liberties, the Federation of Legal
Centres, the Children's Welfare Association of Victoria, the International
Commission of Jurists, the National Children's and Youth Law Centre, the
National Children's Bureau of Australia, the Human Rights Commissioner
and the Criminal Justice Coalition strongly objected to the proposals. A pub-
lic hearing was conducted by the Scrutiny of Acts and Regulations
Committee on 5 August 1993. Subsequently, the first Crimes (Amendment)
Bill 1993 was withdrawn and replaced with a second Bill. The Crimes
(Amendment) Bill (No. 2) was introduced in the Legislative Assembly on 21
October 1993. The Attorney-General, Mrs Jan Wade, suggested that exten-

sive community consultation had been conducted and had resulted in several significant policy changes. However, there were few differences between the two Bills. For example, Lane (1993b) noted that not one word had been altered in the clause pertaining to police powers to obtain names and addresses. This clause had been subject to the most strident criticism. The *Crimes (Amendment) Act 1993* was granted royal assent on 14 December 1993 and came into operation on 1 June 1994.

The *Crimes (Amendment) Act 1993* enables police to demand the name and address of a person if the police believed on reasonable grounds that the person had committed or was about to commit an indictable or summary offence, or could help in the investigation of an indictable offence which had been committed or was suspected of having been committed. Failure to comply with the police request means that the person has committed a summary offence and is liable to be fined. The Scrutiny of Acts and Regulations Committee (1993e) suggested that the expansion of police powers to obtain names and addresses constituted a reduction in rights. Indeed, these provisions attack the individual right to privacy and the right of individuals, who have not committed an offence, to conduct their business without police investigation. The Act removes the right to silence and the right of individuals to decide whether or not to involve themselves in police investigations. The Victorian Council for Civil Liberties submitted to the Scrutiny of Acts and Regulations Committee that :

> the legislation is tantamount to creating a positive duty on the part of citizens to provide information about themselves and others to government enforcement agencies, even where there is no suspicion that they themselves have been involved in a breach of the law. (Victorian Council for Civil Liberties 1993c: 5)

Moreover, the Act may lead to the unnecessary criminalisation of the community and may foster an acceptance of police harassment and abuse, especially of youth and ethnic communities. The Victorian Council for Civil Liberties (1993c: 4) postulated that:

> we are all too familiar with the offences of 'indecent language' and 'offensive behaviour' which have in the past systematically arbitrarily been used as nuisance offences in order to bring the authority of the police to bear on groups that they have found to be undesirable.

The Act also enhances the fingerprinting powers of police at the expense of the rights of Victorian children in what appeared to be a knee-jerk reaction from the Attorney-General to the murder of James Bolger by two 10 year old boys in the United Kingdom. Police have historically been unable to fingerprint children under 10 years of age and a court order has been required to fingerprint children aged between 10 and 17 years. However, the *Crimes (Amendment) Act 1993* provides that children between 10 and 14 years of age may be fingerprinted if the police believe on reasonable grounds that the child has committed, been charged with or summonsed to answer charges for an indictable or summary offence. The police must obtain the consent of the child and a parent/guardian of the child. If the consent of both parties cannot be obtained, then the police may apply for a Children's Court order to fingerprint the child. The child, however, may not be party to the application, cannot call or cross-examine any witnesses and only has a limited right of address before the court. The International Commission of Jurists suggested that this breached Australia's obligations to the United Nations Convention on the Rights of the Child which guarantees every child the right to examine or have examined adverse witnesses in judicial or administrative proceedings (Scrutiny of Acts and Regulations Committee 1993e). The Scrutiny of Acts and Regulations Committee (1993e) agreed that these procedures may unduly trespass on the rights and freedoms of children aged between 10 and 14 years and may constitute a breach of international obligations to which Australia is party.

In addition to diminishing the rights of children between 10 and 14 years of age, the *Crimes (Amendment) Act 1993* reduces the rights of 15 and 16 year old children. The Act empowers police to fingerprint adults and children over 15 years of age believed on reasonable grounds as having committed, been charged with or summonsed to answer charges for an indictable or summary offence. Police may use reasonable force to obtain the fingerprints of a person who refuses to give his or her fingerprints voluntarily. These provisions abolish the special procedures which exist for children and treats 15 and 16 year old children as adults. Hence, the Act is in conflict with a general policy of treating young offenders with special care and, according to the International Commission of Jurists, thus breaches the United Nations Convention on the Rights of the Child (Scrutiny of Acts and Regulations Committee 1993e). The Scrutiny of Acts and Regulations Committee (1993e) suggested that these provisions may unduly trespass on rights and freedoms of 15 and 16 year old children. The committee also stated that the use of reasonable force to obtain fingerprints reduces rights of all persons over 15 years of age. Certainly, the use of 'reasonable' force by police to obtain fingerprints appears to be excessive and could potentially be used to justify assaults on individuals in police custody.

The most significant amendment in the *Crimes (Amendment) Act 1993* was the creation of a new offence of loitering by sexual offenders. Two six year old girls were assaulted near a toilet block at Cheltenham Primary School on 17 November 1993. Six days later, in another knee-jerk reaction by the Attorney-General, a House Amendment to the Crimes (Amendment) Bill (No. 2) was introduced which made it a summary offence for a convicted sexual offender (convicted in any Australian state or territory) to loiter without reasonable excuse near a school, kindergarten, child care centre or any public place regularly frequented by children and in which children were present at the time of loitering. A sexual offender guilty of loitering may be punished by imprisonment or fine. Sexual offenders have a high rate of recidivism and therefore children require adequate and ongoing protection (Bruer 1993). Legislation designed to protect children from sexual offenders thus may be necessary. However, this amendment was hastily introduced and overturns a principle of justice which ensures fundamental civil rights and is also difficult to enforce.

This provision undermines the principle of justice that offenders, having served their time in gaol, have paid their debt to society and should then be free to continue their lives. Instead, sexual offenders will be marked for life. Mr Robert Richter QC stated that

> the community can and must be outraged at incidences such as attacks on little girls ... but the government should be responsible and rise above the howls of anguish to consider the consequences of what it is proposing. If not, the whole fabric of our law will erode and these erosions are not easily reversed. (cited in Macken 1994: 25)

On a more practical level, it will be almost impossible for convicted sexual offenders to resume normal lives upon completion of their 'formal' sentences because of the extremely broad definition of 'public place'. The *Vagrancy Act 1966* defines public place as any public highway, road, street, bridge, footway, footpath, court, alley, passage, thoroughfare, park, garden, reserve, place of public recreation, railway station, platform or carriage, wharf, pier, jetty, passenger ship or boat plying for hire, public vehicle plying for hire, church, chapel, school, public hall, theatre, market, auction room, billiard room, open bar, race course, cricket ground, football ground or place of public resort! The Scrutiny of Acts and Regulations Committee (1993e) commented that the width of the definition means that it would be virtually impossible for convicted sexual offenders to remain in any place whatsoever for any length of time. The Criminal Justice Coalition warned that the legislation would prevent sexual offenders from doing simple things such as going on picnics or eating in McDonald's restaurants (Parliament of Victoria 1993d: 2116). The Attorney-General attempted to allay these fears by suggesting that:

> a person who is actually dining at McDonald's will no doubt have a reasonable excuse for being there; but a person who sits in front of a cold hamburger for the whole afternoon will almost certainly not have a reasonable excuse for being there. (Parliament of Victoria 1993d: 2116)

This adds a whole new dimension to the meaning of fast food!

NOT SO FREE INFORMATION: *FREEDOM OF INFORMATION (AMENDMENT) ACT 1993*

Open and accountable government is an indispensable ingredient of democratic societies. Government accountability is contingent upon public access to the information and options available to government decision makers (Flick 1981). Victorians have historically only possessed the privilege to attempt to seek access to government documents, rather than a statutory right to do so. However, the *Freedom of Information Act 1982* gave Victorians a legally enforceable right of access to government information on 5 July 1983 when the Act commenced operation. There were several exemptions to the prescriptions of openness, chiefly applying to cabinet, law enforcement, or commercially sensitive documents. The principles of freedom of information had been an important component of the Cain Labor government's election platform and the legislation received bipartisan support. Federal freedom of information legislation was also enacted in 1982 and other Australian states eventually followed suit.

Ironically, the *Freedom of Information Act 1982* ultimately embarrassed the Cain/Kirner Labor governments with scandals such as the Victorian Economic Development Corporation. Not surprisingly, the Labor government attempted to limit the scope of the legislation by taking 'unwinnable' cases to the High Court of Australia and introducing legislative amendments designed to weaken the Act (Zifcak 1993: 15). However, the coalition-controlled Legislative Council thwarted any attempt to restrict the public's statutory right of access to government information. Instead, the opposition used the *Freedom of Information Act 1982* to its utmost advantage. Ricketson (1993: 11) noted that the opposition made 1683 freedom of information requests in the year preceding the October 1992 election. This was almost 400 more requests than during the previous year. Unfortunately, the Kennett government has not displayed the same respect for the principles of freedom of information in office as it did in opposition. Legislation and regulations which decrease the community's right of access to government information have been enacted.

The Kennett government introduced the Freedom of Information Bill 1993 into the Legislative Assembly on 5 May 1993. The Bill was rushed through both houses of parliament. Mr Jim Kennan MP commented that the Kennett government wanted to

> smuggle the Bill through in the dead of night. This is ludicrous. Many people wonder whether the Legislative Assembly is really a place for debate, discussion or public scrutiny of government legislation. It certainly is not under the Kennett government. (Parliament of Victoria 1993b: 2240)

The *Freedom of Information (Amendment) Act 1993* was granted royal assent on 8 June 1993 and became completely operational on 1 January 1994 (Box 4). A positive aspect of the Act is the extension of the scope of freedom of information legislation to include local government documents. Municipalities had been deliberately excluded from the *Freedom of Information Act 1982* to enable local government bodies to be covered by separate legislation. However, such legislation was never enacted. The *Freedom of Information (Amendment) Act 1993* thus opens up a previously inaccessible category of government documents to the scrutiny and criticism of citizens. This should assist Victorians to challenge local government decisions. Despite expanding the reach of freedom of information legislation to include local government documents, the *Freedom of Information (Amendment) Act 1993* reduces the ability of citizens to challenge state government decisions by expanding the cabinet document exemption and implementing a user-pays system.

Box 4: *Freedom of Information (Amendment) Act 1993*

•Amends the *Freedom of Information Act 1982.*

•Establishes a legal right of access to local government documents (with a similar exemption to that applying to cabinet documents).

•Expands the cabinet document exemption.

•Introduces a $20 application fee, removes the $100 ceiling and gives government agencies the discretion to require a deposit.

•Permits government agencies to refuse to process repeated requests and voluminous requests which may substantially and unreasonably divert the resources of the agency from its other operations.

•A regulation separately establishes a $150 fee for freedom of information applicants who go the Administrative Appeals Tribunal to test government claims about secrecy.

A cabinet document exemption originally applied to all documents specifically prepared for consideration by the cabinet. Dr Spencer Zifcak of La Trobe University argued that this exemption was essential to prevent public disclosure of the views and votes of individual cabinet members. Such public disclosures would erode the notion of collective ministerial responsibility which is a basic tenet of the Westminster system of government (Zifcak 1993). However, the *Freedom of Information (Amendment) Act 1993* expands the cabinet document exemption. Ironically, the new cabinet document exemption appears to be remarkably similar to that suggested by the Cain Labor government and vehemently opposed by the coalition Opposition in 1985. The new cabinet document exemption includes any document which has been considered by the cabinet, used to brief ministers in relation to issues considered by the cabinet or to prepare cabinet submissions, or contains ministerial opinions which pertain to an issue discussed by the cabinet. Documents containing purely statistical, technical or scientific information are explicitly excluded from the exemption. The broad scope of the cabinet document exemption will enable the Kennett government to become more secretive. Documents relating to sensitive political issues may feasibly be stapled to the back of a cabinet submission, but not be considered by the cabinet. However, these documents may be declared to be exempt from freedom of information legislation. The Kennett government has already used the extended cabinet document exemption to deny access to documents relating to the controversial decision to abandon plans to construct a museum at Southbank and to the TAB sell-off.

In addition to widening the cabinet document exemption, the *Freedom of Information (Amendment) Act 1993* abolished the $100 statutory limit on the charge for any one request and introduced a $20 application fee plus the 'reasonable costs incurred' by government agencies making the documents available, i.e. photocopying. Exemptions to these provisions are possible on the grounds of hardship. Charges may also be levied for the time it takes for documents to be found.

The Kennett government's justification for the implementation of a user-pays system was the substantial cost of processing freedom of information requests. The Attorney-General stated in her second reading speech that:

> at a time when Victoria faces enormous financial problems as a consequence of the former government's irresponsibility, it is imperative that all areas of government activity—including the processing of FOI applications—be conducted on as near a cost-recovery basis as is feasible having regard to the nature and character of the activity. (Parliament of Victoria 1993a: 1738)

Ricketson (1993: 11) noted that such requests cost the Victorian government $2.9 million each year. However, the removal of the $100 ceiling and the institution of a user-pays system undermines the effectiveness of the original Act. The substantial costs incurred in obtaining government documents under freedom of information legislation will deter poorer citizens and non-profit public interest groups from exercising their statutory right to access government information. The Scrutiny of Acts and Regulations Committee (1993b) concluded that these amendments represented a reduction in rights.

The accessibility of government documents under freedom of information legislation has also been limited in other ways. For example, the Kennett government proclaimed a regulation on 7 December 1993 which imposes a $150 fee on appeals lodged in the Administrative Appeals Tribunal against government refusals to release documents under freedom of information legislation. The regulation excludes requests relating to personal information and became effective on 1 January 1994. Dunlevy (1993) noted that the regulation was proclaimed without a regulatory impact statement establishing the social and financial effects of the fee, alternatives and reasons for rejecting such alternatives. An impact statement is usually required when a government approves regulations which introduce fees. However, the Premier, Mr Jeff Kennett, invoked a rarely used power of veto to waive this requirement. The greatest impact of the appeal fee, like that of the implementation of a user-pays system, falls on poorer Victorians and non-profit public interest groups. Such groups will be less likely to challenge government decisions pertaining to freedom of information requests. If government decisions about freedom of information exemptions remain unchallenged, then the openness of government is stunted.

UNEQUAL OPPORTUNITY: *EQUAL OPPORTUNITY (AMENDMENT) ACT 1993*

An election platform of the Kennett government was to reform the Victorian equal opportunity system to increase the efficiency and accountability of discrimination complaints. The Attorney-General suggested that the (then) Commissioner for Equal Opportunity, Ms Moira Rayner, and the Scrutiny of Acts and Regulations Committee had recognised the lack of accountability in the equal opportunity system (Wade 1993). However, Ms Rayner has denied any such acknowledgment (personal communication, 14 December 1994). Whatever the case, the Kennett government enacted the *Equal Opportunity (Amendment) Act 1993* to alter the equal opportunity system (Box 5). Ms Fay Marles, Commissioner for Equal Opportunity from 1977 to 1987, suggested that the amendments may prevent unnecessary delays in settling complaints and expand the education and research roles of the Equal Opportunity Commission (Marles 1993). However, it appears that the Kennett government has instituted changes which tip the balance of power in the complaints process in favour of respondents and removed an independent statutory official.

The Hamer coalition government enacted Victoria's original anti-discrimination legislation. The *Equal Opportunity Act 1977* created a Commissioner for Equal Opportunity and an Equal Opportunity Board to investigate, conciliate and determine discrimination disputes (on the basis of sex or marital status) and to promote equality of opportunity between men and women. The Act was repealed and replaced by the *Equal Opportunity Act 1984* which broadened the grounds for unlawful discrimination and outlawed sexual harassment in employment, education and the provision of goods and services and accommodation (Scrutiny of Acts and Regulations Committee 1993c).

Box 5: *Equal Opportunity (Amendment) Act 1993*

•Amends the *Equal Opportunity Act 1984*.

•Provides for the speeding up of the hearing of certain complaints, usually involving the implementation of policies or programs.

•Abolishes the position of Commissioner for Equal Opportunity.

•Creates a position of Chief Conciliator.

•Creates an Equal Opportunity Commission comprising five members appointed by the Governor in Council, including the Chief Conciliator.

•Empowers the Equal Opportunity Board to order that the costs of an action are normally borne by the loser.

The Kennett government introduced the Equal Opportunity (Amendment) Bill into the Legislative Assembly on 27 October 1993. The Victorian Council for Civil Liberties, the Victorian Bar Council and the Women's Electoral Lobby were extremely critical of the proposals. The Scrutiny of Acts and Regulations Committee (1993d) recommended 33 alterations to the Bill. However, the legislation was rushed through the Legislative Assembly (during the middle of the night) and the Legislative Council in barely one month. The *Equal Opportunity (Amendment) Act 1993* was granted royal assent on 7 December 1993 and was enforced on 1 March 1994. Only six of the Scrutiny of Acts and Regulations Committee's recommendations were fully incorporated into the legislation, while two were partially implemented. The remaining 25 of the committee's amendments were not incorporated into the *Equal Opportunity (Amendment) Act 1993*.

The most serious aspect of the legislative changes emerges from alterations to the cost provisions. Each party has historically had to pay their own costs. However, the Attorney-General initially planned that the amendments would provide that the loser in an equal opportunity action would *automatically* pay the costs of that action. Following public outcry, however, she altered the proposals and, in a House Amendment, gave the Equal Opportunity Board greater discretion to award costs. The *Equal Opportunity (Amendment) Act 1993* provides that the Equal Opportunity Board 'must fix a sum which reflects the costs reasonably incurred by the person in favour of whom the order is made and any other pecuniary loss incurred by that person', unless there are special circumstances. In other words, the cost of an action before the Equal Opportunity Board will normally be borne by the loser, including any indirect financial loss stemming from the complaint (Marles 1993). These provisions expose the complainant to a significant financial risk. Given that individuals with discrimination complaints are often poor and relatively powerless and that respondents are commonly corporations, institutions or governments, the new cost provisions mean that it is less likely that complainants will pursue equal opportunity actions. Hence, the provisions undermine the accessibility of equal opportunity legislation. Mr Alan Goldberg QC, (then) President of the Victorian Council for Civil Liberties, argued that

> people who are discriminated against on the basis of sex, age, race or physical or mental abilities are often the most disadvantaged members of our community. To suggest that they be required to challenge the government, an employer or provider of goods and services, with the unprecedented number of financial risks involved, makes a mockery of a system which was designed specifically to provide the least privileged members of the community equality of opportunity for the just resolution and elimination of discrimination in this State. (Goldberg 1993: 14)

The Act also encourages respondents to an expedited complaint to apply to the Equal Opportunity Board to bypass conciliation and have the complaint heard by the Board without the complaint going to conciliation. An expedited complaint is a complaint which the Equal Opportunity Commission has decided may be resolved by conciliation and in which the complaint relates to a policy decision of the respondent. There are no provisions for a complainant to initiate an expedited hearing. Although these provisions may decrease the amount of time equal opportunity complaints take to be resolved, they alter the emphasis of equal opportunity actions from cheaper and user-friendly conciliation to more expensive and adversarial arbitration, and make complainants liable for large costs. Marles (1993: 18) suggested that:

a game of bluff in which forcing complainants either to go to the board or drop their complaint could well become a successful gambit. The opportunity for respondents to bypass conciliation ... also has the potential to burn off complainants. It can be increasingly expected that legal advice to respondents will include an argument for going down this track.

So, bypassing conciliation in the hope of 'burning off' complainants is a strategy which could be employed by respondents, including governmental respondents.

Currently, 30–35 per cent of discrimination complaints are made against government agencies (Rayner 1993: 2). However, it is likely that this figure will decline because citizens without access to adequate financial resources will be unwilling to challenge government policies alleged to be discriminatory. Thus, provisions enabling respondents to bypass conciliation may enable the Kennett government to avoid scrutiny and criticism of its policies.

In addition to altering the balance of power in equal opportunity complaints, the *Equal Opportunity (Amendment) Act 1993* abolished the position of Commissioner for Equal Opportunity. Ms Moira Rayner was appointed as Commissioner for Equal Opportunity in May 1990 for a five year term. She embarked on a widespread education campaign which saw equal opportunity expectations heighten, especially in the workplace (Richter 1993). During the financial year 1993/94, 1616 formal equal opportunity complaints were received, a 43 per cent increase from the previous financial year (Figure 1). It was also the highest number of formal complaints recorded in one year since the Office of Equal Opportunity was established and began keeping records in 1978. Richter (1993) suggested that Ms Rayner had engendered a culture where people could complain and refuse to tolerate discrimination and injustice. The widespread support for Ms Rayner was demonstrated by the huge attendance (700 people attended and 300 people were turned away) at a dinner held in her honour in February 1994 to raise money for a fighting fund for women wishing to pursue equal opportunity complaints in the future. Ironically, the function was held 15 years to the day after the first equal opportunity action was launched in Australia.

Figure 1: Registered Number of Equal Opportunity Complaints
Source: Rayner (1993: 11) and Equal Opportunity Commission (1994: 12).

AREA	1992/93		1993/94	
	No.	%	No.	%
Employment	842	74.7	1414	87.5
Goods and Services	184	16.3	148	9.2
Accommodation	30	2.6	27	1.7
Education	61	5.4	22	1.3
Clubs and Sport	11	1.0	5	0.3
TOTAL	1128	100.0	1616	100.0

However, the Kennett government was less concerned with Ms Rayner's creation of a culture which encouraged individuals to be intolerant of discrimination than with her criticisms of government decisions and legislation. She had sought interim injunctions to prevent the removal of women from Fairlea (the only metropolitan prison for women), Tarrengower (where women could keep young children with them) and Barwon into Jika Jika, a specially designed segregation facility for dangerous male offenders within Pentridge (Rayner 1993). She had also suggested that the Kennett government's enactment of the *Employee Relations Act 1992*, which precipitated the largest public demonstrations witnessed in Melbourne since the Vietnam Moratorium marches in the 1960s, had contributed to the increase in discrimination because some small employers had misunderstood the legislative changes (Rayner 1993). These comments incensed the Minister for Industry and Employment, Mr Phil Gude.

It appears that the abolition of the position of Commissioner for Equal Opportunity was a direct attempt to remove a vocal critic of the Kennett government's policies and practices from office rather than being concerned with accountability and efficiency. If this was not the case, then the Attorney-General should have personally suggested that Ms Rayner apply for a position on the Equal Opportunity Commission to avoid suspicion being cast over the Kennett government's real reform motives. The Scrutiny of Acts and Regulations Committee (1993d) was concerned that the termination of the position of Commissioner for Equal Opportunity may trespass against the rights of the (then) current office holder. Dr Ken Coghill MP commented that the:

Commissioner for Equal Opportunity was appointed by the government to carry out a statutory defence of the civil and human rights of Victorians. Because criticisms about prisons and small employers happen to make the government uncomfortable, it decided it would not stand by these basic principles of human rights. It has taken vindictive, contemptuous action against the individual and the institution with which the individual is associated. (Parliament of Victoria 1993c: 1957)

Unfortunately, the practice of removing 'troublesome appointees from office by the simple expedient of abolishing their office' is a well-entrenched and bipartisan one in Australia (Murphy 1994: 31) (Box 6). Even so, this tradition cannot be condoned because it compromises the independence of statutory offices and encourages office bearers to make decisions to secure their positions. Independent statutory officials, like judges, need to be able to execute their duties without fear of reprisal or hope of preferment from the government of the day (Kirby 1994).

Box 6: Removing Troublesome Appointees (Kirby 1994)

1976   Dr Venturini, unlike his fellow commissioners, was not reappointed when the Trade Practices Commission was abolished by the Fraser coalition government. He had been critical of the Trade Practices Commission's failure to pursue what he called a cartel in zinc production.

1981   The Federal Court of the Northern Territory was abolished and reconstituted without its judges.

1988   Justice James Staples was the only member not reappointed when the Hawke Labor government replaced the Australian Conciliation and Arbitration Commission with the Australian Industrial Relations Commission.

1988   Five judges of the NSW Court of Petty Sessions were not reappointed to a reconstituted court after being denied the opportunity to respond to a secret report which was central to their dismissal.

1992   The Victorian Accident Compensation Tribunal was abolished and 11 judges were not offered alternative judicial positions. These judges have commenced legal action against the Kennett government.

1992   Victorian Law Reform Commissioner was removed from office when the Law Reform Commission was abolished.

1993   Victorian Liquor Licensing Commissioner was not reappointed.

TINKERING WITH PUBLIC PROSECUTIONS: *PUBLIC PROSECUTIONS ACT 1994*

The Kennett government attempted to reform the Victorian prosecution system with proposals contained in a document called the 'Public Prosecutions Bill 1993'. The Kennett government claimed that the document was only a cabinet draft bill when it was leaked to *The Sunday Age* in December 1993 and caused public outcry. The proposals were strongly criticised by the (then) Director of Public Prosecutions (DPP), Mr Bernard Bongiorno, who threatened to resign if the proposals were implemented. Opposition was also voiced from senior members of the judiciary, the Victorian Bar Council, the Law Institute of Victoria, the International Commission of Jurists, DPPs throughout Australia, the Victorian Council for Civil Liberties, legal academics and even Liberal Party backbenchers and rank and file members. The proposals were supported only by the Police Association, a trade union to which police may belong, and a lobby group called the Victims of Crimes Assistance League. Although the Attorney-General eventually capitulated to public demands for the proposals to be altered on 16 March 1994, the contents of the original Bill are significant because they were proposed, defined and defended by the Attorney-General as a desirable agenda for reform (Connor 1994). An examination of the original Bill thus highlights the Kennett government's disregard for the need for public prosecution processes to operate independently from party politics (Corns 1994).

Responsibility for prosecutions in Australia historically lay with the Attorney-General until the first independent office of the DPP was established in Victoria in 1982. The Cain government hoped to establish a more efficient prosecutorial system and to prevent undue influence by police and politicians over decisions to prosecute citizens. In other words, the aim was to provide a safeguard against politically motivated prosecutions or non-prosecutions (*Australian Financial Review* 1993). Justice David Harper, President of the Victorian division of the International Commission of Jurists, posited that:

> the liberties of a democratic society disappear if the administration of justice is not independent of the executive government. Decisions to prosecute or not to prosecute are an important aspect of the administration of justice. They must be made by a person whose independence is beyond doubt. (Harper 1993: 14)

The benefits of an apolitical and independent prosecutorial arm have been widely recognised since the Cain government initiative. An office of the DPP has been established federally and in every state and territory in Australia. In Victoria, similar to other statutory bodies, the DPP has been responsible to the Attorney-General for the performance of the office of the DPP. In practice, however, it has been widely accepted that the Attorney-General should not intervene in prosecutorial decisions and polices, and that 'to do so would undermine the raison d'être of the office of the DPP' (Corns 1994: 277).

However, the Kennett government placed such independence and freedom from political interference in jeopardy with proposals contained in the 'Public Prosecutions Bill 1993' to alter the Victorian prosecutorial process (Box 7). Harper (1993) argued that the office of the DPP would

---

Box 7: The Original 'Public Prosecutions Bill 1993'

•Repealed the *Director of Public Prosecutions Act 1982*.

•Established a restructured Office of Public Prosecutions.

•Created a Deputy DPP appointed by the Governor in Council for seven years.

•Created a Committee for Public Prosecutions comprising the DPP, the Deputy DPP, the Solicitor for Prosecutions, the Solicitor-General and a person appointed by the Governor in Council to ensure that the prosecutorial system operated economically, effectively and efficiently.

•Provided that prosecutorial personnel must have regard to the special concerns of victims.

---

be emasculated in three ways. First, the administrative aspects of public prosecutions (i.e. control of office staff who perform the actual prosecutorial function and the budget which pays for it) would be placed under a separate Office of Public Prosecutions. The head of this office, the Solicitor for Public Prosecutions, would be subject to the *Public Sector Management Act 1982* (i.e. a contracted public servant) and thus dependent on the government of the day.

Second, the creation of the position of Deputy DPP would undermine the independence of the DPP. The DPP would be required to seek written consent from the Deputy DPP on certain things, including to bring contempt proceedings, issue guidelines with respect to prosecutions, overrule a crown prosecutor and to have a police prosecution referred to the DPP. Clearly, the Deputy DPP's power would be greater than or equal to the power of the DPP, essentially giving the Deputy DPP the power of veto over the DPP's actions and decisions. This would effectively strip the DPP of his independence, but not of his office. Serious implications stem from this proposed power arrangement considering that the Deputy DPP would be responsible to the Attorney-General (rather than the DPP) for the execution of his or her powers and functions. The social and political aims of the government could potentially exert a powerful influence over the decisions of the Deputy DPP, thus allowing party politics to influence prosecutorial decisions and structures (Corns 1994).

Finally, the Bill proposed to subject the DPP's operations and decisions to the scrutiny of a Committee of Public Prosecutions comprising the DPP, the Deputy DPP, the Solicitor for Prosecutions, the Solicitor-General and a person appointed by the Governor in Council. A majority controlled committee would hold real power over the DPP, including the power to instruct police regarding offences and classes of offences referred to the DPP for prosecution (*Australian Financial Review* 1993). Moreover, this committee would meet in private and would not be publicly accountable for its decisions.

It is possible that the proposed changes to the public prosecutorial process were designed to undermine the independence of Mr Bongiorno who, like Ms Rayner, had antagonised the Kennett government. He had threatened to charge the Premier with contempt over statements about the Frankston murder case. The Attorney-General had allegedly pressured Mr Bongiorno not to proceed with these charges against the Premier. He had also earned the wrath of the Police Association after charging eleven police officers with murder-related offences over the shooting of two criminals. Furthermore, Mr John Elliott, former Elders IXL chief executive and a prominent Liberal Party member, allegedly called for Mr Bongiorno's dismissal and an investigation into his office.

Claims that the Kennett government had plotted to tamper with the independence of the DPP and to force Mr Bongiorno from office where strengthened on 10 April 1995. Ms Ann Collins, a former lawyer of the Justice Department, alleged on the ABC's 'Four Corners' program that Mr Greg Craven, the Attorney-General's principal adviser, had instructed her and another officer to prepare legislation to curtail the powers of the DPP on 6 October 1993. Mr Craven allegedly described Mr Bongiorno as a publicity-hungry megalomaniac. These revelations resulted in calls from the Law Institute of Victoria, the Victorian Bar Council and the state opposition for an independent inquiry into the DPP affair. However, as Mr Robert Manne, editor of *Quadrant*, suggested, a full public inquiry will only occur if someone in the Victorian cabinet or on the government backbench is willing to stand up to Mr Kennett (Manne 1995). Without an independent inquiry, it is difficult to ascertain whether the proposed changes were intended to interfere with the independence of the DPP. However, the fact that the Attorney-General did not inform Mr Bongiorno about the proposals before they were leaked, coupled with her and the Premier's public criticisms of the DPP, lends weight to the suggestion that the proposals were intended to undermine the independence of an outspoken statutory official.

Public prosecutions need to be, and need to be seen to be, independent of political party considerations. Public prosecutions need to be made on the merits of the case (Connor et al. 1993). Dr Chris Corns of La Trobe University and the Victorian Bar postulated that if the reforms were implemented, then

> the degree of appropriate political independence of the system of public prosecutions would be lost. The potential for party political considerations to influence prosecutorial decisions would be enormous. Even if that potential was never acted upon, the existence of mechanisms and procedures enabling political interference is unacceptable. (Corns 1994: 281)

Public outcry about the proposed reforms forced the Kennett government to abandon the radical proposals and an 'official' Public Prosecutions Bill was introduced in the Legislative Assembly on 20 April 1994. The *Public Prosecutions Act 1994* was assented to on 7 June 1994 and commenced operation on 1 July 1994. Almost all of the provisions which had been criticised in the original Bill were removed. The position of Deputy DPP was abolished and replaced with the requirement that the DPP consult with a Director's Committee on certain decisions defined by the Act. The function of the Committee for Public Prosecutions was altered from a monitoring role to an advisory capacity. Interestingly, the Act also makes new provisions with respect to the manner of dealing with certain contempts of court. However, the Solicitor for Prosecutions remains in control of the administrative aspects of public prosecutions.

Mr Bongiorno (who resigned as DPP on 27 October 1994 after occupying the position for four years) suggested that while the Act preserves the DPP's independent decision making function, it removes the DPP's control over the office staff and budget. He argued that this lack of effective administrative control renders the independence of the office of the DPP meaningless (Office of Public Prosecutions 1994). However, Xavier Connor QC, a retired judge of the Federal Court of Australia postulated that 'the effect of this administrative change is not easily predicted ... [and] it remains to be seen how the new Victorian system will work' (Connor 1994: 491). He concluded that the *Public Prosecutions Act 1994* 'appears to be a workable and rational solution to the problems of balancing considerations of independence and accountability. It is seen to be acceptable by the legal community and with the caveat mentioned above, by the Director himself' (Connor 1994: 491). Similarly, Mr Alan Goldberg QC was pleased with these alterations because:

> they preserve the integrity and independence of the office of the Director of Public Prosecutions which is fundamental to our criminal justice system. The changes are also a recognition of the importance of the community speaking out when a government proposes litigation which impinges on civil liberties and has the potential to erode the fundamental principles which underlie our system of justice. (Goldberg 1994: 2)

CONSULTATION UNDER THE KENNETT GOVERNMENT

Consultation has not been an important item on the Kennett government's agenda. The Kennett government failed to conduct adequate community consultation about legislative changes which affected many Victorians. It did not consult independent statutory officials about changes to their offices or legal experts concerning complex legislative reforms. Instead, legislative bills were secretly prepared and debates within the media and the community only commenced once the bills had reached parliament (if they had not already been leaked). However, the speed with which legislation was enacted limited the ability of citizens and community organisations to participate in debates.

In addition to the lack of adequate consultation, the Kennett government often ignored the concerns raised when consultation was conducted. Legislative changes were implemented regardless of the community's legitimate concerns about the erosion of civil and political rights. For example, the Scrutiny of Acts and Regulations Committee held six public hearings to provide a forum for the articulation of community concerns about particular legislative bills. In the public hearing about the first Crimes (Amendment) Bill, considerable community concern was expressed about the Bill's provisions to increase police powers to obtain names and addresses. The Scrutiny of Acts and Regulations Committee (1993e) agreed that the provisions reduced the rights of citizens. However, the Kennett government ignored both community and committee concerns about the erosion of rights and freedoms and the provisions to enhance police powers to obtain names and addresses were not altered.

The dismissal of the Scrutiny of Acts and Regulations Committee's recommendations about the impact of legislation on civil and political rights is a strategy which the Kennett government has frequently employed. This committee was established on the recommendation of the Legal and Constitutional Committee (1987, 1990) by the Kennett government on 17 November 1992 as an all-party committee whose role was to act as a 'watch dog' on human rights (Parliament of Victoria 1992: 841). That is, the raison d'être of the committee was to establish whether primary or secondary legislation unduly trespassed on rights and freedoms and to review legislation referred to it. Wallace (1994) stated that although the Scrutiny of Acts and Regulations Committee does not intervene in the parliamentary process, it is an important vehicle for principled persuasion.

The Attorney-General argued that the creation of the Scrutiny of Acts and Regulations Committee reflects the Kennett government's philosophical and ideological commitment to achieving civil liberties (Wade 1994). However, this commitment appears to be somewhat superficial because the Kennett government has ignored many of the committee's recommendations. For example, the Scrutiny of Acts and Regulations Committee (1994: 11) considered 130 bills and commented upon 71 of these bills during its first year of operation. The committee concluded that 38 of the bills commented upon may have breached the committee's criterion, yet the Kennett government only amended or undertook to amend 13 (34%) of these bills. The remaining 25 (66%) bills were implemented regardless of the Scrutiny of Acts and Regulations Committee's concerns about their impact on civil and political rights.

Clearly, consultation has not been a high priority of the Kennett government. It has inadequately consulted the community about reforms, dismissed many concerns which have been voiced and ignored the recommendations of a committee which was specifically established to provide advice about the impact of legislation on rights and freedoms.

CONCLUSION

The coalition parties released few details about their policies and intentions prior to the Victorian government election in October 1992. In retrospect, this was a sensible strategy because it is unlikely that Victorians would have elected the coalition parties to government had they been aware of the explicit details of the proposed changes. Whatever the case, the coalition parties' lack of detailed policy statements was not the central concern of Victorian voters. Rather, they were worried about rising interest and unemployment rates and the collapse of financial institutions. It was the public's perception that Victoria was experiencing a severe financial crisis and that this crisis was caused by the Cain/Kirner governments' economic mismanagement that led to the coalition parties' landslide election victory. Rayner (1994: 12) appropriately commented, however, that 'Idi Amin could have won that vote'.

The Kennett government immediately commenced implementing radical reforms. No corner of Victoria was left untouched as the Kennett government effected what Bernstein (1994: 46) suggested is widely perceived to be an 'economic–political revolution'. This paper has examined five of the Kennett government's actions, namely changes to sentencing practices, police powers, the accessibility of government documents, the equal opportunity system and the public prosecution process. This exploration of these changes has revealed that civil and political rights (as distinct from socio-economic rights) have been eroded in Victoria. The content of the legislative changes coupled with the manner in which they were introduced have resulted in the degradation of the rights and freedoms of all citizens. The task which remains is to attempt to explain how and why this has occurred. Hence, the rest of this paper is concerned with two questions:

1. How has the Kennett government been able to implement changes which have eroded civil and political rights in Victoria?

2. Why has the Kennett government enacted legislation and adopted particular practices which have eroded civil and political rights in Victoria?

The how question

The Kennett government has been able to implement changes which have eroded civil and political rights because of its numerical dominance in parliament. The Kennett government holds 61 out of 88 seats in the Legislative Assembly and 30 out of 44 seats in the Legislative Council. This means that it can curtail parliamentary debate and ensure that legislative bills are passed in both houses of parliament, regardless of the impact of such bills on the rights and freedoms of Victorians. Although the parliament has historically been responsible for the protection of rights and freedoms, Campbell and Whitmore (1973: 405) recognised that 'it is clear that Parliament has the barest minimum influence over the government in power with a comfortable majority'.

The why question

It is more difficult to explain why the Kennett government has implemented reforms and adopted particular practices which have eroded civil and political rights. However, several explanations have been articulated. It has been suggested that the Kennett government was given a mandate in a free and fair democratic election to economically and politically reform Victoria.

Commentators have postulated that the Kennett government has merely been using this mandate to improve the situation of all citizens (Bernstein, 1994). Alternatively, it has been argued that the Kennett government's actions reflect its leader's personality: his intolerance of criticism from the party, the parliament or the public; and his aversion to consultation. For example, an editorial in *The Sunday Age* likened the government to a bully and suggested that this reflected:

> essentially the flaws of leadership: a want of requisite balance, judgement and consideration at the top. This would be a better Government, and Victoria would be a happier place if Mr Kennett's energy, enthusiasm and boldness was matched by sensitivity, compassion and understanding, a greater willingness to listen and heed, and a deeper respect for proper ways of pursuing his goals. (*The Sunday Age* 1993: 14)

Although there is some truth in both these accounts, neither provides a sufficient explanation of the Kennett government's activities. Rather, it appears that the Kennett government has been motivated by other factors, including a desire to be perceived as a strong conservative government and a determination to reform Victoria economically.

The Kennett government has been concerned with appearing to be a strong and socially conservative government. The coalition parties campaigned for election on a traditionally conservative platform of stronger law and order enforcement policies. On attaining office, the Kennett government has appeared to be concerned with fulfilling its election commitments and reinforcing its authority to govern, rather than implementing principled reforms. Such attempts to maintain the illusion of order and government control have resulted in the erosion of basic rights and freedoms. For example, Fox (1993: 414) stated with reference to the:

> *Sentencing (Amendment) Act 1993* that the Kennett government was elected on a platform of strong law-and-order enforcement policies and the purpose of this legislation is the declaration of that commitment to do something about crime, rather than a principled effort to reform the process of punishment. Unfortunately, the symbolic benefit is attained at the cost of some basic principles of justice.

In addition to displaying its strength, the Kennett government has consistently been concerned about getting Victoria on the move. It has argued that Victoria languished in a financial crisis when the coalition parties were elected to power in 1992. Crooks and Webber (1993) disagreed with this analysis and suggested that the sense of crisis has been created by the Kennett government itself in order to introduce and legitimate its policy agenda. Whatever the case, the Kennett government has maintained that harsh economic measures were required to rescue Victoria from financial ruin. These harsh measures have sometimes meant that it has been necessary to sacrifice civil and political rights. However, the Kennett government has argued that these changes will ultimately benefit all citizens. In other words, the Kennett government considers that the erosion of rights and freedoms is an unfortunate side effect of the medicine administered to cure Victoria of the economic ills caused by ten years of 'hard Labor'.

Victoria was experiencing financial difficulties when the coalition parties were elected and economic reforms were clearly necessary. The Kennett government commenced this task with missionary-like zeal, intent on transforming the government into an economically efficient and business-like operation. Bernstein (1994) suggested that the Mr Kennett has often proudly stated that Victoria is the fifth largest business in Australia, following the federal government, the NSW government, Coles-Myer and BHP. Unfortunately, this enthusiasm for efficiency and an unswerving faith in economic indicators as measures of performance have blinded the Kennett government to the repercussions of its changes on civil and political rights.

For example, according to economic indicators, the diffusion of power between different organs of government renders decision making time-consuming and inefficient. Thus, Zifcak (1994) argued that the Kennett government limited the Supreme Court's jurisdiction to review parliamentary and ministerial decisions and decreased the independence of statutory offices in an attempt to increase the economic efficiency of decision making. However, the Kennett government ignored the fact that although it may be economically inefficient, the diffusion of power between different organs of government is essential to ensure that power is exercised responsibly rather than arbitrarily.

Similarly, the Kennett government's obsession with economic efficiency has been reflected in the inadequacy of its consultation about changes. Community consultation can be costly and time-consuming, and usually produces a plethora of different points of view. Some of these opinions will inevitably conflict with the government's objectives, including important economic objectives. Zifcak (1994: 4) suggested that the Kennett government 'has taken a very hostile stance towards interest groups with different points of view in the belief that they compromise the Government's economic endeavours and, in doing so, undermine the logic of the market'. However, effective democracy is contingent upon political participation both at *and between* elections (Zifcak 1994). Thus, citizen involvement in the development and implementation of legislative changes and consideration of views in opposition to those of the incumbent government are essential if democracy is to operate satisfactorily in Victoria (Chadwick 1994).

Finally, the Kennett government's concern about Victoria's economic recovery has been demonstrated by its tendency to dismantle legislative provisions which may impede its ability to govern and the ability of businesses to operate. It has decreased the likelihood that citizens will pursue equal opportunity complaints against the government, reduced their ability to obtain access to government documents and decreased the probability that they will challenge government decisions pertaining to freedom of information requests. The Kennett government appears to believe that involvement in equal opportunity or freedom of information disputes merely distracts it from its more important tasks of economic reform. However, the Kennett government has ignored the fact that dissent is both an element and condition of democratic societies. It is essential that citizens are able to challenge government decisions, policies and practices. Moreover, Zifcak (1994: 5) rightly stated that 'it is both mistaken and dangerous to confer on economic freedom a claim that is prior to political liberty. For political liberty is not merely incidental to but is the essential precondition for the achievement of economic freedom'.

The coalition parties were elected to government in October 1992 with an agenda to politically and economically reform Victoria. It is difficult to believe that the Kennett government could not have implemented many of its changes without trespassing on the rights and freedoms of its constituents. However, the Kennett government's desire to be a strong conservative government and its narrow focus on economic achievements have meant that the impact of its radical changes on rights and freedoms has been ignored. This has resulted in the degradation of civil and political rights. If we value fundamental rights and freedoms and Victoria's record in acknowledging and protecting them, then the erosion of civil and political rights by the Kennett government is cause for immense concern.

REFERENCES

Australian Financial Review 1993 Justice and the state of Victoria, 15 December: 14

Australian Labor Party 1995 *Might versus Rights. The Kennett Government's Attack on Democracy* Victoria: Australian Labor Party

Bailey P 1990 *Human Rights. Australia in an International Context*, Australia: Butterworths

Bernstein D 1994 Crashing through *The Independent Monthly* November: 46–7

Bruer M 1993 Think before we allow arrest for loitering *The Age* 19 November:18

Campbell E and Whitmore H 1973 *Freedom in Australia* 2nd edn Sydney: Sydney University Press

Chadwick P 1994 Letter to the editor *The Age* 4 October: 14

Commonwealth of Australia 1987 *Report of the Advisory Committee on Individual and Democratic Rights Under the Constitution* Canberra: Canberra Publishing and Printing Company

Connor X, 1994 Victorian Director of Public Prosecutions *The Australian Law Journal* 68, 7: 488–91

Connor X, Kirby M K, Nicholson A, Charles S and Meldrum M 1993 Letter to the editor *The Age* 21 December: 10

Cooray L J M 1985 *Human Rights in Australia* Australia: ACFR Community Education Project

Corns C 1994 The politics of prosecution *The Law Institute Journal* 68, 4: 276–81

Crooks M L and Webber M 1993 *State Finances and Public Policy in Victoria, Bulletin of Society and Economy—1* Northcote: The Victoria Foundation

Dunlevy L 1993 No reason offered for fee to appeal against FoI rulings *The Age* 13 December: 14

Equal Opportunity Commission 1994 *Annual Report 93–94* Victoria: Equal Opportunity Commission

Flick G 1981 *Civil Liberties in Australia* Australia: The Law Book Company

Fox R G 1993 Victoria turns right in sentencing reform: the Sentencing (Amendment) Act 1993 (Vic.) *Criminal Law Journal* 17, 6: 394–415

Goldberg A 1993 Letter to the editor *The Age* 17 November: 14

Goldberg A 1994 President's report *Civil Liberty* 10, 1: 2

Harper Justice D L 1993 Letter to the editor *The Age* 16 December: 14

Jones M 1990 The fundamental freedoms in J Wallace and T Pagone (eds) *Rights and Freedoms in Australia* Australia: The Federation Press: 2–13

Kingston J 1993 Letter to the editor *The Age* 16 December: 14

Kirby Justice M 1994 Address to the Moira Rayner Dinner Regent Hotel, unpublished speech

Lane D 1993a Letter to the editor *The Age* 7 May: 12

Lane D 1993b Crimes (Amendment) Bill (No. 2) 1993 Notes for the Inquiry by the Scrutiny of Acts and Regulations Committee, unpublished

Legal and Constitutional Committee 1987 *A Report to Parliament on the Desirability or Otherwise of Legislation Defining and Protecting Human Rights* Melbourne: F D Atkinson Government Printer

Legal and Constitutional Committee 1990 *39th Report to the Parliament: Report upon the Constitutional Act 1975* Melbourne: L V North Government Printer

Macken D 1994 There oughta be a law *Good Weekend* 2 April: 22–6

Manne R 1995 The Premier, the DPP and the facts *The Age* 26 April: 13

Marles F 1993 Equality left in the balance *The Age* 25 November: 18

Murphy D 1994 No mercy for fair go monitor *The Bulletin* 1 March: 30–1

Office of Public Prosecutions 1994 *Eleventh Annual Report of the Office of the Director of Public Prosecutions for the Year Ended 30 June 1994* Melbourne: Office of Public Prosecutions

Office of the Premier 1994 *Victorians Creating the 21st Century—A Progress Report* Melbourne: Office of the Premier

O'Neill N K F 1987 A never ending journey? A history of human rights in Australia in L Spender (ed), *Human Rights—The Australian Debate* Australia: Redfern Legal Centre Publishing: 7–23

Painter J 1993 Hopes of peace hover over bloody protest scene *The Age* 14 December: 1

Parliament of Victoria 1992 *Legislative Council Hansard* 20 May Melbourne: L V North Government Printer

Parliament of Victoria 1993a *Legislative Assembly Hansard* 7 May Melbourne: L V North Government Printer

Parliament of Victoria 1993b *Legislative Assembly Hansard* 19 May Melbourne: L V North Government Printer

Parliament of Victoria 1993c *Legislative Assembly Hansard* 18 November Melbourne: L V North Government Printer

Parliament of Victoria 1993d *Legislative Assembly Hansard* 23 November Melbourne: L V North Government Printer

Rayner M 1993 *Report of the Commissioner for Equal Opportunity for the Year Ended 30 June 1993* Melbourne: L V North Government Printer

Rayner M 1994 What Kennett and my chinchilla have in common *The Age* 26 September: 12

Richter R 1993 Letter to the editor *The Age* 26 October: 12

Ricketson M 1993 Free information—at a price *The Australian* 10 May: 11

Rozenes M 1992 *Police Powers: Arrest, Search and Seizure, Electronics Eavesdropping and Telephone Interception* Legal Studies Discussion Paper No 6 Melbourne: Victorian Council for Civil Liberties

Scrutiny of Acts and Regulations Committee 1993a *Alert Digest No 8* 13 May Melbourne: L V North Government Printer

Scrutiny of Acts and Regulations Committee 1993b *Alert Digest No 9* 19 May Melbourne: L V North Government Printer

Scrutiny of Acts and Regulations Committee 1993c *Review of the Victorian Equal Opportunity Act 1984 Interim Report* L V North Government Printer

Scrutiny of Acts and Regulations Committee 1993d *Alert Digest No 17* 16 November Melbourne: L V North Government Printer

Scrutiny of Acts and Regulations Committee 1993e *Alert Digest No 19* 22 November Melbourne, L V North Government Printer

Scrutiny of Acts and Regulations Committee 1994 *First Annual Report* Melbourne: L V North Government Printer

The Sunday Age 1993 The best of times, the worst of times 19 December: 14

Statute Law Revision Committee 1979 *Progress Report on the Constitution Act 1975. A Bill of Rights* Parliamentary Paper D-No. 9/1979 Melbourne: Parliament of Victoria

Victorian Council for Civil Liberties 1993a *Warnings on Sentencing Bill,* press release 14 May

Victorian Council for Civil Liberties 1993b Press Conference November

Victorian Council for Civil Liberties 1993c *Scrutiny of Act and Regulations Committee Crimes (Amendment) Bill—1993 Submission on Behalf of the Victorian Council for Civil Liberties* Melbourne

Wade J 1993 Media Release 26 October

Wade J 1994 A liberal executive *Law Institute Journal* 68, 9: 833–834

Wallace J 1994 The Attorney-General and civil liberties *Civil Liberty* 10, 3: 4–5

Weeramantry C G 1990 Human rights in J Wallace and T Pagone (eds), *Rights and Freedoms in Australia* Sydney: The Federation Press: 240–55

Zifcak S 1993 The FoI Act: closing one cabinet, opening another *The Age* 11 May: 15

Zifcak S 1994 Kennett governance *Civil Liberty* 10, 2: 2–5

Parliament and Political Power

Ken Coghill

A more equitable distribution of political power has been one of the enduring objectives of democratic socialist and social democratic political parties
throughout the world, including the Australian Labor Party. The labour
movement was founded to enhance the bargaining position of working
people in relation to those who control the economic resources of work-
places. It was soon realised that it was essential to exercise power within political processes if labour parties were to achieve a more equitable distribution
of resources.

Some political movements were founded to obtain political power and
exercise it on behalf of one or more sections of society. They did not admit
that members of society should exercise any control, democratic or otherwise, over the movement when it was in government. Political power was top
down from an all powerful, all knowing central committee. These political
movements have generally failed to match or sustain the improvements in the
lives of members of the general community which democratic systems have
achieved (although those in positions of power often did very well). These
movements failed the central purpose of delivering political and economic
power to people at large.

POWER AND EFFECTIVENESS

It is now beyond question that democratic structures of government are the
most effective means of achieving and sustaining more equitable distribu-
tions of resources and of resolving conflicts within society. There is ample
empirical evidence pointing to the advantages of democratic systems in generating more equitable social and economic environments.

A clue to the reasons for the apparent success of political systems which
disperse political power is to be found in complexity theory. (For a review of
this work, especially that of the Santa Fe Institute, see Waldrop 1992; Gell-
Mann 1994.) This theory suggests that the optimum performance of physical, economic and biological systems occurs at a point part-way between
order (rigid control) and chaos (absence of control). At this transitional point
a system is more complex and adaptive to its environment than when it is in
a static ordered state or in a state of chaos (disordered). This is a useful con-
ceptual framework within which to consider systems of government. It supports the commonsense view that economies and other complex systems

work best when there is a balance between the extreme positions of central control and the total absence of regulation.

Regulation of the economy is a major function of the political system. Accordingly, policy about the distribution of decision - making and administration is relevant to the effectiveness with which the economy achieves its objectives. These objectives are, of course, ultimately social objectives.
The political systems which appear to perform best are those in which a balance is maintained between the power of central control and the power of individuals and small/local groups. Systems which impose rigid central control tend to stifle the adaptation of society to changing circumstances—witness the failure of the eastern European command economies to match the improvements in standards of living and in environmental protection of the democracies of western Europe. Societies in which there is little effective central government are unable to provide the social and physical infrastructure necessary for advances in social conditions—Somalia is an extreme example.

Among the various democratic systems, there are less dramatic distinctions which can be analysed in a similar way. An example is Putman's (1993) analysis of the relative development of the regions of Italy since the establishment of regional governments in 1970. Putman identified the presence of a civil society as the key feature that distinguished northern regions in which regional government has been a more effective agent for change from the southern regions which had retained a more feudal culture. This analysis provides further evidence of a subtle relationship between social and economic progress and the level of complexity of a social system.

Other distinctions between democratic systems can be identified. Lijphart (1991) has classified democratic systems into:

•presidential (people elect a president who chooses an executive. A separately elected congress puts controls on the executive's actions) and

•parliamentary (people elect a parliament which then chooses an executive from its members. Australia has a parliamentary system and the proposed republic would be parliamentary, too). Parliamentary systems may be

   —majoritarian (with single member electorates) or

   —consensus (with proportional representation).

Lijphart claims that equitable societies are more likely to develop under parliamentary systems of government than under presidential systems. It may be, however, that parliamentary systems using proportional representation, like MMP (mixed member proportional representation) which is being introduced in New Zealand, have achieved more equitable societies than our majoritarian system.

Presidential systems concentrate power in the hands of an individual—a central focus of power. Rather than the power of the United States President being balanced by the power of the Congress, the separation of powers has, in practice, institutionalised deadlock between the two. Since Congress has no executive power, it has not developed blocs and members of Congress have become vulnerable to influence by special interests. Neither the United States President nor the Congress have been able to deal with major issues such as gun control and the chronic budget deficit.

Australia's majoritarian systems, by integrating the executive in the legislature, have avoided deadlocks between the two, but in so doing have concentrated power in the hands of the executive. The executive's power has grown to be equivalent to that exercised by the absolute monarchies (hereditary dictatorships) which they succeeded. Majoritarian electoral systems in parliamentary democracies have led to the emergence of strong, cohesive political parties dominating the composition of parliaments.

- •In parliaments, a high proportion of government members serve in executive positions.

- •Control over the chamber's proceedings is exercised ruthlessly by majorities supporting the executive.

- •Governments use their majorities to resist the forms and levels of accountability to the parliament which are essential to the maintenance of responsible government.

- •Question Time becomes mere theatre, auditor generals are unable to expose waste and corruption and laws are made without real examination or debate.

Our elections have increasingly become periodical events to determine the personalities who will comprise elective dictatorships rather than being part of a truly democratic process involving the members of society in the decisions affecting their lives.

Australian states have seen far too many examples of parliaments which have failed to take executive governments to account. The Fitzgerald Report on the Queensland government and the WA Inc. Royal Commission Report are merely two of the most recent chapters in a sad history. Modern European parliamentary systems may have reduced these problems by integrating not just the executive but also major decision making and the scrutiny of government administration into their activities. Proportional representation means that majority government is less certain and less frequent. It tends to force a more consensual style of decision making, which in turn discourages an adversarial, divisive style in which the policy pendulum swings from one fad to another. The appointment of premiers/prime ministers and in some cases cabinets is subject to parliamentary approval. Parliamentary committees monitor departmental activity and expenditure.

However, corruption came to be institutionalised in all major Italian parties under the former system of proportional representation using list voting. This experience highlights the potential pitfalls of proportional representation.

CHECKS AND BALANCES
Checks and balances are institutionalised in parliamentary democracies elected by proportional representation; checks and balances exist in Westminster

majoritarian systems only in so far as they are respected by the majorities. They can be ignored or overturned by decisions of the majority, except in jurisdictions where they are entrenched by referendum.

Checks and balances are the means of restraining the tendency of people in power to exercise authority in the interests of themselves and their associates. Checks and balances are at the heart of the key constitutional questions which have faced our system of government since it was shaped by the 1688 Bill of Rights in England. That Bill of Rights concerned the rights of the parliament over the monarchy. It established the parliament as sovereign—as the ultimate source of political power. It had little to say about any rights of those subject to the parliament's authority. The concept of popular sovereignty, in which the people have ultimate power, was not contemplated. That archaic heritage continues to underlie Victoria's system of government. It is appropriate to review this heritage, given constitutional development and practice in other places and the recent history of civil rights in Victoria.

In Australia, the rigid hierarchy of responsibilities of national, state and local government is giving way to a complex and fluid range of relationships. The Commonwealth deals directly with local government and sponsors regional organisations. Victoria enters into sister state relationships with provinces in foreign countries and our instrumentalities market services internationally. Melbourne and other cities enter into sister relationships with foreign cities. Local public and private institutions exchange information and personnel with interstate and foreign counterparts, bypassing Victorian government. Local governments tender for contracts in other municipalities. The Victorian parliament and the Victorian government no longer enjoy singular authority within the limits of their constitutional and other statutory powers. They must adapt to a political environment in which governance occurs through the complex interactions of many loci of power and influence.

The system of government must be recognised as the mechanism through which society regulates its affairs and allocates resources. As the complexity of society increases, so the system of governance must evolve and develop to cope with that complexity. The system of government must be adapted to keep pace. Its role must be prevented from declining to the extent that the Victorian community loses the benefits of complexity and tends towards chaos.

The changes which could improve the operation of Victoria's system of government are significant but evolutionary. There is no reason to suspect that revolutionary change would be desirable.

The Victorian Constitution
The system of government in Victoria is established by its basic law which is included in the (Victorian) *Constitution Act 1975* and some related legislation including the Constitution Amendment Act.

•It provides for a constitutional monarchy in which the Queen is the head of state, represented by the Governor.

•The parliament includes the Governor and the two houses of parliament, each of which must approve legislation before it can become law.

•The head of state appoints the premier and ministers, technically as members of the Executive Council. This is an anachronistic relic of the origins of Westminster as a council to advise the monarchy.

More recent constitutions of parliamentary democracies provide for the (house of) parliament to determine the premier by a vote of confidence or similar procedure. In some cases, the cabinet is subject to similar endorsement by the parliament. Such provisions are inherently more democratic and properly free the head of state from being forced into a position of resolving essentially political disputes.

Recent events have shown that the constitution is hopelessly inadequate to protect the democratic rights and freedoms of Victorian people. The Constitution Act can be changed by majority votes in both houses of parliament. A number of other Australian state constitutions and the constitution of the Commonwealth of Australia require referendums at which the people must vote to approve major changes to the power of governments and the way in which they work.

The Commonwealth Constitution was developed by Australians through a series of constitutional conventions before being submitted for approval by a referendum in each of the then colonies. Victorians have never been asked to vote in a referendum to approve the state constitution or any changes to it.

A constitutional convention should be elected, separately from the parliament, to review the Victorian Constitution. The convention would be required:

•to publish discussion papers on major constitutional questions, to call for submissions and publish submissions and to hold public hearings at major centres throughout Victoria

•to prepare advisory referendums on key options to be put to the people by the Victorian Electoral Commission. The results of advisory referendums would not be binding, but would be expressions of opinion to guide the convention

•to prepare a final report proposing a new constitution to be submitted for approval at a referendum not later than the following election

•to consider a number of specific proposals. These would include:

–provision for the premier to be determined by a resolution of the Legislative Assembly, the provision to be entrenched so that it could not be amended except by a referendum approved by a majority of those eligible to vote

–entrenchment of key constitutional safeguards which could not be amended except by a referendum approved by a majority of those eligible to vote, e.g.

> freedom of speech
>
> representative parliamentary democracy
>
> rights to local government
>
> one vote one value
>
> electoral system for each house
>
> independent control of electoral boundaries and elections
>
> ministerial responsibility to the parliament
>
> independence of the judiciary, the auditor general and the ombudsman
>
> trial by jury for major offences
>
> freedom of information, and, of course
>
> amendment of the requirement for referendums

- methods of changing other constitutional provisions
- right of the Supreme Court to review actions of the government and the parliament
- subsidiarity (see below)
- relationships of local government (and other democratically appointed local authorities) to state government
- reform of the Legislative Council—role, size and electoral system, and
- right of public servants to speak publicly on government policy and administration

SUBSIDIARITY

There is a balance to be struck between local control of government activities and centralisation for economies of scale, while providing for redistribution in the interests of equity. Subsidiarity offers a well tried political principle on which to base that balance. It is used by the Europe Union as a central tenet of the division of responsibilities between the EU and national governments, having been first put forward as a principle by the Catholic Church last century. It provides that responsibility is to devolved to the most local practicable level.

Subsidiarity has the potential to be used within Australia and within Victoria to ensure that decisions and administration which could be left in the hands of local government is not appropriated by more remote and alien sources of power. It must be a central theme of a vision for the future of Victoria and Australia. Subsidiarity would give people increased control over decisions affecting their lives, reverse creeping centralism, take power back from Canberra, and force local government to lift its game and be effective and accountable.

In practical terms subsidiarity might involve a provision in the Victorian *Constitution Act 1975* both declaratory and providing appropriate opportunity for enforcement by the Supreme Court through action initiated by citizens or local government, and appropriate amendment of the Local Government Act and other relevant legislation such as planning law.

Subsidiarity need not create exclusive legislative authorities, except in obvious cases such as defence. Subsidiarity would create a hierarchy of standards, so that in a case such as environmental law, the national government would have authority to determine the principles such as national minimum standards, the state (or territory) would have legislative authority subject to those principles within its region of Australia and local government would have a general competency subject to consistency with national and state law. For example there could be:

- •a national standard limiting greenhouse gas emissions in accordance with the Montreal Protocol obligations

- •a state law requiring land use and building controls to serve the objectives of the national standard and

- •local government responsibility for applying and meeting the objectives of the national and state legislation in a manner reflecting local circumstances.

The Constitution should provide that, unless amended by referendum, decision making and administration is to be delegated to the most local practical level.

LOCAL GOVERNMENT REFORM

The Kennett government's municipal amalgamations will be a pointless exercise if they do not enhance the performance of local governments beyond the claimed cost cutting. People want quality service more than the mirage of reduced rates. More fundamentally, the reform process has demonstrated the powerlessness of local government despite its recognition in the Victorian Constitution Act.

Local government leaders can be expected to support policies which give them more authority and revenue-raising capacity within overall state and national objectives set by the respective spheres, subject to greater accountability to their own communities. Local government should be guaranteed a democratic basis, power, autonomy and accountability through entrenched provisions of the Constitution. Within those guarantees, the principle of subsidiarity should enable a local government to adopt its own local constitution. Any fundamental change to the specific local constitution of a municipality should likewise be subject to entrenchment in the same way as provisions of the Victorian Constitution Act.

Also important is provision for ward committees or some such local consultative/advisory democratic bodies within the larger local governments that have been formed by amalgamations. Citizens would have the right to petition for their council to delegate decision-making power or a council could initiate such delegation, again subject to accountability through the council.

A bill of rights?

Debate over a Victorian Bill of Rights focuses on both the concept and the content. The debate over the concept is ignored here. Content is important, since a number of specific rights have been shown to be vulnerable to actions of the Kennett government. These rights were always protected by conventions—norms of behaviour—under previous Victorian governments. The Kennett government has shown that conventions count for nothing to a regime with the power, the arrogance and the determination to impose its will. Victorians have no guaranteed democratic rights and freedoms. It is essential that fundamental rights are entrenched in the Victorian Constitution so that no government can ever again undermine or remove them. This section explains the rights at risk and the entrenchment required.

Trial by jury

Victorians do not have protection from subversion or removal of the ancient right of trial by jury for major offences. The Kennett government has undermined the right by removing the principle of 'guilty beyond reasonable doubt' through the introduction of majority verdicts. The Constitution should be amended to provide that, unless amended by referendum, people in Victoria are guaranteed the right to trial by jury for major offences.

Freedom of speech; freedom of information

Victorians employed by the Kennett government have had existing constitutional powers used to silence them. Government employees are prohibited from public comment on any matter of government policy and administration, not just those things to which they may be privy in their work. Other Victorians have no guarantee of freedom of speech. The Constitution should be amended to provide that, unless amended by referendum, people in Victoria be guaranteed freedom of speech. The Constitution should also be amended to provide that, unless amended by referendum, people in Victoria are guaranteed freedom of information except, subject to appeal to the Supreme Court, to the extent desirable to protect personal privacy, criminal investigations and prosecutions and other specified circumstances.

Just compensation

The Victorian government can compulsorily acquire or confiscate personal property and rights without any compensation, unlike the Commonwealth government which can only acquire property on 'just terms' because of a safeguard in the Commonwealth Constitution (S. 51 (xxxi)). There have been literally dozens of new laws in which the Kennett government has removed the right of Victorians to go to the Supreme Court to seek compensation for the possible loss of some right to property, economic use or other right for which a value could be calculated. In many cases the denial of rights to claim compensation has been quite unnecessary—no one had any reason to lodge a claim, but still the Kennett government insisted on a catch-all prohibition just in case someone used the Supreme Court to try to halt a project. In other cases, the denial of normal legal rights was quite deliberate and calculated, as in the case of Albert Park. Not content with denying the right to claim compensation to home owners whose houses were damaged during construction of the car racing circuit, Mr Kennett rubbed salt in the wound by making arbitrary offers without any right of review. The Victorian Constitution should be amended to provide that, unless amended by referendum, just compensation is to be available for any reduction or removal of rights.

Parliament

The Premier of Victoria, Joan Kirner, said in a Ministerial Statement on 18 March 1992:

> There is a widespread perception and concern expressed both in the community and in the Parliament that the standing of Parliament is low and still declining. It is not too far fetched to apply Chifley's words and to conclude that democracy has been dealt some harsh blows by actions on all sides of Parliament which have damaged public respect for Parliament in Victoria.

Factors which Mrs Kirner identified as having changed the parliament, affecting the perception, included:
- more disciplined political party systems in parliament
- use of parliament by all parties as theatre to influence media and public opinion rather than as a forum for substantive deliberation
- increasing legislative and policy dominance of the Commonwealth in the federation and consequent reduction in the power and influence of state parliaments
- greatly increased policy and managerial resources available to executive governments since the 1970s
- increased numbers of parliamentarians and increased time spent on parliamentary duties, in accommodation which is now inappropriate to their role and functions

The Fitzgerald Royal Commission dealing with political corruption in Queensland and other reviews in Australia have highlighted the dangers to good government when parliament becomes a mere rubber stamp for a domineering executive government. If the parliament is prevented from holding government accountable and from properly considering legislation, government inevitably becomes more and more arrogant and likely to pursue the interests of its own members and friends rather than serving the public interest.

The Victorian parliament was making progress to reforming and strengthening its role in the years prior to the 1992 election of the Kennett government. The clock has been turned back by the treatment of the parliament since that election. The Governor committed the Kennett government to continuing the reform process in his speech on 26 October 1992 when he officially opened parliament after the general election. Sadly, the Governor's words and the parliament have been treated with contempt since that day. Members, including government backbenchers and the opposition, were denied any reasonable opportunity to examine and consider legislation which fundamentally changed the rights of Victorian men, women and children in the spring 1992 sittings. The legislation included powers for government ministers to make sweeping decisions which are usually reserved for the parliament itself.

•Debates which would normally have been spread over six or eight weeks were crammed into the 11 sitting days, many being long or even all night, of the three week session.

•Members been given as little as ten hours notice before bills were scheduled for debate and decision, and that after a succession of extraordinarily late nights!

•Debate was savagely restricted by use of the guillotine more often in the first ten weeks of sittings than in the past twenty years. The guillotine was applied

> once in the first session after the 1973 election
>
> once in the first session after the 1976 election
>
> not at all in the first session after the 1979 election
>
> three times in the first session after the 1985 election
>
> once in the first session after the 1988 election
>
> and 25 times in the first session after the 1992 election!

•Members had no opportunity to cast properly informed votes as required by their constitutional duty.

•Ministerial responsibility to answer to parliament has become a mockery, with some of the longest and most irrelevant answers to questions without notice heard in the Victorian parliament in many years. The Speaker, faced with a strong-willed Premier having a two-thirds majority, has abandoned previous guidelines for ministerial answers and failed to impose any meaningful limits on them.

•Freedom of information (FOI) has become a hollow concept except for those with the wealth to use it. The very principle of open government has disappeared for many agencies now exempted from FOI.

•Ministers have refused to provide information in answer to written questions on notice, thumbing their noses at a fundamental principle respected in other parliaments.

•The fundamental principle that the lower house has exclusive power to initiate legislation to raise or spend revenue was established in Victoria in hard fought battles last century and written into the Constitution in 1975. It has been cast aside by the government: legislation to raise funds and authorise spending has been introduced first into the Legislative Council (Victoria's equivalent of the House of Lords).

•The authority of the Speaker of the Legislative Assembly as the most senior officer of the lower house has been severely reduced, and the President of the Legislative Council treated similarly.

•The Standing Orders Committee, chaired by the Speaker, did not meet after the election for about a year. It has not resumed the valuable work undertaken in 1989–92, and the all-party Joint Select Committee on the Parliament has never been re-established.

•The government three times refused to allow debate to refer the important issue of the programming of parliamentary business to the Standing Orders Committee, and then forced through its own proposal without reference to the Standing Orders Committee.

•The government abandoned the principle of bi-partisan parliamentary committees, increased the number of committees and gave all the chairmanships to favoured Liberal sons (no women, no National Party members and no Labor opposition members).

PLANS FOR REFORM

During 1989–92 wide-ranging initiatives were taken through unanimous reports of the all-party Standing Orders Committee (chaired by the Speaker) and with the support of the Labor government. These were intended to improve the way in which the parliament works, so as to improve the quality of government. The thrust of the recommendations was supported by Premier Joan Kirner's Ministerial Statement 18 March 1992. The recent contemptuous treatment of our system of government and the parliament demand action to restore public confidence and to establish standards of excellence in the way Victoria is governed.

Opportunities for reforming the structure and operations of the parliament of Victoria include the following.

Roles of houses

The Legislative Council fought many actions by the Legislative Assembly last century which led to the Assembly establishing its financial privilege, that is, its exclusive right to initiate money bills that raise revenue or authorise government expenditure. In Victoria, the principle was confirmed in the *Constitution Act 1975*. Nonetheless, the Kennett government challenged the principle with its Legal Profession Practice (Guarantee Fund) Bill which appropriated money from the legal profession for expenditure at the discretion of the Attorney General.

The Legislative Council has been reduced to a mere rubber stamp since the election of the Kennett government with a majority in both Houses. It has not made one significant amendment except at the government's initiative. The Legislative Council has been prevented from carrying out its democratic review role.

Broad issues of the relative powers and roles of the two houses arise. The two houses have been elected by an identical franchise since 1952 and their powers are not significantly different except in respect of money bills and the requirement that the Premier be a member of the Legislative Assembly. Logic suggests that each house have a distinctive role. The Legislative Council must be restored to its role as a house of review to curb the excesses of governments like the Kennett government.

The Constitution should be amended to provide that, unless amended by referendum, the Legislative Council's role is the review of legislation and the operation of government, without power to force an early election, to block or delay supply and appropriation bills or to delay other legislation beyond a specified reasonable period (e.g. six months) after which the question could be submitted to a joint sitting.

Systems for election of houses

There is no safeguard to protect the public from the introduction of electoral systems which would gerrymander one or both houses of parliament. Victoria has the only mainland upper house of parliament not elected by proportional representation of one form or another. The Constitution should be amended to provide that, unless amended by referendum,

- all votes in all elections shall be as nearly as practicable of equal value

- the Legislative Assembly is to be elected by preferential voting to single member electorates

- the Legislative Council is to be elected by proportional representation, either by a number of multimember electorates as proposed in the 1988 Bill or one single electorate.

Number of MPs

The number of MPs in the Victorian parliament should be lowered by reducing the size of the Legislative Council in line with its changed role which would reduce the electoral work load of members of the Legislative Council. A reduction in the number of members of the Legislative Council from 44 to 31 would reduce the number of Victorian state MPs by approximately 10 per cent.

Fixed term parliaments

The Governor can now select (on the advice of the Premier) the date on which the parliament is dissolved and a general election called. This is a historical anachronism. It derives from the time when parliaments were convened by kings to provide advice. The rise in power of the executive (headed by the Premier) at the expense of the monarchy has left the initiative and discretion with the Premier. This creates an advantage to the government in manipulating the timing of elections which has no basis or rationale in democratic principle.

Fixed terms exist in the United States and a number of other countries including Norway. Norway has a constitutional parliamentary democracy not unlike Victoria's system. The NSW parliament is now bound by a referendum fixing its terms at exactly four years. Early elections are possible only in limited circumstances which could not be orchestrated by the government for partisan advantage.

Provision should be made for fixed terms of four years for the Legislative Assembly (as in NSW) and, for the Legislative Council, two terms of the Legislative Assembly, through amendment of the Constitution.

Grievances

Making representations on behalf of individuals, groups or areas—expressing grievances—is one of the roles of MPs. Grievance debates in the Legislative Assembly (they do not occur in the Legislative Council) are intended to be opportunities for members to raise any matter of concern.

The right and opportunity to raise grievances have been severely reduced by the Kennett government. Under standing orders, grievance debates are scheduled for each third Thursday whether or not the house is actually sitting. Under the sessional order introduced by the Kennett government, grievance debates occur only at the discretion of the Government, removing yet another opportunity for members to carry out their role. In a number of sessions since 1992, less than six hours was provided for grievance debates, compared with sixteen hours which would have occurred if standing orders had been allowed to operate.

Grievance debates should be guaranteed on a regular and frequent basis, by amendment of standing orders.

Parliamentary committees

The present structure of committees is a gross departure from the form which existed successfully for the previous ten years, although it has not been without some redeeming features. The establishment of the Scrutiny of Acts and Regulations Committee has proven to be a worthwhile initiative.

However, the standard structure of an uneven number of members, with a government majority and a government party chair leaves all the committees open to manipulation. The government's partisan interests can prevail over the parliament's scrutiny of government. A number of key committee reports have been disgracefully partisan and lacking in evidence or sound argument to back up their claims.

Furthermore, the structure fails to enhance the parliament's general scrutiny of government administration in the manner which is increasingly common in the parliaments of other countries (including New Zealand and the United Kingdom). Many other parliaments now have departmental or policy area committees which liaise with and monitor the administration of their allocated government departments. They report on relevant legislation after its introduction into the house and before substantive debate. In a reformed Victorian system, each committee would be responsible for a 'super ministry' or group of portfolios.

Question time

Many of the criticisms which members of the public make of the conduct of Parliament arise from the televised reports of the highlights (or the low points) of question time. In part the conduct is a product of the emotional atmosphere which questions without notice generate, but the rules also contribute.

Questions and particularly their answers in the Legislative Assembly can be deliberately lengthened for tactical reasons—usually to limit the number of questions which have to be answered. That problem is eliminated in the Legislative Council by giving the President authority to extend question time if too few questions have been asked. The Speaker should have a discretion to allow question time to be extended if opportunity for asking an adequate number of questions is not available.

A more serious issue is the nature of answers to questions without notice. The Westminster principle of ministerial accountability to the parliament was lost in Australia when early Speakers established the rules to apply to questions without notice and their answers. Ministers were not and are still not obliged directly to answer questions without notice, whereas they must always answer in other circumstances (except for a right to refuse to answer on grounds such as national security). As a consequence, question time develops into a farcical exercise in talking around questions, attempting to remain relevant while 'failing' (refusing) to answer the thrust of questions that may embarrass the minister or the government.

Suggested solutions to this problem were recommended in the 1992 report of the Standing Orders Committee, with the effect of limiting answers and questions in accordance with Westminster principles. Standing orders should be amended in respect of questions without notice as recommended in 1992:

•A member asking a question must not offer argument or an opinion on the matter, or give facts or names of persons, except those strictly necessary to explain the question.

•When a member gives facts or names, he or she is responsible for their accuracy. When the matter is of sufficient importance, the Speaker may require prima facie proof of accuracy.

•In answering any question the minister or member must be directly relevant and responsive to the question; must be reasonably succinct; must not introduce matter extraneous to the question nor debate the matter to which the question relates; and must comply with the same rules and practices as apply to the asking of questions.

Speaker

The current Speaker has been placed in a degrading and humiliating position and the office of Speaker demeaned by the contemptuous treatment he and his office have suffered from the Premier and the government. One of the first actions of the government was to announce a reduction in the salary and hence the status of the presiding officers while the government forced through fat increases for its own members.

Fundamentally, the authority of the Speaker reflects the respect with which he and his office are treated. More than by any other action, the Speaker was made to look like the servant of the Premier over the date of the Broadmeadows by-election. Mr Kennett deliberately kept the Speaker waiting for three weeks for comment on the date for the Broadmeadows by-election. If Mr Kennett treated the Victorian Speaker, Mr Delzoppo, with the respect which the United Kingdom Prime Minister reserves for his/her Speaker, Mr Delzoppo could act with a confidence and authority reflecting the high regard in which his chairmanship was held until he assumed office.

Members of the house must uphold and enhance the respect for and authority of the Speaker and the office of Speaker. The Speaker's salary and entitlements must be restored to parity with ministers.

Use of parliamentary privilege

The fundamental principle that members should be free to speak in parliament without fear or favour necessarily creates parliamentary privilege under which members can make statements that could otherwise give rise to proceedings for slander or libel by individuals who believe they have been wrongly maligned. Many people believe that as a matter of fairness, individuals who believe they have been wronged should have some right to put their case on the public record.

The Australian Senate has introduced a procedure whereby a person who believes that they were wronged by a statement in that house can have a statement presented to the house if it is approved after a thorough examination. Such a procedure should be adopted in Victoria, by amending standing orders.

Crown privilege

Among the devices used by the executive government to avoid accountability to the parliament is the claim of crown privilege. Crown privilege is the claim by the executive that it may determine not to disclose certain information or categories of information to the parliament; it arises from the executive's historic origins as the instrument of the crown rather than of the parliament. The concept of responsible government has never totally severed this historic link. Indeed, the Australian Constitution is drafted on the premise of the executive being a creature of the crown. The frequent use of the term 'crown privilege' in this context reflects the link between the executive and the crown and is vulnerable to Marchant's colourful claim that ministers in the use of

their royal prerogative powers [are] absolute monarchists who seek to reform the state in the form it was in the age of Charles I ... when strong executive government ... was claimed would benefit all the nation. (Marchant 1991: 61)

If the executive were totally responsible to the houses of parliament, there would be no question but that the executive must comply with any lawful order of the house or a committee acting with the authority of the house. The issue arises because of the unresolved contradiction between the constitutional provision for the executive's appointment by the crown as the instrument of the crown and the convention that the executive is responsible to the houses of parliament. The assertion by the executive of immunity challenges the very concept of ministerial responsibility. If a minister refuses to recognise the authority of the parliament to hold him or her accountable for actions taken under his/her responsibility and the parliament declines to act, can 'responsible government' have any meaning?

The claim that certain categories of information are immune from the parliament's right to know stands directly counter to the one principle by which Hyde distinguishes government norms from those of the commercial world. He wrote :

> governments should have no secrets from their own citizens. Certain matters of national security aside, through their parliaments the public are entitled to know what their governments are up to. (Hyde 1993: 22)

In Collins' (1978: 366) words there are three axioms:

1   that ministers are responsible to parliament for the conduct of their departments

2   that in relations between ministers and officials, ministers have the last word

3   that officials are accountable to the public only through the accountability of ministers and cabinet to parliament.

However, this traditional view of the responsibility and accountability of ministers and the public service to the parliament is widely regarded both as a false description of the how the system of government actually works and unrealistic in practical terms.

As Professor Hugh Emy and Dr Owen Hughes (1988: 309) have put the issue:

> What is required is an attempt to rethink and reconceptualise the relations between the executive and legislative branches especially, or the organisation of the large public power of the state, in an era of large governments supported by large bureaucracies, exercising very large powers of discretion.

Who determines whether it is public interest that certain information should not be disclosed is the central question to considered in claims of crown privilege.

1.   There should be a presumption of disclosure, so that all information

should be available unless it is in the public interest that it not be.

2. The principle of 'responsible government' remains intact if it is the parliament which determines whether it is in the public interest that certain information should not be disclosed by the executive or alternatively that it should be disclosed on a confidential basis (i.e. in closed sessions similar to those which may be used by courts of law) to the parliament through a committee. In practice, the house(s) could choose to delegate the right to make determinations in respect of a particular inquiry. Any further publication would be a matter for the parliament.

3. Parliament must have a reserve power to deal with any refusal to submit to the authority of the parliament. Each house of the parliament must establish its ultimate authority for parliamentary officers to search and seize information which it is seeking from the executive, through direction to officials authorised by the house, if necessary.

The exercise of such a power should never be necessary except in the sense that the mere potential for its use would virtually guarantee the furnishing of the information sought.

Numbers of sitting days

The government scheduled only 51 sitting days for Victoria's Legislative Assembly for 1993. A further five were added later by the Premier as a political stunt associated with Aboriginal land rights. There were only 47 Assembly sitting days in 1995!

Despite the government's total control of the programming of parliamentary business through overwhelming numerical superiority in both houses, the eight weeks of the 1993 autumn sittings were utterly inadequate. As a result, the Assembly sat for extraordinary hours. The scheduled winter parliamentary recess was to have been one of the longest ever.

The parliament should be scheduled to sit more days and more hours in total each year. Session dates should be fixed by sessional order for the same weeks in each year (except as affected by Easter), subject to variation by decision of the respective house and to the Speaker having the right to call additional sittings on the request of the government.

Sitting hours

Victoria's irregular and extraordinary sitting hours are largely a result of poor management of parliamentary business. Nonetheless its sitting hours compare poorly with well-managed parliaments and other decision-making bodies. The sitting hours are currently subject to sessional orders which trigger the adjournment at 10.00 pm except when a motion is moved for (unlimited) extension of the sitting. Such motions are invariably supported by government MPs, no matter what their private misgivings.

The parliament should be scheduled to sit for reasonable hours on each day fixed by sessional order, with provision for one extension of the sitting limited to a further one hour on the vote of a simple majority, or a specified longer period of debate with the cooperation of the opposition.

Management of the parliamentary business program

In 1992 the Legislative Assembly Standing Orders Committee issued an options paper following extensive investigation and debate. It described the arrangements adopted in the House of Representatives, the Senate, the South Australian House of Assembly and most European parliaments. Those arrangements vary in the procedures used, but all have adopted ways of managing and programming parliamentary business in a far more professional and effective way than the tyranny of the majority applied in Victoria recently.

The existing sessional order affects only government business and allows the government to effectively override the program as the whim takes it. It makes no provision for private members (i.e. mostly opposition) business and bills. Despite the limitations of the sessional order, the political parties and members are learning to use it to improve the functioning of the house. It is important that the parliament takes the further steps needed to establish a system which advantages both sides of the house and the good government of Victoria.

Set times for debates

Members of parliament can have little idea of when a particular major debate will occur, and interested members of the public can have almost no idea. Set times for the resumption of second reading debates should be established, through a provision in the standing orders. The motion customarily used when debate is adjourned should provide for debate to resume at a particular time on a specified date, e.g. 3.00 pm on Tuesday 28 November 1995. If appropriate in a particular case, the motion could also specify the period to be set aside for debate, e.g. 'That the debate on the second reading of the ...(name)... Bill be adjourned until 3.00 pm on Tuesday 28 November 1995, two hours to be set aside for debate'. It would then automatically take precedence over any other business then before the house which would be automatically deferred.

Standing orders presently provide for a maximum of 30 minutes for most speeches, whereas most members can put a case in a fifteen to twenty minute address. The thirty minute limit tends to encourage members to use the available time, effectively forcing later sittings or reducing the opportunity for other members to use the house's limited time.

Fitness for office

It is difficult to demonstrate that account is taken of the fitness for public office of prospective MPs, and the evidence suggests that this is a problem affecting all major parties at least at a state level. Past NSW parliaments have been peppered with members against whom serious allegations have bee lev-elled and, in a number of cases, proven. The Victorian parliament has, thus far, been spared the presence of little crooks, at least in recent years. At the very least, candidates for preselection could be required to sign declarations disclaiming corrupt activity.

However, lack of fitness for parliamentary office is not limited to criminal activity. A number of leading MPs have failed to demonstrate an understand-ing of fundamental issues of propriety such as the need to separate private interests from public duty. Neither of the political parties nor the parliament offers any meaningful education or training in parliamentary principles and practice to new or continuing parliamentarians.

The preselections of each major political party are compromised by its small membership which is a tiny fraction of those who generally support and vote for that party. This limits both the fields of potential candidates and the representative nature of those voting in preselection ballots. In some ways, the domination of preselections by combinations of special interests isolated from mainstream party activists and even more so from supporters outside the party has elements of the discredited ancient British institution of 'rotten boroughs'.

The imminent introduction of the MMP (mixed member proportional representation) electoral system in New Zealand is reportedly affecting the range of people interested in contesting elections—some are showing an interest in serving as parliamentarians, keen to serve in the parliament and its committees, rather than harbouring ambitions of being government minis-ters. Victoria's combination of an absence of interest by talented leaders and a lack of concern for the integrity of members of our system of government provide fertile ground for the seeds of outright corruption such as that which bedevilled Queensland and Western Australia in recent years.

These weaknesses of the existing preselection system invite consideration of alternatives. One model is the system of primaries used in the United States of America. A voter may register as a voter for one of the parties and may then vote in a primary election which determines the candidate from that party who will contest the following general election. However, the system has its costs which create other weaknesses (favouring those who can afford to contest primaries).

Independence of statutory appointees

The powers available to any Victorian government with a majority in both houses to override or change the Constitution enable it to overturn any fund-amental constitutional principle which gets in its way. As Victorians found with the removal of Equal Opportunity Commissioner Moira Rayner, the constitutional sovereignty of the parliament can be abused to subvert the independence of judicial and quasijudicial offices. Similarly, the Supreme Court has been removed as a source of appeal for justice for Victorians in dozens of pieces of legislation.

The problem is not just the powers available through the Constitution.

The Kennett government has disregarded the customs, traditions, practices and conventions central to the checks and balances on which good governance depends. The usual remedy is to codify these matters in statutes and institutions, but these can be overturned.

Good government requires that there be a conscious policy within the government and the public service of inculcating an appreciation of the principles of good governance and an understanding of their relevance to issues such as protecting the independence of statutory appointees from political intervention. The Constitution must be amended to provide that judicial and quasijudicial offices cannot be abolished except by referendum and that holders of such offices cannot be removed except by Act of parliament for specified forms of incapacity. The Constitution must be amended to provide a guarantee of the right of appeal to the Supreme Court except to the extent abolished by provisions approved by referendum.

Citizen initiated referendums

More fundamental than many of the suggested reforms of the Constitution Act and the parliament is a re-examination of the distribution of power between the people and their democratic institutions. There is worldwide interest in the concept of democracy as a vehicle for providing individual needs and freedoms. This interest in democracy in its purest form has manifested itself in various guises.

In Australia, the concept of citizen - initiated referendums (CIRs) has been marginalised as a political issue through its hijacking by various movements including the extreme Australian League of Rights and one launched under the banner 'Voters' Veto'. This latter movement called for citizen initiated referendums on constitutional reform and legislative initiatives, giving the right to veto legislation as well as to force the resignation or 'recall' of MPs.

However, variations on all or some of these processes have a respectable record in a number European countries including Italy and Switzerland and a mixed history in some states of the United States. Countries founded on the Westminster tradition like Australia, have not normally been receptive to concepts of 'direct democracy', as these movements are sometimes described. Despite the ephemeral character and marginal impact of the voters' veto movement in Australia, it is informative to look at the impetus for such a movement.

In Italy, a form of direct democracy relating to referendums has been in operation since 1970. Acts may be repealed in whole or any part (except categories imposing tax, dealing with international treaties and providing amnesty for prisoners). Ten citizens may lodge a request for such a referendum with a particular court. They must then obtain 500,000 signatures of eligible voters (estimated to be about 7.5 per cent of the total) in support between 1 January and 30 September. The Constitutional Court checks the legality of the proposal by 10 February of the following year. The President of Italy and the Council of Ministers must then separately issue orders for the referendum. If a majority of those entitled to vote (35 million) do so and a majority of those voting support the referendum, it passes. In this way direct democracy can provide different groups access to the agenda setting process, and act as a political safety valve. In the period 1970–89 inclusive

- 33 referendums were requested
- 19 were found to be admissible
- 14 proceeded and
- 5 were passed.

The relatively high threshold of 500,000 petitioners appears to limit use of the provision. A citizen initiated referendum was the major trigger in the recent political reforms which followed exposure of the corrupt political control of government in Italy.

In practice, it can be argued that the citizens' initiative model tends to encourage sectionalism and to work against unpopular minorities. The ideal of political pluralism is, in the process, diluted into parochialism. The representative process of the Westminster system has a moderating effect and provides for equitable access to diversity. A wider, cross-sectional consistency in policy and public accountability is, in this way, afforded greater protection.

It has also been argued that the notions of direct democracy as espoused by Voters' Veto and the Citizens' Initiated Referendum Party are inconsistent with the principles of responsible government. The Westminster system provides for the concerned citizen to be actively engaged in the political process through parliamentary petitions, through active lobbying of local members and through membership of political parties. Moreover, where there is widespread and sustained support for a particular change to the law or opposition to a proposed law, it is generally taken up by one of the mainstream parties. In this way, single issues do not become the property of professional initiative sponsors who seek to market policy as a commodity. A most important tradition of the political culture of the Westminster system is the tradition that the government of the day should be given all the powers it needs to carry out its policy—each party expects to pursue its course without undue hindrance when it has the reins of power.

However, the very concept of the parliament having a higher status than the citizenry whose interests it is intended to serve is offensive to our understanding of democratic principles. To that extent, provision for citizen initiated referendums has the potential to contribute to the substitution of popular sovereignty for the outdated concept of parliamentary sovereignty. It is the potential of such movements to distort the democratic process that is disturbing. However, with adequate safeguards drawing on the experience of other countries, a provision for citizen initiated referendums could be a valuable addition to people's democratic rights. Safeguards should include:

- public education in the role of referendums as a part of general information in the operation of the system of government

- •definition of the acceptable subject matter of referendums, e.g.
  - –must be limited to one question
  - –must be limited to a matter within the constitutional jurisdiction of the Commonwealth/state/local government
  - –must not relate to a specified individual natural person or incorporated body
  - –must not relate to an administrative action
  - –must not bind the parliament to enact a certain law or take a certain action
  - –may approve a certain enactment as if that enactment had been made by the parliament
  - –may in certain cases (e.g. constitutional matters including the structure of the judiciary, the parliament, electoral system) be entrenched so that it could only be amended by another referendum
- •a requirement for review and approval of proposed petitions for referendums by a specified independent authority, e.g. the Electoral Commission (similar checks to Italy)
- •an adequate threshold of voters petitioning for a referendum (expressed as a percentage, e.g. 7.5 per cent of enrolled voters, with some questions such as key constitutional provisions requiring a higher threshold), signatories to be checked by the Electoral Commission
- •minimum periods of at least several months between lodging a petition for a referendum and the conduct of the referendum, the period to be related to the significance of the proposed question, corresponding to the petition threshold requirements (a higher number of signatories could be the basis for a reduced minimum period in some cases)
- • limitations on the timing of referendums to separate them from general elections
- •a requirement that a referendum question be approved by a majority of all eligible voters.

CONCLUSION

A range of provisions such as these could assist in creating a culture for the responsible use of CIR and a more democratic society. Improving the conduct of parliament, entrenching the rights of Victorians and providing more initiative to citizens: these are all means of empowering and protecting our rights. All the recent evidence is that we need all the protection we can get.

REFERENCES

Collins H N 1978 What shall we do with the Westminster model? in Smith R F I and Weller P (eds) *Public Service Inquiries in Australia* St Lucia: University of Queensland Press: 366
Emy H and Hughes O E 1988 *Australian Politics: Realities in Conflict*

Melbourne: Macmillan

Gell-Mann M 1994 *The Quark and the Jaguar* London: Little, Brown

Hyde J 1993 The unbusiness of politics *The Weekend Australian* September 4–5

Lijphart A 1991 Constitutional choices for new democracies *Journal of Democracy* 2, 1

Putman R D 1993 *National Civic Review* 82 2: 101–7 reprinted in *IPA Review* 1994 47: 31–4

Marchant L R 1991 in O'Brien P and Webb M J (eds) *The Executive State: WA Inc and the Constitution* Perth: Constitution Press

Waldrop M M 1992 *Complexity—The emerging science at the edge of order and chaos* New York: Simon & Schuster

PHOTOGRAPHERS T

It was a stray invoice that prompted fate to brin
them brothers-in-law and photographers: three men, ...

Harry Ord Thompson, Walter Percy Collier and John Samuel Hart all shared a passion for photography, though only Harry, the eldest of the three, had been in the photographic business all of his working life. Having secured a five-year apprenticeship with Frederick William Morgan of Durham, Harry was fortunate enough to become a photographer's assistant for Matthew Auty of Tynemouth, one of the outstanding photographers of the North. He travelled widely to build up an extensive collection of scenic views and landscapes but the phenomenal rise of the postcard came several years after his untimely death on 29th July 1895 at the age of 45. Harry would always recall with great affection the part that Matthew Auty had played in advancing his own career as a professional photographer.

Matthew Auty inspired Harry and Harry inspired his two brothers-in-law to embark upon careers in photography. Walter had served his apprenticeship as a draper and John was a groom turned soldier. In 1903, Walter and John opened a tailoring business at 62 Liverpool Road, Great Crosby, but soon changed their careers to become photographers, firstly in Great Crosby and later in Formby, until they were persuaded to join Harry in Newcastle upon Tyne. The three worked together between 1908 and 1912 as Harry built up a fine collection of photographs of rural Northumberland that could be turned into postcards. The legacy of the three photographers exists today in the photographs that they have left.

LIVES OF THE THREE PHOTOGRAPHERS

16.02.1871	Birth of Harry Ord Thompson	(HOT)
20.07.1875	Birth of Walter Percy Collier	(WPC)
19.07.1881	Birth of John Samuel Hart	(JSH)

24.12.1898	Marriage of HOT to Beatrice Isabel Dudley Collier
13.09.1902	Marriage of JSH to Flora May Collier
26.12.1905	Marriage of WPC to Catherine Florence Poynor

1908–1912	WPC and JSH with HOT in Newcastle upon Tyne
20.12.1910	Death of Catherine Florence Collier

07.09.1937	Death of Walter Percy Collier
21.11.1950	Death of John Samuel Hart
18.12.1950	Death of Harry Ord Thompson

INTRODUCTION

Victorian Photography   The growth of photography in the 19th century had been phenomenal, a factor not lost on Alice Mary Hughes (1857-1939) who was one of the outstanding lady photographers of the day. In 1899, she revealed her thoughts in an article in the Harmsworth Magazine: *Of the many arts and crafts which have seen an extraordinary development during the sixty years of the reign of our Most Gracious Queen, there have been few which have undergone a more complete transformation than that of photography. Who is not familiar with the daguerreotype taken during the thirties and forties? There the unfortunate sitter appeared as in a glass darkly, grotesquely like and yet unlike; and, it need hardly be said, with no attempt to procure a charming, still less an ideal, portrait. Then came the carte-de-visite in which a whole family appeared grouped on three by two inches of pasteboard. Nowadays, photography can claim to be an art and most people would prefer to have a fine photograph than an indifferent portrait.*

Even Queen Victoria and Prince Albert dabbled in the new art. Indeed, after the death of Albert on 14th December 1861, the Queen entered a period of prolonged mourning and employed photography to ensure that his private rooms and personal effects were kept just as they were during his lifetime.

The example of Queen Victoria and Prince Albert helped to promote the popularity of photography. The Victorians developed a passion for dressing up and having their pictures taken. During the second half of the 19th century, small cartes de visite (3½ x 2¼ inches) and larger cabinet portraits (5¾ x 4 inches) were produced in their millions. Many were carefully arranged in albums with heavy card mounts and often fastened with a clasp and lock to keep the contents away from the prying eyes of servants. It is a shame but understandable that few of these portraits carry the name of the person or "sitter" as those, who had their photographs taken, were called. By the time that the three brothers-in-law were working in the first years of the 20th century, the postcard (5½ x 3½ inches) had replaced the carte de visite and cabinet portrait. This would remain the standard format for photographs of people and places for the remainder of the 20th century.

Postcards   On 1st October 1870, the Post Office introduced its own official postcards, measuring 4¾ x 3 inches, designed for brief messages and sold pre-printed with a halfpenny stamp. Its willingness to accept any other form of postcard was slow but, on 1st September 1894, it allowed privately printed picture postcards, 4½ x 3½ inches, as long as they had an undivided back, with the picture and message on the front and the address on the back. On 1st November 1899, it allowed picture postcards, 5½ x 3½ inches, with similar undivided backs. Picture postcards became objects of interest that could be collected and displayed in postcard albums, though most of the postcards were printed in Germany, with room to write just a few words around the picture. Newspapers were full of the new craze. The Shields Daily Gazette of 5th April 1900 proclaimed: *The day of the scrap book is over and one can part with it without a pang, for it was a mass of irrelevancies ... Nowadays, its place is gradually being taken by the postcard album; and there is much to be said in favour of preserving the cards adorned with really artistic views of foreign towns that are sent home by friends abroad ... On the Continent, last season, post-card albums were all the rage and they could be obtained cheaply in England towards the end of the summer.* The Golden Age of the picture postcard dawned on 1st January 1902, when the Post Office allowed postcards, 5½ x 3½ inches, with divided backs. These new postcards had the picture on the front and both the message and the address on the back, allowing the picture to be viewed without an intrusive message.

The 1851 census lists the names of 51 photographers (50 men and 1 woman). The 1901 census, however, records 17,268 photographers (12,335 men and 4,933 women) with the 1911 census listing 19,068 photographers (13,205 men and 5,863 women). These figures do not take into account those for whom photography was not their registered occupation. In August 1905, the Daily Mail estimated that there were four million amateur photographers in Great Britain, roughly one tenth of the adult population. In 1893, Kodak had introduced The "Kodak" Girl and, a few years later, published How to make Good Pictures for the amateur photographer. In 1923, the first edition of The "Kodak" Magazine appeared and, in 1925, The "Kodak" Fellowship was created, which encouraged members to wear the Fellowship badge to promote "camera comradeship" among photographers.

Unlike printed postcards, real photographic postcards could be produced at home by an enthusiastic amateur in the darkroom and many villages had an amateur photographer, who took family portraits and sold postcards of the local area. Postman and mechanic Roderick James Thompson of Bellingham was skilled in portraiture and flash photography; postman James Edwin Hamilton of Haydon Bridge produced postcards of local views, events, sporting teams and weddings, many of which appeared in the local press; John Lancaster, a signalman at Whittingham, who later became the ferryman at Haughton, produced cabinet portraits of local families; and schoolmaster Herbert Hearfield of Harbottle produced cabinet portraits and a series of pictures recording the damage caused by flooding on 9th June 1907. Printed postcards were produced by commercial firms in large quantities for distribution over a wide area and might carry the name of the local retailer who sold their cards. A good deal of business was done during the summer months at seaside towns like Whitley Bay. A family trip or school outing to this popular resort might consist of a visit to the Spanish City, building sandcastles on the beach, having fish and chips and, if time and money allowed, a visit to the photographer's studio, where families would be photographed in their Sunday best clothes. People dressed up for a day out in those days.

Northumberland   With the exception of the Roman Wall, rural Northumberland had seen relatively few visitors in the early years of the 20th century. Redesdale, however, attracted several photographers, especially during the construction of Catcleugh Reservoir, but their names are largely unknown and the quality of their photography was variable. One photographer who came to Redesdale in the 1920s was Thomas Carlton Wood (1880-1970) who produced an attractive album of twelve postcards of the training area. He also published postcards of the Redesdale Arms, a popular rendezvous for the army, with its legendary landlord, Benjamin Prior, known as *the man who never forgot a face.*

By the time that Harry Ord Thompson discovered Redesdale, the navvies, who had built the reservoir, were long gone. They were replaced by soldiers, training on the new Redesdale artillery practice camp, which opened in 1911. There was plenty of demand from the volunteers, who would want a postcard to send home to friends and family during their fortnight of training. One dedicated writer was Arthur Henry Bradford, a regular soldier in the Army Service Corps, who sent a series of Collier postcards from Redesdale Camp during the summer of 1914 to Florence, his wife, who was living in Herefordshire. Another unposted card records W. P. Collier and J. S. Hart at Carter Bar, the border between England and Scotland.

The 1906 Kelly directory of Northumberland lists 80 photographers, most of whom specialised in portraiture work, though some published postcards, notably brothers Richard Emerson Ruddock of Newcastle, an artist turned photographer, and John Candlish Ruddock of Alnwick, an engraver turned photographer. Others included three photographers based in Whitley Bay: Gladstone Adams, who had been an apprentice of Matthew Auty, Godfrey Hastings, who acquired the business of Matthew Auty, and Burton Graham, who had a busy studio at 5 Esplanade. John Pattison Gibson (1838-1912) of Hexham, a dispensing chemist, was a noted Victorian photographer who took dozens of photographs of the Roman Wall, which were later sold as printed postcards. Postcard production was lucrative but required more time, travel, manpower and marketing than studio portraiture.

The years following the First World War saw a dip in the demand for postcards. Gone was the passion for collecting the attractive continental cards of the Edwardian Age, many of which had been printed in Germany. Even some of the card mounts that Matthew Auty had used were printed in Berlin. The cost of postage doubled from ½d. to 1d. on 3rd June 1918 and more people used the telephone to send messages. Despite the depression, however, which followed the Great War, more people began to visit new places. Such tourists created a market for good quality local postcards, which were a convenient way of recording their travels. Buying a postcard was instantly satisfying and infinitely more reliable than taking a photograph, which might not "come out" when you got back home.

HARRY ORD THOMPSON

Early Years   Harry Ord Thompson was born on 16th February 1871 at 22 Askew Road, Gateshead, eldest of the three sons of George Henry Thompson, who was a barrister's clerk in the Grainger Arcade, Newcastle, and Elizabeth Thompson (née Ord). He held a respected but poorly paid position and, when he died, aged 53, on 30th May 1882, he left just over £89, which put Elizabeth and her three sons, Harry (11), Frederick (9) and Frank (7) under considerable financial pressure. To make ends meet, Elizabeth tried to get Harry accepted as a choral scholar at Durham Cathedral School, where his education, board and lodging would have been provided free of charge. Harry would have made a good chorister. He was very musical and had a good singing voice but, as he was approaching his twelfth birthday, was considered too old for training. Frank, however, the youngest of the three brothers, was accepted as a choral scholar. Though pleased for his brother, who could look forward to at least five years in the choir, Harry would often recall the days when he went to school with stomach cramps through hunger.

His mother set about devising other means to keep the family. She started a modest business knitting wool in Durham but it was not very successful because, it was said, of its poor location. The 1891 census, however, records her as a dealer in photographs, living in Durham with her two younger sons, Frederick and Frank, at 47 Sadler Street. It cannot be a coincidence that 46 Sadler Street was the premises of photographer Frederick William Morgan, who would play a life-changing role in the career of young Harry. In her later years, and with failing health, Elizabeth left her home in Gateshead and came to live with Harry at 202 Portland Road, where she died, aged 76, on 14th December 1916, deeply mourned by the members of her family, especially Harry, who had never failed to support his mother through thick and thin all of her life.

Apprenticeship   It was Frederick William Morgan (1859-1932) who offered Harry, now aged almost 15, a five-year apprenticeship on 7th December 1885. In return, Harry undertook that he would *well and faithfully and diligently serve the said Frederick William Morgan as his Apprentice in the business practice of a Photographer for and during and until the full end and term of five years.* For this, he would receive a reimbursement of £10. 8s. in the first year, rising to £26 in his fifth and final year.

The eldest son of Frederick Morgan, an established Durham grocer and wine merchant, Frederick William Morgan began his working life as an architect's assistant and he appears as such in the 1881 census, when he was living comfortably at 1 Sadler Street, Durham, with his widowed father, two younger siblings, Dora and Alfred, and two servants. Like many young men of the Victorian age, however, he was drawn to photography and, with or without paternal blessing, quickly became an established photographer, who was able to take on an apprentice in the person of Harry Ord Thompson. He did not carry on with the family grocery business following the death of his father on 23rd January 1888 and, later that year, on 11th October, married Dannetta Mary Turner, the daughter of James Edward Turner, a Surrey wine merchant, at Holy Trinity Church, Penge.

The 1891 census names Frederick William Morgan as a photographer and picture frame maker who had premises at 1A and 46 Sadler Street, the latter being the shop of his late father. It is uncertain how long his photography business lasted. The 1901 census records him as an architect's assistant in Newcastle and he had moved to London by the time of the 1911 census. He was a fully qualified architect when he died, aged 72, on 2nd March 1932, leaving the sum of £2,245 to his younger brother, Alfred John Morgan, who was an exceptionally successful chartered accountant. He had become managing director of Cameron's Brewery, Hartlepool, in 1920 upon the death of Captain Watson Cameron, brother of the founder Colonel John William Cameron, and succeeded multi-millionaire Sir John Ellerman as chairman in 1932. He left £20,170 when he died, aged 72, on 8th August 1935.

Matthew Auty   Having become a qualified photographer, Harry crossed the River Tyne to work for Matthew Auty of Tynemouth. The 1891 census records that Harry, now aged 20, was a photographer's assistant, boarding at 12 Percy Street, Tynemouth, which was a stone's throw from the photographic studio of Matthew Auty at 20 & 21 Front Street.

Matthew Auty (1850-1895) began his career as a tobacconist but soon turned his interest in photography as an amateur into a profession. He opened a studio at 20 Front Street, Tynemouth, around 1885, founding a business that would continue for the next eighty years. He later expanded his premises to include 21 Front Street. One of his apprentices was Gladstone Adams (1880-1966) who later opened his own studio at 18 Station Road, Whitley Bay, a popular venue for day-trippers, who would combine a trip to the seaside with a visit to the photographer's studio. Gladstone Adams may be credited with the invention of the windscreen wiper and, during service in the Royal Flying Corps as a photograph reconnaissance officer, Captain Gladstone Adams was one of those responsible for the burial of the "Red Baron" flying ace, Manfred von Richthofen, on 22nd April 1918.

Many photographers installed skylight windows to convert the top floor of their premises into a studio where they could make the best use of natural light for exposures that might require several seconds in summer and even more in winter. Such premises ideally had three storeys, one as a reception area and for displaying photographs, one for developing and printing, and the upper storey for use as a studio, which was likely to be the lightest room of the building. Following the example of film studios, Matthew Auty built a glasshouse in the rear garden of his premises in Tynemouth so that ladies and the infirm would be spared the ordeal of climbing flights of stairs to have their picture taken – and leaving them out of breath, trembling and incapable of remaining still for long enough to ensure a successful exposure. This innovation proved very popular and it was in this studio that Harry would have spent much of his time.

Even so, studio portraiture was very limited during the winter months. Until electricity was installed to produce better illumination, studio portraiture depended on the availability of natural light for taking photographs. Many photographers installed electricity from the 1880s and claimed that they could take pictures whatever the weather and time of year. The lighting, however, in these "electric studios" was rarely able to produce enough illumination for reliable portraiture and most photographers resorted to magnesium flash power, which was hazardous even in the most experienced hands and often resulted in severe burns.

Photographic studios were busy places and the Victorians loved to dress in their finest clothes and have their photograph taken. The studio of Matthew Auty in Tynemouth would have been busy enough but a large, fashionable studio in London, like that of Alice Mary Hughes, was definitely designed to impress. One of the most interesting features of her fine reception rooms was a number of beautiful Louis XV screens, covered with exquisite specimens of her work, though many of the photographs, it was admitted, were neither for sale or reproduction. As photographer to royalty and the gentry, the daughter of the renowned portrait painter Edward Hughes, she was one of the leading lady photographers of the Victorian age, who specialised in portraits of women and children. She was proud of the fact that she never photographed men. *Now of course I employ an immense number of people – during the season as many as sixty at a time – but, when I first opened my studio, I did everything myself, even to the retouching and spotting ... I fancy very few people realise the immense trouble taken – over every photograph properly produced. People always want their proofs in a great hurry but I have always set my face against sending out any hurried work, and every one of my photographs passes through the hands of about fifty people before it finally reaches the sitter.* (Harmsworth Magazine 1899).

Matthew Auty might have looked with some admiration on a photographer like Alice Hughes. He did not have fine reception rooms with a number of beautiful Louis XV screens or as many as sixty people working for him but he appreciated that the success of his business depended largely on the love that the Victorians had for the carte de visite and cabinet portrait. He was, however, one of the first of the Northern photographers to produce scenic view cards, modelled on cabinet portraits. A dozen of these views could be mounted on stout cards and formed into books. These opened like a concertina and became popular with increasing numbers of Victorians who began to visit places of beauty or culture. Many of his views were later produced as postcards but the phenomenal rise in the sale of picture postcards and albums was a development that Matthew Auty did not live to see. Within a few years of his death, the postcard format, 5½ x 3½ inches, had replaced the format of both the carte de visite and cabinet portrait. On 1st October 1870, the Post Office had introduced its own postcard, designed to be used for short messages, and it was keen to maintain its monopoly. After Post Office regulations changed, however, on 1st January 1902 to allow the divided back, the picture was no longer spoilt by the message, which formerly had to be written below or around the view. This was a small change but one that heralded the Golden Age of Edwardian picture postcard collecting, with nearly every home investing in a postcard album.

Many years later, Harry Ord Thompson recalled how Matthew Auty *set off each summer to some new location and, after taking pictures under the most favourable conditions of light and weather, returned with a set of negatives of a quality superior to anything previously on the market.* Six of his sample books still survive, with the most popular locations being the city of Durham and its Cathedral and, straddling the border of Northumberland and Cumberland, the village of Gilsland, where the Shaw's Hotel made it a popular Victorian spa resort.

Rebuilt and enlarged after a disastrous fire on 27th August 1859, the Shaw's Hotel offered over 100 rooms for the visitor or invalid seeking to exchange the fumes of the city for the fresh air of the country. Occupying high ground overlooking the village, the new hotel became a fashionable hydro and featured several lounges, a library, newsroom, billiard and bagatelle tables and a ballroom. A major attraction consisted in its hot and cold baths, which satisfied the Victorian craze for all forms of the so-called water cure. The hotel had a pumping engine to bring water up from the sulphur well by the River Irthing, where there were picturesque walks, shops and bazaars. The hotel prospered for forty years and was purchased on 1st February 1902 by the Northern Co-operative Society as a convalescent home.

The sheltered serenity of Gilsland attracted not only visitors but also photographers like Matthew Auty, who had a large display of his view cards at Gilsland Post Office. Others included Brampton photographers J. S. Farrer and G. Parkin, who set up studios in Gilsland and specialised in portraiture, and Fred Lee of Haltwhistle, who specialised in taking pictures of couples and individuals on the Popping Stone, the romantic spot beside the River Irthing, a short walk from the hotel, where tradition relates that Sir Walter Scott proposed to his fiancée, Charlotte Charpentier. He married her on 24th December 1797 after a courtship of three weeks.

It was on 29th July 1895 that Matthew Auty died of heart failure, his untimely, but not unexpected, death depriving the North of an outstanding photographer who had won many prizes, at home and abroad, which were recorded on the reverse of his cartes de visite and cabinet portraits. An obituary duly appeared in the Shields Daily Gazette on the following day. *The deceased gentleman, who was only 45 years of age, served his time with Mr. John Harvey, tobacco manufacturer, and afterwards commenced as a retail tobacconist on his own account at Tynemouth. Mr. Auty, who proved very successful as an amateur photographer, eventually commenced business in Front Street, Tynemouth, as a professional photographer. This departure turned out to be a perfect success and so excellent were the productions that emanated from his studio that in time prizes from all parts of England, Scotland, Ireland and Wales were awarded to the Tynemouth photographer at exhibitions held in various places; while in 1887 a similar honour was forthcoming from the exhibition at Florence.*

His marriage to Elizabeth Cecilia Everatt, seven years his junior, on 8th November 1877 had proved childless and the terms of his will, in which he left almost £3,375, spawned a legal tussle between his blood relatives and his widow, who would receive an annual allowance on the condition that she did not remarry. A widow of just 38 years, with no ties, might still entertain the prospect of a second marriage. As the result of a relationship she formed with Robert Archibald Heaven, the manager of Matthew Auty, she gave birth to a boy on 1st December 1896. Marriage followed in Edinburgh on 13th April 1900.

The business of Matthew Auty, including its name, goodwill and its photographic plates, was acquired by Godfrey Eldon Hastings, a stationer and photographer of Whitley Bay, who continued the studio portrait business while expanding the commercial postcard side. He may have read the article in the Sunderland Daily Echo of 3rd January 1901 on Messrs. Raphael Tuck and Sons of Moorfields, London, who *are making a speciality of picture postcards and have sent us some specimens, which are a perfect dream of beauty; indeed, it seems almost a sacrilege to commit them to the rough hands of the stamper and postman.* Since 1900, Marion & Co. of Soho Square, London, had been producing photographic paper for the amateur in the postcard format with the required postal regulations pre-printed on the back.

Much of what is known about Matthew Auty comes from Harry Ord Thompson. Harry became a member of the Society of Antiquaries of Newcastle upon Tyne on 20th November 1930 and made frequent gifts of books and artefacts to the Library and Museum of the Society. On 25th March 1942, he read a paper entitled "Matthew Auty and the Auty collection of photographic negatives" which had been presented to the Society by Miss Edith Anne Hastings, sister of Godfrey Eldon Hastings (1871-1914) and Jonathan Drewry Hastings (1872-1940). The Society added that the bequest also included the plates of Godfrey Hastings. Edith died, aged 71, on 15th July 1946, the youngest and last surviving of the three children of Eldon and Esther Hastings, none of whom married.

Chance Encounter   It was while he was still working for Auty & Co. shortly after the death of its founder that Harry had a life-changing experience. It seems that a stray invoice had been received from photographic material suppliers F. K. Hurman & Co. of Newcastle, where Beatrice Isabel Dudley Collier, elder sister of W. P. Collier, was working. Harry was sent to have the matter rectified and consequently met Beatrice, who would become his wife for the rest of his life. Harry and Beatrice, always known as "Bertie" by the family, were married by the Reverend John Wilkinson on 24th December 1898 at St. Peter's Church, Newcastle upon Tyne, where Harry was a member of the choir. They spent their honeymoon in Norwich with Uncle Fred Collier and would have met his fiancée, Sarah Coxford, a young widow, whom he would marry on 2nd April 1899. Frederick William Collier (1856-1917) and Henry James Collier (1844-1902) were two bachelor brothers who came to Norwich in the late 1870s where they built up a successful business, H. and F. Collier, manufacturing dog biscuits and foodstuffs for poultry, pheasants and other game. Members of the Collier family could always be sure of receiving a brace of pheasants every Christmas until the outbreak of the Great War.

His marriage to Beatrice encouraged Harry to further his ambitions and he appears in Kelly's directory for 1900 as a photographer. He was probably working for Photochrom when his daughter Mabelle Flora Dudley Thompson was born on 27th March 1901 at 145 Portland Road. The 1901 census, taken four days after her birth, describes Harry as an undermanager for a photographic view company. Founded in Tunbridge Wells in 1896, Photochrom specialised in photographic views in plush frames and later began publishing sepia postcards. In 1902, the family moved to 74 Bolingbroke Street. Harry proceeded to gain further experience by working for Kodak before deciding to start his own business. In 1907, he moved to 91 Helmsley Road and took a house in 54 Portland Road to use as a workshop, having borrowed five pounds from the Reverend John Wilkinson, who had conducted his wedding eight years earlier.

Independence   Much of his early work as an independent photographer was influenced by his time with Matthew Auty. Apart from studio portraiture and bespoke photographs, he was already exploring the idea of taking artistic views, which could now be turned into picture postcards. Whether by accident or design, Harry was in Bellingham on 22nd September 1906 and witnessed the ceremony of Riding the Fair, also called Riding the Boundary. Although the importance of this custom, once part of St. Cuthbert's Fair, had declined over the years, the Hexham Herald reported that *several horsemen turned out, headed by Mr. Charles Tomlinson, the Duke of Northumberland's steward at Bellingham, with Mr. William Gardner as standard bearer. They marched round the Fairstead to the music of the bagpipes, played by the Duke's piper.* Placing his photographic bag in the shade of a tree, Harry proceeded to take several pictures of the ceremony as it made its way along the main street.

During his visit to Bellingham, Harry probably looked around the shops, for which Bellingham was famous, with a particular interest in the postcards on sale. One such would have been the shop of newsagent and stationer Elizabeth Mary Smith (1869-1952) who published her own postcards (E. M. Smith) and sold those of others, including James Valentine & Sons of Dundee and James Beaty & Sons of Carlisle. Both firms concentrated on the picturesque waterfall of Hareshaw Linn and the village of Bellingham, which was a popular destination for visitors in the summer months and had claims, like Allendale, to be a health resort.

At the time that Harry was surveying the postcard market, many national photographers were producing printed postcards of the main local landmarks and beauty spots, which could yield lucrative sales, such as the Tyne bridges in Newcastle or the Hareshaw Linn in Bellingham. Most of these postcards were colour-printed and looked attractive enough on the postcard stands. Harry had no designs on competing with the larger firms, who had the resources to sell their cards, cheaply and in large numbers, to shops, post offices and other outlets over a wide area. He realised, however, that there was a gap in the market for real photographic cards, especially those of the more remote locations. These were uneconomic for the larger publishers, which tended to concentrate on the locations that tourists, with a limited amount of time, were likely to visit. Although lacking the immediate appeal of colour-printed cards, black and white postcards had no rivals in terms of definition and quality.

For the moment, Harry had two of his photographs of Riding the Fair published as sepia-printed postcards, which carried H. O. Thompson, Newcastle-on-Tyne, on the reverse. It is not known whether he was pleased with the results but he returned to the same area when he took a picture, again published as a sepia-printed postcard, of the new church of All Saints at West Woodburn, around the time of its consecration on 1st November 1907. Harry perhaps sought something of the quality found in his bespoke or studio photographs, which were produced in small quantities for individual clients. Printed cards, however, which were produced in large numbers for the commercial market, could never achieve the detail of real photographs. Photochrom specialised in printed postcards but even these, which were of superior quality, could not match the definition that a photographer could achieve in the darkroom. Producing photographs for a client in small numbers was one thing; producing and distributing postcards for the commercial market in larger numbers was another. The demand for postcards, however, was expanding and lucrative. If the commercial side of his postcard business were to become successful, assistance would be required.

Combining business with pleasure, Harry began to make a series of forays into rural Northumberland, hoping to find reliable outlets for his postcards in the shops and post offices of villages like Matfen, Humshaugh, Barrasford, Wark, Falstone, Otterburn, Rochester and Harbottle. Many of these areas were difficult of access but, as a man used to horses from his service in the Volunteers, Harry had no hesitation in hiring a horse and trap. These travels proved to be an eye-opening experience. Published on 6th January 1908, Ward's directory of Newcastle upon Tyne is the first to locate Harry at 202 Portland Road and to describe him as a technical, <u>outdoor</u> & publishing photographer.

The Final Move The seven years following the birth of his daughter had seen Harry and his family change house several times. By the spring of 1908, however, the final move had been made to 202 Portland Road, where Harry would remain for the rest of his working life. With its nine rooms, this property, which had stood empty since the departure of Alfred Bradfield three years earlier, gave Harry ample scope to expand his photography business. Five rooms were used by the family and four for photography. His great nephew, Harold Hetherington, who was born on 31st July 1919, recalled that he once ventured into the basement, where Harry had his photographic workshop. Being a helpful young lad, he swept the floor and threw the sweepings into the boiler. There was a sudden explosion. Some shavings of magnesium, used for flash photography, had been spilt on the floor and went off with a bang. The explosion rocked the house from top to bottom. The incident had its funny side but shows the risks of using such techniques to produce the light that Harry might need for interior photographs.

Harry enjoyed taking high quality photographs of rural Northumberland. He understood the financial potential but soon realised that it would require more than one photographer to take pictures on location, process them in the darkroom and sell them in the market place. Harry would not have to look far for two partners. Shortly after setting up his business at 202 Portland Road, Harry turned to his family with a proposition. In Lancashire, since around 1904, his brothers-in-law, Walter Percy Collier and John Samuel Hart, had been evolving from tailors into photographers. From their tailoring business at 62 Liverpool Road, Great Crosby, they had been producing dozens of high quality real photographic postcards of the local area in relatively small numbers and without the use of machinery.

Some of these were sold to local retailers to be published as printed postcards, including Stephen S. Cushing of Great Crosby, Mary P. Newcombe of Waterloo and George H. Henshall of Bootle, where the distinctive titling of W. P. Collier appears alongside the titling of the printer. These printed postcards were of acceptable quality and certainly good enough to carry a message or be displayed in a postcard album but did not have the definition of a real photograph. Harry Ord Thompson probably felt the same when he saw the printed versions of his photographs of the Bellingham Riding. The hallmark of a professional photographer would always be the labour intensive and time consuming production of photographic postcards, the product of the darkroom rather than the printing press.

Working Together   Walter and John accepted the offer of Harry to put the postcard side of his business on a commercial footing and to do on Tyneside what they had been doing on Merseyside. Each gave up their photographic interests in Lancashire and moved to Northumberland. Shortly after Harry had established himself and his family at 202 Portland Road in the spring of 1908, they found that they too were travelling to the most remote areas of the county, taking photographs for the increasingly popular and lucrative postcard market. It is almost impossible to identify who took the original photographs as it was Harry who did most, if not all, of the titling. The presence of Walter in Harbottle, however, is confirmed by a postcard of Harbottle Castle, with the trees in full foliage, which was posted on 24th June 1909, dating the original photograph to the summer of 1908. It carries the titling of W. P. Collier. Another card of Harbottle Village, posted on 18th February 1910, carries the titling of H. O. Thompson. It is likely that much of the marketing and distribution was left to John, who obtained a motor licence in 1909.

Over the next four years, the three brothers-in-law worked together in building up an extensive collection of high quality photographs of rural Northumberland. They continued to concentrate on the more remote areas where good quality black and white postcards were rare or non-existent. They took pictures of the North Tyne Valley and Upper Coquetdale and travelled the road through Redesdale, marked by its marching line of telegraph poles. The increasing number of bars carrying the wires gives some help in dating the sequence of the pictures. W. P. Collier took a picture of J. S. Hart at Carter Bar, 1,372 feet above sea level, where the main road from Newcastle crosses the Border into Scotland. The route was well supplied with hostelries at Otterburn and Horsley, shops and post offices at Otterburn and Rochester, together with the Redesdale artillery camp, where soldiers were sent for training after its establishment in 1911. Many photographers did good business at the training camp, notably Joseph Elliott & John Harvey Thomas, who formed the firm of Elliott & Thomas of Hexham. Many of the shops and post offices put large wooden frames outside to display the postcards they had on sale.

Separate Ways   By 1912, however, W. P. Collier and J. S. Hart had decided to go their separate ways. John had run his own photographic business at 95 Rothbury Terrace, Heaton, for a short time before he moved to Norwich, the home of Frederick William Collier, the uncle of his wife Flora, and became a photographer in the village of Newton St. Faith. Walter opened a shop in Bellingham, the village where Harry had taken pictures of Riding the Boundary six years earlier. Family tradition records that Harry gave Walter £100 to help him start his new venture and, as a bonus, freedom to photograph rural Northumberland as he wished.

With this gesture, Harry deprived himself of a lucrative source of income but could now concentrate on the commercial and technical side of his photography. Ward's directory of Newcastle upon Tyne for 1912 reflects this change of emphasis and describes him as a technical, <u>commercial</u> & publishing photographer.

Two years later, however, events took an ugly turn when Britain and Germany went to war on 4th August 1914. The threat of further enemy action after the bombardment of Hartlepool, Scarborough and Whitby by German warships on 16th December 1914 put the whole of the East Coast on a war footing. Harry was not daunted by the prospect of military service. He had always been a devoted member of the Volunteer Force, which had been created in 1859 as a part-time rifle, artillery and engineer corps. In 1908, he was awarded the Edward VII Medal for 20 years' service in the Volunteer Force, which was then re-organised as the Territorial Force. His unit was a mounted battery of artillery and would ride out into the surrounding countryside at weekends to conduct exercises. Harry confessed that he would often fall asleep in the saddle on the return journey. Once a year, his unit boarded the train at Newcastle Central station with their horses and guns and travelled to the firing ranges at Lydd in Kent.

Military Service   On 12th September 1914, Harry enlisted in the 63rd (2nd line Northumbrian) Division of the Army Service Corps. He was almost 44 years of age, 5 feet 9¼ inches tall, and recorded his occupation as a commercial photographer. The Army Service Corps (now the Royal Logistic Corps) was formed in 1888 to supply the army with technical and military equipment, transport and general supplies such as food, water, fuel and building materials. It was to the Transport Section that Harry was transferred on 18th June 1915 with promotion to the rank of Acting Staff Sergeant Major. It was intended that units of the 2nd Line should remain at home but on 26 July 1915 orders were received that any men could be taken for service overseas. With the exception of two weeks' leave, Harry served in France from 1st March 1917 to 18th May 1919, putting a great strain on his wife Beatrice and missing the wedding of his daughter Mabelle to Horace James Hetherington on 15th January 1919. As protection, he left them "Leader" a foxhound which he had bought as hunting was suspended during the War. "Leader" proved to be a faithful and much loved guardian of the family.

One bonus of his service abroad was that Harry, as a photographer, was posted to a section that processed aerial photographs of the Front and made them into maps. The deadlock of trench warfare was a catalyst for aerial reconnaissance, since the traditional use of cavalry to reconnoitre the enemy was impossible. Millions of aerial photographs were taken of enemy positions, with R.A.F. squadrons alone taking 2½ million photographs during 1918. Harry was one of the unsung heroes who used their photographic skills to save lives and shorten the war.

Return to Photography   After his discharge on 17th June 1919, having been awarded the coveted Territorial War Medal for Voluntary Service Overseas, the Great War for Civilisation Victory Medal 1914-1919 and the British War Medal 1914-1918, Staff Sergeant Major H. O. Thompson returned home to 202 Portland Road. The techniques that he had learned while on military service encouraged him to bring new ideas to his photographic business as he expanded and developed what was termed Commercial and Technical Photography.

Victorian printers had found it difficult to produce photographs and text together and relied on engravings because photographs were invariably dark and lacking in contrast. The photograph that Henry Waitt (1862-1904) of Bellingham took of the opening of the new road bridge at Reedsmouth on 24th September 1904, for example, was printed as an engraving in the following edition of the Hexham Courant. As printing techniques improved in the later 20th century, however, the photographer gained greater access to the printed page and the Guide to Newcastle, printed in 1905, displayed an equal number of photographs and engravings. By the time that Harry returned from military service, printing relied on photographs rather than engravings or wood cuts and industrial Tyneside offered many opportunities for the photographer, though competition was intense. For this purpose, he invested heavily in expanding his business at 202 Portland Road. The five basement rooms became photographic workshops and the two attic rooms were used as a copying room and spare darkroom. The front room on the ground floor was used as an office. Harry and Beatrice occupied the remainder of the house.

The purpose of what is now called Industrial Photography was to produce photographs of industrial premises, equipment and products for books, catalogues, directories, newspapers, trade journals, exhibitions and advertising. This entailed visits to factories, coal mines, shipyards, power stations and public buildings. Regular customers included C. A. Parsons & Co. (turbines and generators), A. Reyrolle & Co. (electrical switchgear), Hugh Wood & Co. (mining equipment) and Sir Howard Grubb, Parsons & Co. (astronomical instrument makers). Harry also compiled a large collection of Newcastle street views and buildings, including war memorials and churches, many of which he produced as postcards.

On these expeditions, he travelled alone by public transport, starting on the tramway, which passed his front door, and then by bus or train. A leather bag carried the camera that he had selected for the job, usually a whole-plate model, 8½ inches x 6½ inches. His favourite camera was a Sanderson with a good selection of lenses, dark slides loaded with glass plates and a focussing cloth. He carried his wooden tripod separately. He used personal experience and judgement alone to calculate the length of exposure and account for any other factors in order to get the best possible picture. On his return, he processed the exposed plates himself, leaving the routine developing & printing to his staff. His preferred materials were Ilford plates and Gevaert or Kosmos papers. For personal use, his favourite camera was an Ernemann hand and stand camera, in which he used Agfa film packs, 3¼ inches x 2¼ inches. All processing solutions he made up from basic chemicals to his personal specifications. The results in terms of definition, gradation and grain could not be bettered today. He even used to grind his own lenses by hand.

In addition to his commercial and technical work, Harry became one of the photographers who did developing & printing for Boots the Chemists, one of the national firms that catered for the photographer. As long as chemicals were used to produce pictures, chemists were inextricably linked with photography and for many families "sending the film away" for printing was part of the ritual after returning from holiday. Boots sold chemicals, cameras and equipment, with processing being outsourced to local photographers. They also offered a picture framing service. Despite providing a steady stream of work for several years, with the consequent increase in staff, competition from other photographers was always very fierce and the work later became unprofitable. The use of his professional talents to produce a snapshot rather than a photograph jarred upon the innate desire that Harry had to produce the perfect print. Even Walter, who did developing & printing for a wide area around Bellingham, was forced to admit on one occasion that he had done his best with the films of Bessie Hall, a keen photographer, who lived on the remote farm of Carshope in Upper Coquetdale, adding in a note "perhaps the light was not good or taken rather late in the day, the cause of them being so dull."

The 1920s witnessed the evolution of the snapshot camera in the hands of the amateur photographer, who often possessed more enthusiasm than expertise. To encourage amateurs to process their own films, firms like Kodak of Kingsway and Johnson of Hendon offered kits with equipment and chemicals to get the amateur started. Everything was supplied, except experience and expertise, and the instructions made it all look so easy. The "Kodak" Magazine was aimed at the amateur photographer and promoted competitions with tempting prizes. Even smokers could get a start in photography. Many products offered tokens which could be exchanged for a camera, though cigarette smoke was one of the pollutants that became engrained in the surface of the finished photograph, along with smoke from domestic fires and industry. Microscopic specks of dust and smoke stuck to the glossy side of a wet print and were pressed deep into the emulsion when the print was rolled on to a glass plate to enhance the glossy surface.

In addition to his passion for restoring grandfather clocks, Harry was a keen local historian, with a strong interest in architecture and archaeology. It was, however, the Roman Wall that really captured his imagination and provided a good deal of photographic work. In 1912, Harry produced a series of postcards on the excavations of the Roman fort at Wallsend. In the 1920s, he would often be seen along the main road to the west of Newcastle. This had been built on the line of the Roman Wall by General Wade after the second Jacobite rebellion of 1745. As sections of the Wall were uncovered in preparation for road widening and house building, Harry would be called out in all weathers to make a photographic record of the excavations before they were filled in. Excavations of mile castles, sections of the Roman Wall still standing, the Roman sites of Corbridge and Housesteads, and other Roman military works required more photographs. After his death, his negatives were donated to the University of Newcastle.

Legacy   Harry made a comfortable living as a photographer and succeeded in achieving his life's ambition as the prime mover in founding the Newcastle branch of the Professional Photographers' Association, now the British Institute of Professional Photography. Exhibitions in the 1930s regularly displayed his pictures, such as the interior of Dunston Power Station, a miner drilling holes for shot-firing and the modernised interior of a Northumbrian Pele Tower. Bound by a strong code of personal ethics, however, he did not advertise his business, holding that, as a professional photographer, it would be unethical to employ such methods, apart from putting, on occasions, his name and address on the back of his pictures, or his initials HT or HOT on the front.

The departure of his brothers-in-law led Harry to concentrate on expanding the commercial and technical side of his photography but he did not entirely abandon the business of producing postcards. He published a notable series of pictures of the Training Ship Wellesley which was destroyed by fire at North Shields on 11th March 1914. After his return from military service, he visited Matfen to take a picture of the war memorial, unveiled on 1st May 1920, and took pictures of two war memorials in Newcastle upon Tyne, the Commercial Battalions Memorial, unveiled on 5th July 1923, and the 6th Northumberland Fusiliers Memorial, unveiled on 29th November 1924. Many of his postcards were published by Andrew Hogg Herries, a stationer and newsagent of Newcastle upon Tyne and president in 1914 of the Federation of Retail Newsagents, Booksellers and Stationers.

Harry retired, aged 65, from full-time photography in 1936 but still continued to have his photographs published. He was a member of the British Legion and secretary and vice-chairman of the Newcastle upon Tyne branch. He was proved right in his conviction that it would not be long before another war came and, upon the outbreak of the Second World War, he joined the Civil Defence as an Air Raid Warden. It is sad that neither Harry nor Beatrice lived to see the end of war-time rationing and shortages. Harry died of a heart attack at 15 Stratford Grove on 18th December 1950. Beatrice died at Lemington Hospital on 6th December 1952, her death being registered by her brother-in-law, Frank Thompson.

On 20th December 1950, his obituary appeared in the Newcastle Journal. *The death has occurred at the age of 79 of Mr. Harry Ord Thompson of 15 Stratford Grove, Newcastle. For 60 years in business as a photographer, he was a member of the Institute of British Photographers and exhibited several times. He was also a member of the Society of Antiquaries. Mr. Thompson held the Volunteer Long Service Medal and served with the Army Service Corps in the 1914-18 War. He was at one time a vice-chairman of the Newcastle branch of the British Legion and was also for many years a chorister at St. Peter's Church, Oxford Street, and later at St. Andrew's Church, Gallowgate.*

In a career spanning 60 years, Harry saw many changes, especially the transition from the artistic and portraiture work of photographers like Matthew Auty to the technical and commercial photography of the 20th century. It is a shame that many of his pictures are lost in trade magazines and catalogues - or in the photograph albums of Boots customers. Some, however, can still be seen in the publications of learned societies like the Society of Antiquaries of Newcastle upon Tyne.

One thing that did not change, however, was the love that Harry had for rural Northumberland, whether it was the "picture postcard" village of Matfen, 20 miles from Newcastle, or the lonely farm of Low Bleakhope, nestling at the head of the Breamish Valley, miles from anywhere. It is fitting that one of his last pictures to appear in the Newcastle Weekly Chronicle of 15th April 1939 was a landscape of the Cheviot Hills, a favourite location for many of his photographs.

Harry and wife Beatrice (right) with daughter Mabelle, son-in-law
Horace Hetherington, and grandchildren Mavis and Harold c. 1925

Riding the Fair, Bellingham, printed postcard
H. O. Thompson 22nd September 1906

Riding the Boundary, Bellingham, printed postcard
H. O. Thompson 22nd September 1906

Country: idyllic Post Office, Cambo
H. O. Thompson c. 1907

Town: fashionable Highbury, Newcastle upon Tyne
H. O. Thompson c. 1909

St. Barnabas Church, Jesmond, opened 1904, closed 1978
H. O. Thompson c. 1909

St. Barnabas Church Workers
H. O. Thompson 31st July 1909

Confined places: High Level Bridge, Newcastle
H. O. Thompson c. 1910

Open spaces: Low Bleakhope, Breamish Valley
H. O. Thompson c. 1910

The farms of Barrowburn and Windyhaugh, Upper Coquetdale
H. O. Thompson c. 1910

The farm and shooting lodge of Carlcroft, Upper Coquetdale
H. O. Thompson c. 1910

Fox and Hounds Inn, West Woodburn
H. O. Thompson c. 1910

Bay Horse Inn, West Woodburn
H. O. Thompson c. 1912

Elsdon Mill on the Elsdon Burn
H. O. Thompson c. 1910

Joseph and Matthew Hall of Elsdon Mill
H. O. Thompson c. 1910

Platelayers near Bellingham
H. O Thompson c. 1910

Bellingham Station, looking north
H. O. Thompson c. 1910

Rochester Picnic and Sports, Redesdale
H. O. Thompson 18th June 1910

Falstone Show, North Tyne Valley
H. O. Thompson 11th October 1911

Flooding at Bellingham 14th May 1911
H. O. Thompson

Flooding at Bellingham 14th May 1911
H. O. Thompson

Coronation Festivities on Wark Village Green
H. O. Thompson 22nd June 1911

Dance in Colwell School Room
H. O. Thompson 1st December 1911

Bardon Mill Brass Band outside the Public Hall
H. O. Thompson 1912

Throckley Bank Top Football Club
H. O. Thompson 1912

Matfen war memorial, unveiled 1st May 1920, and Temperance Hotel
H. O. Thompson c. 1921

Commercial Battalions war memorial, unveiled 5th July 1923
H. O. Thompson c. 1924

Attaching a pony's shoes, underground stables, Ashington Colliery
H. O. Thompson c. 1930

Bringing a pony from the coal face, underground stables, Ashington Colliery
H. O. Thompson c. 1930

Titling of Harry Ord Thompson
with erased titling of J. S. Hart on the left

Titling of Harry Ord Thompson
with erased titling of W. P. Collier on the left

JOHN SAMUEL HART

Early **Years** John Samuel Hart was born on 19th July 1881, the son of Samuel Hart and Annie Holmes, his second wife, at South Otterington, five miles south of Northallerton. His father was a coachman for Robert Aikenhead (1822-1895) of Otterington Hall, a 21-room mansion, where Samuel was still in the employment of Robert Aikenhead when he died on 5th July 1895. After the death of her husband, Frances Aikenhead, 23 years his junior, would remain at Otterington Hall until 1909 but with a reduction in her retinue of servants. In due course, Samuel became landlord of the Station Hotel, Northallerton. He left in 1903 and died, aged 69, on 20th February 1909, with John being present at his death.

Soldier On 24th February 1900, John went to Richmond to enlist in the Corps of Dragoons of the Line, giving his occupation as a groom. This was a cavalry regiment and recruits with an experience of horses would have been particularly welcome. The army was dependent upon horses not only for tactical manoeuvres but also for the movement of troops and equipment. On 3rd March 1900, John found himself at the Curragh Camp in County Kildare, Ireland, adjacent to the Curragh Racecourse. It was, however, a condition of enlistment that a recruit might be posted to another regiment and, on 2nd January 1902, John was posted as a gunner to the Royal Garrison Artillery at Seaforth Barracks, Lancashire, whose duties included manning the coastal artillery Battery at Bootle, part of the Mersey defences. This stood at the end of the street where Flora May Collier, the younger sister of Walter Percy Collier, was living. Bootle Battery was demolished in 1927 prior to the completion of Gladstone Dock, still an important working dock, one of 43 docks which once stretched for 7½ miles along the Mersey Estuary from Seaforth to Dingle and which were connected by the Liverpool Overhead Railway. The line, known as the Dockers' Umbrella, opened on 6th March 1893 but soaring maintenance costs forced it to close on 30th December 1956, much to the dismay of the local communities along the line. It was owing to the importance of its docks that Bootle would suffer some of the heaviest bombing of the Second World War.

It was not long before John met Flora May Collier and, on 13th September 1902, the couple married at St. Leonard's Parish Church, Bootle, a stone's throw from where Flora (and possibly Walter) was living at 29 Shakespeare Street, one of the many streets named after poets in this area of the Lancashire town. It was the marriage of Flora to John Samuel Hart that changed the career of Walter Percy Collier.

Seaforth Barracks had opened in 1882 as a cavalry barracks with ample accommodation for officers and other ranks, married men and stabling for 80 horses. The census of 1901 records 550 names, including soldiers, wives and children. After their marriage, John and Flora Hart set up home at 44 Cyprus Vale,

Great Crosby, where their first child, John Percy Dudley Hart, was born on 19th June 1903. Flora was keen that her husband should leave the army. With a gift from Harry Ord Thompson and a modest legacy from Uncle Fred Collier, who had died on 13th February 1902, she was able to raise the required £18 to buy him out and John returned to civilian life on 17th July 1903.

Photographer   The career of John Samuel Hart changed three times over the next few months: insurance agent, tailor and photographer. Tall, fair-haired and handsome, the ex-soldier was the ideal salesman and for a few months worked as an insurance agent, during which time the family moved to 5 Endbutt Lane, Great Crosby, a larger terraced property with six rooms. By 1904, however, he had joined his brother-in-law, Walter Percy Collier, to begin a new career venture. The Liverpool directory for 1905, published in 1904, records the firm of Collier & Hart, tailors, at 62 Liverpool Road, Great Crosby, with the two brothers-in-law taking over the premises of John Dolan, a master tailor, who moved to 6 Liverpool Road. As a qualified draper, Walter would deal with the technical side of the business while John might visit local houses with his wares and sample books, canvassing on the doorstep, as was usual in those days. His regular contact with customers may well have made him realise the potential of photography to create additional income, whether from studio portraiture or by selling postcards of the area. People might like to have a portrait of themselves in their new clothes or even a picture of their own house. One lady sent a postcard of her house in Jesmond to her nephew on 25th August 1904 with the words "Have you had a photograph of our little house yet? A man came this morning and took some and came to see if we would have them." It is quite likely that the man was none other than Harry Ord Thompson.

Walter had been aware of the potential of photography ever since the marriage of his elder sister Beatrice to Harry Ord Thompson, who was building a successful career as an independent photographer on Tyneside. One of the earliest postcards that Walter produced, dating to the autumn of 1903, was that of Mrs. Jane Chisnall, fruiterer and greengrocer, taken outside her shop at 5 Islington, Great Crosby, a short distance from 62 Liverpool Road. The optimistic titling "A Merry Christmas and Prosperous 1904" belies the fact that her husband James, a blacksmith, had died on 15th June 1903 after a long illness and her clothes suggest that she was still in mourning. Another card, posted on 1st July 1904, is of the Royal Court Pierrots at Blundellsands. Walter probably took both pictures with a quarter-plate camera (4¼ x 3¼ inches) and printed them on the postcard format of 5½ x 3½ inches. He later used a half-plate camera (6½ x 4¾ inches) with the picture being cropped, as required, to postcard size.

The picture postcard market had blossomed since the change in Post Office regulations in 1902 allowing the picture to occupy the whole of one side with both the message and the address written on the reverse. The attraction of such "divided back" postcards meant that they were keenly collected in specially produced postcard albums, which became as popular as the heavy, leather-bound photograph albums of Victorian times. Although postcards were intended to communicate a short message quickly, many cards found their way straight into postcard albums by courtesy of collectors of all ages. One Bellingham writer added (1905) the message: *This is one of the new postcards* and, several years later, another, sending a card of Matfen Hall, produced by W. P. Collier, wrote on the back: *I thought you would like to have this card and it would not be wise to send it through the post.*

Great Crosby   The tailoring firm of Collier & Hart lasted for about two years. During this time, both men were showing an increasing talent for photography and began taking views of Great Crosby and the surrounding area, which they published as postcards, produced in the darkroom and not on the printing press, with Walter doing the titling in his own distinctive style. The large attic rooms at 62 Liverpool Road, with skylights and dormer windows, provided enough natural light for both tailoring and photographic work. Postcards were individually developed and printed by exposing them to natural light in wooden frames, which held both the glass negative and photographic paper. There were no machines. Output was measured in dozens rather than hundreds. The quality was excellent and, though labour intensive, the profits were all their own. Additional income could be created by selling the copyright of photographs to local retailers, including photographer George Herbert Henshall of Bootle and Mary Phoebe Newcombe of 89 St. John's Road, Waterloo, who had become a successful stationer and newsagent after the death of her husband Thomas on 1st February 1894.

It is not easy to distinguish the work of the two photographers. Neither put their name or initials on their pictures and it seems that Walter, who had exquisite handwriting, did the titling for John. The writing of a title, using a photographic pen and ink, on a glass negative could make or break a photograph and required a steady hand and lots of practice. The distinctive horseshoe motif, however, which recalls John's background firstly as a groom at Otterington Hall and then as a soldier in the Dragoon Guards, on many of the Great Crosby postcards may indicate the work of John rather than Walter. Except, perhaps, for a reference number, no titling was required on bespoke photographs or studio portraits when the place or person would be known.

Formby   Within two years, the brothers-in-law had gone their separate ways. The Great Crosby directory, published in June 1906, lists W. P. Collier as a photographer at 62 Liverpool Road. There is no mention of J. S. Hart. John was a fast learner and, by 1906, felt that he had gained enough experience as a photographer to start his own business. He and Flora moved to 9 Raven Meols Lane,

Formby, where he set up a studio in one of the six rooms. His second son, Alfred Neville, was born there on 28th March 1907, with John giving his occupation as a photographer. It was about the same time that Walter and Catherine left the shop at 62 Liverpool Road and moved to 14 Formby Street, Formby, a large semi-detached property, just around the corner from the Hart family.

It is difficult to judge the success of the two photographers. Formby was an expanding commuter town especially as it was served by the Liverpool, Crosby and Southport railway, which was fully electrified on 5th April 1904. W. P. Collier produced a large number of postcards of Formby, Freshfield, Hightown and Altcar, as he had done in Great Crosby, including several of Eccles level crossing and Formby station, which was only a minute's walk from his house. J. S. Hart probably concentrated on portraiture and studio work. There appears to have been limited competition from other local photographers, such as Samuel Bevan Reynolds, who also had a stationery shop, but equally, perhaps, limited demand from other shops and customers.

Newcastle upon Tyne   It was Harry Ord Thompson who brought the two brothers-in-law to Newcastle upon Tyne with an exciting proposal to produce real photographic postcards of rural Northumberland. Picture postcards had become highly collectable in their own right after the change in Post Office regulations in 1902 had allowed a picture to occupy the whole of one side of the postcard without being spoilt by an intrusive or personal message. By the time that he was established at 202 Portland Road in the spring of 1908, Harry had already been expanding his photographic collection of rural Northumberland and saw the potential in producing high quality bespoke photographs and postcards of an area that had hitherto remained relatively undiscovered. One postcard writer, indeed, had apologised for the quality of a printed postcard of the village of Wall that she sent on 6th January 1908 to her friend in Edinburgh, her words "photographers are few up this way" suggesting that there were few photographers producing high quality topographical postcards as opposed to studio portraits.

The two brothers-in-law joined Harry during the course of 1908. They would put their bicycles on the train to visit many of their locations, especially the road through Redesdale, where Walter took a picture of John at Carter Bar, the border between England and Scotland. The photographers worked well together but Harry knew from personal experience that such associations always tended to be fragile. Some twenty years earlier, on 31st March 1892, Matthew Auty and Richard Emerson Ruddock had dissolved their partnership, with Matthew continuing the business in Tynemouth and Richard starting his own photographic studio and postcard business at 2-8 Pilgrim Street, Newcastle, until moving to Bristol and then migrating to America in 1914 where he died, aged 68, on 21st November 1931.

History repeated itself firstly with John and then with Walter. John had accompanied Walter on many of their forays into rural Northumberland and was probably responsible for much of the marketing as the 1911 census describes him as a canvasser and photographer. He had obtained a motor licence in 1909, which gave him greater independence and the chance to start his own business. For a couple of years, he had his own photographic business at 95 Rothbury Terrace, Heaton, but then moved with his wife and family to Norfolk, leaving his plates with Harry, who duly printed them with his own titling. His name first appears on the Norwich electoral register of 1913, which would indicate that he was living in the city when the register was compiled in the summer of 1912. It was with great pleasure that Mabelle Thompson recalled the two glorious summers that she spent on holiday in Norfolk as a young girl. Everything changed, however, on 4th August 1914 when war was declared on Germany. At this time, John was living as a photographer in the village of Newton St. Faith, a few miles north of Norwich.

Norfolk   John had been living in Norfolk for a couple of years when Britain and Germany went to war. In less than a week, John, true to his colours, had volunteered for military service. On 10th August 1914, at the age of 34, he enlisted in the 1st East Anglian Brigade of the Royal Field Artillery, recovering £8 of the £18 that had been paid to buy him out of the army eleven years earlier. He was promoted to corporal on 30th September 1914. For the next year, he served at home, receiving promotion to sergeant on 14th August 1915. With bases in Norwich, North Walsham and Great Yarmouth, the Norfolk Batteries were used to guard against the threat of German attack from warships and Zeppelins on the towns along the coastline of Norfolk and Kent. He may have been stationed in Margate doing the same work as he had done in Bootle, twelve years earlier. On 15th November 1915, however, he was posted abroad with the British Expeditionary Force. He missed the birth of the third of his three children, Renee Flora Dudley Hart, on 28th February 1916 at 111 Alderson Road, Great Yarmouth. He saw service abroad until 1st July 1917 when he returned to Britain and was discharged on 24th September 1917 as being "no longer physically fit" for military service. He had given his profession as a photographer upon his enlistment but was not required to use these skills, unlike H. O. Thompson and W. P. Collier.

For the second time in his life, John left the army to become a civilian but, as with many men who returned from the War, family life did not return to normal. John was one of thousands of ex-servicemen who returned from conflict and slaughter on an industrial scale and found it hard to adjust to normal life. After serving in the forces for over three years, with just over half of these abroad, he found that he could return to neither family nor photography. John turned his back on Northumberland and Norfolk. The county where he chose to spend the rest of his life was Kent and the town that he chose was Margate.

Margate   John used his motor licence to become a taxi-cab proprietor in Margate and appeared as such in the Thanet Advertiser and Echo of 14th August 1920. He found himself in court for allegedly disregarding the signal of a police constable on 1st August requiring him to stop while driving along the Marine Terrace on a busy Bank Holiday Sunday. John confirmed that he was lodging at 66 Victoria Road, Margate, and argued that he had no reason to defy the constable, whose signals had been unclear. He had held a motor licence for eleven years and had never had so much as a complaint made against him let alone a conviction. He proudly recalled his military career until his retirement from active service in 1917 with the rank of battery sergeant-major. The Court found that he had no case to answer and acquitted him. Driving in Margate, especially during a Bank Holiday weekend, was not for the faint-hearted and policemen did not have a universal system of hand signals. Although motor licences had been introduced in 1903, it was not until 1st April 1934 that the driving test was introduced, three years after the first edition of the Highway Code appeared on 14th April 1931.

The years following the First World War were not prosperous. The promise of a Land Fit for Heroes did not materialise and many people took the decision to migrate to Australia, Canada or the United States. Following the example set by Isabella, her mother, and her brother, Alfred Edmond, almost 25 years earlier, Flora decided to seek a better life in America. It would appear that, for several years, Flora and John had been living separate lives in Great Yarmouth and Margate.

On 31st March 1923, Flora May Harte, as she now wrote her surname, left Great Yarmouth and travelled to Liverpool. There, she and her two youngest children, Alfred Neville, aged 15, and Renee Flora, aged 6, boarded the S.S. Andania and sailed to America, their final destination being San Diego in California. John did not accompany her. It was H. O. Thompson, her uncle, whom she named as her "nearest relative" in the country of her departure. Harry Ord Thompson and his family had survived the upheaval of military conflict. Flora knew that others were not so fortunate. She secured employment as a nurse and then became a housewife. She was present at the death of her mother on 10th October 1931. Flora herself died on 29th November 1942 and was buried in Daytona Memorial Park, Florida.

A New Life   The life that John led in Margate consists of a series of snapshots, with John losing contact with his wife and children in America. On 19th November 1930, at the local Register Office, he married Mary Jane Keeley, a widow since her husband Philip, a shop keeper, suffered a fatal heart attack on Christmas Day 1914 and died, aged just 34. John gave his profession as a builder's yardman. John was present at the marriage of his eldest son, John Percy Dudley, to Gertrude Eileen Lea on 6th July 1935. He was a staff sergeant major with the 7th Hussars at Hounslow Barracks. This was a military wedding. John gave his profession as a soldier on his son's marriage certificate. For the whole of his life, John remained proud of his military background and neither family nor photography could quite fill the gap when he returned to civilian life.

The 1939 Register describes John as a car park superintendent and light car driver, living at 26 Westbrook Avenue, Margate. He and Mary later retired to Pear Tree Cottage at Harbledown, near Canterbury. In his later years, John was not a well man and died, aged 69, of heart problems on 21st November 1950. His profession was given as a chauffeur. Mary died of old age in Margate on 7th December 1955.

The photographs of John Samuel Hart are the least well known among the three photographers. His photographic career spanned rather less than ten years and during most of this time he was working with Walter Percy Collier and Harry Ord Thompson. He did have a connexion with Lancashire, however, and produced a series of postcards of Holcombe, near Bury, bearing the same horseshoe emblem and titling that appeared on the postcards of Great Crosby.

John was a soldier first, a photographer second and then a family man. Had not the Great War intervened, however, the photographs of J. S. Hart might have become as well known as those of H. O. Thompson and W. P. Collier.

Seaforth Barracks, Claremont Road, opened 1882, closed 1958
Wright & Co. c. 1900

Liverpool Road, Great Crosby
J. S. Hart c. 1905

Aerial view of Great Crosby
J. S. Hart c. 1905

Carnegie Library, College Road, opened 1905, closed 2013
J. S. Hart c. 1905

Moor Lane, Great Crosby
J. S. Hart c. 1905

"Teas, Refreshments and Minerals", Little Crosby
J. S. Hart c. 1905

St. Mary's Roman Catholic Church & Convent, Little Crosby
J. S. Hart c. 1905

East Wilkwood, Upper Coquetdale, and the Dunn family
J. S. Hart c. 1910

West Wilkwood, Upper Coquetdale, and the Anderson family
J. S. Hart c. 1910

Picture of J. S. Hart
taken by W. P. Collier c. 1910

Picture of W. P. Collier
taken by J. S. Hart c. 1910

WALTER PERCY COLLIER

Early Life   Walter Percy Collier was born on 20th July 1875 at 77 Elswick Row, Newcastle upon Tyne, the son of draper Walter Dudley Collier and Isabella Thompson, who had married on 24th July 1872. Walter and Isabella had four children, two girls followed by two boys. Thanks to having two sisters, Walter would acquire two brothers-in-law, Harry Ord Thompson, an experienced photographer, and John Samuel Hart, a soldier who became a photographer. It was the marriage of Beatrice Isabel Dudley Collier to Harry Ord Thompson on 24th December 1898 that would bring Walter into contact with photography and a career spanning 35 years, the final 25 of which were spent in Bellingham.

Isabella   On 8th November 1891, Walter died, aged 41, of tuberculosis and Isabella found herself a widow of 42 years. She was too young to spend the rest of her life in mourning. A couple of years after the death of her husband, she left Beatrice in charge of the family at 184 Doncaster Road after securing the position of a lady's companion to Mrs. Pendleton, a wealthy American. This was one of the few openings available to a middle-aged Victorian gentlewoman living in reduced circumstances. She might be employed by an unmarried woman living on her own, by a widow, or by an unmarried woman who was living with her father or another male relation but had lost her mother and was too old to have a governess.

A companion would be needed by a wealthy society woman, who had no daughter or niece available for companionship and who needed a gentlewoman, preferably somewhat younger than herself, who was prepared to work, read, play music, and walk or drive with her. She might be required to prepare the menus for a forthcoming dinner, to help entertain visitors or to arrange flowers in vases, any light duties, in fact, that would normally fall to an unmarried daughter of the house. The annual allowance (as a salary was called) paid to a companion might fall between £25 and £100, though a travelling companion, as Isabella became, might receive anything from £150 upwards. All in all, it was not a bad way of life.

This association brought Isabella to the United States in 1902 and she became a naturalised citizen in 1907. Two years later, she married William Nolden, 15 years her senior, who had migrated to the United States from his native Prussia about 1857. For both, it was their second marriage. For the first five years of their married life, the couple ran a fruit farm in Rock Creek, California, where Isabella wrote to her family in England describing her skill in raising chickens. They then moved to San Diego, where they ran an apartment block and later a hotel. The hotel was rather run-down but the couple built it up. William died, aged 89, on 9th April 1923, a week after Flora May Harte, the younger of Isabella's two daughters, and her two youngest children set sail from Liverpool for America. In the 1920s, California, like most of America, was enjoying a booming economy and Isabella, like many other Americans, took on various financial investments. The Wall Street Crash of 1929, however, proved that it was all too good to be true. Fortunes were lost overnight as America entered the Great Depression. Many of the investments that Isabella had undertaken went bad and she was forced to appeal to her family in England for help. She survived, albeit in reduced circumstances, and died, aged 82, on 10th October 1931 in Eustis, Florida, the home of Flora May Harte.

Draper   Shortly after reaching his 15th birthday, Walter Percy Collier secured an apprenticeship as a draper with Hutton's of Newcastle. Five years later, he qualified as a draper, an occasion that was marked by the gift of a book (Character by Samuel Smiles) from John William Tickle, a draper's clerk, of 11 Woodbine Road, Gosforth. This book was very special and Walter kept it for the rest of his life. He duly inscribed it, in his beautiful copperplate handwriting, with his name and the date, December 1st 1895, which he underlined with the distinctive wavy line that would be found in the titling of some of his earliest postcards.

Manchester   Having completed his apprenticeship as a draper, Walter continued his career in Manchester. People travelled long distances to find work in those days. Cotton was King in this city, which was surrounded by mills, all producing materials for the clothing trade. He had probably left Newcastle shortly after the marriage of his elder sister Beatrice to Harry Ord Thompson on 24th December 1898. The 1901 census records him as a hosier's assistant, living with his younger sister Flora May at 30 Deyne Avenue in the Rusholme district of South Manchester. It was a neat, five-room, end of terrace house, a short distance from the busy road from Manchester to Wilmslow. His brother, Alfred Edmond, the youngest of the four children, had probably gone with them. On 29th May 1899, he started work as a goods porter at Manchester Central station, headquarters of the Manchester, Sheffield and Lincolnshire Railway, known from 1st August 1897 as the Great Central Railway, after the company began its London extension from Nottinghamshire to Marylebone. He left on 14th September 1899 and arrived in New York on 4th June 1900 where he began work at the West Side Foundry as an iron-moulder. At some stage during his working life, he lost three fingers from his left hand. By the time that Flora May married John Samuel Hart on 13th September 1902, she was living at 29 Shakespeare Street, Bootle, Lancashire.

If the marriage of his elder sister Beatrice to Harry Ord Thompson on 24th December 1898 had shown Walter the door to photography, the marriage of his younger sister Flora to John Samuel Hart on 13th September 1902 opened it. The two brothers-in-law, Walter and John, went into partnership as tailors at 62 Liverpool Road, Great Crosby, but soon exchanged fabrics for photography. They began to learn the business of photography together.

Great Crosby   By 1905, W. P. Collier had become a proficient photographer, as proved by his pictures of the train crash at Hall Road, a station on the Liverpool-Southport line, less than two miles from his shop. At 4.37 p.m. on Thursday 27th July 1905, a Southport-bound express train collided with an empty local service, resulting in 20 deaths and 48 injuries. Both drivers jumped clear before the impact and survived. He soon arrived at the scene of the accident and produced several graphic photographs of the mangled carriages, one of which was published in the Liverpool Echo on the following day. He later returned to take a picture of a forlorn carriage, now shrouded under a huge tarpaulin, which was published in the Formby Times on Saturday 5th August. Another of his pictures, enlarged and carefully titled, was sent to King Edward VII and Queen Alexandra, who had been "greatly shocked" by the terrible railway accident.

Formby   Walter was the last of the three photographers to get married. He was living "over the shop" at 62 Liverpool Road when, on 26th December 1905, he married Catherine Florence Poynor, a Bootle girl of Catholic background, describing himself as a photographer on his marriage certificate. Six months later, during the summer of 1906, the couple moved to 14 Formby Street, Formby, joining John Samuel Hart and his family who had made Formby their home a few months earlier and were living just around the corner at 9 Raven Meols Lane. Their new house was in a row of spacious semi-detached properties, a stone's throw from Formby station, and two of their three children were born there, Florence Muriel on 12th August 1906 and Edith Millicent on 25th July 1907. Walter duly set about producing a collection of postcards of Formby and the surrounding area, including Freshfield and Altcar, and was a frequent visitor to Formby station, which lay at the north end of Formby Street.

From the day of her marriage, Catherine found herself the object of increasing family pressure. She came from a Catholic family but had married a non-Catholic in the local Register Office. The first two of their three children, Florence Muriel (1906) and Edith Millicent (1907) were born within eleven months of each other at 14 Formby Street. Harry Ord Thompson was keen that his two brothers-in-law should join him in his new commercial enterprise on Tyneside. Her father John Thomas Poynor died on 16th August 1909 and shortly afterwards her mother Annie began to suffer from a chronic neurological paralysis, requiring constant nursing care, which would lead to her death on 15th April 1911.

Newcastle upon Tyne   It had probably been arranged that Walter and John would join Harry shortly after he was established at 202 Portland Road in the spring of 1908 and Walter would not allow family circumstances to compromise this commitment. He left for Newcastle as Catherine and her two young children moved to 11 Browning Street, Bootle, the home of her parents. Among the earliest postcards that can be attributed to W. P. Collier, as he began working with H. O. Thompson, is a printed postcard of Harbottle Castle, carrying his distinctive titling and posted on 24th June 1909. The fact that the trees are in full foliage suggests that the original picture, which was also published as a real photographic postcard, was taken in the summer of 1908. The period between late spring and early autumn was the season for travelling and taking photographs, which would be processed as postcards over the winter months and put on sale the following spring. Even lighting was essential for producing a good postcard: too much bright sunshine would produce a negative of high contrast which might prove difficult to process. To around this time may be ascribed a postcard that Walter sent from Woodburn to his wife Catherine who was living "care of" 11 Browning Street, Bootle. *Hope you got letter and are all keeping well. Love to you and children and all at home. P.* Percy rather than Walter was the name used by the family.

On 15th September 1910, Catherine gave birth to her third child, John Percival, at 11 Hemans Street, the home of her brother Albert and his wife Mary, a couple of streets away from her mother's house. Shortly after registering his birth at Bootle on 22nd October 1910, she joined Walter at 106 Chillingham Road, Newcastle.

Family Tragedy   Their reunion was short-lived. On 20th December 1910, Catherine was taken to the Royal Victoria Infirmary, Newcastle upon Tyne, where she died of heart failure. Walter was present at her death. Baby John was barely 13 weeks old. Earlier in the year, on 26th January 1910, Catherine had expressed concerns about her heart when she wrote to Sarah Reid, a friend of her sister Annie and a fellow schoolmistress, who later boarded with the Poynor family. It is not known the extent to which emotional stress had contributed to her condition but it was a question that would haunt Walter for the rest of his life, forcing him to concede, in his darkest hours, that he might have put photography before family. Catherine was buried in Heaton Cemetery, Newcastle upon Tyne, but was also commemorated on her parents' memorial in the Catholic Church of St. Peter and St. Paul, Great Crosby. Father, mother and daughter had all died within three years of each other between 1909 and 1911.

Despite the death of his wife, Walter carried on with his commitment to build up the commercial side of the postcard market for Harry. His passion for pictures remained undiminished. The 1911 census, taken on 2nd April, records that Walter was staying at the Temperance Hotel in Whalton, which he was using as a base for taking pictures of the village and neighbourhood, including Gallowhill Hall, near Bolam, which was the subject of several postcard publishers. The same census records that his sister, Flora May Hart, was "in temporary charge of Mr. Collier's house" at 106 Chillingham Road, which consisted of her husband, their own two children and the three children of Walter, including baby John.

Such a situation could not be sustained. The children were divided among their maternal aunts, with Muriel and Edith going to live in Bootle with Annie Edith Poynor. Annie was a spinster schoolmistress at the local Catholic School and brought the girls up accordingly. Baby John was sent to live in Farnworth, near Bolton, with Marguerite Poynor, a schoolmistress, who had married Joseph Brown on 14th September 1908. The couple already had a young baby, Frederick Gerard Brown, the first of their three sons, who was born on 19th July 1909.

Within 18 months of his children being relocated, Walter had left 106 Chillingham Road and had become an independent photographer once again. Family tradition recalls that Harry gave Walter £100 to help him set up his own business in Bellingham, the capital of the North Tyne and a popular rendezvous for increasing numbers of visitors, who would come by road or rail for the shops, a stroll or picnic on the banks of the picturesque Hareshaw Burn, or for their holidays. On Sunday 14th May 1911, however, the village had been the scene of a major flood when a freak thunderstorm caused the Hareshaw Burn to burst its banks and spread destruction in its wake. It was a young Bellingham photographer, Roderick James Thompson, who had been brave enough to produce a series of photographs of the flood as it surged through the village. Harry Ord Thompson was one of several photographers who produced a series of postcards of the aftermath of the flood, though it was probably Walter who travelled to Bellingham to take the original photographs. A view of the damaged houses, taken by Elliott & Thomas of Hexham, appeared in the following edition of the Hexham Courant.

Bellingham   With the financial and professional support of Harry, Walter was established in Bellingham by the spring of 1913 and was renting a former butcher's shop in Lock-Up Lane. The front of the shop was small but it had a large area to the rear, originally used for meat preparation and storage, which had a good water supply, essential for washing photographs and postcards. He sold tobacco, sweets, stationery and general goods, which proved popular with locals and the increasing number of tourists who would visit Bellingham. Not that photography was forgotten. Within a few weeks of opening his shop, he was taking pictures of Bellingham and the surrounding area, including two local events, the Falstone Show on 9th October 1913 and the visit of Captain G. W. Dawes in his biplane to Otterburn Hall on 25th-27th October 1913. Walter soon became a familiar figure as he travelled along the quiet roads of rural Northumberland, with his large, old-fashioned half-plate camera strapped to his back, tripod and all.

Harry tended to take photographs of villages that would be sold in local shops or post offices. The bespoke pictures that he took of individuals had no titling except for a four-figure reference number, usually ending with a B for bespoke, signifying that they were not for commercial production as postcards. Walter, however, would produce postcards of almost every village, farm or house that he passed on his journeys. Some of these, such as those of Hadrian's Wall, were sold in their thousands. Others had a more limited circulation but they satisfied his ambition of having a picture of every location within a forty-mile radius of Bellingham. In this respect, he was like Francis Frith (1822-1898) who undertook to photograph every town and village in the United Kingdom. Initially, he took the photographs himself but, in due course, hired people to help him and established the firm of Francis Frith & Co. of Reigate, which published over 300,000 photographs and sold them to tourists as souvenir view cards and later as postcards. Within a few years, over two thousand shops throughout the United Kingdom were selling his pictures.

On opening his shop in Bellingham, Walter was free to take whatever pictures he wanted, no matter what the likely financial return, as he had done at the beginning of his photographic career in Great Crosby and Formby. He put pictures before profit and some of his pictures, perhaps the most rewarding, would have been sold as postcards in very small numbers. Each glass plate, however, was kept in a paper envelope, with the number of copies carefully recorded. After he returned to being an independent photographer, he took his own pictures of the locations that he and John had visited for Harry, several years earlier.

The declaration of War on 4th August 1914 did not affect Walter immediately except that he took a series of pictures of the local volunteers as they paraded in Bellingham before leaving for the Front. In fact, the years between 1913 and 1917 saw him producing the core of the "Collier Collection" of photographs of Bellingham and the surrounding area, including the North Tyne Valley, Upper Coquetdale and Redesdale. Bellingham, indeed, like Allendale, was seen as a tourist destination and was particularly popular for its shops, especially during the summer, when the influx of visitors often led to a shortage of accommodation. The Hexham Courant of 11th September 1915 reported that 500 or 600 visitors had been staying in and around Bellingham on a recent occasion, which was testimony enough to the popularity of the neighbourhood as a health resort. The summer season in Bellingham, however, was short and Walter needed the sales of stationery, tobacco, sweets and general goods to carry him over the long winter months when the numbers of visitors and the sales of postcards were reduced.

In addition to running his own business, Walter, who could always tell a good piece of cloth, may have assisted at least one of the Bellingham tailors & drapers, Richard Pigg (1864-1915), William John Waugh (1857-1943) or Thomas Hedley (1876-1955) as, upon enlistment in the Army on 26th May 1917, he gave his occupation as a draper's assistant (temporary). One local draper had complained to the Appeals Board that he could not afford to lose a vital member of staff who had been called up for military service. His appeal was rejected.

Royal Flying Corps   On 26th May 1917, Walter enlisted in the army and on 14th July 1917 was transferred to the Royal Flying Corps as an aerial photographer, whose duties included the taking and processing of many thousands of pictures of the German military dispositions. His elder daughter Muriel, aged 11, who was living in Bootle, was named as his next of kin. The Royal Flying Corps became the Royal Air Force on 1st April 1918. After he was discharged on 10th March 1919, he returned to Bellingham and quickly acquired three local offices, showing the regard in which he was held. He became secretary of the Bellingham branch of the Comrades of the Great War, registrar of marriages for the Bellingham area and branch manager of the Ministry of Labour Employment Exchange. He also served as secretary of the Bellingham Burns Club and proposed several toasts at the annual Burns Night ceremonies. He liked nothing more, however, than to enjoy his pipe and a pint with his friends in the Rose & Crown in Manchester Square. This was literally his local as Walter lived in an apartment next door before moving in 1927 to the elevated cottage of Pinch Me Near, a mile from Bellingham, which had fine views of the village and the North Tyne Valley. His children were frequent visitors but it was in 1923 that Edith came to live in Bellingham with her father and helped with the developing & printing side of the business until her marriage to George Roland Heppell, an engineering mechanic, on 7th June 1930. She would still help out, however, if needed, and became a talented photographer herself.

Return to Photography   The First World War changed the availability of many of the traditional postcards. Many black and white photographs, taken in Great Britain, had been sent to Germany to be printed as colour postcards. The printer and his printing press had been producing pictures for hundreds of years before the photographer and his darkroom and the printer could produce pictures in colour and not just in black and white. Germany had a high reputation for its advanced standards of colour printing but the Great War put an end to this trade and the attractive postcards that had been produced in the first decade of the 20th century were no longer on sale. Walter, however, carried on regardless with his pictures of rural Northumberland and would soon find that the postcard market was changing in his favour. After he returned from military service, he found that there was a growing demand for good quality topographical postcards among the increasing numbers of tourists who took to the road and wanted a reliable record of their travels. Even in the hands of a good amateur photographer, buying a postcard of a favourite location was a safer option than taking a photograph, which might or might not "come out" after being developed and printed.

It is only in 1934, however, that Walter uses "photographer" instead of "stationer" as his entry in the Kelly directory. This is not surprising as it was the stationer rather than the photographer who sold postcards but it may also have been out of regard for local photographer and entrepreneur Roderick James Thompson (1890-1982).

For several years before Walter arrived in Bellingham, Roddy, as he was known, had been producing fine studio portraits, where he was skilled in the use of flash, and taking some excellent photographs of local events, such as amateur dramatics, leek shows and the Bellingham Flood on 14th May 1911. He enlisted in the Royal Air Force on 25th June 1918, stating his occupation as a motor mechanic and, on his return, started the first bus service in Bellingham. The Kelly directories of 1914 and 1921 record him as a photographer. He saw his future, however, in the motor car and later took over the garage of his father, John Thompson, which he ran until his retirement in 1966. Ironically, after the death of W. P. Collier on 7th September 1937, Roddy turned his premises into a fish and chip shop. Another local photographer was Robert William Huntington (1881-1973) who became postmaster of Bellingham after the death of Margaret Horner on 17th February 1914. Described as a postmaster and photographer in the Kelly directory of 1914, he migrated to Australia with his family on 3rd December 1920, before settling in New Zealand, where he died, aged 91, on 7th June 1973. Neither of these two Bellingham photographers produced postcards on a commercial scale.

Many thought that the postcards of W. P. Collier were too good to be posted and put them straight into their postcard albums. Many of his photographs were used in local guidebooks or estate catalogues, such as those printed for the sale of the 11,816-acre Kidland Estate in 1923 and 1925. He never put his name on his postcards. Only the presentation folders that he used for portraits or pictures of special occasions, such as weddings, carry his name. Not that he had much need to advertise. *Everyone knew Mr. Collier and Mr. Collier knew everyone.* Even Lock-Up Lane, where he had his shop, was known as Collier's Lane.

Legacy   As the capital of the North Tyne, Bellingham always had at least one photographer in residence. Walter Percy Collier, however, stood out as the most prolific of at least five local photographers: John Brown Richardson (1847-1896), Henry Waitt (1862-1904) and Eliza Jane Waitt (1864-1930), Robert William Huntington (1881-1973), Roderick James Thompson (1890-1982) and Edward Dobbin (1897-1980). On 20th October 1927, Edward Dobbin married Jane Charlton Smith, the niece of Bellingham newsagent and stationer Elizabeth Mary Smith (1869-1952) and found that he had gained not only a wife but also the shop of her aunt. He quickly expanded the business and his name appears in the 1929 Kelly directory as a *newsagent, stationer, tobacconist, fancy goods, patent medicine vendor, china & glass & wireless accessories dealer.* After the death of W. P. Collier, Ted, as he was known, acquired many of the glass plates that Walter had taken of Bellingham. Indeed, the plates were among the few items to survive the closure of his shop. As well as reprinting many of these plates, Ted, who was a keen photographer, used to travel around the area in his Riley car and produce his own postcards, mainly of Redesdale, the North Tyne Valley and Bellingham.

In a career spanning almost 35 years, the last 25 of which were spent in Bellingham, W. P. Collier produced thousands of high quality black and white postcards, easily recognised by their distinctive titling, whether in Lancashire or Northumberland. After his death on 7th September 1937, his shop was dismantled and many of his photographic plates were given to the shops and post offices that had sold his postcards. Many of the plates have survived. A collection of a dozen plates was found in a shop in Newcastleton in Liddesdale and includes views of two planned villages, Newcastleton, created as a weaving centre, and Riccarton, created as a railway junction for the Waverley Route from Edinburgh to Carlisle and the North British Railway from Hexham to Riccarton. Another collection of over five dozen plates came into the possession of John Robinson (1926-2005) of Falstone and consists of views of the North Tyne Valley, including many of the farms now submerged beneath Kielder Water and the remote village of Plashetts, created in the 19th century to house the miners at Plashetts Colliery.

Northumberland was a picture postcard paradise where W. P. Collier could carefully compose the pictures that he would sell from local outlets or at his little shop in Bellingham. All of his postcards and photographs were contact printed from glass plates and have outstanding definition. The legacy of the Collier Collection is a definitive view of Northumberland in the period between two World Wars.

Edith, John and Muriel Collier outside the shop
of their father in Bellingham c. 1922

Comrades of the Great War

Within days of the declaration of war on 4th August 1914, the ladies of Bellingham (and other local communities) were sending home comforts to the local Territorials at the Front. Shirts were particularly needed, or the money to buy them, and many ladies set about knitting socks, as individuals and in groups. Territorials did not get these supplied by the Government. W. P. Collier arranged for a letter of thanks to be published in the Hexham Courant of 3rd May 1919 for Mrs. J. P. Elliot of Holmwood, the secretary of the Bellingham Ladies' Working Party. Margaret Scott Elliot (1866-1933) was the wife of John Peter Elliot (1857-1920) who succeeded his father as a respected and dedicated doctor at Bellingham. After her husband died, aged 63, of pneumonia on 22nd October 1920, Margaret returned to her native Roxburghshire, where she died, aged 66, on 8th April 1933.

Dear Madam, At the first general meeting since the formation of a Post in connection with the Comrades of the Great War, the feeling was expressed that we should in some way convey our sense of appreciation to the Ladies' Working Party, and all who in any way supported them in their efforts to brighten the lives of the boys who have served in the army. Men in all parts of the world and in all ranks of the service participated in the benefits of your labours, and the letters and cards we sent in acknowledgement very feebly and inadequately expressed the real sense of our gratitude we felt towards your workers. Nothing was left undone to ensure our comfort and well-being. We were regaled with tobacco, cigarettes, chocolates, sweets, cakes and Oxo, and, at Christmas time, we had your delicious homemade plum puddings. Over and above these, you distributed among us more than 10,000 articles of underwear, gloves, etc, etc. Such effort must have called for great self-sacrifice, both in time, money and material, and we want you to know that your endeavours on our behalf touched our hearts and many times helped us to stiffen a lip and stifle a grouse. Such gifts were often very opportune, particularly when the army "menu" was reduced to "bully and biscuits" and the underwear reached us when the remnant of all we possessed had accumulated a motive power almost to enable it to a route march on its own account, to say nothing of the increased comfort of homemade woollens in biting weather, as experienced with army issue, or sometimes no issue at all. We know we are also bespeaking the thoughts of our comrades, who are retained in the army to ensure the acceptance of a just and lasting peace, as also of those heroic men who have given their lives for the cause. Since our inception, you have further contributed to the "Comrades" £15 from your funds and tea money. We also beg to acknowledge, through you, the receipt of 15s. each from Mr. George and Mr. Robert Foster. In order to give a wider publicity to our expression of gratitude, you will pardon our taking the liberty of publishing a copy of this letter in the local press. Believe us to be, Madam, Yours, most sincerely, (signed) W. S. Telfer (Captain), W. P. Collier (Secretary).

Obituary of Walter Percy Collier
20th July 1875 - 7th September 1937

Covered by a Union Jack, the remains of Mr. Walter Percy Collier were taken to their last resting-place in Bellingham Cemetery on Saturday afternoon 11th September for interment in the presence of a large gathering of mourners.

He had resided in the Border Town since about 1910. He served his apprenticeship with Messrs. Hutton, drapers, of Newcastle, but later took up photography in partnership with his brother-in-law, Mr. H. O. Thompson, of Newcastle. He developed the commercial side of the business and built up an extensive wholesale and retail trade. He was one of the best-known photographers of the North and beyond the Borders, and his postcard views were obtainable over a wide district.

He saw service with the Royal Air Force during the Great War and took a keen interest in the British Legion and the local Burns Club. He was Registrar of Marriages from 1920. Greatly interested in the Roman Wall, he paid many visits to that great memorial of the Roman Occupation and his collection of views of Housesteads and of other stretches of the Wall is considered one of the finest in the North.

In his death, Bellingham had lost a much-respected townsman. When people first met Mr. Collier, they were struck by his whimsical humour and attractive personality. He was a man who seemed to have tasted bitter experiences but he was determined not to let them embitter him. He had found out the weaknesses of humankind and seemed to have resolved to master them in himself. Thus his quiet strength came to be respected. The lines of suffering, mental as well as physical, all too clearly shown in his face, were evidence that life had not been easy but, whatever blows he had received, he was "game" to the very end of the struggle.

He had started his life on an entirely different career. He was led to take up photography in such a way that he looked upon it as a definite calling. None would deny that, in that calling, he was faithful. The talent given him he cultivated and used with utmost fidelity to the great advantage of the neighbourhood.

As the arrival of the coffin was awaited at Bellingham, the night before, a vivid rainbow arched the sky – a symbol from time immemorial of the Eternal Mercy.

Hexham Courant Saturday 18th September 1937

Jane Chisnall outside her shop at Great Crosby
W. P. Collier autumn 1903

Royal Court Pierrots at Blundellsands
W. P. Collier posted 10th July 1904

Hall Road Train Disaster near Great Crosby
W. P. Collier 27th July 1905

Hall Road Train Disaster near Great Crosby
W. P. Collier 28th July 1905

Formby Station, looking towards Southport
W. P. Collier c. 1906

Formby Street, looking towards Formby Station
W. P. Collier c. 1906

Alt Cottage, home of John Johnson, veteran of the Crimean War
W. P. Collier c. 1906

Altcar Camp, opened 28th July 1860 as a rifle training range
W. P. Collier c. 1906

Sheep pens at the Falstone Show
W. P. Collier 9th October 1913

Sheep pens at the Falstone Show
W. P. Collier 9th October 1913

Dated postcard of W. P. Collier
25th - 27th October 1913

Dated postcard of W. P. Collier
25th - 27th October 1913

Redesdale Artillery Practice Camp
W. P. Collier c. 1914

Officers' Mess, Birdhopecraig Hall
W. P. Collier c. 1914

Chollerton war memorial, unveiled 21st August 1920, and St. Giles Church
W. P. Collier c. 1920

Wark war memorial, unveiled 26th March 1921, and village green
W. P. Collier c. 1921

A shepherd driving his sheep at Rochester
W. P. Collier c. 1925

A soldier driving his tank at Rochester
W. P. Collier c. 1925

Chollerford Station, renamed Humshaugh 1919, closed 1956
W. P. Collier c. 1915

Tarset Station, North British Railway, closed 1956
W. P. Collier c. 1915

Bellingham Station, looking north, closed 1956
W. P. Collier c. 1920

Bellingham Station, with North Tyne added 1926
W. P. Collier c. 1926

Dawston Viaduct and Saughtree Station, closed 1956
W. P. Collier c. 1930

Riccarton Junction Station, closed 1969
W. P. Collier c. 1930

King George V Silver Jubilee
W. P. Collier 6th May 1935

King George V Silver Jubilee
W. P. Collier 6th May 1935

MATTHEW AUTY AND THE AUTY COLLECTION OF PHOTOGRAPHIC NEGATIVES.

By H. O. Thompson.

Read on 25th March, 1942.

The late Matthew Auty, like many other of our more successful professional photographers, was not originally trained in that business but went into it from the amateur ranks. He served his apprenticeship as a tobacconist, and as a comparatively young man had a business of his own in a long and narrow lean-to shop which some of our older members may recollect, on the road from Tynemouth to North Shields beside the present Tynemouth Goods Station, which was then a passenger station. When the railway from North Shields was continued to Cullercoats and Whitley, and the present Tynemouth station established, Mr. Auty removed into new premises on the bend running from the new station into Front Street. It was during these times that his passion for photography developed, and he used to take photographs of views of Tynemouth and that locality, Cullercoats fisher people, and so forth, for sale in his shop ; and at the same period he became a member of the old Newcastle upon Tyne and Northern Counties Photographic Association—a body which ranked high among Photographic societies in those days. It may be of interest if I quote the names of the Council for 1895, which incidentally was the year of Mr. Auty's death. President— J. Pattison Gibson. Vice-Presidents—M. Auty, W. Parry, J. S. B. Bell, J. Hedley Robinson. Council—W. Errington Cowan, J. E. Goold, George Hall, J. J. Kirkwood, Edgar G. Lee, T. O. Mawson, Captain Sayers, G. L. Snowball, John Watson, L. Williamson. Treasurer—F. Park. Secretary— James Brown. Assistant Secretary—W. Parker Brewis. The meetings of the Association were held in the Central Exchange Art Gallery, now a thing of the past.

It was through his membership of this Association and his growing friendship with our member the late Mr. J. P. Gibson that Mr. Auty was encouraged to launch into photography as his principal vocation, although he still kept up a connection with the tobacco trade and ran, right up to the time of his death, a tobacco business in King Street, South Shields.

He acquired a double-fronted house in Front Street Tynemouth, and effected a good deal in the way of altera,

tions to adapt the premises for the running of a photographic business. A large Studio was built in the garden at the back—this, being on the ground floor, was both novel and advantageous, as there was no stair to climb in order to reach it ; but as Mr. Auty was shrewd enough to recognise that landscape and view publication work was his strong suit rather than studio portraiture, he employed an operator for this latter and devoted himself to the task of building up year after year the series of negatives of local subjects which have now, by the generosity of their last owner, come into the possession of our Society. Somehow it seems to me, looking back over the space of more than half a century, that in the summer periods of those days we were favoured with a much larger proportion of really fine weather than we get now ; at any rate Mr. Auty would set off each summer to some new pasture and come back with a series of negatives, taken generally under most favourable conditions of light and weather and of a quality superior to anything previously on the market. A good salesman, he never experienced any difficulty in finding shopkeepers who were only too pleased to be supplied, and in some places he would arrange for more or less exclusive agencies. Those were the days when the picture post-card had not come in and so adversely affected the view-publishing business ; and year by year the collection was added to—Durham, Gilsland and Brampton, Alnwick, Warkworth, Bamburgh and the Farne Islands, Holy Island, Richmond (Yorks.), Bellingham and the North Tyne, and so forth, as demand arose and work could be taken in hand. This led to a need for increased accommodation ; and about 1892 Mr. Auty purchased the adjoining premises, No. 21, Front Street, and adapted them as work rooms.

Up to the latter part of 1894 Mr. Auty used personally to go round and keep in touch with customers, booking up their requirements and freshening his series of negatives ; but towards the close of that year the heart trouble which was gradually bearing upon him became so bad that he had to enter a nursing home, and he passed away on July 29th, 1895, at the early age of 45. The business which he had founded and which had been steadily progressing under his guidance carried on for a while by its own momentum ; but eventually the publication side and the collection of negatives were taken over by the late Mr. Godfrey Hastings, of Whitley Bay. ; and it is gratifying to know that the series of negatives, and especially the earlier ones taken by Mr. Auty himself, are now in the safe keeping of our Society, whose thanks are due to all who have contributed to bring this about.

If I may conclude by going somewhat into technical matters; I would say that in Mr. Auty's work he was never satisfied unless he had secured a negative at least as good but preferably better than anything of the same subject already in existence ; yet some of his working methods were decidedly original and occasionally unorthodox. He used to contend that the man was not born who could invariably give a plate the correct exposure and, as under-exposure was of no use whatever, he used to expose his interiors very fully indeed and then develop the plate slowly and tentatively. Some interiors he took of the Keep were secured by setting up the camera on a Saturday afternoon, leaving it exposing all day Sunday, and shutting it off on the Monday morning. Despite all this, his negatives were of an extraordinarily even quality and standard of excellence. He was one of the first photographers to succeed in securing negatives of lightning flashes—a thing which has been accomplished often enough since, but wasthen a novelty. Frequently when taking interiors of such places as Durham Cathedral he would use instead of a tripod a pair of steps, fitted so that three cameras could be placed upon them—a 12" x 10", a whole-plate, and a half-plate ; and thus secure at the same time three original negatives in different sizes. For the same purpose when working out of doors he would use a 12" x 10" camera for which he had adaptor backs for whole-plate and half-plate slides, so that by changing his lenses he would get three successive exposures on the one subject but in different sizes, which meant that the prints were all made from original negatives, not from reproductions. He also evolved a method of dry-mounting photographs, many years in advance of the present shellac-tissue system.

Gifted with more than the average store of energy, and deeply in love with his work, he never spared himself ; and the long hours he used to put in both at his photographic business and his other activities, coupled with his keen interest in swimming, at which he was an expert, doubtless told upon him in the long run and aggravated if it did not actually give rise to the heart trouble from which he died at, as already mentioned, the age of 45.

SHISHA PANGMA

The alpine-style first ascent
of the South-West Face

To Jean and Sarah

DOUG SCOTT & ALEX MacINTYRE

SHISHA PANGMA
The alpine-style first ascent
of the South-West Face

Originally titled *The Shishapangma Expedition*

BÂTON WICKS · LONDON
THE MOUNTAINEERS · SEATTLE

also by Doug Scott
BIG WALL CLIMBING
HIMALAYAN CLIMBER

in preparation
ALEX MacINTYRE'S CLIMBS
compiled by John Porter

The Shishapangma Expedition was first published in Great Britain in 1984 (Granada, London).
republished privately by Doug Scott 1994.
Copyright © by Doug Scott and Jean MacIntyre, 1984 and 1994

The book, retitled *Shisha Pangma – The alpine-style first ascent of the South-West Face,*
is published in Great Britain and America in 2000
by Bâton Wicks, London and The Mountaineers, Seattle.
Copyright © by Doug Scott and Jean MacIntyre

All trade enquiries in Great Britain, Europe and the Commonwealth (except Canada) to
Bâton Wicks Publications, c/o Cordee, 3a De Montfort Street, Leicester LE1 7HD

All trade enquiries in U.S.A. and Canada to
The Mountaineers • Books, 1001 SW Klickitat Way, Suite 201, Seattle, WA 98134

British Library Cataloguing in Publication Data
ISBN 1-898573-36-0 A catalogue record of this book is available in the British Library

United States Library of Congress Catalog Data
ISBN 0-89886-723-1 A catalog record of this book is available at the Library of Congress

Printed and bound in Great Britain by Butler and Tanner, Frome.

PUBLISHER'S NOTE

Shisha Pangma – The alpine-style first ascent of the South-West Face
is a retitled and adapted version of *The Shishapangma Expedition* (Granada,
London, 1984). The book was the first winner of the Boardman Tasker
Award for Mountain Literature*, and has since been an invaluable reference
source for those visiting the mountain. It was reprinted privately in 1994.

The peak has been variously named Gosainthan, Shishapangma,
Xixabangma but most publications have now settled on Shisha Pangma which
is the form used in the new title and other additions to this book.

Shisha Pangma is one of the most interesting and accessible of the 8000-
metre peaks. Its popularity as a mountaineering objective has greatly increased in recent years with the introduction of direct access from Nepal to
Tibet, eliminating the expensive approach via Beijing. Most expeditions concentrate on the routes using the original Chinese approach from the north but
a growing number of climbers are opting for the safer (albeit more technically
demanding) southern routes. The first expedition to the southern side, which
penetrated an unexplored valley and completed three major new climbs (including a route of descent), forms the exciting subject matter of this book.

In the earlier years there was some confusion about the heights, naming
and positions of the various summits of the mountain. MacIntyre and Scott,
on reaching the summit, and with clear conditions and time and energy to
spare, crossed most of the ridge between the Main and Central summits and
took valuable photographs, some of which are reproduced in this volume.
The uncertainties about the summits have now been resolved but their legacy
may have been that many climbers who considered that they were ascending
Shisha Pangma actually headed for Central Summit and settled for this lower
top when confronted with the difficulty of continuing to the true summit.
Recently Central Summit has become the main target for northern ascents
and it is understood that the Chinese authorities are issuing certificates to
Central Summit climbers stating that they have climbed the mountain – an
unfortunate development. That these trends are linked to the increased
commercialisation of the Northern Route is a further matter of concern.

The minority interest in such matters dictates that the original, monochrome
book is reprinted rather than a more elaborate new edition. However some

---

* In 1983 no prize was awarded. In 1984 the prize (to its full value) was awarded to the authors
of two books – *The Shishapangma Expedition* and *Living High* by Linda Gill.

5

critical improvements have been made for this edition. A chronicle of important expeditions to Shisha Pangma has been added, along with comprehensive lists of summit climbers, fatalities and an updated bibliography. Some maps have been adapted and there are new diagrams as well as eight pages of colour photos depicting the facets of the peak and its summits.*

Taken together these additions should add greatly to the understanding of this fascinating mountain, its topography, its difficulties and its dangers. They may also counteract the growing "obfuscation tendency" by some of those claiming ascents of this and other 8000m peaks (e.g. Cho Oyu and Broad Peak) where the final section of an ascent presents awkward problems that are convenient to ignore. The summit of a mountain is its highest point and, though the ascent of an individual route can quite properly be noted and respected, to claim a summit ascent when the party has stopped short of the highest point (often for sensible reasons) is both disruptive and unnecessarily misleading. A major attempt on a high peak is usually an achievement in itself, even in the event of failure. Sometimes a failure in difficult conditions is more memorable than a routine success. The greatest success of all is to return unscathed after skilfully negotiating the ascent and descent.

* Many of the photographs from the original book have since appeared in colour and in larger format in Doug Scott's *Himalayan Climber* (Diadem, 1992, reprinted by Bâton Wicks, 1997, also published in North America, France, Italy, Germany, Spain and Japan.)

ACKNOWLEDGEMENTS The original edition of the book made note of the numerous companies and organisations that gave the expedition greatly appreciated support. Help, advice and services linked to the production of the book were provided by: Michael Aris, Joan Barson, Anders Bolinder, John Cleare, Dr Jim Duff, Norman Dyhrenfurth, John Everard, George Greenfield, Dennis Hennek, Pamela Hopkinson, Tsunemichi Ikeda, K. Ishihara, Reinhold Messner, Nick Prescott, Rhona Prescott, Audrey Salkeld, George Scott, Jan Scott and Keiichi Yamada.

In this new version of the book Doug Scott, Jean MacIntyre and the publisher wish to record their thanks to the following: Xavier Eguskitza for bringing his encyclopaedic knowledge of Himalayan facts to assist with the new appendices and the bibliography; Lindsay Griffin for further historical and technical advice; Pavle Kozjek for photographs and information; Warwick Anderson, Tony Charlton, Frances Daltrey, Geoff Gabites, Lindsay Griffin, Brian Hall, Rhona Prescott and Keiichi Yamada for new photographs and other photographic help; Margaret Ecclestone, Ruth Ennemoser, Elizabeth Hawley, Sigi Hupfauer, Norbert Joos, Karl Kobler, Hajo Netzer, Renato Moro, Marcus Schmuck, Susi Steckbauer and Reinhold Messner for additional mountaineering information; *Mountain, High, The Iwa to Yuki, The Alpine Journal, The American Alpine Journal, Desnivel* and *The Himalayan Journal* as consistent and reliable sources of information.

To all of these people, companies and institutions, we offer our humble thanks.

Contents

New Colour Photographs for the 2000 edition

between pages 306 and 307

Photodiagrams

Maps and Diagrams

Corrigenda for the original book

The heights given for Main, Central and West Summits have all been remeasured – see note on p303; the caption on p197 should note the north-western summit; Keiichi Yamada should be credited on p260; on p262 Mustagh Ata was first climbed in 1956, not 1959; on p288 the third ascent party was led by Hans Mautner, not Dr Paul Alf; on p289 the movements of the Molomenqing team are confusing – refer to p304; in the index Shi Ching should be Shuh Ching and the Iranian Expedition noted in the Shisha Pangma entry actually attempted Everest.

Author's Note

DOUG: On the Friday before leaving for Tibet Alex MacIntyre and I signed a contract to write a book about our forthcoming expedition. On the Saturday we boarded the plane, secure in the knowledge that, with the publisher's advance on royalties, we had finally raised the funds for our estimated budget.

Here is the book, but first a brief explanation as this is, in some ways, an unusual expedition account. We had decided that the book should include contributions from all members of the team – Roger Baxter-Jones, Paul Braithwaite, Elaine Brook and Nick Prescott, but with Alex and myself writing the bulk of it. I opted to write something about the people who have lived around Shishapangma and the travellers, missionaries and mountaineers who have been in the vicinity of our mountain. Alex would write an account of the actual doings of our group, on the journey and on the mountain itself. On our return Alex gathered together his extensive diaries of the trip with several taped interviews with members of the team and went off to his little farmhouse on the flanks of Kinder Scout, just above the village of Hayfield in Derbyshire. More or less continuously, for two months, he wrote his account of our two-and-a-half-month trip.

This expedition was a hard one. We were for ever worried about an escalating budget, frustrated by red tape in Peking and again in Lhasa, exhausted by the journey across the plateau in an open truck which proceeded in its own dust cloud – in fact we could hardly relax at all until the last yak-man had turned his back on us at Base Camp. The team itself was an interesting mixture of people with, at one extreme, Alex – ambitiously directing his energies to ever-steeper Himalayan Faces with Tibet, for him, very much a secondary consideration – and, at the other, Elaine – whose reason for coming with us was to see Tibet and to spend time with the inhabitants, and with no ambition to climb high. The rest of us fell into place between.

It is incredible really that there are not more times of tension and displays of negative emotion on expeditions, considering that members spend two and a half months very much in one another's company, unable to walk away from any conflicts that may ensue and with no distractions to take the heat off. And as regards the mountaineering, as Alex joked, we would be hard-pressed to write an article for *Mountain Magazine* because on summit day everything went so well.

At twenty-eight years of age Alex was either the young upstart of the expedition or a breath of fresh energy; whichever he was, or was perceived to have been, he held strong views and, with his lawyer's logic and intelligence and his basic honesty, he could put them over well. It is no surprise that Alex has written provocatively – and deliberately so, to provoke the rest of us into adding our own comments.

Briefly, when Alex had completed his first draft of the manuscript he left for Nepal, where he lost his life on the huge South Face of Annapurna. Elaine's commentary was written before he died. Nick and Roger added theirs afterwards. I remember feeling indignation and injured pride at some of his statements and at first I hoped to persuade him to alter some of what he had said. But the more I read and the more I thought deeply of what he had written, the more I understood and the more I liked it. This was fortunate because, with his passing, it is now impossible to alter his text, apart from editing by Alex's friend Terry Mooney and by Mark Barty-King of Granada Publishing. My own comments are substantially those I noted immediately after first reading Alex's account and although, with different feelings for him now, my love and respect have moderated what I wrote earlier, I have tried not to eulogize; he would have hated that.

Diary of Events

1979
Mar   Nick Prescott first wrote to CMA general query on climbing in 'Chinese Himalays'
Aug   Approaches made through Thomas Cook's to CMA in Peking by Doug Scott (unaware of approaches made by N.J.P.)

1980
25 Mar Reply sent with application forms and 1st edn of reg's (N.J.P.)
27 Apr Application sent for Shishapangma for spring 1982 (asked for route from north but offered to try south if north booked up) (N.J.P.)
24 June Application accepted for "South Ridge" (?) route (Protocol set for summer 1981) (N.J.P.)
25 Aug Application for Everest and Shishapangma both in 1983, spring (D.S.)
26 August
26 Aug Peak fee paid to confirm booking (N.J.P.)

1981
April   Doug takes over Nick's application for Shishapangma (Doug, Georges Bettembourg, Paul Braithwaite and Jim Duff with Nick and Dr John Minors in support)
27 Apr Chinese agree to negotiate with Al Rouse when he is in Peking on Kongur Expedition
25 July Protocol signed in Peking (Al Rouse representing us)
2 Nov   Deposit paid (20 per cent of estimated costs to CMA as agreed in Protocol)

1982
2 Apr   Finally have enough money to go!
3 Apr   Depart Heathrow
4 Apr   Arrive in Peking (via Rawalpindi)
5–7 Ap Negotiations with CMA over costs
8 Apr   Fly to Cheng Dhu and buy most of food
9 Apr   Fly to Lhasa
10 Apr Drive Lhasa to Shigatse
12 Apr Drive Shigatse to Zegar
14 Apr Drive Zegar to Nyalam
17 Apr Yaks arrive in Nyalam
21 Apr Alex and Doug reach site for Base Camp
22 Apr Doug descends to Nyalam to sort out food and liaison officer
24 Apr Gear and full party (excluding LO) arrive in Base Camp
28 Apr Advance Base set up by Paul, Alex and Roger
1 May   Doug and Alex have to go down valley to argue with LO

4 May   Full party leave Advance Base to climb on Nyanang Ri (Nick and Paul retreat)
5 May   Elaine retreats from 19,000 ft
10 May Paul leaves for Britain; storm
12 May Storm
13 May Storm
14 May Storm
15 May Doug, Roger, Alex and Nick to Advance Base; high winds
16 May Same party on up to establish 'Castle Camp' on ridge beneath Pungpa Ri couloir; Elaine leaves for Dingri
17–19 May Doug, Roger and Alex climb Pungpa Ri (1st Ascent)
22–23 May Nick goes up to Advance Base and tries to solo Ice Tooth on the second day – gets part way up and retreats back to Advance Base where Doug and Wu arrive
24 May Doug, Roger, Alex and Nick to Castle Camp
        Shishapangma to bottom of route and go up to 1st bivouac at 19,500 ft
26 May Nick back to Castle Camp and Doug, Roger and Alex on up S.W. Face; bivouac at 23,000 ft, bottom of snow pod
27 May Bivouac at 25,000 ft part way up snow pod
28 May Up to couloir and along S.E. Ridge to reach the summit at two pm; bivouacked at 24,900 ft part way down S.E. Ridge
29 May Descent to Castle Camp, met by Nick
30 May Cleared Castle Camp and down to Base Camp; yaks waiting to take us down to village
31 May Nick and Nyima dismantle Advance Base; packing up Base Camp
1 June Leave Base Camp at 1.30; reach Smaug's Lair at six pm
2 June Nyalam: Communist Youth Fête in progress
3 June Drive to Shigatse, lunching at Zegar on the way (meet Adrian Gordon and Charlie Clarke and hear about accident on Everest)
4 June Rest day; telegrams sent to UK
5 June Drive to Lhasa via Gyangtse
6 June Visit Sera Monastery and Jo Khang Temple (Dalai Lama's birthday)
7 June Lhasa–Cheng Dhu flight
8 June Cheng Dhu–Peking flight
9   Negotiations with Chinese
11 June Leave Peking for home
12 June London

11

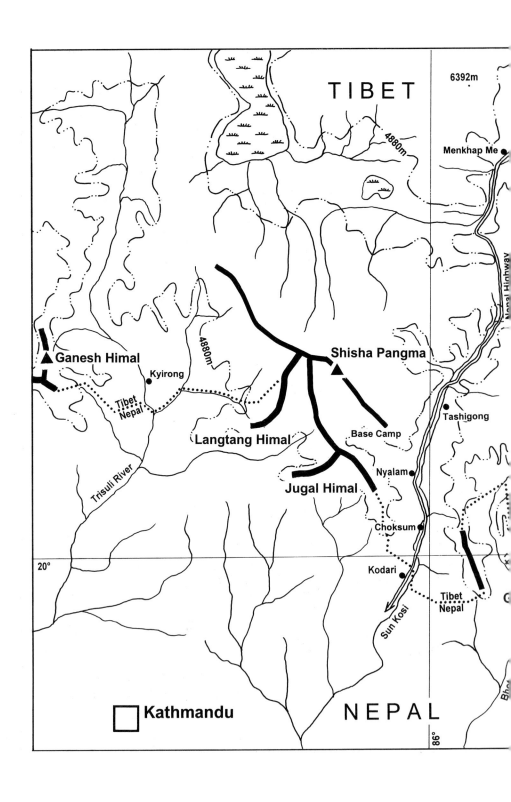

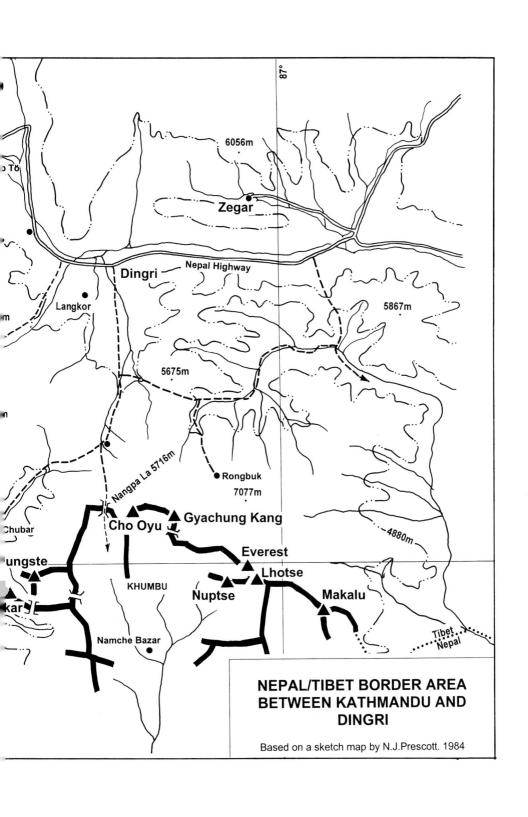

NEPAL/TIBET BORDER AREA BETWEEN KATHMANDU AND DINGRI

Based on a sketch map by N.J.Prescott. 1984

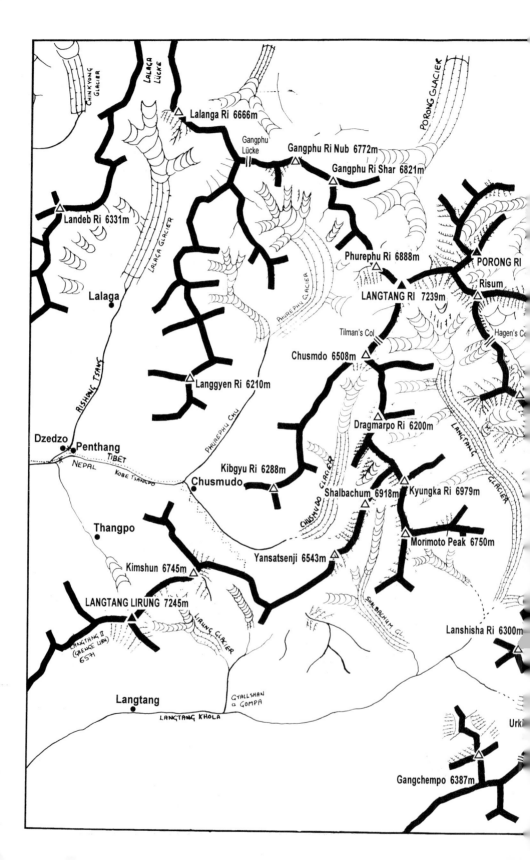

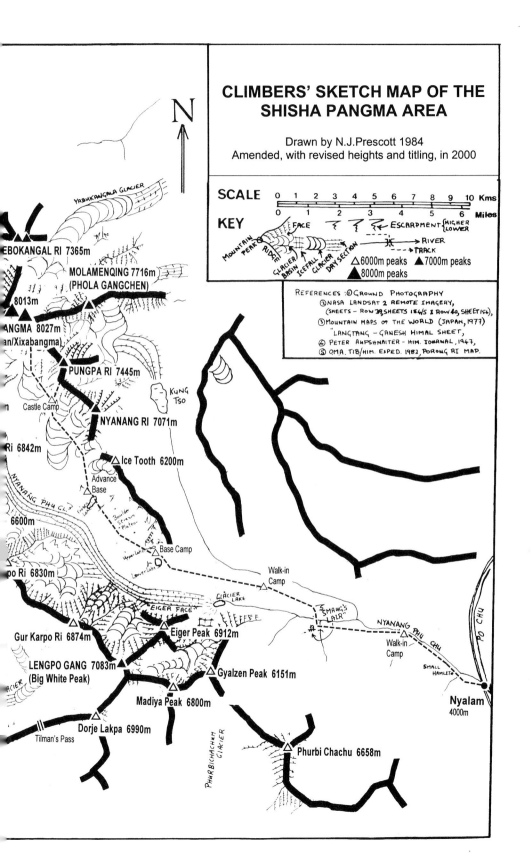

CLIMBERS' SKETCH MAP OF THE SHISHA PANGMA AREA

Drawn by N.J.Prescott 1984
Amended, with revised heights and titling, in 2000

SCALE

0 1 2 3 4 5 6 7 8 9 10 Kms
0 1 2 3 4 5 6 Miles

KEY

FACE   ESCARPMENT {HIGHER LOWER}
MOUNTAIN PEAK   RIDGE   RIVER
GLACIER BASIN   ICEFALL   GLACIER   DRY SECTION   TRACK
△6000m peaks ▲7000m peaks
▲8000m peaks

REFERENCES : ① GROUND PHOTOGRAPHY
② NASA LANDSAT 2 REMOTE IMAGERY,
(SHEETS – ROW 39 SHEETS 154/5 & ROW 40, SHEET 156),
③ MOUNTAIN MAPS OF THE WORLD (JAPAN, 1977)
"LANGTANG – GANESH HIMAL SHEET,
④ PETER AUFSHNAITER – HIM. JOURNAL, 1947,
⑤ QMA. TIB/HIM. EXPED. 1982. PORONG RI MAP.

YABUKANGALA GLACIER

EBOKANGAL RI 7365m

MOLAMENQING 7716m
(PHOLA GANGCHEN)

8013m

ANGMA 8027m
an/Xixabangma)

PUNGPA RI 7445m

KUNG TSO

Castle Camp

NYANANG RI 7071m

Ri 6842m

△Ice Tooth 6200m

NYANANG PHU GL.?

Advance Base

6600m

Boulder Strewn Plateau

Upper Lake

Base Camp

po Ri 6830m

Lower Lake

Walk-in Camp

GLACIER LAKE

EIGER FACE

SMAUG'S LAIR

NYANANG PHU CHU

PO CHU

Gur Karpo Ri 6874m

Eiger Peak 6912m

Walk-in Camp

LENGPO GANG 7083m
(Big White Peak)

△Gyalzen Peak 6151m

SMALL HAMLET

Madiya Peak 6800m

Nyalam
4000m

△Dorje Lakpa 6990m

Tilman's Pass

PHURBICHACHAM GLACIER

Phurbi Chachu 6658m

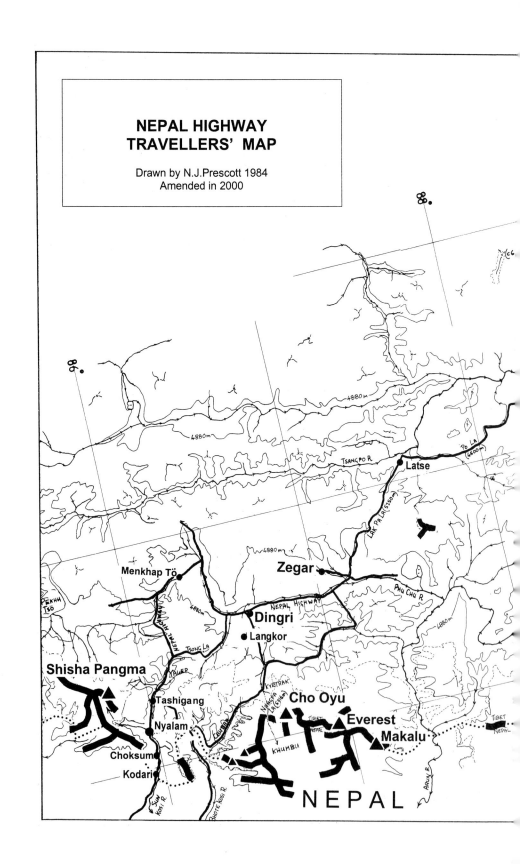

**NEPAL HIGHWAY
TRAVELLERS' MAP**

Drawn by N.J.Prescott 1984
Amended in 2000

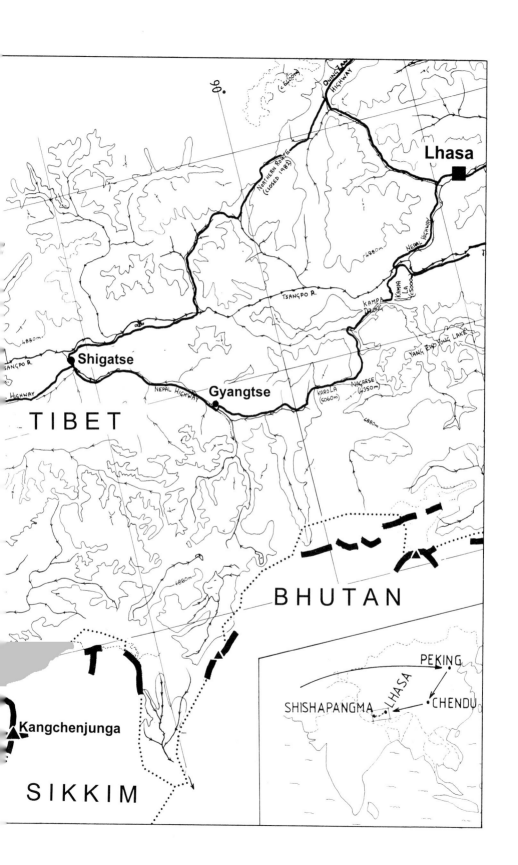

CHAPTER 1
Preparations

ALEX: In the spring of 1982 I managed to inveigle my way on to an expedition. It was going to Tibet, with permission to climb a mountain called Shishapangma, but I would have as readily gone to Harlem for what that expedition had to offer!

On its southern flanks this largely unknown, elusive, barely pronounceable mountain of uncertain altitude boasts a huge, spectacular, visually formidable (and consequently tantaliz-ingly attractive) mountain wall over two and a half kilometres high and twice as broad – an unclimbed, unvisited Alpine playground. To climb it became an ambition, but not just to climb it, we had to make the ascent with style, as light, as fast, as uncluttered as we dared, free from umbilical cords and logistics, with none of the traditional trappings of a Himalayan climb. The wall was the ambition; the style became the obsession.

The tale properly begins in the more obscure regions of the mind of a young man from Belfast. Nicholas John Prescott is a tall, eager, agitated Irishman possessed of fair, aquiline features, an irrepressible buoyancy, eyes framed in gold-rimmed spectacles, a brash and sometimes misplaced con-fidence and a method of speech that can reduce all but the most hard-nosed listener to a confused resignation. It was in the summer of 1979 that Nick formed the opinion that he would like to climb in China.

In the accessible big mountain ranges of the world, climb-ing is currently undergoing something of a mid-life crisis. The problem is that almost all mountains worth their salt have been climbed, sometimes by a whole handful of different routes. Virginity has fallen out of vogue with the virtual extinction of the unclimbed summit. It is increasingly difficult to maintain the pioneering spirit in the face of instant informa-tion, the need to book a peak well in advance of a projected expedition, the probable presence of a couple of other expedi-tions at the base camp (and more than likely swarming all over your mountain), and the multifarious trekking groups, cake shops, hotels and hippies on the approach routes. The mountaineer observes himself as part of an industry and, incongruously, it is the tourist industry he is a part of. He may be a somewhat more independent, long-term, purposeful tourist perhaps, but a tourist he is nevertheless. There, is, of course, much to be said for the newly evolving order. The mountains are readily and frequently accessible without the need for big sponsors or 'independent means'. Any number of interesting, inspiring and demanding climbs are there to be tackled and the skills synthesized from ever-increasing familiarity with high mountains allow the mountaineer, should he choose, even greater freedom to roam in an exhilarating environment. The possibility for adventure is no less – indeed for the individual the opportunity is probably greater than ever and, if you have forgotten the tin opener, there is a good chance of borrowing one from the expedition next door!

However, even the most hardened socialite can occasionally entertain a feeling of nostalgia for the pioneering spirit and a desire, just once, to avoid the queues and practise his sport amongst rarely climbed, uncluttered mountains in unmapped, infrequently visited valleys. Such promise was perceived in China. Add to that the sense of mystery, the attraction of the forbidden, almost mystical atmosphere engendered by the revolution and subsequent self-imposed isolation of that country, then the excitement generated by the possibility of this slumbering giant's unbolting a few of her doors is obvious. A billion untapped consumers, a thousand unclimbed summits – the mountaineering world took its place alongside the radio manufacturers, the watchmakers, the fridge salesmen, and pushed. China became the property of the world's climbing establishments, of politics and contracts, through businesses and meetings with Vice-Premiers – facts to which Nick Prescott remained blissfully ignorant.

Possessed of the commendably futuristic notion that – as Nick put it – 'it seemed possible that if they had built this highway [the Nepal Highway between Lhasa and Kathmandu] they were going to do something with it', in 1979 Nick wrote to the relevant Chinese authorities to enquire whether he and some friends might drive over and attempt a couple of modest mountaineering objectives in Xinjiang. An

Iranian expedition had recently been granted permission to climb in China, which did seem to confirm the general sense of expectancy regarding her emerging accessibility, but no reply to Nick's letter was forthcoming, no more permits were being issued and so the project was forgotten.

The following Easter a large envelope arrived on Nick's Welwyn Garden City doorstep from an organization called the Chinese Mountaineering Association. It contained an address in Peking, a schedule of charges, details of those areas where foreigners would be permitted to climb and an invitation to make an application for a mountain. China had, indeed, opened up though not quite in the way Nick had envisaged. Climbing in China was going to be very expensive; the rates being charged were – and are – prohibitively high. Nick had never been on an expedition in his life, but notwithstanding this fact he decided to head for Tibet. If you were only going to be able to go to China once, then the opportunity to see Tibet had to be seized!

In Tibet two mountain massifs were being made available to the foreign climber – the Everest Massif and the Shishapangma Massif.

NICK: Of the two, Shishapangma looked the most reasonable. The route from the north appeared to be straightforward and, of course, it was lower than Everest. The original application form required that you list three alternatives. There are two glaciers which flow from Shishapangma's northern side, so one can put down two routes from the north. Probably the best thing would have been to have left the third alternative blank, but we looked at the map and there seemed to be a big valley going up the south side, so we put that down as our third option . . . we never seriously thought about climbing it from the south.

ALEX: That, however, is exactly what Nick received permission to attempt. The permit was for the spring of 1982. What had begun as a boozy conversation amongst friends from the Bristol area, regarding a possible overland adventure culminating in a modest mountaineering objective, was now an expedition to one of the world's highest mountains, to tackle one of the world's outstanding Himalayan Faces, all on the dubious merit that the mountain was lower than Everest and had been climbed once, from the north, without too much difficulty by a Chinese expedition of one hundred and sixty-five members! Nick's sense of optimism was even further underscored by the fact that, in spite of all his good intentions and commendably entrepreneurial instinct, his Alpine climbing experience was scant. Facing a budget in excess of fifty thousand pounds, Nick had now moved into the rarefied world of high altitude and high finance for which his best qualification was an impressive faith in himself.

For a while plans revolved around the possibility of making a film with the Bristol-based climber and film-maker, Jim Curran, and an experienced team began to assemble from amongst Jim's climbing friends and acquaintances, but as it became apparent that Nick was no monetary alchemist, these melted away. By the end of March he was on his own again. In the first week of April 1981 Nick rang Doug Scott and offered to hand over the permission. Doug accepted immediately.

DOUG: With an average elevation of 15,000 feet, Tibet has aptly been called the 'roof of the world'. As the rainfall is on the low side and evaporation high, there are numerous puddles in the form of lakes both great and small, mostly without outlet, this being a somewhat flattish roof. In the south precipitation is heavier and melting Himalayan snows all help to form river systems such as the Indus and Sutlej in the west and the Arun and Tsangpo (Brahmaputra) to the south and east. All these rivers break through the main Himalayan divide, pouring their waters on to the plains of the Indian subcontinent. There are many other lesser rivers spilling off the edge of the plateau; these plunge down deep gorges, through rhododendron thickets and coniferous forests to the more humid south. Thus, the Himalaya is carved up into blocks of mountains grouped together under local labels.

At about the centre of the Himalayan chain are the Langtang Himal and Jugal Himal. The highest peak in this area is Shishapangma, ten miles north of the Jugal. It is separated from the Ganesh Himal to the west by the Trisuli/Gandaki River which flows by the town of Kyirong, and from the Kosi section of the Himalaya – which includes Gauri Sankar, Cho Oyu, Everest, etc. – by the Po Chu/Bhote or Sun Kosi Valley,

24

passing by the town of Nyalam. It is along these valleys and their well-established trade routes that travellers have always approached Shishapangma in the past, and twentieth-century mountaineering expeditions also followed these lines of communication, probing the defences of this 'mystery mountain'.

The naming of Shishapangma reflects the cultural and religious influences of this region. At first there was no debate. It was simply given a number, 23, by the Survey of India during the 1850s. A few of these survey figures survive, principally K2 (K for Karakoram), but the Survey Department did try to find local names for their maps. Until recently the Sanskrit Gosainthan had been used on most western maps, 'Gosain' meaning 'God' and 'than' meaning place or abode. Obviously, there is a connection between this name and that of the venerated Hindu pilgrim centre, Gosainkund, some thirty-two miles to the south-west in Nepal and only four days' walk from Kathmandu. Gosainkund is also the name given to the foothills to the south of the shrine and the holy lakes to which pilgrims go in large numbers. It was (and still is), according to Perceval Landon in his monumental book *Nepal* (1928) '. . . the most important religious centre outside the Kathmandu Valley'. In a footnote he mentions that '. . . the frontier line, as traced on Nepalese maps includes access to the summit of the mountain', i.e. Gosainthan. However, the mountain itself is several miles north of the main Himalayan divide and wholly in Buddhist Tibet. There it is known as Shishapangma, which would seem to be the most appropriate appellation, and the one used in this book.

According to Toni Hagen,[1] Shisha or Chisa is the word for comb or range and Pangma the feminine for grassy plain or meadow. This is exactly how it looks when travelling to it from the north, the 'range above the grassy plain' of Southern Tibet. The Chinese have recently used several different spellings, including Hsi-hsia-pang-Ma Feng[2] and now, in the 1980s, Xixabangma, which makes it more difficult to pronounce than to climb. Ji Zixiu of the Chinese Academy of Sciences, whilst 'unravelling the mysteries of Mount Xixabangma', interpreted the Tibetan meaning as 'the mountain with the severe climate'. He writes that it was known to explorers and mountaineers as the 'Black Virgin'.[3]

After carrying out triangulations during the period from

1846 to 1855, the Survey of India gave Number 23 a height of 8,013 metres (26,291 feet), which made it the lowest of the fourteen 8,000-metre peaks. Further survey work by the tireless Indian surveyors during 1925 established that Shishapangma stood well to the north of the Himalayan watershed. The Chinese give a height of 8,012 metres. They have a reputation for very accurate survey work and the fact that they were taking off a metre says a great deal for their trust in their calculations. After re-calculating Shishapangma in 1978, the Survey of India put it at 8,046 metres (26,398 feet).

During our visit the Chinese mentioned that the peak was being re-calculated and have now informed Erwin Schneider that, by their reckoning, the height is 8,027 metres but none of this matters very much in relation to the actual climbing of the peak, nor has it anything to do with the fact that the Himalaya are still imperceptibly isostatically uplifting, due to the erosion and perhaps the recession of ice from their flanks.

I had Shishapangma very much in mind when I first met Alex MacIntyre in the autumn of 1981 at the Base Camp of Makalu in Nepal. Alex was attempting a new route on the West Face of Makalu, in my opinion one of the most technically difficult and demanding Faces in the world. With two Polish companions he nearly pulled it off, but was defeated by sheer technical difficulty at 7,700 metres and had to retreat; but what an attempt it had been, on a new route in Alpine style, climbing steep rock, battling with powder snow and then safely retreating down some 1,800 metres of fifty-degree snow and ice! I had already voiced the opinion to my wife, Jan, that it would be good to have Alex on our Shishapangma expedition when Alex told me I should take him. I told him that I thought so too, providing it was OK with the rest of the team.

In the summer of 1976 Alex had done two new routes on the Grandes Jorasses, one of them a fine line right of the Walker Spur which had been previously attempted unsuccessfully by Chris Bonington and Dougal Haston in winter. During the following autumn Alex made the first Alpine-style ascent of the direct route on the Eiger with Tobin Sorenson and, in so doing, established himself as one of Europe's foremost Alpinists. So he had already had a taste of

26

high standard Alpine climbing when he made a six-day Alpine-style first ascent of the North-East Face of Koh-e-Bandaka (*c.* 22,500 feet) with an Anglo-Polish expedition in the summer of 1977. After climbing the South Face of Koh-e-Bandaka in 1967, I had had a look at the North-East Face and given it 'short shrift', knowing then that I was not up to tackling 2,000 metres of what looked to be unstable snow and rotten rock. In 1978 Alex joined an Anglo-Polish expedition to put up a new direct route on the South Face of Changabang. It still is the most technically difficult route ever climbed on that mountain. Again, this ascent was in impeccable Alpine style. In 1980 he was back in the Himalaya, this time in Nepal climbing a route as steep as the North Face of the Courtes in the Mont Blanc Massif, but here 8,167 metres high on Dhaulagiri's huge East Face.

By now Alex had earned for himself a fine reputation as a young and innovative Himalayan Face climber, but his contribution to climbing was also seen in other departments, principally in helping to establish a solid connection between Polish climbers and ourselves. He had also brought a touch of realism to the bureaucratic procedures of the British Mountaineering Council, of which he had been National Officer for three years. Alex was educated at a Jesuit school outside Sheffield, arguing one day a point and the next day counterpoint, good training for the study of Law he took up at Leeds University.

Alex was 'all out front', forthright in his opinions on matters which concerned him and about which he had given much thought; then again, when he was not sure of his ground he knew when to keep quiet, to watch and to learn until he was sure. He was of the punk generation with that devastating honesty and lack of hypocrisy. I see Alex as a bit like Monkey, the hero in the exciting Chinese mythological novel *The Pilgrimage to the West*; he, too, has a clear definition of what is right and what is not and acts accordingly for the most part. Alex had a reputation for being abrasive and very ambitious, saying that he wanted to achieve the status of Chris Bonington *now*, not when he was forty – and there is nothing wrong with that, providing he could reconcile himself to the competition. Problems of ambition only seem to arise when climbers seven years younger are snapping at the heels of

27

those in the way. There is no real difficulty between those who are two generations apart, and with Alex I felt no threat, for it was obvious that he would soon outstrip my climbing record – if he had not already done so. And I hoped that I would be no opposition to him either.

Roger Baxter-Jones was climbing with me and Georges Bettembourg on Makalu that autumn of 1980; we climbed three small peaks of 6,000–6,800 metres with our friend Arianne Giobellina, and then went on to Kangchungtse (7,640 metres), five days up and down, before setting out on the six-mile-long South-East Ridge of Makalu with the intention of traversing over the summit (8,475 metres) and down the North-West Ridge. We almost pulled it off, but a four-day storm had us pinned down at 8,000 metres for two nights, where Georges developed a pulmonary embolism forcing our retreat. It had been a marvellous expedition with us all supporting one another and in agreement on the ways and means of our climbing. We had been out nine days on the ridge, in and out of storms and high winds – a big breath of fresh air.

Roger lives in Chamonix, guiding when he can and working on the roads when he cannot. He made a strong impression amongst the Himalayan climbing fraternity by his ascent of Jannu with Rab Carrington, Brian Hall and Al Rouse via the French Route, but in a twelve-day Alpine push as opposed to the two-and-a-half months needed by the French twenty years ago. He can carry his load and more, if necessary, which is essential when pushing on up in Alpine style. In fact, he is one of the strongest Himalayan climbers I have been with, and one of the more modest. He read philosophy at Sheffield University and has a philosophical bent, for it hardly troubles him that his exploits do not always hit the headlines. His abiding interest is for the 'Inner Game' approach to sport, particularly skiing, which he applies also to life. Through the Inner Game discipline he is able to step back from the complexities of the daily round and see what is actually going on from a radically altered perspective. To those of us locked in the frenzy of organizing an expedition, comments from Roger can be quite shattering. Living in Chamonix, oblivious to the ever-present worry of trying to tie up too many loose ends, phone ringing, letters to write, family to care for,

Roger's lackadaisical approach and sometimes critical statements on the preparations have irritated me at times. However, having been shocked out of *my* normal routines, I see on reflection that his comments usually help me to move in a better direction.

Roger's ready smile and good humour, coupled with his natural exuberance in the pub or on the mountain are renowned. He is a true cavalier of the mountains.

When I came back from Makalu, Alan Rouse invited me to join him and a team he was getting together for the North Side of Everest. He had booked Everest with the Chinese whilst in Peking. The leadership of that expedition, however, went to Chris Bonington and subsequently Alan was excluded, which was unfortunate for I had seen a way to revive the plan which Paul Braithwaite and I had hatched two years earlier and to which Al had given his tacit approval – for us to go ahead with Shishapangma and combine it later in the same season with a lightning Alpine-style climb on either the Kangshung Face or North-East Ridge of Everest.

Paul Braithwaite shared my enthusiasm for this approach to the big mountains. He, too, had found the big, siege-style expeditions lacking in the fundamentals of climbing, namely to be involved in all stages of the climb from early preparations and planning and to have the freedom to move fast once the climbing is under way.

Paul had excelled in the Alps, notching up most of the *grandes courses* in spectacular time by travelling light, moving together and sometimes solo, particularly in the Mont Blanc Massif but also up the Matterhorn and Eiger North Faces amongst others in Switzerland. He and I had climbed continuously for thirty-six hours up the 1,200 metre East Pillar of Mount Asgard on Baffin Island in 1972 with Paul Nunn and Denis Hennek. We were back again to Baffin Island in 1973 and then, in 1974, went up the unclimbed North-East Ridge of Peak Lenin in the Pamirs with Clive Rowland and Guy Lee. Paul had been a key member of the 1975 Everest South-West Face Expedition, for it was he and Nick Estcourt who first climbed through the gullies of the Rock Band to 8,200 metres, paving the way to the summit. He and Nick would have repeated our climb to the summit had the expedition not been abandoned after Mick Burke's disappearance.

I first realized what a fine ice climber Paul was during a visit to Mount Kenya in 1976. He always excelled on rock, winding his gangly body up, even after long absences, to climb the hardest routes of the late 1960s and early 1970s. On ice he was in a class all his own, as on the vertical head wall of Mount Kenya's Diamond Couloir, where he and I did an early ascent with him out in front on the crux, like a giant tarantula, back arched, head up, picking away through icicles and overhanging ice with his 'terrordactyls' and front points constantly in motion – as smooth as the glistening green ice he moved over.

On the Saturday night we had been bemoaning the fact that the Japanese had refused to allow us into the Western Cwm to try Nuptse that autumn and so decided to go to Kenya and left the following Wednesday. It all fell together beautifully, climbing new routes in Hell's Gorge and a new route on the steep East Face of Mount Kenya before going north to Tanzania to attempt the Big Icicle on Hell's Gate of Kilimanjaro. This was weeping wet due to the heat of the still partially active volcano, and so we had to abandon that one and instead walked on scree and cinder to the summit.

Paul has a natural talent for business. From his base at Delph in Greater Manchester he operates three climbing equipment stores and at the same time helps his wife run a dressage shop. In recent years he has found the same excitement from taking part in eventing that he has always got from hard rock climbing. After contracting a lung allergy during the ill-fated 1978 K2 Expedition, he had been out of high-altitude climbing, channelling his energies into his business enterprises and into eventing, where he seems to enjoy the contrast in social life – Cliff Phillips on Saturday, Mark Phillips on Sunday!

During the summer of 1979 Paul and I had decided to approach the Chinese Government to allow us on Shishapangma and Everest in the same season. He hoped that by the time all the preliminaries had been arranged his lungs would be completely cured. John Hunt had agreed, as always, to be our patron whilst letters of support were kindly written by the Secretary of the Royal Geographical Society – John Hemming; the Mount Everest Foundation – David Edmundson; and the British Mountaineering Council – Dennis Grey. Lord Rhodes of Delph, a neighbour of Paul's, agreed to help through his business connection with China. We had applied for access to Shishapangma South-West Face for March and April 1983, and Everest's East Face for May and June – a grandiose plan.

Now, during our annual visit to the Alps over Christmas and New Year 1981–2 we had an expedition meeting in Georges Bettembourg's flat in Chamonix, at which Paul, Roger Baxter-Jones, Alan Rouse, Georges and myself discussed our plans for Shishapangma. The meeting centred on our need to raise a vast amount of money, and we hoped that Nick Prescott, whom no one knew then, would wave a magic wand and produce it. We agreed that if anyone dropped out Alex could join us, and indeed early in 1982 our doctor, Jim Duff, had to drop out as his wife was expecting their first child. Whilst we all welcomed Alex it was sad to be losing Jimmy, for me in particular as I always valued his company both on and off the mountains.

Over the next few weeks Georges and Paul wrote off to the manufacturers for climbing equipment whilst I amassed general equipment and all the food that we could take with us, and attempted to help raise the necessary funds. Whilst food and equipment was generously donated, money in Britain was very tight and the list of charges issued by the Chinese clearly indicated any expedition to a peak above 7,000 metres in China would cost at least five times the amount needed for a comparable peak in Nepal. Yet to approach the Himalaya from the south is much longer and more arduous than the journey to Everest from the north, where the wide open valleys of the Tibetan Plateau allow for easy road communications even right up to Everest Base Camp. Hotel charges, we learned, would be a hundred times more expensive for foreigners than they are for the indigenous population.

However, Nick Prescott accepted the challenge and at the end of the day was responsible for about half the donations to the expedition from sources that had never been approached before, using his connections in the world of construction and big business, as well as his Irish contacts, to good effect.

One setback during the early spring was Alan's resignation from the team; he had decided to cut down on some of the climbs he was planning for 1982 because, having already been to China and knowing how expensive it would be, he preferred to go to the Karakoram and to Nepal instead. Another body blow occurred when Georges dropped out because of domestic and financial difficulties only ten days before departure. By then Nick, who was handling all the negotiations in China through John Everard in the British Embassy in Peking, had put down six members on the list. At the British Mountaineering Council Conference at Buxton we went around some of our climbing friends, touting for another member, but it was just too late. No one could raise the £1,500 minimum contribution.

There was, however, one person I knew of who had an abiding interest in Tibet and its people and religion – Elaine Brook who, although from Britain, is a naturalized citizen of Canada. She had just returned to North America and was in Colorado when I sounded her out about the trip. Without a moment's hesitation, she agreed that she should go, but then stopped to enquire what role she would play on the expedition. I told her that Roger, Alex, Paul and myself were very keen to climb the South-West Face of Shishapangma in Alpine style, but that during our acclimatizing period I had expected to be climbing with Nick. If Elaine wanted to climb then she could join Nick and myself and maybe the others, as they wished. Whilst we were on the South-West Face I thought it would be possible for her to spend time with the Tibetans, put into practice the Tibetan that she had learnt and find out all she could about them. After only a week back in North America, she caught a plane home again and joined the expedition a few days before departure.

Back in 1976 Elaine had been on one of our expeditions to Baffin Island, and she had walked-in with Reinhold Messner and my family to Makalu in 1981. Often we found ourselves locked in combat – she being a fellow Geminian, I think I saw mirrored in Elaine my own faults – but in general I valued her company and many of her attitudes to the mountains. She had, in fact, been a very good rock climber and for a time in the early 1970s foremost amongst the small group of women rock climbers in the country. Latterly she has turned to climbing and trekking in the Andes and in Nepal. During the spring she climbed Mount McKinley as a member of a medical research programme. Primarily though, it was her fascination for Tibet and leanings towards Buddhism that made me think of asking her to come along. On this expedition my own interest was divided equally between Tibet and Shishapangma. Also, going off with the boys again is all very well, but with two expeditions a year six months of all-male company can be a bit wearing, so I hoped that the presence of Elaine would help soften the atmosphere. Her involvement with this expedition would, of course, be subject to the approval of the rest of the team. Alex said he had no objection, in fact he always found female company in the mountains an advantage. Roger, too, was positive, but with a reservation that Elaine should not get in the way of his climbing the South-West Face. Nick saw in Elaine the possibility of a partner for various excursions he hoped to make whilst the hard-core were climbing routes from which he would probably be excluded, this being his first visit to the Himalaya. Paul said that if it was all right with the others it was all right with him, and so we had a team of six.

Nick and I now went flat out to raise the rest of our projected budget. The Mount Everest Foundation and British Mountaineering Council gave us grants totalling £2,000, and we also received the Bass Charrington Award from the Mount Everest Foundation. I had negotiated to write articles for the *Doctor* magazine and the *Illustrated London News* but we were still a long way short of our target.

ALEX: Seventy-two hours prior to our scheduled boarding of the plane the expedition started to fall together. It happened as Doug had always promised it would but could never quite explain and as Nick, for all his explanations, could never quite promise. Indeed, explanations had been a bit thin on the ground of late. Whether we went or not was now down to Doug; everyone else was clean out of ideas. Doug was holding the trip together; he wanted to go. The rest of the team hung on, hoping his optimism and his name could bridge the gap. The whole of Nottingham knew that Doug was off to Tibet. My phone calls to Nick elicited the information that we were ten thousand pounds short. Doug swore blind it was 'only' four thousand two hundred pounds. Neither could reconcile the other's figures.

'Don't worry, youth, something's bound to come up.'

Questions. I had acquired the nasty habit of asking questions. How much something? . . . from where? . . . what notional sums of money had slipped into the accounting which were not guaranteed? Doug seemed perturbed. After all, he had been on enough expeditions. Where was the optimism . . . the faith you needed to live this life to the full? Why wouldn't I devote my energy to phoning up other people and asking them for money? Why wasn't I helping? We were not particularly helpful. The budget had been slimmed beyond recognition. Experienced China hands told us, quite reasonably, being no spendthrifts themselves, that we would be doing well to get away with twelve per cent over the original budget, which had in any case been agreed for only five people. We were now six, and looking at the prospect of a personally crippling debt.

The expedition was due to fly on the Saturday. On the Wednesday I delivered a car-load of equipment to Paul's house in Delph and then we found ourselves discussing Alaska. Could we arrange to get off to Alaska if the trip fell through, which seemed at least fifty per cent possible even in our most optimistic moods. Everything had focused on the possibility of a book contract with a cash advance. Trying to synchronize revenue and potential expedition was fast becoming a hopeless task, but with a book we would, just, have the barest conceivable minimum to enable us to depart. Now, with two and a half days to go, despite the occasional tentative nibble, we had nothing. The book contract was our emotional traffic light, and it had stuck on stop.

That morning I had left Karrimor with some equipment for the expedition and a parting shot to Mike Parsons, the Managing Director: 'If I don't phone on Monday, you'll know I'm in Peking.'

For the last few weeks my life had resolved into a familiar, hectic dash around the equipment companies, pleading and cajoling: 'Can you make?'

'For when?'

'Next week.'

'Alex, you're crazy!'

Phoenix produced windsuits with inspiration – when asked for our measurements over the telephone we suggested they could perhaps just remember what we looked like! The suits were Red-Starred to Nottingham on the Friday.

Troll produced bivouac tents from a detailed technical specification to 'imagine you have to sleep in it'.

As the date for departure approached and the uncertainty increased Doug's admonishments no longer sounded so comforting; the nightmare thought of driving back up the motorway with a car-load of gear to return and a restless soul adrift in the spring was depressing.

On Friday lunchtime Paul told his wife Jane he was not going. At about the same time I arrived at the office of the literary agent, George Greenfield, situated off Fleet Street. Down in the small, spartan, cream-coloured basement I found Nick in his element, knee-deep in papers and plans, photographs and projections, the attention of two journalists in the flesh and any number of inquisitive people telephoning. The immediate impression was that we were conducting the Battle of Britain all over again. I readily joined in the fray.

It was apparent that the trip had undergone a metamorphosis. George had clinched a book deal, the *Illustrated London News* would buy two articles, the *Daily Express* would chip in a little, a medical magazine wanted to know how we performed at altitude. Doug Scott was going to Tibet, and people wanted to know. Doug's and Nick's figures finally added up to the same thing: we might just possibly have enough – we were on our way.

Roger arrived in the office, having driven over from Chamonix on hope and faith, when we were still bankrupt.

ROGER: In Chamonix, the French contingent wavered. Both Georges and I had recently committed ourselves in new relationships. We both knew well that expeditions are paid for not only in cash and risk but also in broken affairs. Georges talked himself out of the expedition and I talked myself in. The news from England was confusing: 'It's on', 'It's off', 'It's on'. So, with the gas, the rope, the axes and head lamps plus 17,000 borrowed francs, I arrived early on April Fool's Day to help Nick in his telephone begging. I had already been on one of Doug's trips. You know you're going when the plane takes off, not before.

ALEX: Now on the phone again, Roger was speaking to Doug. 'It's feeling much better today, it's feeling good.' Paul phoned – how was it?

35

'It's on. We've got enough, kid. It's all on.'

Finally it all became a little overwhelming and we repaired to the pub to re-run the calculations before going our separate ways to settle last-minute chores. At my mother's house the afternoon's packing dissolved into a million tangents. That evening my girlfriend Sarah arrived from Manchester. We bought some wine, and chaos reigned. Up in Saddleworth Paul told Jane he was going after all.

Except for Paul, who would fly direct to Heathrow from Manchester, the team were due to rendezvous at Nick's house in Welwyn Garden City the next morning. Doug rolled up with Elaine in the afternoon but then no one expects Doug to be on time. A day's packing was achieved in an hour. The expedition lay strewn about home and garden. All manner of essential items were left behind, any number of luxuries sneaked on board. A mountain of grotesquely stuffed kit bags grew on the lawn at an alarming pace, complemented by an assortment of foam pads, radio cassettes, ropes, batteries and books. This then disappeared into the innards of Roger's mother's VW, Doug's Cortina, Nick's brother-in-law's Allegro and Nick's own Capri for an independent, outer-suburban dash – Watford, Denham, Slough and, finally, the familiar bedlam of Heathrow's Terminal Three on a Saturday afternoon.

Paul's gaunt, fraught face appeared. The human *mêlée* swallowed us up and the equipment mountain reappeared near a check-in counter. A final flurry of activity ensued, with ever more passionate exhortations from Doug to avail our-selves of yet more hand luggage, possessed as he is with a morbid aversion to paying excess baggage dues. Sporting a Walkman, hand-rolled fag, and bouncing to Bob Dylan, he zeroed in on the weight scales and check-in counter, prevail-ing upon officials, speaking eloquently of the joys of rounding down figures, terrorizing the weighing machines, willing them to see our point of view. An Austrian friend of mine, Robert Schauer, stopped by for a chat *en route* by car from Graz to taste some ice-climbing in Scotland, and we mused over possible future plans and the fate of mutual friends in Poland.

'This is the final call . . .'

A tearful goodbye with Sarah, and then that final dash for

the plane, labouring under our illusions of cabin baggage, through disbelieving Security.

'Can you tell me what is in this package, sir?'

' "Rise and Shine" drink.'

'And this?'

'Fox's Glacier Mints.'

'And this?'

'Batteries.'

'And this?'

'Postcards.'

'This?'

'Karabiners.'

'Climbers are you?'

They know, don't they? We raced through the duty free (PIA planes are dry), exhorted by airline officials to 'hurry please, the plane is leaving', and requests from the press photographer (much more readily complied with) to pose. Our seats were in the upstairs compartment. I couldn't get myself and baggage up the stairs and when I finally reached my seat the aircraft was already rolling. Off the ground and up, we banked over a sunny, springtime London; next stop Peking.

Notes

1. *See* Dyhrenfurth, p. 156
2. See *Times Atlas of China*
3. See *High Mountain Peaks in China*, p. 19.

CHAPTER 2
Peking to Nyalam

DOUG: By the end of 1981, Shishapangma had been climbed five times. All the routes had, more or less, followed the one pioneered by the Chinese in 1964; and none of them had been accomplished in Alpine style. But this is one of the problems of climbing in China. To go 'Alpine' means to leave the base of the mountain self-sufficient and to move up the route continuously without further contact with the ground, i.e. without fixed ropes and support parties. The weight factor makes it impossible to use bottled oxygen. Therefore the team needs to be fully acclimatized, but in China this is a real problem for a low-budget expedition. Ideally, it would help to stay at such towns and villages as Zegar (4,280 metres) or Dingri (4,100 metres), but the cost of accommodation, which cannot be avoided, and excessive parking fees for retaining onward transport makes this prohibitive. To book smaller peaks on which to acclimatize before the big one is also time-consuming, entailing more expense.

One advantage of climbing on the South-West Face of Shishapangma, as opposed to the Northern side, was that the walk-in would start at about 3,800 metres and be sufficiently lengthy to help acclimatization. Another factor was the much shorter distance from a base at the foot of the South-West Face to the summit of the mountain; once acclimatized, such a route would be feasible in Alpine style, providing the technical difficulties were not too severe. There were also unclimbed peaks in the vicinity on which we could acclimatize and above all here was a mountain flank and valley that would excite our curiosity for no one had ever been anywhere near it before. We were at long last en route on a voyage of discovery.

We stared in wonder at the open, airy airport at Peking, all decked in marble and with none of the rush of Heathrow or the noise, bustle and humidity of Islamabad where we had changed planes. In the foyer we were met by Mr Chen Changren San, a protocol officer of the Chinese Mountaineering Association, who told us he had been to the summit of Shishapangma in 1964.

We were whisked along broad boulevards into downtown Peking and to the Chiennen Hotel, built, like so many of the others we saw, in the 1950s' Russian mausoleum style. During dinner, we met various dignitaries of the Chinese Mountaineering Association (CMA) with whom we were to have a great deal more contact. At six o'clock the following morning we went out with a temporary interpreter to find that the broad pavements were full of people, mostly elderly, performing Tai Chi. We stood watching them making beautifully precise movements of their limbs. Such was their concentration that they seemed oblivious to the presence of gawking Westerners. We left them moving in slow motion, backwards and forwards, a kind of moving meditation exercise, and continued on our way to a nearby park.

As it was rush hour the streets were filled with cyclists going to work. All we could hear was the constant whirr of bicycle chains. Everyone seemed to be dressed in the same

Tai Chi on the Boulevard of Peking
Doug Scott

drab green or blue cotton Mao suits, young and old. Since the recent swing to more liberal attitudes it is no longer the law to conform to clothing models, but obviously old habits die hard. Despite the lack of motorized transport, which consisted mainly of overcrowded trolley buses, there seemed to be quite a pollution haze hanging over the town, either from the many factory chimneys belching out acrid smoke, or from the dust blown in from the interior. At the entrance to the park were groups of locals attacking imaginary adversaries with broad-bladed swords in the course of practising Kendo, one of the martial arts, of which Tai Chi is an offshoot. The

The team on the Great Wall. Left to right: Roger Baxter-Jones, Alex MacIntyre, Elaine Brook, Doug Scott, Paul Braithwaite, Nick Prescott
Chinese Tourist

park was crowded despite the early hour; opera singers were sounding off from a pavilion, individuals were doing their Tai Chi or sat around reading, couples were learning lines of verse and a few Westerners in shorts and T-shirts jogged, head and shoulders above the Chinese.

Then began three days of negotiations with members of the CMA. These negotiations in Peking and subsequently in Lhasa were to take up a great deal of our time – especially for Nick the treasurer, Alex the lawyer and myself as official leader. They precluded much in the way of sightseeing in Peking, but we did make the mandatory two-hour drive to the Great Wall.

I was expecting just another tourist attraction, but what an attraction it is! To stand on the Wall, knowing that the section we could see sweeping up and round on the very crest of the hills continued beyond for a total length of 4,200 miles, I found quite staggering. It is wide enough for two horsemen to pass each other and is between thirty and sixty feet in height. The Wall is one of only two man-made offerings seen by astronauts from Space; then I remembered that the other is the pollution haze hanging over Los Angeles.

There were few other foreigners amongst the throng of Chinese laughing and jostling along the ramparts. Groups picnicked on the turrets looking out across the plain to the north from whence Tartar and Mongol horsemen once came galloping, bent on pillaging the northern cities of China. Now, of course, that frontier lies many miles to the north and today the importance of the Wall is the boost it gives to the Chinese tourist industry, and to the Chinese pride in their heritage.

The gentlemen with whom we negotiated in Peking were themselves mountaineers and members of the CMA. They had begun climbing during the period of friendly co-operation with Russia. Alex, who took copious notes in his little red book during our discussions, describes them later. But as background information, the reader may be interested to know something of the principal characters.

There were several reasons why our expedition was involved in negotiations far more protracted than any other. No one had been to the south-west side of Shishapangma before and the Chinese could not be expected to foresee all the

41

problems we old hands envisaged, so a good deal of time was spent going over problems concerning yaks, yak-men, porters, mail runners, food supplies, etc. Also, apart from always operating the law of 'not parting with any money until the last possible moment' when dealing with expedition finances, there were areas where we might legitimately cut our enormous budget. Al Rouse had given us a few tips on his return from Kongur, such as taking only one vehicle instead of the two recommended. We understood that camping was a possibility in Lhasa, thus saving enormously on hotel charges. So for these and other reasons, although we missed out on the sightseeing, we did have a first-hand, in-depth experience of the Chinese under negotiating pressure.

The star Chinese performers numbered six. The Gang of Six, as they became affectionately known to us, had all started their climbing in the 1950s. Chen San was not only the Protocol Officer for the CMA, he was also a climbing coach. He did not take a very active part in the debate but sat quietly, listening for the most part, putting in a word now and then. To me he epitomized Chinese climbing attitudes. He was very diffident when I asked him what he had climbed, not because he was under orders not to divulge such information and not because he had nothing to declare. He had, in fact,

Negotiations with Chinese Mountaineering Officials. Left to right: Peking interpreter, Wu Ming, Paul Braithwaite, Alex MacIntyre (with Little Red Book), Dr Li Shuping, CMA interpreter, expedition interpreter Wu   *Nick Prescott*

climbed Elbruz in the Caucasus in 1956, Peak Lenin in the Pamirs two years later and Mustagh Ata in 1959. He had reached 8,100 metres on Everest in 1960 and 8,200 metres in 1975. In 1964 he had been Deputy Leader and summit climber on Shishapangma. Not many Western mountaineers hold such a record of high mountain climbs under their belts. He may have been elsewhere, but these are all the facts I could prise out of him. After the Chinese climb on Everest in 1960, the Vice-Premier at the time, Ho Lung, 'called on the climbers to sum up their experiences, conscientiously refrain from getting conceited, carry forward their style of hard work . . . to make fresh contributions to China's socialist sports and high-altitude exploration'. Although I suspect that modesty may be a national characteristic of the Chinese anyway, this sound advice seems to have been adhered to impeccably.

The Gang of Six could not have done more. Mr Wu Ming, who was a geologist and hydrologist during the early attempts on Shishapangma and on Everest, did everything possible to meet our demands, as did the 1975 Everest doctor, Dr Li Shuping. They were at all the meetings and bore the brunt of the ensuing work, such as contacting the semi-autonomous Lhasa section of the CMA for their reaction to our demands. Wu Ming was a sort of Roy Jenkins character, quietly but firmly making shrewd compromises. Whenever we reached deadlock, however, Shi Zanchun, the Vice-Chairman of the CMA, was called in to arbitrate. He had been leader of the 1960 Everest Expedition. His name was absent from the list of climbers on subsequent expeditions until 1975, when he appears to have been leader again. In China I think 'leader' can be interpreted loosely and may well be a position shared with others. Shi was very much the politician, and not at all given to compromise.

Chang Chun-Yen usually attended all the meetings and functions the Chinese laid on for us. He was tall for a Chinese, about six feet and, at fifty-one with a family of three children, very fit and strong-looking. He told us a lot about Shishapangma, which he had climbed, warning us of the snow we could expect on the south side and genuinely admiring our intention to climb the Face with only four climbers and in Alpine style. They did seem to have grasped the concept of climbing in Alpine style.

At a banquet given in our honour, Hsu Ching presided. He had led his team to the top of Shishapangma in 1964 and he had also served as Deputy Secretary of the Communist Party Committee on that expedition. He had been deputy leader on the 1957 Minya Konka Expedition and on the 1960 Expedition to Everest, and had also climbed Mustagh Ata twice.

ALEX: We had received the most stringent instructions to be on time for the banquet, just this once. The system adopted for foreign expeditions in China rests on the concept of a single leader issuing clear instructions to his team, whose main preoccupation is to be available, wherever they should be, at the time they have been asked to be there, their main occupation being eating. Lacking any such leader, with no great grasp of time (no one had a watch), and possessed of the ability to be going in a multitude of different directions at once, we did not always measure up to the high standards set by our Japanese cousins. On this occasion, however, we did make it on time, except for Roger, who was lost somewhere in the city.

Much time was taken in stressing etiquette to us as we approached in the minibus. The Big Chiefs (Doug and Nick) would sit at the top table, the hoi polloi (Paul and Alex) would sit at the bottom. The hoi polloi took great delight in informing Elaine she would have to eat in the kitchen, but in the event she sat with Doug and Nick!

Sumptuous food was served in a bewildering array of courses, while young ladies kept the alcohol flowing – which it does liberally on such occasions. Periodically, dignified members of the banquet would stand and propose a toast on whatever appropriate pretext came to mind. This would be a signal for a 'down-in-one' of the liquor in front of you, which was promptly topped up again. Needless to say, the team took to this like ducks to water.

The negotiations, when resumed, went something like this: 'Now, about camping in Lhasa . . .'

'There is no camping for foreigners permitted this year.'

'What? But, look, your regulations specifically refer to the possibility. They even give a price.'

'The authorities in Lhasa will not permit foreigners to camp in Lhasa this year!'

'Can we sleep in the back of the car?'

'There is no possibility but to do according to the regulations and arrangements of the Chinese Mountaineering Association. There is no room for bargaining about the rest of your accommodation.'

'But this is outrageous, absolutely outrageous. Just to sleep, just to put my head down, ninety pounds. Wake up in the morning, phew . . . ninety pounds gone. . . Ask him if we can keep walking all night!'

Our negotiations in Peking were vital to us. Barely three days away from the Forbidden City, just a week away from our first glimpse of Shishapangma, and a mere twenty-four hours away from the unthinkable, ignominious return to London – the most expensive sightseeing tour of Peking ever undertaken – wagging tongues, a thousand 'told-you-sos'. In the main it was Doug who swept the debate on to the CMA. Twenty years of worldwide mountaineering experience sustained on inadequate funds ('Inadequately funded climber savages Chinese Mountaineering Official!' – *Daily Express* exclusive), against almost every major form of authority devised by our present-day world have left a hardened nerve and a tenacious, stubborn resilience that would compliment a mule.

'The regulations are not made only by the CMA. The CMA cannot change the regulations.'

'The CMA is representing China. We are talking to China!'

'Yes, we do represent China, but you should have had everything arranged beforehand.'

'Look, this problem comes about because we thought we were going "economy" after what our telex told us, and because you will not allow us to camp in Lhasa.'

'We cannot understand your protest.'

'About the ridiculous price we have to pay?'

'If the price is too high, cancel it!'

The fundamental, absolute and feared bottom line. From time to time you may hear theories that this or that establishment body in one or other of the main climbing countries was the driving force whose cunning negotiations and political contacts opened China and Tibet to the world. This is not so; political change in that country opened the door. The climber is a source of foreign exchange. The reasons why we are

45

allowed to buy our way in are in a stratosphere far beyond the ken or persuasion of the climbing world. You don't need contacts, you need cash, and our lack of this fundamental commodity was a novelty in this land.

In all, we spent an unprecedented fourteen hours in negotiation with the CMA. They are used to dealing with relatively docile, disciplined expeditions backed by a sponsor or sponsors more interested in the publicity, good relations, 'mutual friendship' and the quiet life. As we hadn't found such a sponsor, our debate ranged far and wide, conducted with a passion through specifics and politics, pursuing points through a dozen polite, exasperated negatives, along a dozen obscure tangents, pushing on every door, probing for flexibility, fighting against the possibility of the often-commented-upon 'inspired inaction' of the Chinese system that would send us home or into heavy debt.

Our negotiations began in Room 311 of our hotel, a small sitting room in a double apartment. When it became apparent that life was not going to be simple they switched venues to a conference room in another hotel, the Tintan Sports Hotel, in a different, amorphous part of town, where they brought in a higher official, Mr Shi.

In the room of the Tintan Sports Hotel we spent eleven hours in crisis management, brinkmanship and tea-drinking. The negotiations developed with the pace of a brilliant, furious and finely balanced cricket match. Mr Wu Ming and Dr Li defended their wicket from a small settee set at the far end of the rectangular room, beneath a small portrait of Mao and, with studied competence, used every stroke in the Chinese bureaucrats' book to quite deadly effect – the 'anzhoo womendi guilu' (according to our regulations), the 'fuza' (complicated), the 'kaolu kaolu' (we are looking into it) and the ultimate, impenetrable appeal to 'Chinese-British friendship' – an anagram for your paying them lots of money.

Doug opened the bowling at silly mid on, on a small armchair to their right, but soon squeezed into an impossibly close first slip, right up beside Wu or Li on the settee itself.

'Bloody hell, Doug, if he sees you there he'll do his nut.'

Towering over his spectacles, he would sweep back loose strands of hair, take a last puff of a rabid cigarette and, quivering at the apparent inflexibility of the defence, hurl another telling bouncer, well-aimed, but nevertheless swept for six. The remainder of our team took up positions in armchairs close to the wicket, Paul giving worried directions on position and strategy, Roger shouting the rising score (i.e. unbudgeted cost escalation). Nick ducked as the sixes whistled over his head and his neatly tabulated rows of figures crumpled before him. By lunchtime they had scored a double century and we were not going anywhere.

We had been given to understand from a telex from the British Embassy that the Chinese had agreed to charge us at 'economy rate'. This, it turned out, was a mistake. Economy class was reserved for accredited students. Polite assurances to 'do everything to help us economize' had been misunderstood. The second blow was the information that all our foodstuffs, which were to have been purchased by the CMA and await our arrival in Lhasa, had not yet been bought but would be accompanying us airfreight – at our expense, naturally. My diary recorded:

Again, this is our mistake. The Chinese system does not volunteer information, it simply assumes you intend the consequences of your actions and they dictate those consequences. Why was it assumed in our budget that this stuff would go overland at minimal cost? Nick's accountancy is screwing up because his assumptions do not fit a Third World system, and they certainly don't fit this one. His lack of experience in expeditions shows in this budget of his.

Mind you, it must be said, if Nick had understood the system and accounted on that basis, we would never have gone in the first place. So perhaps we have to bless that budget!

'Before you have come to China we want to make everything satisfactory.'

'Well, you know what you can do.'

'But we must abide by the regulations.'

To the rest of the team there were times when Doug's sense of proportion seemed obscure. While we were reeling under the disastrous news of the air freight costs, he set off on a conversation about beans – which, it appeared, we could not afford to freight anyway. On being told there were no beans in China he rounded on the interpreter with cold eyes, speaking very slowly: 'I don't think Dr Li knows what I mean. Every country in the world has beans. I think you had better ask him again. Two months is a long time without food!'

There were also times when the Chinese must have perceived they were dealing with lunatics, such as when we insisted we would bicycle to the Great Wall. They were incredulous. (It took us two hours in a minibus.) But fundamentally I think it was the novelty of negotiating with someone who pleaded abject poverty from the start which stumped them.

Finally, they gave up the defence and threw the ball back. 'How much did you plan to spend in China?'

Nick added and subtracted for what seemed an age. Everyone waited with bated breath. 'Fifty thousand, nine hundred and sixty yuan over and above what we have already deposited with you.'

Worried Chinese faces looked glum. We caught the mood and looked glummer. Dr Li ferreted around an inside pocket of his drab blue Mao jacket and produced two thin, neatly folded pieces of paper, put on his glasses and pondered. We pondered with him. Were we going home?

Clearly, our hosts were not happy. 'How much have you paid already?'

'Fifteen thousand, nine hundred and forty yuan.'

In what amounts? On which dates? Did we have the receipts? It was moving too quickly now. Nick could not find the information or the receipts. London – here we come? A minute ticked by. A minute is a long time.

'Pheewhee!' Dr Li's grinning face expelled air and sank back, relaxed. The payment had been located. There had been no instructions as to who had sent it, an anonymous donation!

'Bloody hell, Nick.'

Suddenly business was in the air; we were all on the same side.

'How much weight of equipment do you have with you?'

The weight estimate, perhaps a touch optimistic, drew some expressions of disbelief. We tried to explain light-weight, Alpine-style climbing to blank faces. 'We climb like Reinhold Messner.'

That did the trick. Dr Li doubled back over his paper, scribbled on another, making swift calculations. We all had

48

some more tea. He finished and sat back. 'Mr Wu has a solution to your budget. As you have *already* arrived in China and with little money, and it seems you are quite strong and can bear hardship, we will try to help you spend less.'

And they did. Every effort would be made to change arrangements in Tibet; they would try to make sure we only needed to use one truck if it would take all the equipment; they would try to help us spend only one night in Lhasa; they would try to help us reduce our numbers of yaks and yak-herders. We would buy the bulk of our foods ourselves in Cheng Dhu and freight it from there, we should take big 'hand baggages'; we should carry large loads to the Base Camp ourselves as an exercise for high altitude.

'That's a good idea?'

New regulations were produced. Certain things were cheaper this year, certain problems easier to deal with. 'We now believe you can operate within your budget, but you must prepare yourselves for the rigours ahead. It is not as comfortable in a truck as in a Toyota! Now you are new friends to us and you are welcome to visit China in the future. We await good news from you in Peking. Your route is very hard, but we believe you are all stronger than Messner.'

To this there was general consent!

The system was flexible. The CMA in Peking had decided to give us the green light, now that we were *already* here. I sometimes wonder whether they did not sit and deal with past expeditions in almost total disbelief that, as another few thousand yuan slipped on to the budget, everyone smiled and talked of 'Chinese-Somebody Friendship'. I don't think a Chinese would fall for that one. During the three days of talks the telephone and telegram wires to Lhasa had buzzed continuously as we put up ideas for reducing costs.

'We will make representations.'

'Will you make strenuous representations?'

'Yes, we will make strenuous representations.'

DOUG: On 8 April we flew to Cheng Dhu, tired from our negotiations but enlivened by our excursion to the Great Wall and socializing at the British Embassy. It was there we had heard of the gathering storm, thousands of miles away in the South Atlantic. Embassy officials had quietly given us a good deal of support behind the scenes, particularly John Everard who had exchanged dozens of telex messages with Nick before our departure. We looked forward to seeing them all again in two months' time.

At Cheng Dhu we changed planes and in dense cloud flew on towards Lhasa surrounded by a quantity of hand luggage which amazed even us. Sitting on vacant seats were 450 eggs, a hundred pounds of sugar, sacks of vegetables as well as five thousand postcards, plus a good deal of our personal belongings. Nick took great delight in informing us that our plane was an 'illusion' (Ilyushin). It was certainly of 1950 vintage, shaking horribly as it took off and vibrating among the foothills leading up to the Plateau of Tibet. Through clearings in the clouds we could see heavily wooded valleys and snow-capped peaks below. The further west we travelled the more extensive grew the vista of peaks stretching away in all directions to the horizon. Such a sight certainly made a nonsense of 'Munro bagging'. However, we all agreed that one peak we would like to bag was Namcha Barwa (7,756 metres), one of the highest unclimbed peaks in the world and

Flying on to the Plateau of Tibet – in the background Namcha Barwa, one of the highest unclimbed peaks in the world
Doug Scott

the most easterly peak in the Himalayan Range. Tibet's famous river, the Tsangpo, changes direction at Namcha Barwa, turning due south – from west to east – to flow down into Assam where it is known as the Brahmaputra. After three hours we had passed over the wooded country, over peaks covered in spring snow and glaciers winding in between. Now we looked down on to the dry, semi-desert countryside surrounding Lhasa. The Himalayan Range – Kangchenjunga, Everest, Shishapangma and all the others – disappeared into the distance marking the southern edge of the plateau. So here we were, coming into Tibet.

ALEX: We touched down into a parched, barren landscape at around 9.45 am. A single, wide, dusty strip obviously able to accommodate larger and heavier aircraft served as the runway. There was no taxi-ing, no request to remain seated for the long jerky ride through distant outfields to the terminal designate. The plane simply turned right after a brief trundle and halted near some parked vehicles. We waited while it discharged its other bustling, laden passengers and then proceeded to manhandle our hand baggage on to the tarmac below, blinking at the barren hills that surrounded our wide, flat valley floor, reeling from the rapid and immediate change in altitude, for we were now at a height of around twelve thousand feet. Our eventual aim would be to climb at heights over twice this altitude, but for the moment it was a shock. How the tourist reacts, paying their ten thousand dollars, I wouldn't like to think.

At the edge of the runway, a few feet away from us, sat two clean white Toyota minibuses. We loitered and awaited some directions, our team, resplendent in scruffy, travel-worn hand-me-downs, contrasting with a party of Japanese who had travelled on our plane handsomely arrayed in bright colours of red and blue with various yellow golfing caps, all new, all expensive and all over which they insisted we wrote our autographs, scrawled in indelible black ink, while we photographed them photographing us signing them. A curious bunch of lads!

At a single instruction they promptly fell into a Toyota and disappeared. The other vehicle was apparently for us, and various attempts were made to usher and exhort the team into it, a far more difficult process than that we had just witnessed. At the runway we were introduced to our liaison officer, Pemba.

Rumbling down the last stretch of dusty road for the final forty kilometres to Lhasa, the tourist system swung into action. After twenty kilometres we reached a small, newly painted and probably newly repaired monastery, at which we bundled to a halt.

'The monastery is closed today, the monk is in Lhasa.'

In a spirited attempt to photograph the building to advantage, the roof of a neighbouring earth house was precariously occupied.

'If a bunch of Tibetans turned up in Delph and began clambering all over my roof I'd do my nut.'

Doug and Elaine disappeared on the inevitable quest for the ever more illustrious, definitive photograph. The rest of us were treated to an example of how things should be done. Another minibus, full of West Germans, drew to a halt, the windows slid back and cameras clicked on motordrive. Some sweets were tossed out to scrounging children. A couple of more adventurous males dismounted and gathered around the doorway, photographing the children begging, then the whole caboodle vanished in a cloud of dust, down the road to lunch no doubt.

Our driver was unhappy. We had been more than five minutes; we would be late for lunch. Meanwhile, our shop steward had absented himself from view, a dream fulfilled, a Tibetan monastery in his foreground, Tibet in the background. Dolma, the tourist guide, Pemba and the driver were puzzled at this obviously unique situation.

'Why can't your leader no bring him back?'

'He is the leader!'

Time in Lhasa was precious to us and, at nearly ninety pounds per person per night, unforgettable. We could afford to spend only one night there and would have to leave on the back of a truck, a minibus would cost about £4,000 extra. As we did not have the money for these expenditures we were anxious that our liaison officer should understand our predicament. Much time was devoted on the way in to explaining to him our status as 'a personally financed and relatively impoverished expedition'. Many smiles and sympathetic assurances that it would all be fine and he would help us to his utmost were forthcoming. However, as we got down to specifics over lunch, about the two vital items that Peking had promised to push on our behalf, it soon became painfully apparent that Pemba was going to be a disaster.

'But Pemba, it is vital we only spend one night in Lhasa.'

'Mayo, it's just not possible.'

'But why not? It's OK by us.'

'Mayo,' and with that he would grin his toothy grin, shake his head and chuckle to himself. It was as if he felt he were dealing with errant children who would soon understand and do things his way – the liaison officer's way.

'And another point, Pemba, we are only going to use one truck. One truck is quite sufficient for our expedition.'

'It is impossible.'

The afternoon wore on as we tried to get our liaison officer's co-operation, which, we had been assured in Peking, was the vital factor regarding our requests. We sat in the courtyard of one of the hotel's compounds, arguing and pleading with one of the most inarticulate, stubborn and unintelligent men it had ever been anyone of the team's misfortune to deal with. He was not at all interested in our plight, except inasmuch as it affected him. There would be no bright new clothes or expensive Western trinkets. We would not be buying his affection, but rather would be expecting him to do a job.

'Mr Pemba says if you don't have enough money, go home as others have done before!' Wu, our interpreter, spoke.

It was so simple for this man to say such a thing – to display such total lack of interest. Tempers frayed. Pemba produced his liaison officer's paper of authority for all to see – stamped and signed!

'Now look, we are a very small expedition. We will all easily fit on a truck.'

'No, no, everything cannot fit on a truck.'

'Ask him, Wu, how can he know that, he doesn't know how much equipment we have.'

'It's very uncomfortable and dusty to ride on a truck.'

'But we know all about riding on trucks. We have ridden thousands and thousands of miles in trucks. We have ridden in Afghanistan, Africa, Pakistan, India, Turkey . . .'

53

'It is forbidden for foreigners to ride in trucks this year.'
'That's not true.'
'Mr Pemba says he has a suggestion to help you halve your minibus costs. You can take a jeep, but everyone will not fit in the jeep.'
'So someone will have to ride on the truck.'
'Yes.'
'So it can't be illegal.'
'But this is for Chinese–British friendship!'

The final rock-bottom answers; it was time to go to the CMA office. Liaison officer support or not, Pemba quite obviously wished to ride in a Toyota for his own comfort and, in hindsight, perhaps to do some profitable trading along the way, selling off supplies granted to liaison officers and interpreters for expeditions.

DOUG: The plateau of Tibet, in the heart of Asia, is fifteen times the size of the British Isles and, at an average height of 15,000 feet, all of it is above 10,000 feet. Those of us who go to the mountains will recall reaching those heights above the level of the trees where there are grassy Alps dotted with Alpines below, the crags of ice and rock. It is at those heights, in the clear cold air, that spirits rise noticeably and cares and worries subside. So it is perhaps not surprising that the Tibetan plateau is steeped in religion or that until recent times one in seven of its three and a half million inhabitants lived and worked in the monasteries, the number of which has been variously estimated at 2,500 and 3,500. It is hard to imagine such an arid land being able to support the building and sustenance of monasteries on the scale of those we saw on our 500-mile journey to the peak of Shishapangma and back.

Thubtem Jigme Norbu recalled from exile the effect of his native Tibet:

The countryside itself helps perhaps. I know that those of us who have had to leave Tibet feel a real loss, not being able to see our mountains and feel our winds and breathe the clear cold air. It is a countryside that takes our thoughts directly to a state of existence far above our own. Its very size and splendour make a man's thoughts turn inward. In Tibet we lived with the world around us, not just in it. In itself it seems part of our blessedness.[1]

Now we drove through an arid land of strong contrasting

colour, a Salvador Dali landscape of windblown sand piled up against dark red rocks vibrant against the blue sky. Pemba was shouting out rules and regulations, Wu was interpreting, Dolma, the hard-working tourist guide, spoke English and was answering our questions. She was grey with fatigue. How many times already had she told Westerners that she was at school in Darjeeling before the 1959 uprising, and 'yes, it was mostly Tibetan Red Guards who had damaged or destroyed the monasteries. Yes, they were repentant now. Yes, the Cultural Revolution of 1966–8 was a hard time for us all.'

To change the past into the present she pointed to a haze-covered hump on the flat valley floor: 'You will see the Potala soon,' she said.

As the bus rounded a bend on the stabilized gravel road we caught sight of the Potala in the distance through the superstructure and smoke of a cement factory.

We were driven straight to our hotel, still five miles from Lhasa. We ate a splendid lunch but ended up with indigestion through indignation at being told that the driver was not available again until the evening. With the prospect of only one day in Lhasa, we wanted to spend every minute actually in the town. Soon we were locked in debate with Pemba over our cost-cutting schemes once again. Alex gave it all his lawyer's logic. Elaine took photographs. Roger strutted about, furious. Paul slept that one out. Poor old Wu was hard-pressed, interpreting. I was checking a pile of air-freighted equipment when I heard the debate reaching a crescendo, a babble of high-pitched voices that suddenly stopped. Our driver had changed his mind, and we were off to the CMA Headquarters in downtown Lhasa.

We drove down metalled roads, past Chinese-inspired buildings, into the compound of the CMA. Immediately, Pemba aimed for a group of similarly attired Tibetans. Their black leather coats, swarthy skins and dark sunglasses gave them a slightly sinister appearance, like members of some Mafia gang. It was obvious they were debating our proposed cut-down on time in Lhasa and the exclusion of the minibus. Elaine, speaking Tibetan, soon found the one man who could help. Jigme had been a national football coach and did speak some English. Elaine put our case to him and to another Tibetan sporting a ratting cap. He set off for the main office,

The Potala
Doug Scott

where Alex and Roger had gone to organize the stamping and
franking of our five thousand postcards.

ALEX: We waited in a small, clean office until finally an official
arrived, a short, stocky darkish man of practical manner, a
bearing that implied experience in the field, and a flat cap
under which cropped black hair protruded. He motioned for
us to remain seated and pulled up a chair opposite us. Dolma
translated.

'We would like to cancel the minibus and use only one
truck.'

'Yes.'

We nearly collapsed. I asked Dolma to enquire what position he held and whether we needed to meet a higher official to
confirm this – this man bore no obvious air of authority.

'He says he has authority on certain matters and can decide
this.'

I turned to Roger. 'Let's not get too excited, some higher
official will probably walk in and we will need to begin all
over again.'

'Can we pack this evening and leave tomorrow?'

'Yes. And my men will help you pack.'

Unbelievably, within half an hour we could suddenly afford our expedition. The wealth of telegrams and phone calls from Peking, exhorting the Tibetans to facilitate our passage, had done the trick – Pemba notwithstanding.

DOUG: Meanwhile, in another part of the compound, the rest of us checked out the Thomas Cook Lhasa cache of camping equipment stored there for trekking groups. Roger Balson from Cook's China and Searcher Office had kindly arranged for us to borrow eight Vango Base Camp tents, stoves and kitchen gear.

The mood amongst the leather jackets grew decidedly hostile. Pemba was, to put it mildly, not being a very good ambassador. His main grouse was nothing to do with us, although it arose from his realization that he was not going to receive a set of clothing, mountaineering and camping equipment from us; we were taking advantage of a change in the rules which allowed us to make a cash settlement to the CMA instead. They would then arrange for Pemba to hire whatever he needed from them, to be returned later. Because of this, and the lack of a minibus which meant an uncomfortable ride for him, and maybe also a lack of status, he was definitely turning against us. We were to suffer Pemba's always unhelpful and at times hostile attitude throughout the expedition. Fortunately, in Wu we had a superb interpreter – highly intelligent, absolutely honest and one who managed to arbitrate between us and Pemba.

Opposite the Cook's cache we checked our food order. That was also ready and complete. Suddenly the reek of rotting cabbages wafted in from an adjoining room. Mindful of our lack of fresh vegetables, we set off to investigate. To our delight, piles of carrots, sweet potatoes, onions and parsnips as well as the cabbages were stored under mounds of soil. We bought the lot. It was an invaluable addition to the rather spartan diet we were expecting. Another find was ten cases of Budweiser beer, left by an affluent American expedition. We bought this as well. But I could contain myself no longer and set off with the others to see Lhasa.

It was like stepping back a thousand years into medieval

Tibet. The whitewashed walls of three-storey houses sloped back and up to tiled roofs jutting out over the road and a jostling throng of Tibetans. What a crowd they were! A vibrant energetic horde of wild-eyed nomads, just off the steppe, weatherbeaten with a splash of turquoise, amber and coral colour strung around their necks, poking out of chunky sheepskin jackets, greasy brown. The smell of Tibet was all around them.

Down the centre of the road pilgrims were prostrating themselves, lying out flat, standing up, eyes fixed in front, oblivious of the crowd and the crowd not paying them much attention either. They walked a few paces forward to where their hands had reached, and down they went again with arms stretching out once more. They continued all day round the perimeter of the Jo Khang, the town's cathedral. Buddhist pilgrims are said to build up merit in this way by prostrating themselves round the base of Holy Kailas – a distance of some thirty-five miles – which, of course, takes several weeks. One old man with a lovely toothless laughing face wore a full-length leather apron to protect his knees and carried clogs to put over his hands whilst prostrating. He hired himself out to those Buddhists who were too busy to build up their own merit and wealthy enough to engage him.

At the entrance to the Jo Khang there were about a hundred pilgrims prostrating themselves before making an entry. It was only in the last two years that the iron gates fixed here by the Chinese in 1959 had been taken away. Now Tibetans from all over the plateau flocked into Lhasa to worship at this ancient, sacred place. There was so much devotion in the air, far more than I ever expected after reading of the devastation brought to this country by the Chinese overlords. We had read the tourist brochure:'Tibet is no longer medieval.' How wrong they were – certainly about this part of Lhasa.

After making some purchases from the many stalls laid out on the narrow pavements, dhal from a Nepalese trader, garlic, onions and beans of uncertain age from Tibetans, we returned to the CMA Headquarters to finalize arrangements for the mail and the stamping of postcards, which Dolma undertook

Professional prostrator, Lhasa
Doug Scott

to organize ready for our return. After a protracted argument with the bus-driver, we managed to squeeze in a few more hours that evening in Lhasa. I walked around with Wu, who was showing the strain of the last few days. He said that it had been a long day. I said that he could have fifty-two lying on his back at Base Camp, but added that we had never before had an interpreter work so hard 'above the call of duty'. Alex was with us as a Tibetan lady walked by, with the traditional 108 plaits in her hair and wearing the traditional clothing, silver and turquoise ornamentation. He wondered whether she took it all off when she got back home at night, sitting down with her feet up and saying: 'Ah well, that's another hard day's work done – looking traditional.'

'I couldn't live here,' said Alex.

Although obviously still spinning from our travels, we were able to feel the calm of this place – like walking back down a time-warp with the Potala rising above it all. In 1966 the Potala had been within a few days of destruction and only

Tibetans prostrating themselves before entering the Jo Khang
Doug Scott

the timely intervention of Chou En Lai prevented its being demolished during the Cultural Revolution.

How much I regretted the shortage of time and money that prevented our visiting other monasteries in the area such as Drepung Monastery, once the largest in the world with 10,000 monks in residence before 1959 – in 1980 there were 240. Neither did we enter the School of Tibetan Medicine with its magnificent tankas, nor the Summer Palace with its walls covered in murals, some depicting Tibetan history.

Back in the hotel courtyard we checked out all our food and gear. Everything accounted for, we marvelled at the Chinese efficiency in these matters. It would never have arrived so fast and so completely at Lukla (the Nepalese airstrip on the Everest approach). That evening we talked with a Tibetan who had returned as a tourist on a German visa after a twenty-year absence in exile. He told us just how much of the old town had simply disappeared – pulled down as it began to disintegrate. The Chinese would not allow the Tibetans to repair or decorate their homes for twenty years after 1959. He had just met Heinrich Harrer who had recently revisited Lhasa. Ironically, the authorities would allow him only seven days in Tibet this time. Alex twiddled the knobs on the radio, anxious to know what was happening in the South Atlantic as the Generals in Argentina attempted to find external solutions to internal problems. They could do with some of the Lhasa energy beaming over Buenos Aires.

At dawn on 10 April we left our hotel. A cold, crisp, dust-laden breeze blew down the road as we drove away, wriggling around on the sponge mats in the back of the open lorry, trying to find a position that was comfortable on top of the fuel cans, kit-bags, boxes of food, etc. Just at sunrise we came to a bridge with the sun coming up behind it. Chinese soldiers came racing across from a nearby barracks and at bayonet point we got back on to our lorry and roared off down the road in a cloud of dust. Apparently foreigners were not allowed to take photographs here!

The dust was a constant feature and one that had Paul worried. He hoped to protect his lungs by wearing an industrial mask. The rest of us had white silk scarves, purchased in Cheng Dhu, tied across our faces. We were now on the Nepal Highway, which links Lhasa with Kathmandu.

62

There were many other trucks trundling along, and we braced ourselves for the extra dust cloud joining our own. After crossing the Tsangpo River we began to climb slowly up a pass with the lorry engine spluttering to a halt about every half mile. During these halts Tibetan children would run across from nearby villages. Their parents would come along too and offer us chang from earthenware jars, very welcome in the dust; we would give them Chinese chocolate in return whilst the children were scrambling over the lorry, inspecting us and our gear. There were huge grins of delight whenever they put on our 'Walkman' headsets. Pink Floyd did seem to have them somewhat confused, but they responded very positively to the tape of temple music which I had bought at the hotel.

It was whilst Elaine and I were both plugged into the same cassette, listening to this music, lulled half asleep by the gongs, pipes, cymbals and drums as well as the wailing, singing and chanting, that I realized I was understanding the words of the singing for they were coming across in English in a Lancashire accent. Still half asleep half awake, almost floating as in a dream – but not the sort of dream you have in the middle of the night – I saw face after Tibetan face passing one in front of the other, brown, red, weatherbeaten faces, strong faces, pleading faces. Then I woke up with a jolt. The lorry was juddering to another stop – the fuel injection system clogged with dust.

Later that evening Elaine commented on the music. In passing she said that she had understood the words, for it had come across to her in French. Much later, on our return, we met a party of trekkers at Shigatse. Jo Sanders, the leader of the group, had been into the Tashi Lunpo Monastery where the music on our tape might well have been recorded. She had just spent two hours there and was looking dazed and somewhat distant. When I asked if she was feeling all right she explained that, whilst she had been sitting quietly at the back of the temple, listening to the monks, drifting in and out of sleep, she had understood the chanting for, to her, it spoke not only in English and French but in other languages which she understood. Sven Hedin the Swedish explorer had visited Shigatse in 1907. The chanting had a profound effect on him. He found it led 'the listener away to the land of dreams and hope'. I had the certain feeling that something eternal and universal was locked away in the temple music.

After crossing a pass about 16,000 feet high, we came across the huge Yang Zho Yong Lake nestling in the brown-mauve hills. We came down to the town of Kampadzong and only after a fairly violent argument would Pemba agree to stop the lorry. His attitude was doubly irritating, for not only were we being rushed at an unreasonable speed through this fabled land and missing out on interesting places, but the vehicle broke down continually and always at some insignificant, boring stretch of road, miles from anywhere. Pemba would allow us to stay for only half an hour at Gyangtse, though fortunately on the return journey we did manage half a day there. Now we could see the ruined battlements of the fort to

Monastery in the shape of a mandala, Gyangtse
Doug Scott

which Younghusband had laid siege with his howitzers in 1904. It was ten o'clock in the morning when we limped into Shigatse. The vehicle would only go as far as a hundred yards before it spluttered to a halt. Then the driver got out, topped up the carburettor and we continued for another hundred yards. It was quicker to walk the last two miles into the town, the second largest in Tibet.

On 11 April we woke early to take advantage of our enforced stay here, for we insisted that the mechanic did not leave until the vehicle was in running order. At our hotel another interpreter-cum-local guide with the name of Chou had been assigned to us for our stay in Shigatse. He helped with our haggling at the market, where we bought more foodstuffs, turquoise necklaces and other bits and pieces similar to those that can be bought over the border in the main Sherpa town of Namcha Bazaar.

Up above the town of Shigatse stands the Tashi Lunpo Monastery, which was built in the fourteenth century by the first Dalai Lama. There were said to be three thousand monks there before the Chinese 'liberators' arrived; now six hundred have again taken up residence. It is a huge complex of buildings covering some three thousand square yards, all very extensive and impressive, with gold rooftops and a huge prayer wall down which prayer flags are lowered during religious festivals. Part of the monastery was destroyed between 1966 and 1968, but it is being patched up by carpenters and construction workers busy everywhere. We decided to explore the monastery the following day.

Meanwhile we walked a mile out of town to the Summer Palace, where the Panchan Lama used to reside. Since Liberation in 1950 he has been on some Standing Committee in Peking. Despite banging on doors we were refused entry. Elaine, Roger and I wandered round the outside of the Tashi Lunpo Monastery and there came across a group of nomads and two monks sitting around campfires by their yak-hair tents. We were invited to sit amongst them and given Tibetan tea. If your palate is prepared for something like thin vegetable soup, then it is no surprise to gulp down salt tea with globules of rancid butter floating on the surface. Roger drank his from a human skull, a symbol of impermanence! It was in this circle that our heads stopped spinning from the ride; we

65

'Clowning monk' from the Tashi Lunpo monastery
Doug Scott

seemed immediately to sense and feel the peace of these nomads and the monks who had joined them. One very handsome lad with strong features and a complexion weathered almost black gave us tsampa soaked in tea and butter. Tsampa flour reconstitutes in hot water as it is in fact ground roasted barleycorn, the traditional food of Tibet. The elder of the two monks was forever clowning around and had us in stitches of laughter; he was completely unselfconscious; months in isolation, locked away from all the cares and worries of the world, had certainly not made him introverted. I envied Elaine her knowledge of Tibetan, as Roger and I could only smile and gesticulate.

Early the next morning we met Jake from Calgary and a friend of his from Leeds; they had been in China for three

Having Tibetan tea with nomads on the outskirts of Tashi Lunpo
Doug Scott

months, having entered via Hong Kong. They were travelling outside the regular tourist system, with obvious advantages. They were staying in the same hotel as ourselves, but at local rates – 1.60 yuan per night, while we were paying 120 yuan. They had been ten days in Lhasa at 1.50 yuan each – we had paid out 210 yuan per person a night! We all wandered down into the monastery with Chou, who had only slightly more tolerance than Pemba for our dawdling and interest in all things Tibetan. We did, however, spend a little time in a hall where about eighty monks in khaki velvet cloaks and blankets knelt chanting. We were all moved by the intensity of their devotion.

We watched a group of young novitiates renovating an ornamented door lintel, then questioned Wu carefully after he had had a conversation with an elderly monk. It seemed that novitiates were now being introduced into this monastery. There were four between the ages of ten and fourteen and thirty older monks between fifteen and thirty. Most of the other monks there appeared to be well over fifty, but at least

Fortified monastery at Zegar (Shegar Dzong or the White Fort referred to in the Everest Reconnaissance [1921] as having a population of 400 monks, now a ruin)

Doug Scott

these figures illustrate that the monastery was being allowed to re-establish itself.

All too soon we had to go. The lorry had been ready for some time and Pemba was working himself up into a mad frenzy. At noon we set off for Zegar. The lorry was now in better shape and we easily crossed over a 4,500-metre Pass, the Pola. We stopped there for a picnic by a walled adobe brick village, then off again. All around the pale blue moor was tinged with light brown; overhead in a blue sky dragon clouds floated by, as we passed a nomad encampment with yaks grazing beneath ruined forts and monasteries right on the edge of crumbling clifftops.

At Zegar we had a rest day on 13 April. As the town is at

Nomadic horsemen, off the Dingri plain. Ruins of Mongol forts at Menkhap Tö in the background

Doug Scott

4,280 metres our acclimatization had really begun. After so long in the lorry it was good to walk in the direction of the fortified monastery, built right to the summit of a thousand-foot hill – definitely one of the wonders of Tibet. During the Cultural Revolution most of it had been dynamited into rubble. From the hills above Zegar we caught sight of Everest, Makalu, Cho Oyu and maybe Shishapangma. The air was clear and the hills and mountains all around mauve with the wild mountain thyme covering their slopes.

At Zegar Elaine heard, from a villager, of an Indian pilgrim who had been found delirious, suffering from frostbite after having crossed the Himalaya to the north of Dingri. He had been taken to the local hospital where we went to make an offer of antibiotics. There we found a Chinese doctor with ample supplies of medicines, but working in the most atrocious conditions. His surgery was the patients' room, a damp, concrete structure with water swirling around at our feet and a bucket overflowing with bloody bandages, swabs and amputated toes. But clearly the Chinese 'bare-foot' service

Our first view, from near the Tsongla Pass, of Shishapangma with banner clouds blowing off the summit. This photograph illustrates the accessibility of the Himalaya from the north

Doug Scott

Shishapangma (centre) East side with Phola Gangchen (right),
Pungpa Ri (left, beneath Shishapangma) and Nyanang Ri (the rock
tooth, left)

Dennis Hennek, from Gauri Shankar

works in Tibet, for this doctor was obviously dedicated to his
profession and cheerfully doing all he could for the benefit of
his patients.

On 14 April we left Zegar by the way we had come in. After
a few miles we were back on the Nepal Highway, heading
west down broad valleys through wonderful country of
contorted twisted red rock high upon the mountainsides to
the north; to the south, on lower hills, ancient castles were
crumbling back into the slopes. Two hours later we rounded a
bluff and the valley widened into a huge plain stretching right
up to the very base of Cho Oyu and the Nangpa La Pass. On
many occasions we had looked up from the south as we
approached Everest Base Camp in Nepal and seen that side of
this Pass. It is the main trading route between Khumbu and
Tibet, and from our Sherpa friends we knew that trading had
been resumed via this route. They had told us how they
travelled up the glacier, over the 5,716 metre Pass and down as

far as Dingri. Suddenly we realized that the settlement we could now see on the east side of a large rocky prominence poking out of the Dingri Maiden (field) was Dingri itself. What a contrast this northern side of the Himalaya is compared with the southern slopes, where steep mountainsides heavily wooded with conifers and rhododendron forests plunge down to raging torrents. Here, far away from any roar of water, only the wind blows across the flat plains over the yellow grassy furze of vegetation. In the north the traveller can so easily reach the foot of the Himalayan mountains, a wall of snow reaching up to blue skies with white clouds hanging over them.

We followed the road west and north. After crossing the high Tsongla Pass at about 5,480 metres we could see Gauri Sankar and Menlungtse and, for the first time, were treated to a fine view of the north-east side of Shishapangma – a cockscomb of peaks above the plains with wisps of cloud wrapped around them. Driving south round sweeping horseshoe bends following the Po Chu River (Bhote Kosi in Nepal), we passed Tashigong on the other side of the river and drove down into the town of Nyalam.

Note

1. *See* Norbu, p. 37.

CHAPTER 3
Nyalam to Base Camp

ALEX: We reached the village on 14 April, with the lengthening shadows and creeping cold of a wintry evening at twelve thousand feet in the Himalaya. A substantial bridge over a small mountain torrent marked the entrance to the town. In Peking we had been told explicitly that Nyalam was forbidden to foreigners, but the truck rolled over the bridge without hesitation and halted on the far side. Wild, wind-battered, dusk-caked faces peered from the back of our truck; a few quizzical, bemused faces peered back. The inevitable inquisitive children clambered up the tailgate to stare and wonder at the nature of our baggages. Naturally, having been told that Nyalam was out of bounds to foreigners, we set off to explore, a curiosity compounded by necessity with the silent disappearance of Pemba. One group, Doug, Elaine and Nick, demonstrated considerable instinct in managing to locate, in the dusk, the completely unadvertised and quite unobvious only teahouse in town. The remainder discovered the cinema.

'What's that sign, youth?'

'Sausage, egg, chips and beans. £1.50p. Breakfast served all day,' we translated.

'It's the cinema, but it's too late now, it has already started.'

Paul summed up the initial reaction. 'There must be booze in a place like this, eh? We'll be all right here. Wallop, egg and chips and a cinema – not bad at all.'

Less accurate predictions must be rare. The place was almost deserted, most people presumably being in the cinema, but one errant individual was spotted and intercepted by Wu. The local promptly disappeared and returned some minutes later with The Leader.

The Leader was the man with authority over the region, not merely the town itself and, by China's standards, he was a good leader, keeping well out of the way of potential trouble whenever possible. Within that context he was most helpful to us – indeed, we seemed to have been expected. We were shepherded into a small meeting room, rectangular with peeling whitewashed walls, a cracked cement floor, lit by the inevitable bare, low-wattage light bulb which cast eye-straining shadows. Around most of the walls were wooden benches, somewhat uneven and crude in construction but solid and well draped in blankets and cushions for comfort. Beside them stood long simple tables on which the inevitable and welcome tea appeared. So, eventually, did the teashop team, our liaison officer and a whole company of village notables who crowded in to stare at the barbarians – especially the blonde woman and the big man with a woman's hair. Minions were reduced to peering in through windows.

'Pemba says we will stay in this conference room tonight.'

'That's very nice of Pemba to arrange this.'

'It will cost twenty yuan per person per night.'

'Wait a minute, Wu. Tell Pemba we cannot afford to pay this sort of money. How many times must we impress upon him we are not a typically wealthy expedition to China. We're poor. We cannot afford this money. We must camp.'

'Camping is not permitted; local regulations forbid this.'

I could not believe this, it was all too convenient – to have been expected where we were not supposed to be, then be refused permission to camp outside the town as we had previously been told to do – what deals were being worked by Pemba? Subsequently, we were to discover in Peking that Pemba had the authority to ignore any such local rule, even if it did actually exist, but he was quite unconcerned about helping us. If we were 'poor', then so far as he cared we could simply go home. In the meantime, if a few yuan could be made, all well and good. At any rate, that was the nature of my suspicions. Now, faced as we were with the need to pay to stay here, it was imperative that we depart tomorrow.

'Can you ask The Leader if the yaks are here?'

'The Leader says they are not here yet.'

Tired minds sprang to the alert. Doug's eyes narrowed just that perceptible hint.

'Well, Wu, I think we had better ask him where they are.'

'The Leader says they are about forty kilometres north, back along the road that you came.'

'Why?'

74

'They do not think you can go to Shishapangma from this village.'

'If they did not expect us to go from this village why did they expect us here?'

Unfortunately, such Western logic seems more apt to confuse issues in China than to help. We now found ourselves in the unbelievable situation of having to justify and persuade the assembled dignitaries that we were indeed going to Shishapangma from their village. Consternation and an excited babble ensued. Indian fluster and Chinese bureaucracy seemed to merge into the volatile deliberations of this group. Everyone, everywhere seemed to want to be in on the act, to have a say in what we could or could not do, but at Nyalam we had reached the final straw.

'The Leader says you cannot possibly go from the south. It is very steep, it is unknown, no one has ever been that way before. The route is from the north, there must be some mistake surely. He says you do not understand.'

We did understand, we understood their morbid fear of not following the crowd, the fear of being 'the nail that stands up' which permeates this culture. For the first and only time the system helped us. Our permission, as we pointed out, was from the south. We had to explain to these people, so used to delivering opinions on all manner of subjects about which they so often do not have a clue, in the only way they could grasp, that the authority which said our route would be via their village from the south – and only from the south – was far greater than theirs. Who would challenge it? There was no point in trying to explain mountain climbing.

In the event we were sentenced to spending three nights in Nyalam waiting for a second team of yaks to assemble. Whether the system worked with any speed or concern for us we do not know, but we had by now lost all faith in it – and in Pemba. Our unnecessary opportunity was taken to explore, behind the town, the valley up which we would move towards the south side of our mountain, and to explore the town itself.

What we experienced did little to endear the place to us. Where it borders the road the front of Nyalam consists of characterless, modern, alien military and civil type administration buildings, at best resembling one of the seedier ends of a cheaply built, makeshift small-time ski resort after the snow has vanished. Behind this modern aspect sat the old village, nestling on and around protruding bare rock, squeezed for space on the valley side. It had an almost nightmarish quality, narrow twisting alleys ankle deep in oozing mud and refuse, everywhere littered with bones and the severed heads of sheep or goats. Crumbling houses concealed fleeting, hidden faces and ragged mongrels. Nyalam – known in the past as Kuti – had a reputation as a place not to be in, and something of its unsavoury past still lingers here; it was unsettling.

Fundamentally more unsettling was the abysmal food. Interesting ingredients were destroyed by the kitchen and conjured into a cold, greasy, indigestible and unvaried diet, served in ever diminishing quantities as we became increasingly unable to face it. Thankfully there was some palatable chang, and the evenings could always be enlivened by varied debate, the friction qualities of varied bricks on various climbing walls in Yorkshire, next year's K2 expedition, the value or immorality of the multi-national corporation, and any number of slights against vegetarianism, Buddhism and taking Sony Walkmans completely to pieces with a Swiss Army knife. The last three were invariably aimed at Doug, who would overcome all opposition by smiling healthily, reposing peacefully and reassembling the Walkman without a hitch.

'It's no problem, just a matter of experimenting, getting inside and playing around.'

There isn't much Doug can't fix with a penknife. He also nearly managed to die from hypothermia on a first reconnaissance expedition up the valley.

DOUG: I awoke early, as I had to, with 'Rise and Shine' music blaring out from loudspeakers attached to the highest buildings. This was no Butlins Holiday Camp; all I wanted to do at Nyalam was to leave it, especially as all the negotiating and hard travelling had put an edge on the internal relationships of the team. Nick had developed a bad cold and cough, walking around our concrete bunker in bare feet with Alex chiding him for not looking after himself better. There was Paul with his gourmet palate, incredulous at the recurring rice, spinach and potatoes. Elaine was fretting for hot water to wash the dust from her tangled blond hair, Roger was withdrawn and Wu a worried man at the prospects of spending six weeks with Pemba and his bullying tactics. It was time to take a walk up the valley.

I walked out of the door, passed The Leader busily shovelling rubbish into a bucket that had emerged from under the melting winter snow. I told him, 'You wouldn't get Council officials in Britain doing that', but then, on looking at his hands, I could see that they were red and blistered. He seemed a kindly man, perhaps not unlike a typical District Commissioner who had served the Indian peoples during the days of the British Raj.

At the outskirts of town I passed a new hydroelectric station, one of over eight hundred dotted around Tibet, so I had read. There had been only one small generator before 'liberation', the one which Heinrich Harrer described during his stay in Lhasa and which provided electricity for the Mint and to light the houses of some of the nobility. I passed on, thinking that maybe such hydro schemes as well as all the other material advantages which the Chinese had brought to Tibet would encourage the return of refugees from the south; indeed many of them were beginning to infiltrate back over the borders, helped along by resettlement grants provided by the Chinese Government.

Soon I put all these thoughts behind me. It was so good to be able to stretch my legs and to stride out past the last rude fields and over grass, blueberry shrubs and juniper poking out of the melting snows. Already butterflies were darting about and the smell of spring was in the air, giving bounce to my steps as I set off up the valley past a cluster of yak-herders' huts and on alongside the river for about seven miles. I climbed up a 1,000-foot hillside to have a better look around. Having forgotten to bring the photographs and maps, and with afternoon cloud gathering around the mountain tops, I could not see Shishapangma and the thought occurred to me that maybe The Leader was right, maybe we should be forty miles north. Dismissing the thought, I continued along a ridge top which dropped down to my left on to an undulating plateau dotted with frozen lakes and snow fields, stretching up to Phurbi Chachu in the Langtang. So far the route I had taken had been reasonable for yaks, and apart from patches of deep snow I thought they would be able to continue up the valley for as far as I could see. I glissaded down snow streaks lying in hollows and came to the river, trying to cross the icy waters which came up to the pockets of my jeans and then up to my armpits as I had to reach down to the slime- and ice-covered rocks to keep my balance. Once up the far bank, I collapsed behind a stone circle, finding shelter there from the wind which was worrying its way down the valley and through my Helly Hansen jacket. The sun was now hidden behind the clouds and I began to shiver as the cold wind penetrated the million holes of the nylon pile. I raced along a stony track which occasionally lost itself in patches of snow. To keep warm and to keep my spirits up I sang old songs at the top of my voice. Then I came to a field where there was a hut and a young lad in green by the entrance cutting some wood. He looked up in some surprise to see and hear me coming down from the direction of the mountains. I had been clutching the folds of my jacket across my body to stop the wind; now I let it go and walked into the hut through a low doorway covered by a thick yak-hair blanket. I did not want the lad to think I was a softie, but I was glad to reach out my cold blue hands towards the fire. I had seen only the fire at first, until my eyes had become accustomed to the dark smoky interior. Water was bubbling from a blackened teapot and soon I was clutching a mug of Tibetan tea as steam rose from my drying clothes. After three more cups of tea the Tibetan lad produced a cloth bag of tsampa, which was welcomed by my shrunken stomach. It was not long before I ran out of the few Tibetan words I had gleaned from Elaine, and with the silence the lad produced a three-stringed fiddle. After tuning the strings he played a lively tune – something between country and western and temple music. I thought of home and being with my family but got a grip and put the thought aside, knowing that I had got to be here, body and soul. When I did concentrate my attention upon it, the music had a strange calming effect that warmed my whole body. After chewing some garlic and drinking another cup of salty tea I continued on down the valley much revived, to find the others at our Nyalam 'hotel'. My faith had been restored at finding that young lad up there tending his cows and yaks in the way of his fathers. That was my first day in the mountains – not much of a day, but a good day which had taken me up to about 16,000 feet and put me in better spirits. We were all in good spirits – those of us who had got out of the village and up into the hills.

ALEX: On the evening of the sixteenth a young boy and an older man, who appeared to be his father, materialized in the room. It seemed the young boy was to be our yak-driver and a second boy would join him tomorrow. Apparently they had nine yaks. The overall enthusiasm the young lad exhibited at the prospect of spending time with us in the hills was that of a person assigned to dig his own grave; they seemed to be of the impression that the yaks shared a similar sense of urgency.

'How many days does he think to Base Camp?'

They began by suggesting ten days, about two kilometres a day – what might be best described as 'the slow grazing approach'. At such a rate, bearing in mind that two runs would be needed to get all the equipment to Base Camp, this would be completed in one month's time.

'Please ask The Leader why it is that his communist yaks are

At Nyalam, the roadhead, we had our preliminary negotiations with the yak boys through the Chinese commune leader
Alex MacIntyre

so hopeless compared with the capitalist yaks a few kilometres away over the border in Nepal.'

In the end we extracted a shady, reluctant promise 'to work as hard and as long as the yaks could in any one day', and to try to get to Base Camp in two days. In Nepal two days would have been more than adequate but here there was clearly no incentive to do more than the absolute minimum. Given half a chance they would have taken a month, and an inexperienced team would probably not have made it to the mountain. It has always been the one proud claim of the Chinese System that once you have paid your price you have only to sit back to be whisked efficiently at maximum speed to your base. Away from the beaten track to Everest and possibly Shishapangma's northern side, the system patently breaks down. It also had absolutely no concept of responsibility. It fails – you pay!

The yaks arrived at ten o'clock the following morning.

At first it had been suggested that we should manhandle all our baggage a quarter of a mile or so, in order that the easily startled yaks could avoid the traffic, but this notion was dropped when Doug offered to close the main road instead. The vision of Doug, singlehandledly closing such a strategically important highway did not seem to agree with The Leader's concept of a peaceful life and the yaks duly arrived the following day, late, outside our room. At least, eight did – one had managed to avoid all attempts at capture.

For over two hours we set about loading these pensive, suspicious, horned animals noted for the occasional goring they can serve up on the unsuspecting herder. They are, above all, extremely strong animals and the loading is in reality a great confidence trick perpetrated by humans on the confused or better part of their nature. The yak is persuaded to stand still by whatever means are most appropriate to its trust in and the disposition of its handler, which, in the case of our yak-boys, meant every trick under the sun. Rope would be used to lasso one of the horns. A roped nose ring and roped feet completed the equilibrium. An expedition member would then be volunteered to hold this assortment of ropes, eyeing his yak at least as warily as the yak eyed him. A yak-boy would then pick up a kitbag, generally weighing over twenty kilos, and stagger towards the yak, hoisting the load on to its flanks, whereupon its legs would buckle a touch and the animal would emit a disgruntled groan. The second boy would attempt to repeat the process from the far side and the loads would be roped to the yak in counterbalance – except that at about this time the yak could be counted on to have a go at the peculiar-smelling individual holding the ropes in front of it. Once yak, expedition member and loads could be reassembled in close proximity again the process would be repeated.

As a result it was a bruised, sorry-looking team that limped, late – at around midday – with the final eight yak-loads out of the village, following a wide path through cultivated paddy-fields on the river bank to a small shack at the perimeter of the agriculture, an hour's walk away. Our yaks were not a strong team, sorry and unfit and seemingly unused to the work which was now required of them, and our fears were confirmed when, at the shack, we had to abandon one yak and its loads. It was too ill to continue.

A brief ten minutes past the shack our caravan collapsed. We had just encountered our first ground snow as we moved on to a narrow track contouring over a bracken- and boulder-strewn hillside that ran down into a narrow gorge below where the constricted river boiled, terrain in which yaks are supposed to be at home. One yak went berserk and headed uphill, dragging its load along behind it. The remainder, seizing on this initiative, scattered in each and every direction, contriving wherever possible to shed the loads. Sugar and flour bundled downhill in slow tumbles, but miraculously survived.

In the meantime the weather had deteriorated to damp afternoon mist, a strong breeze and wet snow. The scene began to assume the desperation of the flight from Culloden. Havoc reigned as disgruntled expedition members took to the hill in pursuit of yaks and loads, stalking and herding while avoiding the unhelpful attentions of one yak which had taken to charging people as it evaded all attempts to capture it. The yak-boys were totally fazed and out of control. Paul found one at the back of the caravan sitting behind a boulder, laughing at the chaos. When scolded, he burst into tears.

We called a halt at the first suitable camping ground we could find, stunned by the realization of what today meant in terms of our prospects of coaxing yaks and boys to Base

Camp. We were a mere one and a half hours above the village. A damp, sodden camp was pitched on the marshy, uneven ground. The multitude of equipment behind us was retrieved from the hillside, with the exception of one load which had vanished, and we huddled under our Red Army tarpaulin for our evening meal, not the most content of expeditions.

The following morning it was straight back to Nyalam to see The Leader and institute a post-mortem. Once again we assembled in the room, accompanied by the Head of the Commune, our liaison officer, the yak-boys and a variety of odds and bods from the village. One yak-boy opened the fray by claiming that Paul had assaulted him. This patent lie was of no concern whatsoever to The Leader, who told him that if Paul had, he would not have been all that surprised, considering they took six hours to get as far as they did. Then followed much earnest problem-solving on behalf of our hosts who eventually accepted our original suggestion that we should continue with the five good yaks, and that The Leader should locate another five strong yaks as quickly as possible. Another lunch was inflicted upon us and we finally got away by four pm, our whining yak-boy replaced by an older, slightly more confident lad.

The morning of 19 April dawned miserable. The misty, inclement weather persisted; inside the tents life was damp, outside everything was saturated. Flurries of wet snow swept across the camp. That morning Paul returned to continue packing and await the promised yaks. Doug, Roger and I coaxed our five yaks and two yak-boys off up the valley, crossing the river at an adequate bridge about an hour upstream. On a small area of flat grazing ground, situated close by, was a small stone yak-man's summer hut. The boys had previously insisted it would be a day to the second bridge from our camp. Furthermore, no one had volunteered the information about the hut, which would have been such an obvious target to aim for; but then, I doubt if much information is ever volunteered in China.

Over the bridge an old moraine slope, now grassy and well anchored, rose steeply for nearly two hundred metres. On the ridge crest some cairns beckoned, and we reached these via an indefinite twisting path, to be greeted with the view of a snow valley behind, which seemed to swing to the north and vanish into small, indistinct hills. The ridge was particularly exposed to the wind, which whistled along it, driving spindrift in its wake. Soon all views became obliterated by encroaching cloud creeping up the valley from Nyalam.

We followed the ridge for about half an hour, until one yak simply sat down with a resigned grunt and refused to move. The three of us divided its load between us and struggled the short distance to a site where a large boulder and some flattish ground clear of snow presented a place to camp. The altitude, now around four thousand metres, was taking its toll, and we were happy to dump the gear and turn back. Paul had returned from Nyalam empty-handed – except that Wu had come up with him. Elaine and Nick were ill, and it was a cold, empty kitchen that greeted us.

The following morning began apathetically, but rapidly assumed the proportions of a farce. The yak-boys insisted that they could not go on, the yaks had to rest. Doug and I persisted and then a conversation ensued regarding how many yaks were well enough to continue and who would go up. The debate became more and more complicated as first Roger then Paul seemed to become inclined towards a rest day, whilst Doug and myself insisted that the current altitude was not sufficient to warrant a rest and, anyway, we could not afford one as time was slipping away. All this, in the midst of our argument with the boys, meant that the packing was short-tempered and haphazard, our slow pace and indecision worrying. The boys, meanwhile, continued to insist that no yaks could continue, and then that the two sick yaks must stay but that they could not be left alone in the valley, because of the danger from wolves. We told them that one boy could stay with the two yaks if they wished. Then they insisted that one boy could not herd the yaks on his own and they were afraid we would beat him when he failed us.

The situation was becoming frustratingly absurd. It seemed that any and every trick and opportunity was designed to hinder our progress, with every extra day meaning another wage to be paid. Finally, we had four yaks loaded and away with one of the boys, Nyima, when, through the mist, came a sight for sore eyes, five more well-laden yaks, accompanied by a small, bandy-legged old man with a gnarled, mischievous face and sympathy for and control over his animals.

He carried straight on through, up the bank on the far side of the river whilst Doug and I had lunch at the yaks herder's hut.

DOUG: Alex and I sat huddled on the sheltered side of the hut against the driving mist, munching boiled eggs and grain bars. Alex steered the conversation towards expedition organization in general and ours in particular as far as it had developed. He was quite frank, as usual, saying that he felt the need for the formal organization that was characteristic of the expeditions he had been on with the Poles. On those expeditions everyone had a specific job and the leader made certain the jobs were done. Alex was in favour of a structural approach, rightly pointing out that the Polish climbers had been very successful over the years. I knew that planning and organization from leader down through a hierarchy of subordinates was one way to success. But what is 'success'? The importance of what we do is not in standing upon the summit of our peak but what happens along the way.

Not much happens when a strong leader takes control, immersing himself in the planning, preparation and running of the trip to the detriment of his own enjoyment of being there; because of the pressure he is under he cannot be himself. The interest and actual involvement in the expedition's progress by the other members is proportional to the power of the leader. The stronger the leader, the less enthusiasm the majority of the expedition will have for it. They go to sleep. This of course depends upon the character of the leader. Usually an older, more experienced leader's awareness and standing will be at a level sufficient for him to know the old maxim that to 'rule truly is to serve'.

I admitted to Alex that I was not equipped to lead nor did I want to be led. As far as our trip was concerned our best chance lay in a flexible approach with everyone on their toes, ready and prepared to do what needed doing when the opportunity arose. I hoped that such flexibility would allow for the vast range of ability and experience in our party. On the SW Face of Shishapangma we both knew that there would be no problem, for those attracted there would draw on similar experiences and arrive at the same conclusions.

(I had a conversation along the same lines with Roger in our

84

hotel in Lhasa, as he too favoured more organization as a result of his experiences with the Inner Game of Skiing Group. To both of them, the essence of my reply was that we must expect each to take responsibility for himself and for each other. If we cannot do this on an expedition of only six friends, when can we do it?)

I picked up a bucket of 300 eggs and followed Alex, carrying a large pole, up the bank to our rock.

ALEX: We set up camp then. Roger had remained at our first camp with a tight chest, and Paul, Nick and Wu had returned to Nyalam for the day to make some more arrangements. Pemba, by this time, was beginning to feel that perhaps he should make an effort to join the trip, but we had no yaks to spare yet for our liaison officer. When Paul finally left for the camp he appeared and started to moo and make puzzled yak imitations. Unfortunately, we had already gone on ahead and Paul was unable to explain the situation.

Their tent that night was a crowded, damp, sloping affair, all three in one tent and Roger – in whom periods of rest while the rest of the team is operative tend to cause grumpiness – was now pursuing a 'quest for exactitude', mainly at the expense of Nick, who had the habit of making sweeping assertions.

The following morning dawned fine and sunny. Doug and I went in search of the Base Camp, a long day spent wandering along the ridge top up this beautiful valley. To our left, spring avalanches cascaded over the mountain walls. We picked out an ice line on a superb two-thousand-foot rock wall opposite us. Seconds later an avalanche obliterated it, a salutary reminder. The packed snow betrayed evidence of a teeming wild life, with tracks everywhere. The ridge was obviously a recognized route with the winter snow still on the ground, and some tracks were the size of a fairly substantial cat. After about four hours, turning up away to the right, underneath a small rock peak, we found our Base Camp site. My diary records it as: '. . . an excellent place, south facing in a beautiful mountain with a still-frozen lake and flat places to camp.' Continuing past the lake we struggled up deep snow to the plateau above, and to our first sight of Shishapangma, retaining its mystery, surrounded in cloud, but nevertheless, thankfully, there, about six miles away. It was at least the right valley.

We got back to the small boulder camp at about seven pm. The rest of the team were now in residence after a valiant and heavily burdened struggle up the slope, labouring under the loads that the two remaining yaks had refused point-blank to carry. At last Base Camp was in sight. We would make our first ferry tomorrow.

Our team were most definitely having problems in getting up in the mornings. The alarm clock was still down in the village, and Nick's frequent claims to have another one tucked inside his head were not proving true. Some improvement was achieved at about 7.15 am. Elaine vanished into the kitchen, Doug and I began to pack yak-loads. Numerous exhortations that the yak-men should also get up were falling on deaf ears; they were exhibiting a most marked reluctance to do anything until the sun reached the tents. China, which actually spans four time zones, has made the decision that all time is Peking time, with the net result that when it is about midday in the Nyanang Phu Valley, it is a more sensible nine o'clock in the Langtang Range, just over the way in Nepal. We never did adjust to this. It was almost inevitable that before anything could be organized in the morning we had reached midday, and yet even with the knowledge of the time difference, an irrepressible urge to consider five pm as the immediate precursor of nightfall could not be shaken off.

Today, by some miracle, we had the nine yaks away by eleven o'clock, with the old man, Namgyal, the boy Nyima, Doug and myself. Almost immediately we were involved in a tug-of-war with regard to the amount of snow on the ground and, unbelievably, the correct way to get to Shishapangma. With a slow, plodding reluctance we made our way along the ridge top for a couple of hours, the old man grumbling and finally drawing to a halt. Doug tried everything he knew, neither could understand the other. Both knew what he was on about. Finally, in desperation, Doug seized two hundred yuan, waved it under Namgyal's nose and exclaimed: 'Two hundred bloody yuan, you go Base Camp, paid in Beijing, two hundred yuan, it's a fortune, now GET A BLOODY MOVE ON!'

An hour later, without warning, the yaks were turned

down into the valley on our right. We persisted that this was wrong, we must go along the level ridge; there was deep snow in the valley, no good for the yaks. This was accompanied by a peculiar miming act to illustrate the imagined impact of deep snow on our small company. The old man was unmoved. He was still convinced that the way to Shishapangma was up the valley on our right side and he vanished into the thigh-deep snow. The yaks went through like ducks collapsing on ice. Within two hundred yards the caravan had ground to a halt, tempers had snapped, loads were being dropped, then a horn went into the cooking oil and oil leaked on to the snow.

'Now, you, listen; why the bloody hell don't you listen? I told you it's no bloody good this way. Me, him, come yesterday, looking, looking, now get back on that bloody ridge.'

Back to the ridge we struggled, the yaks remaining stoic and patient throughout this display of mankind's futility, the futility of climbing mountains, the futility of their burdens, of their leader, and of our arguing. Souls in purgatory! Our two-hundred-yard excursion had cost them one and a half hours in exhausting, belly-deep snow.

The perambulation continued along the ridge crest once again amid a non-stop friction between ourselves and the old man, who seemed to be of the opinion that we should return to Nyalam and wait a month. We longed for the solid

Our loads being carried up to Base Camp in typical weather
Doug Scott

Nepalese yaks which would have had us at our Base Camp days ago. Finally, we came to a halt on a barren ridge, down the far side of which we would have to descend. The camp was about twenty minutes away. The yak drivers called a halt; it was as far as they wanted to go. We wanted them at least at the bottom of the slope, from whence we would be able to ferry to the camp. Tempers exploded, the old man dumped a load and insisted that his yaks could not go down. We knew full well they could. I dropped on all fours, insisted he did the same, and set off down the slope. He obviously thought we had now cracked up completely. He began to assert again and again that this was not the way to Shishapangma and threatened to return to Nyalam.

Doug blew a fuse. 'Bloody well go back to Nyalam then, see if I care, go on, go back, go home, you go eating, sleeping, screwing. Doug, he goes up into the cold snow, climb Shishapangma, poor poor Doug, now GET THOSE YAKS DOWN THE HILL!' Doug's gesticulations left nothing to the imagination.

A stiff breeze whipped damp mist over the hillsides. It could have been a Glencoe November. I was still on all fours, halfway down the hill. Doug was bouncing with rage, the old man was beside himself with anger and the yaks were looking worried. And then the tension snapped. If we wanted to go the wrong way – so be it. The yaks were driven to the bottom of the hill, the loads dumped and we turned for camp, a tiny, steady, quiet caravan, walking back into the gathering dusk, covered by a thin veil of cloud, brushed by light snow. The bells of the yaks struck a mournful note. The yak-man accompanied them by whistling a tuneless, repetitive ditty. Down in the valley the lightning played on more distant ranges.

After a day's rest we made our second run to the Base Camp on 24 April, without a hitch, this time to stay.

CHAPTER 4
Trouble at Base Camp

ALEX: The almost reflex drive towards Base Camp lent to our team a cohesion formed by a total unity of purpose, an identifiable and obvious goal desired by all. There were, however, some particular problems inherent in the make-up of our team which, once our Base Camp was established, needed to be faced. As we were over a week behind schedule in reaching the camp, the increased urgency of our future timetable underlined our differences by leaving less time to climb and, consequently, less room for compromise.

From the day Nick's original climbing companion, Dr John Minors, had dropped out, the expedition had become unbalanced. The original proposal had been for the Face climbing team of Doug Scott, Paul Braithwaite and Georges Bettembourg to accommodate Nick and John Minors within their acclimatization plans as far as was reasonable, with a view to the fact that these two compatible climbers would then be able to enjoy their own devices in the area at a standard and speed dictated by their abilities. When personal circumstances forced Dr Minors to withdraw, plans shifted towards Nick's ambitions being accommodated with the help of Georges Bettembourg, who had become increasingly interested in a ski descent of the mountain, rather than an ascent of the South-West Face. So it was hoped that, should Nick successfully accompany the other members of the team over the acclimatization programme, he would be able to accompany Georges over an easier flank, at least as far as an intermediate camp established during the acclimatization climbing, and possibly even to the summit if the terrain and Nick's ability suggested this would be reasonable. However, it was always unlikely that such an ambition could be fulfilled. Doug put it to Nick quite succinctly.

'You can't expect to keep up with us. Some of us have been doing this sort of climbing for the last twenty years. It's our trade if you like. I don't expect you'll be able to climb on the

South-West Face of Shishapangma, and you certainly wouldn't expect me to be able to design an oil rig.'

Some of us were a little more basic. 'You'll be lucky to get to Base Camp!'

Through the months preceding our departure Nick had become increasingly bullish about his prospects on the mountain. From the comfort of Britain, photographs of the Himalayan Giants can appear deceptively innocent, especially to the inexperienced. At high altitude, even on the easiest snow slopes, a high degree of stamina and competence is demanded. Without the logistic emphasis of the classic Himalayan style of mountaineering, more than ever the climber needs the depth of experience which ensures that his climbing is second nature to him, almost completely reflexive, for the slightest error can have the gravest consequences. At the very least, the danger of frostbite is a constant and very ready companion. However, in the deceptive ease of the pre-expedition socializing, the Alpine-style 'fast-talk', the mountain's flanks were at times being endowed with an almost playground atmosphere, and Nick, not unnaturally, hoped for great things for himself. When Georges dropped out of the expedition, trying to accommodate Nick's ambitions was once again a primary consideration, and amongst the several reasons for Doug's invitation to Elaine was the hope that, as a second support climber, she would be able to share in some climbing with Nick.

On 13 April, in Zegar, the question had its first real airing. Until that time it had been overlooked, almost embarrassingly, while the experienced team sought to avoid the issue by postponing it until the effects of altitude had made themselves known. The problem was pinpointed during a discussion about a second, intertwined but less-vital current of tension – the different degrees of emphasis placed by each member of the team on the amount of time and effort we should afford for seeing Tibet itself. In the bare, spartan, concrete eating hall of our hotel at Shigatse, with its peeling whitewash and decaying atmosphere, we had considered our onward timetable. With their passionate interest in Tibet and its people, Doug and Elaine wanted to stop and camp at the village of Dingri. This village had a long history of association with the Sherpa people of Nepal, and their Sherpa friends had often talked of it. The remainder of the team were more concerned with moving straight through to the roadhead, a more blinkered drive direct towards the mountain, in order that we might maximize our time there. This conflict of opinion was heightened somewhat by the inclusion of Elaine, whose scholarly interest in the country and its people was, for her, perhaps the pre-eminent reason for deciding to come along. She had hoped to undertake some climbing during our acclimatization programme and then to travel in Tibet while the climbers turned their attention towards the South-West Face.

By the time we had reached Zegar, it was fast becoming apparent that the costs incurred in the towns, due to the high prices and the restriction on camping, meant that the expedition had to minimize time spent in such fabled cities as Lhasa. Moreover the System absolutely prohibited any deviation from the regulated path along the route. Doug and Elaine may also have been perturbed at the dominance of drive towards the mountain exhibited by the majority of the team. The debate was becoming a little heated around our rusting metal table, at which an almost untouched breakfast still lingered. Elaine, unhappy with the aggressive atmosphere as she perceived it, got up to leave the table.

'Hang on, Elaine, you can't just walk off like that when things get awkward, you know. You've got £1,500 tied up in this trip as well; you have to say what you think – aggressiveness or otherwise.'

'Well, I'm mainly interested in Tibet, as you know, and I'm not going to hang around Base Camp for three weeks while you do your Face.' The cat was out of the bag!

Roger spoke: 'But we thought you would be climbing with Nick while we were on the Face.'

This was the impression shared, not without some concern, by Paul, Roger, myself and Nick. Elaine was not so sure. The differences in personality between herself and Nick ensured they were not an obvious match as close friends; and Nick's lack of experience meant, as she quite sensibly pointed out, that such an approach was probably unrealistic.

'It's been done before [climbing as a team of two on eight-thousanders], but only by a few, very experienced climbers. It's just not on for Nick and me.'

The realism was greeted with some relief by Paul, Roger and myself, but with some considerable worry by Nick, who pointed out that he had been under the impression that he and Elaine would climb together, and that he was anxious to maximize the amount of time he climbed above Base Camp.

'Look, it's no insult to Nick, this. I've no idea about his climbing; it's just plain crazy for two inexperienced climbers to go on an 8,000-metre peak.'

NICK: Having become committed to the idea of this Tibetan expedition my approach was to think positive and concentrate on making it all work. I would take more care another time to have a list of potential stand-ins. However, even if I had prepared such a list, it is probable that none would have been available at the ten days' notice we had when Georges dropped out just before we left.

My personal commitment was not just a bullish dream of starting Himalayan climbing with an 8,000-metre peak. It just happened that this was the trip I set up in order to get the opportunity to climb in Tibet. Alex's calculating mind and the application of his merciless lawyer's logic was a necessary ingredient in the field. However, on any trip the outcome is frequently at odds with logic. In the country which epitomizes the heart of Buddhism I was prepared to let my fate lead me, not a mindless animal to sacrifice, but a thinking man to a new experience.

ALEX: There had never, of course, been any intention on Doug's part to have inexperienced, unsupported members of the party wandering about over high Himalayan ground. He had hoped, rather, to share his joy of and experiences in these mountains with everyone over the first few weeks, making time and himself available and taking developments as they came. He feels keenly that the ambitious Alpinist should try to make room in his plans for the less experienced climber. I hold to a contrary, less patient approach, that a person should work his way through the mountains, should he wish to, on the back of his own experience rather than accept any degree of shepherding. I think it would be fair to say that, to a greater or lesser extent, Paul and Roger share this view. There would, therefore, have been a certain unwillingness to make available too much extra time to accommodate the slower pace of Nick and Elaine, even without the additional hindrance of the extra time consumed by the approach to our Base Camp. Inevitably, this created an undercurrent of potential tension at the Camp, which was considerably assisted by the fact that it turned out to be one of the most unrelaxing, almost miserable Base Camp sites that any of us could remember. The snow never melted; the lakes remained frozen for the duration of our visit; the sun was rarely seen and, when it appeared, it was usually feeble, the atmosphere, very hazy, creating a sense of consternation. Could this be the self-same sun that was so pleasant in Nepal, and might even burn the unwary to a frazzle? The overall effect was dispiriting. The wind would blast the snow around our amphitheatre, wreak havoc with the tents and kitchen, and nibble away at our morale.

The kitchen, which is generally the focal point and social centre of any expedition, was our tarpaulin, which we had borrowed from the Red Army down in Nyalam, draped at one end over a large boulder and secured at the front to two stout crossed poles. From outside it looked like a curious animal from the Magic Roundabout. Inside it was a squalid affair. The slope of the ground ran alarmingly and with icy certainty downhill, towards the rock. Spindrift whistled through the front and slipped in through the sides where the stores had been stacked to provide some ballast and protection from the winds. The tarpaulin was not over-large and any movement within the kitchen had to be conducted at an acute bow, which was at least useful in that the eyes, if open, were guaranteed to be looking in the right direction to pick a way through the minefield of pressure cookers, stores and plates that slid about the icy floor before migrating towards the rock. Had we been pitched in the bows of an ocean-going tramp steamer, life could not have been much more awkward. At times the entire construction strained violently as a particularly severe gust slammed in through the front and attempted to inflate the tarpaulin sufficiently to achieve a vertical take-off. Huddled in one-piece duvet and Goretex windsuits, with feet freezing even in double boots, eyes down against the spindrift, one could have been forgiven for harbouring the illusion that we were an Orc road-mending crew high in the mountains of Mordor.

The poor weather also mitigated against the possibilities of sunbathing, so that much time was spent in individual tents, with the result that social intercourse was at a premium. Nick was feeling the effects of altitude and now subject to a bad cough, Roger was in love and wondering why he bothered climbing the Himalayas, Paul was worried for his chest, Elaine was feeling the uncertainty of her exposed position on the team, and Doug was finding himself in the awkward and unrewarding role of expedition intermediary; we needed prolonged bad weather like a hole in the head.

On 26 April Doug elected to return to Nyalam with Wu, to organize the transport of the remainder of our equipment with Pemba, to make arrangements for the collection and delivery of our mail and to purchase meat.

DOUG: As mist, blown by a cold wind, swirled around the site we had allocated for Base Camp, Roger arrived carrying the eggs in a wicker basket, teetering from boulder to boulder, a pole across his shoulder with Nick knee deep in soft snow supporting the other end. Alex was carrying a pole too, with the snow right up to his crutch. They flopped down by the tents that we had erected whilst Paul was pulling boulders towards a kitchen site. Elaine was producing cups of tea in the porter tent. Whilst I was cooking some rice Elaine came over angrily, telling me to let the lads prepare their own meat. This was the result of the banter that always goes on in the presence of vegetarians, usually in light-hearted vein although when the going gets tough maybe an aggressive edge creeps into their comments. Being grumpy, as my wet clammy clothes had rapidly cooled and there was everything to do, I snapped back telling her not to complain about moaning meat-eaters. She went to her tent.

Later I went over to see her and to find out that she was fed up with the lads' aggression. I went across to the lads and told them not to grumble about the food to her, putting on a show of anger that soon evaporated as we continued eating, drinking and joking, celebrating our arrival long into the night. Early next morning, whilst I was putting the brew on and washing last night's dirty pots, I talked to Elaine about the previous evening, trying to reassure her that all would be well once we settled in. 'It's just a stage in the game and you shouldn't misinterpret the lads' boisterous behaviour.'

She replied, 'I cannot stand the aggro.'

Outside, Alex was saying to Roger, 'This has been a great trip so far,' and Roger agreed.

Inside, Elaine was saying, 'It's their language I can't stand, and their constant moaning about the lack of meat.'

I knew there was more to it than this but could not quite put my finger on the reason for Elaine's obviously distraught condition.

There was work to do. We were at this time having so much trouble with Pemba that we felt we could not rely on him at all. Before going on any further I decided that it would be best if I tried to clarify his position on the expedition with The Leader at Nyalam. At the same time, we could purchase tins of Chinese meat from the People's Store there and, if possible, any fresh vegetables that had been brought up from the south. We still hoped to receive mail at Nyalam and so, for this reason too, I went down to arrange mail runners. Feeling pretty depressed, I set off with Wu. At such times homesickness always wells up.

On the way Wu and I became separated in the mist. I went back up to look for him but, after a couple of hours searching the valley floor, I reasoned that he must have continued down valley. Finally, I arrived at Nyalam to discover Wu tucked up in bed with all his clothing strewn around in front of the stove drying. It turned out that he had failed to locate the logs spanning the torrent and had fallen into the river whilst wading across. He had thought his end had come. He was so relaxed after his ordeal, so glad to be alive. There was no mail.

On the twenty-sixth, after a solid nine-hour sleep, I awoke to the loudspeaker music. During the day I purchased cases of meat, wrote letters home and spent a lot of time with Pemba hoping to win him over by discussing (with Wu interpreting) his climbing activities on Everest, where he said he got up to 8,000 metres. Pemba said that he was forty-six years old and was born a peasant boy near Shigatse. He said his parents were slaves and that they had to give half their crop to the landowner every year, also that they could not leave their land without his permission. His father had some yaks which ate the landowner's crops, so the landowner beat Pemba's father, putting him in bed for a week before he died from his injuries. A few weeks later Pemba's mother died – he was then sixteen years old. He had three sisters and two brothers, all older than himself. One of the sisters was a nun. He continued to grow crops, tending the yaks and then, in 1960, after helping transport loads for the 1960 Chinese Everest Expedition, he joined the CMA as one of the first recruits. He went on three expeditions to Shishapangma's north side. It was in 1975 that he reached 8,000 metres on Everest, and the following year went up to the base of K2 from the north. He spent most of his time instructing other climbers from China and Tibet. He reckoned he was well off, having a farm and two yaks a few miles north of Shigatse which were being looked after by his wife with their two children, a girl aged four and a boy aged eight. He had money in the bank (3,500 yuan) and a radio and considered himself much better off than his parents. I asked him about his religion. He said that he did believe in a lot that the Buddhists had told him but what he tried to do was to work hard for his country and be honest. He said a lot more than the seven monasteries we had heard of were still functioning out of the three and a half thousand being used before liberation. There were plans, he claimed proudly, to restore the Rongbuk monastery near Everest over the next two years, with the Chinese providing all the materials.

Just then the Party Secretary for Nyalam poked her head through the door to talk to Pemba. She was a big woman dressed like the Sherpas and with one very large tooth poking over her bottom lip. She seemed a rather nice lady and I wondered how the Tibetans and the Chinese got along together, for here in Nyalam there are not only Chinese officials but also the military, this being a frontier town. In 1959 many Tibetan people fled from the Chinese along this valley to find sanctuary. Pemba said they need not have fled because the Chinese did not do all the dreadful things that were expected of them. Now they all worked together as brothers; in fact, Pemba said, the Tibetans hold high positions in the running of their affairs. For instance, he said, Lodse, who climbed Everest in 1975, is now in charge of the CMA in Lhasa and his wife is Chairman of the Tibetan Financial Committee.

By now it was late at night and the snow was coming down outside. Quite a crowd had gathered in my room and one by one they left, leaving me with my thoughts and dreams.

On 28 April we left Nyalam, having suffered for three days the worst food I have ever had; rice, spinach and boiled potatoes for breakfast – and for lunch – and for dinner. The left-overs were recycled for the next meal at the communal kitchen serving the Chinese workers who do not have a wife with them.

Pemba said he would move up to a yak hut, the highest building on this side of the mountain and later christened by Elaine 'Smaug's Lair'. He said he would do his best for us but I had absolutely no faith in the man. He was only concerned about himself.

Wu and I walked to the yak-herders' huts an hour and a half from Nyalam, where inside one of them we found three young Tibetans who offered us tea. Wu talked to the older woman in Chinese, a language she had learned although she had never been to school. We got into a conversation about contraception. In China, Wu said, they are only allowed to have one child in the cities; if they live on a farm they can have two, whilst in Tibet, which is reckoned to be under-populated, a family may have three children. Once you have achieved the limit you are supposed to be cut. I asked him to find out as much as he could about the lives of the Tibetans. Apparently they are allowed to own three or four yaks, and all the rest belong to the commune, who give them 300 yuan a year each for food. He was not able to say much more than is put out by the government agencies.

It was a pleasant interlude, a nice contrast to sit among these calm, gentle people after three days in Nyalam. They told us that many Tibetans now inter-marry with the Chinese; in fact the lady, Pandgo, who climbed Everest in 1975 had married a Chinese sportsman who was a Leader in Lhasa. It did seem to me that Everest had given a big boost to Tibetan and Chinese co-operation and perhaps also a lot of pride and stimulation to get the place moving.

We walked off, up valley to Base Camp, the frost on the ground twinkling orange while birds flew in droves flitting this way and that with a flutter of feathers as they dipped and dived above us. This time we went further along the valley before climbing up the moraine. There were several birds with long curly beaks, which no doubt fed on the shoals of fish – some of them two or three inches long – that swam in the cold, clear streams meandering over the flat valley bottom. Dwarf willow catkins stuck out of the snow and we saw many cat tracks crisscrossing our route.

From the moraine crest I could see our mountain; it seemed a long way off in time but I found comfort in the thought that all the running around this valley would help me to acclimatize for the virgin South-West Face. By the time I reached camp I was feeling confident that we would climb it. I knew it would have to be on the first attempt and in Alpine style.

I staggered into camp – only Nick was there, 'How's Mr Scott?' he said in his Irish drawl.

'Obviously better than Old Nick,' I replied, judging by the way he was coughing.

Elaine was off on a walk around to the east, whilst Paul, Roger and Alex had gone up to find a site for Advance Base Camp. They all returned more or less together, full of enthusiasm as they gulped down their tea. They reckoned the South-West Face of Shishapangma looked feasible and the peaks upon which we were hoping to acclimatize seemed reasonably accessible.

On 29 April we all set off to carry loads to Advance Base Camp after a meal of rice-porridge, eggs and chips. Elaine, without much enthusiasm, decided to come along too. Alex and I went up front, breaking trail in the soft snow. We stopped to climb one of the superb boulders dotted around the undulating country between Base Camp and Advance Base Camp. Elaine plodded by as we were engrossed in our climbing and walked on into the mist. It was on the tip of my tongue to tell her to wait but I left it as she seemed withdrawn and moody. Fifty minutes later when we arrived at the Advance Base site, a friendly place in a little hollow amongst grass and boulders, there was no sign of her. We dumped the gear and food then, yelling 'Elaine' at the top of our voices, headed all the way back to Base Camp. It was like a walk on the Cairngorm Plateau and now just as wild as the Cairngorms are in winter – snow, wind and bad visibility. We hoped that Elaine was back in camp but when we arrived there at 5.30 pm she was still absent. We sat around having a beer, and then put our boots back on to go and look for her, when she staggered in obviously very distressed. I went over to comfort her but she pushed me away saying that she had been crawling around for two hours, vomiting. Poor lass. Elaine did not eat that evening. I suddenly realized that she was very dehydrated, which accounted for her vomiting; it is so easy to become dehydrated, especially for someone as slight as she is.

I fed her tea and orange drinks and tried to jolly her along without much success. She talked to me about the backbiting that goes on about Nick. For Alex she had only contempt, saying that he always spoiled a good atmosphere with his aggressiveness and took the others along with him. Without realizing it, they changed from sensitive beings to oafs. I suggested to Elaine that she put all her energy into climbing now, then into Tibet later; it is impossible to be in two places at the same time.

The following day did not start much better, for it was whilst I was making tea and preparing breakfast with Roger that I talked to him about Elaine's comments. Roger denied that there had been any backbiting; they had simply been discussing how they could get Nick up a climb and about the share-out of camera gear after the expedition.

Elaine came into the kitchen, having heard our conversation from her tent, and saying: 'You have no right to bring that up.'

I told her, 'It is necessary for the trip.'

We take off in a violent argument, both reverting to type: mechanical man, mechanical woman, out of control; me going on about her moods and the edge she was putting on the trip, calling her a stupid bitch, and her yelling at me to shut up. Paul comes and goes, Alex arrives and says it has been a good trip and adds: 'The only fly in the ointment was the woman who could not take it in a man's world.'

Finally I retired to my tent and Elaine came over with a mug of lemon juice and we laughed at our argument and then talked about all the good trips that we had known and what had made them so. She had met Alex after our argument and they had had a talk.

'Did it help?' I asked.

'He was brutally to the point,' she said.

Later, Alex told me that during this conversation he had told Elaine that he did not want her to come between him and

Shishapangma. He asked her what was her reason for being here. Was it just to follow Doug about like a puppy?

Alex told her, 'You are the problem of the trip – if you were not here there would be no problem.'

I felt like the pig in the middle whilst all this was going on, trying to grasp an answer that might reconcile the two extreme elements of the trip. I could see both sides quite clearly but could think of no solution. Alex, with a single-minded drive for the mountain, a person great to be with whilst everything proceeds in that direction; and Elaine hoping to enjoy a climb that would take her above the valley to have a good look around, and then to go down to spend time amongst the Tibetans with whom she empathized so well. As soon as either Alex's or Elaine's expectation appeared to be in jeopardy the negative energy that was generated put a dampener on the whole of the enterprise. I blamed myself for not having foreseen this problem. The only reconciling factor possible was a bit of love but there was none – not between Alex and Elaine, they had both put up their shields.

May Day dawned bright and clear; at long last the weather seemed to be improving. Elaine, her old affable self, was already in the kitchen cooking breakfast. Roger and Paul had 'the runs', which didn't improve Roger's temper or his liking for Nick's strange ways. Roger talked to him in his clipped manner, ordering him about the camp on errands, to which Paul just smiled and joked: 'RBJ calling water boy; RBJ calling water boy.'

It was time to go. Alex was champing at the bit.

ALEX: It had been our hope to push to Advance Base Camp today in order to start our acclimatization climbing, but both Paul and Roger had become quite ill overnight and so that they would have a chance to recover the remainder of the team settled for another carry. On my way back, in order to start a competition which I knew Paul at least would find irresistible, I raced back as fast as I could manage, running over the last hill, leaping in unsteady bounds down the final slope before collapsing into camp. Forty-five minutes to get there, and fifteen minutes' horizontal coughing after that.

Back in camp, another problem was developing. Eight yaks and our two yak-men had appeared in camp, carrying –

unbelievably – one load between them! As if that were not enough, Pemba, who had engineered this masterstroke, had taken up residence in the small shack before the second bridge and announced his intention to proceed no further. With the yak-herders came two similar letters, both addressed to Wu. We were to remove our Base Camp immediately.

We were, to say the least, incredulous. The complete and total lack of understanding of mountaineering and mountains was frustrating to the point of tears. This liaison officer was no more interested in our expedition than in the price of a wet suit in Bradford. We were to withdraw because our camp was too high, the highest base camp ever established in China, even higher than the Everest Base Camp, which should be the highest as Everest was the highest mountain! Our height, he asserted, was 5,400 metres at least, and possibly 5,600. This seemed somewhat unlikely from our point of view, as the rock summit high above our camp was only 5,400 metres on the map. However, Pemba assured us, all this was against regulations and Wu was to withdraw from our camp immediately while negotiations were opened. Pemba's note stated that regulations did not permit camps above 5,000 metres. This was doubly frustrating as, first of all, it was unlikely that we were higher than 4,900 metres but, more importantly, there was no such regulation. The regulation and the altitudes were being plucked out of thin air to suit a purpose – that purpose being essentially, we believed, the comfort of our liaison officer. Indeed we believe, and not without reason, that there is a simple conspiracy among liaison officers in Tibet to keep base camps as close to the roadhead as possible for their own convenience. After all our time and effort in getting to our camp, with our attentions finally directed towards the climbing, we were, unbelievably, being menaced once again by the System in the shape of this unsympathetic, selfish man. Reaction was immediate, if not always helpful.

'Hang him!'
'Inform the *Express*!'
'Sack him!'
'Ignore him!'
Someone would have to go down, but who? Once again, the ugly tentacle of lost time was rearing in our direction. Doug would go down. Who would go with him?

'Alex?'

'Not me, I'm going climbing.'

Even as I said it, I knew I wasn't. If the business were to be done quickly, we were the obvious choice. Nick was intent on sacking Pemba, but this was simply, obviously, not possible. No matter how aggrieved one might feel, it is a dangerous course to make a move which stakes your version of events against that of a government official and then expect 'justice'. Any such action would put the position beyond our control; new, unknown elements would be introduced into the equation with who knew what results. Doug was right; we had to go down.

There was a half moon that night. Wu, Doug and I grabbed a hasty supper from amongst the evening meal's preparations and left at about ten pm through the beautiful, cold savagery of mountains lit by moonlight and valleys dark in their shadow, a blackness into which we plunged off the far end of the moraine ridge. For the final half hour of the approach, down towards the sleeping shack, dogs had sensed our coming and barked their warnings. Armed with this knowledge and a fistful of stones we crossed the bridge and approached the den. Agitated and angry, the dogs' eyes gleamed in the periphery of our torch vision, but they sensed our mood, felt the occasional projectile and slunk quietly away.

The small, ill-fitting, stubborn wooden door that was the entrance to the shack yielded to a kick. Inside, startled exclamations greeted us, peering eyes blinded by our torches. Pemba was at the far right wall; Gandhi, the dismissed yak-boy, slept beside the fire, opposite the door.

'Pemba, get up!'

For over two and a half hours we argued in that damp, smoky, desolate shack. Pemba sat on his bare wooden bed with his thick army coat pulled close over his shoulders, rubbing his knees in a slow pantomime fashion, looking (he thought) at once troubled and concerned, understanding and hurt, and consequently, in our eyes, like a cunning child caught doing wrong. I sat on Pemba's right on a small earth bench while Doug alternated between sitting on his left and on an inoperative wood-burning stove and attempting to pace about the den which was still filled with solid banks of winter snow. Gandhi made efforts to prepare tea from damp twigs. Much blowing and puffing produced an impenetrable smog, but little in the way of tea. Wu sat on my right and tried to keep some sanity as the argument developed through him, thick and fast.

'Now Wu, tell Pemba that he is a menace, in all of the twenty expeditions I have been on I have never had a worse liaison officer. He is a total hindrance, always mayo, mayo, mayo (no), we can't stay just one night in Lhasa, we can't cancel the minibus, we can't stop for pictures, he can't manage the yaks . . .'

'Mr Pemba says he has done his utmost . . .'

'Utmost!'

'Utmost to help you and you simply don't appreciate it.'

'Mayo, mayo, mayo, what good's that?'

With maps and photographs we demonstrated as convincingly as we could that our camp was not above 5,000 metres, but Pemba continued to insist it was impossibly high.

'Mr Pemba says you are mountaineers. You will be very tired and when the weather is bad you will need to rest. You must come down to this place to rest; your camp is too high!'

A willingness to give advice on matters that are quite beyond the ken of the adviser seems to be a habit in this part of the world. We tried changing tack to an approach more in keeping with the realities of the Chinese System.

'Tell Mr Pemba that we are very important people, as he must realize for such a small team to be invited as guests of his government to such a large mountain. Tell him I am the third most important mountaineer in the British Mountaineering Association, Doug is Mr Everest who discovered the Chinese tripod, Paul is the biggest retail man in our country and Roger is a very important mountain guide. Tell him we are writing a book. If this mayo mayo persists, we will have to report him to the CMA, to Peking, to our Embassy and to London. He will be a man to be avoided at all costs.'

'Mr Pemba says he has been on several expeditions and has never had any trouble. He will tell all his future expeditions about you. You are the worst expedition ever to come to China. Mr Pemba says he is a citizen of the People's Republic of China and you should not treat him like this.'

You know you are at the bottom of the barrel when 'citizen

of the People's Republic of China' comes up in the conversation, but still it went on. Pemba had to come to Base Camp.

'Doesn't he even have the basic curiosity of a mountaineer to get two days up a yak-track?'

'Mr Pemba says his knees are too bad to go up to the camp, and that he has a bad chest.'

'What's wrong with his knees?'

'Arthritis.'

'Advise Mr Pemba to stop eating meat!'

In the end it was agreed that Wu would return with us to Base Camp, which was vital as, without him, we would have no one to secure our tents in our absence whilst climbing. Pemba would follow, he assured us, as soon as his knees permitted. There was no more argument about rules and regulations, no reference to altitudes, it all boiled down to claimed arthritic knees which, when we looked at them, did seem pretty bad. Why had the CMA sent such an unhealthy man to an unknown base camp? I slept outside that night, unable to stand the interior's squalor. The following morning we made a weary return to camp. Having forgotten my sunglasses, I had to wander back with my scarf tied over my face, a sort of a breadline production of the Elephant Man. We were greeted by coffee and pancakes, congratulations and tales: 'Number three mountaineer – that must make me number one!' and a good dinner into which considerable thought had gone.

The camp was resplendent. Roger had donned his organizational cap and harassed anything on two legs. There were even different bags for organic and inorganic waste. It was unlikely to last.

At last we were free to turn our minds to acclimatization. Our intention was to climb the South-West Face of Shishapangma in Alpine style. As explained earlier, this means that the climbing team approaches the foot of its objective intent on climbing that route in one single push, without any support from fixed ropes, previously placed camps or previous presence on the route. It is a major aspect of the recent trend in Himalayan climbing towards lightweight climbing, though lightweight climbing is not necessarily Alpine style. The crux of the Alpinist's approach is his desire to avoid setting foot on the proposed route until he is sufficiently acclimatized by climbing elsewhere to contemplate climbing that route in one single acquaintance.

The process of acclimatization, by which the climber adapts his body to the rarefied atmosphere and lack of oxygen at higher altitudes is, perhaps, best understood by taking the process backwards. While the planning varies between individuals, their experience, level of fitness and stamina, and the nature of the climb, my thinking for such a climb as the South-West Face would run along these lines. The summit is just over 8,000 metres; it is a fairly technical climb by modern standards but will probably allow a fast ascent by a rapidly acclimatized team. Ideally, the team should have bivouacked previously around 7,000 metres and climbed above the bivouac the following day, perhaps enjoying three highish· bivouacs on the overall trip. In order to be fit enough to do that without going over the limit and exhausting themselves for the Face, they will need to have bivouacked at 6,400 metres on a previous climb, climbed above that for some distance and, again, enjoyed two or three bivouacs on that climb. The climber will then look around the area on which he is and try to fit the theory into the places available to him to climb. It is also often a good idea to use acclimatization to check out and leave some supplies on a proposed descent line.

Acclimatization theory and practice differs widely between climbers, but for our team on this occasion the above approach was approximately agreed on, and the area seemed to fit the bill perfectly. To the right of the South-West Face was a shoulder which I have subsequently discovered had a name, Pungpa Ri, at 7,445 metres. (Anders Bolinder, the eminent Swiss cartographer, had passed on to Doug this information gleaned from an original map by Peter Aufschnaiter.) This was also on a possible descent route. A climb in this area would prepare us for an ascent of the Face. In order to be fit enough for this climb, we could utilize the easier slopes of Nyanang Ri, a mountain of 7,047 metres. To the right of that again was a snow and ice slope on the ridge that led from Nyanang Ri eventually to our Base Camp, the highest hump of which was around 6,200 metres and upon which we might also have enjoyed useful first-day climbing. This first day would have been particularly useful for Nick and Elaine, who, with less experience and stamina than the rest of the team, would need a longer run-in at acclimatization. However, we had by now lost even more time, and so, in the kitchen on the evening of 2 May, I proposed that we did not have the time to accommodate this and should move directly on to the slopes of Nyanang Ri. Paul and Roger were in immediate agreement. Doug did not dissent.

CHAPTER 5
Acclimatization Climb

ALEX: The first acclimatization climb wrought havoc with our team. Within a minute of leaving the Advance Camp Nick was ill, bringing up his breakfast. Fifteen minutes up our small rocky valley, below a steep snow and boulder slope that led up to the plateau fifty metres above, we stopped and waited for him to join us. The first major crisis was about to explode. White and ashen, Nick was approaching in slow zigzag up the incline, picking a forlorn path amongst rocks and snow patches, dictating a pace at which we could not expect to spend the next night – even should we care to – more than an hour above our Advance Camp. At these altitudes, illness is extremely debilitating and recovery difficult. The body is quickly drained of all reserves, exhausted, activity eats into the very soul. Nick was already higher than he had ever been before, and now the pace dictated by our acclimatization programme was presenting him with a hopeless task under a heavy rucksack. Fundamentally, Nick had not logged enough hours slogging through Scottish bogs in winter blizzards, lumbering through the frantic, non-stop twenty-four-hour exhaustion of the Alps, to lend any foundation to the initial optimism that, somehow, it would 'be all right on the night'.

Like a pack of pursued wolves with a badly wounded mate, the experienced climbers smelt the inevitable 'Nick's had it'. To go on was exhaustingly pointless. Any one of us would have cut loose and lost altitude as quickly as possible, but for Nick it was not such a simple choice, for he did not have the experience to be able to contemplate shaking the illness and catching up with our progress independently. Once he turned around he would be out of the reckoning with no partner with whom to attempt the lesser peaks, yet the more he tried to push on the more irrecoverable would be his exhaustion and the greater our lack of progress.

Cold calculations worked back from the recesses in my mind: how many days would it take to reach that goal, and how many more days did we have? We were hoping for four days away on this trip with three days' rest afterwards, five out on the next with another three days' rest, and all-told, the Face would, with luck, consume a week. Twenty-two days, which put us on to 26 May without any allowance for a particularly bad patch of weather or illness in the camp, and our acclimatization programme was already quite ambitious. In my mind it all added up to going now, and going without those unable to sustain the pace. Nick reached us.

'How're you doing, Nick?'

'Not so well.'

We remained for another couple of minutes and then moved off, up the steep slope above, to wait once again at the top.

'That slope will kill him.'

'I wonder if he realizes we don't normally acclimatize at this pace?'

Roger and I pushed on for another ten minutes over a small, flat, snowy plateau and up on to some more moraine above, where we sat and waited again, hoping to show that Nick was dictating the pace and that we were not in the habit of making such frequent stops. The sun was strong today. From our boulder, looking back over the way we had come, we could see down the valley where we had struggled with the yaks and, beyond that, the Himalayan ranges to our east, Gauri Sankar and Menlungtse, a Tolkienesque beauty so shapely from that angle that an accurate painter would have been accused of misrepresentation. Tired of the waiting after nearly half an hour, Roger left his rucksack and descended to see what now was causing the long delay. A little later Elaine appeared at the top of the slope and came over to join me.

'What's happening?'

Elaine said little, sensing the cold edge in me and the sympathy towards it by the majority. How long before this self-made argument would revolve over her head?

Another twenty minutes passed until finally two more figures appeared, Doug and Paul, 'Looking-Glass' characters, the gentle, shuffling bear and the emaciated, strutting turkey, deep in conference.

'What's up?'

Paul told me that he and Doug had had a long chat with

Nick. Not having been well that morning he would have liked a day's rest but was unwilling to ask for it. 'He won't get very far, he's knackered.'

'Yes, but how far?' I was looking at Doug. 'Look, this is fast becoming ridiculous. It's obvious that Nick's had it, we haven't got the time, we're on a bloody tight schedule and at this rate of travel we are only going to get to the edge of the glacier today. A day's walk, an hour's progress, we may as well go back to Advance Base for supper! And anyway, you know how stubborn Nick is, if he was dead he'd only admit to a slight limp.'

'Look, Alex, just relax and give him some time to sort this out for himself, let him make the decision.' It was Doug.

Roger came into view, carrying a rucksack, and then Nick, unburdened, meandering, almost stumbling, painfully slowly in our direction, like an actor trying to imitate the last steps of an exhausted person lost in a blizzard but without the props. When he reached us no one seemed willing to say anything, but the sight of Roger carrying the sack was, for me, the final straw. If it must be me, then so be it.

'Nick, as far as I'm concerned you've had it, you might as well go down now.'

He told me about his stomach, how all he needed was another day.

'Nick, you're just clutching at straws. You don't have all the years of slog necessary. I'm sorry, but charity ends at five thousand metres.'

I thought back to the same argument underneath Makalu the previous spring, when a friend had slowed perceptibly and fallen behind. Then, on a barren moraine, I had shouted to a colleague: 'Look, you stupid Pole, give him a couple more hours!'

That time it had been me demanding time for a friend, but I knew him well enough to realize that he would have already reached his decision; he only had to catch us up to tell us. With Nick, I sensed too much optimism, too little grasp of what I saw as reality. What about the others?

'What do you think, Paul?'

Unknown to me, Paul was on the verge of a shattering decision of his own. He agreed with me; charity did end at five thousand metres.

'Roger?'

'Well, I agree with you but Nick's got to reach his own decision.'

'Bloody hell, Roger! Don't be such a bloody amateur. These are mountains you know. They kill people.'

ELAINE: I looked down the valley; wisps of cloud filtered between the peaks, the distant ranges were blue and hazy. Down below, in the green and purple shadows, people were living and working, weaving tales, seeing their world in a way very different from ours.

The arguments were still buzzing back and forth, crowding and pushing against the timelessness of the mountains. Why was it not enough just to be here, feeling the energy of this place? I was living in a different world; images of mountains, snow and sun, that subtle touching of minds sharing exhilaration and dangers in the thin air. But somehow the dream had turned into a military exercise with no room for dreamers. I knew I was questioning why I climbed at all. I knew I was climbing here because of Doug, because I could pick up on his enthusiasm and love of challenge, in the same way that his sensitivity allowed him to share my perceptions of the people we had met.

The valley beckoned, filling my head with the tales Namgyal had told me as we followed the yaks along the ridge, of traders and smugglers, adventures in the mountain passes, of lamas and hermits. It was only my stupid stubbornness in wanting to finish a job once started that was keeping me going.

I turned and walked up the moraine before even that evaporated.

ALEX: Elaine left, worried for her future. She would not be able to match our pace if we moved quickly, and then the same questions would be levelled at her. Her departure made me even angrier. Why did she have to melt off at the first hint of trouble; why did she have to be such a pained, quiet and bloody martyr! Doug and I fell at each other.

'If I was the leader of this trip I'd tell Nick to go down.'

'Well, fortunately, Alex, we are not all like that. Why don't you just calm down and let things take a natural course? Why do you have to push it?' He was speaking in his school-masterly manner.

'But it's so bloody obvious, man; if Nick can't see this now, how the hell can you expect him to see it later? I've a lot of respect for you, Doug, but I also reckon that some of your trips have failed to realize their potential because of your happy-go-lucky approach.'

Poor Nick, what did an hour or so matter – why not let the situation become irresistibly obvious? Now his personal trauma was becoming nothing more than a battleground over which Doug's character and my own could skirmish.

NICK: In the spring I had been too busy with organization to visit the Alps for my final pre-expedition training, and by the time I got to Nyalam I was wiped out from recurring sore throats and spent most of the time there laid up. I had been lucky to recover quickly enough to go up to Base Camp with the others and had been trying to make up for lost time by doing as much as I could. But I was not fully attuned to pacing myself at high altitude and was still thinking of Himalayan as being just super Alpine, not allowing for the recovery time needed between bouts of exercise in the early stages of acclimatization, particularly when I found myself slow to acclimatize.

I had been running out of puff very easily, which was predictable enough, and also my stamina was very low so that I recovered very slowly and needed a lot of sleep. I was still groping around in the dark and in my own mind relying on others to tell me what to do. Sensibly enough they refrained from doing so. The most encouraging thing was that I was sleeping very well, though I was feeling the cold, which is a sign of slow acclimatization. None of us could ever match Doug for not feeling cold. It was a very cold spring.

My diary for 30 April reads: '29th was coldest night yet'. It was on the 1st that I began to show signs of overdoing it and acclimatization slowed down again. My diary reads: 'I arrive back from Advance Base Camp feeling whacked and sick. Early to bed with chronic wind followed by diarrhoea in the night.' The night before records that Paul and Roger had stomach trouble. I had seemed to recover but should have waited at least another day before going climbing.

111

But I was worried that the others would not wait for me and I would get no climbing done. The situation reads very clearly, but mountains are all about decisions – the climbing is the easy part! When I got back to Advance Base Camp I would start sorting myself out. My diary reads here: 'very dehydrated'. No wonder. I must have emptied out the contents and linings of my stomach and guts behind every twentieth boulder over the last half-mile stretch of mountainside.

ALEX: Finally, Nick said he would go down.
  'Is it your decision, Nick?'
  'Well, it seems to be "our" decision.'
  'It's not good enough. It must be your decision.'
  With that I gave up in disgust and stomped off after Elaine, muttering darkly about the ridiculous and the obvious. Over the rise I saw her moving straight on and tried to catch her attention, knowing that her way would soon be blocked by a glacial wall and that we had to turn right here to get on to the

Beneath Nyanang Ri: the debate – should Nick go on? Left to right: Paul, Nick, Roger

Doug Scott

glacier at its nearest point. I shouted several times, but she didn't hear me. Perhaps she didn't want to hear me?

'Oi, woman!' I screamed in my most deprecatory tone; surely she would hear that. She turned and I beckoned her in my direction. The glacier was quiet and smooth, falling gently from a col above us on the right, between Nyanang Ri and the smaller six-thousander we had originally hoped to climb on.

It looked so safe, but we had not been on it and it had a comprehensive covering of snow that could be obscuring a potentially lethal crevasse, so for our first passage we would want to go roped. I don't think Elaine was very happy at the thought of being roped to me.

ELAINE: Alex was uncoiling the rope.

'Better tie on for this one.'

He was smiling, the aggression gone and replaced by an instant boyish charm. It was too sudden. I groped for excuses not to go with him, but even as I did so, I realized it was pointless. By the very fact of being there, I had become a very small rung on his ladder of success which would take him to the summit of the mountain as quickly as possible.

I was slow, perversely and deliberately so.

His dry sarcasm reached me from the other end of the short rope. 'Did they teach you to kick the snow off your crampons like that?'

I changed the subject. 'You thinking of climbing that?' pointing to the steep rocky ridge above us.

'Yes, that's the kind of Himalayan climbing we do. But you have to remember there's only a few world-class climbers who are capable of that kind of thing. Just because we talk about it as if it's easy, you shouldn't think it *is* easy.'

We untied at the far side of the glacier and Alex disappeared over the moraine without a word.

ALEX: It had been our intention to make a rising traverse across the steep boulder slopes of the rognon that forms the lower part of the ridge leading up towards the summit of Nyanang Ri, and then to continue in the same fashion over the wide snow and ice slopes beyond, aiming eventually to reach a col on the ridge between Nyanang Ri and Pungpa Ri, from which we would try to work our way back towards Nyanang Ri. At

113

the far side of the boulder slopes we found ourselves peering out into space, struck dumb by the presence of a sheer rock wall that plunged down to the icefields over two hundred feet below, very comprehensively obstructing our path. The four of us were now together. Paul had gone down after Nick. Doug and Roger were subdued, describing their friend's demise brought on by the pain in his lungs.

DOUG: All of us were feeling quite depressed at Paul's decision. I felt an enormous sadness for him and some responsibility too, for having encouraged him to come on this expedition when I knew that underneath his confident exterior there lurked a nagging doubt as to whether his involvement with Shishapangma was worth the sacrifice that such a trip entails. I felt so miserable for him, made worse perhaps by how well he was taking it. There was plenty to do in the Alps, he said, and he could look forward to a season of show jumping. I could have burst into tears for him. He explained how he had been using an inhaler to relieve the congestion in his lungs. It had worked fine to start with, but day by day its good effects diminished and by the evening the lower parts of his lungs were giving him a lot of pain. It was obvious that he could no longer treat the symptoms but had to do something about the cause of this problem. That meant a descent to lower levels out of the cold, biting winds, where he would not have to breathe so hard in an effort to wring out from the air all the oxygen the body needs. As Paul staggered off down to catch up with Nick I plodded on in the steps of Alex and Elaine wondering why it had to be that first Jimmy Duff, then Georges and now Paul, the three people I have enjoyed being with most in the mountains, were no longer with me on Shishapangma. I knew that for me it was to be a hard trip.

Rather than descend we opted to continue up the ridge, scrambling along it until we met ice. At this point we bivouacked. We chose a small, narrow, snowy col just behind a rocky gendarme that marked the end of the scrambling. We were now enveloped in cloud and exposed to a wind which was increasing in intensity and threatening snow. We scrabbled amongst the rocks, rejecting the larger ones and packing the prized, flatter slates into small, gravel-packed ledges on which we would sleep. To our left steep mixed ground

114

disappeared over sharp rock walls; to our right a smooth, concave ice slope petered out of sight. Once the self-made ledges were large enough and smooth enough to contemplate sleeping on, the bivouac sacs (tents) were dug out of rucksacks, billowing and unruly in the wind. With no back wall of rock or ice to pitch them, we had to string them awkwardly off ice axes and guy lines like slack, square-rigged sails, and then open one of the side zips to pass in our rucksacks before crawling in ourselves.

My first bivouac of the year. A tired and sluggish mind began groping for a memory of the routine required to make of this curious pastime the disciplined, second-nature routine that it would have to become. Boots, socks, gloves, sweaters, cameras, batteries, Gaz cylinders, sleeping bag, duvet, food, snow, stores, rucksack and Karrimats. Hunched up in that wildly flapping red cocoon, by the light of a torch, some order had to be made of all this. Wet gear had to be removed and dried; dry gear put on and protected. Sleep? Just a few moments of precious sleep, and it would be all right. No, you must fight that desire, there can be no sleep now, it is hours away. Above all we must organize and cook, melt the snow and ice outside for the precious water that it is imperative we drink in order to maintain any fitness at all at these altitudes. The non-stop battle against dehydration cannot be won, the trick is to lose it slowly.

A snow-encrusted head thrust itself through the zip on the far side, followed by a body and an unwelcome volume of snow. The feet, vigorously banged together to remove packed snow from the soles, came in last. For a moment, Roger and I relaxed in the luxury of being out of the wind, but with the desire to sleep creeping on it was time to work again.

A valiant attempt was made to clear the snow out of the sac. Karrimats were laid on the floor and rucksacks unpacked. Havoc reigned within our cocoon. Neoprene overboots were peeled off the plastic double boots and, folded inside out, placed under a Karrimat. Boots were removed and damp socks changed for dry ones. The damp socks were then placed inside the outer layers of clothing for the night and all the following day, whereupon they would be dry enough on the next bivouac to go back on the feet. After a couple of days you begin to smell like ripe Gorgonzola! Gloves used that day were also placed next to the body to facilitate drying. The plastic boot outers were put into a stuff sack to keep them free from snow. Later they might serve as a pillow. The Alviolight inners were replaced on the feet. The one-piece windsuit was removed and duvets (or one-piece duvet suits) put on if they had not already been worn during the day. Finally, you can squeeze into the sleeping bag, along with batteries, Gaz cylinders, torch, lighters, spare gloves, etc. . . . and try to cook! This whole contorted, restricted programme can consume up to three hours.

The food on our first acclimatization run was not good, consisting in the main of herbal teas, chocolate bars and tinned fish. We had, by force of circumstance, come superlight to Tibet and had only a limited amount of good climbing food which we were unwilling to commit in any quantity to this climb.

Outside our tents that night nearly a foot of fresh snow fell. By morning it had ceased. The valley floor below had taken on a very wintry hue but the ridge above was relatively clear of the worst effects of the fresh snow, having been blasted by the wind throughout the night. Gradually the two teams gathered themselves and emerged, blinking, from their hibernations. After a brief discussion we chose to continue up the ridge. The alternative was a traverse from our spot on to the snow slopes beyond, via a delicate mixed ramp of loose rubble that looked decidedly Matterhornish.

ELAINE: We made brews and drank them for the next two hours, lazily discussing different ideas which had come to us in past climbing experiences. I had never before had such a strong awareness of Doug's feelings about climbing. Although his strength and experience were so far beyond mine, our ideas were so close and he no longer had the need to prove himself, being quite content to carry some of my gear and slow his pace to mine; trimming his style to fit mine became just another dimension to the way he climbed.

Tomorrow, it seemed there would be small chance of my continuing. This would leave Doug caught between conflicting loyalties.

ALEX: We set off independently up the ridge, crampons on, scrambling over rock steps, steep snow and hard green ice, pleased to be making upwards progress over Alpine terrain at last. Roger, away first, set a good pace. Doug set off next but found himself forced to tarry, waiting for Elaine. I overtook him a hundred metres above the bivouac site, waiting astride a rock just above the first appreciable snow-ice bulge. Having had to help Elaine pack that morning and carrying the majority of his team's gear, Doug was not happy. I climbed on, but after some fifty metres a shouted conversation got under way between Roger, who was by now sitting waiting a little further up the ridge above a second steep little ice bulge out of my sight, and Doug below, out of my hearing.

'Doug says can you go down and collect the technical gear from him.'

Dumping my pack in the snow, I bundled off down, quickly losing the laboriously gained ground, to reach an unhappy, unmoved Doug. We sat and waited for Elaine, who was moving slowly towards us, forced to resort to the front point technique where, on the first bulge, the rest of us had passed quickly using the more relaxed French style.

'What are you going to do, kid?' Doug asked.

'Look, I'm OK. I'm not having any particular problems. I can carry on like this for the rest of the day, but I can't possibly go on at your pace. If this was a plodding day I'd be OK, but it obviously isn't.'

I spoke. 'Well, it's not going to be a plodding day for Roger and me. We want to push on as far up the ridge as possible today. It's up to you and Doug what you do.'

ELAINE: The first effects of altitude soak into you like heavy treacle, slowing body and mind until the sense of time becomes distorted. I had experienced this with my friend Judy Sterner during our explorations of the Andes, and we had spent such days resting or casually exploring, glad of the excuse to enjoy the mountain without the guilt of feeling lazy.

Now I was forced to haul my sluggish limbs up a small step, the pack pressing me into the ice. Alex's angry voice came from somewhere above.

I thought, 'Well, this is it.' There was no decision to make, really, but still it was hard to give up, although I was not really sure why.

'You gave it a good try,' said Doug, looking at his boots.

117

As we redistributed the gear, I saw with sudden painful clarity that he was waiting for me to ask him to rope me across the glacier, steeling himself to do it, knowing it would put him out of the acclimatization climb, and set him back seriously when he came to tackle the Face with the other two. He had already done so much to keep us all together.

I took a deep breath. 'If you can come with me down the exposed part of the ridge for a few hundred yards, I'll be fine the rest of the way.'

Thirty minutes later, I was alone at the edge of the ice, watching three tiny figures moving slowly into the mist above.

ALEX: Eventually Elaine decided to descend. Doug accompanied her down the ridge past the bivouac site to the end of the ice, while I plodded up the slope once again, with his rucksack this time, and Roger dropped down to pick mine up. Eventually we reassembled over a brew on Roger's small, rocky knoll.

Doug had rejoined us quickly, without the impediment of rucksack: 'I'd just like to say one thing. It's a great pity that we ambitious, strong climbers can't make a bit of room for the others, rather than cut them out.'

Through the middle part of the day we wound our way along the flatter, central section of the ridge, teetering over hard wintry ice, shuffling over cornices, a cheval up rock edges, peering to our right down the disconcertingly vertical wall that ran off in hard ice to the glacier over two thousand feet below. Two gendarmes were negotiated on the left-hand side, rocky and loose, and a final abseil put us on a col above which the ridge rose steeply, challengingly, up compact rock to the summit of Nyanang Ri. From these close quarters we had to concede that further progress in this direction was unreasonable, and we were forced to turn left on to the open snow slopes in a rising leftwards traverse where the crevassed slopes ran up high towards the summit ridge connecting Nyanang Ri with Pungpa Ri. Eventually, Doug disappeared into the first substantial serac on our route and announced it sound. We could sleep there tonight.

'Bloody hell, Doug, no way!'

Over my head half a huge cathedral dome leaned crazily

towards the daylight. It seemed inconceivable to me that such a vast and apparently unsupported ice mass could remain in place for the following twelve hours, even if it had managed to do so for the past ten years. Doug, much amused by this wanton display of cowardice, took to leaping about in the back of the cavern, thumping the resounding roof above him with his hammer and exclaiming as to its indestructible qualities. I was not particularly reassured. I knew Reinhold Messner had spent one night in a crevasse with Doug on Chamlang and had sworn never to do so again, it having been in his opinion at the time, the most dangerous thing he had ever done!

But if it did stay put? Outside, a fair storm had kicked up, and the flat floor at the back promised an easily constructed, quick bed place. Roger joined Doug, took a mighty swing at part of the roof, and this collapsed with a resounding crack to even more rejoicing from Doug.

'There you are, youth, it's even safer now.' Democracy being what it is, I had to stay.

Next morning, much to my suprise, we awoke. Doug, blaming old age, was in action first on the breakfast, which consisted in the main of tea and Mars bars. Outside there was no hint of last night's snow, though in the mountain's shadow it was bitterly cold. We continued our rising leftwards traverse until, after an hour, we found our way barred by a large bergschrund. The most promising point of access to the upper slopes was on our left, at a point where the berg-schrund's mouth narrowed to a gap over which it would be possible for a stretching climber to plant his ice tools and attempt to haul himself across. Carefully we traversed towards this point on unstable snow. Below, the slope fell almost immediately into another hole created by a large serac and crevasse, while further down more of its brethren waited to swallow the unwary or unlucky. To the left large blue seracs blocked progress. Above lay hard green ice we wanted to gain.

Doug, the actual 'rock-man' of the party, worked his way down a snow ramp below the gap that barred our entry to the ice for about ten metres, and then, standing on top of the ramp, reached, hit and hauled himself on to the slope above. The two 'ice-men' in the party maintained a discreet presence,

Nyanang Ri. Roger (left) looking across to Alex on the lower slopes
Doug Scott

away in the crevasse from which Doug had begun his descent, and their experienced hesitation was duly rewarded when Doug, finding the texture of the ice hard, suggested he might take a rope on up the rest of the way.

While we worked above, however, Roger began to suffer from inertia and hauled himself on to the slope at a point a little further along from that used by Doug in order to avoid falling ice chunks. As Roger set up after him I contemplated my navel in the freshly arrived sun and belayed Doug, who had now placed an ice screw. Suddenly, with a most desperate croak not dissimilar to that of a half-strangled crow, Roger's much maligned throat and tonsils attempted to wrap themselves around that most descriptive and alarming of words.

'Avalanche!'

Peering up from his ice slope, Roger had been perturbed to see a considerable and agitated white slurry heading in his direction. Doug, a fair way above his ice screw now, was directly in the path of the avalanche's main mass. I dived into the ice gap, trying hard not to pull Doug off, waiting for him to drop in at any moment, while up above, for nearly twenty seconds, he hung on to his axes for dear life, one foot's front points teetering on the ice, the other completely adrift.

DOUG: As Roger croaked his warning I looked up to see a frothy mass now cascading down towards me. Until that moment I had not been able to make much of an impression on the hard brittle ice with my ice axes – but then I did! First one pick then the other in quick succession went right in up to the shaft. I hung on by the wrist loops as the white tide surged over me, trying to present as low a profile as possible by pushing my body into the slope. I emerged spluttering, thanking my lucky stars there had been no ice and rock mixed up in the powder.

ALEX: Out on the left Roger, though blessed with a foot-ledge and being out of the main stream, was unroped and spent anxious moments wondering if he would be swept into the increasingly irresistible white tide that was rushing over him. Finally it stopped, and frosted white figures, registering their continued adhesion with whoops and exclamations, appeared once again on the slope. The pitch was finished, snow was reached and we continued on our way with half an eye cocked on another evil brew of afternoon weather boiling up over in the Langtang Himal.

Against this backdrop of a broody, stormy Himalaya we continued our rising leftwards trajectory unroped, again on firmer snow arching over the top of the highest bergschrund on the Face, unknowingly approaching the zenith of our orbit while the rock wall above constantly revised our opinions leftwards. And then, from above, came another rifle-like retort. Stonefall!

The redundant brain now burnt rubber. Ears, always alert, attuned to the sounds of danger by years of straining to decipher the sounds of the mountains, knew long before the eyes could confirm that the load was coming our way. Then the eyes picked up the oncoming missiles and plotted these surface skimmers, finely calculating trajectories in times only understood by nuclear physicists. We were open, bare on the slope, being strafed by grapeshot granite. We ducked and dodged and the emphasis of the fall passed some twenty feet to our left.

The danger passed, time resumed its normal speed and so did we. Roger was still keen to gain the ridge by a steep narrow gully line of ice above, but as I called out the hours of daylight left it soon became apparent we would not be further than a pitch up the gully before nightfall, and we could expect at least another two pitches before a chance of a bivouac.

'Only four hours left.'

'It's going to be two, just to the foot of the gully.'

'Surely it's only one?'

'No way, Roger.'

'And anyway, it's miles up there to the ridge; you won't get further than a couple of hundred feet before night on that ice!'

We tried to go further left at our present height, but almost immediately hit hard ice again. Hard ice – every move strains the muscles, every muscle strains the mind. At these angles it is too time-consuming at high altitude to rope, but without rope security is tenuous, with axe and hammer picks and crampon points barely biting, forcing the climber to balance precariously, unwilling to move for the strain of another step yet unhappy to stay for the stress of remaining put – a sorry dilemma that did not appeal to our tired bodies. We decided to bivouac in the bergschrund, now fifty metres below us. Our capsule had reached the natural limit of upward progress. Tomorrow we would have to descend.

For the purposes of our acclimatization programme, we had achieved enough, though the climbing, strenuous, dangerous and without obvious reward, was not to our liking. Of the three of us I probably felt this the least, content to be able to consider one of our acclimatizing steps satisfied. Doug, who in spirit belongs more to ridges than to calculated altitudes and calendar-dictated pace, was not happy. Then, in our bivouac tent, with all the cooking finished and the team settling down for the night, the frustrations welled up. As the most vocal pusher of our current approach, I was rounded on. In the dark a bombshell exploded in the tent.

'I'm just not going to operate in this cold, calculating

manner, Alex, and follow your decisions which have been inflicted on this team by force of personality.'

'What on earth are you talking about, Doug?'

Doug gave as an example the decision to drop the first acclimatization climb which had led to our struggling for adequate progress on the slopes of this mountain. At the root seemed to be an objection to my relentless calendarization of the climbing.

Angry, I refused to accept this. 'Look, Doug, you're talking crap. There is just no way I can go around dictating to the likes of Paul or Roger – or you for that matter. The problem is that for the first time you are not necessarily getting things done your way under the guise of democracy by the force of *your* personality!'

Doug pursued this point in the dark.

'Look, Doug, there is absolutely no point in harking on to me like you do to officials. You're not going to wear me down, so you might as well drop it until Base Camp.'

Doug's head was a foot away to my left, separated by the foot-end of Roger's sleeping bag, his presence pinpointed by a small red glow of a cigarette end. His smoking is a fascinating ritual that begins with a determined rummaging through the top pockets of his pile jacket in search of stray tobacco strands which appear finally with a magician's touch and flourish, rescued from past, crushed cigarettes that disappeared in their own smoke long ago. The search would then continue for suitable papers. Once into a climb, the focus of such combustible material almost inevitably centres on such wonders as the camomile tea-bags, heavily favoured for their gluing qualities. In contrast, the John West tinned salmon wrappers were a source of near-total desperation, being impossible to stick and almost as impossible to burn.

Following our dam-burst we entered slightly calmer waters, a longer, detailed calendarization of our climb. I was of the opinion that our present schedule was the only feasible one, given the time available. Roger agreed that it seemed sound. However, we ran back over the dates, searching for a gap to fit some other venture, such as a trip to Hagen's Col, with Nick and Elaine, into our schedule, until, with Roger correctly insisting this was all a waste of time and we should leave it to Base Camp, we drifted off to sleep.

ROGER: This bivouac in the ice cave saw the birth of the timetable. Gone the freewheeling approach where we would climb around our chosen mountain until one day we sensed that permission was given and the final pilgrimage would begin. We had to be on top by 2 June. The climb would take six days so we should pass so many days at this altitude and so many days at that. This was logical but death to a certain spirit we sought in the hills. Only later did I realize that the Chinese bureaucracy had really taken control of our expedition; in resisting the System we had come to share it. I felt that my task was to show the Chinese that the anarcho-Alpine approach could also succeed. But in wanting to display this spirit I had already lost it.

ALEX: The following morning we left after just one cup of tea. There was little Gaz left. The wind had got up in the night and was now whipping snow directly into the cave. It was bitterly cold. We roped together, with myself, the lightest and consequently easiest to fish out of crevasses, in the lead followed by Roger and finally, at back stop, Doug. The slopes had been stripped clear of excess snow and our descent was marked by good snow and ice at an angle in the upper reaches of about forty degrees. I turned my back tentatively towards the slope and faced away from it. The crampons bit well and I was able to zigzag down, fingers freezing in the wind, down, down, down at a fair pace with Roger behind. He was even more in his element over such terrain, watching the rope and sharing the sense of exhilaration that comes with descending quickly down unknown ground, guessing from above the correct line, a cunning line through and around seracs, a little left when the inexperienced senses would have sent you rightwards, all maintained at a stimulating pace in a savage wind.

Doug, the least experienced at descending the steepest slopes facing out, in the earliest stages found himself facing in towards the slope, and less able to watch the rope, which sneaked out and coiled close to Roger's feet – a source of danger. Becoming agitated, Roger started shouting at Doug to maintain greater control. Doug was shouting back – what was the hurry? We had all day, we should take care. Finally, we reached the glacier below, a disjointed, disorientated team. Doug was worried. The spectre of another K2 venture haunted him, and I was apprehensive regarding what, to my mind, was his 'irrationality' on the last bivouac. We made our own separate ways back to the Advance Camp. Here the wind prevented us from lingering.

I left the Advance Camp first, moving down the valley and out on to the plateau. At a large boulder which marked the approximate halfway point on the journey between the two camps, I stopped and waited. Doug arrived five minutes later.

'Show me this new route then.'

He did, and I couldn't do it. In the traversing of our boulder-strewn plateau I had evolved the habit of going across a little lower than usual and had, in the course of such travels, discovered some excellent boulders. We now tramped together across the snow while I showed him the best ones. Roger joined us at an excellent low rock simply brimming with good problems. Doug was purring now.

'From the ridiculous to the sublime'

It was a happier, more together team that bounded into camp with the last of the evening light to a feast of jam pancakes, rice and that king of dishes – egg and chips.

The weather, in the meantime, remained awful at the Base Camp. Indeed, it had become apparent that it was worse here than further up the valley. Long tentacles of grey cloud would sweep up from Nyalam, engulfing the camp almost without fail, while further away, at the foot of Shishapangma, the sun could shine for hours yet. The early exhortations not to wash or swim in the upper lake, as this would pollute the drinking water, were mocked by a foot of ice.

Paul summed it up. 'The only other place I know like this is Delph in winter – misty and miserable!'

CHAPTER 6
Pungpa Ri

ALEX: May 8th was a long, tiring and decisive day, not helped by a general absence of sun, save for a couple of hours in the morning, and an early onset of the cold, biting wind, the cloud and the snow. In our difficult little kitchen we assembled in dribs and drabs over a disjointed, uninspired breakfast and then turned our attention to the state of our trip.

Paul had decided to leave. He had continued to entertain some slim hope of salvaging his climbing chances, even after the decision to turn back from the first acclimatization run on Nyanang Ri. Indeed, on the evening of the seventh he had told us that he had not given up all hope; but in the cold light of this following morning he announced, in his matter-of-fact way, the collapse of an ambition. His chest had continued to grow tighter, the medicines were offering only a brief illusion of relief and to stay was to risk another long, debilitating illness that would ruin the remainder of the year at the very least. The realization that Paul would probably not climb again on the world's highest mountains was a blow keenly felt by his friends.

Since his return Nick had been taking brief exercise, a little more each day. He was still very keen to do some mountaineering and, above all, to establish that he could acclimatize to these altitudes with a view to future plans. He would see the expedition – in so many respects his 'baby' – through to the end, and assist the Face climbers as much as possible with the tedious though much welcomed task of load-carrying. For Elaine, the eighth was probably one of the most depressing days of the expedition. Doug was still casting around the calendar for any possible way of guaranteeing her some involvement. The most obvious project was to go with her and Nick up to Hagen's Col, and possibly climb around on some of the slopes in that vicinity. This was an attractive proposition, holding a principal advantage for even the most ambitious Face climbers in that it would permit a detailed reconnaissance of the Face and its approaches. But cast around as we might, we could not guarantee the time for a trip to Hagen's, and certainly not before the ascent of the South-West Face. This position was hopeless for Elaine. There was no future for her in hanging around for climbers who might just be able to afford her some time, and she had absolutely no interest in doing so. A major reason, possibly the pre-dominant one, for Elaine's being there was to see Tibet, to try to get close to this land and its people. She and Doug had talked enthusiastically about this aspect of the trip when he had phoned to ask if she was interested in coming, and that, she now proposed, was what she would do. In this she must have felt almost betrayed.

'Look, you can't just wander off around Tibet like that, Elaine. You've seen the place. They won't permit it and you can expect to be visited by officials within a couple of days. Everywhere is connected by phone and road, and you can at least expect to be held pending the end of the expedition, let alone the problems you'll cause for us with one member unaccountably wandering around in a sensitive zone.'

This, from the point of view of the remaining members of the trip, was perhaps the crux of the matter. If Elaine left the expedition then there was a good chance that it would find itself in hot water, for the Chinese System did not recognize the possibility of such individual action. We had permission as a single entity to follow a prescribed path, and from that path no single part of our entity could deviate without risking some retribution against the whole. But what about the promises on the phone? What about the enthusiastic words from Doug which had brought her here at such expense? She could not, surely, be expected now to brood for a month in this miserable, sunless hollow whilst we pursued our own selfish goals.

'You'll have to persuade the authorities to change your status to tourist.'

We broached the problem with Wu, who, in the crucial absence of Pemba, would have to assist us to the best of his ability now with advice beyond the call of the interpreter's role.

'The chances of Elaine changing her status are not good. We can try hard to help her, but it is not easy.'

Elaine's position was invidious. It was unlikely the authorities would be easily persuaded to alter her status, yet at the accommodation rates charged to expeditions she would not be able to afford to linger in the towns to present her case. The remainder of the team, comfortable in the knowledge of a predetermined future, pressed on her the need to be more optimistic, to press for a visa which she might well obtain. But that would entail aggression, and aggression was not in Elaine's character. Nor was there any guarantee that the Chinese would be persuaded. Elaine was depressed. Her prospects seemed as bleak as the cold, squalid kitchen. She had come to climb, but did not fit in with our plans; she had come to see Tibet, but it now appeared she would not be able to do so. Doug's optimism was falling flat in the face of Tibetan realism. Perhaps she might as well go home? Once on the road at Nyalam all she risked was a fast return home.

This now left Doug, Roger and myself in the climbing team, and in the kitchen Doug broached a question: 'About our team up on the Face, did you feel there was something wrong? Was there something wrong between us?' What was Doug getting at? What did he want? I certainly did not know. 'Maybe you don't quite understand what I'm trying to say. Was there something bugging you?'

Roger said the rope-work on the descent bugged him at the time.

'Yes, Roger, now about this rope-work. You're better than me at some things and one of them's rope-work. You do that every day of your working life and I do it once in a blue moon, so you have got to accept that I won't be so good. I just don't like the feeling of being guided – treated like a client.'

'But it was dangerous.'

'It's all very well rushing down in front, but if you were playing at being "anchor man" as I was, you would have been slower. Really, I get this feeling that somehow you regard me as an old fart.'

'Let's face it, Doug, you are an old fart!'

Big grins broke out everywhere. We pored over maps and plans for an hour, debating and re-debating our various options in order to evolve an agreed prospectus. Roger and I were in favour of going on to Pungpa Ri immediately, trying for the top but if necessary being content with bivouacking at above 7,000 metres. Doug was still very much interested in climbing Nyanang Ri, and suggested the prospect of easy terrain on the northern slopes of the mountain, similar to that on the north side of Shishapangma. This, he suggested, would permit us to contemplate climbing to the col between Pungpa Ri and Nyanang Ri from our side, but then conducting a fairly simple traverse on the back side of the ridge. It was agreed to reconnoitre the ground on the east side of Shishapangma, the Phola Glacier, which would show us this back side and also the descent from Shishapangma itself, and to draw up our battle plan after that. The BBC World Service informed us that an eruption of a volcano in Mexico, El Chinchonal, was affecting the weather in Asia. We regarded the falling snow ruefully.

Roger's reconnaissance to the Phola Glacier the following day revealed that the east side of Shishapangma was not suitable for a descent, but that it would be reasonable enough for us to attempt to return to Base via Pungpa Ri. The upper reaches of the east side, just behind the east ridge, were fairly open slopes descending into a snow bowl at around 7,600 metres. This would allow us to lose vital altitude quickly, an important consideration for the Himalayan climber coming away from a summit, especially over unknown ground. The northern side of Nyanang Ri was spectacularly steep; there was no prospect of easy traversing in this area. We would have to concentrate our all on Pungpa Ri. That evening we feasted on bean stew.

The following morning I awoke, wretchedly ill. The old, half-cooked beans had disagreed with my hungry gulping and I was well on the way to being poisoned. By mid-afternoon the intensity of the pain was excruciating and living was an exhausting ritual of lying collapsed in a damp tent, drained and feverish, until the need to vomit had grown overwhelming. Outside snow was settling thick and fast. Each wretched diarrhoeic trip outside left me colder and damper, reducing still further rapidly depleting reserves and jeopardizing my chances of climbing as the vital stamina and energy drained away and I started to dry up like a prune. The team were worried. Doug made frequent excursions to my tent and later Roger took over the mothering role. Candles appeared to heat the tent, a whistle to summon help. Was I all right on my own? Would it not be better if I moved to another, less damp, more central tent? Perhaps Roger should stay with me overnight? Was there anything at all I might like to eat? The following morning I was no longer actively ill. Wasted, washed out and drawn, but thankfully still in line to climb; Doug, on the other hand, was expressing personal doubts.

The climbing on Nyanang Ri had not been very satisfying, more of a job of work than a source of inspiration, and some aspects of the climb were now troubling Doug – the descent especially. This had been fast, by Doug's standards a 'mad dash down', which had left him uncomfortable and feeling exposed at the back, unable to control events that might occur, obviously less at ease with the techniques of facing out and walking down a slope. Marooned at the back of the rope, he also found himself rarely included in debate about the direction to take, while Roger and I had a fairly obvious rapport going, enjoying the speed and execution of the descent. All this, coupled with Roger's annoyance at the rope snaking around his feet as Doug, facing in, attempted to match the pace between pleas to slow down and take care, meant that Doug was left to ponder his value to a team from which he was beginning to feel excluded. When we had reached the rognon below the Face and the symbolic rope was removed, and with it all outward sign of our mutual dependence, his internal dispute sharpened.

'Not again. Not another K2.'

Was he getting in the way? Why was there no rapport between us? Did he matter? Did it matter to him what he did, visit Tibet or climb Shishapangma? Surely if he was out of sympathy with me and Roger, if climbing the mountain was going to be an aggressive, individualistic ego-trip, then fine, he would go to Tibet. He wanted to climb Shishapangma, but did we *really* want him to come along on the climb? With Paul leaving for home – the only man in the party with whom Doug had total rapport – and Elaine's dreams crumbling, it was a difficult, exposed period for Doug. If he wasn't wanted then there was no point in climbing the route. It was Roger who was first made privy to the idea of Doug's not going to the summit, on the afternoon of 11 May. I knew nothing about it, no hint was dropped when he came down before dawn to check my state or when he brought the tea and boiled

130

egg a little while later and assured me he knew just how I felt. I learned of the question on the following day, when I finally re-emerged from my tent into the kitchen.

'I'm thinking of not going on the climb but going on a tour of the whole massif and then around Tibet with Nick and maybe Elaine. Would that be OK for you?'

The previous afternoon Roger's reaction had been one of some sympathy. He also doubted the value in climbing these Himalayan Giants and was engaged in a debate of his own that our slog on the slopes of Nyanang Ri in contrast to the joy of climbing in the Jorasses North Wall the previous winter had sharply highlighted. Should he quit, maybe after his planned ascent of K2, maybe even after Shishapangma itself? He knew now he could do it, but did he want to do it – slog up these all-demanding mountains? Now I was telling Doug it was OK. Two of us could tackle the Face as well as three. He could do whatever he felt his destiny required him to.

I am not the best person to pose a question to, by someone hoping for some grasp of the underlying confusions that prompt it. My mind does not have the intuition for this. I could sense that Doug was searching for something – but what? Who was I, at twenty-eight, to tell a man of his record when to climb on? Roger and I began to consider packing as a two-man team. I did not understand Doug's doubts because I had never shared them. I was better at walking down snow; Doug was better at climbing up rock. So what! I would not be sensitive enough to feel out of sorts if I were holding the team up on the rock. I would probably demand and expect a rope. Doug, in contrast to all the teaching he had tried to instil in himself, was unable to see our situation in its overall context; he could not see his stamina, his experience, his selflessness on the mountain; he could only worry about whether he was still fit enough to climb with the 'youngsters' (even if this particular youngster had been the least fit of the team). We wanted him to come. Roger told him quite explicitly that he wanted him along.

I wandered up to Doug's tent that afternoon to find him talking with Elaine. Doug told me later that she, who probably understood the true nature of his question, and who had probably the most to gain from a decision by him not to go on Shishapangma, was convinced that he should climb. Now I

131

stuck my drained face and unruly mop through the entrance. 'Above all, you're a climber, you're not a tourist, you can't go bumming around Tibet!'

Not only was he not a drag on the team. We wanted him along.

ROGER: Doug's suggestion that he should retire was a shock. I blamed myself for getting angry about his rope-work on Nyanang Ri. Doug has done as many hard firsts in the Himalayas as any man, and perhaps nobody has so many doubts about his own value. He has survived broken bones, storms and broken teams and is worried about being slower than us on steep ice. Probably Alex and I could climb the mountain without him, but it would be an incomplete team, we would be sure to feel a shadow tied on to the rope. I wanted him along badly, and told him. He said he needed time to think, but I was sure he'd come. The man's a climber.

DOUG: When it became obvious that Roger and Alex *did* want me along, that I would not be in the way of their expectations, as I felt I had been on K2 in 1980, all other ideas evaporated into the past. My proposals for a traverse around the mountain with Nick and Elaine rather than a vertical ascent of it were posed not just to reveal the true feelings of Alex and Roger (although I admit to having been put out by Alex's attitude to Nick and Elaine, for whom I felt some responsibility, and by Roger's coldness to me as he switched from climbing companion to patronizing guide). It was nothing to do with descending a thousand foot of easy angled snow and ice as Alex supposed. The truth of the matter was that I had still not come to terms with my own ambitions.

I certainly longed to see as much of Tibet as possible, the dream of which had diminished with every problem that had arisen, but I still hoped to visit some of Milarepa's caves and holy places after the climbing. The climbing of Shishapangma's South-West Face was my real problem, more so after having seen it. Here was a major Himalayan wall that no other climber had attempted – no information, no close-up photographs, certainly no ropes strewn around from half-hearted attempts. No climbers had even set foot in the approach valley before. An ascent of it would satisfy, for at least the time being, every ambition. It would be recognized as a great success, a big step forward in world Alpinism, to which I am so obviously attached. I knew that as good as these feelings felt, they were a form of madness. I had to know for myself whether I was attracted to the Face for the pure enjoyment of the climbing and its aftermath or whether I wanted the recognition. At the time I did not reason this out as I have done on reflection. My emotional response was a gut reaction to the fact that I still could not take it or leave it as I knew in my heart I must.

Before all the major climbs I have made there has come a time when I have had to reconcile myself for one reason or another – bureaucracy, weather conditions, illness in the team or whatever – to failure. Curiously, almost immediately after I had let go of my ambition a change in circumstances usually worked to my fulfilling that ambition, but in humility. This was not something I became aware of until after I climbed Everest. Climbing Everest may have moderated my ambition enough to see this; or simply that by then I was old enough to understand my ambition. It is always worth my while remembering the intensity of my ambition when I was in my late twenties and early thirties, especially as now most of my climbing friends are much younger than me since so many of my contemporaries are no longer climbing. The emotions involved must be at the very least confusing and probably upsetting to my companions. Fortunately for me, in Alex and Roger I had two friends who were tolerant of such questioning as mine. I now *knew* we were in for a good climb together. The altered state of consciousness which comes from such struggles at high altitude would not be squandered. So I now looked forward positively to sharing this climb with Roger and Alex, giving and taking, and in so doing cutting through the junk – locating something more durable and worthy of the name, man.

ALEX: The debates about calendars and plans started to assume some harmony; the effort was channelled in one direction, to the South-West Face, and now all we needed was the weather.

On the thirteenth we were supposed to be heading up the hill to establish a second Advance Base and attempt Pungpa Ri. This effort never materialized. At 11.30 am the zip on my front door rasped up its metal sliders and Nick produced a welcome cup of coffee. 11.30! I was furious. What had happened? Why were we not already up on the plateau, *en route* for Advance Base and beyond? Roger had our solitary alarm clock. Where was he? ('I seem to remember switching it off!') What had happened to Nick's oft-proclaimed 'internal alarm clock', and why, oh so suspiciously, hadn't Doug got us up? He must have been awake early, he must have been hoping Wu would return to the camp today with mail. How could anyone jeopardize a climb for letters!

'And what about you?'

'Me?'

'Yes, you, lying in bed, reading Ustinov since nine-thirty this morning. Why didn't you get up and rouse the camp? Why didn't you produce the first brew? Why on earth are you so grumpy?'

Despite the obvious irrationality I stomped up to Doug's tent, tetchy, almost angry at our inability to generate momentum. The kitchen was deserted again. How could someone have got up, made a brew, and gone back to bed again on a day we were supposed to be away? Why do we have this ridiculous system without clearly defined responsibility for the kitchen and getting the day under way? Why does Doug insist on believing in the essential goodness of human nature? I put on some water for tea and eggs and eventually some semblance of a team began to appear in the kitchen. Though windy, the weather was still sunny. If we could not get out and use such weather we would never get up the route. I was generally feeling insufferable.

At about 2.30 pm, whilst I was packing personal belongings in my tent, Doug arrived: 'I reckon you had better collapse the tent before we go up because of the risk of it being damaged by this wind.'

'Sure! Sure!'

I emerged to find a blizzard in progress. Resplendent in windsuit and double boots I ploughed back to the kitchen. 'I don't really fancy collapsing the tent in this weather.'

Two pairs of suspicious, uncomfortable-looking eyes peered out of the dim light. 'Ah well, now you should mention that . . .'

I grasped a certain impression. 'If you think I'm the hard nut to crack, you're wrong. I'd rather stay here.'

There is nothing like a blizzard to induce an air of realism. A carnival atmosphere ensued and a major cook and binge session commenced. Potatoes, rice and chapaties were all produced with varying degrees of know-how to be taken up the hill. Complete havoc raged while the elements battled their way through our kitchen – a skid row shelter full of men and one woman, bunched over stoves and bottles of alcohol, Budweiser and Bacardi, resplendent in duvets and windsuits, double boots and gaiters, discussing heroes – Captain Scott's romantic dash against Amundsen's calculated flair, while the wind whipped around our boulder, underneath the skirting of our tarpaulin, covering the occupants in spindrift and theatening to lift our cover away, rip it off and throw it in the lake below. Unseen avalanches echoed from the surrounding mountain walls; thunder growled. The alcoholic merriment began to degenerate into infantilism. Two soups were produced for instant consumption, along with a giant egg and chips for the survivors, Roger, Nick and myself. Doug and Elaine retired in the face of increasing idiocy. Roger and I started a potato-peeling competition that rapidly degenerated as we appointed ourselves founder-members of the McSpud-peeler Clan and adopted a habit of conversation and mental aptitude thereupon that we could not elude for the rest of the evening. Nick was written off as a rabbit and, finally, we found ourselves alone in our merriment, harassing anyone or anything that ventured near.

Doug came in then beat a retreat via Elaine's tent. 'They're pissed.'

'I know. I can't cope, that's why I'm here!'

The weather improved a little during the night, but by 9.30 the following morning conditions were once again terminal, with spindrift ripping into the kitchen, blasted there by a gale. A Vango was plundered of its fly sheet in order to erect some sort of barrier to the elements. A huge, vividly lit thunderstorm got under way, intermixed with the redoubled rumblings from the avalanches. That morning we thought the kitchen would disappear for good, or at least the poles would snap. But thankfully it held.

Roger disappeared with his skis. 'I'm just going out for a walk.'

And then that evening a blue sky emerged; a sharp light

emphasized the majestic white mountains now standing proud out of the sea of cloud that surrounded them and a revivalist spirit emerged from the climbers. Now we simply had to climb the mountain!

The South-West Face of Shishapangma runs down on its eastern side to a shoulder at an altitude of 7,400 metres. This shoulder – Pungpa Ri – the expedition christened Punk Peak. On our first acclimatization exercise on Nyanang Ri we had attained an altitude of around 6,500 metres, with two bivouacs at around 6,300 metres. This exercise would not be sufficient to allow us to move on immediately to attempt the South-West Face without risking considerable exhaustion and illness on its upper reaches. From past experience we did know that we could now expect to climb to within the vicinity of 7,500 metres with an acceptable margin of safety, and with the result of improving our condition for an attempt on the Face. Furthermore, it appeared likely that we would descend from the peak to the south-eastern side of the mountain. Pungpa Ri was, therefore, the obvious choice, being of the correct altitude, fairly interesting to climb and comprising a substantial chunk of our descent route from the summit, should we turn right at that place. We would even be able to protect our descent by leaving a small cache of Gaz and food on Pungpa Ri, which we would be able to aim for in the likely event of our having run low on or out of supplies after climbing the Face.

Our most bedevilling problem was still that of time. It was now 15 May. We were due to leave Base Camp on 1 June, but as yet in our rather dramatic time in Tibet, only three of us – Roger, Doug and myself – had managed a miserly total of three days' climbing. The possibility of weather continuing in the vein that had harassed us since our arrival at Nyalam was barely thinkable. Failure is an inevitability for the Alpinist; he will always experience it and in the greater ranges of the world he may experience it with depressing frequency; but surely not on this trip? Not after so much hassle, so much striving against the Establishment? Yet paradoxically, those elements of the team that had been pushy and ambitious were more relaxed now that the leeway in the calendar had almost vanished. The outcome was now down to the weather – and about the weather a mortal can do nothing. So there was no point in fretting. I was feeling good.

On 15 May we finally got away from camp as planned. The day dawned blue and clear after our week of snow. Over in Nepal we could imagine that many a climber would be digging out his tent on some mountainside or other, relieved to be still there, alive, constantly surveying the prospects of avalanches. For our part we managed some momentum, even the battered stoves volunteered to work first time. We gradually put it together, adding cups and spoons, plates and petrol to our previously prepared food store, finally leaving camp independently sometime after mid-day. Elaine was also going today, down to Nyalam and, hopefully, Tibet.

ELAINE: Within two hours of waking to a better day, my gear was sorted and repacked for travelling through Tibet. A set of warm clothes, emergency bivouac gear, sugar and tsampa and a pile of books – on Milarepa, Tibetan history and Buddhist philosophy, plus the heavy volumes of Tibetan grammar, all crammed in with socks and canisters of film. I felt the tightening of the stomach which comes with excitement. In a kind of limbo between the mountain and the unknown came a rare moment of prescience and I knew I was on the edge of greater dangers and deeper insights than I had previously known.

ALEX: For we four remaining climbers it was upwards, a long slog through plentiful fresh snow, out over the plateau towards the Advance Camp. We made our way independently, as was our habit, each starting in his own time, ploughing a furrow through snowdrifts at times three feet deep. Shishapangma's wind-stripped, black countenance gave a brief, mischievous wink and was swallowed up by the relentless grey mass of cloud boiling over from the Langtang cauldron. The first flakes of snow stung our exposed faces. All the other peaks behind put on cloud caps. Fast-moving, high cirrus scudded overhead and on towards Everest and the far horizon. On the Walkman Bruce Springsteen's more forlorn numbers kept me company.

The Advance Camp was in disarray, though thankfully only one tent had actually collapsed, unfortunately the one containing Doug's mountain sleeping bag, which was saturated. While I was digging out the site and the equipment the others joined me and we decided to stay put. Doug's sleeping bag needed to be dried out, the weather was poor, Nick, last in, was looking pretty tired and we had our work cut out in these conditions to select our food, equipment and medical kit and secure our camp.

The following morning we were away by eleven. Despite the previous débâcle I was once again assigned to the food. This time we could spare more for each man and did better. Fish, cheese, soup, tsampa, tea, milk, Rise and Shine, lemon, garlic and chilli, together with vast personal treasures of chocolate and carob bars, joined our pre-cooked potatoes and rice carried up from Base Camp. The climbing equipment was easier.

'Deadman?'

'No!'

'Heavier rope?'

'No.'

As we continued our way across the snow, tufted grass and boulders behind the camp and up the steep slope on to the old moraines above, the elements took another tack. The fine, clear skies were complemented by hurricane winds, ferocious and doubly bitter, whipping out of the north and mocking our aspirations. Could we dare contemplate climbing in such conditions? High above us the once-snowy flanks of Nyanang Ri were being stripped relentlessly down to a polished green ice. Great white plumes streamed from all the surrounding summits. Already we were dressed in everything that had been appointed to the rucksacks with a view to combating a climate three thousand metres higher. The thought of trying to erect a bivouac tent in these conditions was unbearable, and this was only May! The Himalaya in winter? It was a sobering thought. Our current predicament must be nothing compared with the cold desperation of living on and among these mountains in winter.

At the top of the rise we crossed to the entrance of the glacier and in a slightly descending traverse line we made the boulder slopes beyond, envious of Roger who had brought his skis and now reaped his reward for the labour of carrying them as he glided over the knee-deep snow and out of sight. At the other side of the boulder slope, beyond the glacial tongue, we stopped for a brew, sheltering from the wind behind large rocks and rejoicing a little in the sun. Then we moved out on to the second glacier, passing underneath the point at which we had descended from Nyanang Ri, and continued in a gradually ascending line for some hours, once again watching Roger vanishing into the distance to a rock ridge beyond. This ridge, which runs out into the main glacial valley from the foot of the ridge running down from Pungpa Ri, maintains a shattered rocky crest mounded by a litter of moraine, polished boulders of granite and quartz, steeper on the far (west) side, than the east.

Roger reached the boulders first, dumping his skis and angling up left, towards the crest and along this a little way out into the main valley to observe the approaches to the South-West Face from a good vantage point. Doug and I, wading along in the parallel tracks of Roger's skis, reached the moraine some forty minutes later and struck rightwards, towards a small rock turret beneath Pungpa Ri which we had christened the Castle, but which in reality resembled more a nuclear submarine's conning tower, its bow end carved in the manner of an Indian Chief. We reached the crest of the ridge a few feet to its left, to see clearly Hagen's Col, towards which the sun was now setting, and below us a snow slope plunging nearly two hundred feet to the next glacier which then rose gradually towards yet another crest of rock ridge and moraine that marked the right-hand boundary of the South-West Face proper. We appeared doomed to angle for ever up a series of tilted shelves which, at their far end, greeted us with a steep drop to the altitude we had enjoyed some hours before. Just past the conning tower the backbone of the ridge upon which we now stood turned through an angle of fifty degrees and ran straight, true and well-defined, towards a snow plume which we assumed to be in the vicinity of the summit.

Out of the cold wind, in the shaded lee of our rock crest, I found Doug engaged in his favourite pastime – building a den. The Titan in him hurled rocks about the place with gay abandon while the more angelic aspects of his character extolled the virtues of warm rock and sunrises. Roger appeared below us and was of the opinion that Doug was wasting his time as one minute away, under the Castle, was a flat floor covered in snow. Doug redoubled his exhortations regarding the rocks' heat-retaining properties, but the politician in him offered an unhappy Roger the large, flat-topped rock that alone had sufficient area to accommodate the two-man Salewa tent. Nick arrived at about eight o'clock. It had always been intended that, as far as was practicable, he would transport a quantity of food and Gaz for us before returning to Advance Camp and projects of his own. Cajoled thus far, he was now without a sleeping bag. We three being in possession of quite excellent sleeping bags, much Dunkirk spirit and stiff-upper-lip advice was offered to Nick regarding the prospect of sleeping in Doug's one-piece duvet suit – a fate already shared by a number of his friends who had survived similar predicaments in such places as Everest's South-West Face at 26,000 feet.

'Aye, youth, but look what happened to him afterwards.'

'Terrible, terrible it was – poor bugger emigrated to Australia.'

There was a notable reluctance to lend Nick a Karrimat. Eventually we settled down for the night.

'Doug, brew . . . Doug, brew . . . Doug, BREW!'

Unbelievable! Someone was trying to rouse us at only seven am, and insistently so. In our bivouac tent there was incredulous disbelief, coupled with a reluctance to budge. It was an evil trick. Coughing, rasping, dry throats would do much for a cup of tea, but get up? Surely not! Roger had thrown in the towel over Nick's cold, restless antics in their Salewa at about 6.30 and now expected our unit, which had seemingly only just got to sleep after a heavy night on the Walkman, to get up. Seven am – an early rise, bitter early morning shadows, sun glinting on only the highest snow-capped peaks, frozen fingers, real Alpinism. I could have shot Nick.

We were sorted and packed by 10.30, stumbling down the boulders in our ridged plastic boots to the ice behind the conning tower. We put on our crampons and set off up the easy snow and ice slope above, waving a last goodbye to Nick, who would come no further on this jaunt, before reaching the wide couloir that ran up the right side of the ridge descending from Pungpa Ri. The couloir finished at a col about a thousand metres above us, from which we would move left up on to the ridge itself and, hopefully, on towards

CASTLE
CAMP

Our route and bivouac sites on Pungpa Ri
Doug Scott

the summit. For much of the day we moved unroped, each
individual at his own pace – for myself a quick dash and pause,
for Roger and Doug a more studied, steady rhythm. After a
couple of hundred metres we roped up to pass over an
uncertain crevasse. There was some temptation to keep the
rope on, Doug being of the opinion that it was OK and would
not cost us much in time, while I muttered away to his left
about this being ridiculous and that even he and I would be

141

skiing on such terrain in the Alps. Meanwhile, Roger was running out the rope above, but after twenty metres Doug conceded that it was beginning to look a bit daft, so we put the thing away until we reached an icy three-pitch narrows some two-fifths of the way up the couloir.

'I'll lead this if it's OK.' I was already tying on to the first rope.

'Sure, want the second rope?'

'If you can uncoil it in time!'

In a jiffy Doug had it uncoiled while I was still faffing about with the gear. An understandably caustic remark was lost in the wind.

At the far end of the ice narrows, in the last crevasse, we stopped for tea before continuing up the wider snow couloir above. The day was most notable for its down winds, which periodically whistled down the couloir and slammed into us, peppering us with irritating, occasionally dangerous grapeshots of ice fragments. We leaned into the slope, teetering a little uncomfortably on crampon points, straining with the concentration needed to remain stable in the face of such raw brutality and wary lest a truly irresistible blast, not

Alex climbing steep ice at the start of our climb on Pungpa Ri
Doug Scott

without precedent in these mountains, should be the next to be heralded by the approaching express train whoosh. That day Doug went especially well, seeming almost to gather pace towards the evening. He enthused about various breathing techniques that were working wonders for him but left me a gulping, gasping wreck. Roger moved with a steady, studied pace throughout the day, comfortable on the crisp, firm neve, probably dreaming about skiing.

I lost my rhythm completely and then my stamina in the upper reaches of the couloir and privately rued the bean episode. A short distance below the col, as it broadens towards the ridge, the couloir has a large buttress of rock intruding into its central area, producing a Y-shaped split. Doug reached the rocks first, on the left-hand side of the buttress about half way up, and disappeared around the prow out of view. I reached the rock and sat gratefully on a small ledge, facing out, the weight of the rucksack supported by the ice behind, and exchanged pleasantries with Roger who was approaching fast. Together, we found Doug about a hundred feet higher, on the prow of the rock ridge, on a small icy slope below a stubby, loose rock wall about twenty feet high which provided a barrier against the worst excesses of the wind's gusts. He was flailing at the ice with his axe, at peace in the setting sun. Liberated chunks slid down the slope to another, more exposed ledge some ten metres below – an awkward, rubbly mess. We chivvied away at our eyrie for over an hour while the sun dipped away towards the western mountains, casting long shadows and a cutting chill across our couloir.

Excavating ledges from ice is a chore made no more agreeable by the number of times in the past the climber has beavered away in the night to fashion a bed while his body desires only a warm drink and sleep. The temptation to cut corners and be satisfied with a ledge less than comfortable is great, but any such suggestion would be condemned by Doug as unworthy of our traditions and heritage. I swear he only climbs big mountains for the rock and the den-building!

When we had a ledge sufficient to sleep three abreast, pitons and ice screws were tapped tentatively into the rock above and the bivouac sac gingerly suspended from these. The rock was loose and I wished I had taken a helmet. We cooked into the night, not finishing until around eleven pm. Roger sat on the right side of the tent, attempting to cook in a small alcove outside, fashioned by our chivvying into a corner where the rock jutted out at the end of the ledge. Doug proclaimed the beauty of the sunset over Hagen's Col whilst leaping in and out of the sac in his stockinged feet, exclaiming on the rapidly falling temperature and rearranging the tent's suspension points. It was a little like camping with a scoutmaster who is more keen on the finer aspects of scouting than on his charges.

The following morning Doug made his first spirited attempt at the dreaded chilli, cheese, tsampa opening gambit. I replied with a successful 'incredulous compromise defence' and ended up with a tsampa Ready-Brek on my plate instead. Doug swears by his awful concoction, an evil brew which Roger claims to find OK. I don't believe him and am inclined to the opinion that he only eats it because it is so awful he thinks it must be doing him good. They ate it together on Makalu – but then, they didn't get up that.

Having thus breakfasted we abandoned our eyrie, together with some of our food and Gaz. The purpose of carrying so much weight up this route was to leave supplies at bivouac spots we could aim for on the descent. Gaz and drinking materials are especially vital in this respect. With such safeguards climbers can pare to a bare minimum the loads they take on their main climb. Our bivouac site was about fifty metres below the col. Here, for the first time, we were confronted by that most exciting and mysterious of views – to stand on the very edge of the Himalaya and gaze to the west, over range upon range of fairytale snow mountains, and to the east, down a final precipice and out over the infinity of the brown, alluring, wild Tibetan Plateau, from this distance stripped of its corrugated iron roofs, concrete houses, telegraph poles and road – restored to its barren, mythical wonder.

Immediately opposite stood the shapely pyramid summit of Phola Ganchen, first climbed by a New Zealand party from the north in 1981. Its southern precipice fell steeply and tantalizingly to the Phola Glacier below, the top third com-

Alex and Roger moving up easy ground above the Ice Narrows on Pungpa Ri

Doug Scott

prising a sheer, almost vertical rock wall cut in places by the thinnest and most tenuous ramps. To our right the North Face of Nyanang Ri offered a similar intricate and excellent Face, while behind it mountains whose shapes and names we knew so well – Everest, Lhotse, Gauri Sankar, Menlungtse – stood proud in a choppy ocean of peaks.

From the col we moved leftwards along the snow crest towards the flank of the rock ridge that runs down to the Castle Camp, up steepening snow towards a small rock buttress where a halt was called, ropes produced and Roger volunteered for leadership. For a while Doug and I savoured the luxury of a halt with rucksacks removed, while Roger forced a way up the steepening ground to the mixed terrain of snow and ice a rope length above. Sat astride a small rock knoll facing out, I fed out Roger's ropes, attached to nothing more than a faith that he would not slip and a brief contemplation of the curious leftwards flip that would put my boulder into the position of a running belay should any mishap occur to the leader. The ropes ran out, a belay was hacked out of iced rock, and we were called to 'come on' – Doug and I, fifteen feet apart on our separate ropes, moving together.

Doug reached Roger first and claimed the tiny foot ledge upon which the belay stance had been taken. I found myself marooned at the end of a lead of rope about ten feet to the right, standing on hard ice, exchanging and alternately cursing calves on the inadequate foothold hastily chopped for the purpose. I watched Roger, now at work on the mixed climbing above. All the while I was worrying about the possibility of a rock being dislodged by the rope trailing behind him. Suddenly, I was not happy. The situation was quietly serious. The undercurrent of danger that prevails with every step in this inhuman environment through which we choose to pass edged a little closer to the surface. That rock above looked brittle and unstable. What if the structure he was teetering on to collapsed? To be hit by rock here, to swing unconscious, to hang beneath Doug, battered and bruised . . .? What was the prospect of a retreat from here? Meanwhile, Doug was fretting, wanting to lead, to be out

Doug and Alex climbing on Pungpa Ri during the second day of the climb

146

in front exploring the new ground where time does not hang so heavy.

Roger reached the ridge with the last stretch of the rope and belayed. We followed to a point a little below his stance where we angled right, up towards a snow ramp. The terrain behind Roger on the ridge crest was difficult and rocky, a fact which in its turn made it awkward to persuade Doug not to go there. The ramp was pleasant, leaning out to the right, giving views down the steep, fluted powdery eastern flanks of our ridge and the glacier below. On the south side of the crest we could see our bivouac spot of the night before and then follow the sweep of the couloir down through the hour-glass narrows and on to the Castle Camp, now twelve hundred metres below.

The ridge itself was excellent, rising like a single roller-coaster track directed up a hill, the track itself being ten feet wide and inclined at a forty-degree leftwards tilt. At the bottom of the tilt steep mixed ground disappeared from sight over rock walls that fell unseen to the glacier below, while to the right, beneath the cornices of the ridge, the unstable fluted columns of snow mimicked this process. The clouds were rolling along the Langtang Himal to our left, while from the Phola Glacier gusts of wind swept up and blasted thin white wisps of cloud hundreds of feet above our heads. But the main force of the wind swept in from the west, eddying around the cornices and snow flutings, causing us to turn our heads away and bend low to make progress. At one point the conditions drove us out to the right, into the snow flutings. Roger found himself wading up fifty-degree powder snow, waist deep, struggling to regain the security of the ridge above while his two tailenders watched and prepared to dive into a crevasse if necessary. But the slope stayed put and we made the ridge again.

At over 7,000 metres now we were weary, feeling the minimal amount of acclimatization so far undertaken, but overjoyed to be going somewhere fresh and unknown. We finally stopped in a small, windblown hollow sculpted from the side of a boulder on the west side of the ridge, a frozen image of a disappearing whirlpool, tempted there by tiredness and the prospect of some shelter. Having identified a site some half an hour previously, Roger had wanted to stop there and bivouac. Then it had been about five pm and we opted to carry on a while. But now Roger was keen to stop here. I was tired, and liked the idea but not the place, which looked cramped and cold; but this time Doug agreed with Roger and there was no choice.

The team were now feeling weary from their exertions. Doug had acquired the beginnings of a severe cough and his back was aching from last night's digging. Both Roger and I were run down. We stashed equipment beneath the boulder and sculpted a wall out of the snow opposite. A floor of sorts was produced, the tent erected and one of the worst bivouac nights of the trip ensued. We had made a poor decision. The boulder gave us no shelter, but rather funnelled the wind into our alcove. It was impossible to open the left-hand zip, as the spindrift would rapidly invade the tent and saturate the occupants. Throughout the night Doug pleaded with me to open the door. I wanted to, I very desperately wanted to, but had no energy to explain this, muttering only a feeble 'can't', which was taken to mean 'won't'. We could open the right-hand zip a little, but the cooking had to be done inside the sac. Originally a two-man bivouac sac, it was now accommodating three people and their two cookers, and sited in a place where the winds seemed to suck away the oxygen so that the atmosphere rapidly became nauseating. As the sparse oxygen that exists at that altitude is used up, the Gaz fails to burn properly and the tent quickly becomes poisoned. A nauseating headache, at least, is guaranteed. Our tent was also poorly pitched, suspended too high from the back wall, which seriously reduced the available room inside, whilst the rear wall failed to provide adequate support for our backs as we sat against it, three abreast, trying to cook. The effects of the nausea mitigate against prolonged cooking, and as a result inadequate amounts of water are melted, and without replenishment of fluids a vicious circle begins, for the climber who does not drink enough will find it much more difficult to recover himself for the next day's efforts. The inside of the sac seemed to become more hoar-frosted than ever and the inevitable damp began to creep through our down equipment.

The temptation to do nothing was resisted through the need to do so much in this bivouac. We were exhausted and were reluctant to change even from our cooking to our sleeping positions, but attempted instead just to slide down and collapse. But there was not enough room, and weary, half-sleeping bodies were forced to move again, to lift legs and pivot around, shifting sleeping bags and Karrimats until it was possible to lie lengthways in our tent which had shrunk with the very manoeuvre and now crushed us together like sardines. Doug took the dog-kennel, Roger the right-hand wall and myself the centre, but there was no clear rectangle after our evening's digging, and we had to lie in contorted shapes across one another. I was lying head downhill, in an excruciatingly uncomfortable, almost intolerable position. My continual moving caused Doug to complain, though his real complaint was the painful aching in his legs from past injuries, from which our cramped position permitted no relief. The frozen fibreglass hoop arcing across the inside of the tent shifted as we did, and showered us with frost. It was cold!

The following morning the wind had steadied to a quite spectacular strength. A feeble effort was made to melt more water and we then limped out of our battered nylon shell, thankful not to have to pack. From here we would try to reach the summit and return inside the day. It was 19 May and throughout the mountain landscape similarly clad climbers would be emerging from similar homes and, bent against the wind, going about this most obscure business of climbing mountains – dozens of kindred spirits with the same dreams and aspirations, the same cold toes! And as we progressed on our way the landscape became more stunning as ever more recognizable giants came into view – Dhaulagiri, Annapurna, Manaslu, Peak 29, Himalchuli to one side, Cho Oyu, Everest and Lhotse to the other.

We reached the summit at about 1.15 pm, after little more than two hours' effort; Doug patiently rallied the troops at the pace they could afford – a pace dictated in the main by myself, the slowest member of the party, whose inevitable, unyielding tug on the rope halted the front man. The summit was an

Doug Scott on the summit of Pungpa Ri, with Shishapangma's rocky SW Face in the background. The eventual route of descent was down where the rocks meet the snow

Alex MacIntyre

uncertain affair, a high point where the ridge turns left and runs down to a col before running away up to the summit of Shishapangma. The very top was astride a cornice and, being the lightest of the party, I was accorded the dubious privilege of crawling over it on all fours to see if it would collapse. From our vantage point we were able to spy out our proposed descent line, down the back side of Shishapangma's South-East Ridge. Also, we spotted a possibly higher point on our own ridge, some fifty metres to our left, and so we subsequently climbed that to make sure we had reached the highest point.

By 2.15 pm, after a celebration of photographs and Crunchy bars, we were ready to descend. A nagging question started to make itself voluble. Should we, could we, get all the way down tonight? Had we done enough to put us in condition for the Face, or did we need another bivouac on the mountain?

Down? Suddenly the air seemed thicker, the point of the exercise more tangible, a spacious bed and a lingering sunny morning awaited the man who got off this hill tonight. I recalled that glorious day a year ago, on Dhaulagiri, where after pushing up to the summit from 7,500 metres we made it back to the col at 5,700 metres in time to enjoy afternoon tea with the Swiss Expedition. Of course we could get down.

We bundled away along the ridge, conducting a public debate on our chances. The second bivouac hindered us only long enough to pack the sac and leave some Gaz canisters and chocolate bars under the boulder. The evening sunshine caught us with a hurried drink of Rise and Shine at the first bivouac. A thousand metres of snow couloir tempted the eyesight down to the Castle, and we went for it in long, loping zigzags, facing out with the relaxation that tiredness brings, bundling down the slope, rappelling through the ice narrows, remembering the whereabouts of the first uncertain crevasses, while a mass of huge black clouds built up over us and a blood-red glow from the setting sun filtered through its base, creating an atmosphere of doom. Snow flurries whipped into our faces. If the Nazgul had appeared it would only have been fitting. We had taken only six hours to descend.

CHAPTER 7
The Climb – Lower Half

ALEX: We awarded ourselves three days' rest and repair at Base Camp. Life here was more tenuous than ever. The lake was frozen, banks of cloud and mist rolled relentlessly up the valley and over our corrie, it still snowed and a thick carpet of snow covered the ground. If conditions were any warmer at all, they simply made the snow heavier, clinging, more difficult to walk through. An insidious dampness became increasingly irresistible. With the three climbers from Pungpa Ri tired and lethargic and Nick still not well-acclimatized and, in any event, away on projects of his own after the first day, life in the camp was disjointed. No one was particularly inclined to take charge of the cooking, which, consequently, assumed a *laissez-faire* status. Those not in the kitchen were not catered for, a turn of events felt most keenly by Roger, who was of the habit of taking to bed and not emerging until the late afternoon, whereupon a determined effort on his part to generate an organized interest in a large evening meal would be greeted by the kitchen-dwellers with well-fed apathy.

'Why didn't you give me a shout when it was time to eat?'

But it was never 'time to eat', because we were in the kitchen and eating all the time. 'Why didn't you come down? You know we're here, you can hear the row. Why are you lying in your bed all day? What are you getting so grumpy about. . .? If you don't like the organization, don't stay in bed all afternoon, moping about it. Get up and change it!'

And Roger would be left to conduct a lonely vigil into the night, chipping and frying eggs and perhaps brooding just a little on his apparent martyrdom. Hints of exactitude sur- faced, together with a spicing of grumpy antipathy towards the rantings of myself and Doug about the breakdown of the Chinese climbing system, for whose inefficiencies and mis- takes, we assured ourselves, we were not going to pay. In the main the electricity flowed between Doug and Roger, I having been identified – probably quite rightly – as insensitive to the issues.

ROGER: What I did best at Base Camp was sleep. In the morning I could hear the others in the kitchen, chatting, and I would feel a little hungry, but laziness would get the better of me and I would snuggle down and pull the sleeping bag cord tight. Getting sentimental about Christine back in Chamonix passed many hours. Base Camp life is perfect for the lazy man. I could justify any amount of doing nothing on the grounds of rest and recuperation. The difference here was that we had no staff, no smiling face at the tent door in the morning with a mug of tea, '*Chai, sahib*'.

One of the rare occasions when we were all together was to listen to the news. We could pick up an Australian programme which was full of stories of the Falklands War. These seemed like tales from a distant planet to me. Men were dying for what? Apparently for a landscape a little like the one we were living in. It didn't help my humour.

The kitchen was squalid and draughty. The stoves, fed on dirty petrol, were constantly in need of cleaning, and cooking took a long time. Sometimes I would crawl out of my tent

Without cooks we never did get Base Camp kitchen sorted out
Elaine Brook

only when the others were settled in for the night and would rattle around the kitchen, cursing the icy floor, the others who had not cooked for me, the petrol and the terrible weather. We never shared the long days of sunshine and idle chat that make for a good Base Camp life. Doug's style was improvisational and mine organizational. It used to annoy the others that I would attempt the organization of the camp when they had already retired. I did my best to make my life miserable and then blamed the others. It was a pleasure to leave that camp for the mountain. The only social highlights were visits 'chez Alex' to drink rum and listen to music and chat.

Sometimes, when I left my tent late at night, the clouds had lifted to reveal the mountains around us. I would sit on a rock and stare at the starlit arêtes. Around me the candles inside my friends' tents made them glow orange. Inside one Elaine used to do her Tibetan lessons, Nick in another tucked into *War and Peace*. Paul's was empty, Wu asleep, and I could imagine Doug scribbling into the night, listening to Dylan on the headphones for the nth time – 'There's a slow train . . .'

ALEX: On the second day Nick left for Advance Base, intent upon climbing the icy snow peak behind it, which, with its summit in the vicinity of 6,500 mettes, would establish his ability to acclimatize to respectable altitudes and lay a foundation for future plans. He was also talking of attempting to climb the initial couloir of Pungpa Ri to the col between it and Nyanang Ri while we made our Face attempt, thus securing experience up to 7,000 metres. Doug, always hopeful that Nick should realize some of his climbing ambitions, had been giving advice on getting high. Now he counselled diplomatically against this second project.

"Well, there are several pitches of green ice in the narrows, Nick, pretty tough for soloing and even worse for descending. I'm not sure it's a good idea solo.'

No doubt Doug, in his quiet way, would have dissuaded Nick from this more ambitious climb, but unfortunately 'The Ogre' was in the kitchen, feeling mean, his advances towards a reluctant primus stove roundly spurned. Nick voiced the opinion that he felt he could tackle the green ice, he had Alpine experience of soloing ice up to eighty degrees and he had a 'Chacal' with him.

'When the bloody hell have *you* been soloing eighty-degree ice? You haven't got a clue what eighty-degree ice is. You're talking rubbish and you'll probably kill yourself to boot. "Chacal!" Christ, Nick, it's the experience of the bloke wielding a tool that counts at altitude, not the bloody tool. You're acting like an idiot and idiots die up here.'

'Well, Alex, you're wrong. I have actually climbed steep ice solo.'

'Oh aye! Where?'

'The North Col of the Frendo North Face.'

'You mean the Col du Plan?'

'Yes.'

'Nick, the bloody Col du Plan's been skied!'

'Not down the buttress it hasn't. I was in the chimneys on the buttress.'

'Nick, you're talking garbage.'

NICK: My memory of our exchange was somewhat different, and certainly I was never dumb enough to think of steep green ice as anything but serious and intimidating. The Ice Tooth, the 6,500-metre peak I was hoping to climb, was a bit 'shiny' and black all over – clearly it had lots of green ice. I rarely think two climbs ahead immediately before going on a route, and do not remember discussing possible further climbs with Alex at this stage.

The argument arose simply over which ice tool I should take. I ventured to discuss this with Alex. He uses, and likes, 'Charlet Moser' hardware and seemed unable to understand anyone liking anything else. I had brought my 'Chacal' ice axe because I had found the Charlet tools uncomfortable to use. I mentioned to Alex that the most exciting tool I had used was a Hummingbird ice axe. An American friend had insisted on lending it to me in Chamonix the previous summer, before I went on the solo climb Alex refers to, and I had been very impressed with it. Alex found this ridiculous, as the climb does not usually involve any particularly steep ice and he seemed determined to pour scorn on my basis for liking the Hummingbird. I had found the axe so good that I had climbed the ice in the back of the short cleft on the lower section of the buttress in preference to climbing a short section of wet and possibly icy rock. According to Alex it was all in my mind, I

156

was wrong and a fool into the bargain. His lawyer's logic does not always show through at times like this! Doug quietly soothed tempers.

ALEX: Alpine-style climbing in greater mountain ranges is not dissimilar to some aspects of conventional, or perhaps even guerrilla warfare. Long periods of lazy inactivity lead with an inevitable sense of increasing urgency towards a short, frantic, dangerous engagement on the front line, the mountain wall. The climber enjoys many advantages over the soldier; he is his own general and his own private – the carnage, the destruction, the imperative of killing does not haunt him. But the same brooding, electrifying tension is in the air, the same inevitable advance towards the appointed hour for going over the top, and if in the close proximity of strong minds and tired bodies tempers become a little short and nerves a little frayed, the context must be understood.

NICK: I had tried approaching the north side of the Ice Tooth when the lads were on Pungpa Ri. This little peak was supposed to have been our first acclimatization climb, but instead Doug and the others had gone for Nyanang Ri. They were short on time and needed to get some nights out above 6,000 metres. The top of the Ice Tooth was about 20,500 feet, only just over 6,000 metres.

The first approach to the Ice Tooth had been discouraging. I had not got away early enough in the day, had taken too much gear and had gone very slowly. I found that on my own, with no one to pace me, I was just crawling along. However, little by little I was showing signs of some acclimatization. I was not feeling the cold so much and was finding breathing easier. I have done a lot of distance running in the past, and have a fairly slow pulse rate. I tend to breathe slowly and deeply. Even at the highest Alpine altitudes, my breathing only quickens a little, except when I am unfit, and I can usually breathe slowly enough to get a reasonable lungful at a time. However, even our Base Camp was higher than the highest point in Western Europe, and in the early stages of the trip I was bothered by my very fast breathing. It was very quick and shallow and I was getting slight fits of gasping from time to time.

Gradually I had begun to notice that everyone gasped a bit,

and I found that by deliberately gasping faster during a gasping fit it went away much more quickly and I didn't even have to break my pace.

So, I felt ready to try again to get some climbing done, but I had to go alone as the others were fully committed to their programme to climb Shishapangma. Doug, Alex and Roger planned to go for the Face in three days' time. I would be needed to get as much food as possible to the bottom of the Face, but in the meantime I had a day for soloing. I intended to try the Ice Tooth again, but approaching from a different direction this time. I planned to meet Doug and the others in Advance Base in two nights' time, ready to go up to Castle Camp with them.

I set off in the early hours of the following morning under a starlit but moonless sky. After an hour and a half's walk from Advance Base I arrived at a high frozen lake beneath the glacier from which I would approach the mountain. It was still pitch dark with no sign of first light. It is said that the loneliest time is the hour before dawn, and I will never forget the experience of staring out as far as the eye could see, up the valley, down the valley, across to the ridges on the other side and seeing only the gaunt dark shadows of mountains. Nowhere was there any sign of man, not even a distant friendly glow in the sky. I remembered the wolf's tracks I had crossed below Advance Base the afternoon before, and shivered. When some time later the peaks grew into shapes from shadows, I welcomed the dawn as I had never welcomed it in my life before. I realized also the reassurance of seeing some lights on another route in the Alps when setting out solo.

The rest of that day was a little disappointing. I got on to the glacier and, baked by the hot sun in the south-facing, windless valley, crossed to the foot of the Ice Tooth at last, and without disappearing into any crevasses on the way. The night before it had snowed heavily and the Face was plastered except along a thin line in the centre, where it had avalanched.

My plans had focused on the sides of the Ice Face and I had no intention of going out alone on the open Face on what would have been sustained front-pointing on green ice. Instead I headed for a gully on the right side of the Face where there was a series of small buttresses. Unfortunately, when I got into the lower sections of the couloir, the ice under the snow ran out and I found myself on about twelve inches of uncompacted snow on a dry couloir base. Furthermore, the couloir looked as if it could go on like that for much of its length. The rock was uninviting and I headed back down to Advance Base. The difference in time between ascending and descending in the Himalayas is vastly greater than in the Alpine altitudes, and despite leaving the Ice Tooth in the mid-afternoon, I arrived at Advance Base only just after Doug and Wu, who had come up from Base Camp. Roger and Alex were going straight up to Castle Camp the following day and would join us there.

ALEX: Nick left camp on the twenty-second, and his ability with the pancake mix was sorely missed. Doug disappeared the following afternoon with Wu, being less keen than Roger and myself on making the long haul from Base to Castle Camp in one day, and a little anxious to leave the atmosphere at Base behind.

For our third day of 'rest', the weather was fine.

'Roger, the milk is mixed for your Jordans!' A suspicious amount of rice and beans had disappeared into the innards of Doug's rucksack. He and Wu were just about to leave when anxious eyes spied a small, lone figure approaching us over the snow covering the lower lake. Mail!

Since reaching China we had received no mail; word from home is a precious jewel to the expedition climber, yet for seven weeks we had endured an unaccustomed silence, suspecting some collusion by the authorities to deprive us of the letters we knew had been sent – perhaps to underscore the inadvisability of refusing to hire the usual expensive mail jeep for our stay and relying instead on the normal service as far as Nyalam. It had to be mail. Doug *knew* it was mail.

'I wouldn't get too excited, youth. It could just be a note from Pemba or Elaine, or just a letter for Wu.' But Doug was certain.

'Roger! Roger, it's mail! It's Nyima, it must be mail.'

Mail it was, but only for the happy Wu – a cruel blow further exacerbated by an unhappy note from Elaine. She had fallen in the river. Doug's camera and lens were soaked, his film at least was ruined.

Wu was jubilant. Word from home. Doug and Wu departed for the Advance Base.

'Just keep telling him how happy you are, Wu!'

With the letters arrived a small piece of prime cooked meat and fresh spinach. Roger and I repaired to the kitchen for yet another round of havoc – steak, egg and chips, spinach cheese scrambled eggs, lychees and chocolate sauce, potato pancakes and, finally, triumphantly, the fruitcake we had made for the climb! We talked about the K2 trip. Would Roger come? Did the Himalayas provide value for money for all the time and effort – a value that was so readily found in the Alps, especially in winter or in fast unencumbered ascents of the hard rock climbs in summer. Roger was finding the camp depressing – which was not surprising.

The following morning I awoke none too early, with indigestion. Miraculously, I also managed to get up just after dawn. The first sun found me huddled over our two remaining operational stoves, trying to get a morning brew under way. Tea and muesli were provided for Roger in bed, as he had once again beaten the aspirations of the alarm clock. I left finally at about eleven am, weighed down under a quantity of fresh food and cold beer, my stomach bubbling. Once on the plateau, Shishapangma beckoned from beneath a sunny, calm sky, this time for real. Our intended route could be easily traced. What would it be like crossing the rock barrier? Could we find a good bivouac there? Would there be any stonefall? Today we would have to get all the way to Castle Camp. Tomorrow we would be on the Face.

I met Wu shortly before the Advance Camp. He had moved up to the beginning of the glacier with Doug and Nick a couple of hours before, so there was no chance of catching them.

DOUG: I wonder if any interpreter has ever done more for an expedition than Wu. Against all the odds, this frail young man from the south of China, miles from the mountains, had camped and carried a heavy load up to 6,000 metres and remained cheerful to the end, despite every imagined and unimaginable problem that had come his way. The first time we had set eyes on him was at the CMA Headquarters in Peking – all skin and bone in his ill-fitting Mao Tse-tung suit.

160

Paul burst out laughing at the thought of him up here and then into a parody of the George Formby song 'Oh Mr Wu, what can we do with you?' We did all right, having Wu along.

ALEX: At the Advance Camp I found a second mound of food concealed within the flap of our Vango outer tent, together with an accompanying instruction in an unmistakable Scott scrawl to take it through to the Castle. Doug had been at work, preparing all manner of rices for the hill. I left most of it hidden, to make sure Roger would not make the mistake of taking Doug's instructions literally. Then I carried on in the now-sweltering heat, regretting just a little the previous afternoon's gluttonous binge and the can of Budweiser I had just consumed. The snow was soft and I grew increasingly tired. By the moraine at the beginning of the second glacier I was reduced to six breaths for every step and a rest every ten steps. On the moraine at the far end of the glacier that rest stop was promoted to a lengthy, sit-down affair – hardly the stuff of which supposed Olympic athletes are made. I wilted into camp at about eight pm.

'Where's Roger?'

'When I left at eleven he was still sewing on the addition to the bivi tent. He said he would be a while yet.'

He certainly was. Indeed, we had all but written him off. It is an indication, perhaps, of the independence of purpose accorded to the individual on an Alpine-style trip of this nature that we finally decided that Roger was not coming. An incredulous 'Don't believe it' conversation ensued. The weather was right. The people were right. And now, after all the struggle and effort, human error! Perhaps he had decided to retire now. Perhaps he had decided to go home. Had the mail arrived at last – a letter from an unfaithful lady? Early on in the conversation, as we consumed large quantities of Doug's pre-cooked vegetables, I had ventured the occasional 'perhaps he was late in leaving Base Camp – after all, we thought it was a six-hour walk, but it's turned out to be nine.'

However, as time wore on and no light could be observed on the far end of the glacier, such obvious – and, as it transpired, accurate – reasoning was enthusiastically rejected. Roger, we eventually concluded, had fallen asleep again, burnt down his tent, been attacked by a wolf, broken his leg and decided, quite unreasonably, to go home. We collapsed with laughter and indignation, imitating a brooding Roger and calling to each other the now time-honoured phrase: 'Water carrier calling Roger Baxter-Jones!'

I don't recall any plans to descend on the morrow to investigate the possibility of his having been run over by a boulder, but I hope we would have got around to that by the morning. Instead, we considered the prospects of going on the Face tomorrow without him, and plans were drawn up for a two-man ascent of the Face, utilizing the small Salewa tent rather than the bivouac sac. Blissfully unaware of his declining reputation, Roger, who had left Base Camp at four that afternoon, finally rolled into camp at midnight, to the strains of Fauré's Requiem on his Walkman, and to a general reluctance to afford him a bed. We were glad to see him.

At last we were within striking distance of realizing our ambition. The three Face climbers were fit enough to tackle the mountain with some optimism; the weather had settled into a more reasonable pattern and, above all, there was now a total unity of purpose. Nothing existed to distract us from the climb; no more ruthless decisions had to be made and problems of calendarization, of ambition or of ego had now vanished. Individual method and madness was being channelled into a united drive, the variety of skills and experience in our three-man team could be collectively pitted against the Wall. The question 'why?' – at times so prevalent on our trip – could be shelved. Tomorrow evening we would surely be bivouacking in a serac just beneath the rock band, contemplating the breakthrough into the couloir above that would lead us irresistibly to the summit.

Unfortunately, it did not quite work like this. The following evening found our happy, non-questioning, united group strewn over a large, comfortable rock ledge, sunbathing, only a couple of hours further on from the Castle and at the foot of the Face. The one thing that had proven irresistible was the attraction of remaining in bed in the morning. Perhaps it was the long effort of the previous day which had taken its toll; perhaps the late arrival of Roger had mitigated against the earliest of starts, but I think our fundamental problem was the absolute inability of anyone to get up. Belying our supposed warm-blooded status, we dozed, reptilian, until the sun, long since up, was able to coax the lethargy out of our bones. Equipment lay draped over every convenient boulder. Food sat perched on every available flat top, and Roger was still sewing up the additions to the bivouac tent. The image of the Himalayan Alpinist as an incisive, wilful person, ruthlessly calculating his project in grammes, centimetres and seconds, dissolved in a scene not too far removed from a seaside picnic. We even considered hanging on at the Castle for another day, but in the end the need for some sort of momentum forced us out of camp and off, towards the route. Three and a half hours later we were sunbathing again.

From the Castle Camp the South-West Face of Shishapangma is approached almost at right-angles from the east. To reach the Face the climber has two principal choices. He can descend a couple of hundred metres down a tongue of snow immediately behind the Castle Ridge which would then permit him to work a way low across the glacier but necessitate regaining the lost altitude on the far side; alternatively, he can attempt a continuing traverse from the Castle site to reach a gently rising snow shelf leading to a route underneath the southern Face of Pungpa Ri and the first facets of the Shishapangma Face to the proposed start of the route, without losing valuable height. Unfortunately, immediately above the shelf a horizontal rock strata was visible, and directly above that sat a long active serac wall of such uniform nature that it had an appearance more of being constructed by human hand with the intention of keeping barbarians off the upper snow slopes than a phenomenon of a mountain landscape.

None too keen on losing height, it was the latter alternative which principally attracted our team. However, to reach the snow ramp, first we had to negotiate our way down a short but extremely steep rock wall which neatly dissected our path. The rock was loose and, in parts, vertical but a brief inspection revealed the possibility of passing this obstacle in one abseil, which we subsequently did. Then we crept, me first then Roger, Nick and Doug with the abseil ropes, independently, quietly, underneath the ice rampart for nearly two hours, mesmerized by the weird shapes and unlikely structure of this blue-white wall, all the while scrambling over and around the debris that served as a constant reminder of the tenuous nature of a body's existence in this unpredict-

163

Our route up Shishapangma's SW Face, showing the minor variation
and bivouac sites

Doug Scott

able environment. Not even Doug, with all his years of mountain experience, could recall passing for so long, so close under one such single serac wall.

DOUG: I said that it was nearly as bad as the Khumbu Ice Fall.

Roger complained bitterly to me, 'It's stupid coming this way.'

'I don't suppose you'd bring your clients here,' I replied.

'No, and we shouldn't bring Nick either.'

'But he's not a client,' I reminded him.

Nick came staggering along, rubbing his arm. 'I've been blooded,' he said with some concern and some pride. 'A bloody great chunk of ice broke off and caught my elbow.'

'Yes, it was a poor decision,' I agreed. 'As Alex puts it, "Gambling time and effort against the prospects of infinity." '

Nick took all this in his stride, and seemed to be coming into his own. He was well-pleased with his performance – as indeed we all were that day.

ALEX: We made our desultory pace through the sweltering open oven that a high Himalayan glacier becomes in late May. Finally, with relief, our snowshelf ran out from under this immediate threat as the rock bench finished and we were greeted instead by the sight of smaller and hopefully more stable brethren running up the steepening slope above us and into the rock of the extreme right-hand edge of the South-West Face.

I was out in front, and it was sobering to watch the imperceptible pace of the small black dots behind, still beneath the serac wall. In the heat, the weight of the rucksacks was dispiriting, perhaps twenty kilos in all. Axe, hammer, ropes, crampons, ice screws, pitons, sleeping bag, clothing, socks, gloves, film, camera, Gaz and, above all, food – cooked potatoes, rice, lentils all added on and above what we might normally have carried, what I would most definitely have taken only to ensure that we would eat well tonight. Nick was coming along with us to the foot of the route and his rucksack also bulged with an assortment of Gaz and goodies of which we would have to relieve him in a few hundred metres. Finally, I reached the point at which the snowshelf ran out against the Face. A much-practised judo throw thumped the

165

rucksack into the soft snow; I sat on it and observed.

We had come out at a point almost two hundred metres above where the South-West Face plunged into the glacier below. I was sitting on top of a huge scrac, and only feet away from a prominent fracture line at its edge. Above and to the left a chaos of rock towers and ice fields, tenuous snow gullies, long striking ridges and cunningly placed, defensive ice walls threw down a confused, irresistible gauntlet. Directly above, our chosen line merged into steep rock and disappeared out of perspective into a hazy white sky. In the immediate foreground lay a thin barrier of rocky towers, grouped in three main series. Separated by sharp ice arêtes, guarded on the right by the inevitable seracs and on the left by a shimmering blue ice field which suggested agony to anxious calf muscles, they led upwards towards the rock wall which would be the key to our climb. From this, an ominous, familiar rattle was under way.

Anxious searching eyes soon picked out a posse of stones, each and every one a potential man-eater, leaping and bounding down the route. At the highest pillar they had a choice, to bound rightwards and off down the blue ice field, or to keep left and down our first few hundred metres, just to our right of the rock towers. To a man they turned left. Our minds burned rubber briefly, but decided they would pass and watched with relief as they did so, some ten metres away.

The mountain was alive in the sweltering heat. A veritable London bus of a rock trundled out of the central section of the Face, gathered pace and executed a giant leap off the ice field and out over the last five hundred metres in an emotion-numbing 'Whirrr'. I was reminded of a hot August afternoon spent at the foot of the Croz Spur on the North Wall of the Grandes Jorasses. Could we stop here? Roger reached me and I was disappointed to learn the time was only two o'clock – not even midday over in Nepal. Dare I suggest being content with such inconsequential progress as that made today? Instinct insisted we should not push on.

I put a case to Roger. At our current pace and with the rucksacks we would be carrying, we would be unlikely to climb for more than another four hours. At that rate of progress the yield of the afternoon would be minimal. Anyway, Nick would not reach here for another hour and once we had taken on board the food he was carrying our loads would, in my opinion, be too heavy. But above all, we would be exposed to stonefall. On the other hand, if we were to stop now, eat as much as possible, dump some of the rest of the food and travel light after an early start tomorrow morning, we would probably spend the next night as high up the Face as we might manage with the slightly higher, probably more cramped and more lethargic start that continuing today would give us. The crux of the problem was our loads. By my standards, the quantity of food we were carrying on the mountain was vast, torn as we were between the desire to eat well on the first bivouac and a reluctance to commit ourselves to a super-light schedule for the Face until we had come to grips with the rock band.

Doug arrived. What did he think? Perhaps we might just move further up the Face for a while, to the top rock tower behind which we could probably bivouac in comfort. I mentioned the stonefall and the mountain duly obliged as we considered Doug's thoughts on the matter, a couple more large stones whipping alongside the potential bivouac site! We opted to stay put and soon a brew was well under way as we basked contentedly for a time in the luxury of a day's work nearly done. Nick joined us with tales of harassment from the serac wall.

Eventually, we considered the question of where to spend the night. I suggested one of the seracs immediately above us and Doug led off towards it. Upon reaching it, however, in an intuitive brainwave, he pushed up another fifty metres over on to the rocks to locate a quite superb eyrie, one of the truly great bivouac sites of the world.

Thus by three-thirty – barely past midday just five kilometres across the border in Nepal – we were in residence. Nick, who had accompanied us to the eyrie, would now, according to the plan, turn back for the Castle, taking a safer descent route on to the glacier for photographs of the Face. Instead, equally impressed by the excellence of the site and the incongruity of relaxing and sunbathing at the foot of such a mountain wall – as if on a Mediterranean cruise – he opted to stay and enjoy the experience of yet another cold night out in Doug's one-piece duvet suit.

Enthusiastic construction ensued in a determined attempt

to secure the flattest and most comfortable of floors, an exercise most memorable for more of Doug's Titan stone-throwing exercises as he battered embedded rocks with equally large counterparts until luxury was created in the floor of a unique rock pulpit a little larger than the base of our bivouac sac. Equipment, clothing and climbers were draped out in the sun once again; a tan was the principal objective of the afternoon and an expansive mood swept through the camp, generating some sympathy for my rabid rantings about the food and going light. I was permitted into the food bags. On the Face we took the following: three types of tea, sugar, milk powder and packet soups, salt, garlic, lemon, processed cheese, tinned fish (salmon and tuna), a handful of chocolates, tsampa and chilli for that horrendous cheese and chilli mix. Minimal food was packed for three days, Gaz for four.

Bivouac at the foot of the SW Face of Shishapangma, overlooking the afternoon clouds filling up the Nyanang Phu Glacier. In the background are the Jugal Himal peaks of Phurbi Chachu (on left), Lengpo Gang, Dorje Lakpa (behind) and Gur Karpo and at the front the unclimbed Eiger Peak (6,912m), only noted previously by Aufschnaiter. On the right Pemthang Karpo Ri and the frontier ridge
Doug Scott

Doug Scott, Alex MacIntyre and Roger Baxter-Jones at the foot of
Shishapangma SW Face on the evening before starting the climb
Nick Prescott

Everything else was out and the bag packed for Nick, including spare clothing, socks, Doug's duvet suit, ice pegs, food
and Gaz. The Gaz calculation was the most vital. Without
melted snow water, a climber's days at altitude are extremely
limited. By any bivouac standards, a munificent feast then
emerged and we retired to bed content, the Face climbers into
their well-pitched tent and Nick outside under a dazzlingly
clear night sky crisply illuminated by a half moon, an icy
landscape of mountain shadows.

Mornings are the bane of a mountaineer's life, especially the
cold, pre-dawn start into which he is traditionally supposed to
rouse himself. For once we managed to adhere to this bar-
baric, though necessary custom, brought about by the fact
that in the cold of the night the mountain is often at its safest.
A creeping light from the east lent substance to the mountain's
shadows, a steely grey glacier began to emerge from the
valley below and, in our pulpit, grumpy figures moved
listlessly in the cold. What to take; what to leave; did the
decisions of the previous evening seem right in the hard reality
of morning?

By seven we were away, Nick down to the glacier below

with surplus gear and a 400-mm Pentax with a lens to record our progress before making a detour back to the Castle, and the remainder up into the wall above, moving well and luxuriating in our progress up snow ice to the immediate right of the rock towers.

'An hour at this time is worth three in the sun,' I was babbling.

'Are we there yet?'

After a while this accommodating terrain dissipated into steeper, hard blue ice and we were faced with a choice, either to move rightwards and attempt to wend our way through the seracs, looking for snow, or to move left towards the rock pillars which held the promise of a ribbon of snow on their immediate flank. We chose to move left.

Doug was now in front. He reached the pillar but his activities there revealed thin snow over polished grey ice, a mean medium for travel. Roger and I observed the barely biting crampons and changed tack, heading directly up our icy slope while Doug, peeved at this betrayal, moved on to the rock and fast disappeared from view. Every now and then a head would appear above us to extol the virtues of rock or demand poses while pictures were snapped.

DOUG: There were several interesting points brought out by this mix-up, and the emotion it aroused stamped the incident for ever, it would seem, into our minds. Whilst it should be a case of 'every case on its merits' it never is so entirely. When Alex and Roger opted to go straight up the ice-snow couloir after we had decided to go up the rock arête, I did feel somewhat 'peeved and betrayed', harping back in my mind to the law lodged firmly there that we do not move until there is agreement as to how and where, then we go for it in unity of effort and purpose. Now there was indecision and, to my mind, danger in it. Rocks had bounded down the couloir the day before and chunks of ice were poised for take-off some thousand feet above, a situation which I try to avoid if there is an alternative. There was another possibility – one, admittedly, more to my liking. Long stretches of hard ice or snow are all very well, but for me inherently boring. Even after

Roger and Alex in the ice couloir
Doug Scott

170

enjoying a superb day on Ben Nevis, soloing 'Orion Face' and 'The Curtain', I sensed a certain lack of variety in the climbing, finding it somewhat repetitive. Ice climbing is a bit like riding a bike, once you can do it, all you can do then is go faster or for longer. Rock climbing is never quite like that. You never know quite how it will be, certainly not on new ground. Best of all, I like to combine them both and that is what the arête held in store for a thousand feet – ice, slabs of rock, hard snow and rock buttresses. I can think of nothing that I enjoy more in the mountains than moving fast over such ground with freedom to experiment, to rest to weigh up the next bit, ice and rock, one after the other.

I came up on to a ledge overlooking the couloir to see Roger and Alex some two hundred feet below. My feet ached at the thought of me out there, tiptoeing up, hour after hour, with a heavy rucksack. I have never liked cramponing all day since breaking my ankles on the Ogre in Pakistan in 1977. I sat scanning the rest of the Face where elegant buttresses and arêtes lay parallel to mine. They were steeper and would provide exciting lines for the next expedition to this side of the mountain. We could have been there – too late now, I told myself – still, this wasn't so bad. Maybe Roger and Alex would come over.

I yelled across: 'Why don't you come over here? It's really good rock, better than that boring couloir.' I had meant this to be a light-hearted invitation, but Alex's reaction indicated that he had not taken it that way. Maybe he felt it was his turn to feel peeved that I was now sitting comfortably, ensconced on a rock ledge, taking photographs, looking down on him – or maybe there was a note of triumph in my voice which got his back up.

ALEX: Roger and I persevered and soon reached snow, up which height was quickly gained, while Doug, now facing more compact rock, re-emerged to enquire the nature of our future prospects – a bearded, bonneted, icy, Carringtonesque face grinning at us from round a corner and enquiring, 'What's it like, youth?'

'Snow for another fifty metres, then more ice for about a hundred metres to the ridge behind the last tower. It looks good from there to the rock band.'

Doug, suspicious of metres, let alone ice, was unhappy. Hard ice imposes tremendous strain on the lower joints of the leg and Doug now had pinned joints following an abseiling accident on the Ogre. 'Why don't you two come over here for a change, instead of climbing that bloody boring stuff.'

A certain contempt for the ice, and by implication the people who chose to climb it, was unmistakably evident. Perhaps intended to jar or embarrass us into joining him, it had the opposite effect on me. Not at all unsympathetic to a change of rhythm and the idea of rock climbing, I was, however, personally unsympathetic to the tone which became more apparent as I grew increasingly reluctant – a reluctance I believed to be well-founded. From my vantage point it appeared that, in a short while, anyone who wished to make progress would be forced by the compact nature of the towers above to move back on to the ice, and no time would be saved – in fact it might well be lost. But Doug was now harping determinedly, in an almost talking-down fashion that had no place in a team like ours on a Face such as this.

Why couldn't he just say his legs hurt and ask, the bloody old fool? 'Quit talking to me like a child, Doug.'

'Why not, that's the way you talk to Nick.'

What! Is he serious, does he really want to get into a personality clash here? I started to boil. 'Bloody hell, Doug. Nick *is* a child in this terrain; at least I don't treat him like a puppy!'

Another thirty metres or so higher I could see clearly that Doug would be back on ice – and harder, more polished-looking ice than I would be climbing. Why couldn't he just accept my judgement? Why distrust me?

Roger was starting to move over to his left to oblige the insistent Doug. I shouted down to him as he began to negotiate thin snow over rubbery ice.

'I don't think there is any point, Roger, the last pillar is detached from your rock by an icy col, and it's not worth climbing, or even easy if he does want to climb it.'

Meanwhile Doug, secure in the knowledge that he had at least one rock partner, was firing questions at me *vis à vis* his possibility of progress.

'Well, I reckon you can move around the right side of that pillar if you want, but there's nothing doing above.' And with that I changed a mental gear and continued my now independent way up the ice, which rapidly became more brittle and easier on the legs, making quick progress up past the final tower, up past the snow arête – which I moved over to join for its last few metres – and up another short stretch on to a comfortable rock ledge, there to sit and await events below.

Roger had reached the rock and clambered up to Doug, where he discovered an intention to climb a hard, steep layback crack above. Discussion ensued, Roger wanted to return to the ice – he saw no point in climbing this rock. Doug insisted it was faster, and anyway if he had not been waiting for us he would be hours ahead, but Roger's persistence eventually seemed to draw from Doug a reluctant agreement to return to the fold. He moved back out on to the awkward hard ice that abounds on the sides of such rock, at the same time glancing back to see Doug fast disappearing up the layback. The expedition now had a petulant child! Realizing that that child would need to climb ice sooner or later, and might need a rope then if not before, Roger continued up beside the pillar and moved back left and on to a ledge upon which Doug promptly landed himself, gasping after some alarmingly hard moves off a jammed block up a steep granite crack – the hardest moves of the climb.

A look at the tower above revealed a thin, compact structure of overlapping rock slabs and they found themselves forced out right, Roger leading over the hardest ice of the climb to the snow arête above.

I munched a Mars bar in the luxury of the morning sun and sucked the odd icicle. Roger appeared at the side of the tower, his red jacket an identifiable point of moving colour.

I yelled, 'Ice is nice and will suffice!'

'Right on, brother.'

Doug reached the snow arête, tired by the ice and now with the confusion of some responsibility of holding us up, of feeling out of sorts. He had even mentioned going down to Roger. Always honest in such emotions, he shouted up an apology, but the warming sun and a second (tomorrow's) Mars bar had melted the antagonism. We were making good progress and the dispute had been more about our characters than the chances of success.

While the others moved up the arête towards my ledge I set off up the ice above.

'What's it like?'

'This is good snow ice which seems to run to the barrier about a hundred metres above me. That looks like interesting mixed ground. You'll get your rock soon enough, youth!'

A brief passage through an icy narrows permitted a right turn on to a small, narrow rock ledge. The area we were now entering was showing increasing evidence of stonefall; the ice was pitted with fist-sized rocks, but the day did not seem to hold any hint of threat. It was time for a brew in this advantageous viewpoint, where we could re-group, pause and take stock of the wall above.

Gingerly, I ferreted around in my rucksack, unpacked the Gaz stove and pan I was carrying, carefully made a small ledge for it on the snow, wrapped the Karrimat around to keep out the breeze and began to melt water. Sitting facing out, legs dangling over the drop below, I watched for the impending arrival of Roger and Doug. On our precarious perch we enjoyed a milky tea whilst discussing our progress so far, the weather and our probable line through the wall above. Which way would take us to the unseen couloir above? Which way would unlock the key to the route?

The lowest point of the rock band was now about fifty metres above us. It seemed to tempt us leftwards with a hint of hidden, but interesting gully climbing providing a direct link to the couloir. Roger was the most interested in this move, in at least crossing over to peek around the corner, but neither Doug nor I was keen to go this way. We knew this area well from our observations at the Castle, or on the slopes of Pungpa Ri, and these suggested that we should now move right under the band, up to and over a bergschrund which was visible to us and which we knew would give access to an out-of-sight ice field beyond. Roger insisted, quite correctly, that the left-hand way looked extremely interesting. Doug confirmed this by saying that it had appeared to be acutely steep green ice from the ridge beyond the Castle, while I was unhappy about climbing in a narrow gully because of the danger of rockfall, dislodged either by the leading climber or his ropes or from above. There was an awful lot of mountain above, from which rocks could be gathered into the couloir,

which, in its turn, would funnel them directly into the gully. We opted to play the percentages and moved right.

The bergschrund proved an interesting little pitch, consisting of an insubstantial snow bridge over a deep hole, with exit barred by a steep and awkward little ice wall. Roger led over this obstacle, sidling over the snow, placing an ice screw at the base of the ice wall and then, with firm blows with his ice tools, swung himself up and over the lip and out of sight. The rope snaked out. Shouts of 'What's it like?' went unanswered and the first clouds drifted in to surround us, putting a chilly edge on the air.

'Stones!' An urgent shout from Roger.

I dived behind Doug. Doug dived for the ice wall.

'OK. They embedded in the snow up here.'

When Roger was secure at the end of the pitch, Doug and I followed some four metres apart on the same rope. With Doug just over the lip, I was forced to stop and work at removing the ice screw, which was well placed and would require considerable effort. This caught Doug with an unprepared, enforced stop on ice above, only a couple of feet away from the more relaxing snow. He wanted to move, a bull straining on a leash. Snow and ice lumps cascaded down from his efforts to get more comfortable.

'Christ, Doug, what are you doing, cut it out, man.' Below, not dressed against spindrift, I was furious. It wasn't professional, I wanted to scream at him. A fresh wave of agitated soft snow landed on my head. 'Hell, Doug!'

'It's only frozen water, youth. The rope's cutting through it above anyway.'

When at last the screw came out the heave over the lip brought no respite. Doug was anxious to be off and I needed a rest. I untied at a canter and followed at my own pace to Roger, who was standing on good snow ice at the left side of a small ice field, belayed to his ice axe, hammered, shaft down, into the surface. The snow field was the shape of a concave triangle, the upper point prematurely truncated by a grey bastion of rock which towered above our heads into the mist, while our team had assembled in the lower left corner and

Roger climbing to the ledge where we had lunch
Alex MacIntyre

177

therefore had a snow arête running left to right across the line of vision. We could see neither round the arête nor above the rock bastion. Which way now?

Observations from below had again suggested to me that the way was to the right of the rock, up an obvious ice gully which would by-pass the buttress and lead to a traverse line back left into the couloir. Doug's ideas tied in with this, but Roger was keen to see if we could traverse into the couloir from our current height, and certainly the structure of the ground to the left did suggest the possibility of easy access. We moved up the snow arête to peer over and into the visage of a steep Alpine gully dressed for the depths of winter. We turned right, Doug leading now, hungry for the promise of rock in his hands, awkwardly across a steep ice slope and then with great confidence over loose and difficult flakes, around a corner and out of sight while Roger and I began to move up to give more rope.

Above the belay a narrow ice tongue led up through the mixed ground above, but the ice was brittle and broke away in large plates when hit, and Doug was quickly out to his right on to the rock. This was loose and awkward to start and seconds burned in indecision while, up the ropes, a critical electric tension raced towards Doug from his seconds, to whom the ice tongue was the obvious, simple passage.

'Forgive an old man just one mistake.'

A straight leg was swung up and over a prow of rock, the body shuffled after it and finally he was established, almost sitting on his precious rock, and then away up a long mixed granite pitch of delicate, fascinating intricacy for such altitudes, finally stretching the ropes in pursuit of a belay. Below, we grumbled at the need to remove our pitons and stand naked on tottery flakes and, when that was not enough, on brittle ice, waiting for the dim sounds of a hammer beating metal that would tell us he had found a place to stop, and that we would all soon be safely attached to this mountain. They duly came and we moved into the ice tongue, but the ice plates made life a misery for the second climber, and none too

Alex with Roger (behind) climbing the mixed ground on a double rope during the evening of the first day

Doug Scott

comfortable for the first! Soon we were picking our way up the rock, keeping close together and moving with an awareness of the vulnerability of the lower man – in this case Roger. We finished independently, to the left and right of Doug, enjoying the experience and dreaming of the Alps again.

'Well, youths, you seem to have managed to second that almost as fast as the old man led it.'

The evening shadows were now creeping over us, the sun fast disappearing in the direction of Hagen's Col and the sun-kissed rock dissolving upwards out of our reach. Our principal concern was now becoming the location of a place to sleep for the night. To the left the mixed ground led to a snow-banked ledge that disappeared around the buttress in the direction of the couloir, and I was tempted to head that way. Doug, however, was sure that the traverse line we wanted was higher, above and around the top of another compact rock tower, and we accepted this judgement as he had fast disappeared upwards at an ever-quickening pace, suggesting slightly easier terrain. I hung back off the piton at my belay stance, shuffling and shivering and dreaming of the warm clothing to be found only inches away, burdening my shoulders and back. If only I could take off the rucksack for a moment, just to relieve the weight; if only I could sit down and maybe sleep a little. The body was beginning to feel the impact of the long day. What altitude would we be at now? Nearly seven thousand metres? We must have travelled more than a thousand metres today – exhilarating, unprecedented progress that now suggested sleep. Above, the sun receded beyond reach and it was cold.

ROGER: It had been a great day, we had solved the key passage of the Face on the first day, on the first attempt, but now I had eyes only for the bivouac. I sized up every ledge, every snow slope. All I needed was one square foot of flat ground to park my ass and sleep would follow. But no, the home-builder was looking for a construction site, and I climbed tetchily up into the night after him.

ALEX: A shout from above interrupted my dozing. The rope had run out and Doug was shouting down that we should all move together now, it was easier up there. We undid our belays, I beat out the piton, shoved my ice axe over my

180

Climbing on the rocks before entry into the 'pea-pod' couloir, anxious to find a bivouac place before dark

Doug Scott

shoulder through the strap of the rucksack harness and followed Roger up that next delightful two hundred feet. This method of climbing demands confidence. The first man climbs ahead, taking advantage of those places where protection can be arranged fairly readily, a tape sling over a rock flake for example, while the rest of the party follow behind at similar speed, removing the equipment as they come to it. Should a mishap occur, there is some chance it might be contained.

I reached the ledge at last, welcoming the chance to stop moving for a moment, but perturbed by the talk of a bivouac here on this awkward, uneven, chaotic and, to me, singularly uninviting seat of rock. Roger favoured staying here, where at least we could guarantee some sort of a sitting bed, while any attempt at further progress would, in all probability, see us caught by the impending dark in the middle of nowhere. Doug was keen to push higher, confident in his intuition that another pitch up the rock would find us a place to sleep behind

181

yet another granite brow, but to me the rock above looked, if anything, even more compact and I could understand Roger's reluctance to continue in that direction.

'Has anyone looked round the snow bank?'

Immediately on our left a snow arete obscured all further view. Doug untied and moved round the corner while I belayed him and cursed my fate at not being able to remove my rucksack. Whoops of delight drifted back to us.

Roger summed up our hopes. 'He must have found a bivi ledge de luxe. That's the only thing that prompts such emotion from him!'

But the whoops were at the discovery of a stunning sunset, and the immediate proximity of the couloir.

What about a place to sleep?

'Well, there is some sort of possibility just below me at the end of this snow bank.'

Roger, not keen on 'some sort of possibility' when he was set on a definite one, made his opinion known to Doug.

'Roger, you're a right bloody Jonah on bivouacking, always the bloody pessimist, always unwilling to go on. You'd bivouac after breakfast if you could.' Then Doug disappeared to investigate further. Roger and I degenerated into bickering.

'I don't want to sleep here, Roger. I want to lie down.'

'Sitting down's not so bad, we've all bivied in worse places.'

'Yes, and that's why there's no way I'm staying here – it's crippling, dossing in a place like this.'

Meanwhile the light grew dimmer, unfed, exhausted bodies colder. Muffled exclamations were now reaching us regarding life on the far side of the snow bank. Perhaps we could get into the couloir now, perhaps we could dig a ledge below. Doug summed up the options as Roger moved off, unroped, to check on Doug's eyesight. We had four choices – to stay put, press on up the rock, bivouac round the corner in a similar place to our current ledge, or force an entrance into the couloir and climb this for a hundred metres or more to a place where a col behind one of the huge towers of rock on the far bank offered the possibility of a site.

DOUG: At last I could see that we could bring this very long day to a close. From my high point it looked as though we could lower Alex (being the lightest) down on to the snow of the couloir. From there he could go up and belay us across to him. Another two hundred feet of easy snow should bring us up to a flattish snow arête sticking out from the Face on the opposite side of the couloir. The sky was mauve, turning deep purple. It should be a good day tomorrow, but what a day this had been – snow, ice and rock, 3,500 feet of it; a journey from the known to the unknown in every sense, physically, psychologically and emotionally, for we had run the whole gambit through tiredness into second wind, from security to uncertainty with a commitment to more of the same, and a whole range of emotions, fear, pride, anger and joy, had surfaced down in the depth of the now dark couloir. We had made good progress, but there was still much to do.'

ALEX: Everyone returned to the belay, and we opted for the couloir. A sense of urgency took hold; we were committing ourselves to climbing into the night in search of an uncertain home and, above all, we wanted to be in the couloir before it grew pitch black. While the others sorted themselves out and removed the belay I, in my turn, moved off round the arête, exhorted by Doug to hurry to catch the last glimpse of the sunset. I followed the snow round and peered into the dim couloir below.

A tricky series of moves over loose slabby rocks lying like uncertain rooftiles in a small rocky corner cried out for caution. The belays now removed, the others were away round the arête behind and moving after me, maybe seventy feet of rope between us and no runner to safeguard against any error. I reached a small ledge and crept left to Doug's high point under a bulging rock wall, to peer into the gloom below. We were on top of the right-hand retaining wall of the couloir.

'We'll need to rappel about seventy feet.'

With the onset of nightfall the inevitable mountain breeze struck up and my tired body felt this as a cutting cold that sent shivers racing around the skin while inside the furnace, low on fuel, turned over to the pilot light as it had done so many times before. I sat on the edge of the ledge, feet dangling over the top, attempting to bury a piton behind a reluctant rock.

'What about this?' Roger had reached the ledge and was fingering an excellent crack in the wall above.

'Christ, I'm sorry, I didn't see it!'

Roger hammered in a piton, clipped in a karabiner and began to lower me down into the couloir, out over the wall, leaning well back, crampon-points scraping and sparking against the frozen rock. I passed over a small overhang, a brief second in mid-air, then crampon points bit happily into crisp, frozen, receptive snow. No ice lurked here.

'What's it like?'

'Good snow, absolutely brilliant.'

'Can you test the ropes?'

The other end of the rope whistled down in the darkness. A sharp pull confirmed the rope was running freely through the sling attached to the piton and the last man would have no problem in retrieving it once he had slid down it to this point.

Meanwhile, above me Doug had discovered that the piton Roger had placed was the prized titanium peg he had found on the Abbruzzi Ridge of K2 in 1980. The sight of this old faithful friend securely embedded in its last resting place troubled him. He began hitting it.

'What the bloody hell are you doing?'

'I always place the peg I abseil on.'

'Now Doug, that's just not true, and anyway such an egocentric approach is not possible in a small team like this.'

'Well, it's titanium. It's very expensive and unique.'

'It's also nine o'clock in the evening!'

The piton stayed. I was now moving up the couloir. The couloir, in a day, perhaps eleven hundred metres of progress over high and difficult Himalayan terrain. Only in our wilder speculations had we hoped to be here tonight; we would have been satisfied just to have reached the foot of the rock band. Now we were through it, the crucial obstacle that might have so seriously delayed us. Years of experience peering up into rock bands on other mountains had been brought to bear and we had slipped through on the perfect line. We were a cohesive entity now; only the sheer professionalism and trust within the operating parts of the whole permitted the luxury of debate over the price of titanium! In a cold, hostile world we were warming to the sensation of control, over ourselves, our actions, and adaptation as we merged with and moved through this strange environment – a capsule of humanity passing over a wild, uninhabited, unique universe.

The snow arête upon which we had hoped to find our good bivouac site was a disappointment. It was very icy and extremely narrow, while the slope on the other side vanished steeply into another unseen gully. To sleep here we would have to work into the night to fashion a ledge. Down in the blackness below, two pinpricks of light appeared as the others switched on their head torches. On the slope above, the moon-cast shadows tempted with the promise of flatter places, of ledges perhaps on the couloir's left side. I ambled on up for another couple of hundred feet, chasing the shadows but finding no respite in the angle, no place to sleep. In the valley below and the mountains beyond the bright half moon illuminated a steely cold world. How many other climbers on those mountains over there would be blessing this settled weather as they looked out on the self-same clear, clear night and dug for ledges at this late hour. A fair few I was prepared to guess.

'Anything up?' Doug's voice broke into my wanderings.

'Nothing so far.'

'Bad luck. Well, come down, you've done enough. We'll sleep here.'

I tumbled back into the darkness, towards the bobbing lights that marked our bed-to-be. Doug was already at work, wielding his axe against the ice, his unfathomable strength and patience a gift to anyone fortunate enough to have him digging their bivouac site. I sparrowed about, getting in the way rather than doing much helpful work, while ice chips showered us with a cold coat. Roger struggled into his one-piece duvet suit and then began the precious job of making some tea. Standing on the snow slope below us a few feet away, perched over a tiny alcove he had scraped from the snow, he melted snow for the brew that would seduce parched, rasping throats and trickle some warmth into our dehydrated, chilled cores, our frozen souls. The tea, when ready, was gulped thankfully but all too quickly. It takes so long to transform snow into boiling water in the night at seven thousand metres in a cold breeze.

All three of us then redoubled our efforts against the arête, intent on fashioning a place where we could lie side by side along the top, three feet wide and six feet long, a precarious park bench perched over thousands of feet of ice falling away both to left and right. We danced around and over this place, hammering and chipping like crazed carpenters, cursing cold toes and numb fingers and taking a masochist's delight in this world in which we now lived. No fixed ropes snaked out behind to offer an umbilical connection to the ground. We would not pass a day fashioning ledges and building spectacular little cities from which the logistics machine could erect another layer of the pyramid. We were just three people, a nylon bag and an evolving perch, totally involved in our climb.

When the ledge looked as if it might just accommodate the three of us I fished out the nylon (Goretex) sac from my rucksack, together with the fibreglass poles which, when pieced together and erected in a curve across the inside of the sac from diagonally opposing corners, give it a shape. Doug, crampons off, disappeared through one of the zipped side panels and I pushed the poles in after him. Much threshing and cursing ensued as the frantic red bag writhed in a curious fit around the space in question and threatened to career down the mountain at any moment. Perhaps it was eating Doug? This seemed the most apt explanation. In the fracas fibreglass poles shot out of the other unzipped side panel and vanished down the slope, while the writhing reached a climax and a confused, indigestible Scott was rudely regurgitated.

The contraption being my responsibility, I was summoned to make the second attempt. With no backing wall of ice or rock to suspend it against, the tent had a mind of its own. The remaining, half-erected fibreglass poles flailed around the sac and disappeared like crossbow bolts. With all doors closed, the thing was finally tamed with the remaining poles and pinned to the floor and slopes with ice screws and ice axes.

'OK!'

Rucksacks bundled through the door, followed by cold, cramped climbers, and the familiar struggle against the limited space began. It was a wretched night, we were too tired to do much cooking and compromised on the vital intake of fluid. Parched throats rasped on thin air while Doug's cough grew worryingly incessant and bronchial. The tent was heavily frosted on the inside and down in the dog-kennel, with a single layer of material between myself and the slope, my sleeping bag was becoming seriously damp.

DOUG: I had felt the first signs of laryngitis down at the bottom bivi. It certainly added another dimension to this climb for me, for after bouts of coughing I felt completely drained and the lack of sleep was a nuisance and an embarrassment. I was concerned that I was keeping Roger and Alex awake and that I would not be able to equal the efforts of the others. I did have the chance to solo back down on the first day, but not now. I was committed to go for the top to get off an easier way. This realization gave me added strength, which I sorely needed. The search for this bivi before dark had me climbing like a madman, covering the 700 feet of mixed ground to the couloir and then hacking a platform. I'd let myself become oblivious to one of the golden rules of high-altitude climbing: to pace myself.

CHAPTER 8
To the Summit

ALEX: Next morning we remained cocooned, waiting for the sun. It is hard to grasp the splendour of this life-giving force unless you have sat and frozen, waiting for the first lightening of the far horizon and the final, triumphant blaze of gold as the topmost part of the orb comes into view. Any climber caught out in a desperate forced bivouac on Alpine mountains can well understand why this deity was worshipped of old. Although our grasp on life was pretty firm and our bivouac neither forced nor particularly bad, we had all waited for those first streaks of light on other occasions and we were thankful for the sun. We warmed and worked on the cooking, trying to replace some portion of the liquid lost, the calories exchanged for our upward passage, and then bailed out of the tent in a gleeful celebration of yesterday's progress, photographing the tent and ourselves with the determination of the archetypal Japanese tourist. Our only blight was Doug's cough.

ROGER: Doug's daily retirement ceremony came early that day. His cough was terrible and had been all night. I reassured him that he was not holding us up and even if it did finally take longer because of his health we were all in this together. He consented to try another hundred metres and, shortly afterwards, overtook me and started breaking step. It was easy to follow his line, even on ice, as the bloody mucus he was coughing up marked the path.

ALEX: Now that we were through the rock band we decided to abandon even more equipment and stake all on speed. A couple of pitons, three ice screws, a little food and our one and only helmet were abandoned, carefully tied to one of the ice screws in case we should need to have recourse to them in the unforeseen emergency of a descent down this route. The couloir above our bivouac was narrow and twisted left out of sight behind the ridge, obscuring our view of the ground above as it ran through a veritable gorge of towering rock

Alex by the first bivouac, showing the view across to the Nyanang Phu Glacier where it turns beneath Pemthang Karpo Ri. The prominent 'fluted peak' on the skyline just left of centre is Ganchempo

Doug Scott

structures on the right and a delicate, defined, gendarmed, steep-sided ridge on our left. We kept to the right as we moved into the gorge, creeping up under the right retaining wall, hugging it close to minimize the risk of stonefall funnelled from the unseen ground above, chasing the shadows as the sun grew hotter and the still air became stifling. How high were we? Opposite us, identifiable mountains whose heights we knew refused to dip below our line of vision. Surely we must be over seven thousand, but why then would the seven-thousanders not slip below us? The question of our height was to remain a topic of conversation for the rest of the climb. Could we really have climbed so far yesterday or had we merely been mistaken in our estimates of the height of the rock band?

Above our narrow gorge the couloir suddenly broadened into a wide snow pod, at the entrance to which, on some rare ledges on the right, we stopped to melt snow for water.

Hot or cold water? This was not so much a question of preference as logistics. Up here, above twenty-four thousand feet, a man without fuel to melt the snow is living on rapidly running-out, borrowed time. We had two spare Gaz cylinders and two almost new ones in the stoves, enough, with care, for two more bivouacs and a desultory brew on the next day, possibly. By opting for cold drinks, we would use up less fuel and in the warmth of the day could drink a little more precious water. Not that snow water is particularly good, it is pure, almost distilled, and without essential additives, but it is always welcome.

ROGER: Himalayan climbing is about putting one foot in front of another and breathing whilst doing so. Keep doing this and you'll make it. Like Doug I play breathing games, changing rhythms, counting steps, directing the inhalation to wherever the strain is. Silly mind games help too, such as imagining you are moving the mountain down with your feet as you stay at the same height. Often enough the mind spins off into protracted fantasies, the lone survivor battles on to safety. Only when you stop can you look around and see the Himalayas. We were now beginning to look over the frontier ridge into Nepal and perhaps tomorrow we would peer over the Tibetan plains. Here, as nowhere else, the climber sees the immensity of the world – on the earth but not of it, playing games with gravity amongst all that beauty.

ALEX: We languished on our ledges for nearly an hour. A wind was starting to get up and, above us in the pod, it echoed and whirred in a fashion not dissimilar to the sound of far-off but fast-approaching stonefall, an unwelcome additional strain. And one stone did pass. I was slouched on a ledge, lethargic under the relentless sun, when attentive ears identified a confirmed, incoming missile amongst the wind's purrs. Reflexes took over. There was no shelter, not that I had particularly arrived here looking for shelter; it is simply that at every moment on the mountain the climber will automatically assess his exposure and the possibility of shelter – which way do you dive, jump or roll? I dived against my ledge, curling tight as a ball beneath the rucksack which had mysteriously appeared in my hands and over my head, a centurion with all too short a shield. The projectile struck a glancing blow a few feet away to the left, and passed harmlessly into the void below while we collapsed into our lethargy again.

Over the Langtang that afternoon the clouds built anvils which then drifted with their threat of storms in our direction. Doug had noted the slightly changed cloud formation low over Nepal that morning, and remarked on this. Now, once again, he was watching a familiar deterioration in the weather pattern that might come to nought or might mark the onset of storms experienced in the past, such as that which had swallowed the upper slopes of Everest and with it Mick Burke. We eyed these anvils warily as we set off up into the pod, crabbing our way up 'French technique' diagonally leftwards, still close under the right retaining wall. Clouds now began to swirl over our mountain. The winds encompassed us, blasting mist and cloud up from the gorge below, whipping it up into the pod and obscuring us from one another. The wall grew a little more grey and a little more sombre as the first snowflakes stung our faces.

As evening approached we came to a huge rock buttress split down the middle by an impressive chimney. Beyond that the couloir closed to a spectacular narrows again and vanished from our sight. I had moved out on to the right wall itself underneath this tower, along a line of snowy ledges, looking for a bivouac site while the others progressed through the mist below to the point at which I had turned on to the rock.

'Where is he?'

The situation was looking worse, windsuits were being donned and we urgently needed a place to shelter.

'Over here.'

'What's it like?'

'With a bit of digging we can have a fairly good ledge, I think.'

'But what about protection against snow?'

The area I was investigating was part and parcel of a huge field of compact slabby rock. Slabby rock is a desperate place on which to be marooned for a night when the weather breaks and the snow begins to fall. Cascades of spindrift sweep down and over anything in their path, building up behind bivouac sacs in an attempt to push them and their occupants off, and thundering down on top of them with a suffocating pounding, eventually to seep in through unimagined gaps in the tent and cover the inmates in a fine white dust that soon melts and saturates everything.

I was angry with myself for even considering sleeping here. It is sometimes too simple to blame the inexperienced for doing inexperienced things. A brief conference was called and we settled on a site identified by Roger, over on the other side of the couloir, a little higher on what looked to be – when you could see it – soft wind-blown snow beneath a steep section of broken yellow rock. Roger led off, still unroped as we had been all day, towards it and by the time I reached him he was already at work, excavating under the rock into a small alcove. The snow was soft and our one shovel made short work of providing a spacious ledge. I dumped my rucksack in a small, wind-scoured snow eddy and scrambled up the loose snow to join them, utilizing holds on the steep rock wall. However, some concern was apparent, especially from Doug, regarding the appearance of a horizontal fracture line below us.

Were we digging into a detached slab and, if so, would we soon be off on a ride down the mountain? A debate ensued while Doug scrabbled around our immediate vicinity for somewhere else and I procrastinated by removing myself from the ledge, but at the same time telling Doug I didn't think much of his proposed alternatives. There was nothing else obvious, and the ease with which Roger's surface was yielding luxury was a telling argument against Doug's continued insistence. All three of us examined the crack like monkeys struck dumb, prodding with axes and thumping with feet. The point was finally settled when the site's main backer leapt up and down on the thing with frustrated vigour (though not without first attaching himself to a piton driven into the loose rock ceiling above his head). Two anxious pairs of eyes carefully analysed this curious activity at seven thousand-plus metres until, satisfied that nothing had moved except Roger, we rejoined him in the effort to scour out a substantial crib.

The tent was erected with loving care and the rucksacks gingerly passed up by human chain to be deposited safely inside, followed immediately by their owners. The threatening outside world was exchanged for a new horizon, yellow and flapping just a foot or two away from the Face, a world preoccupied by the need to melt water, the amount of tea and sugar left, the amount of Gaz remaining and thirst. We enjoyed camomile tea, and China tea, Rise and Shine and packet soup with a little cheese added. A tin of salmon was opened and heated over the flame, but for the rest of our solids we had to rely on the remaining chocolate bars and boiled sweets. How we regretted our missing potato powder, sitting amongst the heather or in some yak-man's house. How many calories had we burned today? How many would we take in? It didn't seem to bear thinking about and so we didn't.

Roger and I passed the night in tolerable comfort; for Doug it was an exhausting torment of racking coughing.

The following morning the principal topic for discussion as we peered out of the unzipped roof in our tent was the small matter of where exactly were we? Always an optimist on this score, Doug was sure we were at the top of the pod, at about 7,800 metres. Roger and I, however, were unwilling to believe this and, after eyeing distant summits, guessed that with luck we might be in the region of 7,500 metres. Doug shuffled through his belongings, pulled out a plastic bag and produced the photograph of the Face. A careful study revealed the unmistakable landmark, a striking, distinct rock buttress split by a deep chimney and guarding the right-hand exit from the couloir. We were looking straight across towards its base! Yet I was still reluctant to believe – perhaps higher up would be an even more striking rock buttress; perhaps we had not yet even entered the pod? The seven-thousander over the road looked suspiciously high. To believe we were at seven-eight now, and go through that narrows to see a couloir stretching ahead would be a blow. Don't trust the photograph, beware the bitter disappointment.

The threatening weather of the previous day was nowhere to be seen in the clear cold sky over our mountain, though once again the layers of cloud were building already in Nepal, with a promise of snow this afternoon. We packed and left, unroped, scrambling down from the ledge and stepping out into the couloir which narrowed immediately and passed, curling slightly around a right-hand bend, snaking through a deep chasm down which a bitter cold wind whistled. In the relative calm of the bivouac we had not put on windsuits and

193

now, in stark contrast to the previous morning, we found ourselves chasing rays of sunshine up that dark alleyway, nursing cold extremities. Where were we? How had all this looked from below? Was Doug really right?

A hopeful mind tried to recall how the finish had looked from so far below; the pictures changed with the angles we had viewed it from, but there was never a finish like this. Never mind, we would reach the summit tonight and, after all, we had planned for three days, or even four. Doug had stopped and sat down on some snowed-up rock higher up the couloir, just above the bottle-neck; Roger was joining him and I was cursing my fingers roundly, as I had for the past half-hour, enough for Roger to enquire about them. It's good to be part of a team.

'They're all right, just a little damp (the gloves) and not woken up yet.' I pulled out of the neck of the gully and stopped below them. Above, and to the left, steep walls; to the right more gentle ground ran round a rocky brow – to where?

'What's up, Doug?'

'We're there, youth!'

The Face was done, we were just a couple of minutes from the ridge. I sat beside them in the bitter wind, emotions numbed. So many barriers, so much work, protocol and precipice. If only Paul could have shared this with us today!

The final two minutes brought us to a col on the ridge and to the edge of the Himalayas. Before us stretched the seemingly endless Tibetan Plateau. To the left a crested snow ridge snaked up towards the summit. The last of the sugar went into the tea, windsuits were donned, rucksacks carefully stashed together in the snow, a single rope grabbed. Slowly, we set off up the ridge, almost savouring the final half hour of labour, working up slightly to the right of the crest on the northern slope by two short steps, peering down a concave snow slope that vanished in a line of sight to reappear in jumbled glaciers far below which melted, in their turn, into the arid brown lands beyond.

Roger followed by Alex coming out of the 'pea-pod' couloir. The 'Eiger' peak is directly beyond the couloir

Doug Scott

The ridge stopped, we were now on the north side of the summit. A careful step over a potential crevasse led to a small snow basin. At the far side of this a snow ramp led out across an icy serac wall, a final heave over the lip and I was looking at the Langtang again, a last couple of steps and I could peer back down the South-West Face. The summit! But which summit – the rocky protuberance just above, on our end of the ridge, or the shapely snow point some 250 metres along the ridge?

Doug reached me and we agreed it must be the one above, but how to be sure? Below on the ridge, Roger, suffering from the over-rapid consumption of a tin of frozen fish down on the col, was making slower progress. While waiting we would go along and check this other candidate. The ridge grew increasingly narrow and sharp. The north side was powdery and steep, impractical and dangerous to traverse; the south side was steeper, vanishing immediately into a jumble of rock and sugary ice, offering awkward purchase for the feet and no security for the axe. We called a halt and sat astride a small point on the crest some thirty metres before and just below our intended objective, the summit of which was no more than a couple of metres above us, whilst the one in the other direction, from which we had come, was a good thirty metres higher. Which one did the Chinese climb?

Doug followed by Roger at 7,900 metres with Phola Gangchen behind

Alex MacIntyre

Alex with Doug (behind) on the middle (north-easterly) summit at 7,996 metres

Roger Baxter-Jones

DOUG: There is nothing like a summit ridge to bring out that little extra energy. I had heard somewhere that there was some doubt as to which summit the Chinese had climbed so I readily agreed to Alex's suggestion that we go along in a westerly direction towards the two high points of this cor-niced summit ridge. Alex was moving well now, much better than down in the Narrows. Having left our sacs behind was probably helping all of us. He swung his boots into the soft snow and moved crabwise across to the first summit. I had never been on such a summit, for beyond the snow and Alex there was nothing to be seen until my eyes focused on the blue puddle of Lake Peku filling a hollow on the purple plateau. Alex went to within 60 feet of the far west summit but retreated, not wanting to ride a collapsing cornice down the northern flanks. Thick clouds that had nestled in the valley bottom all morning were now racing over the summit break-ing up and sending smoke signals north into the interior. Roger sat patiently waiting our return just below the main summit and the one climbed by the Chinese. As tired as I was I registered feelings of exhilaration to be there up amongst the clouds and with the company I kept.

ROGER: The exaltation of arrival was cut down for me by a dubious tin of sardines that left me nauseous. I hobbled up the final ridge, doubling over now and again to throw up in the snow. It was a bad joke. When I raised my eyes I saw the glaciers of the North Face dropping directly on to the infinite brown plains, whereas behind I could see from Makalu to Manaslu via Everest, but I could only look through sardine eyes. I waited on the saddle until Doug and Alex had decided which summit was THE summit, then I dragged myself on top of it just to make sure, with Doug and Alex who wrote two thousand in the snow. We got £2,000 more for this book because we reached the top. I was very happy to be there though; now we could start going down.

ALEX: It was two pm. The grey visage that had hung over Nepal for the last few hours was now venturing over to

The view of the main summit of Shishapangma from the middle summit. The tiny figure of Roger can be seen to the right of the summit

Doug Scott

entertain us for the afternoon, while above it towering white anvils strained the neck. From the northern glaciers billowing cumulus swept up and over the ridge, while the wind, now increasing in intensity, raced and eddied along it, drawing mischievous whirlpools of snow in its wake. Along the ridge and eastern snow slopes towards Pungpa Ri, our line of descent was fast disappearing from view. Time to descend!

We paused briefly at the rucksacks to rope together and consider directions and then probed tentatively into the clouds. Roger, the second on the rope, was the most studied in our descent with his observations from the Pungpa Ri. I broke the trail to his directions, a little left, a little right, a meandering path past barely glimpsed, unfamiliar landmarks. From our rucksacks a rock outcrop served as the first marker, leading us towards the ridge. A brief way down this we found ourselves peering, confused, down a quite considerable and totally unexpected rock wall. This forced us into a wide detour to the left, around and down into a flat plateau below, where we sank thigh-deep into the snows that had collected in this lee-side basin. We struck out into a horizonless world in which we hoped that somewhere to our left the East Face tumbled away in its giant seracs and avalanche slopes, and to our right sat the South-West Face.

Finally the South Ridge itself appeared once again out of the grey. Doug, plagued by his exhausting cough, wanted to bivouac, tempted by a rock outcrop on the right, but neither Roger nor I was keen to go even a little way uphill, and we continued to contour and ignore the rock until we sat down on the snow above the South Face, which plunged below, out of sight into a swirling cauldron. What to do? Doug was keen to halt and Roger was a willing accomplice if we could find a site. I was hesitant, keen to shake off the altitude, to drop another couple of hundred metres. I walked up and stood on a small snow prow to investigate the surroundings.

Down below, a steep rocky drop led to another snowy col. What the hell – why not stop! The loss of altitude was not worth the fight over such terrain. Doug's cough was worse; it had been a long day. A crevasse winked down on our eastern side; it offered shelter under its lip, and we piled in. Soft snow yielded an acceptable platform after fifteen minutes' shovelling. I was accorded the remaining glass fibre poles and the limpid sac took form under the snowy lip. Karrimats were thrust impatiently through the side entrances and laid out to cover the floor; rucksacks were flung in and the remaining bodies followed immediately. The outside world zipped out, we were now suddenly tranquil and quiet, bodies no longer whipped and stung by the gale now surging across the slopes.

The rigmarole and routine of settling down for the night was now second nature. Roger lent me his one-piece down suit as my sleeping bag was now saturated. The wind blasted into our sac from the left, where Roger sat for the purpose of cooking. I sat centrally and Doug to the right, our rudely constructed cooking annexe served as the kitchen, allowing us to keep the fumes out of the main tent and preventing our precious oxygen from being consumed by the stove. Doug had insisted on the cooking seat, but now, racked by coughing and shattered from the inability to sleep for most of the Face climb, he was too tired to afford the task his usual diligence and managed only one brew.

Bickering ensued while I changed places and continued, but we were low on fuel and the choice of drinks, without sugar or interesting flavours, had become sterile and we could not drink much that night. With three people inside a cramped bivouac tent and the zips closed against the elements, the already-thin oxygen content falls perceptibly, claustrophobically. Doug put his head in the annexe to sleep, but the winds whipped snow under the flaps and forced him out of there. At the other end snow steadily accumulated through a partly open zip and a ghoulish atmosphere began to evolve. Lying in the darkness, with nylon slapping close to or in your face, on the borderline of oxygen deficiency, your world covered by a white, hoary frost as you lie cocooned in damp layers of material, it can be difficult at times not to wonder at the sense of it all.

The following morning the nylon was flapping and straining as wildly as ever while the peppering blast of snow continued to slam into us. Newly awakened senses still deep in their sleeping bags recorded the sounds and made little effort to stir. Today we had to fight a blizzard. Why hurry to that uncertain fate? Finally, consciousness gained the upper hand and suspicious heads poked out of gaps yielded reluctantly by frozen zips to be confronted by a clear blue sky and the plains of Tibet, while great gusts of wind carrying freshly fallen snow ripped across the plateau in a devil-dance. This was our blizzard!

ROGER: We passed a miserable night in a certain couldn't-careless spirit. After all we were on our way down.

During breakfast Doug made an announcement: 'Do you know, lads, it's my birthday today, I'm forty-one.'

'Well done, Doug, happy birthday, let's get the hell out of here!'

ALEX: Tantalizing views of the Everest region basked clear in a morning sun. We were looking east, and at a welcome sun that warmed us with the promise of a good day – a good chance to reach our camp far below. I made the worst cup of tea ever produced, which did little for my reputation but did inject some mental vigour into my companions, who searched happily for new ways to damn my culinary capabilities. Leaving all the sad remains of our food-store where it was, and taking only a couple of tea-bags and a stove, we packed our tent and set off down.

The steep rock band of last night immediately barred the way, but we struck a line between this and the huge serac wall to its left, down steep powdery snow, facing into the slope, myself at the front leaping over or into crevasses, cautiously eyeing the seracs above, the unstable snow hollow, until we had lost height to a point where a diagonally rightwards wade would lead down to the col below Pungpa Ri. A slow, steady progress was forged towards this goal, wondering all the while at the ground Himalayan climbing requires you to travel, wondering at the stability of the snow slope down which we had no alternative but to descend.

The col! Above us, some two hundred metres away, stood Pungpa Ri and known ground, caches of Mars bars and Gaz, and an unwelcome, uphill plod to reach its summit. We could expect to labour for at least another nine hours in that direction. To the right a rocky gully led into a facet of the South Face. In the far back it contained a small, hard, thin snow runnel which appeared to lead down into widening snow fields and a flattish col below, scattered with seracs through which a way ran diagonally left – we thought, especially Roger – to the slopes and seracs we had passed over just after leaving Castle Camp! An unknown, tempting line home. Roger had spied out this line most keenly from below. We stood on a small promontory in a biting wind. It looked OK, Scottish twoish I felt, but then it disappeared from sight. Roger began talking about pitons.

'I don't fancy abseiling, Roger, if it's down to that. I'd rather go over Punk; after all we know that.'

'I suppose it's Punk then.'

We withdrew from the edge and began to prepare for the uphill slog. Doug sat in the snow, was roused by the news to peer over. A tower of strength, still on the go when most of us would have been shattered by his chest ailment, he was now, as he told me later, feeling increasingly divorced from the two comparative youngsters who no longer seemed to be consulting him. Unused to not having a full say in decisions, used to being the driving force, he wondered if perhaps we had decided against the descent because of *him*!

DOUG: I wondered what they would do if I had not been there or if I had been as fit as I was on Kangchenjunga. I looked down. 'It doesn't look so bad,' I ventured – at least, I thought, not as bad as plodding all the way up Punk. I opted to go anchor man, not that I had much say in the matter for Alex was off down into the wind tunnel of a gully as soon as the decision was made.

ALEX: I looked at Roger. What the hell! We piled into the wind tunnel of a gully as if into a Jules Verne adventure, while ice particles blasted by a driving upwards gale whipped by into the space beyond. It was exhilarating leaning out into that wind, moving out on to unknown ground, guessing the way down over crisp, firm snow and rotten shattered rock. The snow lifted by my crampons slammed back up into the lads behind. I was festooned with our remaining slings and pitons, instructed to secure protection where possible, but the rock yielded little more than the odd sling on a shattered block until finally we arrived at the first snow field. Forty-five degrees at first, we faced in and worked down in a series of hurried movements and lingering rests, but as it relented we dared ourselves to face out and rely on our feet on the superb snow. Maybe forty degrees here to being with, the snow fields were interrupted by short rock walls, but we sidled through them

202

with cunning and without difficulty, out on to the last field which led to the bergschrund which guarded the entrance to the shelf below. Perhaps sensing our euphoria, it yielded an easy jump. I bundled down the snow below and sat laughing, waiting for the rest to join me. We would be in the camp tonight – almost certainly!

Roger arrived and, a minute later, there was Doug. To brew or push on? Our momentum was now irresistible. Doug, the one man with a water container, pushed soft snow through the nose and shook it violently. Tucked next to the belly under the layers of warm, windproof clothing, it would melt a little and those minute trickles of water were offered round and poured delicately down disbelieving, tormented throats.

Back on less steep ground now, with the prospect of hidden crevasses, we roped up once again and continued our right-wards downwards drive. On the final slopes we had hoped that a thin snow sliver over harder ice, which had been spied while passing underneath *en route* for the Face itself, would offer the chance of continuing a descent without having to resort to the ropes. I arrived above the slope, making a few wary, tentative steps with blunted crampons out on to the slope, then stopped. We would have to abseil.

Our last, expensive ice screws were abandoned without a moment's hesitation as we fixed the ropes and then slid down them, three times repeating the drama of placing the single tube of metal into the ice surface, threading the rope through a small sling attached to the eye of the screw, throwing down the ropes and sliding down for fifty metres, one after the other to rope's end – there to repeat the procedure. Our last ice screw took us to snow deep enough and adherent enough to permit us to turn out and continue unroped, almost leaping now, down to a gap that led us simply over the serac rampart before making a last bounding dash through the snow to a place where a small trail of footprints, days old and wilting in the sun, passed across us rising left to right, heading towards Shishapangma. They were our own tracks. We had squared the circle!

But the rock wall was too great an obstacle on the way back to camp, so we continued our descent to the foot of the rib. Then, with Roger leading and Doug coughing along a little at

Doug (background) and Roger nearing the foot of Shishapangma's SW Face after descending some 6,000 feet of steep 45° ice and snow on the last day

Alex MacIntyre

the rear, we ploughed gradually back up the snow towards the home we knew waited just on the other side of our spectacular rock Indian Chief, Castle Camp.

A final euphoric drudge, out of danger, had us heading for home, for Lhasa, for Peking, for London, up the slopes, counting steps and counting days. Above, a small figure was suddenly visible, moving awkwardly over the unstable boulders towards the snow. A shout. It was Nick. Had we done it?

'Yes.'

'Good line?'

'Yes.'

'Have you got a pan and some salt?'

We ploughed up the snow, over the boulders, around the conning tower and finally, incredibly, into camp. We were back.

CHAPTER 9
Return

DOUG: We stumbled around Castle Camp like sailors returning to land after months at sea. It felt so strange to be walking on the horizontal – not that we walked far. We flopped down by our tents, which Nick had erected, took off our boots and sweaty socks and stretched out on our foam mats. The stove was spluttering away as Nick produced brew after brew to rehydrate our emaciated bodies. Delicious moments, these, of returning strength and clear head after so much effort and concentration. I lay there dozing in and out of sleep, as tired as I had ever been. It had been a hard climb. Dosing myself with antibiotics, I hoped my hacking cough would quickly clear before we went through the dust of the plateau. Whilst dozing I became aware that I was visualizing my thoughts; I could see scenes from my past, scenes I did not expect. One stood out vividly – I was approaching a Tibetan Gompa and through the huge doorway I could see a prayer wheel about twenty feet high and ten feet across. As I went towards it, with others, it burst apart to reveal a bright light shining from within. I walked up into the prayer wheel to be greeted by Tibetan monks in their maroon yak-hair cloaks. They were smiling benignly, with beatific welcoming expressions on their faces. The vision ended as Alex passed me another mug of tea. I asked him if he ever felt different after such efforts as these?

'Bloody tired,' he said.

We slept for about ten hours. Next morning we were off down the valley, clearing Castle Camp and Advance Base before we staggered into Base Camp. The high winds blew streamers of snow off the peaks in the Langtang. The mountains were so sharp and clearly defined everything was clear and I was at peace with them and myself.

For a time at least we three were content, but what next? Where had our ascent of Shishapangma taken us? For Alex towards Annapurna. For me K2, a traverse of Lhotse and Lhotse Shar and Cho Oyu next year with other vague plans to climb other mountains during the coming years. I knew that unless my climbing led to a greater and more lasting peace of mind, no amount of climbing one peak after another was going to bring me anything but ephemeral satisfaction.

Last night Nick had talked of having another go at the peak he referred to as 'The Ice Tooth'. I wondered if he was all there, grasping at straws just before the arrival of our transport home. He was still fretting for the unobtainable but I no longer worried but still felt sad for him that he had not had the chance to know these mountains and to see beyond them as we had.

On 31 May Nick and the yak-boy, Nyima, went back to collect the rest of the equipment from Advance Base as we sorted our gear into loads at Base Camp. We burnt all our rubbish and put aside quantities of flour, rice and cooking equipment as a gift to our yak-men. On 1 June we sauntered off downhill, back on to the green as clouds were swirling on top of the Langtang and over Shishapangma and Pungpa Ri. We reached Smaug's Lair in the evening, as the sun cleared to reveal a perfect sunset. All was peace and contentment until we met Pemba and discovered that he had misappropriated a lot of the food we had left with him and most of the food we had bought in Peking for Wu.

On 2 June we arrived at Nyalam after a splendid walk down the valley, stopping to admire the primula and splashes of colour from other flowers unknown to us. A China Youth Day Festival was in progress outside the village and chang was flowing freely. A better atmosphere pervaded the town. With some surprise we learned that Pemba had ordered a minibus. After discussions with The Leader, we agreed that this was nothing to do with us and Pemba would have to explain later why it was here. We knew why it was here – Pemba had loads to carry that were earmarked for his friends in Zegar and Shigatse. Pemba seemed infected with all that is bad in the West, a man in a hurry, avaricious, materialistic, power hungry, forever pulling rank, demanding respect without deserving it, but he had forsaken traditional Tibetan values.

Having said goodbye to The Leader, who had done all he could to assist us, on 3 June we wound our way up the Po Chu Valley, back on to the plateau – now only four of us and Wu lying out on the sponges. Then we drove straight past Zegar

Driving back across the plateau, Roger, Wu, Nick and Alex
demonstrating that we were successful in bringing back all our
fingers (and toes)!

Doug Scott

and arrived at Shigatse at nine o'clock that evening. Out of the
shadows, behind one of the barrack-like buildings of the hotel
complex, the two familiar figures of Charlie Clarke and
Adrian Gordon approached us. We thought they were still on
Everest. They told us the awful news that Joe Tasker and
Peter Boardman had disappeared high up on the North-East
Ridge of Everest. Roger's reaction was shared by us all.

ROGER: We had rolled into Shigatse triumphant, the mountain
was climbed, Pemba was banished with the unordered
minibus and we were successfully maintaining our reputation
as the worst foreign expedition ever to reach Tibet. Here,
also, I could tell my story. But there was another story to
listen to. Joe and Pete were dead. In the courtyard of the hotel I
met the remains of the British Everest Expedition, 1983.
Charlie Clarke and Adrian Gordon told the news and my joy
vaporized. I had never climbed with Joe and Peter and from
our mountain had looked towards theirs with a feeling of
rivalry, and some envy. But there was always the feeling that
they were 'one of us', the small band of Himalayan pushers.

207

There was nothing left to do but for the survivors to get drunk together.

Once again I felt the mixed emotions produced by death in the hills. Firstly, the glamour – look, what I do is important, fatally important – and then the emptiness – what on earth do we run these risks for? The glamour showed the most that night as the group of travellers and trekkers partied together, but the emptiness was felt in the long ride the next day.

'Why, what for, why them and why not us?' No answers were to be had from the desolate Tibetan plains.

DOUG: It was a very subdued group who drove on through Gyangtse to Lhasa. *En route* we were given various notes left by Elaine and Paul. What a contrasting retreat from the mountain these two had had. Paul, who had gone through the System, enjoyed a completely trouble-free journey to Peking and back home. Elaine, on the other hand, trying to spend as much time in Tibet as possible, had met nothing but problems with the authorities. We had crossed the bridge where Elaine had fallen into the river and seen the ten-foot pool where she had almost drowned. At Zegar she had been bitten by a dog and after her return to England she was haunted by the thought of possible rabies. But hers is another story, and one she may well tell in a book of her own.

After a day and a night's discussion in Lhasa we flew off to Cheng Dhu and then Peking, where we tied up the expedition satisfactorily with the Chinese Mountaineering Association.

Our last evening in Peking began with a visit to the British Embassy grounds to drink the Queen's health, on her official birthday, with the Ambassador and about three hundred other dignitaries. For a couple of hours we strolled around the gardens of the official residence, drinking from a seemingly endless supply of cold bottled beer which was welcome on a warm day, but doubly so as negotiations had been finally brought to a satisfactory conclusion. At last we could relax from the constant tension we had been under since entering Nyalam. This, I knew, was a time for caution, having seen before even old hands collapse into the bushes at such functions as this Embassy gathering. I warned the lads to pace themselves, for we were due at a dinner in our honour with the Chinese Mountaineering Association.

Our taxi took us along to the Suhcai San Guan Restaurant, which specialized in vegetarian food. Already seated round the table were the now-familiar figures of Wu Ming, Dr Li, Shi Zhanchun, Chang Chun-Yen, Chen San, Hsu Ching and Wang Fu-Chou, with whom we immediately got into conversation. Wang Fu-Chou was one of the three climbers reported as having been to the top of Everest by the North Ridge in 1960. Hsu Ching, the leader of the first expedition to climb our mountain, was Master of Ceremonies, pouring wine and Maotai in small glasses one after the other throughout the meal. It was excellent, quite the best vegetarian food any of us had ever had. We wolfed down ribbons of bean curd that resembled beef, Chinese pickles, seaweeds, bamboo shoots, soya bean concoctions and several varieties of dried mushrooms, some indigenous and some not, and capped every course with a magic Maotai potion in narrow thick-glass tumblers, which loosened our tongues. General bonhomie prevailed as we toasted one another to the end. A pile of certificates was produced, confirming the fact that we had ascended Shishapangma; one by one, on somewhat shaky legs and with some amusement, we arose from our seats to be thus certified. We thanked the CMA for their hospitality and walked out to our taxi, pairing off with our Chinese friends. Wu Ming told me I should apply for other peaks.

'Do you really want us back, Wu Ming. Haven't we caused you enough trouble?'

'You are good boys, come again!' He seemed to mean it.

None of us was ready for bed so we decided to go to the 'Disco for Foreign Guests' advertised in our hotel lobby. No one can recall where this event took place, for we arrived by bus, having given our taxi driver the night off. There was an imposing building dominating a large square in front. We walked up palatial steps to find only four or five other foreigners inside, although highly amplified music was booming out across the strobe-lit dance floor. Out of habit we gravitated towards the bar and collapsed, legless, at one of the tables.

Roger and Alex, with energy to spare, went cavorting across the floor, dancing with each other for lack of more suitable partners, whilst Wu, Nick and I sat that one out. Alex

209

came across and pulled me off my seat and we whirled around, Alex off the floor in my arms until I let him go as I swung round and he slid along the polished wood on his backside. I don't know why I just let him go like that – maybe I thought it would be amusing – or possibly I felt some aversion to his pretty face next to mine – I don't know – but I dropped him. Alex's mood changed from hilarity to anger; the next moment we were locked in combat, tearing at each other's cotton T-shirts and rolling around the floor, much to the consternation of the others. Quickly they tried to part us and we stood glaring at each other, Alex screaming, 'You're just an old fart – you're past it', and me thinking, 'Is this where I put the nut in?' But I didn't butt him with my head – the only appendage which was free to move – I couldn't do that to him; but I warned him that he had better watch out, for when Nottingham lads get roused they can hurt.

By now we had been edged out to the door by Nick and Roger, both two inches taller than me and about six inches taller than little Alex. There on the steps, his taunts ringing in my ears, I lunged out at him. He broke free from Nick and came up yelling, 'I've been trained to kill,' and I was thinking, 'Those Jesuits have a lot to answer for' when wham – right between the eyes came Alex's fist and down went my glasses, which usually keep me out of such tricky situations, now broken into little pieces on the concrete.

'Let me get at the little bugger,' I yelled, though I could hardly see where he was – or anyone else except Roger, who had his giant arm round my neck, pulling me towards the taxi.

Alex yelled, 'You're finished, you miserable old sod.'

I yelled back, 'Well, you've finally shown your colours – how'd you keep it bottled up all this time?'

We took separate taxis back to the hotel, me blubbering to dear old Roger about the need to soften these trips with the presence of women. I said a lot of other things to Roger too. 'There have been times on this trip when I've hated you, Roger. Your off-hand remarks all seemed unjustified as you will not really get involved with the hard work of organizing and negotiating. But Roger, just stay as you are, you're a great bloke, just don't change one bit.'

Suddenly, I saw how different we all are, yet how much we

all need one another. Back at the hotel Roger and I sat talking, when in came Alex and Nick. They had gone walking round the block to cool off and, for once, Nick found himself in the position of Alex's confidant. Alex wasn't sure what would happen when he got back to the hotel, but told Nick he was ready for anything. Nick came across to my room to see how I was. I felt drained and thoroughly miserable at the turn of events. Then Alex came across, sobbing away, declaring, 'I never wanted this to happen, never meant any of those things I said. I love you, I love your family, you've just got me up an eight-thousand-metre peak. I'm sorry.'

At the same time I was muttering that I hadn't wanted it to happen either – where did it all come from? But wondering if he really meant it, then deciding that he did.

It was time for bed but I had one last call to make. I went across to see Wu. He was sitting on his bed, reading.

'Well, Wu, I hope we didn't embarrass you. I hope you won't get into trouble for all this. We like and respect one another really, you know. If anything, we're too much alike.'

'In China we do not show our emotions . . .' and then he stopped and thought it out, concluding in his sing song voice 'I think your way is better.'

Somewhat hung over, we went down for a final Chinese breakfast, during which we said our goodbyes to Jo Sanders and her amiable group of trekkers who were staying in the hotel. We left in the taxi, as usual half an hour behind schedule, this time for the final debriefing at the CMA Hotel.

'By the way, Alex,' I said, 'what's this about your being trained to kill?'

'Well, I've been doing karate lessons,' he said.

'Oh, that's OK then – still, you were lucky I didn't land you one.'

We walked into the office, Alex and I, chatting about points to be raised and caught the merest suggestion of inquisitiveness in the eyes of our Chinese friends. Perhaps they were expecting us to jump on each other again. If so, they were too polite to show it – too inscrutable to let on that they knew. I signed various bits of paper which amounted to the CMA's owing us £1,200, which was sent on a month later. All's well that ends well, as this meeting did, with further exhortations to sign up for another Chinese campaign. We said we would when we could afford it, and especially if they were to open up other ranges and peaks in Tibet to foreigners, not to mention Namcha Barwa. Wu Ming told us they had plans to open it up, but first, he said, 'We Chinese are planning to go there after reconnaissance that is taking place right now.'

'You ought to have an Anglo-Chinese Expedition.'

'Not possible,' he said. 'Namcha Barwa very attractive, yes?' he added. 'Americans especially interested, offering big bribes, very funny.'

'Did you take them?'

'No – here first come, first served.'

We believed them. They are honest, these CMA officials, straight down the line within their terms of reference, and they took them to the limit to help us out. We left wondering whether we would ever make it back again.

We headed off downtown, to purchase presents in the large stores; apart from books, thick cotton track suits, Chinese teas, fans and chopsticks there was not a great deal of choice. Somehow we got behind schedule again and arrived very late for the afternoon flight to Islamabad. First, we had to be searched and various Tibetan trinkets we had bought at Shigatse were taken away from us with no chance of ever seeing them again. This seemed a bit mean, as they had hardly any value and had involved us in hours of bargaining down to prices comparable with those in Nepal. But at least the Tibetans had been paid for them.

Then we moved into the sphere of Pakistan International Airlines, to find a very strict regime in control, allowing no excess baggage to go through free, despite letters from PIA in Britain suggesting that this would be a good idea. Finally, with the plane revving up on the tarmac and only five minutes to go before take-off, we said 'Take it or leave it' and slapped down half the amount requested – about £300 – and tore off down the marble corridors to the waiting aircraft.

For Alex and me our return signalled the start of a mammoth writing session. Alex also had to plan and prepare for Annapurna South Face in the autumn with John Porter and René Ghilini. Three days before he set off he came up to Cumbria with Terry Mooney to hand in his writings, which had taken him a solid two months, working away in his little cabin below Kinder Scout. He said he would make a few alterations, add a bit more after Annapurna and generally kick it into shape with Terry's help. Most of his brief visit was taken up with talking about our plans for 1983; not only had I booked K2 for the spring, but also Lhotse South Face for the autumn and the South Face of Cho Oyu for the winter. Alex, Georges Bettembourg and myself would be going out together in the autumn and winter, with our families and Alex's girlfriend, Sarah.

Back in Nottingham, we had already met to discuss some of the finer points that Alex was bringing up in the book, about the internal relationships on the expedition. We projected ourselves back on to the plateau and on to the flanks of Shishapangma in an effort to recall as accurately as we could our feelings and thoughts at the time. In searching for the truth we renewed our respect for each other. When my wife, Jan, came into the room to remind Alex he had an appointment in London, she asked us what we had been doing, for, as she said, we were glowing. We had got very close to each other – the ultimate endorsement of what we do together. We planned to go over the book on Alex's return from Annapurna and bring the others into the discussions. Perhaps we could end up with an expedition book the likes of which had not been done before.

On 17 October 1982 Alex and René Ghilini were retreating from the South Face of Annapurna, after a fine attempt, when a solitary stone hurtled down and struck Alex, killing him and knocking him down 800 feet.

In November Terry Mooney and Alex's mother organized a memorial service, which was attended by many of Alex's relatives and friends; there was a lot of love between us all that day in Hayfield. His life and death had brought us all much closer together. Once again, I was reminded of Thornton Wilder's *Bridge Of San Luis Rey*, as I was after the deaths of Mick Burke, Dougal Haston, Nick Estcourt, Joe Tasker, Peter Boardman . . .

But soon we shall die and all memory of those five will have left the earth, and we ourselves shall be loved for a while and forgotten. But the love will have been enough; all those impulses of love return to the love that made them. Even memory is not necessary for love. There is a land of the living and a land of the dead, and the bridge is love, the only survival, the only meaning.

Postscript

ROGER: I heard about Alex's death in the postscript of a letter from Nick. I refused to believe it. Alex and I had discussed our futures and he had been quite clear that he would survive another five years of dangerous Face climbing and then take on the job of simply 'being famous'. Death was for much later. Paul confirmed Alex's change of plans by phone, but these were simply words: 'hit by a single stone whilst coming down . . . fell 800 feet . . . body in a crevasse.' I had Alex's words in front of me, the draft for this book, and they were

Alex in the Old Town of Lhasa
Nick Prescott

full of life. He had told me he'd last a while yet; he'd worked it out and I believed him – most people did, for Alex told the truth.

I finally felt Alex's death driving to work very early on Monday morning. I broke down – he'd lied to me, the bastard – it wasn't possible – all that vitality taken out by a single stone – we had things to do, mountains to climb. No, no, no and no. I thought of him sitting in bed, in a squalid room in Nyalam, Walkman on, watching the absurd debate between us and the Chinese Army over a rotten piece of canvas. I was outraged – he was simply amused; he knew it wasn't important. I thought of him when he walked through the hotel door after the fight to tell Doug he loved him, no justification, no blame, just letting his friend know what was in his heart.

The deaths of Joe and Pete touched Alex; he decided to reduce his risks and withdrew from an attempt to climb Everest in winter. But he still left for Annapurna in the autumn, having written his part of this book. By now Alex's mother will have put up a stone at Annapurna Base Camp which reads:

It is better to live one day as a tiger than a hundred as a sheep.

Alex was a lucky man, he did well what he wanted to do – climb big mountains – and he did it with a full heart. I miss him.

APPENDICES

by Doug Scott

I
Early Buddhism in Tibet and Milarepa

The ancient myths indicate that, at first, there was a void from which the earth was formed; then, after a passage of time, there was great flood from which land emerged. In the South of Tibet humans were born through the blessing of Chenresig, Lord of Mercy, and Dolma, his Consort. They sent their incarnations on to the earth, one as a monkey bound by the vow to be celibate and to live alone in meditation, and the other an ogress. She became lonely and so approached the monkey who at first refused her until he was overcome by compassion. He returned to Chenresig for advice, which was that it was time for Tibet to have children and that he should take the ogress as his wife. (Modern tourists can now visit the Summer Palace in Lhasa and there beautifully painted murals depict the evolution of earth and humankind.)

Humans developed from apes. The humans began to eat the fruit (fat) of the earth and the more they ate the more they lost their power and descended from light into darkness. There was, at first, enough food for all without their having to work for it, then the rot set in, with greed and subsequent theft of one another's food. Now people had to work, organize and defend themselves. They had to work hard for others; they became ill, went hungry, lost control of their lives to administrators, fought battles and got on to the daily round of 'Samsara', going round in circles in a cycle of death and rebirth, so that appearances hid the reality.

Humanity was now locked into the round of suffering, the wheel of life. Shamanistic beliefs grew. Gods and spirits were seen in the rocks and trees, in the air, on the mountain tops – in everything as a means to provide answers and a way out of the confusion that now existed for the human race. Out of this grew a religion which much later came to be called Bön and which persists to this day amongst Tibetans and amongst neighbouring communities. The priests and devotees of this pre-Buddhist religion, who are known as Bönpo, recognized a hierarchy of external powers with which they attempted to come to terms. They gave offerings to the gods. Shamans took control of the religious practices that developed. They exorcised spirits which were thought to cause sickness and insanity.

During the sixth century AD, Buddhism made its appearance in Tibet and grew alongside the earlier faith. Whilst both borrowed from each other they continued to develop separately, and so whilst they have much in common they are recognized as two distinct beliefs to this day. Songtsen Gampo (557–649), whose name means 'He who is powerful and profound', is popularly credited to have been the first Buddhist ruler of Tibet and the person who established the Buddhist faith there; he became the 33rd King of Tibet in 634.

He first entered a phase of conquest during which he subdued rival kingdoms, and having done so he moved his capital from Yarlung westward to the centre of his newly formed nation. He built a fort on top of 'Red Hill' in Lhasa, which is now the site of the Potala. From here he consolidated his gains and, looking to the future, married two Buddhist princesses – one Chinese and the other Nepalese. They were in addition to his three Tibetan wives.

As R. A. Stein points out in his scholarly *Tibetan Civilization*, Songtsen Gampo's reign was the start of Tibetan history. From then on, records exist with a fair degree of accuracy. It was certainly an era of great renaissance in learning, material welfare, philosophy and religion. Stein quotes from the Thangyig Chenmo, in which Songtsen Gampo was said to have borrowed techniques from the four points of the compass: '. . . in the East, from China and from

The statues of Songtsen Gampo (centre), Princess Wen Cheng (right) and Princess Tritsun; photograph taken in the Jo Khang temple

220

Minyak he took books of technology and of divinatory calculation. In the South, from India, he translated the Holy religion. Westward in the land of the Sok and in Nepal he opened the treasuries of foodstuffs, wealth and goods. In the North, from among the Hor and Yugur, he took books of laws.'[1]

After Songtsen Gampo's death, Tibetan power and influence continued to spread. Military activities during the reign of the 33rd King had led to the defeat of several important regions of China and for a time China even had to pay a tribute to Tibet. With increasing contact being made with not only Buddhist China but also to the south with India and Nepal, the Buddhist nucleus, which was centred on the royal family, spread out into the towns and villages of the Tibetan Plateau at the expense of the ancient beliefs. For a time they continued to co-exist, side by side with each other without major upsets, possibly because the Bön adopted certain Buddhist precepts. Power struggles between royal relatives, however, were eventually to bring down the royal lineage.

The Indian sage Padma Sambhava was invited to spread the dharma in Tibet by King Trisong Detsan during the eighth century. Padma Sambhava was well-versed in magic and also Tantric Buddhism, which he is said to have studied in Eastern India. He used magic to great effect when confronted by the Bönpo. He too incorporated certain Bön beliefs into the Buddhist system. He was then able to further his cause without major conflict. Padma' Sambhava assisted the King in establishing the first big monastery in Tibet, at Samye.

Although the Buddha had always advocated a middle way between extremes, he had always allowed that, for a few who were well advanced and had the perfect teacher, Tantric Yoga could be employed as a short path to enlightenment. The Buddha had, generally speaking, been addressing the broad mass of the people and not just an élite few. By following his teaching the people, instead of suffering their lot, now had the means to do something about it. As regards the élite, the man whom the Tibetans later regarded as having filled the role of the perfect teacher of the Tantric School of Buddhism was Padma Sambhava; being a very accomplished practitioner himself, he is said to have been able to create demons to defeat other demons. He also had the power of materialization and dematerialization as well as other supernatural talents. There is a common misconception that Tantric Yoga permits aspirants all kinds of bodily pleasures, including the practice of sex magic. In fact the way is through rigorous self-training and strict discipline. Only the strong and dedicated can follow this dangerous path and the followers of Padma Sambhava, when they

221

gained great powers, could use it for one purpose only, and that was for the good of the rest of humanity.

Legend holds that the power of the Bönpo priests had been checked by Padma Sambhava, but before many years passed the pendulum again swung in favour of the Bön, and a violent conflict ensued. During the reign of the last King, Langdasma, Buddhism had to go completely underground and many of the monks fled into exile or were killed. Internecine quarrels came to a head when the King's two sons quarrelled and the Kingdom disintegrated. Eventually, the country was reunited under the rule of the Lamas, firstly in the 13th century by the noble family of Lamas associated with the monastery of Sakya in Southern Tibet, and again much later by the Dalai Lamas from Lhasa after 1642. Whilst temporal power suffered vicissitudes too numerous to mention here, religious power and organization prospered greatly after the restoration of Buddhism in the 11th century.

Atisa (982–1054), the great reformer and conciliator of divergent schools of thought within Buddhism, led the revival. Buddhism – and particularly Tantric Buddhism – had become debased. One of his reforms was to state clearly: 'that the Tantra should only be followed by those who had passed through the previous stage of ethical training and philosophical reflection and that the actual practice of Tantra was a purely spiritual affair in no way calling for female counterpart or the use of intoxicants and in no way permissible for the selfish goal of self-advancement.' He also stressed the importance of welding together the physical, emotional and mental parts of man into one whole as a means to spiritual progress. Atisa founded the Kadampa Order which evolved into the Gelugpa Sect, the most powerful branch of Lamaism which has continued through to this day, for the Dalai Lamas are of this sect.

One of Atisa's contemporaries was Marpa (1012–1096), who thought that the Tantric Yoga System had been diluted. Marpa and his pupil, Milarepa (1040–1123), laid the foundations for the Kagyü-Pa (Kargyupa) Sect. It may be confusing to the casual student of Buddhism that there are so many lineages and orders within Tibetan Buddhism. Perhaps, through following the evolution of the Kagyü-Pa Sect, more light will be shed on this; it is also very much part of the background story to Southern Tibet and the area around Shishapangma in particular.

Marpa came from the area north of Bhutan, whilst Milarepa was born under the shadow of Shishapangma. The lineage which they founded has continued to the present day and the reader is recommended to follow up this outline account by reading Chögyam Trungpa's books *The Myth of Freedom* and *Cutting through Spiritual*

Milarepa: from a wood-cut print

Materialism, as he is of the school descending from the Marpa and Milarepa and can put the 'flesh upon the bare bones' of the outline that follows.

Buddhism has often been kept pure and alive not in the big monasteries but in the caves and isolated sanctuaries of Tibetan aesthetes and saints. We see parallels of this in other faiths, as with the Gnostics in Christianity, who sought inner knowledge, as opposed to the Christian Church dogma of faith and intellectualism. The Sufi sought Allah through the inner path by leading a simple, austere life rather than through reaching 'out there' for the prophet, as in traditional mainstream Islam. The Yogis of India play the same role amongst the Hindus. All of them sought to attain spiritual insight (Buddhahood) in their lifetime in order to help the rest of mankind to the same realization. It is not academic information that is passed on from teacher to pupil but the actual inspiration, alive as it was in the beginning. This is what is meant by the oral tradition. The guru awakens his pupil as he himself was awakened to the reality behind appearances – although the actual details of the teaching depend upon the individual requirements of the novice. All this becomes clearer through tracing the course of Milarepa's initiation and eventual elevation to Buddhahood.

Marpa was born at Lhotrak, an area to the north of Bhutan and south of Lhasa and the Tsangpo River. It is one of the more fertile areas of Southern Tibet where his parents owned both agricultural and pasture land. Marpa's parents took good care of their son and were wealthy enough to send him away to the guru Drogmi's school, partly to cure him of his bad temper, which he later conquered in a positive fashion in his efforts to enlighten Milarepa. He went to India, where he furthered his studies. He stayed there for several years and then returned home for more gold to finance further education and to bring back books and ancient manuscripts from India to Tibet. He became known as 'Marpa the Translator', and returned once again to set up as a wealthy farmer and to rear a family.

In fact he married several wives and, to all outward appearances, was simply a translator of ancient religious documents and a farmer expanding his land and property. But during his time in India Marpa, after sustained periods of study, had received an initiation from Naropa, the great Indian guru, who in turn had been initiated by Tilopa. There is no record of any earthly teacher having enlightened Tilopa who, therefore, is said to have received the secret teachings by divine intervention. The teachings are so powerful that the disciple who receives them orally is sworn to secrecy. An act of faith was obviously required on the part of the pupil. Marpa tested the faith of his pupils, and of Milarepa in particular, to the limit. He was neither in appearance nor manner conventional, being corpulent, bad tempered, sometimes drunk and generally unsaintly, choosing to go against fundamental Buddhist laws when it suited him. All this was but a disguise of the enlightened Marpa.

Whilst Marpa was seeking initiation as a young man of twenty-eight, Milarepa was born in the village of Kya Ngatsa (or Koronsa) which, according to W. Y. Evans-Wentz,[2] is situated in the Province of Gungthang, on the Tibetan frontier of Nepal, a few miles east of the modern Kyirong, about fifty miles due north of Kathmandu. Approximately, then, his home was some three hundred miles west of that of Marpa and on the flanks of the Shishapangma massif – the area that Heinrich Harrer and Peter Aufschnaiter were to find so attractive nine hundred years later.

His parents were comparatively rich and influential in the area and all went well for Milarepa until he reached the age of seven, when his father died, leaving all his possessions: 'herds – yaks, horses and sheep – at the head of the valley; fields at the bottom of the valley; cattle-cows, goats and asses on the ground floor of the house; and upstairs furniture and utensils, gold, silver, copper, iron, turquoise, silk, and the corn loft.'[3] The father left all this in the care of his younger brother, as was the custom, and the brother would then hand it over to Milarepa when he achieved manhood. The uncle, however, abused the trust placed in him. For the next seven years, recalled Milarepa: 'in summer, when the fields were cultivated, we were my uncle's servants; in winter when the wool was carded, we were my aunt's servants. They fed us like dogs and worked us like donkeys.'

When he was fifteen, Milarepa's mother invited all her relatives to a feast and asked that Milarepa's land and property now be restored to him. Milarepa's uncle and aunt were consumed with avarice and stupidity and refused to part with anything. In turn, Milarepa's mother was filled with anger and hatred and determined to destroy her brother-in-law and his wife. She had just enough money to send Milarepa off in search of a sorcerer so that he might learn the black arts to reap vengeance upon the wicked relatives. After finding one teacher unsatisfactory, Milarepa found another who initiated him into the black arts after intensive study. He went back to his village and there, on the day of the wedding feast of his uncle's son, Milarepa worked his magic and the roof collapsed on to the wedding guests. Later, he brought hail down on to the crops of the villagers who were angry at Milarepa's mother for encouraging her son to bring about the deaths of thirty-five of their neighbours!

Some time later, Milarepa experienced a conversion, rather like Saul on the road to Damascus and, like him, Milarepa now brought into the cause of good all the power that he had previously devoted to evil. 'I was filled with remorse for the evil I had done by magic and by hailstorms. My longing for the teaching so obsessed me that I forgot to eat. If I went out, I wanted to stay in. If I stayed in, I wanted to go out. At night sleep escaped me. I dared not confess my sadness to the lama or my longing for liberation. While I remained in the lama's service I asked myself unceasingly and passionately by what means I might practise the true teaching.'[4] Eventually, Milarepa was directed to go out and seek the teachings from Marpa.

On the day before Milarepa's arrival, Marpa had a prophetic visitation by Naropa. Marpa's wife had a complementary dream which caused Marpa to think to himself: ' "These dreams are very much in accord," ' and his heart was filled with extreme joy but to his wife he only said: "I do not know the meaning since dreams have no source. Now I am going to plough the field near the road. Prepare what I need." '[5]

Milarepa was surprised to find Marpa ploughing the field:

a tall and corpulent monk, with large eyes and awesome look. . . I had scarcely seen him when I was filled with unutterable joy and inconceivable bliss. Stunned for a moment by this vision, I remained motionless. Then I said: 'Master, I have heard that the learned Marpa the Translator, personal disciple of the glorious Naropa, dwells in this region. Where is his house?'

For a long time he looked at me from head to foot. Then he said: 'Who are you?'

And Milarepa went on to tell him what a great sinner he had been. Marpa agreed to Milarepa's request and took him on as a student, provided he first atoned for his sins. Then began an ordeal which has caught the imagination of the Tibetans and everyone else who has heard of it.

Marpa instructed Milarepa to build a round tower. When it was half-finished, and after great labour, Marpa told him casually to tear it down again and put the stones and earth back to their places of origin, because he had not really thought the matter out properly. Then he told Milarepa to build a semi-circular tower on the crest of a mountain and again, when it was half-finished, Milarepa had to tear it down, replacing all the earth and stones, for Marpa said that the other day he was drunk and had not given the right directions. Then Milarepa was instructed to build a triangular tower which, again, had to be pulled down, for Marpa asked Milarepa who had told him to build it in the first place, for he had not.

Marpa's wife, Dakmena, was Milarepa's spiritual mother

throughout these trials and she herself gave him certain teachings known as the Mahamudra. Milarepa then had to build a square tower, nine storeys high, Marpa promising him again that on completion he would give him the teachings for which he craved. Milarepa entreated Marpa to confirm this before witnesses, which he did before his wife. And so Milarepa began building the square tower but then, when he reached the second storey, Milarepa noticed a large boulder in the foundations and, because he had received the help of Marpa's other three disciples, Milarepa had to remove the stone. After demolishing the building he took the rock back to its place only to be told by Marpa to fetch it again and put it back as the corner stone. On completing the tower he went to the Lama and asked for the initiation and instruction which he had promised. At this Marpa lost his temper and slapped him, grabbed him by the hair and threw him out.

Next morning, after the Lama's wife had consoled him, Milarepa was put to work by Marpa, building a covered walk at the base of the tower. Just as he was about to finish this he was called away to receive the teachings. On seeing that the initiation gifts that Milarepa had brought were, in fact, his own property, being furnished from his own household by his wife, Milarepa was cursed and kicked and thrown out once again. And so it went on, building and abuse, until the open sores on his back became infected and he was sent back to work with a pad to protect his wounds from the rocks. Milarepa was now in complete despair. He still had 'faith in the Lama and I have not a single word in rebellion; on the contrary I believe that I am in darkness on account of my sins. I am the author of my own misery.' He wept.

After more trials Milarepa was ready to kill himself, hoping that he would be reborn with a body worthy of religion. He had reached rock bottom. Not only had he atoned completely for his sins, he had also surrendered all expectations and ambitions in life, and it was at this point that Marpa now gave him the necessary initiations and instructions on the secret path.

Is it not the same for us all? At some point along the way we have to come to terms with the fact that our aspirations and plans may prove fruitless. In a minor way I can see that this happened before I climbed Everest and Kangchenjunga, as well as before climbing other peaks and certainly before Shishapangma, when all the indications led me to believe that circumstances counted against us. I have so often had to let go of my expectations completely – yet almost immediately afterwards there have followed a series of incidents and events which have allowed me to proceed to the summit of these mountains with great confidence and also humility. One of the few times when I did not let go but pushed hard throughout to reach my goal, I ended up with two broken legs! My approach and attitude on that occasion had been far from humble and I went for my objective oblivious to the dangers – as happens when ambition outstrips ability.

After his initiation into the Tantric mysteries, Milarepa, full of love and veneration for his master and his wife, parted company with his guru. He now entered the meditative period of his life, living in isolated caves in the region lying between Shishapangma and Mount Kailas. How difficult it is for us to imagine how Milarepa could spend more than half his lifetime in solitude, denying himself nearly all the worldly comforts that we take for granted. But then Milarepa had seen earlier on in life the misery and suffering which people had to bear and he discovered an effective means to achieve permanent peace, drastic though it was. This is the advice he gave to his followers:[6] 'The nature of samsara is such that wealth which has been accumulated is dispersed, houses that have been built are destroyed, unions are broken, and all that is born must die. Since inevitably one suffers from one's acts, one must abandon worldly aims and give up accumulating, building, and uniting. The best remedy is to realize the ultimate truth of reality under the direction of an enlightened lama.' In his *Myth of Freedom*,[7] Chögyam Trungpa suggests that:

We may appreciate this desolation if we are an occasional tourist who photographs it or a mountain climber trying to climb to the mountain top. But we really do not want to live in those desolate places. It is no fun, it is terrifying, terrible.

But it is possible to make friends with the desolation, to appreciate its beauty. Great sages like Milarepa relate to the desolation as their bride. They marry themselves to a desolation, to the fundamental psychological aloneness. . . They do not need physical or psychological entertainment. . . Ultimate asceticism becomes part of your basic nature, we discover how samsaric occupations feed and entertain us. Once we see samsaric occupations as games then that in itself is the absence of dualistic fixation, nirvana. Searching for nirvana becomes redundant at that point.

It was in his cave that Milarepa confronted the gods – pleasant emotions and perceptions – and the demons – painful emotions and perceptions. He did not do this blindly, in any kind of self-righteous way, nor did he try to put a lid on them. It was only when he saw them for what they were that he could let go of them and transmute the energy behind them. Gradually, stage by stage, he was able to see the world as it really is. Surely this is what we all do. After years of repeating errors, discovering – usually by accident – that to let go of our ambition, of our anger and hatred of those who

228

stand in the way, of our accumulating power, is a way to avoid a lot of pain and further suffering. After the expedition we have to let go of our anger and frustration about what others have said and written about us by feeling our way to the source of such negative emotions, owning up to them if necessary and finally watching them evaporate, transmuting them into love – at which point feelings of happiness and contentment well up from a source never previously suspected.

Sad to say, we will never reach the heights to which Milarepa took this discipline and save ourselves a lot of hard slogging and suffering intense cold by flying through space as he flew to the cave of the 'evil shadow' where he meditated until 'an intense power of Tumo radiating warmth and bliss' arose within him 'immeasurably superior to any such experience [he] had in the past'. However, his life is an inspiration at least to take a step in his direction. Milarepa's spiritual development is a 'Pilgrim's Progress' where, like Christian, he is often tempted from the path. At one point his former tutor's son congratulates him and suggests that now he is doing well as a religious devotee why carry on – why not settle down, repair his house and marry Zessay, the girl he was betrothed to in his youth? And Milarepa at another time sees a vision of Marpa and yearns to be with him and his wife. In the same vision, Marpa in typical fashion tells him in no uncertain terms to get on with his job, reminding him why he became his pupil and took the religious path. This is exactly what we have to do on Himalayan climbs when the going gets tough, with storms raging, supplies diminishing and worries about the unknown difficulties ahead; inwardly we have to steel ourselves and be reminded why we came to the mountain in the first place. If we went down when there is still a margin of safety because of our fear of discomfort and the uncertainties above, without taking ourselves to the limit, what agonies we suffer for having never known the experience and value of commitment and the strength and peace that may follow. Even though this is often short-lived how important it is, as the great American climber Willi Unsoeld suggested, to keep it going and let it infuse our daily lives.

Milarepa was able to let go of the need for a personal guru by realizing the universal nature of the guru and seeing guru or Buddha in all things. As an example of Milarepa's compassion at this time, he was able to thank his uncle and his aunt for starting him out on the path of liberation. He prayed unceasingly for their enlightenment 'as a token of my gratitude'. He came to realize that his worst enemy was really his best teacher. To let go of our resentment and anger at what some other equally ambitious climber has said or

229

written, even if it is only on one occasion, is enough to understand Milarepa's 'gratitude'.

Months and years passed by as Milarepa spent his time in solitude, moving from one cave to another whenever the people in the valleys below began to impinge on his isolation and distract him from his meditations. There were many occasions when they sought to tempt him from his path, but he seems to have resisted them all easily. His sister, Petta, entreated him to give up the life that had reduced him to skin and bone. Zessay paid him a visit. She was horrified at his appearance and said: 'I have never seen a religious devotee like you. You look even worse than a beggar. What kind of Mahayana is this?'

Milarepa replies: 'It is the best of all. It throws the Eight Worldly Reactions to the winds in order to realize Enlightenment in this lifetime. This appearance of mine conforms with that tradition.'[8]

She asked him why he could not study religion as others do.

Milarepa replies: 'First of all, those who can only think of worldly goals are content with studying a few religious books. They rejoice in their own success and in the failure of others. In the name of religion they amass as much fame and wealth as they can. They take holy names and put on yellow robes. I turn away from them and always will.' He tells her that they can never marry but that he will pray for her salvation.

Milarepa decides to repair to a more remote cave at Chuwar, near the Nepalese border. As he is getting ready to go he breaks a pot, his only possession apart from the tattered remnant of cloth that is tied around his body. It was the pot in which he cooked his nettle broth.

I consoled myself that all composite things are impermanent. Understanding that this too was an exhortion to meditate, I first marvelled at it; then becoming certain, I sang:
At the same moment I had a pot and I did not have a pot.
This example demonstrates the whole law of the impermanence of things.
In particular, it shows the human condition.
If this is so I, the hermit Mila, will strive to meditate without distraction.
The precious pot containing my riches
Becomes my teacher in the very moment it breaks.
This lesson on the inherent impermanence of things is a great marvel.[9]

As he was singing several hunters arrived and commented upon his melodious singing and marvelled at his body so thin and green. They attempted to stop his work.

Milarepa replied: 'In your eyes I may seem exceedingly miserable. You may not know that there is no one happier and more sensible than I in the world.'

For everyone who comes to tempt him off the path he has only compassion – for his aunt, his sister, for the woman he was betrothed to, to the hunters and other laymen that happen to find him in his sanctuaries – and offers prayers for their deliverance.

Mountaineers, especially, may identify with his need for solitude. Is it not one of the great joys of expeditioning, where our lives are less cluttered and more simple, where we can rest in the present, content that at least for a time the future will take care of itself and the past seems not so important? In our task of climbing the mountain, with all its inherent dangers and hardships, we concentrate the mind and stop it wandering. The higher we go the less we carry the less we have to worry about as we climb, grateful to be there on the mountain. All this is possible providing we are not blinkered by blind ambition and imagined rewards. This is how Milarepa put it:[10]

> Selfish desires stir up the five poisons.
> Temporal desires separate the dearest of friends.
> Self-glorification evokes resentment in others.
> Keeping silent about oneself will prevent conflicts.
> By maintaining tranquillity and avoiding distraction,
> In solitude you will find your companion.
> Humility leads to the highest goal.
> He who works with care will quickly achieve results.
> Renunciation brings great fulfilment.

If, in adopting – even for a short time – some of the ascetic practices of the hermits such as Milarepa we can quieten our minds and find in the space between thoughts more love and compassion than we knew formerly, because we are so grateful to be alive and full of life, and if we can then bring this home with us, our climbing is not entirely selfish – not if we have renewed our zest and enthusiasm for life.

In his splendid book *The Way of the White Clouds* Lama Anagarika Govinda poses the question about religious ascetics: '. . . whether such tremendous effort and achievement would not have benefited the world more if the hermit had returned to the haunts of man and propagated the wisdom which he had acquired.' Then he goes on to say that this is not the hermit's way and yet he may be just as effective as those spiritual leaders who did go out into the world to propagate their wisdom. He gives us an example how the Gomchen of Lachen, to the north of Sikkim, did propagate his wisdom through his chella (pupil) who was none other than the famous Western scholar, orientalist and explorer, Alexandra David-Neel. After putting her through three years of hardship and isolation he imparted to her the profound knowledge that she, in turn, related to the West through her books. She arrived at the profound understanding of the visionary nature of the guru's work: 'Mind and senses develop their sensibility in this contemplative life made up of continual observations and reflections. Does one become a visionary or rather is it not that one has been blind until then.'

This visionary or mystical experience is not just the property of the ascetic but is something which occurs spontaneously to many people. Indeed, it may happen to everyone to some degree. For those that are given a glimpse of a 'separate reality' it often means a profound change in their lifestyle. Sir Francis Younghusband, towards the end of his successful military expedition to Tibet in 1904, had a profound mystical experience on a mountainside above Lhasa:

I was naturally elated at having brought to a successful issue a most difficult and dangerous mission. I was naturally full of good-will, since my former foes were converted into stalwart friends. But now there grew up in me something infinitely greater than mere elation and good-will. Elation grew to exultation, and exultation to an exultation which thrilled through me with overpowering intensity. I was beside myself with untellable joy . . . And henceforth life for me was naught but buoyancy and light.

Such experiences are only too rare; and they are all too soon blurred in the actualities of common life. Yet it is in those fleeting moments that God is made real to us. We glimpse the true reality of things. In those moments we really live. Each is worth a life time. Those who are thus privileged are convinced forever of the utter worthwhileness of life, however hard it may be. To them all life is sacred. What hurts one hurts all.' (*Francis Younghusband* pp. 248–9.) (He went on to found the World Congress of Faiths. He had seen Buddha in all things and now attempted to bring the different religions together.)

Finally, Milarepa's earthly race with time was won and he spoke to his disciples: 'Men of Nyanang (Nyalam) and Dingri and all benefactors and followers, prepare a ritual feast and gather round me, let all other men in the region who have not seen me and wish to meet me come also.'

Milarepa was now in his eighty-fourth year and his disciples and followers and many other people gathered at Chuwar, on the southern slopes of the Himalaya near the Tibetan/Nepalese border. At Drin there was a rich and influential Lama named Geshe Tsakpuhwa, who tried to cross swords with the Master. He hoped to challenge Milarepa with his learned arguments but was unable to do so. Out of jealousy he poisoned the Master. Milarepa began to show the ill-effects of the poison over the next few days.

The Geshe refused to acknowledge that he was the source of

Milarepa's illness until Milarepa transferred half of his pain and suffering to the Geshe, at which point he collapsed in pain, paralysed and choking. He was on the verge of death when Milarepa removed the affliction, at which point the Geshe became a ready convert and sincerely begged for forgiveness, which he was given.

The Repas [Milarepa's followers] asked: 'Can we engage in an active life if it proves beneficial to other beings?'

The Master answered: 'If there is no attachment to selfish aims, you can. But that is difficult. Those who are full of worldly desires can do nothing to help others. They do not even profit themselves. It is as if a man, carried away by a torrent, pretended to save others. Nobody can do anything for sentient beings without first attaining transcendent insight into Reality. Like the blind leading the blind, one would risk being carried away by desires. Because space is limitless and sentient beings innumerable, you will always have a chance to help others when you become capable of doing so. Until then, cultivate the aspiration toward Complete Enlightenment by loving others more than yourselves while practising the Dharma.'[11]

Milarepa continued to let the poison run its course, refusing to save himself or to receive medicines offered by his disciples. As he passed out of his earthly form, 'There appeared in the firmament above them an inconceivable variety of offerings from the gods, such as rainbows and five-coloured clouds, forming themselves into parasols, banners, canopies, bunting and billowing silk'[12] and the Master passed into Nirvana.'

Milarepa is a key figure in the history of Buddhism in Tibet. His importance is summoned up in the words of Lobsang P. Lhalungpa: 'Never, in the thirteen centuries of Buddhist history in Tibet, has there been such a man, who not only inspired an intellectual élite and spiritual luminaries, but also captured the imagination of the common people. . . Throughout pre-Communist Tibet, Milarepa was held in universal veneration. It was so in the past and is still so among the thousands of refugees in the settlements of northern India, Bhutan and Sikkim.'[13] Milarepa's compassion for fellow human beings is reflected even today in the extraordinary love and devotion they give to his memory.

The turbulent times that followed the renaissance of the eleventh and twelfth centuries may be followed elsewhere, for we are only concerned here with the characters that have predominantly affected or passed by the area around Shishapangma.

Notes

1. *Tibetan Civilization*, p. 52
2. *Tibet's Great Yogi Milarepa*, ed. W. Y. Evans-Wentz (Oxford, 1982), p. 52
3. *Tibetan Civilization*, p. 114
4. *The Life of Milarepa* by Lobsang P. Lhalungpa, p. 41
5. ibid., p. 44
6. ibid., p. 163
7. *The Myth of Freedom*, p. 151
8. *The Life of Milarepa*, p. 111
9. ibid., p. 130
10. ibid., p. 172
11. *The Life of Milarepa*, p. 171
12. ibid., p. 173
13. ibid., p. vii

II
European Advances into Tibet

Periodically, from the twelfth century onwards, Europe found cause to revive the myth of Christian kingdoms in Cathay and their legendary king known as 'Prester John'. Despite the advancing Mongol hordes, missionaries such as Friar John Carpini and merchants, of whom Marco Polo was but one, penetrated far into Asia in a futile effort to discover the whereabouts of these communities. Partly as a by-product of this quest, some of these travellers reached Northern Tibet.

In 1324 the Franciscan ascetic, Odorico of Pordenone, set out from Canbaluc (Peking) with the intention of returning home to Europe overland. In 1330 he completed this remarkable journey, claiming to have passed through Tibet and other fabled lands and implying that Lhasa was on his route by giving a description of it. This was probably gleaned from fellow travellers as noted by MacGregor. His journal contains reports of the Tibetan Plateau, which were to be the last to reach Europe for nearly three hundred years.

During the sixteenth century Portuguese merchants established themselves in Goa, on the west coast of India. They were followed by Jesuit missionaries who, in the course of their work, came to hear of Tibet and its inhabitants. They discovered that the Tibetans were given to pious works and carried out religious rites which bore a strong resemblance to those of the Catholic Church. Speculating that there might be enclaves of Nestorian Christians surviving beyond the Himalaya mountains, the Pope supported several expeditions to explore the region, known then as Cathay, with the purpose of reclaiming these isolated Christian communities for the Church.

During this period, in 1590, Father Anthony Montserrat produced the first reasonably accurate map to the Himalaya. He had accompanied Rudolph Aquavivas on a mission to the Moghul Court of Akbar the Great, who ruled most of Northern India from 1556 to 1603 and had invited the Jesuits into his domain in a spirit of friendship and academic enquiry. Curiously, this was at a time when, in England, Elizabeth I was putting Jesuits to death.

In the seventeenth century there was great confusion amongst

European geographers as to whether or not Cathay and China were separate entities or one and the same. Benedict Goes, who made the first of these great Jesuit journeys from the south (1603–7), finally linked China with Cathay and also defined, approximately, the region of Tibet. He travelled north from Kabul through Badakhshan and crossed the Hindu Kush Mountains to Sinkiang. Thus he was able to connect India with Cathay and the Jesuits of Peking. Sadly, the hardships of the journey resulted in his death at Suchow, several hundred miles west of Peking.

Several more journeys were made by these intrepid churchmen, who suffered great privation and physical danger in the crossing of the great Himalayan divide. In 1624, Father Antonio de Andrade and a lay brother, Manuel Marques, set off from the Mogor Mission to convert the Tibetans to Christianity and to find the lost flocks of Nestorian Christians which they still believed to be in Tibet. Four months after leaving Agra, and after imprisonment in the Garhwal, floundering through snowdrifts and fighting off blizzards, dehydration, frostbite and snow-blindness on the Mana Pass (18,400 feet), they crossed into Tibet where they were greeted with surprising friendliness by the Tibetan authorities. Andrade eventually established a permanent mission at Tsaparang. This was possibly the first crossing of the main Himalayan divide by Europeans, and the first authentic penetration into Tibet. On his return Andrade was able to outline, first hand, some of the problems of Himalayan travel. Of mountain sickness he noted: 'according to the natives, many people die on account of the noxious vapours that arise, for it is a fact that people in good health are suddenly taken ill and die within a quarter of an hour. . .'[1] This sounds like pulmonary oedema, although Andrade thought the sickness was due to 'the intense cold and the want of meat which reduces the heat of the body'. Between 1624 and 1640, twelve more missionaries were to repeat the crossing.

The Jesuits at the Tsaparang Mission gradually pieced together something of the geography of Tibet, sometimes from their own observations but mostly from the tales told by passing merchants. Andrade was ambitious to extend the Jesuit influence to the province of Utsang, to the south of Tibet, some six weeks' travelling east of Tsaparang.[2] It was at his prompting that Father Estevão Cacella and Father João Cabral approached Utsang from Bengal. In doing so, they were the first Europeans to set foot in Bhutan, and the first to journey to the land of the Dalai Lama. By 3 January 1628, they had made their separate ways to Shigatse and were well received by the king of the province and by the Great Lama. At first they were allowed to preach and were given ample food and shelter but, over the next two years, their position weakened in the face of opposition from individual Lamas. Several journeys made from the Shigatse Mission brought Europeans close to the Mount Everest Region for the first time. In all their writings, the missionaries make little of the Himalaya mountain ranges, referring to them only as 'lofty mountains' and they also make light of the terrible hardships they must have endured. In trying to establish a more suitable route to their mission stations in India, Cabral, young and strong, set out on a journey to the south-west and crossed over the Himalaya divide, probably passing through Nyalam and Shishapangma. He did this in early February, when the Himalayan wind and cold are at their worst, travelling on down to Kathmandu and Patna and continuing south to Hugli in India. In the course of this remarkable journey, he had made the first European traverse of Nepal.

During 1630, Cacella made a return journey south, and then back north to Shigatse via the Chumbi Valley. This brave missionary died from the rigours of his journey seven days after his arrival. Cabral repeated the journey the following year. In 1640 the Tsaparang Mission failed because of the vagaries of local politics and was abandoned.

In 1661 the German Jesuit, John Grueber, and Albert d'Orville from Belgium were the first Westerners to cross the High Plateau of Tibet from the north to the south – and probably the first, discounting Odorico's implications, to visit Lhasa, which they did on 8 October. They were received there, as elsewhere in Tibet, with typical Buddhist tolerance of strangers and hospitality to travellers. Their journey, which had begun in Peking, was to continue south towards India. On the way to Kuti (Nyalam), when only four days' journey from Lhasa, they came to: 'the Mount Langur. This hill is of unsurpassed altitude, so high that travellers can scarcely breathe when they reach the top, so attenuated is the air. In summer no one can cross it without gravely risking his life, because of the poisonous exhalations of certain herbs.' Langur is a local generic term for mountain and Grueber is probably referring here to the heights of Katambala, which are about fifty-seven miles from Lhasa, as Perceval Landon points out in his book *Nepal*. Landon also notes that: 'the rarefication of the air . . . is always put down by the Tibetans to the existence of maleficent dragons and things which breathe out foul odours and miasms.'

Grueber and d'Orville continued westward, most likely over the Tsong Pass (17,981 feet) to the town of Nyalam under the great peak of Shishapangma. Grueber commented upon the difficulties of the route here, where they had to traverse the tremendous precipices of the gorge. The fathers then followed the Bhote Kosi south, into Nepal on their way to Kathmandu. They eventually completed their journey at Agra during March 1662. Their notes have survived to show the route they followed which, unfortunately, is not the case with Cabral's earlier journey. It is only guesswork to suppose that he took the same route, although Nyalam would have been the logical way.

D'Orville died at the Mogor Mission at the age of thirty-nine, but Grueber went on to Rome, travelling across Persia and Turkey, to make his report. It has proved to be a considerably full and accurate contribution to geography although, surprisingly, he did not describe the landscape or say much about the ordinary Tibetan people. Most of all it was, and remains, an astounding journey accomplished in the face of every difficulty imaginable. They passed within some fifteen miles of Shishapangma in mid-winter. It was not until Father Wessels unearthed these and earlier notes from the Archives of the Society of Jesus in 1921 that the real importance of these great missionary travellers was fully appreciated.[3]

Forty-six years were to pass before the next missionary attempt was made. The Capuchin Fathers d'Ascoli and de Tours arrived in Lhasa in 1707 and were also hospitably received. In 1716 the Italian Jesuit Ippolito Desideri crossed over from Kashmir to Ladakh and then followed the Upper Indus and Tsangpo rivers to Holy Lhasa. He was accompanied by a Portuguese Jesuit, Emanoel Freyre, who had been appointed official leader of the expedition. However, he left Lhasa after only a month's stay. Desideri commented, 'My companion had always lived in hot climates and feared the intense cold and thin air.' Once there he discovered that the Capuchins had temporarily abandoned Lhasa 'for want of the necessaries of life'. Six months after Desideri three Capuchin fathers entered the capital via Nepal. He looked after them for the next six months, although they made it plain that only they had the right to convert the natives. In fact, they sent messages to Rome requesting confirmation of their exclusive rights. After five years the affirmation arrived from Rome, and Desideri, sadly, had to depart.

During the waiting period, however, Desideri had not been idle. Having agreed not to take part in ordinary missionary work, he set about learning the Tibetan language, at the same time gaining an insight into the Tibetan religion and customs which was not equalled for two hundred years. In 1721 his work was finished and he showed it to the Tibetans. Basically it was a studied condemnation of Buddhism and a justification of his own faith: the work caused a great stir and: '. . . my house suddenly became the scene of incessant comings and goings by all sorts of people, chiefly learned men and professors, who came from the monasteries and universi-

238

ties . . . to apply for permission to see and read the book.' He had written it in the Tibetan language. He found the Tibetans: '. . . by nature kindly, virtuous and devout . . . they speak about [their belief] often with great affection and conscientiousness . . . they have the greatest esteem, veneration and respect for their Lamas and monks; would to God that the Christian Catholics showed one-hundredth part of such sentiments to the Prelates, Ecclesiastics and Religious of our Holy Catholic Church.'[4] He confessed that he was: '. . . ashamed to have a heart so hard, that I did not know, love and serve Jesus . . . as this people did a traitor, their deceiver.' At this time the Buddhist faith was going through another period of revival and it remains something of a golden age for Buddhism and for Tibetan culture and influence generally.

Leaving Tibet via the Kuti (Nyalam) road, Desideri entered Nepal. He wrote an interesting description of his crossing of the 'Langur' mountain, which probably took him across the Tsong La (17,981 feet), lying between Dingri Dzong and Nyalam and only thirty miles west of Shishapangma. This route had now been taken many times by the Catholic fathers.

Everyone [Desideri writes][5] suffers from violent headache, oppression in the chest and shortness of breath during the ascent, and often from fever, as happened to me. Although it was nearly the end of May there was deep snow, the cold was intense and the wind so penetrating that, although I was wrapped in woollen rugs, my lungs and heart were so affected that I thought my end was near. Many people chew roasted rice, cloves, cinnamon, Indian nuts, here called Sopari and Arecca [Areca nuts] by the Portuguese and others in India.[6] As the mountain cannot be crossed in one day, there is a large house for the use of travellers. But the difficulty of breathing is so great that many cannot remain indoors and are obliged to sleep outside. Only a short time before our passage, an aged Armenian merchant, who was on his way to Lhasa, died in this place in one night. All these ills cease when Mount Langur has been left behind. Many believe such discomforts are caused by exhalations from some minerals in the bowels of the mountain, but as until now no trace of these minerals has been discovered, I am inclined to think the keen penetrating air is to blame; I am the more persuaded of this because my chest and breathing became worse when I met the wind on the top of Langur, and also because many people were more affected inside the house where the air is made still thinner by the fire lit against the cold, than when sleeping in the open air. It would have been the reverse had the illness been caused by exhalations from minerals or pestilential vapours from the earth.[7]

Desideri left Nepal after gathering more information for his book, which also contained a short account of the Kingdom of Nepal. He continued into India and Agra, arriving there seven years and seven months after first setting out for Tibet. He then sailed from Madras to Europe for a well-earned rest after suffering years of physical hardship. He died in Rome, aged forty-eight, in 1733, leaving a legacy of monumental intellectual efforts.

Desideri must stand as one of the great Asian explorers of all time. Though only a young man of twenty-seven, he displayed all the qualities of a veteran, gathering every scrap of information available at the start of his journey in Kashmir and displaying great drive and qualities of leadership amongst his travelling companions.

Unfortunately, his manuscripts were not unearthed until 1875 and were not actually published until 1904. It was only in this century, therefore, that this and other great missionary journeys were fully appreciated.

The Capuchins were finally expelled from Tibet in 1745 because their rather strong, inflexible attitude to religion upset the Tibetan monks.[8] They left few – if any – converts among the 'heathen' Tibetans. After 1720 the Chinese had tightened their grip on Tibet through the new-found power of the Manchu Emperor. Foreigners found access to Tibet increasingly difficult and two generations were to pass before the next Europeans entered Lhasa.

The famous Capuchin cartographer, d'Anville, did, however, produce a rough sketch map of the country to the north of Lhasa, placing a mountain named Tchomolungma in exactly the same position as that of the Everest Group. Whilst the true significance of Tchomolungma would not have been realized, it is, nevertheless, remarkable how much information of Southern Tibet the fathers accumulated.

During the eighteenth century the political problems of access to Tibet grew worse as Chinese xenophobia increased and they tried to create a buffer state between themselves and India. They were troubled by warlike Indian emperors, the aggressive Gurkhas of Nepal, as well as by the British, who were already spreading their power and influence towards the Himalayan regions of their newly acquired domain.

The East India Company received its Charter from Queen Elizabeth I on 31 December 1600. The company was originally set up to tap the riches of the East Indies, formerly a monopoly of the Portuguese but gradually acquired more and more trading stations which were fortified against Portuguese and, later, French competition as well as against the native Indian Princes.

240

After Clive's triumph against the French and the Moghul Viceroy, Suraj-ud-Doula, at Plassey in 1757 the power and influence of the Company moved north, towards the Himalayan states of Nepal, Sikkim and Bhutan, and only ten years after the Battle of Plassey, a small military expedition under Captain Kinlock entered Nepal at the invitation of the King of Patan. The King and the Newari Kingdom were under attack from the expansive and warlike Gurkhas, and the British, fearing a disruption of the profitable trade from India through Nepal to Tibet and worried about Gurkha territorial expansion, agreed to help check the Gurkha advance. However this British intervention ended ignobly with the soldiers suffering horribly from malaria in the fever-ridden Terai region a few miles inside Nepalese territory. They never came to blows with the Gurkhas, who went on to overwhelm the Newari Kingdom.

Nevertheless the Company remained eager to see 'whether trade can be opened with Nepaul [sic] and whether cloth and other European commodities may not find their way thence to Thibet, Lhassa and the Western parts of China'.

The year 1772 marked the start of Warren Hastings's forward policy. As Governor of Bengal he displayed an active interest in promoting Company affairs north of the Himalaya. After a successful military encounter in the little buffer state of Cooch Behar, where a Bhutanese army was defeated, Hastings followed through with a trade mission to the Deb Taja of Bhutan and the Panchen Lama in Tibet. For this delicate operation Hastings selected George Bogle, a 28-year-old Scot, one of the Company's employees, and instructed him to investigate trade relations with Bhutan and with Tibet, as well as to make notes on the lie of the land, the customs of the people and their form of government.

It is difficult to ascertain how much prior knowledge of the proposed journey Hastings and Bogle were able to glean from the Jesuits. Desideri's account remained locked away in Italian archives until two years after Bogle's departure but snippets of information had been published, mostly in French and Italian but also, by the mid-eighteenth century, in English, as in *Astley's Collection of Voyages and Travels, 1745–7*.

The reports of the Capuchin Mission in Lhasa, *Alphabetum Tibetarum*, were published in Rome in 1762. An English version of Father du Halde's monumental work *Description de l'Empire de la Chine* (Paris 1733) had appeared in 1742. This, together with a volume of forty-two maps prepared by Jean Baptiste d'Anville, the French geographer, and produced in 1735, remained the standard work until well into the next century, although the sheets covering the southern part of Tibet were largely based upon the work of Lamas trained to survey and proved to be not so accurate as the more northerly sections. They were reasonably accurate so far as the river Tsangpo was concerned, but other rivers and also mountain ranges were not so well placed. But for the bare bones of the layout of the country, Bogle would have to go and discover the details for himself.

He went through the Assam Himalaya to Paro Dzong in Bhutan, along the Chumbi Valley and over the Tang La to Gyantse and Shigatse, returning in 1775 by the same route. Although Bogle was not able to proceed to Lhasa and had not taken surveyors in order to avoid upsetting the Tibetan authorities, he did nevertheless bring back a detailed report on the structure of government and religion as well as interesting notes on the customs of the people and Hastings expressed his 'perfect satisfaction' with the results of his mission. Strangely, Bogle never had a chance to follow up his first visit and renew his friendship with the Panchen Lama for both died within a few days of each other, Bogle of cholera and the Panchen Lama of smallpox, in 1779.

This same route was again followed by Ensign Samuel Turner in 1783. He was a first cousin of Hastings, who saw in Turner the ideal envoy to follow up and strengthen the rapport which Bogle had begun with the Panchen Lama. However, the course of history was to overwhelm Hastings's plans for free trade. After the newly united Nepalese invaded Tibet, the Chinese drove them out and tightened their grip on the Tibetan frontiers. The British-Tibetan initiative was at an end and the Company seemed to have given up any hope of reviving it. By the early nineteenth century they showed so little interest in Tibet that Thomas Manning, the eccentric British traveller and scholar, was unable to obtain much assistance for his proposed Tibetan visit and received little acknowledgement when he achieved what Bogle and Turner had failed to do and visited Lhasa in 1811. He was the first Briton to do so, and the last until 1904.

However, the notes and journal which Bogle, Turner and Manning left were valuable contributions to the geography of Southern Tibet and were used in the 1860s, when Britain revived its interest in this now 'Forbidden Land'.

The Gurkhas, in 1791, had foolishly raided deep into Tibet. A force of 18,000 men marched up and through the Himalaya at Nyalam, one of the most difficult roads in the world on to the plateau. They attacked and plundered the venerated monastery of Tashi Lunpo by the town of Shigatse 200 miles away. Here resided the Tahi Lama, second only to the Dalai Lama himself in the

242

Tibetan hierarchy. The Chinese retaliated in strength; hordes of them poured through the Himalaya via the Aran Gorge into Nepal in 1792. The Gurkhas appealed to the Company for military help and the envoy William Kirkpatrick was dispatched with a small escort under Ensign John Gerard. By the time they arrived, the Gurkhas had been decisively beaten only twelve miles from Kathmandu and the Chinese troops then withdrew before winter closed the passes. The terms were that the Nepalese would send a tribute of elephants, peacock plumes and rhinoceros horns to Peking every five years. Thus, as far as the Manchu Emperor was concerned, Nepal was now a 'dependent nation'.[9]

Although Kirkpatrick remained in Nepal, under orders from the new Governor-General Cornwallis to negotiate a workable trade agreement, all official Tibetan correspondence had to be shown to the Chinese Governors, known as Amban, who were to be informed, on pain of death, of the presence of foreign travellers.

With trade and exploration impossible during the late eighteenth and early nineteenth centuries, Britain organized Indian spies to unravel the mysteries of Tibet and to keep them informed of political developments between the Chinese and their unwilling buffer state. Meanwhile extensive surveying and exploratory work was carried out on the southern side of the Himalaya since the Surveyor-General of Bengal, Robert Colebrook, encouraged infantry officers to map any new country visited during campaigns and whilst on tours of duty. John Gerard, the Scotsman in charge of Kirkpatrick's escort, had already sketched a map of the route to Kathmandu in 1792; now, between 1801 and 1803, Charles Crawford produced a map of the Kathmandu Valley from his own observations and a smaller scale map of the rest of Nepal from enquiries amongst the local inhabitants.

Crawford was the first to announce the great height of the 'snowy range'[10] while in 1810 Captain William Webb fixed the height of Dhaulagiri at 26,862 feet. This made it the highest mountain then known and the claim was ridiculed by contemporary geographers, who still held that the highest mountains were in the Andes of South America.

William Moorcroft, the great visionary explorer, was one of the first to work out the topography of the north-western boundaries of the Indian subcontinent. In 1812, disguised as a 'fakir', he was the first Englishman to see Mount Kailas and the sacred lakes that mirror its image. Whilst returning through the Kumaun district, he and his companion, Hyder Young Hearsey, an Anglo-Indian, were captured and mistreated by the Nepalese. They were released after the intervention of two influential Bhotia brothers, Bir Singh and

243

Deb Singh. Their sons were to do a great deal more for the British Empire by way of exploring Tibet.

John Gerard had two nephews in the Survey Department, Dr J. G. Gerard and Captain Alexander Gerard, who proved to be every bit as adventurous as their uncle. From 1817 they travelled the Himalaya for four years, crossing nearly 'every pass from Simla into the Baspa Valley'.[11] In an attempt on Leo Pargyal (22,280 feet) in the Zanska Range, they reached a height well over 19,000 feet at a time when there had only been a handful of ascents up Mont Blanc, and when Pillar Rock in the Lake District was still unclimbed. Their route was, according to Marco Pallis who climbed the peak in 1933, probably all on scree, but he thought that to have braved such an altitude in those days was remarkable, especially at a time when travel was so difficult and the peaks more isolated than now. They seem to have been motivated by a keen curiosity to see and to learn. 'They published a diary which shows them to have been honest observers.'[12] They went on to climb several peaks over 18,000 feet and thus became forever associated with the embryonic development of Himalayan mountaineering.

At the close of the Nepalese War the British agreed to respect the newly established boundaries of the country with the exceptions only of a British resident at Kathmandu, and later British Gurkha recruiting officers and, infrequently, a survey officer to make specific calculations. So it was not until 1949 that mountaineers were given the opportunity of approaching Shishapangma from the south.

It was possible, however, to survey the Nepalese peaks from the Indian Plains and to calculate the highest summits. This was achieved by George Everest (1790–1866) who, from 1830 until 1843, was Surveyor-General and Superintendent of the Great Trigonometrical Survey. During this period George Everest, with very few assistants, completed the measurement of the great meridional arc passing from Cape Comorin through the centre of India to the Himalaya which his predecessor, William Lambton, had begun in 1802. From the primary triangulations associated with his arc, it was then possible to work out a framework of triangulation covering the Himalaya, and to plot accurately the positions and estimate the heights of the main peaks without having to visit them.

Everest completed his Great Arc of the Meridian in 1841. It was, as Kenneth Mason, himself a former Superintendent of the Survey of India, says, 'a stupendous achievement. He was a great organizer, a fine administrator and a tireless worker.'

In the second half of the nineteenth century, with a large and prosperous settlement of British in India, interest in the Northern

Frontier and curiosity about Tibet increased. There was concern too about the possibility of the ever-expanding Russian Empire spilling over into the Indian subcontinent. In 1864 Russia had taken Tashkent and it was only a matter of time before they would move up into the Pamir Mountains. It was estimated that during the previous hundred years the Russians had been expanding east and south into Asia at the rate of fity-five miles a day. For all these reasons, the British took active steps to explore and survey Tibet.

In 1862 General J. T. Walker, the Superintendent of the Great Trigonomical Survey, encouraged Captain Montgomerie to train native Indian explorers in the use of surveying instruments and in the art of practical reconnaissance. When fully trained, it was proposed to send them beyond the Himalaya to carry out clandestine surveys disguised as merchants or holy men. Montgomerie, who was now one of the most experienced frontier explorers, undertook their training at Dehra Dun. He selected two Bhotias, Nain Singh and his cousin Mani Singh. It was their father (and uncle) who had secured the release of Moorcroft and Hearsey in 1812. They were not only 'safe' but also experienced travellers, for they had both explored with the Schlagintweit brothers. They also had the advantage of being closely allied culturally with the Tibetans, both in customs and in speech. During their two-year training, they were not only instructed in the use of the sextant pocket compass and how to observe latitude and estimate altitude, but also shown how this might be accomplished and recorded surreptitiously. They were drilled to count every step, using the beads in their rosaries and to keep records hidden within their prayer wheels. They were equipped with hollowed-out walking sticks to carry a boiling point thermometer and a compass disguised as an amulet, worn round the neck. Special travelling boxes were made with false bottoms to take the other instruments and materials with which to change their identity if they were under suspicion.

After many adventures Nain Singh reached the Tsangpo and then joined a caravan that helped him reach Lhasa on 10 January 1866. He returned, crossing out of Tibet into Kumaun, having paced most of his twelve-hundred-mile route.

By 29 June 1866 he was back at Mussoorie. From his calculations and traverse notes, Montgomerie was able to complete a map sixteen miles to the inch of Tibet's main southern trade route, including six hundred miles of the Tsangpo River. So successful had the experiment proved that other native explorers were despatched northwards to feed information to the British. They were the ears and eyes of the Indian Empire and became known as the Pundits. Kenneth Mason writes (in *Abode of Snow*, p. 86):

To my generation, the story of this is fascinating. Kipling has completely caught the spirit of the pundit period, when Harree Baba the Pathan horse-dealer and the Indian Civilian were real and adventurous characters, when the Great Game in Asia was on and when the frontier mists were almost impenetrable. These characters are not overdrawn and Kim himself is a type of youth born in India, adventurous, loyal and devoted, who learnt to do great things.

Not only did the Pundits travel in great secrecy, their training was conducted in the same manner, They were never referred to by name but only by numbers or letters. Nain Singh was 'No. 1' or simply 'The Pundit'. He went on to check out goldfields in Western Tibet and then helped in the training of several more Pundits.

In 1871 Hari Ram, alias No. 9 or M.H., made the first modern circuit of the Everest Group. Starting at Darjeeling, he then went on to cross the Singalila range, following partly in Sir Joseph Hooker's footsteps. After crossing the main Himalayan divide by way of the Tipta La (16,740 feet) he continued over unknown ground and, after many adventures, reached Shigatse. Then he turned south-westward to Sokya Dzong and Dingri Dzong, mapping all the way. He crossed the Tsong La (an early Jesuit route) and followed the Po Chu of Tibet through Nyalam into Nepal, where its name changes to Bhote Kosi, and continued south, through Nepal, to reach India before the end of the year. Hari Ram, therefore, contributed a good deal of information from behind the highest part of the Himalayan range.

In 1903 Curzon resolved to settle any fears of Russian incursion by setting up the Younghusband mission to Tibet, ostensibly to clear up trading problems and end border disputes. The mission was strengthened in the face of Tibetan intransigence until, finally, in 1904 some twelve hundred British and Indian soldiers, sixteen thousand pack animals and ten thousand coolies, armed with artillery and Maxim guns, crossed the fourteen-thousand-foot-high Jelap La and engaged a force of Tibetan soldiers, armed only with matchlocks and swords, at the tiny village of Guru. Although Younghusband was hoping for a bloodless victory, fighting broke out as the Sikhs tried to disarm the Tibetans. Only minutes later, half the Tibetan army were dead or wounded and the slaughter continued even as the Tibetans slowly walked away, heads bowed, ignoring the bullets that continued to crash into their ranks. The British forces suffered six minor casualties. This, the last throw of the dice in the Great Game, was not a glorious chapter in British Empire history.

After a further skirmish near Gyangtse, when the Tibetans were again routed, Younghusband was free to march into Lhasa, the first

Englishman to do so since the time of Warren Hastings. Whilst the mission had been conducted with great distinction and determination, often in desperately cold weather, the British were unable to find any Russians nor to negotiate with the ruler of Tibet, for he, the Dalai Lama, had fled to Buddhist Outer Mongolia. The treaty that was drawn up with the monks of the Buddhist Hierarchy in Lhasa quickly lapsed in the face of political pressure in Europe and, later, with the Anglo-Russian Agreement of 1907. Younghusband, however, showed great moderation during negotiations and established, for the first time, a bond of friendship and trust between the British and the Tibetans. Although it would require several years of political manoeuvring before the way was clear for mountaineers to visit the north side of the Himalaya and to make an attempt on Mount Everest in particular, at least the door was now partly ajar.

One direct result of the Younghusband mission of 1903–4 was the survey journey along the Tsangpo under the leadership of Captain Rawling. Captains Rawling,[13] Ryder[14] and Wood and Lieutenant Bailey were the first Europeans to traverse the upper Tsangpo since Desideri in 1716, yet they never mention the Italian Jesuit.

The closest point they reached to Shishapangma was the ferry crossing at Lelung, 14,400 feet high, by the Tsangpo, although they did make a visit south from their east-west Tsangpo Valley route and establish that the grassland plateau seemed to stretch right up to the Himalaya, giving relatively easy access. A vast area to the south of the Tsangpo watershed remained unsurveyed and almost unknown except for the sketch maps made by the explorer Hari Ram (known as M.H.) in 1871–2 and 1885. However, the surveyors attached to the 1903–4 mission had carried out a detailed survey of the lines of communication through Sikkim, the Chumbi Valley and Tibet, south of Lhasa. During the course of exploring and surveying some 40,000 square miles of territory north of the Himalaya they showed conclusively that there was no mountain higher than Everest. Also Younghusband had gained a tentative agreement from the Tibetan authorities to allow mountaineers into Tibet. He obviously had Everest in mind. All of this was to be of value for the first Mount Everest Expedition, which took place seventeen years after Younghusband's mission withdrew.

Notes

1. See MacGregor, pp. 25–74

2. See Filippi, pp. 19–26
3. See Wessels
4. See Filippi, p. 191
5. See Filippi, pp. 309–12 and notes to the Fourth Book, pp. 426–7
6. See Rockhill, p. 149. (Rockhill says that in Central Asia everyone attributes the painful effects of the altitude to pestilential vapours from the soil. The Tibetans call the sickness 'La dug' or 'pass poison' and account for it partly by the quantities of rhubarb that grow on the mountains. Chewing garlic or smoking tobacco are supposed to be antidotes; garlic is even given to the animals affected by the sickness)
7. See Messner, p. 159. (Messner writes: 'I ate a lot of garlic before I set off for Nanga Parbat, as I had read that it increased the elasticity of the vascular walls')
8. See MacGregor, pp. 92–111
9. In Lhasa a memorial commemorating the campaign was erected. The inscription, translated by Sir Charles Bell early this century, reads: 'The glorious Chinese Army crossed the mountains as if they were traversing a level plain; they crossed rivers with great waves and narrow gorges as though they were mere streams; they fought seven battles and gained seven victories.' (See Morris, p. 185)
10. See Mason, p. 630
11. See Mason, pp. 69–74
12. See Pallis, p. 64
13. See Rawling, pp. 212–15
14. He became Colonel C. H. D. Ryder, Surveyor-General of India

III
Earlier Expeditions to Shishapangma and its Vicinity

The first expedition to Mount Everest fortunately included amongst its members the widely travelled naturalist, Dr A. F. R. Wollaston and the experienced mountaineer and surveyor, Major H. T. Moorshead. Moorshead had been on many survey expeditions during which he 'discovered' Namcha Barwa (7,756 metres) in 1912 and later mapped the Tsangpo River where it bends around this still unclimbed peak. He was also an experienced mountain climber; in 1920 he had attempted to climb Kamet (7,756 metres) on the Indian/Tibetan border, with A. M. Kellas.

Captain C. H. D. Ryder of the Tibet Mission of 1903–4 was now the Surveyor-General of India. Naturally, he was very much in sympathy with Moorshead's intention to survey the area lying between that accomplished along the Tsangpo during 1904, and the Himalaya to the south. This area was still a blank on the map. In fact the Government of India met all the survey costs of the expedition. With his survey detachment of about twenty in all, Moorshead mapped 12,000 square miles of totally unexplored country on the scale of four miles to one inch. What is of specific interest to us is that he became the first mountaineer to approach Shishapangma. On the route he took from Dingri he comments upon the ruins of numerous villages and watch towers: '. . . all of loftier and more substantial construction than the miserable hovels which form the scattered hamlets of today – indicating, apparently, the former presence of a large and warlike population.'[1] The modern tourist, outraged at Chinese-inspired destruction of the monasteries, should not assume that all ruins in Tibet are due to the excesses of the Cultural Revolution.

After passing through the settlement of Menkhap To, he climbed up to the Lungchen La (17,700 feet) from which there are extensive views of the three Lakes on the Peku Plain and the north-east side of Shishapangma, about thirty miles away.[2] As cloud was down, the survey work was completed in the region by one of his team, Gujjar Singh, while Moorshead left to join Wollaston at Dingri. It was there that they were told how Dingri (or Tingri) and also Langkor were so named. As this was recounted first-hand by an old monk, it is worth quoting Wollaston on this:

Many generations ago there was born in the Indian village of Pulahari a child named Tamba Sangay. When he grew into a youth he became restless and dissatisfied with his native place, so he went to visit the Lord Buddha and asked him what he should do. The Lord Buddha told him that he must take a stone and throw it far, and where the stone fell he should spend his life. So Tamba Sangay took a rounded stone and threw it far, so that no one saw where it fell. Many months he sought in vain until he passed over the hills into Tibet, and there he came to a place where, although it was winter, was a large black space bare of snow. The people told him that the cattle walked round and round in that space to keep it clear from snow, and in the middle of it was a rounded stone. So Tamba Sangay knew that the stone was his, and there he made a cell and dwelt until he was taken on wings to Heaven. And the place is called Langkor, which means 'the cattle go round', to this day. The people from many miles about had heard the stone as it came flying over the Hills from India; it made a whistling sound like TING, so the country came to be called Tingri, the Hill of the Ting.[3]

At Dingri they received a messenger from the Dzongpen (leader) of Nyalam, inviting them to visit his district. Although this area was not mentioned in their passports they decided to go, with the approval of the expedition leader, Col. Howard-Bury for, as Wollaston comments: 'By a liberal interpretation of the expression "Mount Everest" we considered it necessary to explore the surrounding country as far as a hundred miles or more from the mountain. . .' There could hardly have been two more experienced travellers than these. Wollaston, supported by private means, had been in the Ruwenzori and Dutch New Guinea, as it then was. During his visit of 1912, he reached to within 500 feet of the unclimbed Carstensz (4,883 metres), the highest peak in Australasia. He was not, however, impressed by the human environment around Dingri, judging from his diary entries to his wife:

We are living in an old Chinese barrack . . . filled with the dust of ages and the dirt of every day; the coolies are vile in their habits . . . These Tibetan people are friendly but very greedy for money. They are invariably dirty and beyond words ignorant and superstitious . . . there are monasteries and nunneries full of people who spend time in prayer and are entirely supported by the active population. It looks like a country that has known better times, for wherever you go are ruins of buildings larger and much more solid than any built in these days. The Lamas of the present day seem to have it all their own way and are opposed to any kind of outside influence which may mean progress . . . I hope all goes well with you and the garden; how I should like some fresh fruit and vegetables!

The last was a familiar lament.

With some relief the party set off for Nyalam, calling in at

Sketch by H. A. Oldfield, surgeon in the British Residency in Nepal from 1850 to 1863. The ancient trade route through the Kuti Pass from Nepal (foreground), passes through the town of Nyalam (Kuti) which is now part of the Kathmandu–Lhasa highway
Courtesy Royal Geographical Society

Langkor Monastery to see the casket containing Tamba Sangay's stone on the way to the Tsong La (18,000 feet). There was a raging blizzard blowing on the pass, so it was not until the descent, when the clouds had dispersed, that they were able to catch 'glimpses of the magnificent twin summits of Gosainthan . . . thirty miles to the west.' They followed the course of the Po Chu, where, to their delight, after spending a month on the bleak Tibetan uplands, 'it was a relief to pitch our tents in a homely green field, alongside a rippling brook lined with familiar ranunculus, cow parsley, forget-me-nots . . . and to feast our eyes on the glorious purple of the wild thyme which dotted the hillside.' But their pleasure in their surroundings ended upon entry into Nyalam: 'where the whole population, a most unpleasant-looking crowd of four or five hundred came out to stare at us . . . a large and very insanitary village which is known under the name Kuti by the Nepalis who constitute the majority of its inhabitants.'[4]

At first there was no reaction from anyone in authority and they had difficulty in finding a place to camp, until they discovered two Chinese Jongpens, appointed in Lhasa to govern the area and collect taxes – as is the custom at places of importance, the idea being that one will help keep an eye on the other to prevent fraud and cheating the people. The Jongpens denied all knowledge of the earlier invitation and made it impossible for the travellers to stay by discouraging the locals from supplying them with necessities. They also gave out false information about the passes in the area and 'had the cheek to send one of his men to our camp demanding the pass'.

251

Whilst Wollaston was busy collecting botanical specimens, Moorshead went downstream to within ten miles of the Nepalese frontier before packing up and leaving Nyalam 'more squalid and evil-smelling than any place in my experience', as Wollaston concluded. It had not improved much fifty years later, as we were to discover.

Despite local opposition from the authorities, they returned to Everest via Tashigong and Lapche, a village sacred to the memory of Milarepa. They met many pilgrims visiting the hermit's cell at the ancient monastery. They were the first Europeans to visit Lapche. Under Gauri Sankar (7,144 metres) they continued down the beautiful Rongshar Valley, over the Phuse La (the Pass of small rats). Eventually they came round to the eastern side of Everest to conclude a remarkable 150-mile journey through unknown country.

On Christmas Day 1944, Heinrich Harrer and Peter Aufschnaiter rode into the village of Jongkha Dzong on a couple of yaks. It was only by chance that they were there, as their intended destination was east to Lhasa. A confrontation with the Tibetan authorities had resulted in their being ordered to leave the main highway along the Tsangpo and to proceed south to Nepal over the main Himalayan watershed, through Jongkha and Kyirong to the border. This was but one of many setbacks that these two Austrian mountaineers had to face during their incredible journey from the British prisoner-of-war camp at Dehra Dun, *en route* to Lhasa. Harrer, of course, was a very experienced Alpinist and had been on the first ascent of the Eiger North Face; Aufschnaiter was the leader of the 1939 Nanga Parbat Expedition just prior to the climbers' internment by the British. What an inspiration it is to read Harrer's book *Seven Years in Tibet*. For our expedition it was essential reading, and our problems seemed as nothing in comparison with those of Harrer and Aufschnaiter. How fortunate to have this account of Tibet before the advance of the Chinese 'liberators', and told by a traveller who had no expedition organization to cocoon him and his companion from contact with the local Tibetans.[5]

At that time Jongkha Dzong, about fifty-five miles north-west of Shishapangma, contained roughly a hundred mud brick adobe type houses surrounding a monastery, but no inn. In all their travels in Tibet Harrer and Aufschnaiter never came across public accommodation, for all travellers were placed in private houses by the authorities. This was worked on a rotation system and was set against taxes. During our visit we rarely found tea-houses or public lodging places like those in Nepal or India. Westerners might put this down to the influence of Chinese Communism, seeing it as a means to prevent people communicating but clearly a knowledge of Tibetan customs is required before any judgements of this kind are made.

After a month at the village they continued south, along the Bhote Kosi, calling in at the monastery above Longda founded in the eleventh century by Milarepa. Each day the climate became warmer and the vegetation was sub-tropical by the time they reached Kyirong, the main village on this ancient and most import- ant invasion and trade route through the Central Himalaya, along which some five thousand coolie-loads of salt pass down into Nepal whilst rice and other commodities are brought up into Tibet. The name Kyirong means 'the village of happiness', and justly so by Harrer's account. He compares the village and its surroundings with his native Tyrol – wooden houses with shingle on the roofs, animals housed at ground level and accommodation for the farmer and his family above. All around were well-cultivated fields, while on the slope beyond the forests of oak, pine and rhododendrons were found to be as varied and beautiful as those in Sikkim.

The staple food here, as in many parts of the Himalaya, is tsampa,

Nepalese troops invading Tibet to reclaim land taken from them in 1792. Reproduced from a painting by H. A. Oldfield, 1885
Courtesy Royal Geographical Society

253

which has, of late, found a place in our high-altitude rations. Harrer described the preparation of this nourishing cereal, which is to first heat sand to a high temperature in an iron pan and then to pour barley corn on to it. When the corn bursts open the sand and the barley are put into a fine-meshed sieve to separate the corn, which is then ground. The resulting meal is made into a dough with butter, tea, milk or beer. Other foods available were rice, buckwheat, maize, potatoes, turnips, onions, beans and radishes. Being a holy place, meat was rarely eaten and then only when the animal was slaughtered in another village.

During their ten months' sojourn in and around the village the two Europeans joined in competitive sports – horse racing, archery, cross-country running and nude bathing parties in the local hot mineral springs and lakes. There were numerous festivals at which drinking chang went on for days at a time. But even though they had heard that the war was over in Europe, the Austrians remained determined to continue to Lhasa and further east to the Japanese lines. In November 1945 Harrer and Aufschnaiter made their way north, secretly, and then north-west, over the 16,000-foot Charkyu Pass, from which they had fine views of the deep blue lake of Peku and the mountains beyond. Aufschnaiter 'took the opportunity of sketching the magnificent panorama of the Pungrong Range, with Gosainthan and Lapche Kang in the background'. As far as they knew they were the first Europeans in this area, though they hardly had a chance to savour the occasion as their fingertips were cold and fresh snow lay all around on this little-used route. After several more days' march, they came into the area visited by Moorshead twenty-four years earlier, and then descended to the Dingri Plain.

Eventually Peter Aufschnaiter parted company with Harrer in Lhasa and returned to Kyirong. In October 1951 he managed to get to within six miles of Shishapangma from the east and took photographs from above the Kong Tso Lake. In 1954 he visited the Langtang area, putting the finishing touches to his map of the whole area by linking his observations from the north with those now made from the south. Along with many others before us, we found this map invaluable – a visible manifestation of great high-mountain endeavour by this modest man, of whom unfortunately we know so little. As his excursions around Shishapangma were in a particularly sensitive area, he may have decided to keep his researches private. His papers are believed to have been lodged mainly with the Völkerkundemuseum in Zürich and some with the veteran Himalayan explorer Paul Bauer. Since Aufschnaiter has passed on, it is to be hoped that the full story of his travels to this part of the world will soon be told. Incidentally, it was Aufschnaiter's opinion that the most promising way to climb Shishapangma was from the north-west.

With the end of the Second World War, the British withdrawal from India and the Chinese Communist threat to Tibet, the Nepalese cautiously opened their doors to foreign tourists in an effort perhaps to remain independent of both India and the Chinese.

In 1949 the British Ambassador in Kathmandu obtained permission for a small expedition to visit Nepal. The approach was made by the Himalayan Committee in London to the Prime Minister of Nepal. Apart from incursions into Nepal from Darjeeling and Sikkim during reconnaissance visits to Kangchenjunga, there had been no European climbers active in Nepal. This request was granted and the British Expedition were allotted the Langtang Himal – to the delight of its leader, H. W. Tilman, who sought not only to 'explore' the Langtang but also the southern environs of Shishapangma – particularly since Tibet was about to 'go into the red', as he put it. Along with his great friend, Eric Shipton, Tilman was, at that time, the foremost Himalayan mountaineer of the pre-war period. He made the first ascent of Nanda Devi and, in 1938, led the last Mount Everest Expedition of the inter-war period.[6]

It was with Everest in mind that the London Himalayan Committee attempted to regenerate British interest for Himalayan climbing, and used the royalties from Tilman's book of the 1938 Expedition to finance him in Nepal. Peter Lloyd, who was with Tilman in 1938 on Everest, was the only other climber in the party. The Nepalese gave their consent to this visit on condition that it undertook some scientific work, and so O. Polunin, a botanist, and J. S. Scott, a geologist, were also members of the party. Their eight-day approach march from Kathmandu to the Langtang Valley at 11,000 feet lay up the Trisuli Valley, a journey typical of those made by many more expeditions in the future approaching the Himalaya from the south – a country of gorges, ravines and swift-flowing streams. They went right up to Rasua Garhi, the frontier post at only 6,000 feet, but within six miles of a 21,000-foot mountain. It was there that they visited an old fort on the Nepalese side of the frontier, a remnant of former incursions into Tibet by the Nepalese and the retaliatory raids by the Chinese who, in 1792, penetrated into Nepal as far as Nawakot, a few miles north of Kathmandu.

The Langtang village, at 11,000 feet was then a collection of thirty houses with cattle – cows, zhos, yaks – grazing on the fine open land beyond the fields of buckwheat, wheat and potatoes. Always a keen observer, Tilman noted the large quantities of butter and beer produced in the valleys: 'Butter enters largely into their religious ceremonies and so does beer, for in the debased Buddhism of these parts, as in Shropshire, "Malt does more than Milton can to justify God's way to man". The butter is burnt in innumerable lamps, drunk in innumerable bowls of tea and images are decorated and human heads blessed with it.'

After spending a week surveying from a base at the Buddhist Gompa beyond the village, they moved up to the glaciers at the head of the valley: 'The major peaks are trigonometrically fixed and up to the level of habitation the maps are good enough to dispel any illusion one might have of being an explorer; but above that they are bad enough to permit of glaciers offering charming surprises and cols unexpected and puzzling vistas.'

From one col in the area, at about 19,000 feet, Tilman, Lloyd and their Sherpa Tenzing, looking north-east, behind a tangle of peaks, could see 'a lump of a mountain with a long flattish summit and a Western Face more rock than snow'. They thought that it was neither high nor distant enough to be Shishapangma and never saw the mountain again, but after Lloyd had computed his survey data they believed that it was, in fact, Shishapangma but failed to show its true orientation.

Mist and cloud continued to keep the big mountain out of sight, and when they eventually climbed up to a col on the great Himalayan divide known now as Tilman's Col, from which they looked down on to a westward flowing glacier, probably the one now called Phuriphu on Aufschnaiter's map, their view east to Shishapangma was blocked by intervening mountains and ridges.

It was during this period that they attempted to climb Langtang Lirung from the north, the highest peak in the Langtang Himal, but bad weather and too many obstacles thwarted their plans at the base of the mountain. They also had permission to visit the Ganesh Himal, further west. Here they climbed a small peak, Paldor (5,928) metres). Later, they returned to the Langtang Valley in August and attempted to climb Ganchempo (Fluted Peak, 6,387 metres). This is one of the most beautiful peaks in the area, with its fluted faces of deep snow, but wet slushy snow lying on hard green ice meant that this attempt was abandoned well short of the summit. After exploring up to the Jugal Himal in the south-west, they departed the area in mid-September without, unfortunately, climbing any major peak but with a wealth of information for the use of future visitors, including confirmation that the monsoon is not the best time to climb peaks of 20–23,000 feet nor is it conducive to surveying. Nevertheless they had opened up the area to the outside world and were able to show that the origin of the Langtang Valley lies much further north than is indicated on the Survey of India Map which they used, although it is, in fact, even further north than indicated by Tilman.[7]

The first photograph to show any detail of Shishapangma from a south-westerly direction was taken by Dr Toni Hagen in the autumn of 1950. This Swiss geologist flew over the Langtang area whilst conducting preliminary geological investigations on behalf of the United Nations. He spent five of the next eight years in Nepal, during which time he made nineteen expeditions, the longest lasting six and a half months. He travelled more than 8,700 miles on foot with just two loyal Sherpas, carrying out an immense amount of field work, visiting every valley in the country, covering not only the geology but also the human aspects of Nepal. Following his surveys of the Langtang area (mentioned below) he recommended that a cheese industry should be established there. After overcoming many problems with bureaucracy and the uncertainties as to whether yak milk could be used for cheese making, a cheese factory was set up in the Langtang Valley after a visit there by a Swiss cheese expert, W. Schulthess, in 1953. This cheese has been a boon to local users, tourists and expedition climbers ever since.

During the autumn of 1952 Hagen trekked into the Langtang Valley accompanied by one of his Sherpas, Aila, and they made their way with relative ease up the Langtang (Tuaga Phu) Glacier to a col at just over 20,000 feet now known as Hagen's Col, and one very close to the South-West Face of Shishapangma. From there it would have been but a stroll down on to the upper Nyanang Phu Glacier to the base of the mountain, only four miles away at this point. His photograph (reproduced in *To The Third Pole*) was actually taken from a snow dome vantage point (6,250 metres), further west and nearer to Tilman's Col, from which he could see more of the mountain than was possible from his col. Hagen also published a sketch map of this area which appeared in 1953.[8]

In the spring of 1955 the first all-women's Himalayan expedition went up into the Jugal Himal. Tilman had looked down into it from the Langtang during his visit in 1949, when no one as far as is known had ever actually penetrated into the range. Monica Jackson, Elizabeth Stark and Evelyn Camrass set out to explore the region and, if possible, climb one of the peaks there. They travelled north-east from Kathmandu, going along the Balephi Khola to the village of Tempathang and then up the Pulmthang Khola to its source, where they established Base Camp not far from the snout of the Phurbi Chyachu Glacier. The three women, Elizabeth Stark a speech therapist from Lanarkshire, Monica Jackson a London

257

Many explorers/climbers tried to penetrate the complex of glaciers in the upper Langtang area and to sight or reach Gosainthan, as Shishapangma is called in Nepal.

The three maps shown illustrate the history of exploration and development of our knowledge of this area between 1949, when Nepal first opened her frontiers to foreigners, up to 1956. None of these maps compare with that produced by Aufschnaiter, which first appeared in 1957. This is still the prime source for identification of peaks in the Langtang Himal, and has been used in the production of Nick's 'Climbers Sketch Map'.

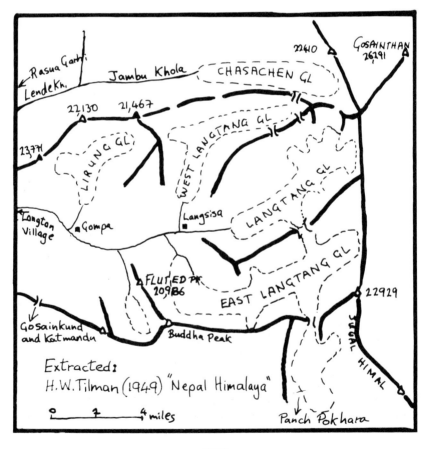

258

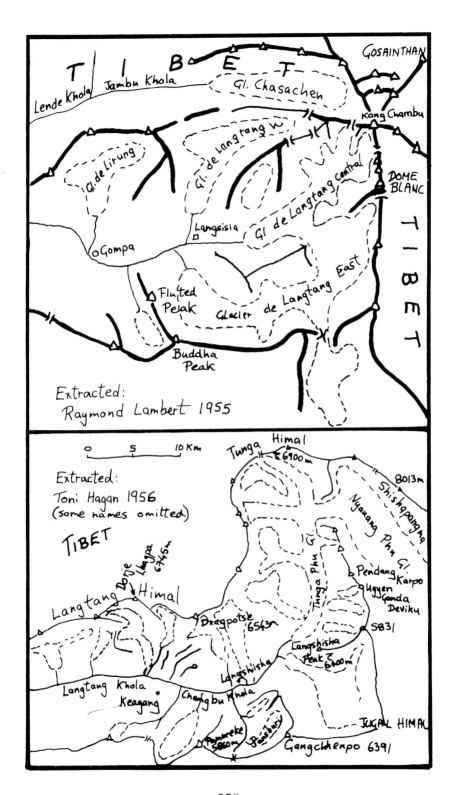

Extracted:
Raymond Lambert 1955

Extracted:
Toni Hagan 1956
(some names omitted)

259

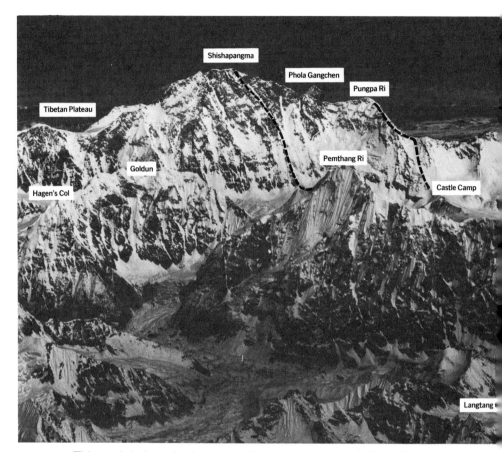

This aerial photo looks across the upper Langtang Phu Glacier basin and the frontier ridge with the SW Face of Shishapangma in the background. On the left of the picture can be seen the glacier going up to Hagen's Col which crosses the frontier ridge into the upper Nyanang Phu Glacier basin

housewife and Evelyn Camrass a doctor from Glasgow, made up a modest expedition that achieved a great deal, reaching several cols during surveying expeditions and making collections of flora and fauna.

On 11 May Stark and Jackson reached the summit of Gyalzen Peak (6,151 metres) from the south and at the head of the Phurbi Chyachu Glacier, the upper section of which has become known as The Ladies' Glacier. They were accompanied by Mingma Gyalzen, after whom the peak was named (although the spelling of which has varied ever since), and Ang Temba. Unfortunately, Evelyn was

260

suffering from high-altitude headaches and had to remain at their last camp and so did not actually make it to the summit. However, later she climbed up on to a ridge near their Base Camp, from where she was able to make further corrections to the Survey of India map. Gyalzen Peak, on the frontier ridge of the main Himalayan divide, was the first peak to be climbed in this area. We were to pass by the steep northern flanks of Gyalzen several times during the course of trekking from Nyalam to our Base Camp under Shishapangma.

After passing the enormous cliffs of Gyalzen, Lenpo Gang and Gur Karpo, we walked up to our Base Camp, opposite the massive snow peak of Pemthang Karpo (6,830) on the eastern side of the Nyanang Phu Valley and on the main Himalayan divide. This peak was first climbed by the Swiss Everest climber, Raymond Lambert, and his Sherpa Ang Norbu, who had been twice to Everest – in 1952 and 1953 – Kami Tsering who had climbed on Manaslu the year before, and Pasang, who was also on Everest in 1953. They climbed up from the south on to the south-east ridge, which they followed mostly on the Nepalese side to the summit on 15 May – two days after the Gyalzen ascent. Lambert had already reconnoitred Langtang Ri, but after inspecting the enormous ice cliffs and cornices from Tilman's Col with the Belgian, Jules Détry, decided against climbing it. The fact that the two of them had personality conflicts may have caused this decision and accounts for the paucity of information about this expedition.

In 1957 a British party from the Yorkshire Ramblers Club walked up into the Jugal Himal to attempt Lenpo Gang (7,083 metres), commonly known as the Big White Peak. Tragically, the leader, Captain Crosby-Fox, and two Sherpas were killed in an avalanche. A week later a doctor in the party, Dan Jones, dislocated his shoulder and Sherpa Lakpa Tsering broke his leg and had to be carried out. The villagers at Tempathang must have been puzzled by this strange Western pursuit of mountaineering.

However, mountaineers came thick and fast. Every year expeditions operated in the Jugal Himal and the Langtang Himal, except for the period 1965–70, when the Nepalese closed their mountains to foreign expeditions. In particular, the Japanese were most prodigious in their expeditioning here as elsewhere in the Himalaya. It was on the first Japanese visit during a reconnaissance of the Big White Peak that they discovered the existence of Aufschnaiter's map. They brought it to Japan, an important result of this 'Pilgrimage to the West'. Possibly as many Japanese as expeditions from all other countries put together now climbed in Nepal. It would need a whole book to relate the details of all the

261

expeditions to this area and so further climbs in this region are listed in Appendix IV.

By 1960 only Shishapangma, the lowest of the 8,000-metre peaks, remained unclimbed. This was not because Shishapangma was the most technically difficult, it was simply the most difficult to reach. The only climbers to have access to this mountain were, of course, the Chinese.

The Chinese began climbing in the mid-1950s, during a period when good relations existed between them and the Russians. They climbed together with the Russians in the Pamirs and in the Caucasus, and the two nations joined in combined operations on unclimbed peaks in China itself. In 1959 thirty-one climbers – nineteen from Russia and twelve from China – reached the summit of Mustagh Ata on the same day – a fine collective effort! By the time this co-operation came to an end in 1960 the Chinese had enough experience and, presumably, equipment to continue mountaineering on their own within China, where there was a vast reservoir of unclimbed peaks and largely unexplored mountains to keep them busy during the next two decades. The main events of this period were the Chinese efforts on Everest in 1960. They claimed that three of their climbers reached the summit at 4.20 pm on 25 May, where they collected nine rock specimens for Chairman Mao. Of course, there were no summit photographs and doubts have been cast on the validity of this claim ever since. After our ascent of Shishapangma we met one of the three, minus the fingers he had lost on that climb – Wang Fu-chou, now Secretary-General of the Chinese Mountaineering Association. He described to us how Qu Yinhua climbed the steep second step on the North Ridge of Everest in bare feet at 8,600 metres – the highest bit of crag climbing ever accomplished.

Whether or not they actually got to the summit – and we have no reason to doubt this claim – there is no doubt at all that they were in the region of the summit; that is all that matters here, for it proves that the Chinese did have sufficient high-altitude experience to explore and to climb on Shishapangma.

There is of course a vast difference between the way climbing is conducted in the West and how it is organized in China. In a country that is attempting to pull its far-flung provinces together by engendering a feeling of national pride, and at the same time trying to move rapidly into the twentieth century economically, culturally and in sporting events, mountaineering is naturally used to further these patriotic ends. As a result the Chinese tend to ignore failures and tragedies and concentrate only on the successes; in the West it is often the other way round. Nothing sells newspapers and boosts

TV audience ratings more than reports of disasters, sensationalized at the expense of the actual achievements. To my mind, both approaches are distortions.

It is no wonder either that error and exaggeration tend to creep into the information put out by the Chinese propaganda machine when accounts are rewritten by non-climbers – probably by people who have never seen a mountain. Also translation errors may occur, especially if reports are translated twice, as when they reach us via Japan.

It was in March 1961 that the first Chinese reconnaissance expedition to Shishapangma took place. They made preliminary investigations, contacting local herdsmen and hunters who were familiar with the lie of the land. The local people, they learnt, regard Shishapangma as a holy mountain:

It is claimed that a monk named Wujenrenpuchi going to Nepal to obtain the Buddhist scriptures was passing over the Yabukangala Glacier of this holy mountain when suddenly hundreds of dazzling snow white seracs appeared. This was Shishapangma mountain. On its sides beautiful designs in red, yellow and black were to be seen. 'Good luck' designs similarly drawn are still found decorating many homes in Tibet today. In the eyes of the local people this mountain is a pure and holy mountain.[9]

They also learnt that the local people's reverence for it is not unfounded, for it is the mountain and its store of ice which waters the pastures as well as the lakes that lie to the north of Shishapangma; these teem with fish which can be caught by merely dipping one's hand into the clear water.

Observations were made from all points of the compass, and the party returned in September to October for further investigations, gaining an impression of the topography of the mountain second to none. Their main discovery was that the most likely way of approach was via the Yabukangala Glacier,[10] which flows north-wards from Shishapangma's north-westerly summit, midway between Shishapangma and Risum. On the basis of this information a large party of mountaineers arrived for the third time at the foot of Shishapangma's northern slopes during April 1963. After crossing a number of crevasses and broad stretches of knee-deep snow, members of this 'reconnaissance' reached a height of 7,160 metres.[11] Here one wonders whether this really was a reconnaissance or, in fact, it was a full-scale attempt which failed.

From 5 to 23 March 1964, some 206 mountaineers, scientists and support personnel arrived at the foot of Shishapangma in three groups. After making intensive preparations for the first month they began their climb.

Shishapangma, this 'Holy Mountain', has another side to its nature, as the Chinese were to find out. It can suffer from terrible winds, massive falls of snow and colossal avalanches, but on the whole they seem to have had reasonable weather on their actual climb as it is described in *China's Sports* periodical (1964, No. 4), written at the time and therefore subject to less distortion through rewrites than later versions.[12] In twenty days the advance party, led by Shih Ching, had completed the task of setting up four camps up to 6,900 metres and stocking them with provisions and equipment by mid-March. Then, at daybreak on 25 April the Base Camp, which must have resembled a small village at 5,000 metres, was bustling:

Amidst the clashes of cymbals and the beating of drums, the mountaineers built a farewell arch with pine and cypress branches to salute the assault party and wish it good luck.

At exactly 10 am Peking time in front of the five star National flag, the thirteen members of the assault party raised their left hands and solemnly pledged . . . 'for the honour of the party and the socialist construction of the Motherland, we pledge to unite as one man, march forward courageously and plant the five starred red flag on the summit.'

After braving dense clouds, drifting snow and piercing cold winds, they established an assault camp at 7,700 metres on 1 May. Three of the team remained there as they were showing signs of fatigue; the

The North side of Shishapangma
Reinhold Messner

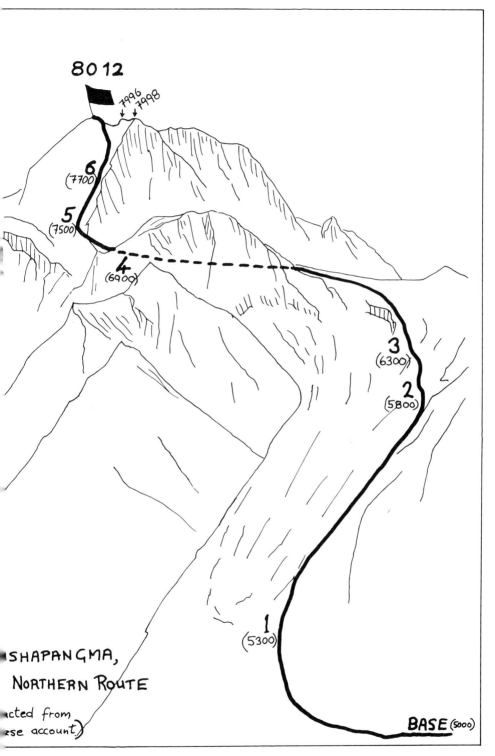

8012

7996 7998

6
(7700)

5
(7500)

4
(6900)

3
(6300)

2
(5800)

1
(5300)

BASE (5000)

SHAPANGMA,

NORTHERN ROUTE

cted from
se account)

Shishapangma, the Northern route

remaining ten continued in three groups with a Master of Sports, Wu Tsung-Yueh blazing the trail. The climbers set out under the leadership of Hsu Ching as one of the radio operators stationed at 6,180 metres called excitedly: 'Hear the battle drum, comrades! Advance! Plant the red flag on the summit!'

Wu Tsung-Yueh led off, followed by Hsu Ching, Sodnam Doje and Cheng Tien-liang; on another rope came Chang Chun-yen, Migmar Trashi and Doje and the third rope consisted of Wang Fu-chou, Chen San (the first Chinese climber we met when arriving at Peking airport) and Yonten. At about 7,800 metres, whilst tackling 'bluish silvery white hard ice', Wang Fu-chou, bringing up the rear, slipped as the icy steps had worn away. Chen San and Yonten whipped the rope around their ice axes and held his twenty-metre fall. Just as the day dawned, the group crawling on all fours over forty-five-degree ice, gained gentler slopes although these were covered in knee-deep snow. In the rarefied air, without using artificial oxygen it seems, they encouraged one another to push on against the strong wind and, finally, they rounded a mushroom of ice and all ten, one by one, stepped on to the triangular-shaped summit at 10.20 am (Peking time).

The Chinese do not write in much detail about their route, they give few directions and have not published definitive photographs from the summit or the summit area. However, there is no doubt in our minds that they did reach the summit. The reasons I am convinced are based on two photographs which they took in the summit area. To take the photograph 'looking east from the 7,800 metre height on Mount Shisha Pangma' the Chinese climbers must have cut diagonally across from their Camp VI at 7,700 metres at a low angle, traversing left across the upper northern slopes of Shishapangma to the upper east ridge that connects with Molamenqing (Phola Gangchen).[13] (In it can be seen the Everest Group, some seventy-five miles away, the Kong Tso Lake, four-five miles below, as well as Molamenqing. It appears to me that the photograph is actually taken from 7,900 metres.) Then . . . 'After traversing this slope [the Chinese] gained a gently sloping ridge to their left, covered in knee-deep snow.' This probably means they cut back right, on to the west-north-west ridge, from where Hsu Ching took another photograph during 'A pause at 8,000 metres'.[14] It shows the two sub-summits to the west-north-west, the nearer being 7,996 metres and the further 7,998 metres. (These figures are based on the summit's being 8,012 metres. The highest of these sub-summits is about four hundred metres away from Shishapangma's Main Summit. I deduce all this from having been to both camera positions and also with Alex to Point 7,996 metres and to a

266

small point of snow between the two sub-summits. During the 'pause at 8,000 metres', the climbers in that photograph are, without doubt, less than a stone's throw from the summit. Anyone who doubts whether or not the Chinese bothered about climbing the last thirty feet does not know mountaineers, and Chinese mountaineers in particular, with all the pressures of the People's Republic behind them and Thoughts of Chairman Mao to spur them on. Two other points worth noting are that on my photograph of the Main Summit, their 'mushroom-like ice pinnacle over a patch of soft snow' down left from the summit can be seen. Also, the top is triangular in shape; there is not that much room on it, however, certainly not enough for nine climbers to pose for their summit photograph, so I would assume that the summit colour photograph published in *Mountaineering in China* is taken from very near the summit but not actually on it.

They stood for forty minutes looking out over 'the majestic scenery of snow-clad peaks and swirling clouds'; to the south-east towered Jolmo Lungma, the world's highest peak, conquered by Chinese mountaineers four years earlier. Wang Fu-chou, who was one of three to climb its summit by the northern slope, stared long and hard at the scene of his earlier triumph. At 11 o'clock they began their descent without mishap and reached Base Camp safely.

The route of ascent had been up the Yabukangala Glacier, approximately from the north to the south, that is, to the head of the glacier before traversing via a corridor eastwards across the upper north ridge that descends from near the summit of Shishapangma. They proceeded on to the snow and ice slopes descending towards the Shishapangma Glacier and from there they climbed upwards to the summit, as outlined above. Despite the fact that the Chinese had so many climbers they had made, for those times, a competent ascent and without the loss of life, despite bad weather, colossal falls of snow and ice avalanches sweeping down from time to time. Another difficulty they overcame was the exceptionally long distance between Base Camp and the summit, a distance of thirty-six kilometres.

This fine achievement was to some extent sullied by the doubt cast by such distinguished experts as Baron Von Sternbach. It is a pity that the Chinese, as so often before and since, published no definitive summit photographs. Those they issued showed nine Chinese climbers against the sky, with no other peaks in sight. Such a photograph could have been taken in the foothills or on a city dump in Peking on a snowy day. Anyone not familiar with the summit terrain and of a suspicious nature, may cast doubts as to where the other photographs were taken in the summit area.

267

A photograph as shown in *Mountaineering in China* (China Publications Centre). The caption reads: 'The forest of peaks as seen from the top of Shishapangma.' The Everest group of peaks can be seen in the far distance (centre). It is interesting to compare the position of the photographer with that of Alex when he took the photo (p. 196) from just below the summit of Shishapangma. Clearly the Chinese are on or within a few feet of the summit.

Sternbach set out his doubts in the German magazine, *Bergsteiger*[15] in a thoroughly scholarly fashion. However there is absolutely no question in our minds but that the Chinese reached the summit of Shishapangma. By a strange coincidence, it was Dougal Haston and myself who proved the doubters wrong about the Chinese claims to have climbed Everest in 1975, with our photographs of the Chinese tripod which they had left on the summit.

It may not be widely known that there were British proposals to climb Shishapangma from Nepal in the 1960s. Michael Ward, of the Alpine Club, did most of the preparatory work, approaching the Mount Everest Foundation for funds and gathering every scrap of information available. The team which was suggested consisted of Joe Brown, Don Whillans, Chris Bonington, Ian Clough and Ian

McNaught-Davis. However, when Ward heard that the Chinese had reached the summit:

. . . and a bust of Mao Tse-tung had been placed there together with the Chinese National flag, that was the end of the British interest in Gosainthan and all that remains of our aspirations are two large and bursting files.[16]

Himalayan climbing was then still in its infancy, where the interest was usually in climbing virgin summits by the easiest routes, rather than for the sake of the route itself.

After the Russian visits in the 1950s, the Chinese did not allow any foreigners to climb in China until 1978. In that year, which was to prove of great significance to Himalayan climbers everywhere, the Chinese granted permission for the Iranians, of all people, to visit Tibet. At that time, however, none of us knew just how far our playground would be extended or who would be able to play in it. A surge of hope and anticipation ran through the climbing world, along with feelings of frustration at the lack of information available and impotence at our inability to emulate this Iranian initiative. The West Germans, however, did manage to match the Iranian performance. Manfred Abelein,[17] a professor of Law and Science and for fifteen years a member of the *Bundestag* was actually in Peking during the spring of 1978 as a member of a German delegation. Whilst there he took the opportunity of approaching the Chinese Mountaineering Association, giving them presents and asking for permission to climb on Shishapangma. The Chinese only smiled and he heard no more about it until he happened to be back in Peking in 1979. He was then told that, since his first approach in 1978, twenty countries had applied for Shishapangma.

Abelein persuaded Franz Joseph Strauss to write to Teng Xiao Ping on his behalf and, in February 1979, he received a phone call from the Chinese Embassy in Germany telling him that he had been granted permission for Shishapangma – but not for 1981, the time most convenient to Abelein, but for 1980. Abelein was invited to go over to Peking to complete the formalities. He was accompanied by Fritz Zintl and Günther Sturm, two very experienced Alpinists and Sturm a prodigious Himalayan climber. They were allowed to go on a reconnaissance of the mountain, during which they reached a height of 5,600 metres, before returning to Germany to make their plans for the following year. Abelein made the now-familiar journey back to Peking in March 1980 with Günther Sturm, Fritz Zintl and the rest of his team. There was Michel Dacher, who had climbed K2 amongst other Himalayan peaks, Sigi Hupfauer, well

269

The first mountaineers to stand
on the summit of Shishapangma:

ABOVE: Hsu Ching (leader of the
expedition)
ABOVE LEFT: Sodnam Doje
(Tibetan)
LEFT: Migmar Trashi (Tibetan)
BELOW LEFT: Chang Chun-yen
(deputy leader of the
expedition)
BELOW: Wu Tsung-yueh

ABOVE: Yonten (Tibetan)
ABOVE RIGHT: Wang Fu-chou
(deputy political commissar)
RIGHT: Cheng Tien-liang
BELOW RIGHT: Chen San
BELOW: Doje (Tibetan)

known for his participation in the Eiger Direct climb in the winter of 1966, Manfred Sturm who had extensive Alpine and Himalayan experience, Erich Reismüller, a cameraman, Dr Wolfgang Schaffert and Otto Wiedemann, who, according to Abelein, was known to be the fastest climber in Germany.

The expedition had decided to approach Shishapangma from the north and to follow in the steps of the Chinese. Dogged by bad luck during April, the team became quite demoralized when Wiedemann became ill with suspected cerebral oedema below Camp I, and when a porter was injured in a crevasse accident. On 24 April, Zintl, Günther Sturm and Dacher announced their intention to try a new route on the North Face; that is, to the right of the Chinese route. Eventually they established a dump of equipment at 7,500 metres, whilst the remainder of the expedition followed the line planned by the Chinese and managed to establish a Camp IV at 7,350 metres, below that of the Chinese Camp V. Zintl went back up to have another look at the North Face route and selected a likely gully as a way through the steep rocks of the Face. However, due to excessive snowfall, the North Face was abandoned and he made a traverse across to the Chinese route. The team were all together at Camp IV by 6 May. On the 7th, Dacher, Schaffert, Günther Sturm and Zintl all reached the summit. On 12 May, Hupfauer and Manfred Sturm also went to the summit. The leader, who had not much climbing experience, was suffering from the effects of the altitude.

An ascent was also made by skis, of a peak to the west of Shishapangma (7,150 metres) on 16 May. The team then went back to Base Camp and eventually home to Germany.

A further ascent of the mountain was made during October of the same year by a team of Austrians. In 1981 the Japanese women arrived and Junko Tabei reached the summit of Shishapangma on 30 April 'with two Chinese assistants'. The fifth ascent of Shishapangma was made by two Tyroleans, when Reinhold Messner, the leader, and Friedl Mutschlechner reached the summit on 28 May. This expedition also flirted with the North Face, but so far no further details have come to light. It is believed that the ascent of the ordinary route made a slight variation of between 7,200 and 7,600 metres. This was Messner's sixth 8,000-metre summit and one which nearly eluded him owing to the strength and viciousness of the winds.

There were two other attempts on Shishapangma in 1981, and both by Americans – one in October and the other in November. The first was defeated by heavy snowfalls and high winds and the latter, the climbers having already extended themselves on the

Kangshung Face of Everest, was also defeated by the terrible winter winds.

A first ascent in the Shishapangma Massif was achieved in 1981. The New Zealanders climbed Molamenqing (Phola Gangchen, 7,703 metres). Their ascent 'via the Yambukangala Glacier to the east of Shishapangma, across the Face of Shishapangma between the North Face and the North Peak, across snow fields to the West of Shishapangma to Molamenqing.' They reported that whilst their route was non-technical, they were stretched to the limit of their logistics, for they had to go a distance even greater than to the top of Shishapangma. Bruce Farmer and Dick Price reached the summit first on 14 May, followed two days later by Warwick Anderson, Ron McLeod, Geoff Gabites, Bruce Clark, Paul Chapman and Tony Charlton. The New Zealand lads had attempted to climb Molamenqing via the Shishapangma Glacier, but after a reconnaissance decided that the route was unjustifiably dangerous. They tried a second line going along the ridge towards the North Peak but, again, found this to be impracticable – especially for continued usage by large numbers of climbers and in the prevailing weather patterns. It appears that this line would be feasible for a fully acclimatized team who could move quickly in Alpine style. The actual route they took to the summit more or less followed the original Shishapangma route, but then skirted underneath the summit of Shishapangma to the western snow slopes leading to the summit of Molamenqing. Their main problems had been 'white-outs' on the broad open snow slopes during storms and periods of high wind. No fixed ropes were used as there were no serious technical difficulties. The main problem, as with all expeditions to China, was the cost – £50,000 for Molamenqing!

Notes

1. *Mount Everest – The Reconnaissance* by C. K. Howard-Bury, p. 321
2. Moorshead's map, produced for *Mount Everest – The Reconnaissance*, names only a pass north-west of Menkhap To – the Yaola
3. See Wollaston, pp. 281–2
4. See Wollaston, pp. 225–9
5. See Harrer
6. See Tilman
7. See *Alpine Journal*, May 1950, pp. 305–12; also *Geographical Journal*, December 1950, article by Peter Lloyd, pp. 172–82
8. See *Les Alpes*, 1956, pp. 165–6; also Dyhrenfurth, Plate 26 and pp. 156–8; Hagen; *N.Z.Z. No. 583*, 14.3.53
9. See *China's Sports*, 1964, No. 4, p. 10
10. The spelling of this name has varied ever since. The Germans (1980) –

Jebokangjale; the New Zealanders (1981) – Yambukangala; the Chinese (in the book *High Mountain Peaks in China*, 1981) – Yebokanggle Glacier; and no doubt there are and will be others. We propose to use the original spelling as in *China's Sports*. We are grateful to Anders Bolinder for making this periodical available to us

11. See *High Mountain Peaks in China*, p. 24. One of the contradictions discussed above appears, for in that volume Xu Jing (Hsu Ching) writes that an altitude of 7,160 metres was attained in September 1961. The high point of 7,160 metres given for 1963 is also suggested by the East-European Himalayan chronicler, Fritz Rudolph, and by Norman Dyhrenfurth in his article in *Mountain Magazine* No. 54, p. 47. It is possible that these two gentlemen obtained their information from the *China's Sports* periodical

12. See *Mountaineering in China*, the chapter called 'The Conquest of Mount Shisha Pangma'; also *High Mountain Peaks in China*, pp. 19–25; and *Alpine Journal*, November 1964, 'The Ascent of Shisha Pangma' by Chou Cheng, pp. 211–16

13. See *A Photographic Record of the Mt Shisha Pangma Scientific Expedition*

14. See *China's Sports*, 1964, No. 4, p. 12

15. See *Bergsteiger*, 1973, pp. 54–5

16. See Ward, pp. 214 and 218

17. See Abelein

IV
Chronology of Climbing Around Shishapangma

Acknowledgement has to be made to Anders Bolinder for unstinted assistance in the compiling of these notes. He has made available a considerable amount of material from his own archives and offered suggestions from his vast fund of mountaineering knowledge. Tsunemichi Ikeda has taken time away from editing *Iwa-to-Yuki* to supply me with information and corrections with regard to Japanese mountaineering activity. John Cleare has shed a good deal of light on the Jugal Himal, having himself made extensive surveys of the region.

Yet I cannot claim these lists are complete, for there are many ascents of the smaller peaks that have gone unrecorded. Also, I have not been able to check all ascents listed where contact with the climbers was not possible.

To avoid more confusion on heights and names of peaks, I have taken both mainly from those used on *Mountaineering Maps of the World* (Japan, 1977) Langtang–Ganesh Himal Sheet, which is a synthesis of previous maps. The long-awaited 'Schneider' Map to this area will be welcomed by mountaineers when it is completed. Until this map appears all heights should be considered provisional. The discerning reader will see from these lists which peaks have yet to be climbed.

Abbreviations:

AAJ	—	American Alpine Journal
AJ	—	Alpine Journal
GJ	—	Geographical Journal
HJ	—	Himalayan Journal
ITY	—	Iwa-to-Yuki
MW	—	Mountain World
NZZ	—	Neue Zürcher Zeitung (Swiss newspaper)

Gur Karpo Ri | Pemthang Karpo Ri (Dôme Blanc) | Goldun | Langtang Ri | Hagen's Col | Porong Ri

Panoramic view from Madiya Peak
K. Ishihara

Chronological List of Mountaineering Attempts on Shishapangma and the Area to the North-West (Phuriphu Himal), South-West (Langtang Himal), and South (Jugal Himal)*

1921

Shishapangma (8,012 m/26,291 ft)

Reconnaissance from the north–north-east (Lungchen La, *c*.17,700 ft) about thirty miles away, by Major H. T. Moorshead and his

* Peter Aufschnaiter recommended that the area be designated Jugal Himal and Langtang Himal (after Langtang Village) for the rest of these mountains. This would overcome the complication of names for 'Phuriphu' that have appeared in Chinese publications e.g. 'Pekhu' Himal, 'Peikukangri Mountain Range' and more recently 'Pinyin Himal'. Aufschnaiter first wrote Langtrang on his maps but later changed this to Langtang after checking local dialects.

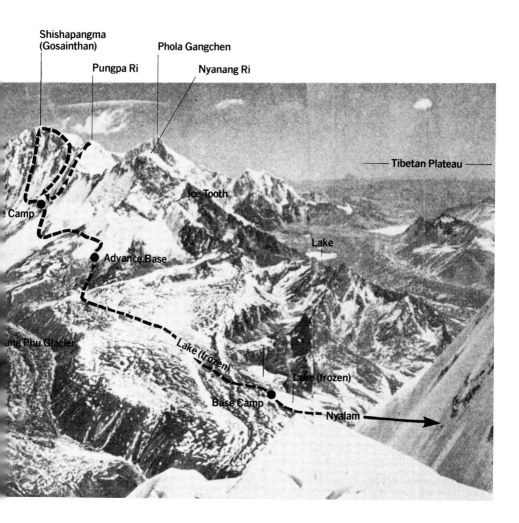

Shishapangma
(Gosainthan)

Pungpa Ri

Phola Gangchen

Nyanang Ri

Tibetan Plateau

Ice Tooth

Camp

Lake

Advance Base

...ang Phu Glacier

Lake (frozen)

Lake (frozen)

Base Camp

Nyalam

survey team during the 1921 Everest Reconnaissance Expedition.
He also sighted Shishapangma from the east with A. F. R.
Wollaston.

Ref: *Mount Everest the Reconnaissance* (Arnold, 1922), p. 322
   A. F. R. Wollaston Letters and Diaries (Cambridge, 1933), p. 229

1945
Phuriphu Himal – Langtang Himal
Reconnaissance from the east and north-east (Kyirong) by P.
Aufschnaiter and H. Harrer during their escape from India to
Lhasa.

Shishapangma
Reconnaissance from the north-west (Charkyu Pass, c.16,000 ft)
Ref: *HJ*, 1947, pp. 116–20
   Seven Years in Tibet: Heinrich Harrer (Hart-Davis, 1953)

277

1949

Langtang

First mountaineering expedition – British. Leader H. W. Tilman with P. Lloyd, O. Polunin (botanist), J. S. Scott (geologist) and four Sherpas. They surveyed the Langtang Glacier during which they reached the col on the main divide at 5,670 metres – Tilman's Col. The survey and the climbing was limited by the monsoon but they found that the origin of the Langtang Valley and Glacier was much further north than was indicated on the Survey of India map. They failed to locate Shishapangma because of the monsoon cloud.

Langtang Lirung (7,246 m)

An attempt made from the north failed to locate a route.

Ganchempo (6,387 m) **(Fluted Peak)**

Attempt via West Ridge abandoned at *c.* 5,900 metres

Ref: Nepal Himalaya: H. W. Tilman (Cambridge, 1952)
   AJ, May 1950, pp. 305–12
   GJ, December 1950, pp. 172–82

1950

Shishapangma (8,012 m)

Reconnaissance from the east by Aufschnaiter (from Kong Tso Lake) about six miles distant. He published an invaluable sketch map of the whole area in 1954.

Ref: Les Alpes, 1959, pp. 194–9

1952

Langtang – Hagen's Col (*c.* 20,000 ft)

Toni Hagen visited the Langtang Glacier during the autumn and the col at *c.*20,000 ft on the frontier overlooking the Nyanang Phu Glacier and the South-West Face of Shishapangma, four miles away. He published the first topographical sketch map of the area the following year.

Ref: NZZ No. 583, 14.3.53 with sketch map
   Les Alpes, Nos. 5, 6, 7 and 11, 1956, pp. 165–6 and *Les Alpes,*
      1959, pp. 194–9: photographs of Shishapangma
   To the Third Pole: G. O. Dyhrenfurth (Werner Laurie, 1955)
      pp. 156–8: Ref. photograph of Shishapangma, Plate 26

1955

Jugal Himal – Gyalzen Peak (6,151 m)

First Ascent: British. Route: south side from Phurbi Chyachu Glacier, 11 May. The first expedition to the Jugal Himal and the first to climb a peak in either the Langtang or the Jugal; this was the

first all-women's Himalayan Expedition: Monica Jackson and Elizabeth Stark (reached the summit with two Sherpas, Mingma Gyalzen – whom the peak was named after – and Ang Temba); Evelyn Camrass, the third member and doctor, supported the ascent up to the last camp (V).
Ref: AJ, May 1956, pp. 60–62 (Monica Jackson)
HJ, 1955–6, pp. 75–81 (Elizabeth Stark)
Tents in the Clouds: Monica Jackson (Collins, 1956)

Langtang Himal – Langtang Ri (7,239 m)
Attempt and reconnaissance by the Swiss Raymond Lambert (leader) and Belgian Jules Détry. Gave up because of dangerous ice cliffs and cornices.

Pemthang Karpo Ri (Dôme Blanc) (6,830 m)
First Ascent: After gaining the South-East Ridge from the south, Lambert, Ang Norbu, Pasang and Kami Tsering climbed the ridge to the summit on 13 May.
Ref: Chronique Himalayenne – Supplément, 1963, pp. 454–9 by Marcel Kurz

1957
Jugal Himal – Lenpo Gang (7,083 m) **(Big White Peak)**
Attempt from the south (Phurbi Chyachu Glacier) by a British party from the Yorkshire Ramblers' Club – including Capt Crosby-Fox (leader), George Spenceley (dep. leader), Don Jones (doctor), Arthur Tallon, Maurice Wilson and W. J. Anderson. The leader and two Sherpas were killed when avalanched near their Camp IV at 5,650 metres on 30 April. One week later the doctor dislocated his shoulder and Lakpa Tsering broke his leg near Camp I. Surveying work was carried out.
Ref: AJ, May 1958, p. 131, also pp. 105–6
Mountain Craft, 1958, No. 38, pp. 2–7
Yorkshire Ramblers' Club Journal VIII, No. 29, 1958, pp. 211–331

1958
Jugal Himal – Lenpo Gang (7,083 m) **(Big White Peak)**
Reconnaissance of the south and south-east side by Japanese Kyuya Fukata, Takehide Kazami, Yuichiro Yamakawa and Kazuyoshi Kohara. This expedition discovered the existence of Aufschnaiter's map and brought it back to Japan.
Ref: Editor, *ITY*

1959
Langtang Himal – Langtang Lirung (7,246 m)
This, the highest peak of the Langtang Himal, has gone under several different names, notably Gangchen Lebrub (local name), Dayabhang (Survey of India maps) and Luri Himal (Nepal-China Boundary Atlas published in Peking).
Ref: AJ, November 1964, pp. 287–8 – a note by Aufschnaiter on the naming of Langtang and Langtang Lirung
Attempt made by Japanese in the autumn via East Ridge by Iida Alpine Club of Japan
Ref: HJ, 1974/5, p. 48
    AJ, 1979, pp. 232–3

Langtang Himal
Confusion has surrounded the Iida Alpine Club of Japan party's claims to have climbed Shalbachum with a height of 6,700 metres after their Langtang Lirung attempt. G. O. Dyhrenfurth has attempted to clear up this confusion. He points out that their Shalbachum should, according to the ridge lines on the sketches, be identical with Aufschnaiter's Phrul Rangjen Ri (6,918 metres), which it now is on the Japanese map (1977) referred to throughout this chronology. Dyhrenfurth continues his investigation: 'However, in the panorama from Gangja La in *Sangaku* (1960, pp. 94–5) the name Shalbachum is attributed to the foresummit (6,702 metres) of Kyungka Ri (6,979 metres). This contradiction between map and picture was not made any easier by correspondence.'

So it remains uncertain which summit the Japanese climbers Hojo, Terahata and their Sherpas, Dawa Thondup and Pasang Temba reached. Dyhrenfurth suggests it could be the foresummit but he cannot be certain. This discrepancy came to light with the Italian Expedition to the area in 1963 who climbed Kyungka Ri.

Nepal: The Jugal Himal
John Cleare

The Japanese claimed it was a second ascent of their Shalbachum. For further information see references.

Ref: Himalaya Chronik, 1963, 1964, 1965
    Sangaku, ACJJ, vol. 55, 1960, etc.

1960

Everest

Climbed by the Chinese from the north. Leader: Shih Chan-Chun. An important milestone in the climbing of the Himalaya from the north.

Jugal Himal – Lenpo Gang (7,083 m) (Big White Peak)

Attempt by Japanese abandoned at 6,800 metres (Camp V).

Jugal Himal – Madiya Peak (6,800 m) (named by Japanese; it means 'Central').

First Ascent: Twenty-nine days after arriving at Base Camp and establishing five camps, Kunitoshi Ishihara, Yuki-hiko Kato and the Sherpas, Pasang Phutal and Chotare reached the summit on 7 May. Ishihara took useful panorama photograph printed in *Sangaku* (1961) showing the south-west side of Shishapangma and the surrounding peaks of the Upper Nyanam Phu Glacier.

Jugal Himal – Gyalzen Peak (6,151 m)

Second Ascent: Via the South-West Ridge from the col between Gyalzen and Madiya Peak. The summit was reached by Kanenori Haruta, Tsuneoh Inagaki and the Sherpa Dawa Thondup.

Ref: Sangaku, JACJ, vol. 56, 1962, pp. 7–8
    Editor, *ITY*

1961

Langtang Himal – Langtang Lirung (7,246 m)

Attempt up the East Ridge by Japanese in the spring met with disaster – two Japanese died, the leader Kaichi Morimoto and Kenji Oshima, with Sherpa Gyaltsen Norbu in an avalanche. Gyaltsen Norbu was the only Sherpa at the time to have climbed two 8,000

Nepal: The Langtang Himal
John Cleare

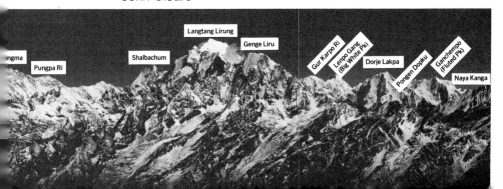

metre peaks – Makalu and Manaslu. The attempt was abandoned at 6,500 metres on the East Ridge.
Ref: HJ, 1961, p. 192
AJ, 1979, pp. 232–3
Sangaku, JACJ, vol. 57, 1963, pp. 13–15

Jugal Himal – Lenpo Gang (7,083 m) **(Big White Peak)**
Attempt by the Japanese, who got to 7,050 metres. The thirteen members were from the All Japan Mountaineering Federation. They then climbed two other peaks:
Gyalzen Peak (6,151 m)
Third Ascent: By the leader, Tokujiro Kajimoto, Hiroaki Bamba with five Sherpas.
Gumasi Peak (6,100 m)
This peak is situated on the ridge between Ladies Peak (6,000 metres) and Phurbi Chyachu (6,658 metres). The name means 'round' in Nepali. Ascent (first?) by Tetsuya Nomura and Takayasu Yamada.
Ref: AJ, November 1961, p. 390
Sangaku, vols. 5, 7, 1963, pp. 15–17
MW, 1964/5, p. 194
Editor, *ITY*

Shishapangma (8,012 m)
Reconnaissance: The first officially acknowledged Chinese reconnaissance took place in the spring, beginning in March. The second reconnaissance was in the autumn from September to October. See text of this book and references given. This peak was now the last 8,000-metre summit unclimbed.

1962
Langtang Himal
A mixed British team visited the area in the spring, led by Lord Glentworth, and including Alfred Gregory and Charles Wylie.
PT (17,750 ft)
First Ascent: Peak west of Shalbachum (Phrul Rangjen) Glacier, on the ridge descending the Yansa Tsenjl (Dragpochhe Ri) (6,543 m)
Tsergo Ri (4,850 m) (North of Jatang)
Climbed by the women members of the expedition and Sherpa Sirdar.
Langshisha Ri (6,300 m)
A circuit was made around this peak.
Col (19,250 ft) was reached near the head of the Langtang Glacier, and on the frontier ridge where they had good views of Shishapangma.

Goldum (6,447 m) (Japanese give 6,947 m)
Attempted by its north ridge to 6,100 m; bad snow conditions prevented further progress. This peak is only four miles from Shishapangma.
Tilman's Col (5,670 m)
Was reached by the women via the Langtang Glacier.
Ref: AJ, November 1963, p. 291
Mountaineering (BMC Journal), September 1962, pp. 9–10

Jugal Himal – Lenpo Gang (7,083 m) **(Big White Peak)**
First Ascent: Sieged by the Japanese from Phurbi Chachu Glacier, across the South Ridge of Madiya Peak to the upper Dorje Lakpa Glacier Basin, on to and up the East-North-East Ridge of Lenpo Gang to its summit on 3 May. 1st Team: Tadashi Morita and Kazunari Yasuhisa; 2nd: Makoto Takashima and Yukihiko Katoh; 3rd: Dr Ishida and Mitsuru Nakano, Masahito Akiyama, both on 5 May. The leader was Akira Takahashi. The route was long and difficult, involving aid climbing near the summit. This was the third time the Japanese had been to this peak.
Ref: HJ, 1964, pp. 43–50, article and photograph of Shishapangma South-West Face
  AAJ, 1963, p. 520
  Sangaku, 1963, pp. 7–9

1963
Shishapangma (8,012 m)
Third Reconnaissance: By Chinese and reported to have reached 7,160 metres via the Yabukangala Glacier on the north side.
Ref: See text of this book and references

Langtang Himal – Langtang II Chenge Liru (6,571 m)
First Ascent: By Canadian Peter Taylor and Pasang Phutar III (Sirdar). Pasang Sherpa went to the top later the same day – 28 May. The ascent from the east had been completed during a total of nineteen days' return journey from Kathmandu. The peak is on the ridge west of Langtang Lirung and above the village of Syabrubensi.
Ref: HJ, 1964, pp. 69–76
  From Cooper's Creek to Langtang II: Peter Taylor
  (Messrs Rigby Ltd, Adelaide)

Langtang Himal – Langtang Lirung (7,246 m)
Attempt by Italians from Turin Section of CAI during post-monsoon. Whilst attempting the East Ridge from the Lirung Glacier, Giorgio Rossi and C. Volante fell at 6,000 metres, prob-

ably because of rockfall. Rossi died immediately and Volante died a few days later at Base Camp.

Langtang Himal – Città di Torino (6,702 m)
First or Second Ascents? Corradino Robbi and Andrea Mellano reached the top of this foresummit of Kyungka Ri (6,979 metres) on 28 October and then went to the main summit without doubt. The Japanese argue that they were not the first up Kyungka Ri.
Ref: *La Scarpone,* 16.10.1963, 16.11.1963, 16.12.1963
  Sangaku, 1960, 1961, 1962, 1965
  Himalaya Chronik, 1963, 1964, 1965

1964
Shishapangma (8,012 m)
First Ascent: Chinese. See text of this book and references below for this first ascent of Shishapangma via the north side.
Ref: *China's Sports,* 1964, No. 4
  High Mountain Peaks in China, pp. 19–25
  Mountaineering in China (China Publications Centre) Chapter on the 'Conquest of Mount Shisha Pangma'
  A Photographic Record of the Shisha Pangma Scientific Expedition (Scientific Press, Peking, 1966)
  AJ, 1964, pp. 211–16
  Bergsteiger, January 1973, pp. 54–5 – Article by Eduard Sternbach *Is Shishapangma climbed?*

Langtang Himal – Langtang Lirung (7,246 m)
Attempt by Japanese from Osaka City University via the East Ridge failed at 18,850 ft, as it was too steep. They did climb two other peaks:
  Urkinmang (6,151 m) **(Buddha Peak)**
  First Ascent: 'Which is located at the south part of the Langtang Glacier (Tunga Glacier), Kiyohara, Ban, Jokei and a Sherpa climbed to the summit on 5 May from South Face.'
  Kyungka Ri (6,979 m)
  Second Ascent: 'Kondo, Sasaki and a Sherpa reached the summit on 8 May from the Eastern Glacier.' They claim a first ascent but Italians had been there in 1963 without doubt.
Ref: *AJ,* 1965, p. 464

Langtang Himal – Langtang Lirung (7,246 m)
Attempt in the autumn by Peter Taylor and party, but after climbing up to *c.*6,700 metres from the west, they gave up through difficulties and lack of experience of the Sherpas and with bad weather approaching.
Ref: *AJ,* 1979, p. 233
  AAJ, 1965, p. 465

284

Langtang Himal – Pemthang Karpo Ri (6,830 m) **(Dôme Blanc)**
Second Ascent: The Japanese Hiroaki Tamura reached the summit via the SW slopes, leaving his two Sherpas, Jangbu and Pemba, at the foot of the final ridge on 22 October

Jugal Himal – Dorje Lakpa (6,989 m)
An attempt by an Anglo-Swiss party, consisting of Anthony, Lord Shaftesbury and Swiss Guides Arci Giroud, Michel Darbellay and Michel Rey. They went up the Trupaiku Glacier and along the West Ridge to *c.*6,100 metres and gave up through heavy snowfall and shortage of time.
Ref: AAJ, pp. 464–5, also for:
  Langtang Himal – Ganchempo (6,387 m) **(Fluted Peak)**
  Attempted by Darbellay and Rey, who were stopped by snow-falls *c.*200 metres from the summit.

1965
Langtang Himal – Dôme Blanc (6,830 m)
Attempted by two Japanese – Ikuo Saeki and Tokumi Yamaguchi – who retreated from high point of 6,000 metres.
Ref: AAJ, 1966, p. 191

1966
Langtang Himal
Royal Nepalese Botanical Survey Team visited Langtang Valley with Mr and Mrs A. D. Schilling and David Sayers.
Ref: See *Journal of Royal Horticultural Society*, May 1969, Part 5, pp. 222–32

There was a ban put upon mountaineering in Nepal by the Government during the latter half of the 1960s.

1970
Langtang Himal – Yala Peak (5,400 m) (exact position unknown)
Ascent during October by a party of seventeen clients guided by Anderl Ernst and organized by Sporthaus Schuster.
Ref: AAJ, 1971, p. 438

1971
Langtang Himal – Langtang Lirung (7,246 m)
Ascent – unconfirmed and unofficial – by solo American climber.

Langtang Himal – Ganchempo (Fluted Peak) (6,387 m)
Attempted by American-Swiss party under the leadership of D. Taylor.

Unconfirmed reports of husband and wife team climbing this peak in 1971.
Ref: HJ, 1971, p. 362

Langtang Himal – Langtang Ri (7,239 m)
Attempt abandoned at *c*.6,000 metres due to faulty kerosene stoves on the South-East Ridge.
Ref: Sangaku, JACJ, vol. 67, 1972, pp. 18–19

Langtang Himal – Urkinmang (6,151 m) Buddha Peak (Baudha Peak)
Various unofficial ascents claimed by a US/Rhodesian/New Zealand party and another by a Swiss party.

1972
Langtang Himal – Urkinmang (6,151 m) (Buddha Peak)
Second Ascent: South Africans – mentioned in *AAJ,* 1975, p. 201

1973
Langtang Himal – Langshisha Ri (6,300 m)
Japanese reconnaissance, during which three died on the Langtang Glacier when struck by avalanche.
Ref: HJ, 1980–81, p. 48
    Editor, *ITY*

1974
Langtang Himal – Urkinmang (6,151 m)
Ascent: Americans Judy Rearick, Larry Derby and Matthew Wells, climbing the West Ridge and using fixed ropes on a 600-ft rock band at 18,000 ft.
Ref: AAJ, 1975, p. 201

1975
Jugal Himal
Mario Fantin of the CAI reports in the *AAJ,* 1976, p. 518, that 'Carla Maverna and Irene Affentranger climbed Jugal Himal in October'. There is no peak called Jugal Himal, only the range of which the Nepalese Government did not allow climbing at that time.

1976
Jugal Himal – Nyakanga (5,846 m)
Unofficial ascent of this peak on Nepalese Trekking list. Many small peaks are often climbed unofficially and no first ascent claims can be entirely reliable.

1978
Langtang Himal – Langtang Lirung (7,246 m)
First Ascent: Joint Nepalese/Japanese – nine-man Osaka City University and four-man Nepalese Tribbuvan University. The route was up the East Ridge from the Lirung Glacier (the same route as attempted by Japanese in 1961 and 1964). The summit was reached on 24 October by Seishi Wada and Pemba Tsering.
Ref: AAJ, 1979, p. 269
ITY, No. 67, p. 145

Chinese to Allow Foreigners to Climb on Everest
For the first time since the Communist Government took control, foreign climbers were invited to climb in China. An announcement was made in the New China News Agency permitting a joint Chinese/Iranian expedition to the North Side of Everest during 1978 or 1979. Fifteen Iranian and twenty Chinese climbers carried out a reconnaissance up to 24,600 ft (21 May) on the North Ridge of Everest in 1978. Although the main expedition planned for 1979 was cancelled because of the revolution in Iran, other expeditions were invited into China.

1979
Shishapangma (8,012 m)
Reconnaissance to Base Camp on the north side by the Germans Manfred Abelein, Fritz Zintl and Günther Sturm, to prepare for their expedition in 1980.

1980
Shishapangma (8,012 m)
Second Ascent: Via Chinese route up northern side by the German Alpine Club's Mountain and Ski School. Leaders – Dr Manfred Abelein and Günther Sturm with Manfred Sturm, Fritz Zintl, Michel Dacher, Otto Wiedemann, Sigi Hupfauer, Dr Wolfgang Schaffert and Erich Reismüller. On 7 May, Dacher, Schaffert, G. Sturm and Zintl reached the summit followed by Hupfauer and M. Sturm on 12 May.
   North Face:
   Attempt by Dacher, G. Sturm and Zintl, but ran into heavy snow and out of time at 24,600 ft on this difficult Face.
   PT (7,150 m):
   Ascent made of a peak (7,150 metres) west of Shishapangma and descent on skis down its north slope on 16 May
Ref: AAJ, 1981, pp. 307–9
   Shishapangma: Manfred Abelein (Lübbe, 1981)

Shishapangma (8,012 m)
Third Ascent: Via Chinese route to about 7,000 metres, then further east than previously to the North-East (Summit) Ridge. The expedition came from Austria (Naturfreunde), led by Dr Paul Alf with Thaddäus Dowbenka, Roman Findl, Egon Obojes, Karl Ölmüller, Kurt Pokos and Ewald Putz. Putz and Obojes reached the summit on 13 October. Further attempts were called off due to the accident of the leader, Alf.
Ref: Der Naturfreund, Vienna, Heft 2, 1981
    AAJ, 1981, p. 309

Jugal Himal – Dorje Lakpa (6,989 m)
First Ascent: Unofficial but confirmed to have taken place in the spring via the West Ridge 'which was not too difficult'. Old fixed ropes were found on the ridge.

Jugal Himal – Kanshurm (6,078 m)
First Ascent: Via East Ridge from Tilman's Pass West of Dorje Lakpa. Unofficial but confirmed.

Langtang Himal – Langtang Lirung (7,246 m)
Attempt on unclimbed 12,000 ft South Face by Michael Searle (Organizer), Mike Stead, Nick Groves, John Marjot, Dr Neil Harding-Roberts, Rod Mackenzie (all British), Shana Parent (Canadian) and Sarki Tsering (Sherpa). The attempt was abandoned more than 3,000 ft from the top on 3 May after climbing a steep rock buttress.
Ref: HJ, 1980–81, pp. 40–48
    AAJ, 1981, p. 257

Langtang Himal – Langtang Lirung (7,246 m)
Second Ascent: First via South-East Ridge, by the six-man free-style Climbing Club party from Tokyo, all reached the summit on 26 October: Iwao Ohtsuka (leader), Tokuo Watanabe, Yutaka Nagai, Shigeki Hirosawa, Gen'ichi Tate, Yasuji Horie.
Ref: ITY, No. 81, p. 171

1981
Shishapangma (8,012 m)
Fourth Ascent: And via Chinese Route by Women's Climbing Club of Japan. The members were Junko Tabei, the leader (Everest Summiter) Setsuko Kitamura, Yoko Mihara, Yoshiko Kato, Keiko Tsurube, Yumiko Kurosawa, Yuko Kuramatsu, Etsuko Otsuki and Noriko Watanabe. Junko Tabei 'with two Chinese assistants' reached the summit on 30 April.
Ref: AAJ, 1982, p. 287
    ITY, No. 88, pp. 181–2

Shishapangma (8,012 m)
Fifth Ascent: And via the Chinese Route by the South-Tyroleans – Reinhold Messner (leader) and Friedl Mutschlechner who reached the summit on 28 May. Other members were the Germans, Dr Oswald Ölz and Gerd Baur. This expedition may have first attempted the difficult North Face, but no further details forthcoming.
Ref: AAJ, 1982, p. 287

Shishapangma (8,012 m)
Attempt on the original route by Americans was defeated by a combination of heavy snowfall and enormous avalanches in September and high winds in October.
Ref: AAJ, 1982, pp. 287–8

Shishapangma (8,012 m)
An attempt on the original route by some of the American Everest Kangshung Face Expedition was defeated by strong winds and a retreat was made from the high point at 23,400 ft on 2 November. Team members were Geoffrey C. Tabin, George Lowe, Lou Reichardt, Eric Perlman and James Morrissey.

Shishapangma Group – Molamenqing (Phola Gangchen) (7,703 m)
First Ascent: And 'via the Yambukangola Glacier to the east of Shishapangma across the Face of Shishapangma between the North Face and the North Peak, across snow fields to the west of Shishapangma to Molamenqing'.

The following members of this New Zealand Expedition reached the summit: Bruce Farmer, Dick Price (14 May), Warwick Anderson, Ron McLeod (16 May), Geoff Gabites, Bruce Clark, Paul Chapman and Tony Charlton (20 May). Also in the team were Mal Lapwood and Ben Noble. The route was non-technical, but logistics were stretched and all load carrying was done by the team.
Ref: AAJ, 1982, p. 288
   To the Untouched Mountain: Warwick Anderson (Reed Ltd, NZ, 1983)

Jugal Himal – Dorje Lakpa (6,989 m)
Second Ascent (First Official): Via the West Ridge. The members of this joint Nepalese/Japanese Expedition were Pemba Tsering, Kazumari Murakami, Eiichi Shingyoji, Kunioh Kataoka and Makoto Anbe, who reached the summit on 18 October. The other member, Tomohiro Uchimura, being tired, stopped a hundred metres short of the top.
Ref: AAJ, 1982, p. 221
      ITY, No. 88, p. 188

289

Langtang Himal – Langshisha Ri (6,300 m)
Attempt via South Ridge of this virgin peak. This joint Nepalese/
Japanese Expedition was led by Isao Yamazaki. Two members
reached 19,300 ft on 9 October, but gave up as the ridge was too
difficult for them.
Ref. AAJ, 1982, p. 221

Langtang Himal – Langtang Lirung (7,246 m)
Third Ascent: Second via South-East Ridge.
This expedition from the Gumma Workers' Alpine Federation of
Japan consisted of Hajime Abe and Sirdar Ang Phuri Lama, who
reached the top on 26 April, and Yasutoshi Kimura, Haroda
Tomokai and Mikio Arai who reached the summit 28 April.
Ref. AAJ, 1982, pp. 221–2
ITY, No. 88, p. 188

Langtang Himal – Langtang Ri (7,239 m)
First Ascent: And via South Ridge by joint Nepalese/Japanese
Expedition led by Hideyuki Uematsu. The following reached the
summit: Noboru Yamada, Makihiro Wakao, Soichi Nasu, Ang
Rinji Sherpa on 10 October; Minoru Iizawa and Isashi Nakaoto on
11 October.
Ref: AAJ, 1982, p. 223
ITY, No. 88, p. 188

1982
Shishapangma (8,012 m)
Sixth Ascent: First Ascent via South-West Face and First Ascent
Overall by Alpine style. British climbers Roger Baxter-Jones, Alex
MacIntyre and Doug Scott climbed the Face from the Nyanang Phu
Glacier in three days to the summit on 28 May. Descent was down
the South-East Ridge to *c.*24,000 ft, then down the South-West
Face (half-mile south-east of ascent route) to a camp by the glacier
on 29 May, where a fourth member, Nick Prescott was waiting in
support. The other members of the team, Elaine Brook and Paul
Braithwaite had departed for home.
  Shishapangma Group – Pungpa Ri★ (7,445 m)
First Ascent: Via South-West Couloir and South-West Ridge by
Alpine style. Baxter-Jones, MacIntyre and Scott climbed this
peak, really the South-West Shoulder of Shishapangma, after
two bivouacs, arriving at the summit on 19 May and descending
the same day by route of ascent.
Ref: Text of this book.

★ This name appears on Aufschnaiter's original sketch map but not the one
subsequently published. We are grateful to Anders Bolinder for making the
original available.

Shishapangma Group – Porong Ri (7,284 m)
First Ascent: Via North Ridge by fourteen-man Japanese party. Tohru Itoh led the expedition of whom Minoru, Wada and Yukioh Etoh reached the summit on 17 May. 'Wada fell in the descent and has been missing.'
Ref: ITY, No. 90, p. 98

Phuriphu Himal – Gang Ben Chen (7,281 m)
First Ascents: By thirteen-man Kyoto University party from Japan. Climbed up the North Face to the top on 21 April by eight members, two other members reached top on 22 April.
Ref: ITY, No. 90, p. 98
  Sangaku, December 1983, pp. 9–10

Shishapangma (8,012 m)
Seventh Ascent: Via Chinese Route. Seven-man expedition led by Makoto Hara, MD, climbed the peak in Alpine style. M. Tomita started from ABC at 5,700 metres at three pm on 10 October and reached the summit at 5.40 pm on the 12th; M. Ohmiya and T. Chiba started from ABC on the 9th and reached the summit at the same time as Tomita. Leader Hara, H. Komamiya and H. Konishi started from ABC on the 7th and reached the summit on the 10th. This is claimed as the second Japanese ascent by Alpine style to an 8,000-metre peak but there had been several attempts: '. . . members randomly rushed on the moderate snow slopes. The summit bids failed three times at 7,400 metres, 7,600 metres, and 7,700 metres, in early October'. No further details are available regarding camps and supplies left on the mountain by these earlier attempts, but clearly acclimatization opened the way for rapid climbing.
Ref: ITY, No. 93, p. 111

V
Expedition Medicine –
A Personal View

Ch'i Po said: 'The utmost in the art of healing can be achieved when there is unity.'
The Emperor enquired: 'What is meant by unity?'
Ch'i Po answered: 'When the minds of the people are closed and wisdom is locked out they remain tied to disease. Yet their feelings and desires should be investigated and made known, their wishes and ideas should be followed; and then it becomes apparent that those who have attained spirit and energy are flourishing and prosperous, while those perish who lose their spirit and energy.'
The Emperor exlaimed: 'Excellent indeed!'
(From the Yellow Emperor's Classic of Internal Medicine)

It is said that the doctors in ancient China were paid to keep their patients healthy. If they became ill payments were suspended, and if the illness became serious the doctor had to pay out for expenses. Prevention, obviously better than cure, was achieved by a holistic approach, for it was known intuitively that man is more than the sum of his parts. They endeavoured to bring order and balance into all facets of their patients' lives so that the Chi energy – the breath of life – could pass through them without interruption. This life force and its power often becomes apparent, spontaneously, during or after severe illness, after emotional trauma, when letting go of attachments, when falling in love, or when a break has been made in habitual routines which may occur through great physical exertion and facing one's fears – as on a demanding mountaineering expedition. It is made manifest through conscious efforts to work on oneself by following any of the many paths mapped out by esoteric doctrines and oral traditions. Anyone who has received traditional Chinese acupuncture will be aware of the vital energy once it has been allowed to run its course through the body.

The Tao, or the way to nurture this life force, is easier for those who live close to nature since they can more easily steer a middle course, avoiding both deprivation and excesses of sensory perception, and can strike a balance between the 'normal' conscious self and the inner voices that reveal themselves in dreams and flashes of intuition. In ancient times the doctor helped his patients to control desire and avoid attachments, all in an effort to let the Chi energy flow. He also paid particular attention to the patient's food, just as in modern times Rudolf Steiner realized that man could more easily make contact again with cosmic energies if the food he ate was grown with the emanations from the cosmos in mind.

On a mountaineering expedition we are isolated for long periods of time and are able to face up to our problems without the usual diversionary constraints of family life and earning a living. Absent are the distractions of TV, spectator sports and the safety valves offered by the pub and weekend crag climbing or participation in other sports and pastimes. It is unlikely there will ever be the perfect mountaineering expedition but each expedition can move in the general direction of understanding and self-awareness at a personal level and can break down the barriers to greater physical achievement.

What follows is a personal view of this two-sided approach to inner and outer freedom on the mountain.

Overwhelming Ambition

Anyone setting off for an 8,000-metre peak is ambitious and, on the face of it, there is nothing wrong in that. Problems only arise if one or more of the team is so attached to the idea of 'success' that negative emotions creep in. To be hooked on the need to impress the rest of the world that you are the hard man of the trip invariably means that petty jealousies, uncontrolled anger, fear, and frustration will prevent a true rapport, to the detriment of the flow of energy (love). Energy goes down the drain and the team down with it. Expedition morale plummets. The attempt is a wash-out, the excuses: weather conditions, snow conditions, illness – anything but the real reason: no love flowing, team going down! Ambition feeds on itself and can never be satisfied. You can only let go of it but it is hard to get off the treadmill.

Going Public

It would take a very advanced team to remain unaffected by the expedition becoming a public event. So often the image we have of ourselves does not match up with the image we feel is being portrayed in the film clips for 'News at Ten', articles going off for serialization in *The Times* or the *Observer*, tape recordings for the expedition book, interviews for the expedition film. With the right team and a bit of common sense it is possible to have your cake and eat it too, providing there is free discussion about these potential pitfalls both during the course of the expedition and afterwards. If

293

we do set off with problems unresolved they will only be magnified at altitude. There are individuals who are hardly affected at all by the commercial side of expeditions but the majority of us find it a problem to some extent.

The root of the trouble lies in our great need to be liked, but in reality the emotion invoked on winning the race or climbing ever steeper Himalayan peaks is not love but jealousy.

Competition

Those of us who see our climbing for what it is – a personal pilgrimage along a path potentially as valid as any other – will act modestly, and even be modest. Which of us can say from our hearts that this need to impress has not been a problem at some time during our climbing careers? It is certainly a fact of life that has to be faced wherever human beings join together and enter the rat race, where the competitors are brought to a standstill in the swamp of institutional boredom and pain as is seen today in all the professions – legal, educational, medical for starters but also at 'grass roots' level – among housing associations, community action groups and wherever hierarchies develop amongst people who join together. So why should we who climb expect it to be different for us?

Age-old Problem

There is another age-old problem, a continuing trend down the years whereby generation after generation of climbers, seven years apart, have snapped and snarled at each other: the younger ones at those who are in the way and those of the older generation at the young energy close on their heels. The 'old farts' should know better, relishing the breath of fresh air, and the younger element must realize that once they have replaced (become) the old guard they can expect the same from the next generation following them. There was one 90-year-old climber still greatly troubled by events which had taken place 50 years before in the Alps – muttering dark thoughts about his rope-mates of the 1930s, and he is not alone in this. Clearly, these problems do not always go away with time, nor is old age a guarantee of equanimity. At such moments it is wise to recall the early days when a healthy spirit of spontaneous curiosity first tempted us to step out into the hills. All of us must have memories of exhilaration and discovery in good company which nothing can tarnish, and which give us the strength to check the rot more effectively, otherwise the whole rotten show will stay on the road for ever or at least make it difficult to attain that spirit and energy needed to enjoy our climbing and everything else to boot.

Mixed Expeditions

Women, by nature or nurture, tend to be less aggressive and ambitious than one's fellow climbers, seem to be intuitively more in touch with their environment and sensitive to emotions. They can help. Recognize the spiritual qualities of a woman and she will help you develop the other side of your nature, but don't become blinded by her beauty – claws of attachment strangle the flow of vital energy. Instead of softening the atmosphere of an expedition, attachments will only arouse negative emotions. Mixed expeditions can be quite interesting.

Homesickness

Overcoming homesickness is to overcome a kind of illness in which feelings of insecurity linger on from childhood pulling us back to the nest for the love and affection that cannot be found out of it. With too many problems left unresolved at home homesickness may be impossible to cure. Is anyone entirely immune from this limiting factor, when even the spirit of the hills may be temporarily dead to the beholder? There are various ways to overcome the depression that results from homesickness – or rather the general insecurity of which homesickness is but a symptom. The usual ways are to hide from it by overwhelming it with ambition, by reaching out for material security, take to alcohol, become a workaholic, sleep around, smoke, eat, escape into books, become a heavy leader, follow some Freudian father figure, take up a 'cause', become 'religious', etc. Some four or five weeks into a well-matched expedition, pangs of homesickness usually subside as the team settle down to share in the common objective and become aware that we are 'but river arks on the ocean brine' until such time as we can feel genuine love for each other.

When this particular sickness has passed the real difficulties of leaving family and friends for two to three months can be faced positively by realizing that it was in their love that they made sacrifices to manage without the breadwinner, father and lover, so that he might do as he had to do. We must do it without useless self-pity and worry, accepting the penalty that they will move on for a time without us. How stupid it is that climbers wish to be away climbing when in the comfort of home, and to be home when uncomfortable on the mountain. To enjoy the mountains fully we must join our bodies in being there. If my thoughts are for ever wandering off out of control it is as if I am blinkered. But we do have the advantage in the mountains that the unexpected continues to shake us out of our routines.

295

Food

Cicero thought that we 'should eat to live, not live to eat' which is a point of view appropriate to expeditions and particularly on expeditions to China in the spring, when fresh foodstuffs are difficult to come by locally and freight charges make the carriage of all foodstuffs a very expensive item. Unfortunately, food assumes an unusual importance on expeditions, owing to the physical effort requiring sustenance which is interspersed by quite long periods of inactivity acclimatizing, weathering storms or resting between climbs, when there is little else to divert attention.

Whilst it is right to take into account the real and imagined terror of there not being the appropriate food for each team member, it might be worthwhile pointing out the advantages of a vegetarian diet. I do not wish to press the issue too far, knowing that amongst meat eaters vegetarian food is the butt of every upset stomach going. The Masai in Africa and the Eskimo of Baffin Island subsist on a diet almost exclusively of meat and have done so for generations. Clearly, however, one man's meat is another man's poison, for there are people who are extremely sensitive to the food they eat. I myself witnessed an arthritis sufferer, who had been confined to her wheelchair, but six months after a radical change of diet was walking normally and full of zest for living. This suggests to me the importance of the food we eat. Since turning to a diet largely free of additives – vegetarian except for occasional fish – I have found that aches and pains from broken and dislocated limbs and fingers no longer ache and are not as stiff as when I was sustained on a 'normal' diet. Whilst this was my motive for a change of diet, I have noticed that at an age (41) when I might have expected my energy levels to drop the opposite is the case. In fact the Latin origin of vegetarian, vegetus, means active and vigorous. Vegetarians claim that the diet helps them sleep more soundly and think more clearly, and I certainly find insomnia is not a problem. Each year since 1978, when I turned to this diet, I find myself more easily adapting to high-altitude climbing. This is a very subjective assessment of complex physiological changes, in which other factors may be involved such as the residual acclimatization from going high twice a year and knowing more about the problems of being high. Hindu pilgrims have recognized that a meatless diet helps them to reduce the effects of 'mountain sickness' whilst travelling over the high passes of the Himalaya. Buddhists and Hindus do not eat meat as they believe that to eat animal flesh will enhance instinctual and animal-like behaviour to the detriment of their spiritual goals. (The boxing profession realize the value of meat not only in building up large muscles but also in making the boxer more aggressive.)

Whether or not meat is taken, chewing garlic is supposed to help acclimatization, as is smoking tobacco! In Tibet garlic was given to animals affected by 'pass poison', according to Rockhill (*Land of the Lamas*). The Sherpas of Nepal favour garlic and chillis for this and other ailments, such as the common cold. Western medicine recognizes that garlic helps strengthen the elasticity of the blood vessels which could presumably be an advantage in acclimatizing to the lack of oxygen. There are many vegetables and herbs that may assist in the acclimatization and general health of an expedition working at great altitudes. The application of homoeopathic medicine for the prevention and cure of ailments merits attention – but not here, as I do not know enough about it yet.

Acclimatization

If, despite applying the suggestions outlined above, expedition members do lose vital energy and succumb to illness, then Dr Peter Steel's handbook on expedition medicine should be consulted. This covers ailments of the digestive and circulatory systems that expeditions may suffer from on the approach march and those of the respiratory system that may arise on the mountain; it is also useful for general first aid. Peter Hackett's book, *Mountain Sickness*, published by the American Alpine Club, is an excellent up-to-date account of the prevention, recognition and treatment of mountain sickness. Further information is to be gleaned from the appendices of the many expedition books produced each year. The main problem of course is acclimatization. There is no substitute for a very slow build-up to enable the body to adapt itself to the lack of oxygen. This is absolutely essential for Alpine-style ascents. To climb on any of the 8,000-metre peaks means we have to be fit and acclimatized from having climbed on lesser peaks first. It is during this period that not only physiological adjustments take place but also psychological factors are put to the test. It is not just a 'Sherpa physiology' we have to work towards but also a 'Sherpa psychology' to survive at great altitudes. They are content to lead uncluttered lives doing a few things well rather than a lot badly. They are economical not only in their actions but also in their thoughts and speech. They usually appear emotionally tranquil, thoughtful and full of grace and good humour.

To some it may seem like a luxury to await the time when all the team experience deep within themselves that intuitive feeling that the time is 'now' to go for it. It is a matter of life and death that we do not go before this moment has arrived. The moment there is

297

unity on which line to take and how this should be followed, when there is agreement that the weather and conditions on the mountain are reasonable, that acclimatization has been achieved and the team members are in complete harmony with each other – then and only then should they commit themselves to the mountain.

(most of this chapter was reproduced in *The Doctor* magazine, Autumn, 1982)

References
Traditional Aquapuncture: The Law of the Five Elements   Dianne M.Connelly
Tao: The Watercourse Way   Alan Watts
Buddhism   Alexandra David-Neel
The writings of Carlos Castenada , Richard Bach, Rudolf Steiner, G.I.Gurdjieff and others

A Note on Mapping

by Nick Prescott

My Climbers Sketch Map of the Shishapangma area sets out some basic information for climbers wanting to go to the upper Nyanang Valley. The adjacent areas were added to relate the map to the adjoining valleys. The heights were produced by Doug after an extensive review of all the data available – maps, notes on mapping and details of climbs made. These showed that a large number of discrepancies existed and where possible these have been reviewed and resolved. Various people were consulted on this – Tsunemichi Ikeda, Anders Bolinder and John Cleare in particular. Even as this book goes to press new heights come in, as they have done every few months since we started this book, from Chinese and Japanese sources, for many of the principal mountains of the area.

The Shishapangma area and the upper Langtang Valley include a complex series of high glacier valleys connected by high cols and passes. The general layout of the area was first unravelled by Aufschnaiter in the late 1940s and early 1950s. Aufschnaiter's original sketch map is dated 21.8.56 and he describes his journey in the *Himalayan Journal*, vol. XIV (1947). The maps produced by other climbers and travellers around the same time failed to reflect Aufschnaiter's grasp of the layout of the mountains.

Surprisingly, the region has not yet been well surveyed. Doubt still exists over the heights of the mountains between the Chusmudo Glacier and the Upper Langtang Glacier. When label-

298

ling the peak to the left of Langtang Lirung, shown on the photograph of the Ganesh area, both John Cleare and Anders Bolinder considered it to be Kyungka Ri. However, given the height of Kyungka Ri (6,979 m), it is inconceivable to me that it would stand above its neighbours from this angle. I consider the NW face shown to be one of the spectacular faces sweeping down to the Chusmudo Glacier and hence have labelled the peak as Shalbachum, the highest mountain along this part of the frontier ridge. It is unfortunate that the Chusmudo Glacier is in an 'inaccessible' part of Tibet and thus the question will remain one of academic interest only, for the time being.

One of the greatest difficulties we had was deciding the exact heights of Shishapangma's summits. In the end we opted for the official Chinese figures of 8,012 m, 7,996 m and 7,998 m. The alternatives for the highest summit are 8,046 m from the most recent Survey of India and 8,027 m from the survey by the Japanese OMA Tibetan-Himalayan Expedition of 1982. In relation to the 8,046 m value, Professor Erwin Schneider suggests that Peaks II and III are 8,030 m and 8,032 m respectively.

The technique I used to produce the map involved procuring 1:100,000 scale black and white prints from the NASA Landsat 2 satellite photographs. 'Photographs' is the wrong word for these since the recording and processing techniques produce a genuine flat image – referred to as remote imagery. Using ground photographs taken on the Expedition and my own knowledge of the area from observations during the trip, the various areas of light and shade can be interpreted from these prints and a map built up. In identifying individual peaks, Aufschnaiter's map was my prime reference, although some of the recent Japanese maps of the Himalaya were extremely useful too.

Our most spectacular 'find' in the Nyanang Valley was the previously unnamed peak I have referred to as Eiger Peak. Aufschnaiter suggests a height of 6,912 m. No one else seems to realize it is there! Its spectacular north face bears a remarkable resemblance to the North Face of the Eiger in Europe, complete with its own White Spider. The Eiger Peak north face is over 2,000 m.

Postscript on Aufschnaiter map references:
Aufschnaiter's first article on his journeys through Langtang in 1944–5 (*Himalayan Journal*, vol. XIV, 1947) included no map. The map itself was produced between this time and 1956 and was first published in that year in *Les Alps* (page 162). A later version was published in *Les Alps* in 1959. However, the version we refer to appeared in *Chronique Himalayenne* by Marcel Kurz (Foundation Suisse, Zürich) in 1963.

Bibliography

With additions since 1984 incorporated by Xavier Eguskitza

Manfred Abelein **Shisha Pangma** Gustav Verlag, Munich, 1980
Alpine Journal, May 1950 and November 1964
American Alpine Journal Regular reports since 1981 plus: 1984 "Shisha Pangma – First American Ascent" by Glenn Porzak; 1989 "Shisha Pangma, my 14th 8000er" by Jerzy Kukuczka; 1990 (the Stremfelj/Kozjek ascent on the S.W. Face); 1991 "New Routes, Cho Oyu and Shisha Pangma" by Wojciech Kurtyka.
Jean Ammann and Erhard Loretan **Erhard Loretan: Les 8000 rugissants** La Sarine, Fribourg, 1996 (all 14 Eight-thousanders) – also published in German by Paulusverlag, 1996).
Warwick Anderson **To the Untouched Mountain: The New Zealand Conquest of Molamenqing, Tibet** Reed, Christchurch, 1983 / Alpenbooks, Seattle, 1983
Gregorio Ariz **Montaña Mágica: Veinticinco años de Expediciones Navarras Extraeuropeas** Txoria Errekan, Arraiot, Navarra, 1996
Peter Aufschnaiter **Himalayan Journal**, 1947
Bergsteiger 1973
Kiku Betelu **Buscando las 14 estrellas: Juanito Oiarzabal a la conquista de los ochomiles** Lur Argitaletxea, Bilbao, 1997 (good photographs).
Kiku Betelu **Los 14 Ochomiles de Juanito Oiarzabal** Desnivel, Madrid, 1999
Elsa and Carlos Carsolio **Encuentro con el Himalaya: La aventura de la esperanza** Fernández Cueto, Mexico, 1990 (the 1987 ascent, good photos).
China's Sports, 1964, No. 4
Alexandra David-Neel **Buddhism, its Doctrines and its Methods** Bodley Head, London (reissue), 1977
Desnivel 82 (1993), 116 (1996), 149 (1999) (illustrated articles of notable ascents).
G.O. Dyhrenfurth **To the Third Pole** Werner Laurie, London, 1955
W.Y. Evans-Wentz (ed) **Tibet's Great Yogi Milarepa** Oxford, 1928
Filippo de Filippi (ed) **An Account of Tibet, the Travels of Ippolito Desideri of Pistoia** Routledge, London, 1932 (with introduction by C. Wessels and an extensive bibliography – scholarly and full of interest).
Geographical Journal, December 1950
Lama Anagarika Govinda **The Way of the White Clouds** Rider, London, 1966
Viki Groselj **Stirikrat osem tisoc** Presernova Druzba, Ljubljana, 1991 (deals with Cho Oyu, Lhotse, Everest and Shisha Pangma ascents).
Toni Hagen **Report on the Geological Survey of Nepal** Fretz, Zürich, 1969
Heinrich Harrer **Seven Years in Tibet** Hart-Davis, London, 1953
Hans Hauntner **Unsere Shisha Pangma Expedition** Der Natur Freund, Vienna, 1981
High Mountain Peaks in China People's Sports Publishing House of China (and Tokyo Shimbun Publishing Bureau of Japan), 1981
C.K. Howard-Bury **Mount Everest - The Reconnaissance** Edward Arnold, London, 1922
Iñurrategi Anaiak (brothers) **Gure Himalaya** Kutxa Fundazioa, San Sebastián, 1998 (impressive photographs of 1996 SW Face ascent.)
Antxon Iturriza **Euskal Herria en los Techos del Mundo – Los catorce ochomiles Vascos** Pyrenaica, Bilbao, 1997 (Basque ascents of all 8000m peaks – good photographs).

Hans Kammerlander *Bersüchtig* Piper, Munich and Zürich, 1999
Zbigniev Kowalewski and Andrzej Paczkowski *Himalalaje Polskie Wyprawy Alpinistyczne,* Sport I Turystyka, Warsaw, 1989
Jerzy Kukuczka *My Vertical World* Hodder & Stoughton, London, 1992. *Mój pionom świat* Sport i Turystyka, Warsaw, 1995 (Polish edition with more photos, maps etc.)
Perceval Landon *Lhasa* Hurst and Blackett, London, 1905
Les Alpes 1956
Lobsang P. Lhalungpa *The Life of Milarepa*
Erhard Loretan *Himalaya. Reflections* La Sarine, Fribourg, 1998
John MacGregor *Tibet* Routledge, London, 1970 (packed with information).
Kenneth Mason *Abode of Snow* Hart-Davis, London, 1955; Diadem, London, 1987
Chantal Mauduit *J'habite au Paradis* Lattes, Paris, 1997
Reinhold Messner *Überlebt alle 14 Achttausender* BLV, Munich, 1987; *All 14 Eightthousanders* Crowood, Marlborough, 1988 / Cloudcap, Seattle, 1988
John Morris *Hired to Kill* Hart-Davis, London, 1960
Mountain 54 March, 1977 *"Shisha Pangma"* by G.O.Dyhrenfurth,
Mountaineering in China Foreign Language Press, Peking, 1965
Thubtem Jigme Norbu and Colin Turnbull *Tibet - Its History, Religion and People* Chatto and Windus, London, 1969
NZZ 583, 14 March 1953
A Photographic Record of the Mt Shisha Pangma Scientific Expedition Scientific Press, Peking, 1966
Oswald Oelz *Mitt Eispickel und Stethoskop* A.S. Verlag, Zürich, 1999
Antonio Ortega (Ed.) *Vascos en el Himalaya 1974-1992: Crónica de una aventura* Pyrenaica, Bilbao, 1992 (1990 Central Summit ascent and various attempts).
Marco Pallis *Peaks and Lamas* Cassell, London, 1939
Mauricio Purto *Everest – La Ruta Lógica* El Mercurio, Santiago, 1992. (Everest and three other 8000ers – shows only the Central Summit was reached in 1991.)
Capt. Cecil G. Rawling *The Great Plateau* Edward Arnold, London, 1905
Gertrude Reinisch *Karawane der Traüme* Rudolf Rother, Munich 1987 (biography of Wanda Rutkiewicz including her Shisha Pangma climb in 1987).
Gertrude Reinisch *Österreichische Frauenexpedition Shisha Pangma* Anton Schroll, Vienna and Munich, 1995 (the Wanda Rutkiewicz Memorial Expedition, 1994).
William Woodville Rockhill *Land of the Lamas* Longman, London, 1891
Fritz Rudolph *Chomolungma und Ihre Kinde* Berlin ddr, 1978
Kiyoshi Shimizu *Shishapangma* (in Japanese) Tokyo, 1992 (the 1991 Japanese tragedy).
George Shiver *Francis Younghusband* John Murray, London, 1952
R. A. Stein *Tibetan Civilization* Faber, London, 1972
Junko Tabei *Shisha Pangma Reflections* (in Japanese) Yama Kei, Tokyo, 1982
H. W. Tilman *Nepal Himalaya* Cambridge University Press, 1952
Times Atlas of China New York Times, 1974
Chogyam Trungpa *The Myth of Freedom* Shambhala, Berkeley, 1976
Walt Unsworth *Everest* Allen Lane, London, 1981
Michael Ward *In this Short Span* Gollancz, London, 1972
Peter Weber *Shisha Pangma* Privately published, Wald, Switzerland, 1985
C.J. Wessels *Early Jesuit Travellers in Central Asia, 1603-1721* Martinus Nijhoff, The Hague, 1924
Krzysztof Wielicki *Korona Himalajów: 14 x 8000 m* Kraków, 1997; *Crown on Himalaya: 14 x 8000* (a simultaneous English edition published in Poland).
A. F. R. Wollaston *Letters and Diaries* Cambridge University Press, London, 1933
Zhou Zheng and Liu Zhenkai *Footprints on the Peaks: Mountaineering in China* Cloudcap, Seattle 1995

301

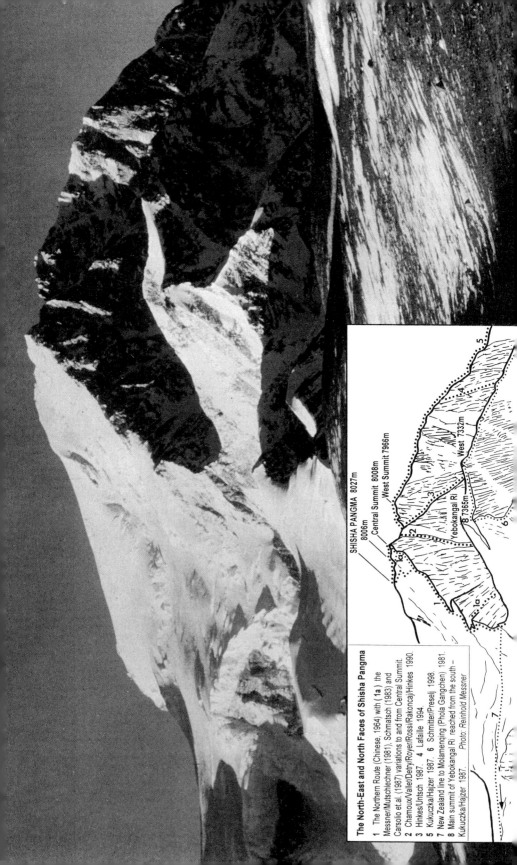

The North-East and North Faces of Shisha Pangma

1 The Northern Route (Chinese, 1964) with (1a) the
Messner/Mutschlechner (1981), Schmatsch (1983) and
Carsolio et.al. ((1987) variations to and from Central Summit.
2 Chamoux/Vallet/Detry/Royer/Rossi/Rakoncaj/Hinkes 1990.
3 Hinkes/Untsch 1987.   4 Lafaille 1994.
5 Kukuczka/Hajzer 1987.   6 Schmitter/Preselj 1998.
7 New Zealand line to Molamenqing (Phola Gangchen) 1981.
8 Main summit of Yebokangal Ri reached from the south –
Kukuczka/Hajzer 1987.   *Photo: Reinhold Messner*

SHISHA PANGMA 8027m
8006m
Central Summit 8008m
West Summit 7966m
West 7332m
Yebokangal Ri
8 7365m

Ascents on Shisha Pangma and associated peaks

This Chronicle updates the original broader history (pp 275-291). It concerns only the immediate Shisha Pangma massif and is compiled from reports in the *American Alpine Journal* and other sources. Xavier Eguskitza and Lindsay Griffin have contributed much additional information.

Initial disparities over both summit naming and heights (in both the *AAJ* and this book) are now resolved. **Main Summit** is now given 8027m / 26,335ft. A short distance away to the north-west **Central Summit** (also called Middle Peak or even West Peak) is now given 8008m / 26,273ft. The true **West Summit** 7966m / 26,135ft is situated on the West Ridge some distance south-west of Central Summit with a pronounced col in between.

The main subsidiary peaks are **Pungpa Ri** to the south-east, **Phola Gangchen** (or Molamenqing) to the north-east, **Yebokangai Ri** to the north and **Porong Ri** to the north-west.

The Chinese first-ascent route gained the North-East Ridge of Central Summit and then, from a height of about 7700m, took a rising traverse across avalanche-prone slopes to Main Summit. Of late many climbers have climbed the ridge directly to Central Summit. A sharp snow arête (often corniced), leads south-east from Central Summit. This can be traversed to gain Main Summit but few opt to use it. Growing numbers of climbers are climbing only to Central Summit. Ascents to either of these summits by the Chinese approach route are given the general title of "Northern Route." In this Chronicle, after 1990, only Main Summit ascents are fully noted except where an ascent or attempt is of particular note, or where an accident is recorded.

Guide to the symbols: The first ten ascents of the Main Summit and other noteworthy ascents or attempts have their initial titling (after the date) **emboldened**.

Main Summit ascents are marked * *Central Summit ascents* + *New routes or variants* §
Ascents where some details remain to be clarified are marked (*) (+) (§)   Female climbers are noted with the prefix "Ms".

1964 North-West Face/ North-East Ridge and Face §* First ascent. The Chinese Hsu Ching (leader), Chang Chun-yen, Wang Fu-chou, Wu Tsung-yueh, Chen San, Cheng Tien-liang and the Tibetans Doji, Migmar Trashi, Sodnam Doji and Yonten, members of a Chinese/Tibetan expedition, reached Main Summit on 2 May without using bottled oxygen.

1979 Northern Route   Dr Manfred Abelein, Fritz Zintl and Günter Sturm carried out a reconnaissance expedition in preparation for their 1980 expedition.

1980 Northern Route* Second Ascent. Main Summit was gained by Michl Dacher, Dr Wolfgang Schaffert, Günter Sturm and Fritz Zintl (7 May) and Sigi Hupfauer and Manfred Sturm (12 May). They were members of a nine-strong German expedition led by Dr Manfred Abelein. A North Face attempt by Dacher, Zintl and G.Sturm failed at 7200m. A 7150m / 23,458ft peak west of Shisha Pangma was climbed (on skis) from the north.

1980 Northern Route* Third Ascent. Ewald Putz and Egon Obojes, members of an eight-strong Austrian party led by Hans Mautner, climbed to Main Summit on 13 Oct. Dr Paul Alf climbed towards the "foresummit" solo at dusk but slipped on the descent and was rescued next day, frostbitten and with broken ankles and ribs.

1981 Northern Route* Fourth Ascent. Ms Junko Tabei with Rinzing Phinzo and Gyalbu (Jiabu) reached Main Summit (30 April). Tabei led an eight-strong Japanese (womens') group.

1981 Molamenqing (Phola Gangchen) § Bruce Farmer and Dick Price (14 May); Warwick Anderson and Ron McLeod (16 May); Geoff Gabites, Bruce Clark, Paul Chapman and Tony Charlton (20 May), members of a New Zealand party led by Austin Brookes, made the first ascent of the main northern satellite peak (7703m / 25,272ft) of Shisha Pangma. They took the Yambukangala Glacier route to gain the plateau north of Shisha Pangma. From here they found a straightforward ascent route up the southern snow slopes.

1981 Northern Route* Fifth Ascent. Reinhold Messner and Friedl Mutschlechner, members of a four-strong group, climbed the peak on 28 May. They gained the North-East Ridge by an avalanche-scoured gully § on the left of the North Face. At c.7900m they traversed across the upper North Face § to gain the Central/Main crest and from there moved to Main Summit. The climb was made in poor visibility. *Details supplied by Reinhold Messner in 1999.*

1981 Northern Route A small American group, led by Gerry Roach, made an attempt in September establishing a fourth camp before avalanche risks prompted a retreat.

1981 Northern Route Americans George Lowe, Lou Reichardt, Eric Perlman, James Morrissey and Geoff Tabin with Wang Fu Chow (fresh from a September attempt on Everest's Kangshung Face) reached 7130m on 25 Oct but high winds made further progress impossible.

1982 South-West Face, Right-Hand Couloir §* Sixth Ascent. Doug Scott, Roger Baxter-Jones and Alex MacIntyre, members of a six-strong British team led by Scott and Nick Prescott, reached the summit on 28 May after a three-day, alpine-style ascent of the face. Scott and MacIntyre then traversed to just short of Central Summit before returning to the Main Summit. The trio then descended by the unexplored South-East Ridge to a col west of Pungpa Ri and thence down the right flank of the South-West Face to their start point.

On 19 May the same trio had made the first ascent of **Pungpa Ri §** (7445m/24,426ft) by the South Ridge and earlier had attempted Nyanang Ri – both as acclimatization climbs.

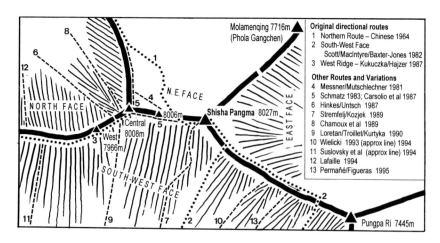

Molamenqing 7716m
(Phola Gangchen)

Shisha Pangma 8027m

Pungpa Ri 7445m

N.E. FACE

NORTH FACE

Central 8008m
West 8006m
7966m
5

SOUTH-WEST FACE

EAST FACE

Original directional routes
1 Northern Route – Chinese 1964
2 South-West Face
    Scott/MacIntyre/Baxter-Jones 1982
3 West Ridge – Kukuczka/Hajzer 1987

Other Routes and Variations
4 Messner/Mutschlechner 1981
5 Schmatz 1983; Carsolio et al 1987
6 Hinkes/Untsch 1987
7 Stremfelj/Kozjek 1989
8 Chamoux et al 1989
9 Loretan/Troillet/Kurtyka 1990
10 Wielicki 1993 (approx line) 1994
11 Suslovsky et al (approx line) 1994
12 Lafaille 1994
13 Permañé/Figueras 1995

304

1982 Northern Route* Seventh Ascent. Japanese climbers Dr Makoto Hara, Hiro Komamiya and Hirofumi Konishi (10 Oct), and Takayoshi Chiba, Motomu Ohmiya and Masaaki Tomita (12 Oct) reached Main Summit – Tomita took two days from c.5800m.

1983 Northern Route+* Eighth Ascent. Gerhard Schmatz+, Josef and Ms Marianne Walter and Dr. Ulrich Schum, members of a seven-strong German/Swiss group led by Sigi Hupfauer, reached Central Summit (Schmatz) and Main Summit on 29 April. Earlier Lhotse veteran Fritz Luchsinger (62) died (pulmonary oedema) during evacuation from a high camp.

1983   Northern Route* Ninth Ascent. Mike Browning, Chris Pizzo and Glenn Porzak, from an eleven-strong American group led by Porzak, reached Main Summit on 30 Sept.

1984   Northern Route* Tenth Ascent. David Howe, Mark Jenkins, Douglas Kelley, Michael Wingert (6 May) and Dr Steven Creer and Michael Lehner (8 May), members of a nine-strong American party led by Joseph Murphy, reached Main Summit.

1985   Northern Route*   Oswald Gassler (first ski descent), Peter Wörgötter, Leopold Schausberger, Balthasar Kendler, Thomas Schilcher (twice), Helmut Wagner, Gottfried Heinzel, Leopold Karner, Hanns Schell, Max Wettstein, Angelo Vedani and Sepp Wangeler, from an Austro/Swiss expedition led by Marcus Schmuck, reached Main Summit (10, 12, 19 May).

1985   Northern Route*   Giuliano De Marchi, a member of an Italian commercial expedition led by Renato Moro, reached Main Summit on 16 May.

1985   Northern Route*   In heavy snow conditions Marcel Rüedi, Diego Wellig and Oswald Oelz, members of a nine-strong Swiss expedition led by Marcus Itten, reached Main Summit on 14 Sept. Skis were used to 7100m and in descent.

1986   Northern Route+   Two large commercial parties from the same organisation, led by Alberto Re and Claude Jaccoux, were active on the mountain in August and September. Eric Escoffier+, Xavier Murillo+ and Takashi Ozaki+ (10 Sept), Michel Vincent+ (19 Sept), Michael Leuprecht+ and Josef Oberauer+ (20 Sept) reached Central Summit.

1987   Northern Route   Attempted by a five-strong American team led by Richard Dietz.

1987   Northern Route+*   Steve Bruce+ and Dick Price+ (16 May) and Mike Perry and Mark Whetu (20 May), members of a nine-strong New Zealand group, climbed the Central and Main Summits. Whetu made a ski descent.

1987   Northern Route+   Alfred Meyer+, Otto Huber+, Klaus Solbach+ and Peter Blank+, of an Austro/Swiss team (ldrs: Hanns Schell / Stefan Wörner) to Central Summit (18 Sept).

1987   Northern Route §+* / West Ridge §+* / North Face §+*   A thirteen-strong Polish/International grouping led by Jerzy Kukuczka climbed a number of new routes:
On 18 Sept. Carlos Carsolio, Ms Elsa Avila, Ramiro Navarrete, Ryszard Warecki and Ms Wanda Rutkiewicz climbed the conventional route to Central Summit and then continued along the sharp snow arête § to Main Summit.

305

After climbing **Yebokangal Ri** § (7365m / 24,163ft), on 29 Aug. Artur Hajzer and Jerzy Kukuczka (using a northern approach) made the first ascent of the difficult and sustained West Ridge § (18 Sept), crossing the West (7966m) and Central (8008m) Summits to reach Main Summit behind the earlier group. After a summit bivouac Kukuczka made a ski descent.

On 19 Sept. Alan Hinkes and Steve Untch climbed the Central Couloir § of the North Face to the Central Summit and then continued to the Main Summit.

This fine expedition formed a suitable finale for Kukuczka's nine-year 8000m peak quest.

1987 Northern Route Oreste Forno's commercial group abandoned its bid on 10 Sept.

1987 Northern Route* Sándor Nagy and Attila Ozsváth (1 Oct) and Zoltán Balaton, Lászlo Vörös, József Csíkos, Lászlo Várkonyi (8 Oct), members of a nine-strong Hungarian team led by Nagy, climbed to Main Summit.

1987 South-East Ridge attempt / **Pungpa Ri** An attempt from the eastern side of the mountain was the objective of a twenty-nine strong British climbing/scientific expedition led by Lt.Col. Henry Day and Col. John Blashford Snell. The East Face was adjudged too dangerous. Luke Hughes and Stephen Venables then (25 Oct) climbed **Pungpa Ri** by a new route (via the Phola Glacier and the South-East Face §) they continued up Shisha Pangma's South-East Ridge to 7700m where deteriorating weather prompted a retreat.

1988 Northern Route* + On 13 May Klaus Gürtler, Peter Konzert and Tillmann Fischbach crossed from Central to Main Summit, and then (rejecting the arête return) descended by the Chinese Traverse. Edward Bekker+, who had stayed on Central Summit, descended alone. Bernd Kullmann, Adolf Metzger, Klaus Schuhmann and Ms Herta Og (14 May); Jürgen Schütz, Thomas Hochholzer, Wolfgang Kunzendorf, Dieter Thomann and Hans Bärnthaler (17 May) gained Main Summit by the Chinese traverse. After snowfall (18 May) Peter Kuge+ and Walter Hölzler+ thought both traverse and linking arête too risky and opted for Central Summit (19 May). All were from an Austro/German/Dutch party led by Günther Härter.

1988 Northern Route* Fausto De Stefani, Sergio Martini and Patrick Berhault (5 Sept) and Pino Negri, Giorgio Daidola and Didier Givois (6 Sept), members of a Franco/Italian group led by Berhault, climbed Main Summit (the final two descending on nordic skis). Berhault had acclimatised at home using a plastic bag and an air pump in a carefully monitored process.

1988 Northern Route* Noburu Yamada, Teruo Saegusa, and Atsushi Yamamoto reached Main Summit on 24 Oct.

1989 Northern Route* Yoshiyuki Tsuji, Kiyohiko Suzuki and Shinji Takamura, members of a sixteen-strong Japanese party led by Michio Yuasa, reached Main Summit on 16 April.

1989 Northern Route+ Almo Giambisi+, Oscar Piazza+, Gino Minuzelli+,Claudio Toldo+ and Angelo Giovanetti+ members of a Swiss/Italian group led by Oreste Forno, reached Central Summit on 4 Oct. Dr Luca Leonardi was swept to his death by a windslab avalanche when just a few metres short of the top while another climber was injured. A large French commercial group (Allibert) abandoned its summit plans to assist the subsequent rescue.

1   The North-East Ridge to Central Summit with the North Face to its right and the West Ridge the right skyline. *Photo: Geoff Gabites*

2   (right) A closer view of the North-East Ridge seen from the lower slopes of Molamenqing. *Photo: Warwick Anderson*

3   The Shisha Pangma massif from the north with (left to right) Pungpa Ri, Molamenqing (Phola Gangchen), Shisha Pangma and Yebokangal Ri. *Photo: Doug Scott*

The East Face of Shisha Pangma from above the Nyang Chu Glacier (above) and an aerial view of the face from above the Langtang Glacier to the south – Molamenqing (Phola Gangchen) and Pungpa Ri are the peaks on the right. *Photos: Doug Scott and Keiichi Yamada*

6 7 (left and above) Andrej Stremfelj during the first ascent of the Central Buttress of the South-West Face in 1989. *Photos: Pavle Kozjek.* 8 (below) Alex MacIntyre on the ridge to Central Summit – unstable cornices stopped his advance when 60ft from the top. The often avalanche-prone slopes on the right deter many Main Summit bids. *Photo: Doug Scott*

9 (above) MacIntyre returning along the Central Summit ridge. Roger Baxter-Jones is seen as a tiny dot on the shoulder below the final humps of Main Summit. 10 (below) Looking east from the summit to Cho Oyu, Everest, Lhotse and Makalu. *Photos: Doug Scott*

.2   (top right)
ing cornices,
Intyre crawls
e high point
mplete the
ascent of
gpa Ri – a
ing/recce
b before the
ha Pangma
"Our descent
e from Shisha
gma is behind
quit this at
earest rocky
h where a
oir (near
) led down
e lower
es." *Photos:*
g Scott

13   Shisha Pangma's unclimbed East Face with Molamenqing on the right. Scott, MacIntyre and Baxter-Jones descended the left-hand ridge from the summit towards Pungpa Ri (left) and then down a gully on the south side of the mountain. The left-hand face of Pungpa Ri was climbed in 1987 by Luke Hughes and Stephen Venables. *Photo: Lindsay Griffin*

1989 South-West Face / Central Buttress §* and other lines §*. Andrej Stremfelj and Pavle Kozjek, members of ten-strong Yugoslav group, made an alpine-style, first-ascent (16–19 Oct) of the 2150m Central Buttress. This was a sustained mixed climb with rock difficulties of IV to V in the upper section. Ice couloirs were followed wherever possible. After going to Main Summit they descended to the Pungpa Ri Col and thence back to base.

On the right-hand side of the face Filip Bence and Viki Groselj made a direct approach to the *British Descent Route* and the South-East Ridge which they ascended to the summit (20 Oct). Illness foiled Stane Belak's and Marko Prezelj's attempt on another new line.

On 12 Oct., Belak, Bence, Kozjek and Stremfelj made the first ascent of **Nyanang Riṣ.** In 1983 Stremfelj and Tone Skarja had made the first ascent of **Ice Tooth §.**

1990 Northern Route+*   Rino Bernhardstrutter+ (11 May), Elmar Fries and Johann Neuhauser (12 May), members group led by Bogdan Brakus, climbed to Central and Main Summits. Milan Cermak and Helmut Daum made a ski ascent of **Yebokangal Ri** (12 May).

1990 Northern Route, North Face §+   After climbing Cho Oyu on 30 April, Benoît Chamoux+, Frédéric Valet+, Yves Detry+, Pierre Royer+, Mauro Rossi+, Josef Rakoncaj+ and Alan Hinkes+ made a three-day ascent of Central Summit (10 - 12 May) by way of a new couloir route on the North Face (left of the *Hinkes/Untch Couloir*).

1990   Northern Route+ A thirty-four-member Japanese Expedition had high-altitude research on its agenda. One project involved monitoring previously acclimatised monkeys. A summary of this is in *AAJ* 1991, p295. Twenty-five members gained Central Summit (17 - 21 May).

1990   Northern Route+   Russell Brice+, Mark Lemaire+, Erik Tryti+, Mark Vallance+ (26 May) and Olav Ulvund+ (27 May), members of an international group, climbed Central Summit.

1990   Northern Route+   Dr Karsten König+ and Reinhardt Tauchnitz+ members of an East German quartet that included Winfried Kraus and Ms Sabine Körbs, reached Central Summit on 26 May. This (impecunious?) group climbed without "official" "Chinese" "permission" to climb in "Tibet" thereby prompting censorious comments from the *"American" Alpine Journal.*

1990   Northern Route In the pre-monsoon period an Italian expedition led by Marco Berti reached 7200m, and a Swiss team led by Fredi Graf reached 7600m.

1990   Northern Route+   Jean Pierre Bernard (leader),+ Charles Davignon,+ Bruno Lascoumes,+ Michel Monnier,+ Ms Emmanuelle Jacquet,+ Ms Annette Nault+ and Ms Brigitte Djajasasmita,+ of a French commercial group, reached Central Summit (25 Aug).

1990   Northern Route+ Using skis to 700m and in descent Juanjo San Sebastián,+ Antonio Trabado,+ José Carlos Tamayo+ and Atxo Apellaniz,+ members of a seven-strong Spanish group led by Sebastián Alvaro, climbed to Central Summit on 30 Sept

1990   Northern Route+ French climbers Jacques Le Hir,+ André-Benoit Lizon+ and George Lombard+ (30 Sept.) and Pierre Lombard+ and Ms Bernadette Lions+ (1 Oct) reached to Central Summit having suspected avalanche danger on the traverse to Main Summit.

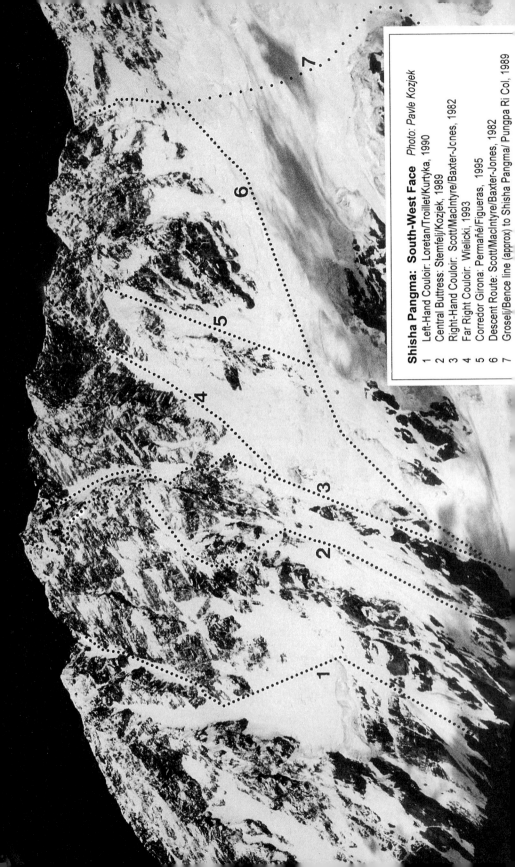

Shisha Pangma: South-West Face *Photo: Pavle Kozjek*

1 Left-Hand Couloir: Loretan/Troillet/Kurtyka, 1990
2 Central Buttress: Stemfelj/Kozjek, 1989
3 Right-Hand Couloir: Scott/MacIntyre/Baxter-Jones, 1982
4 Far Right Couloir: Wielicki, 1993
5 Corredor Girona: Permañé/Figueras, 1995
6 Descent Route: Scott/MacIntyre/Baxter-Jones, 1982
7 Groselj/Bence line (approx) to Shisha Pangma/ Pungpa Ri Col, 1989

1990   South West Face: Left-Hand Couloir §+ Fresh from making a new route on Cho Oyu, Erhard Loretan+, Jean Troillet+ and Wojciech Kurtyka+ made the first ascent and descent of the couloir on 3 Oct. With equipment pared to a minimum they soloed the route at night. Loretan and Troillet reached Central Summit at 10 a.m. and met Kurtyka (who had been delayed on a false line) while descending. Kurtyka gained Central Summit at 4 p.m. The Swiss pair reached the base of the face before dark but Kurtyka (with no bivouac gear) descended to a snow ledge at 7800m and slept well (on a warm night) before completing his descent. The couloir nowhere exceeds 50° and is the most direct and straightforward route up any of the 8000m peaks (albeit to only the Central Summit.)

1990   Northern Route* Miguel-Angel Vidal, Dr Joan Martínez, Maj. Roberto Santaeufemia, Capt. Francisco Gan, Sgts Pedro Expósito and Francisco Pérez, members of a fourteen-strong Spanish Army Expedition led by Major Francisco Soria, reached the Main Summit on 13 Oct. On the descent after an open bivouac in a blizzard, Dr Martínez died from exposure.

1990   Northern Route. A nineteen-strong party led by Eric Simonson abandoned their attempt high on the mountain on 13 Oct because of blizzards and growing avalanche risks. Others failed in similar circumstances: Marc Batard (France) failed at 7500m during a solo attempt; Fabrizio de Francesco (Italy) also reached this height on 21 Sept.

At the end of 1990 ascents of Main Summit totalled 114 with 93 ascents of Central Summit. Thereafter Central Summit ascents proliferated and complete ascents of the mountain became less frequent. Hereafter the Chronicle concentrates on Main Summit ascents. By 1999 Main Summit ascents had risen to 167 whereas Central Summit ascents numbered 464.

1991   Northern Route* Theo Fritsche, Herwig Schnutt, Ms Ottilie Dörrich, Dr Kurt Hecher, Günther Härter and Dieter Porsche members of a nineteen-strong Austro-German party led by Härter, climbed to Main Summit on 20 May, despite the avalanche risk on the Chinese traverse. Two days later Günther Semmler, Werner Braun, Werner Meichsner and Karl-Heinz Thiele headed for Central Summit (having rejected the traverse). Above 7800m there was no further contact and it is thought that the four were hit by an avalanche.

1991   Northern Route In a sobering re-enactment of the previous item, five Japanese climbers, having bivouaced in a snow hole at 7900m were preparing (20 Sept.) to begin the Chinese traverse when an avalanche swept three of them several hundred metres down the face and buried Hidekazu Gomi and Tetsuichi Miyashita who were still in the snow hole. The three avalanched climbers survived though Horikazu Matsuzawa was badly injured. The other two re-ascended but failed to locate the two buried climbers.

1991   Northern Route+ A Chilean/Italian group comprising Mauricio Purto (leader)+, Italo Valle+, Fernando Luchsinger+, Luis García+, Giovanni Mazzoleni+ and Ang Phuri+ reached the Central Summit on 27 Sept. Claims that they continued to Main Summit are considered unreliable because of eye-witness reports and the subsequent statements of Ang Phuri.

1991   South-West Face, Right-Hand Couloir* A South Korean expedition led by Oh In-Hwan repeated the *Scott/MacIntyre/Baxter-Jones Route*. Kim Chang-Seon and Kim Jae-Soo reached Main Summit on 8 Oct.

1992 South West Face, Left-Hand Couloir+ Spaniards Ernest Bladé+, Albert Castellet+, Ms Araceli Segarra+ and Ferrán Latorre+ made the first repeat of the *Loretan/Troillet/Kurtyka Route* to Central Summit on 28 Sept (alpine-style, one bivouac at 6700m).

1993 South-West Face: Right-Hand Couloir* Oscar Cadiach, Manel de la Matta and Ms Chantal Mauduit completed the third ascent of the *Scott/MacIntyre/Baxter-Jones Route* on 4 Oct. and continued to Main Summit.

1993 South-West Face: Far-Right Section / Left Couloir §* An international group of six were on the face: Marco Bianchi and Piotr Pustelnik took the *British Descent-Route* (with *Bence/Groselj* start) reaching Main Summit on 6 Oct. Next day Krzysztof Wielicki soloed the couloir § to the right of the *Scott/MacIntyre/Baxter-Jones Route* encountering exit difficulties from the upper rock amphitheatre but still gaining Main Summit that day.

1994 Normal Route* (+) Cering Doje, Rena, Akbu, Bianba Zaxi, Jiabu (his second ascent of the peak), Wangjia, Luoze, Daqiong and Daqimi of a ten-strong Tibetan expedition led by Sandrub (Song Zhu) reached Main Summit (7 May) reportedly by way of Central Summit.

1994 Northern Route+* Of the remaining fifty-three climbers who reached Central Summit in the pre-monsoon period only Jakob Kirschmer continued to Main Summit (28 May).

1994 South-West Face: Left-Hand Couloir Between 7 - 20 September Ms Catherine Destivelle and Eric Decamp made an ascent of the couloir. On 7 Sept they ascended to 6700m. On 12 Sept they ascended to 7150m and dug a snow hole and descended again. Regaining the snow hole, they sat out a day of bad weather, and on 20 Sept climbed to the col between West and Central summits. Noting avalanche risks they immediately descended.

1994 South West Face: Central Buttress Left and West Buttress § A six-strong Czech group led by Leopold Sulovsky attempted two new routes. On the Central Buttress (right of the *Loretan/Troillet/ Kurtyka Route*) they ascended to 6900m (24 Sept). On the 30th they then completed a new line on the West Buttress to 7200m on the *West Ridge*. While descending they were caught in an avalanche and Zdenek Slachta was killed (1 Oct).

1994 Northern Route+* A fifteen-strong commercial group led by Nikola Kekus placed three members on Central Summit. Kekus crossed the linking ridge to Main Summit (4 Oct).

1994 Northern Route+ / North Face, R/H Couloir § Jean Christophe Lafaille soloed a couloir on the right-hand side of the North Face which contained an 80° section at 7000m. After joining the West Ridge at 7500m, Lafaille continued to the West Summit but, with time pressing, descended his ascent route (9 Oct). Earlier, on the Northern Route, Lafaille and Dominique Caillet had given critical assistance to two climbers avalanched at 7400m. Lafaille+ then climbed Central Summit (7 Oct) but high winds prevented a traverse to Main Summit.

1994 Northern Route / North Face Mark Newcomb made a solo ascent of the *Hinkes/Untch Couloir* on 2 Oct. Having gained the ridge at 7800m west of Central Summit high winds made the final climb to Central Summit unattractive. Newcomb regained his skis at 7600m for a rapid descent. Further bids (with Stephen Koch) got no further than 7000m.

1994 Northern Route+ Tod Gassen, with a US group led by David McNally, died in a crevasse accident near Camp 1 (18 Sept). Three of the team gained Central Summit (9 Oct).

1995 Northern Route+* From the five expeditions attempting the peak from the north in the pre-monsoon period only four climbers gained Main summit. Of note was a rapid ascent by Erhard Loretan who left a camp at 5800m on 28 April and completed a traverse from Central to Main Summit at midday on 29 April. The Central/Main route was also done by Rodja Ratteit (12 May) and Panagiotis Kotronaros (Greece) with Sonam (sherpa) on 13 May.

1995 South West Face: Right-hand Flank § Josep Permañé and Carles Figueras, members of a seven-strong Spanish group, made an alpine-style ascent of the *Corredor Girona* couloir between the *Wielicki Route* and the *British Descent Route* (22- 24 Sept). Deep snow on the summit ridge slowed them and at 4pm they gained a top, but when the clouds cleared it proved to be a fore-summit. At this point they thought it prudent to descent.

1996 Northern Route* There were seven ascents to Main Summit in the pre-monsoon period. Norbert Joos (Swiss), the leader of a commercial group, accompanied one client to Central Summit and then traversed (solo) to Main Summit (1 May). The Chinese traverse was done by three groups: Slovaks Peter Sperka and Stefan Sluka succeeded on 1 May but, after a bivouac, Sluka disappeared during the descent; Christian Zinsli, Bruno Hasler (21 May), Manuel Schneider and Peter Guggemos (30 May), members of a commercial group led by Manfred Lorenz, were the other summit climbers at this time.

1996 Northern Route Viktor Pashtukh and Gennadi Vasilenko, members of a Ukrainian expedition led by Ivan Valenya, disappeared while descending from Camp 2 during snowfall and poor visibility (5 Oct). It is thought that they were hit by an avalanche.

1996 South West Face: Right-Hand Couloir* Spanish (Basque) climbers Josu Bereziartua, Felix and Alberto Iñurrategi completed a two-day ascent of the *Scott/MacIntyre/Baxter-Jones Route* on 11 Oct, climbed to Main Summit, and descended by the British descent route. Earlier, during a training climb on **Ice Tooth** with another Basque group, an avalanche killed José Luis Zuloaga and badly injured Juanito Oiarzabal.

1997 Northern Route+ Three members of a Taiwanese expedition, led by Tsai Jong-Bin, climbed Central Summit in mid May. Here a violent wind gust blew one climber off the ridge to his death.

1997 Northern Route* Six members of two Austro/German commercial groups reached Main Summit by the Chinese traverse on 24 May: Ralf Dujmovits, Gerhard Osterbauer, Karl Hub, Peter Brill, Frank Prasicek and Alois Neuhuber (aged 65). The average age of the last four was 58 drawing attention to the packaged adventure opportunities for older climbers.

1997 South-West Face: Right-Hand Couloir. In early October Slovenians Blac Navranik, Mira Zori and Sandi Vaupoti reached 7200m on the *Scott/MacIntyre/Baxter-Jones Route* (alpine-style, two camps) when a snow storm forced a descent.

311

1998   Porong Ri and Yebokangal Ri (Pt.733m) Theirry Schmitter and Marco Prezelj, members of a Dutch/Swiss/Slovene group led by Reiner Zuidhoff, climbed Porong Ri's East Face § (21 April) and the North Ridge of Yebokangal Ri (Jebo Kangri) to its West Summit (Pt.7332) § (29 April). The main summit at 7365m was not visited.

1998 Northern Route (+) In poor visibility Ukrainians Dr Alexei Bokov, Sergei Bershov and Igor Chaplinsky climbed what they thought was Main Summit on May 1. Circumstances suggest they actually reached Central Summit.

1998   Northern Route+* Christian Kuntner and Stefan Andres, members of an Italian (S.Tyrol) expedition traversed from the North-East Ridge at 7900m and reached Main Summit on 6 May. A similar high line was used (14 May) when the Italians Abele Blanc and Marco Comandona with Waldemar Niclevicz (Brazil) reached Central Summit and avoided the sharp arête by descending a short distance to make the traverse. This joined the arête 70m beyond its sharpest section and thence to Main Summit. This seems to have been the first time that higher traverses were used since the Messner / Mutschlechner climb in 1981.

1998   South West Face: Right-Hand Couloir* A Spanish (Basque) / Mexican / Austrian sextet of Enrique de Pablo, Andrés Delgado, Hector Ponce de León, Juanito Oiarzabal, Christian Stangl and Iñaki Querejeta, climbed the *Scott/MacIntyre/Baxter-Jones Route* and established a camp on the summit ridge. From here Oiarzabal and Stangl (10 Oct) and Querejeta (11 Oct) continued to the summit. All then took the British descent route.

1999 Northern Route+ In the year a total of seventy-six ascents of Central Summit were recorded – forty-five in pre-monsoon, thirty-one afterwards. Main Summit was not climbed.

1999   South West Face: Left-Hand Couloir While moving along the foot of the face to inspect the couloir (5 Oct), Conrad Anker, Alex Lowe and Dave Bridges were struck by an avalanche triggered by windslab sliding off the summit slopes. Anker survived but the other two were buried and others following at a distance were unable to locate them.

A German group that was waiting to climb the face called off its attempt after this tragedy.

Shisha Pangma: Yearly Analysis of Ascents by Xavier Eguskitza
Note: The Central Summit totals include the 31 climbers who continued to Main Summit

Main Summit		Central Summit		Main Summit		Central Summit	
year	total	season split	total	season split	year	total	season split	total	season split
1964	10	(10 + 0)			1990	8	(2 + 6)	60	(41 + 19)
1980	8	(6 + 2)			1991	8	(6 + 2)	14	(5 + 9)
1981	5	(5 + 0)			1992	0		29	(2 + 27)
1982	9	(3 + 6)			1993	6	(0 + 6)	14	(4 + 10)
1983	6	(3 + 3)	1	(1 + 0)	1994	11	(10 + 1)	74	(62 + 12)
1984	6	(6 + 0)			1995	4	(4 + 0)	41	(13 + 28)
1985	17	(14 + 3)			1996	10	(7 + 3)	29	(12 + 17)
1986	0		6	(0 + 6)	1997	6	(6 + 0)	9	(9 + 0)
1987	17	(2 + 15)	15	(2 + 13)	1998	8	(5 + 3)	85	(60 + 25)
1988	21	(12 + 9)	6	(6 + 0)	1999	0		76	(45 + 31)
1989	7	(3 + 4)	5	(0 + 5)	**Totals**	**167**	(104 + 63)	464	(262 + 202)

Shisha Pangma: Summit Climbs

Symbols: § *Participated in new route or variant* + *Visited Central Summit during climb* • *Died during descent*

1964

Hsu Ching §	2 May
Chang Chun-yen §	
Wang Fu-chou §	
Wu Tsung-yueh §	
Chen San §	
Cheng Tien-liang §	
Doji §	
Migmar Trashi §	
Sodnam Doji §	
Yonten §	

1980

Michl Dacher	7 May
Dr Wolfgang Schaffert	
Günter Sturm,	
Fritz Zintl	
Sigi Hupfauer	12 May
Manfred Sturm	
Ewald Putz	13 Oct
Egon Obojes	

1981

Ms Junko Tabei	30 April
Rinzing Phinzo	
Gyalbu (Jiabu) (1st)	
Reinhold Messner §	28 May
Friedl Mutschlechner §	

1982

Doug Scott §	28 May
Roger Baxter-Jones §	
Alex MacIntyre §	
Dr Makoto Hara	10 Oct
Hiro Komamiya	
Hirofumi Konishi	
Motomu Ohmiya	12 Oct
Takayoshi Chiba	
Masaaki Tomita	

1983

Josef Walter	29 April
Ms Marianne Walter	
Dr. Ulrich Schum	
Mike Browning	30 Sept
Chris Pizzo	
Glenn Porzak	

1984

David Howe	6 May
Mark Jenkins	
Douglas Kelley	
Michael Wingert	
Dr Steven Creer	8 May
Michael Lehner	

1985

Oswald Gassler	10 May
Peter Wörgötter	
Leopold Schausberger	
Balthasar Kendler	12 May
Thomas Schilcher (1st)	
Helmut Wagner	
Gottfried Heinzel	
Max Wettstein	
Angelo Vedani	
Sepp Wangeler	
Giuliano De Marchi	16 May
Leopold Karner	19 May
Hanns Schell	
Thomas Schilcher (2nd)	
Marcel Rüedi	14 Sept
Diego Wellig	
Oswald Oelz	

1987

Mike Perry	20 May
Mark Whetu	
Carlos Carsolio §+	18 Sept
Ms Elsa Avila §+	
Ryszard Warecki §+	
Ramiro Navarrete §+	
Ms Wanda Rutkiewicz §+	
Arthur Hajzer §+	
Jerzy Kukuczka §+	
Alan Hinkes §+	19 Sept
Steve Untch §+	
Sándor Nagy	1 Oct
Attila Ozsváth	
Zoltán Balaton	8 Oct
Lászlo Vörös,	
József Csíkos,	
Lászlo Várkonyi	

1988

Klaus Gürtler +	13 May
Peter Konzert +	
Tillmann Fischbach +	
Bernd Kullmann	14 May
Adolf Metzger	
Klaus Schuhmann	
Ms Herta Og	
Jürgen Schütz	17 May
Thomas Hochholzer	
Wolfgang Kunzendorf	
Dieter Thomann	
Hans Bärnthaler	
Fausto De Stefani	5 Sept
Sergio Martini	
Patrick Berhault	
Pino Negri	6 Sept
Giorgio Daidola	
Didier Givois	
Noburu Yamada	24 Oct
Teruo Saegusa	
Atsushi Yamamoto	

1989

Yoshiyuki Tsuji	16 April
Kiyohiko Suzuki	
Shinji Takamura	
Andrej Stremfelj §	19 Oct
Pavle Kozjek §	
Filip Bence §	20 Oct
Viki Groselj §	

1990

Elmar Fries	12 May
Johann Neuhauser	
Miguel-Angel Vidal	13 Oct
Dr Joan Martínez •	
Maj. Roberto Santaeufemia.	
Capt. Francisco Gan	
Sgt. Pedro Expósito	
Sgt. Francisco Pérez	

1991

Theo Fritsche	20 May
Herwig Schnutt	
Ms Ottilie Dörrich	
Dr Kurt Hecher	

Günther Härter
Dieter Porsche
Kim Chang-Seon   8 Oct
Kim Jae-Soo

1993

Oscar Cadiach   4 Oct
Manel de la Matta
Ms Chantal Mauduit
Marco Bianchi   6 Oct
Piotr Pustelnik
Krzysztof Wielicki § 7 Oct

1994

Cering Doje +   7 May
Rena +
Akbu +
Bianba Zaxi +
Gyalbu (Jiabu) + (2nd)
Wangjia +
Luoze +
Daqiong +
Daqimi +
Jakob Kirschmer +   28 May
Nikola Kekus +   4 Oct

1995

Erhard Loretan +   29 Apr
Rodja Ratteit +   12 May
Sonam (sherpa) +   13 May
Panagiotis Kotronaros +

1996

Norbert Joos +   1 May
Peter Sperka
Stefan Sluka •
Christian Zinsli   21 May
Bruno Hasler
Manuel Schneider   30 May
Peter Guggemos
Josu Bereziartua   11 Oct
Félix Iñurrategi
Alberto Iñurrategi

1997

Ralf Dujmovits   24 May
Karl Hub
Peter Brill
Franz Prasicek
Gerhard Osterbauer
Alois Neuhuber

1998

Christian Kuntner   6 May
Stefan Andres
Waldemar Niclevicz + 14 May
Abele Blanc +
Marco Comandona +
Juanito Oiarzabal   10 Oct
Christian Stangl
Iñaki Querejeta   11 Oct

Fatalities on Shisha Pangma

All on Northern Route unless otherwise stated

1983	**Fritz Luchsinger**	Pulmonary Oedema at 6950m
1989	**Luca Leonardi**	Windslab near Central Summit
1990	**Dr Joan Martínez**	Exposure (6800m) during descent
1991	**Werner Braun**	Probable avalanche
	Werner Meichsner	*as above*
	Günther Semmler	*as above*
	Karl-Heinz Thiele	*as above*
	Hidekazu Gomi	Avalanche – buried in snowhole
	Tetsuichi Miyashita	*as above*
1993	**Park Bueoung-Tae**	Fall
1994	**Tod Gassen**	Crevasse fall
	Zdenek Slachta	Avalanche on S.W.Face
1996	**Stefan Sluka**	Missing – descent from summit
	Victor Pastukh	Avalanche at 6300m
	Gennadi Vasilenko	*as above*
1997	**Taiwanese** (unnamed)	Blown off Central Summit
1998	**Andreino Pasini**	Illness at 7200m (21 May)
1999	**Alex Lowe**	Hit by avalanche from S.W.Face
	Dave Bridges	*as above*

314

Central Summit Ascents

Visited Main Summit during climb ·Died during descent
§ *Participated in new route or variant to reach Central Summit*

1983
Gerhard Schmatz § 29 Apr

1986
Eric Escoffier 10 Sept
Xavier Murillo
Takashi Ozaki
Michel Vincent 19 Sept
Michael Leuprecht 20 Sept
Josef Oberrauer

1987
Steve Bruce 16 May
Dick Price
Alfred Meyer 18 Sept
Otto Huber
Klaus Solbach
Peter Blank
Carlos Carsolio* 18 Sept
Ms Elsa Avila*
Ms Wanda Rutkiewicz*
Ryszard Warecki*
Ramiro Navarrete*
Jerzy Kukuczka §*
Artur Hajzer §*
Alan Hinkes §* 1st 19 Sept
Steve Untch §*

1988
Klaus Gürtler* 13 May
Peter Konzert*
Tillmann Fischbach*
Edward Bekker
Walter Hölzler 19 May
Peter Kuge

1989
Almo Giambisi 4 Oct
Oscar Piazza
Gino Minuzelli
Angelo Giovanetti
Claudio Toldo

1990
Rino Berhardstrutter 11 May
Benoît Chamoux § 12 May
Frédéric Valet §
Yves Detry §
Pierre Royer §
Mauro Rossi §
Josef Rakoncaj §
Alan Hinkes § 2nd
Tetsuo Matsuzawa 17 May
Akira Idemizu

Ryu Nagata
Kouzo Tominaga
Shigeki Nakayama
Toshihiro Tsukihara
Masashige Takai
Kouji Fujita
Ms Azumi Shirasawa
Dawa Norbu (sherpa) 1st
Ang Phurba (sherpa) 1st
Arjung Tamang
Ms Tong Lou
Kazuo Hirata 19 May
Qimi (Chimi) 1st
Purbu
Ang Phurba (sherpa) 2nd
Mingma Norbu (sherpa) 1st
Atsuo Saito 21 May
Michiro Nakashima
Kouzo Matsubayashi
Tsuguo Seto
Masaharu Sakakibara
Dawa Norbu (sherpa) 2nd
Ang Phurba (sherpa) 3rd
Mingma Norbu (sherpa) 2nd
Dr Karstan König 26 May
Reinhardt Tauchnitz
Russell Brice
Mark Lemaire
Eirik Tryti
Mark Vallance
Olav Ulvund 27 May
Jean-Pierre Bernard 25 Aug
Charles Davignon
Bruno Lascoumes
Michel Monnier
Ms Emmanuelle Jacquet
Ms Annette Nault
Ms Brigitte Djajasasmita
Antonio Trabado 30 Sept
Juanjo San Sebastián
José Carlos Tamayo
Atxo Apellaniz
Jacques LeHir
André-Benoit Lizon
George Lombard
Pierre Lombard 1 Oct
Ms Bernadette Lions
Erhard Loretan § 3 Oct
Jean Troillet §
Wojciech Kurtyka §

1991
Mark Baruffa 14 May
Ms Gille Pille

Cering Doje 1st
Qimi (Chimi) 2nd
Khtun
Mauricio Purto 27 Sept
Italo Valle
Fernando Luchsinger
Luis García
Giovanni Mazzoleni
Ang Phuri 1st
Tetsuyu Takahashi 4 Oct
Seiichi Kodama
Pasang (sherpa) 1st

1992
Etsuro Hino 6 May
Toyofumi Miyazaki
Ms Magda Nos 26 Sept
Ang Phuri 2nd
Rafael Fuentes
Toni Bericat
Saila Tamang
Toni Vives
Ms Amparo Ortega
Ms Inmaculada Fernández
Iman Gurung 27 Sept
Laurent Lukie
Ernest Bladé 29 Sept
Albert Castellet
Ms Araceli Segarra
Ferrán Latorre
Nam Sun-Woo 2 Oct
Kim Young-Tae
Mingma Norbu (sherpa) 3rd
Nikolai Cherni 7 Oct
Vladimir Koroteev 1st
Ms Irina Vialenkova
Vladimir Shataev 9 Oct
Ms Yekaterina Ivanova
Eduard Lipen
Albert Ishakov
Gia Tortladze 1st 10 Oct
Merab Nemsizveridze
Vladimir Koroteev 2nd 15 Oct

1993
Ed Viesturs 15 May
André Georges 17 May
Marcos Couch 22 May
Nicolás de la Cruz
Um Hong-Gil 1st 29 Sept
Min Kyoung-Tae
Jan Harris 8 Oct
Jim Jennings
Keith Brown
Josep María Maixé
Jaume Garroset
Rafael López
Matej Kranjc 10 Oct
Iztok Tomazin 11 Oct

1994
Floriano Castelnuovo 29 Apr
Ignaz Gruber
Mariano Fulvio
Salvatore Panzeri
Ms Gui Sang
Ms Laiki
Chewang Dorje
Mingma (sherpa)
Phurbu (sherpa)
Götz Wiegand
Frank Gräfe
Uwe Fretter
Heiko Züllchner 30 April
Ms Edith Bolda 2 May
Ms Ewa Panejko-Pankiewicz
Ms Pubu Dschoka
Pasang (sherpa) 2nd
Rena* 7 May
Cering Doje* 2nd
Akbu*
Bianba Zaxi*
Gyalbu*(Jiabu) 2nd
Wangjia*
Luoze*
Daqiong*
Daqimi*
Peter Jungen
Andrew Evans 9 May
Paul O'Bryne
Kazuyoshi Kondo 18 May
Hidetoshi Kurahashi
Takaharu Hayashi
Takehito Ikeda
Iwao Kuwabara 19 May
Yoshinori Kawahara
Pemba Tschering
William Pierson
Alexander McNab
Ang Babu 1st
Jon Tinker 20 May
Ms Brigitte Muir
Lama Jangbu
Stephen Hart 22 May
Michael Smith
Paul Roberts
Paul Carr
Gregory Lindsell
Andy Cave 24 May
David Craven
Ang Babu 2nd
Reinhard Müller 27 May
Dieter Stein
Harald Rössner
Ralf Marsula 28 May
Reinhard Büscher
Alexander Härtlein
Jakob Kirschmer*
Rolf Hass 29 May

Florian Ibel
Karl Veile
Erwin Diesler *1 June*
Ernst Schwarzenlander
Nicola Kekus* *4 Oct*
Jean Chr. Lafaille *7 Oct*
Daniel Alessio *8 Oct*
Richard Forsyth
Larry Hall *9 Oct*
Ted Handwerk
Bruce Hennessey
Cha Jin-Chol *11 Oct*
Han Hwang-Yong
Kim Hun-Sang
Lee Dong-Heon
Um Hong-Gil *2nd*

1995
Erhard Loretan* *29 Apr*
Mal Duff *9 May*
Joe Dalmas
Rodja Ratteit* *12 May*
Sonam (sherpa)* *13 May*
Panagiotis Kotronaros*
Guido Blaschek *24 May*
Lila Bahadur Tamang
Volker Finkbeiner *26 May*
Albert Öffner *4 June*
Ms Martine Farenzena
Helmut Chlastak
Willi Kaltenbacher
Masatsugu Konishi *25 Sept*
Tomiyashu Ishikawa
Tatsuya Harada
Hideki Hoshino
Nima Dorje (sherpa)
Tshering Dorje (sherpa)
Iñaki Otxoa de Olza *28 Sept*
Joshe Mari Artetxe *29 Sept*
Robert Larrandaburu
Didier Minelli
Beat Supersaxo
Reinhold Supersaxo
Karl Huyberechts
Lhakpa Dorje (sherpa)
Kama Tshering (sherpa)
Juan Carlos Gómez *4 Oct*
G.Ladrón de Guevara
Ms Yannick Navarro
Peio Angulo *7 Oct*
Oldrich Rypl
Stanislav Silhan
Tirtha Tamang
Fabio Meraldi *8 Oct*
Josep Ollé
Josef Simunek
Petr Skrivanek *9 Oct*
Juan Corro
Fernando Rey

1996
Arno Mainetti *30 Apr*
Geni Ballat
Gerold Ennemoser *1 May*
Norbert Joos*
Peter Marug *2 May*
Maurizio Lutzenberger *8 May*
Jean Annequin *9 May*
Hans Kammerlander
Anton Buhl *1 June*
Ralf Dujmovits *5 June*
Kami Tenzing (sherpa)
Nawang Thile (sherpa)
Anatoli Bukreev *9 Oct*
Vladimir Bashkirov *10 Oct*
Yevgeni Vinogradski
Valeri Pershin
Boris Sedusov
Nikolai Zakharov
Boris Mednik
Gia Tortladze *2nd*
Park Jung-Hun
Fernando Garrido
Simone Moro *11 Oct*
Silvio Mondinelli
Paolo Paglino
Domenico Belingheri
Adriano Greco
Ms Alexia Zuberer
Jacek Berbeka

1997
Tarcisio Beltrami *4 May*
Sergio De Leo *7 May*
Sergio Magglione *8 May*
Taiwanese climber *mid May*
Taiwanese climber
Taiwanese climber •
Göran Kropp *4 June*
Ms Renata Chlumska
Cyril Destremau

1998
S.Korean climber *26 Apr*
Park Young-Seok *1st*
Kaji (sherpa)
Alexei Bokov *1 May*
Sergei Bershov
Igor Chaplinski
Reinier Zuidhoff *6 May*
Hans Van Der Meulen
Pepe Garcés
Waldemar Niclevicz* *14 May*
Abele Blanc*
Marco Comandona*
Christian Fink
Franz Leitner
Thierry Schmitter *17 May*
Cas Van Der Gevel

Wilco Van Rooyen
Karl Kobler *19 May*
Raphael Chassot
Olivier Pasche
Ms Madeleine Pasche
Bernhard Fahner
Stephan Knorr
Dario Schwörer
Santa Bahadur Gurung
Marc Batard
Ms Ana Collet
Na Temba (sherpa)
Phu Norbu (sherpa)
Serge Bonvin *20 May*
Guido Solinger
Hajo Netzer
Helmut Eibl
Hartmut Stockert
Arne Heckele
Philippe Arvis
Dieter Kramer
Phur Gyaltsen (sherpa)
Rinzin (sherpa)
Edi Koblmüller
Michael Koblmüller
Ms Romy Haller
Andreas Kremsl
Peter Weixlbaumer
Pasang Charka (sherpa)
Pasang (sherpa) *3rd*
Marc Whetu
Ms Ansja De Boer
Geoff Robb
Ralph Pliner
Peter Krug *21 May*
Hansruedi Wirth
Ms Nicole Guntern
Ms Andrea Linauer *22 May*
Otto Pirker
Engelbert Ruetz
Erich Weitlaner
Maila Pemba (sherpa)
Josu Feijoo
Franz Oberlercher *23 May*
Martín Ramos *24 Sept*
Branko Separovic
Sherpa climber
Jan Matlak
Erik Bizon
Marian Cervienka
Pemba (sherpa)
Christian Corneloup
Ms Bernadette Boucaud
Sherpa climber
French climber
Sherpa climber
Gary Pfisterer *25 Sept*
Ms Ginette Harrison
Jozef Janda

Vladimir Paulik
Milan Smilka
Christian Chène *26 Sept*
French climber *6 Oct*
French climber
French climber
Ilgvars Pauls *7 Oct*
José Delgado
Marcus Tobía
Marco Cayuso

1999
Jerzy Kawiak *21 Apr*
Marcin Miotk
Krzysztof Tarasewicz
Robert Wieczkowski
Piotr Henschke *22 April*
Jan Szulc
Doytchin Vassilev *1 May*
Ms Karina Salova
Sven Gangdal *3 May*
Dawa Tashi (sherpa)
Jon Gangdal *4 May*
Dawa Tshering (sherpa)
David Hiddleston *6 May*
Dean Staples
Jim Litch
Kami (sherpa)
Chuldim (sherpa)
Andrew Marquis
Keither Kerr
Doug Mantle
Michael Kropf
Rafael Escandón *7 May*
Silvino Falcón
Romano Benet *12 May*
Ms Nives Meroi
Martin Kung *23 May*
Ms Andrea Boll
Michael Borrmann
Zac Zaharias *25 May*
Andrew Peacock
Brian Laursen
Allen Caldwell
Bob Killip
Steve Simpson
Michael Cook
Tim Robathan
Jamie Hackett *27 May*
Dean Macmaster
David Donaldson
Steve Graham
Brad Reeve
Ms Tanya Bylart *28 May*
Peter Lambert
Carl Johnson
Brian Agnew
Ron Holt *15 Sept*
Robert Anderson

Paul Morrow
Reiji Takahashi
Mr Suzuki
Mr Kata
Japanese climber
Japanese climber   16 Sept
Japanese climber
Adriano Favre   26 Sept
Claudio Rosset
Max Comune
Stefano Percino
Uluocak Ügur
Park Young-Seok 2nd
Sherpa climber
Paolo Obert   27 Sept
Marino Obert

René Ghilini
André-Pierre Rhem
Jean-Philippe Roncin
Thilen (sherpa)
Mingma (sherpa)
Sergi Mingote
Ms Frédérique Delrieu
Vladimir Yanochkin 28 Sept
Edmond Joyeusez
Pierre Sicouri
Frédéric Hasbani
Ms Anne Beauvoir
Austrian climber   29 Sept

Other Noteworthy Climbs

Those who participated in new routes § or early repeats of new routes §r but did not continue to Main or Central summit.   • Died during descent

1994
Eric Decamp §r   7 Sept
Ms Catherine Destivelle §r
Leopold Sulovsky §   30 Sept
Zdenek Slachta § •
Czech climber §
Czech climber §
Czech climber §
Czech climber §
Mark Newcomb §r   20 Oct
Jean Chr.Lafaille §   9 Oct

1995
Josep Permañé §   24 Sept
Carles Figueras §

1998
Enrique de Pablo §r   9 Oct
Andrés Delgado §r
Hector Ponce de León §r

317

Index

Page numbers referring to
illustrations are in italics

319

321